**WITHDRAWN**
WRIGHT STATE UNIVERSITY LIBRARIES

*Casebook of Eclectic Psychotherapy*

**Brunner/Mazel Integrative Psychotherapy Series**
John C. Norcross, Ph.D., Series Editor

1. Handbook of Eclectic Psychotherapy
2. Casebook of Eclectic Psychotherapy

### Review Board

Bernard D. Beitman, M.D.
Larry E. Beutler, Ph.D.
John F. Clarkin, Ph.D.
Windy Dryden, Ph.D.
Joel Fischer, D.S.W.
Allen Frances, M.D.
Marvin R. Goldfried, Ph.D.
Toksoz B. Karasu, M.D.
Arnold A. Lazarus, Ph.D.
Jeanne S. Phillips, Ph.D.
James O. Prochaska, Ph.D.
Paul L. Wachtel, Ph.D.
Esther Wald, M.S.W., Ph.D.

# Casebook of Eclectic Psychotherapy

Edited by

*John C. Norcross, Ph.D.*
Department of Psychology
University of Scranton

BRUNNER/MAZEL, *Publishers* • New York

**Library of Congress Cataloging-in-Publication Data**

Casebook of eclectic psychotherapy.

   Includes bibliographies and index.
   1. Psychotherapy—Case studies. I. Norcross,
John C., 1957-   . [DNLM: 1. Psychotherapy—case
studies. WM 420 C3368]
RC465.C33 1987     616.89′14     86-14770
ISBN 0-87630-434-X

Copyright © 1987 by John C. Norcross

*Published by*
BRUNNER/MAZEL, INC.
19 Union Square
New York, New York 10003

All rights reserved. No part of this book may be reproduced by any process whatsoever without the written permission of the copyright owner.

MANUFACTURED IN THE UNITED STATES OF AMERICA

Dedicated to my parents,

CAROL and GEORGE NORCROSS,

who taught us to love, work, and play

# Contents

| | |
|---|---:|
| Preface | xi |
| About the Editor | xiii |
| About the Contributors | xiii |

1. Introduction: Eclecticism, Casebooks, and Cases  ...  3
   *John C. Norcross*

2. Systematic Technical Eclecticism: Two Depressive Episodes Treated with Very Brief Psychotherapy  ...  19
   *Bernard D. Beitman*
   Commentary: Producing a Temporary Change in the System  ...  47
   *Marvin R. Goldfried*
   Commentary: Making More Use of Our Models  ...  49
   *James O. Prochaska*

3. Systematic Eclectic Psychotherapy: Growing into Separation  ...  53
   *Larry E. Beutler*
   Commentary: Growing into Separation  ...  91
   *Windy Dryden*
   Commentary: An Explicit, Selective, and Consistent Eclecticism  ...  92
   *Stephen C. Paul, Addie Fuhriman, and Gary M. Burlingame*

4. The Case of Julie: An Eclectic Time-Limited Therapy Perspective  ...  96
   *Gary M. Burlingame, Addie Fuhriman, and Stephen C. Paul*
   Commentary: Time-Limited Therapy and the Stages of Change  ...  126
   *Carlo C. DiClemente*
   Commentary: Advantages and Drawbacks of Generic Eclecticism  ...  129
   *Stanley B. Messer*

5. Differential Therapeutics: A Case Illustration  ...  132
   *John F. Clarkin and Phillida B. Rosnick*
   Commentary: Common versus Specific Ingredients in Differential Therapeutics and Psychotherapy  ...  151
   *Larry E. Beutler*
   Commentary: Eclecticism Should Provide Versatility  ...  154
   *Richard H. Driscoll*

6. Antonio—More Than Anxiety: A Transtheoretical Approach  ...  158
   *Carlo C. DiClemente*

Commentary: A Systems Model for a Case of Eclectic Therapy    180
*Edward J. Murray*

Commentary: Approach to Psychotherapy or Theory of Change?    183
*Martin R. Textor*

7. The Teenage Prosecutor: A Case in Pragmatic Family Therapy    186
*Richard H. Driscoll*

Commentary: The Teenage Prosecutor as an Example of Systematic Eclecticism    215
*Bernard D. Beitman*

Commentary: Practicality in Need of Direction    218
*Lawrence C. Grebstein*

8. Theoretically Consistent Eclecticism: Humanizing a Computer "Addict"    221
*Windy Dryden*

Commentary: Reactions from a Multimodal Perspective    237
*Arnold A. Lazarus and Clifford N. Lazarus*

Commentary: Demonstrating Therapeutic Eclecticism    239
*Douglas H. Powell*

9. A Case of Eclectic Family Therapy: "Are We the Sickest Family You've Ever Seen?"    242
*Lawrence C. Grebstein*

Commentary: The External and Internal Context of Eclectic/Integrative Family Therapy    269
*Alan S. Gurman*

Commentary: Eclecticism or Responsiveness?    272
*Stephen Murgatroyd*

10. Functional Therapy: A Case of Training    276
*John Hart and Joseph Hart*

Commentary: Present-Centeredness and the Client-Therapist Relationship    295
*Hugh C. H. Koch*

Commentary: Therapist, Heal Thyself First    298
*Malcolm H. Robertson*

11. Depression and Structural–Phenomenological Eclectic Psychotherapy: The Case of Gill    301
*Stephen Murgatroyd*

Commentary: Why Not More Phenomenology and Less Structure?    320
*Joseph Hart*

Commentary: Is There Truth in Psychotherapeutic Packaging?    322
*Robert N. Sollod*

12. Spontaneous Insight Associated with Behavior Therapy: The Case of Rex    325
*Douglas H. Powell*

Commentary: Some Combinations and Guidelines in Insight and Behavior Therapy    349
*Kalman Glantz*

| | |
|---|---|
| Commentary: When Is Behavior Therapy Enough?<br>*George J. Steinfeld* | 352 |
| 13. Radical Eclecticism: Case Illustration of an Obsessive Disorder<br>*Malcolm H. Robertson* | 356 |
| Commentary: Radical Eclecticism as Directive and Structured<br>*Sol L. Garfield* | 371 |
| Commentary: Perspectives from an Interpersonally Based Behavioral Therapist<br>*J. Kevin Thompson* | 372 |
| 14. A Marital Triangle: How Open Can We Be?<br>*George J. Steinfeld* | 375 |
| Commentary: Marital and Treatment Triangles<br>*John F. Clarkin* | 407 |
| Commentary: Is it Possible to Make a Happy Marriage of Cognitive-Behavioral and Family Systems Approaches?<br>*Michael A. Westerman* | 411 |
| Name Index | 417 |

# Preface

This compendium was designed as an extension and elaboration of the *Handbook of Eclectic Psychotherapy*. The 13 case histories presented herein concretely illustrate the practice of systematic eclectic psychotherapy in its varied manifestations. The positive response to the *Handbook*, requests for detailed cases, and our training experiences all dictated that we address what eclectic psychotherapists actually do, rather than what they say they do or what they recommend to others. As Samuel Johnson once observed, "Example is always more efficacious than precept."

Although intended to complement the *Handbook*, these in-depth cases stand firmly on their own. The cases transcend the indefinite boundaries of eclecticism to address the broader issues of psychotherapy practice and process. The results, in my estimation, brightly illuminate the shadowy figures of psychotherapy's past: reliance on theory rather than human interchange, reluctance to share our work, and discontinuity among clinical theory, research, and practice.

The case contributors deserve special acknowledgment for their perseverance and courage. The Case Guidelines (see chapter 1) required extensive transcripts, therapist remarks, and written patient impressions. More than one irate secretary answered my telephone inquiry to a contributor with a remark on the order of "So, you're the one asking for all these *?#*! transcripts!" Aside from suppressing office rebellions, contributors were asked to present explicit instances of their therapeutic errors, include unedited client comments, bundle it up into a coherent chapter of less than 60 pages, and subject it to the critical eyes of two unfettered commentators. Few psychotherapists, integrative or otherwise, would accept such a challenge, let alone surpass it, as did the contributors to the present volume.

Not a week passes of late without my quietly acknowledging the lifelong contributions of my parents, Carol and George Norcross. Parents frequently advise their children (and occasionally psychotherapists, their clients) that genuine appreciation of loving care develops gradually as the child (or client) matures. This has been particularly true for me with regard to my family, whom I cherish more and more with each day. I thus thank my family—George, Carol, George III, Donald, Philip, Nancy, Rebecca—and Weimaraners—Dagmar, DJ, and Misty. To my stepdaughter, who appropriately felt under-recognized in previous works, I reiterate my appreciation and love. As partial compensation for not highlighting her name earlier, I hereby repeat it boldly three times: Rebecca, Rebecca, Rebecca.

Finally, I am grateful to two groups of people who have convinced me that practicing psychotherapy and writing about psychotherapy are compatible, perhaps even synergistic, pursuits. The first consists of the patients whose private troubles and treatments constitute the content of this casebook. The second consists of the editorial staff of Brunner/Mazel, especially Ann Alhadeff and Bernie Mazel, who provided perfectly timed admixtures of encouragement and direction.

December 1985                      J.C.N.

# About the Editor

*John C. Norcross, Ph.D.*, is Associate Professor of Psychology at the University of Scranton, Research Consultant at the University of Rhode Island, and a clinical psychologist in part-time independent practice. He received his B.A. from Rutgers University, his M.A. and Ph.D. from the University of Rhode Island, and completed his internship at the Brown University School of Medicine. Dr. Norcross is author of over 50 professional articles, editor of the *Handbook of Eclectic Psychotherapy* (1986), and Editor-in-Chief of the *International Journal of Eclectic Psychotherapy*. He lives and plays in the Pocono Mountains of Northeastern Pennsylvania with his wife, stepdaughter, and Weimaraner.

# About the Contributors

*Bernard D. Beitman, M.D.*, is Associate Professor of Psychiatry and Director of Area Studies in Psychotherapy at the University of Missouri School of Medicine. He is coeditor of *Combining Psychotherapy and Drug Therapy in Clinical Practice,* and author of *The Structure of Individual Psychotherapy.*

*Larry E. Beutler, Ph.D.*, is Professor of Psychiatry and Psychology at the University of Arizona College of Medicine. Formerly he had been employed by Duke University Medical Center, Stephen F. Austin State University, Baylor College of Medicine, and the University of Arizona. He is a diplomate of the American Board of Professional Psychology and is Associate Editor of the *Journal of Consulting and Clinical Psychology*. He is author of *Eclectic Psychotherapy: A Systematic Approach* and coauthor of *Cognitive Group Therapy for Older Adults.*

*Gary M. Burlingame, Ph.D.*, is on the core faculty of the Comprehensive Clinic and is affiliated with the clinical psychology program at Brigham Young University. He maintains an active program of research and writing in short-term individual and group psychotherapy and has conducted numerous training workshops in short-term therapy techniques.

*John F. Clarkin, Ph.D.*, is Professor of Clinical Psychology in Psychiatry at the Cornell University Medical College and Director of Psychology at the New York Hospital-Westchester Division. He is coauthor of *Differential Therapeutics in Psychiatry: The Art and Science of Treatment Selection*, and *A DSM-III Casebook of Differential Therapeutics: A Clinical Guide to Treatment Selection*.

*Carlo C. DiClemente, Ph.D.*, is Associate Professor of Psychiatry and Behavioral Sciences at the University of Texas Mental Sciences Institute and an adjunct faculty member at the University of Houston. He is active in both psychology and psychiatry training programs, coordinates an outpatient Addictive Behaviors Treatment Center and conducts psychotherapy and behavioral medicine research. He is coauthor of *The Transtheoretical Approach: Crossing the Traditional Boundaries of Therapy*.

*Richard H. Driscoll, Ph.D.*, is a psychologist in independent practice in Knoxville, Tennessee, and is an associate of the Colorado-based Linguistic Research Institute. He is author of *Pragmatic Psychotherapy* and of several articles on therapeutic issues from an ordinary language pragmatic approach.

*Windy Dryden, Ph.D.*, is Senior Lecturer in Psychology, Goldsmiths' College, University of London and maintains a part-time independent practice in psychotherapy. He is author of *Rational-Emotive Therapy: Fundamentals and Innovations*, editor of *Individual Therapy in Britain*, and co-editor of the *Journal of Cognitive Psychotherapy: An International Quarterly*. His most recent books are *Cognitive-Behavioural Approaches to Psychotherapy* (edited with W. Golden) and *Rational-Emotive Therapy: Recent Developments in Theory and Practice* (edited with P. Trower).

*Addie Fuhriman, Ph.D.*, is Chair and Professor of Educational Psychology at the University of Utah. She is actively involved with training and research in individual and group therapy in the specialty of counseling psychology.

*Sol L. Garfield, Ph.D.*, is Professor of Psychology at Washington University, St. Louis, Missouri. He is author of *Psychotherapy: An Eclectic Approach; Clinical Psychology: The Study of Personality and Behavior;* and coeditor with Allen E. Bergin of the *Handbook of Psychotherapy and Behavior Change*. A former president of APA's Division of Clinical Psychology as well as the Society for Psychotherapy Research, he was editor of the *Journal of Consulting and Clinical Psychology*, 1979–1984.

*Kalman Glantz* was until recently Assistant Professor of Social Science at Lesley College, and is Director of Charlesbank Counseling Services in Cambridge, Massachusetts. He has written several articles on the use of behavioral interventions in psychodynamically oriented psychotherapy and is currently working on a book dealing with the implications of evolutionary biology for psychotherapy.

*Marvin R. Goldfried, Ph.D.*, is Professor of Psychology and Psychiatry at the State University of New York at Stony Brook and maintains a limited practice of psychotherapy in New York City. He is coauthor of *Clinical Behavior Therapy* and editor of *Converging Themes in Psychotherapy: Trends in Psychodynamic, Humanistic, and Behavioral Practice*.

*Lawrence C. Grebstein, Ph.D., A.B.P.P.*, is Professor of Psychology and Director of the Clinical Psychology Training Program at the University of Rhode Island. He serves as a consultant to a variety of agencies and maintains a part-time independent practice. He is an A.B.P.P. Diplomate in Clinical Psychology, author of *Toward Self-Understanding: Studies in Personality and Adjustment,* and has been a Fellow in Family Therapy and Research at the Center for Family Research, George Washington University Medical Center.

*Alan S. Gurman, Ph.D.,* is Professor of Psychiatry and Director of the Psychiatric Outpatient Clinic, University of Wisconsin Medical School. The author/editor of eight books, including the *Handbook of Family Therapy, The Clinical Handbook of Marital Therapy,* and *The Casebook of Marital Therapy,* he is the editor of the *Journal of Marital and Family Therapy,* past president of the Society for Psychotherapy Research, and the recipient of two distinguished career awards for family therapy research.

*John Hart, Ph.D.,* is President of Hart and Associates, a psychotherapy and consulting firm in Los Angeles. He specializes in training professionals in Functional Therapy and in developing school programs for children and youth. He was a contributor to *Modern Eclectic Therapy: A Functional Approach to Counseling and Psychotherapy* and writes a sports psychology column called "Psychological Fitness."

*Joseph Hart, Ph.D.,* is Director of Counseling at California Polytechnic University in Pomona, California. He is also a consultant specializing in occupational psychology, stress management, and wellness programs with Hart and Associates and The University Consulting Group in Los Angeles. He is the author of *Modern Eclectic Therapy: A Functional Approach to Counseling and Psychotherapy,* coauthor of *Psychological Fitness,* and coeditor of *New Directions in Client-Centered Therapy.*

*Hugh C. H. Koch, Ph.D.,* is Top Grade Clinical Psychologist and Specialty Head in Adult Mental Health in the Department of Psychology, North East Essex Health Authority in Colchester, Essex. He teaches and supervises psychological therapies in various postgraduate courses in England and is a visiting Lecturer at the University of North Carolina. He is currently editing *Community Clinical Psychology.*

*Arnold A. Lazarus, Ph.D.,* is a Professor II in the Graduate School of Applied and Professional Psychology, Rutgers University. He has founded several Multimodal Therapy Institutes, serves as a consultant to a number of state and private agencies, and has a part-time practice in Princeton, New Jersey. He has published over 120 scientific articles and 10 books, of which *Casebook of Multimodal Therapy* is his most recent.

*Clifford N. Lazarus* received his B.A. from Rutgers University in 1984 where he majored in psychology and biology. While at Rutgers, Mr. Lazarus was a Henry Rutgers Scholar, received a university research stipend, and conducted extensive research on the stimulus properties of drugs. He is a clinical psychology Ph.D. candidate at Rutgers University where he is currently researching behavioral strategies in the treatment of essential hypertension.

*Stanley B. Messer, Ph.D.,* is Professor of Psychology in the Graduate School of Applied and Professional Psychology at Rutgers University where he directs the psychodynamic track. He is coeditor (with Hal Arkowitz) of *Psychoanalytic Therapy and Behavior Therapy: Is Integration Possible?* and is a consulting editor to the *Journal of Consulting and Clinical Psychology.* Dr. Messer is a consultant to the Office of the Public Defender in several New Jersey counties and maintains a part-time independent practice in psychotherapy and psychological assessment.

*Stephen Murgatroyd, B.A. (Hons.), FBPs.S, M.Phil.*, is Professor of Applied Psychology and Dean of Administrative Studies at Athabasca University, Alberta, Canada. He has worked as a counseling psychologist in a variety of settings and has specialized in adult counseling, crisis counseling, and psychotherapy. Stephen is editor of the *British Journal of Guidance and Counselling* and author of *Helping the Troubled Child—Interprofessional Case Studies, Coping with Crisis* (with Ray Woolfe), and *Helping Families in Distress*.

*Edward J. Murray, Ph.D.*, is Professor of Psychology at the University of Miami and maintains a private practice in psychotherapy. He has published about a hundred articles, chapters, and books on personality, motivation, emotion, and various forms of therapy, including psychoanalysis, transcendental meditation, encounter groups, systematic desensitization, and cognitive-behavior therapy. He has served on the editorial boards of: *Contemporary Psychology; Journal of Personality Research; Psychotherapy;* and *Cognitive Therapy and Research*. He has also served as a research consultant for the National Institute of Mental Health.

*Stephen C. Paul, Ph.D.*, is Assistant Professor of Educational Psychology and Associate Director of the University Counseling Center at the University of Utah. He is also President of Consult West, a firm specializing in organizational consultation and individual, couple, and family counseling.

*Douglas H. Powell, Ed.D.*, is a Psychologist to the Harvard University Health Services. He is President of Powell Associates, consulting psychologists to individuals, schools, and organizations. *Understanding Human Adjustment* and *Teenagers: When to Worry and What to Do* are his most recent books.

*James O. Prochaska, Ph.D.*, is Professor of Psychology and Director of the Self-Change Laboratory at the University of Rhode Island. He also serves as a consultant to numerous institutions and maintains a part-time independent practice in psychotherapy. He is author of *Systems of Psychotherapy: A Transtheoretical Analysis* and coauthor of *The Transtheoretical Approach: Crossing the Traditional Boundaries of Therapy*.

*Malcolm H. Robertson, Ph.D.*, is Professor of Psychology and Director of Clinical Psychology Training at Western Michigan University. He is a Diplomate in Clinical Psychology. He also serves as a consultant to several community agencies and maintains a part-time independent practice in psychotherapy. He is the author of several articles on eclectic psychotherapy and psychotherapy training.

*Phillida B. Rosnick, Ph.D.*, is Assistant Professor of Psychology in Psychiatry at the Cornell University Medical College and Coordinator of Psychology in the Community Services Division of the New York Hospital–Westchester Division.

*Robert N. Sollod, Ph.D.*, is Associate Professor of Psychology and Director of the Clinical/Community Professional Program at the Cleveland State University. He maintains a part-time independent practice as a psychotherapist and consultant. He has published articles concerning therapeutic integration in psychosexual therapy, the relevance of Piagetian concepts for clinical work, and the origins of psychotherapeutic approaches.

*George J. Steinfeld, Ph.D.*, is Director of Consultation, Education, and Family Therapy Training at the Greater Bridgeport Childrens Service Center, Bridgeport, Connecticut. He is also in private practice. He has written a number of theoretical and clinical papers and is interested in bridging the conceptual and clinical gap between individual and family therapies. He is author of *TARET Systems: An Integrative Approach to Individual and Family Therapy.*

*Martin R. Textor, Dr. phil.,* is currently employed by the Hanns-Seidel Foundation in Munich, West Germany. He is author of *Integrative Familientherapie* and editor of *Helping Families with Special Problems* and *Das Buch der Familientherapie.*

*J. Kevin Thompson, Ph.D.,* is Assistant Professor of Psychology at the University of South Florida. He is a member of the Society for the Exploration of Psychotherapy Integration and author of "An Interpersonally-Based Cognitive-Behavioral Psychotherapy" in *Progress in Behavior Modification.*

*Michael A. Westerman, Ph.D.,* is Assistant Professor of Psychology at New York University. He maintains a part-time independent practice in psychology. His publications are in the areas of psychotherapy process-outcome research, studies of family processes related to behavior problems in children, and theoretical issues related to the role played by philosophical assumptions in the practice of psychotherapy.

*Casebook of
Eclectic
Psychotherapy*

CHAPTER 1

# Introduction: Eclecticism, Casebooks, and Cases

## John C. Norcross

The notion of psychotherapy integration has intrigued clinicians for many years (Goldfried, 1982a; Goldfried & Newman, 1986), but it has only been in the last 10 or 15 years that integration has become a specified area of interest. The literature on eclecticism is growing by leaps and bounds, and there is no dearth of theoretical writings on the subject. There is, however, a striking dearth of case histories, particularly verbatim accounts. The *Casebook* attempts to rectify this deficiency and to bridge the precipice between expounded theory and practical application.

The 13 cases in this compendium, all formulated and treated from systematic eclectic perspectives, are detailed. Steps were taken to ensure longitudinal and intensive accounts of integrative psychosocial treatment. The intent is to take the reader into the therapy session—to show what actually transpires, what the therapist is thinking, and how the patient is responding. The goals are to operationalize the therapeutic decision-making process, to discover how interventions are matched to patients and problems, to relate process to outcome, and to discover the breadth of treatment procedures and conceptualizations found in eclectic therapy. These are explored through the multiple and unique vantage points of the psychotherapist, the patient, the interchange (via session transcripts), and fellow clinicians.

The present chapter is intended to review the broad context of eclectic psychotherapy and to consider the role of this *Casebook* within the integrationist *Zeitgeist*. First, I outline several definitions and manifestations of eclecticism with particular emphasis on systematic prescriptive eclecticism. Second, the growing need for and appreciation of casebooks are briefly discussed. Third, I comment on the organization of the book and the preparation of the cases. Finally, several "growing pains" of eclecticism are explicated and a developmental understanding recommended.

## ECLECTICISM

The past 10 years have produced a burgeoning of psychotherapists across orientations and disciplines who claim an allegiance to eclectic psychotherapy. Clinicians of all persuasions are now coming out of their monogamous theoretical closets to proclaim their receptivity to the simultaneous employment of multiple theories and techniques (Held, 1984). Eclecticism has become the modal orientation of mental health professionals, with between one-third and one-half ascribing to it (e.g., Garfield & Kurtz, 1976; Jayaratne, 1978; Norcross, 1985; Norcross & Prochaska, 1982a; Prochaska & Norcross, 1983). Psychologists generally believe that eclecticism offers the best hope for a truly comprehensive treatment approach (Smith, 1982). Historical trends and expert opinions portend increasing reliance on sophisticated integration in psychotherapy theory, research, and practice (Prochaska & Norcross, 1982).

The concomitant openness to contributions from diverse persuasions has given rise to numerous publications and organizations. Specific systems of eclectic practice (e.g., Beitman, 1986; Beutler, 1983; Driscoll, 1984; Garfield, 1980; Hart, 1983; Lazarus, 1981; Palmer, 1980; Prochaska & DiClemente, 1984; Thorne, 1973), influential anthologies (e.g., Goldfried, 1982b; Marmor & Woods, 1980; Norcross, 1986b), and compilations of prescriptive treatments (e.g., Frances, Clarkin, & Perry, 1984; Goldstein & Stein, 1976) have flourished. Several eclectic journals (e.g., *International Journal of Eclectic Psychotherapy*) and series of articles (e.g., Brady et al., 1980; Garfield, 1982; Goldfried, 1982a; Kendall, 1982; Wachtel, 1982) have appeared. Three interdisciplinary and nonideological organizations—the Society for Psychotherapy Research (SPR), the Society for the Exploration of Psychotherapy Integration (SEPI), and the International Academy of Eclectic Psychotherapists (IAEP)—also exemplify the spirit of open inquiry and growing collaboration.

Two serious obstacles to wider acceptance of an eclectic perspective are disagreement over terms and the absence of a generic psychotherapy language (Goldfried & Safran, 1986; Norcross, 1986a). The term *eclectic*, in particular, has been employed indiscriminately and inconsistently. A vague and nebulous term, its connotations range from "a worn-out synonym for theoretical laziness" to the "only means to a comprehensive psychotherapy" (Smith, 1982). In some corners, eclecticism is prized as complex, relativistic thinking by people united in their respect for the evidence and in their willingness to learn about what may be clinically effective. In other corners, eclecticism connotes undisciplined subjectivity, "muddle-headedness," even minimal brain damage. Some have referred to eclecticism as the "last refuge for mediocrity, the seal of incompetency" and "a classic case of professional anomie" (cited in Robertson, 1979). It is surprising that so many clinicians admit to being eclectic in their work given the negative valence the term has acquired (Garfield & Kurtz, 1977).

There is recurrent debate whether eclecticism constitutes another theoretical orientation or the absence of one. Thorne (1973), among others, insists that eclecticism is the active acceptance of an orientation in its own right, albeit broader and more integrative. Garfield (1980), in contrast, uses eclectic to indicate that one is not an adherent of a particular school of psychotherapy. Beyond this, the term does not have any precise meaning. What binds most eclectics together is a stated dislike for a single orientation, selection from two or more theories, and the belief that no present theory is adequate to explain or predict all the behavior a clinician observes (Garfield & Kurtz, 1977).

*Webster's Collegiate Dictionary* defines eclecticism as the "method or practice of selecting what seems best from various systems." Similarly, Brammer and Shostrom (1982) define therapeutic eclecticism as the "process of selecting concepts, methods, and strategies from a variety of current theories which work" (p. 35). If eclectics do indeed choose what appears to work best, few should oppose the movement (Garfield, 1982).

These definitions, though somewhat vague, imply that eclecticism should be *prescriptive* and *systematic*. Prescriptive eclecticism entails going beyond subjective preference, institutional custom, and immediate availability to predicate treatment selection on clinical experience and outcome research (see Dimond & Havens, 1975; Frances, Clarkin, & Perry, 1984; Goldstein & Stein, 1976; Hariman, 1986). Prescriptionism is concerned with that elusive, empirically driven match among patient, disorder, and treatment. With increasing refinement in the categorization of disorders and more precise delineation of change strategies, further advantages of specific treatments for specific conditions may be found. At that point, effective therapy will be "defined not by its brand name, but by how well it meets the need of the patient" (Weiner, 1975, p. 44).

Systematic eclecticism, as opposed to the unsystematic brand, is the product of years of painstaking clinical, research, and theoretical work. It is truly eclecticism "by design"; that is, clinicians competent in several therapeutic systems who selectively choose interventions based on clinical experience and/or research findings. The strengths of systematic eclectic approaches lie in their ability to be taught, replicated, and evaluated.

By contrast, unsystematic eclecticism is primarily an outgrowth of pet techniques and inadequate training. It is eclecticism "by default," lacking sufficient competence for an eclectic approach and selecting interventions on the basis of subjective appeal. Eysenck (1970) has characterized this haphazard form of eclecticism as a "mish-mash of theories, a hugger-mugger of procedures, a gallimaufry of therapies" (p. 145) having no proper rationale or empirical evaluation.

There are multiple manifestations of systematic eclectic psychotherapy, of which three subtypes predominate. Atheoretical eclecticism is an integrative perspective governed by no preferred theoretical approach (e.g., London, 1972, 1986). Synthetic eclecticism strives toward an integration of diverse contemporary theories (e.g., Goldfried, 1980; Prochaska & DiClemente, 1984). Technical eclecticism endorses the use of a variety of techniques within a preferred theory (e.g., Lazarus, 1967, 1981).

These three subtypes are all evident in contemporary practice (Garfield & Kurtz, 1977) and in this *Casebook*. In a survey of clinical psychologists (Norcross & Prochaska, 1982a), eclectic respondents were asked to select the one type of eclecticism that best approximated their own views. Over half (61%) of these eclectics indicated they integrated a diversity of contemporary approaches, 29% responded that they use a variety of techniques within a preferred theory, and 10% claimed that they had no preferred theoretical orientation. Results from a second sample (Prochaska & Norcross, 1983) replicated the order of preference, namely, synthetic, technical, and atheoretical.

Lazarus (1967, 1977, 1981), the most eloquent proponent of technical eclecticism, emphasizes the distinction between the theoretical eclectic and the technical eclectic. The theoretical eclectic draws from diverse systems that may be epistemologically and ontologically incompatible, whereas the technical eclectic uses procedures drawn from different sources without necessarily subscribing to the theories that spawned them. For Lazarus and other technical eclectics, no necessary connection exists between metabeliefs and techniques. It is not necessary to build a composite from divergent theories, on the one hand, or to accept divergent conceptions, on the other, in order to utilize their technical procedures. "To attempt a theoretical rapprochement is as futile as trying to picture the edge of the universe. But to read through the vast amount of literature on psychotherapy, *in search of techniques,* can be clinically enriching and therapeutically rewarding" (Lazarus, 1967, p. 416).

On the other hand, many (e.g., Loew, 1975; Maultsby, 1968; Simon, 1974) have taken exception to Lazarus' technical eclecticism and have emphasized the necessary and important link between theory and intervention. Synthetic eclectics insist that only in theoretical integration can treatments be prescribed in reproducible, testable, and explainable terms. That is, to retain theory in practice is to make psychotherapy more rigorous and consistent (see Held, 1984).

A few final words on the interrelationship of eclecticism and integrationism are in order. Integration refers to the incorporation of parts into a whole. Integrationists, many of whom abhor the label "eclectic," are persons working toward or from an integrative perspective.

Clinical practice can be viewed as a continuum ranging from a single orientation at one pole to an integration of all orientations at the other. The practice of orthodox psychoanalysis or radical behaviorism would represent one end. A hyphenated approach—say, cognitive-behavioral—would be one step further along the continuum. And just how many hyphens constitute eclecticism? Does interpersonal-cognitive-behavioral therapy qualify as an eclectic therapy? There is no arbitrary cutoff on a continuum, of course, and this seems to be a matter of labeling and taste. The ideal of integrating *all* available psychotherapy systems is not likely to be met either. Somewhere between the hyphenated, two-orientation approach and the unattained integration of all theories lie the obscure boundaries of eclecticism.

In my opinion, integrationism is one variant, one manifestation of systematic eclecticism. It should be noted that others believe integrationism is the broader category subsuming eclecticism. In any case, integrationists seek to meld warring therapy factions, typically behavior therapy and psychoanalysis (cf. Arkowitz & Messer, 1984; Marmor & Woods, 1980; Wachtel, 1977; Yates, 1983), into a cooperative and harmonious whole. However, those integrationists restricting themselves to two therapy systems would not technically meet the "three systems or more" definition of eclecticism.

Relatedly, Beitman (Chapter 2) notes that the movement toward bringing together the conflicting schools of psychotherapy has advanced to a point at which two different terms are being used to characterize it. The apparent conflict between the terms "integrationism" and "eclecticism" stems from different intents: a sociopolitical revolution to reduce conflict by recognizing the commonalities in the former, and an attempt to construct one practical and systematic clinical model in the latter. In Beitman's words, "integrationists pave the way by knocking down barriers with attacks on ideological rigidity and systematic eclectics provide the alternative means."

From a different perspective, Gurman (this volume, Commentary to Chapter 9) characterizes eclecticism as adding together techniques and strategies derived from disparate models of therapy. Integrationism, in contrast, involves the careful elucidation of principles by which apparently incompatible views are brought together. Furthermore, according to Gurman, eclectic therapists choose a technique or theory to fit the patient; the integrative therapist chooses techniques or theories in a way that fits him/herself as well as the patient.

Despite the semantic disparities and technical differences, the objectives of integrationists and eclectics are quite similar indeed. Both seek an end to the "ideological cold war" (Murray, 1983) and "dogma eat dogma" (Larson, 1980) environment that has characterized psychotherapy for too long. Moreover, both are devoted to open inquiry, critical dialogue, and reciprocal enrichment among systems of psychotherapy.

## CASEBOOKS

With virtual unanimity, psychotherapy researchers have argued that psychotherapy research should yield information useful for practicing clinicians but has failed to do so to date (Barlow, 1981; Elliott, 1983; Luborsky, 1972; Sargent & Cohen, 1983; Schontz & Rosenak, 1985; Strupp, 1982). As a result, psychotherapy research minimally influences practice—an aloof relationship variously characterized as the dreaded precipice, a crisis of confidence, and an "anaclitic depression" (Parloff, 1980; Strupp, 1981). The standard litany of complaints against conventional clinical research includes irrelevant questions, atypical populations, unrepresentative therapists, unstandardized treatments, unrealistic settings, oversimplification of complex realities, reliance on statistical rather than clinical significance, and concentration on group outcomes rather than individual process-outcome linkages. Indeed, the typical psychotherapist does not engage in research, is reluctant to participate in research, and publishes little (see review by Morrow-Bradley & Elliott, in press).

A shift is needed in psychotherapy research because traditional research methods of experimental psychology—emphasizing isolation, simplification, and aggregate statistics—are not appropriate for studying psychotherapy (e.g., Elliott, 1983; Rice & Greenberg, 1984). Psychosocial treatments are *not* mechanically administered to passive patients, and interventions are *not* discrete, disembodied procedures. Rather, therapeutic skills and techniques are efforts on the part of the therapist to influence the therapeutic relationship and the patient's behavior. We need to turn to the clinical data and ask, as clinicians, "What has happened here and why?" (Butler & Strupp, in press).

Several writers (e.g., Peterfreund, 1971; Schafer, 1976, 1983; Spence, 1982, 1984) have proposed a new mode of clinical reporting which does not rely solely on therapists' recall and which jettisons confusing languages in the service of greater clinical relevance. We need to make a clear break with what Spence (1982) has called the "Sherlock Holmes Tradition" and develop methods of presenting case material which allow the reader to participate in the argument, allow him/her to evaluate the proposed links between evidence and conclusion, and which open up the possibilities of alternative conceptualizations and even refutation. Collectively, this would increase explanatory force and learning opportunities.

Therapists learn about therapy overwhelmingly from their own clinical experience. Second to experience, practical books are the most highly valued sources of clinical knowledge, particularly among experienced practitioners (Clark, Wadden, Brownell, Gordon, & Tarte, 1983; Morrow-Bradley & Elliott, in press; Norcross & Prochaska, 1982b; Sargent & Cohen, 1983).

Systematic case study is a viable research alternative and an attractive pedagogical method. The recent profusion of casebooks reflects both dissatisfaction with conventional research and satisfaction with education through observation. Casebooks attest to the growing recognition of and need for "learning through doing," rather than merely "learning through knowing." Casebooks have now appeared on "great cases" (Greenwald, 1959; Wedding & Corsini, 1979), child psychotherapy (Cooper & Wanerman, 1984), marital therapy (Gurman, 1985), family therapy (Papp, 1977), time-limited dynamic treatment (Mann & Goldman,

1982), multimodal therapy (Lazarus, 1985), and hypnotherapy (Dowd & Healy, 1985). This volume, however, is the first casebook explicitly devoted to systematic eclectic psychotherapy.

When done right, casebooks have much to recommend to the practitioner and researcher alike. Experienced therapists present case histories from beginning to end and provide concrete guidance on the crucial questions of "why, how, and when."

It is case material that grounds soaring metapsychology and translates technical language into "felt experience." Cases provide a "frequent coupling of the abstract with the concrete, a marriage of concept and illustration" (Bonime & Bonime, 1978, p. 38). Theorizing becomes "pragmatic" (Driscoll, 1984) and "consequential" (Berger, 1985)—relevant to what transpires in clinical practice. The clinical data thus render books more readable, interesting, and most of all, useful.

When done wrong—and I fear many earlier efforts were—casebooks become collections of disembodied and anecdotal case material written by speculating practitioners. Specifically, as a practitioner and researcher, I have been frustrated by previous casebooks for several reasons: (a) total reliance on therapist recall (or reconstruction); (b) absence of complimentary or alternative perspectives on the case; (c) incomplete description of the patient and approach; (d) treatment of ideal cases in their pristine form; and (e) lack of therapist rationale for his/her clinical decision making.

First of all, a case should not be presented solely from the therapist's perspective. Distortion, misrepresentation, even falsification are products of theory-bound and appearance-consumed practitioners. It is not the profundity of interpretation that impacts behavior change, but how the material is presented by the therapist and received by the client. Though it is readily apparent that clinical treatment is defined as *received* by the patient, in or outside of immediate awareness, we forget this and rely on what the therapist *thought* he/she provided (Schafer, 1983; Spence, 1982).

Moreover, our sympathy lies naturally with the author. This is particularly true for authors in complete command of the narrative voice and the rhetorical method. The Dora case, as Marcus (1977) made clear, is a clinical *tour de force* in which all significant features of the patient's life are presumably explained. The grounds for these explanations are less than convincing, and yet we come away persuaded and impressed by the clinical reasoning. Freud was able to turn a treatment failure into a literary success (Marcus, 1977; Spence, 1984).

The principal goal of psychotherapy is to bring about change in the patient, not to present a reasoned argument that relies on public data and rules of evidence. When the clinical account is transposed to the public domain, however, it is no longer designed for the benefit of one individual but must now be accessible to all (Spence, 1984). Simply put, it is not sufficient to use the therapist's conviction to impress the reader. Let the "evidence" speak—evidence from different sources (e.g., other therapists, patient, family members) and of different types (e.g., self-report, transcripts, standardized measures).

Toward these ends, case contributors in this volume went beyond mere case study reconstruction by the addition of audio-tape recordings, patients' impressions, and fellow therapists' commentaries. These editorial methods were employed to make the case accounts as complete and valid as possible. The Case Guidelines (see below) required verbatim session transcripts and patients' written reactions in order to facilitate multiple perspectives. Furthermore, two prominent clinicians interested in psychotherapy integration reviewed each case history and provided published commentaries. As presented to the commentators, their comments were "intended to stimulate thought and critical dialogue on the possibilities and varieties of eclectic psychotherapy. Commentaries should embellish a few points, provide complimentary or alternative conceptualizations, relate a transaction to theory or research, and generally discuss the case."

The Case Guidelines were also produced to guard against the remaining aforementioned pitfalls of casebooks, namely, incomplete description of the patient and approach, treatment of ideal cases in their pristine form, and lack of therapist rationale in his/her clinical decision making. The guidelines proscribed mandatory inclusion of salient patient material. Freud (1905/1963, p. 32), the intrapsychic master, cautioned us "to pay as much attention in our case histories to the purely human and social circumstances of our patients as to the somatic data and the symptoms of the disorder." One prerequisite for case contributors was that they had published extensively on their integrative treatment approaches. The *Handbook of Eclectic Psychotherapy* (Norcross, 1986) and auxiliary sources provide detailed information on the underlying theoretical models and clinical reasoning for these eclectic approaches.

Unlike many casebook editors, I was not interested in ideal cases or the pristine application of psychotherapy. The Case Guidelines instructed contributors to select representative cases, to present their therapeutic errors, and to concentrate on the positive as well as negative outcomes of treatment. We have tried to venture beyond the glitter of therapeutic packaging to present psychotherapy as it is experienced in daily practice. What these cases lack in purity is more than compensated by their realism. These 13 cases convey the richness, complexity, and realities of eclectic psychotherapy.

One of the pressing challenges in eclectic psychotherapy is to elucidate and operationalize clinical decision-making processes. Why does one turn right instead of left? At both the microlevel—reflection versus question versus silence—and macrolevel—support versus desensitization versus genetic interpretation—we need to identify individual clinician's rules. This compendium reflects 13 psychotherapists' efforts to do so and, at the same time, attests to the difficulty of the task before us.

The Case Guidelines are presented below in condensed form as a guide to the reader.

## CASE GUIDELINES

These guidelines have been prepared to promote comprehensiveness within cases, to facilitate comparisons across cases, and to answer frequent questions concerning the organization of the case histories. The topics covered here are representative and not exhaustive.

### Case Structure

The guidelines are *not* designed to serve as an outline for the case. The primary goal is to present clear and detailed case histories from eclectic perspectives. Contributors are encouraged to employ whatever structure they feel best presents the required information and their eclectic approach.

It would be appropriate to begin with a synopsis of your eclectic perspective and the reasons for selecting this particular case. Background and theoretical information pertaining to your approach can be summarized here. It would also be appropriate to conclude with several paragraphs on the case, your approach, and eclecticism in general.

### Case Selection

A wide variety of cases is sought, particularly complex cases involving multiple etiologies, modalities, and treatments. The case can deal with practically any problem or diagnostic type amenable to psychosocial treatment. The case should, however, be (1) illustrative of your eclectic approach, (2) completed at the time of writing the chapter, and (3) fairly typical of the types of patients or problems treated by your approach in the past. Additionally, the case requires (4) transcript excerpts (from audiotapes or videotapes) from several sessions, and (5) the patient's written impressions of several critical sessions and treatment as a whole (see Patient Impressions below). Finally, it is suggested that (6) the completed case be between 5 and 25 sessions in length, thereby reflecting the general duration of outpatient psychotherapy in the United States.

*Patient Information*

The case should contain identifying information, chief complaints, and a brief review of salient history. Demographically, include pertinent data such as age, ethnicity, marital status, living conditions, occupation, education, and family composition. The presenting problems, expectations for therapy, psychiatric history, previous treatment, personal and social history, family history, medical history, and referral source should all be summarized. Information brought to therapy with the client—for example, previous test reports—should also be summarized. Certain identifying information must be disguised or omitted, of course, to preserve the patient's anonymity and to meet ethical standards.

*Treatment Information*

The case should clearly present the treatment setting, frequency and length of sessions, and other clinical practices which may influence treatment. Routine psychological test or questionnaire results may be presented in narrative or tabular form. Written contracts, intake questionnaires, and similar forms may also be introduced here.

Starting with the initial contact, describe the processes and outcomes of treatment. Issues pertinent to psychotherapy practice and your eclectic perspective in general should be discussed. Representative topics include:

—intake and assessment procedures
—the process by which you reached a case formulation and diagnosis
—integration of assessment and therapy
—selection and prioritization of treatment goals
—explanation (if any) of your integrative/eclectic approach to the client
—the process of selecting specific treatments for specific disorders
—matching your behavior to the patient's problems
—explanation of your decision to employ a particular intervention at a particular time
—rationale of your behaviors at different points in treatment
—basic interventions and techniques
—the patient's response to treatment, particularly blocks and resistances
—development and evolution of the therapeutic relationship
—different stages or phases of treatment
—evaluation of therapeutic progress or change
—termination process
—outcome and follow-up

*Session Transcripts*

The case should contain numerous excerpts of verbatim session transcripts to illustrate the practice and process of your eclectic approach. Transcripts should ideally be employed to illustrate various phases or processes of therapy. One excerpt, for instance, could reflect the patient's functioning, his/her characteristic behavior, interpersonal relating, and self-presentation. Another excerpt could demonstrate a "critical incident" as judged by clinician or client. A third could trace a therapeutic impasse or specific choice point in treatment.

*Therapist Remarks*

The psychotherapist should describe and explain the sequence of events constituting treatment from his or her eclectic perspective. Particular attention should be paid to the decision-making processes culminating in the case formulation, treatment interventions, and therapeutic relationship. The reader should be made witness, to the extent humanly possible and personally comfortable, to the internal processes (e.g., emotions, cognitions, intuitions) that guide you as an eclectic therapist.

In commenting on the rationale (or lack of) for your therapeutic behaviors, it would be fruitful to discuss both the positive and negative aspects of the case. Presentation of technical errors, mistimed interventions, poorly worded comments, and related mistakes will result in a more balanced case.

*Patient Impressions*

The case should contain the patient's reactions to treatment written after (or during) termination. Patients should be asked to provide critical descriptions of their therapy, concentrating both upon the negative and positive parts of treatment. Further, they should be asked for their candid impressions of critical incidents or transactions presented in the case transcripts. These impressions should ideally be written; however, verbatim remarks from audiotapes are acceptable. Specific patient responses—either spoken or written—are to be encouraged in order that the patient's and therapist's perceptions may be compared.

How are we to evaluate the adequacy of a psychotherapy case? The logicoscientific experimental approach is of minimal assistance. The alternative leads to what has been variously labeled narrative truth or hermeneutic-dialectical truth. It stresses meaning of experiences and their interpretation; it comes in the form of good stories, believable historical accounts, and a proper narrative fit (Messer, 1986).

Sherwood (1969, cited in Messer, 1986) offers three criteria to judge the adequacy of a narrative. The first, self-consistency, mandates that general statements should be consistent with each other. The second, coherence, requires a fit between the parts and the whole and a resolution of the apparent incongruities in the text that are to be understood. The third, comprehensiveness, is the extent to which the narrative account covers the ground. The method is hermeneutic (Westerman, 1986) insofar as it involves perceived meaning and disciplined subjectivity.

In addition, a psychotherapy case presentation should possess "an intelligent and reasonable quality" (Dewey, 1966). Fellow clinicians should be able to assess the potential curative nature of the process and positive outcomes of the work. An *eclectic* psychotherapy case presentation, moreover, should make explicit its systematic and prescriptive nature.

## CASES

Table 1 provides an overview of these 13 cases in terms of integrative approach, therapist names, therapy modalities, client description, presenting problems, and number of sessions. The cases are arranged alphabetically by author. Some readers may wish to order their reading on the basis of an alternative scheme, for example, by type of disorder, format of therapy, or length of treatment.

TABLE 1
An Overview of the 13 Cases

| Chap. Author(s) | Approach | Modalities | Clients | Presenting problems | # of sessions |
|---|---|---|---|---|---|
| 2 Beitman | Systematic technical eclecticism | Individual and marital | Adult female | Depression | 6 |
| 3 Beutler | Systematic eclectic psychotherapy | Individual | Adolescent female | Anger, depression, and narcolepsy | 28 |
| 4 Burlingame, Fuhriman, & Paul | Eclectic time-limited therapy | Individual | Adult female | Dependent stance and incestuous experiences | 10 |
| 5 Clarkin & Rosnick | Differential therapeutics | Individual | Adult female | Depressed mood and dependent features | 20 |
| 6 DiClemente | Transtheoretical therapy | Individual and marital | Adult male | Anxiety and authority problems | 13 |
| 7 Driscoll | Pragmatic psychotherapy | Family and individual | Blended family | Child management and family relations | 10 |
| 8 Dryden | Theoretically consistent eclecticism | Individual | Adult male | Lacks direction, social isolation | 17 |
| 9 Grebstein | Eclectic family therapy | Family and individual | Family (4 children) | Divorcing, multiproblem family | 30 |
| 10 Hart & Hart | Functional eclectic therapy | Group and individual | Psychotherapists in training | Various personal and professional | [a] |
| 11 Murgatroyd | Structural-phenomenological eclectic therapy | Individual | Adult female | Apathy depression | 8 |
| 12 Powell | Integrated behavior therapy and psychotherapy | Individual | Adult male | Performance anxiety | 14 |
| 13 Robertson | Radical eclecticism | Individual and marital | Adult male | Obsessions and generalized anxiety | 9 |
| 14 Steinfeld | TARET systems | Couples and individual | Middle-aged couple | Violence, infidelity, and mistrust | 17 |

[a] Varied according to group member.

The titles of these eclectic models reveal a great deal about their stated purposes and the state of contemporary eclecticism. Several authors (Beitman, Beutler) expressedly emphasize the notion of "systematic" eclecticism, as opposed to the unsystematic, seat-of-the-pants variant. Similarly, Dryden labels his approach "theoretically consistent" and Powell presents his as "integrated." Other contributors, like Driscoll and Hart, stress the bottom-line considerations of "pragmatic" and "functional," respectively. Still others have created novel titles (DiClemente's transtheoretical), intriguing acronyms (Steinfeld's TARET systems), and extreme positions (Robertson's radical eclecticism) to distinguish themselves from the garden-variety integrationism, which has acquired a negative valence in many professional circles.

To my mind, eclecticism refers to the integration of theoretical orientations/techniques *and* to the integration of therapy modalities. However, the former has overshadowed the latter within the professional literature. Efforts to combine individual and marital/family therapy are occurring increasingly at both the conceptual and practical levels. Feldman (1985) has identified four basic forms of this integration: (1) *individually oriented,* in which the predominant format is individual with family interviews being utilized to enhance individual treatment; (2) *family-oriented,* in which the predominant format is conjoint family with individual interviews being utilized to enhance family treatment; (3) *symmetrical,* in which individual and family interviews occur with equal frequency; and (4) *sequential,* in which one approach temporarily follows the other.

Six of the thirteen contributors to this volume combined therapy modalities in their psychotherapeutic work. In two cases (Driscoll, Grebstein), the integration was family-oriented; in three cases (Beitman, DiClemente, Robertson), the integration was individually oriented. In the remaining case (Steinfeld), the format arrangement tended to be symmetrical. In all cases, the same therapist conducted the individual and marital/family interviews.

The case presentations are largely concerned with outpatient treatment of adults. Of the nine individually oriented cases, five pertain to the treatment experiences of adolescent and adult women. The presenting problems run the gamut of common psychopathology, devoid of psychotic disturbances, and are primarily neurotic (nonpsychotic) and functional (nonorganic) in origin. All therapy, to my knowledge, was conducted on an outpatient basis.

Treatment length is multiply determined by numerous interacting forces. These include severity of the disorder, goals of therapy, setting for treatment, reimbursement for services, and the like. In addition, the length of treatment and selection of cases were probably influenced by the Case Guidelines (e.g., recommended duration of 5 to 25 sessions) and pragmatic considerations (such as preparation of transcripts). The reported number of sessions ranged from 6 to 30 and averaged 15. Though somewhat restricted by nonclinical factors, this number is nonetheless consistent with the length of psychotherapeutic services in the private sector. Similar estimates have been proffered by Taube, Burns, and Kessler (1984) for office based visits ($M = 12.5$), by Koss (1979, 1980) for private clinic appointments ($M = 13$), and by Norcross, Nash, and Prochaska (1985) for the number of sessions in independent practice ($M = 15$).

Having now read and reviewed these cases on numerous occasions, I am struck by several recurring themes. For one, there is a venerable potpourri of innovative interventions throughout these cases. They undeniably employ multiple theories, techniques, and modalities. For another, all treatment is unavoidably rooted in and based on an *interpersonal* relationship. These patients' written reactions, like most retrospective accounts of therapy (Gurman, 1977; Strupp, Fox, & Lessler, 1969), highlight the importance of the real relationship and the therapeutic alliance. The comments also reiterate the need for a description of psychotherapy offered to clients. Whether this goes by the name of role induction, expectation enhancement, or formal contract, explaining the nature of treatment is a human and therapeutic move.

Another lesson: psychotherapists need schemes to organize and prioritize the clinical material. Single theories reduce the information load considerably, but this advantage is lost when melding multiple theories. Beitman (Chapter 2) and Burlingame et al. (Chapter 4) emphasize treatment stages, DiClemente (Chapter 6) and Steinfeld (Chapter 14) emphasize levels of change, and Beutler (Chapter 3) and Clarkin and Rosnick (Chapter 5) emphasize the patient's personality style.

The contributors experienced marked difficulty in fully operationalizing their decision-making processes. We still rely largely on unarticulated, perhaps unconscious, rules for determining whether we "turn right or left" in the therapeutic arena. Dryden (1984, 1986), for example, outlines five major clinical decisions in any given case: selection of modalities, establishment of the therapeutic alliance, construction of frameworks to account for client variation, integration of various treatments interventions, and appreciation of changing therapeutic processes over time. Likewise, Frances, Clarkin, & Perry (1984; Perry, Frances, & Clarkin, 1986) organize their "differential therapeutics" around the choices of treatment setting, format (modality), orientation, duration, and frequency.

These clinical cases are presented not as models of perfection to mimic, but as examples of fallible reasoning from which to profit. As in clinical pursuits, "coping models" are likely to be more acceptable and effective than "mastery models." John Dewey wrote (1966, p. 225) that "the method of science means 'emancipation,' it means reason operates within experience, not beyond it, to give it an intelligent and reasonable quality." This might be a motto for all psychotherapies: "an intelligent and reasonable quality."

In this context, my reading of the case commentaries leads me to conclude that they tended to be overly critical of incomplete eclectic models and fallible human practitioners. It is not, of course, our intention to disguise problems or to deny the existence of uncertainty. Nonetheless, our collective impatience with eclectic growth produces, in my judgment, premature criticisms.

This impertinent attitude toward psychological knowledge was eloquently described by Freud (1933/1965, p. 6):

No reader of an account of astronomy will feel disappointed and contemptuous of science if he is shown the frontiers at which our knowledge of the universe melts into haziness. Only in psychology is it otherwise. There, mankind's constitutional unfitness for scientific research comes fully into the open. What people seem to demand of psychology is not progress in knowledge, but satisfactions of some other sort; every unsolved problem, every admitted uncertainty is made into a reproach against it.

Humans possess a nasty penchant for denigrating those who are most open and courageous in sharing their work. I have found psychotherapists to be of no exception in professional matters. If we were to critically evaluate our clients' vulnerabilities as harshly as those of our colleagues, few clinical practices would survive.

Nothing here should be interpreted as condemning critical evaluations and constructive criticism of nascent integrative/eclectic models of psychotherapy. Progress relies on research and reevaluation, and this *Casebook* represents a commitment to such progress. Still, we should heed Freud's (1933/1965, p. 6) warning that "whoever cares for the science of mental life must accept these injustices along with it."

## GROWING PAINS OF ECLECTICISM

Sibling rivalry among theoretical orientations has a long and undistinguished history in psychotherapy. In the infancy of the field, therapy systems, like battling siblings, competed for attention and affection. Clinicians traditionally operated from within their own particular theoretical frameworks, often to the point of being blind to alternative conceptualizations and interventions (Goldfried, 1982b). Mutual antipathy and exchange of puerile insults between adherents of rival orientations were very much the order of the day.

Perhaps these conflicts were a necessary precursor to sophisticated, mature eclecticism. Kuhn (1970) described this period as a preparadigmatic crisis. Feyerabend (1970, p. 209) concluded that "the interplay between tenacity and proliferation is an essential feature in the actual development of science. It seems that it is not the puzzle-solving activity that is responsible for the growth of our knowledge, but the active interplay of various tenaciously held views."

Amid this strife and bewilderment, a therapeutic "underground" slowly emerged (Wachtel, 1977). Though not associated with any particular school and not detailed in the literature, the underground reflected an unofficial consensus of what experienced clinicians believed to be true. Adventuresome clinicians gradually employed strategies and modalities found successful without regard for theoretical origin.

On personal and organizational levels, eclecticism now seeks to define itself like the emerging child. Few universal rules exist, and identity is transitory. Under external pressure, such as a difficult therapy case or a theory-aligned convention, we can succumb to strong regressive pulls back to theoretical purity. Oh, how we can long for the simplicity of one-theory, one-modality psychotherapy!

Integrative theory is rapidly outpacing practice (Prochaska, this volume) and training (Norcross, 1986). How we think and feel about therapy precedes how we practice therapy. Such is the contemporary state of systematic eclectic psychotherapy. And as Prochaska (this volume) aptly notes, changing our therapy practice requires taking action and maintaining this action lest we slip back into old habit patterns.

The integration of therapies, techniques, and modalities *is* a demanding, some would say an overwhelming, task. Thorne (1973) insisted that true eclectics are competent in *all* available forms of clinical intervention; only such a highly skilled and experienced therapist can possess the flexibility to be therapeutic for all clients. Lazarus (1967, p. 415) incredulously inquired, "Who, even in a life-time of endeavor, can hope to encompass such a diverse and multifarious range of thought and theory?"

The expanding demands and boundaries of eclecticism raise profound questions. These demands challenge our tenative identity, test our human limits, and force a reevaluation of our goals. Following are representative questions with which I struggle.

- *How shall we identify ourselves?*

Perhaps as "eclectics," perhaps as "integrationists," or to avoid semantic confusion and ambivalent connotations, a new term derived from Latin or Greek. The issue runs deeper than titles, of course. How shall we feel about this new identity? A coherent identity (the me) requires repudiation of other roles (the not-me), be it psychoanalyst, behaviorist, existentialist, *ad nauseam.*

• *Must eclectic practitioners be competent in all theories, techniques, and modalities?*

A literal computation of all treatment possibilities staggers the imagination. One could make conservative estimates of 10 established theories, 100 interventions, and three modalities (individual, marital/family, group). The resulting combinations (10 × 100 × 3) would be 3,000 possible treatments! The delineation of a central and finite set of change principles or an enumeration of common interventions would reduce the magnitude of the enterprise dramatically.

• *How many interventions or modalities can be integrated profitably within one brief psychotherapy case?*

Several commentators point out that "more is not necessarily better" (Wilson, 1982). An inordinate number or mistimed combination of therapy practices can disrupt the flow and detract from priority goals. A delicate balance must be maintained between therapeutic flexibility and treatment continuity.

• *How do we empirically select among competing treatments?*

Pioneering efforts to operationalize and codify the clinical decision-making processes are underway (see Frances, Clarkin, & Perry, 1984). Comparative outcome research has been, at best, a limited source of direction with regard to selection of specific conceptualizations and interventions. If our empirical research has little to say and if collective clinical experience has divergent things to say, then who is to say do A, not B? We may again be guided by selective perception and personal preference, a situation eclecticism seeks to eliminate.

• *Where is the hard evidence that eclectic psychotherapy is more effective than noneclectic psychotherapy?*

That is a very good question.

In closing, I firmly believe we need a "developmental" understanding of the status of eclectic psychotherapy, that is, to interpret the virtues and limitations of eclecticism within a developmental context. The field, though growing rapidly, is bound by its age, environment, and identity. The answers to these troublesome questions are the ultimate goals of eclecticism; the mediating goals are to explore the possibilities.

## REFERENCES

Arkowitz, H., & Messer, S. B. (Eds.) (1984). *Psychoanalytic and behavior therapy: Is integration possible?* New York: Plenum.

Barlow, D. H. (1981). On the relation of clinical research to clinical practice: Current issues, new directions. *Journal of Consulting and Clinical Psychology, 49,* 147–155.

Beitman, B. D. (1986). *The structure of individual psychotherapy.* New York: Guilford Press.

Berger, L. S. (1985). *Psychoanalytic theory and clinical relevance.* New York: The Analytic Press.

Beutler, L. E. (1983). *Eclectic psychotherapy: A systematic approach.* New York: Pergamon Press.

Bonime, F., & Bonime, W. (1978). Psychoanalytic writing: An essay on communication. *Journal of the American Academy of Psychoanalysis, 6,* 381–393.

Brady, J. P., Davison, G. C., Dewald, P. A., Egan, G., Fadiman, J., Frank, J. D., Gill, M. M., Hoffman, I., Kempler, W., Lazarus, A. A., Raimy, V., Rotter, J. B., & Strupp, H. H. (1980). Some views on effective principles of psychotherapy. *Cognitive Therapy and Research, 4,* 271–306.

Brammer, L. M., and Shostrom, E. L. (1982). *Therapeutic psychology: Fundamentals of counseling and psychotherapy* (4th ed.). Englewood Cliffs, NJ: Prentice-Hall.

Butler, S. F., & Strupp, H. H. (In press). Specific and nonspecific factors in psychotherapy: A problematic paradigm for psychotherapy research. *American Psychologist.*

Clark, H. B., Wadden, T. A., Brownell, K. D., Gordon, S. G., & Tarte, R. D. (1983). Sources of continuing education for behavior therapists: The utility of journals, conferences, and other informational sources. *The Behavior Therapist, 6,* 23–26.

Cooper, S., & Wanerman, L. (1984). *A casebook of child psychotherapy.* New York: Brunner/Mazel.

Dewey, J. (1966). *Democracy and education.* New York: The Free Press.

Dimond, R. E., & Havens, R. A. (1975). Restructuring psychotherapy: Toward a prescriptive eclecticism. *Professional Psychology, 6,* 193–200.

Dowd, E.T., & Healy, J.M. (Eds.) (1985). *Case studies in hypnotherapy.* New York: Guilford.

Driscoll, R. (1984). *Pragmatic psychotherapy.* New York: Van Nostrand Reinhold.

Dryden, W. (1984). Issues in the eclectic practice of individual therapy. In W. Dryden (Ed.), *Individual therapy in Britain.* London: Harper & Row.

Dryden, W. (1986). Eclectic psychotherapies: A critique of leading approaches. In J. C. Norcross (Ed.), *Handbook of eclectic psychotherapy.* New York: Brunner/Mazel.

Elliott, R. (1983). Fitting process research to the practicing psychotherapist. *Psychotherapy: Theory, Research and Practice, 20,* 47–55.

Eysenck, H. J. (1970). A mish-mash of theories. *International Journal of Psychiatry, 9,* 140–146.

Feldman, L. B. (1985). Integrating individual and family therapy. *SEPI Newsletter, 3*(2), 9.

Feyerabend, P. (1970). Consolations for the specialist. In I. Lakatos & A. E. Musgrave (Eds.), *Criticism and the growth of knowledge.* Cambridge: Cambridge University Press.

Frances, A., Clarkin, J., & Perry, S. (1984). *Differential therapeutics in psychiatry.* New York: Brunner/Mazel.

Freud, S. (1905/1963). *An analysis of a case of hysteria.* New York: Collier Books.

Freud, S. (1933/1965). *New introductory lectures on psychoanalysis* (James Strachey, trans.). New York: Norton.

Garfield, S. L., & Kurtz, R. (1976). Clinical psychologists in the 1970's. *American Psychologist, 31,* 1–9.

Garfield, S. L., & Kurtz, R. (1977). A study of eclectic views. *Journal of Consulting and Clinical Psychology, 45,* 78–83.

Garfield, S. L. (1980). *Psychotherapy: An eclectic approach.* New York: John Wiley & Sons.

Garfield, S. L. (1982). Eclecticism and integration in psychotherapy. *Behavior Therapy, 13,* 610–623.

Goldfried, M. R. (1980). Toward the delineation of therapeutic change principles. *American Psychologist, 35,* 991–999.

Goldfried, M. R. (1982a). On the history of therapeutic integration. *Behavior Therapy, 13,* 572–593.

Goldfried, M. R. (Ed.) (1982b). *Converging themes in psychotherapy.* New York: Springer.

Goldfried, M. R., & Newman, C. (1986). Psychotherapy integration: An historical perspective. In J. C. Norcross (Ed.), *Handbook of eclectic psychotherapy.* New York: Brunner/Mazel.

Goldfried, M. R., & Safran, J. D. (1986). Future directions in psychotherapy integration. In J. C. Norcross (Ed.), *Handbook of eclectic psychotherapy.* New York: Brunner/Mazel.

Goldstein, A. P., & Stein, N. (1976). *Prescriptive psychotherapies.* New York: Pergamon.

Greenwald, H. (Ed.) (1959). *Great cases in psychoanalysis.* New York: Ballantine Books.

Gurman, A. S. (1977). The patient's perception of the therapeutic relationship. In A. S. Gurman & A. M. Razin (Eds.), *Effective psychotherapy* (pp. 503–543). New York: Pergamon.

Gurman, A. S. (Ed.) (1985). *Casebook of marital therapy.* New York: Guilford.

Hariman, J. (Ed.) (1986). *Prescriptive psychotherapy.* Springfield, IL: Charles Thomas.

Hart, J. (1983). *Modern eclectic therapy: A functional orientation to counseling and psychotherapy.* New York: Plenum.

Held, B. S. (1984). Toward a strategic eclecticism: A proposal. *Psychotherapy, 21,* 232–241.

Jayaratne, S. (1978). A study of clinical eclecticism. *Social Service Review, 52,* 621–631.

Kendall, P. C. (1982). Integration: Behavior therapy and other schools of thought. *Behavior Therapy, 13,* 559–571.

Koss, M. P. (1979). Length of psychotherapy for clients seen in private practice. *Journal of Consulting and Clinical Psychology, 47,* 210–212.

Koss, M. P. (1980). Descriptive characteristics and length of psychotherapy of child and adult clients seen in private psychological practice. *Psychotherapy: Theory, Research and Practice, 17,* 268–271.

Kuhn, T. S. (1970). *The structure of scientific revolutions.* (2nd ed.). Chicago: University of Chicago Press.

Larson, D. (1980). Therapeutic schools, styles, and schoolism: A national survey. *Journal of Humanistic Psychology, 20,* 3–20.

Lazarus, A. A. (1967). In support of technical eclecticism. *Psychological Reports, 21,* 415–416.

Lazarus, A. A. (1977). Has behavior therapy outlived its usefulness? *American Psychologist, 32,* 550–554.

Lazarus, A. A. (1981). *The practice of multimodal therapy.* Hightstown, NJ: McGraw-Hill.

Lazarus, A. A. (Ed.) (1985). *Casebook of multimodal therapy.* New York: Guilford.

Loew, C. A. (1975). Remarks on integrating psychotherapeutic techniques. *Psychotherapy: Theory, Research and Practice, 12,* 241–242.

London, P. (1972). The end of ideology in behavior modification. *American Psychologist, 27,* 913–920.

London, P. (1986). *The modes and morals of psychotherapy* (2nd ed.). New York: Hemisphere Publishing.

Luborsky, L. (1972). Research cannot yet influence clinical practice. In A. Bergin and H. Strupp (Eds.), *Changing frontiers in the science of psychotherapy* (pp. 120–127). Chicago: Aldine.

Mann, J., & Goldman, R. (1982). *A casebook in time-limited psychotherapy.* New York: McGraw-Hill.

Marcus, S. (1977). Freud and Dora: Story, history, case history. In T. Shapiro (Ed.), *Psychoanalysis and contemporary science* (Vol. 5). New York: International Universities Press.

Marmor, J., & Woods, S. M. (Eds.) (1980). *The interface between the psychodynamic and behavioral therapies*. New York: Plenum.

Maultsby, M. C. (1968). Against technical eclecticism. *Psychological Reports, 22*, 926–928.

Messer, S. B. (1986). Eclecticism in psychotherapy: Underlying assumptions, problems, and tradeoffs. In J. C. Norcross (Ed.), *Handbook of eclectic psychotherapy*. New York: Brunner/Mazel.

Morrow-Bradley, C., & Elliott, R. (In press). Utilization of psychotherapy research by practicing psychotherapists. *American Psychologist*.

Murray, E. J. (1983). Beyond behavioral and dynamic therapy. *British Journal of Clinical Psychology, 27*, 127–128.

Norcross, J. C. (1985). Eclecticism: Definitions, manifestations, and practitioners. *International Journal of Eclectic Psychotherapy, 4*, 19–32.

Norcross, J. C. (1986a). Eclectic psychotherapy: An introduction and overview. In J. C. Norcross (Ed.), *Handbook of eclectic psychotherapy*. New York: Brunner/Mazel.

Norcross, J. C. (Ed.) (1986b). *Handbook of eclectic psychotherapy*. New York: Brunner/Mazel.

Norcross, J. C., & Prochaska, J. O. (1982a). A national survey of clinical psychologists: Characteristics and activities. *The Clinical Psychologist, 35*(2), 1–8.

Norcross, J. C., & Prochaska, J. O. (1982b). A national survey of clinical psychologists: Views on training, career choice, and APA. *The Clinical Psychologist, 35*(4), 1–6.

Norcross, J. C., et al. (1986). Training integrative/eclectic psychotherapists. *International Journal of Eclectic Psychotherapy, 5*(1).

Norcross, J. C., Nash, J., & Prochaska, J. O. (1985). Psychologists in part-time independent practice: Description and comparison. *Professional Psychology: Research and Practice, 6*, 565–575.

Palmer, J. E. (1980). *A primer of eclectic psychotherapy*. Monterey, CA: Brooks/Cole.

Papp, P. (Ed.) (1977). *Family therapy: Full length case studies*. New York: Gardner Press.

Parloff, M. B. (1980). Psychotherapy and research: An anaclitic depression. *Psychiatry, 43*, 279–293.

Perry, S., Frances, A., & Clarkin, J. (1986). *A DSM-III casebook of differential therapeutics: A clinical guide to treatment selection*. New York: Brunner/Mazel.

Peterfreund, E. (1971). Information, systems, and psychoanalysis. *Psychological Issues*, Monographs 25–26.

Prochaska, J. O., & DiClemente, C. C. (1984). *The transtheoretical approach: Crossing the traditional boundaries of therapy*. Homewood, IL: Dow Jones-Irvin.

Prochaska, J. O., & Norcross, J. C. (1982). The future of psychotherapy: A Delphi poll. *Professional Psychology, 13*, 620–627.

Prochaska, J. O., & Norcross, J. C. (1983). Contemporary psychotherapists: A national survey of characteristics, practices, orientations, and attitudes. *Psychotherapy: Theory, Research, and Practice, 20*, 161–173.

Rice, L. N., & Greenberg, L. (Eds.) (1984). *Patterns of change*. New York: Guilford.

Robertson, M. (1979). Some observations from an eclectic therapist. *Psychotherapy: Theory, Research and Practice, 16*, 18–21.

Sargent, M., & Cohen, L. H. (1983). Influence of psychotherapy on clinical practice: An experimental survey. *Journal of Consulting and Clinical Psychology, 51*, 718–720.

Schafer, R. (1976). *A new language for psychoanalysis*. New Haven, CT: Yale University Press.

Schafer, R. (1983). *The analytic attitude*. New York: Basic Books.

Schontz, F.C., & Rosenak, C.M. (1985). Models for clinically relevant research. *Professional Psychology: Research and Practice, 16*, 296–304.

Sherwood, M. (1969). *The logic of explanation in psychoanalysis*. New York: Academic Press.

Simon, R. M. (1974). On eclecticism. *American Journal of Psychiatry, 131*, 135–139.

Smith, D. S. (1982). Trends in counseling and psychotherapy. *American Psychologist, 37*, 802–809.

Spence, D. P. (1982). *Narrative truth and historical truth*. New York: W. W. Norton.

Spence, D. P. (1984, August). When interpretation masquerades as explanation. Paper presented to the American Psychological Association.

Strupp, H.H. (1981). Clinical research, practice, and the crisis of confidence. *Journal of Consulting and Clinical Psychology, 49*, 216–219.

Strupp, H. H. (1982). The outcome problem in psycho-therapy: Contemporary perspectives. In J. H. Harvey & M. M. Parks (Eds.), *Master Lecture Series*, Vol. I. Washington, D.C.: American Psychological Association.

Strupp, H. H., Fox, R. E., & Lessler, K. (1969). *Patients view their psychotherapy*. Baltimore: Johns Hopkins Press.

Taube, C. A., Burns, B. J., & Kessler, L. (1984). Patients of psychiatrists and psychologists in office-based practice: 1980. *American Psychologist, 39*, 1435–1447.

Thorne, F. C. (1973). Eclectic psychotherapy. In R. Corsini (Ed.), *Current psychotherapies* (1st ed.). Itasca, IL: Peacock.

Wachtel, P. L. (1977). *Psychoanalysis and behavior therapy: Toward an integration*. New York: Basic Books.

Wachtel, P. L. (1982). What can dynamic therapies contribute to behavior therapy? *Behavior Therapy, 13*, 594–609.

Wedding, D., & Corsini, R. J. (Eds.) (1979). *Great cases in psychotherapy*. Itasca, IL: Peacock.

Weiner, I. B. (1975). *Principles of psychotherapy*. New York: Wiley.

Westerman, M. A. (1986). Meaning in psychotherapy: A hermeneutic reconceptualization of insight-oriented, behavioral and systems approaches. *International Journal of Eclectic Psychotherapy, 5*(1), 47–68.

Wilson, G. T. (1982). Psychotherapy process and procedure: The behavioral mandate. *Behavior Therapy, 13*, 291–312.

Yates, A. J. (1983). Behavior therapy and psychodynamic therapy: Basic conflict or reconciliation and integration? *British Journal of Clinical Psychology, 22*, 107–125.

CHAPTER 2

# Systematic Technical Eclecticism: Two Depressive Episodes Treated with Very Brief Psychotherapy

*Bernard D. Beitman*

## INTRODUCTORY COMMENTS

*Systematic Eclecticism and Integration*

The movement toward bringing together the conflicting schools of psychotherapy has currently advanced to a point at which two different terms are being used to characterize it. Some call themselves integrationists by which they imply an attempt to meld the warring factions into a cooperative and harmonious whole. Others call themselves systematic eclectics, implying that they are offering a scheme by which diverse approaches may come to bear in the decision-making processes facing each practicing psychotherapist. The apparent conflict in these terms seems to derive from their different intents. Integration is a political and ideological term intended to reduce conflict by recognizing commonality of purpose among diverse groups. It is a call equally well applied to warring religious and to warring political-economic factions throughout the world. There is much to be gained by recognizing common pursuits and interests as well as common means cloaked in differently colored rhetoric.

Systematic eclecticism, on the other hand, implies a more practical approach. It is concerned with the means by which valued results can be reached. Systematic eclectics offer schemes and models by which the contributions from the various schools may be organized for a more rational, more effective psychotherapy.

The intent of both integrationists and systematic eclectics may be very similar. Integrationists pave the way by knocking down ideological barriers with attacks on ideological rigidity, and systematic eclectics provide the alternative means. Ultimately, the result will not be an integration or a systematic eclecticism but rather a clear, usable definition of the psychotherapeutic enterprise.

*The Stages of Individual Psychotherapy*

I have attempted to fulfill the purpose of integration through the stages of psychotherapy. This basic notion provides the outline of a scheme for systematic eclecticism. It is, hopefully, a way to describe psychotherapy that subsumes the schools (Beitman, 1986). Stages provide contexts by which to judge objectives and methods by which these objectives can be reached. The stages may be defined by their objectives: engagement, pattern search, change, and termination.

The objectives of the engagement stage include the building of trust, the formation of a self-observer alliance, and the raising of hope that the therapist is competent to be of assistance. Each of the many schools offers a set of techniques by which these goals may be reached, but there is little evidence that therapists should be restricted to one set. Empathic reception is commonly used across therapies, but trial interpretations are confined to psychoanalytic approaches and relaxation training to behavioral approaches. For some clients either one or both may be useful for accomplishing the goals of the engagement stage.

The objective of the pattern search is elucidation and specification of psychological patterns that, if changed, would bring desired relief and promote enduring change. The content of the pattern search is most variable because the major differences among the schools of therapy lie with their theories of psychopathology and theories of personality development. Some say look to childhood; some say look to underlying attitudes; others say monitor environmental contingencies; still others want to observe patterns of affective expression. Many approaches overlap in their interest in those enduring aspects of human behavior enveloped by the term personality or character style. Therapists tend to be interested in how their patients interact with significant others, including the therapists themselves.

The methods by which information is sought in the pattern search are far more limited. Besides standardized questionnaires, therapists use various forms of listening and questioning to understand how their patients are functioning and what needs to be changed. Therapists may listen to patients as if they are speakers of metaphors, as if their daily speech was a kind of dream production in which utterances are multilayered communications about others and also about the therapist. Patients may also be understood as research assistants, as fellow detectives, trying to comprehend their external reality. They are reporters whose descriptions are taken at face value under the therapist's assumption that significant gaps must be filled. Finally, therapists may listen to their clients as if they are fellow travelers on the road of life—people searching to be experienced, to be understood, to be felt, people wanting to reach and be touched by the existence of another. From this perspective, listening provides access to the inner world of the other, which, for a few minutes, might lead to a community of mood.

In addition to many forms of questions, therapists use homework assignments to gather information. Dream diaries bring the daily unconscious into the therapist's office. Diaries of automatic thoughts bring daily thinking more sharply into view (Beck et al., 1979). Behavioral diaries give rapid, somewhat objective, views of target behaviors. Role playing, hypnosis, interviews with significant others, and direct observation in the environment each carries a different potential for yielding useful information. The therapist's task during the pattern search is to find the most effective means to bring about specification of the patterns to be changed.

The third stage, which is change, appears to have three substages: responsibility awareness, the initiation of change, and the practice (working through) of change. Each of these stages is not necessarily traversed for every patient. Milton Erickson (1976), for example, delighted in not having his patients know what they had been doing to keep themselves dysfunctional, nor did he seem to require that his patients practice their newly initiated changes. Many therapists, however, seem to lead their patients through this sequence. Some techniques seem to be useful for the general sequence (placebo response, desire to please the therapist); some are useful for each of the substages of change (interpretations, exhortation); and some are particularly useful for only one substage. For example, demonstration of repeated patterns is an excellent technique for raising responsibility awareness for psychological dysfunction. In the office, practice is useful for initiating change outside of the office, and behavioral homework is useful during the practice substage.

Techniques appear to offer the means by which therapists can convey their messages to patients about better values and better coping. Although some therapists might hope they are practicing value-free psychotherapy, successful psychotherapy seems to be marked by the convergence of therapist and patient beliefs (Strong, 1978; Beutler, 1983).

Termination is perhaps the most predictable stage since it involves the universal experience of separation for which there are a limited number of forms. The pair can mutually agree; one can initiate it; or it may be forced by circumstances outside the control of each of them. Grief and the desire to avoid the loss are common responses from both participants.

After therapy is ended, the question of maintenance of change and its continuation is raised. In this area, psychotherapy research has ventured very little, but it will become increasingly more important as the practice of psychotherapy receives increasingly more scrutiny by third-party payers.

Each stage seems also to have characteristic interpersonal and process distortions. Resistance or blocks to therapeutic movement appears universal in psychotherapy whether it is psychodynamic or behavioral or humanistic. Unfortunately, labels are ideologically laden and are difficult to apply universally. I use the terms resistance, transference, and countertransference, but others may choose different terms for similar phenomena. For example, some family therapists may ask supervisees, "How does your family of origin influence your responses to this patient?" rather than use the term countertransference.

## Therapist Personal Beliefs

Therapists' tendency to choose responses based on idiosyncratic experiences and values is an understudied element of the psychotherapeutic experience. This description of psychotherapy is no exception. Although the foregoing outline is fairly generic, it is biased toward time and toward process. My background as a therapist is a liberal arts education in a variety of psychotherapy approaches with little formal training in any one of them. I read George Kelly (1955) when I was in college and have remained deeply impressed with the variety of ways there are to look at any given phenomenon. I was deeply touched by Freud and his followers during my medical training, both very positively and very negatively. I had one series of psychoanalytic seminars and one six-month period of psychoanalytically oriented psychotherapy. I became convinced that what I had seen and heard about psychoanalysis was insufficient for an effective practice of psychotherapy. Football and baseball showed me the value of behavioral practice. The pain of the life around me, mystical and religious studies introduced me to existential concerns. I have therefore been open to many different contributions to psychotherapeutic change.

Some therapists come to the integrationist movement from a psychoanalytic base; others are behavioral systematic eclectics. Still others are their own types of therapists trying to find the best blend of theory and technique. We need to respect these differences while at the same time drawing an outline of the boundaries of what psychotherapy is and what it is not. I believe that there is much poor therapy going on in the United States and other Western countries under the name of professional services. A certain variance must also be respected and understood to point the way to future developments and to allow for individual differences among therapists. But some basic, expectable elements should characterize most effective psychotherapeutic relationships. In presenting the transcripts from the case of Mrs. D. G., I hope to show the reader how my personal approach blends with the general definition of psychotherapy described here.

## MRS. D. G.

D. G. first came for psychotherapy in November 1982 at age 51 following the suggestion of her oncologist. He believed that she was depressed and in need of psychiatric treatment. She had her second mastectomy in July 1982; the first was in 1974. In 1972, she had a hysterectomy. Mrs. G. was divorced in 1973 after discovering that her husband was having an affair. She had three children from that marriage who at the time of the initial interview were age 25 (male), age 22 (female), and age 18 (male). The youngest was living at home. She had been married to Mr. G. for four years. He too had been divorced once. She was short and moderately overweight. During the first interview she was very talkative. She demonstrated her depression with occasional bursts of sadness and crying during the interview. Her excessive talkativeness also seemed to be a cover for the depression.

## TREATMENT OVERVIEW

I saw Mrs. G. twice during November 1982. The first session lasted more than 45 minutes (and was not tape-recorded in its entirety since I did not turn the tape over when it ran out). The second session lasted about 15 minutes since we both felt that she was no longer in need of treatment. I saw her four times in December 1984, each for approximately 50 minutes. Her husband was present during the entire second session and for half of the third and fourth sessions. We terminated because she was much improved but also because we were both leaving Seattle in January 1985. She sent me follow-up letters in 1984 and 1985.

Her Beck Depression Inventory Scores for each of her sessions were as follows:

11/5/82—27

11/10/82—Not done but within normal range

11/16/84—40

12/5/84—45

12/12/84—23

12/19/84—13

I saw her as part of a small outpatient practice (between 6 and 12 patient visits per week).

I selected this case because at the time I was asked to contribute to this *Casebook*, I had only this tape available. I had presented it as part of a seminar on cognitive therapy led by Steve Hollon, Ph.D. After

I decided to use it, the patient returned for a second round of psychotherapy.

I have interspersed the dialogue with comments reflecting my own thinking *and* details of the interview lending themselves to succinct expression. These additions are enclosed in brackets.

## PART 1

*11/5/82*

T: Did you have any trouble finding it?
P: No, I just went to the Information Desk, and she told me exactly how to get here.
T: Dr. A. referred you. I wonder, did he give you any idea about what I did?
[I want to know her conception of me.]
P: He said, I think he said that you specialized in counseling cancer patients. I mean that is one field that you are active in. Is that right?
[I believed she felt my reputation was positive.]
T: That's right. I wonder if you have any expectations about what counseling is like?
[I want to get her explanatory model for therapy.]
P: Oh, yeah. I've never been. Matter of fact it really bothers me that I feel that I have to come. That bothers me, because I can't seem to cope with my problems.
T: It bothers you to . . .
P: To say that I have to come to see, to get help. That bothers me.
T: What is it that you say to yourself?
[I introduce a key cognitive therapy question.]
P: Why can't I take care of myself? I mean, why can't I bring myself out of this, these feelings that I have, and why do I have to be so emotional now? I never used to be.
[She takes easily to examining her own thoughts.]
T: So when you say to yourself, "Why can't I do this myself?" what kind of feelings do you have?
[I introduce the connection between thoughts and feelings.]
P: I get very upset with myself. Because I feel inadequate to cope with my problems.
T: And when you feel inadequate to cope with your problems, it makes you upset? And how does your upset come out?
P: Oh, I get angry. I'm very short tempered now and I have a son that's home all the time now, he's unemployed. He's really a good kid, he's very thoughtful of his mother. But, I find that I'm always snapping at him, and I don't mean to.
T: You don't mean to, but you're always snapping at him.
P: I'll just get my breakfast things cleaned up, my kitchen cleaned up, then he comes in and starts having some breakfast and this irritates me. Because I'm not used to having anybody at home in the daytime except myself. He's been home for about a year and a half, maybe not even that. But I enjoy being home. I don't like somebody else around disrupting my routine.
T: Okay, when you see him come into the kitchen, to get his breakfast after you've cleaned it up, what thoughts go on in your mind?
P: I generally will walk out and I'll say, "Clean up your mess, I've already cleaned up the kitchen." He'll take them from the counter and put them in the sink.
T: That's what you say to him, but there's more going on in your mind.
P: Oh, I think I probably just wish that he wasn't there because he's not happy being home either. He'd rather be out working.
T: So, when you see him come into the kitchen, there are a number of thoughts that come into your mind. Like, maybe, you're not always aware of them, but "I wish he weren't here," "I wish he

were working," "I wish I were alone."
P: Uh huh. I like to choose the times I want to be with people, and basically I've always been able to handle being alone very easily, especially when I was working. To me every night I came home to an empty house was a real treat. Because I enjoyed that.
T: So when you see him come in, you say to yourself, "I don't like having someone else intruding on my time, my privacy. I don't like this." So you get mad at him for, even though you shouldn't, for intruding on your privacy.
P: Yeah, I'll snap at him for little things, and my daughter doesn't live at home anymore, but she stops by, oh, about three or four times a week and has lunch on her lunch hour, because she just works down the hill from me. And, even though I enjoy her, we've always gotten along, but he no sooner gets through with his breakfast and then she pops in, and I don't mean I wait on her, but she just helps herself. But for about two hours there, or longer, I've got all these bodies in my kitchen. When I'm used to being in the kitchen by myself. It just . . . I don't say anything too much. I just get irritable.
T: Do you know why you don't say anything very much?
P: Well, I don't know, I wasn't really aware that they were the ones that were actually doing this to me. I would just feel irritable. But I didn't want to hurt their feelings, they hadn't done anything wrong.
[She appears to recognize that talking can bring understanding.]

We discussed her guilt for not working. I was once again able to point out a possible connection between her thoughts and uncomfortable feelings. I then tried to summarize our discussion to that point.

T: What I've tried to show you in this first 5 or 10 minutes here, is something about the kind of questions that I'll ask you, the kind of ways that counseling might help you. Trying to define and unearth the thoughts that you may not be quite aware of in your mind, but still influence the way you behave and the way you feel and the thoughts about your children coming into the kitchen and invading your privacy. Kind of you knew that, but it made it a little clearer to you that you don't want them there because you don't want your privacy invaded.

By this point we were well engaged: I had a positive reputation; she was motivated to participate; she responded well to the cognitive model of therapy I had quickly introduced. She seemed to gain a partial insight concerning the cause of a recurring irritable feeling. I asked her to tell me the history of her current cancer difficulties. She had a second mastectomy in July 1981. The bone scan suggested metastasis to her ribs and skull. Her husband called for the results.

P: I remember my husband called one day and asked the results. Now there's always been this confusion. My husband thinks maybe he heard wrong, but he called me and said, everything's okay. I just talked to Dr. A., and the tests are all negative. I kept saying, "You're kidding, you're kidding." I mean, I couldn't believe that. I didn't feel that good either, and I couldn't figure out how can I feel this way and yet everything's okay. Well, then about three days later, I had to come to see Dr. A. When we came in, we found out that the last slice they took, evidently on this lesion, was positive. So, we didn't find out until we walked in the office that the first diagnosis was right. So I did have metastatic breast cancer, and I just sat there and I looked at my husband and he looked at me and I'm thinking, "You knew all the time."* You know, just these horrible thoughts went through my mind. But we were just both in such a state of shock that I didn't get emotionally upset or cry or like that because I couldn't believe . . . I was just shocked. I had one x ray in December [1981] and it showed exactly the same as the one I'd had in August 1981, which was still good because it hadn't spread any more. And then when I had one in June [1982], six months later, if I hadn't seen those x rays with my own eyes, I wouldn't believe. Like the radiologist said, "You can't tell which is the healthy body. I mean, if you looked at these x rays, you would think it was the body of a healthy person because there is not a mark on them." And, I mean, I was in shock. Really, I just couldn't believe it.

I proceeded to specify her symptoms of depression. She had been overeating, felt as if she could never be full, and had gained 17 pounds in 10 weeks. She felt as she often had during her period—very tense and irritable. She was often unable to get to sleep and not uncommonly woke up to urinate but could not go back to sleep. She was taking a diuretic and an anticancer medication (temoxifin). Later in the hour she described extreme fatigue and lack of enjoyment in activities that usually pleased her. How many of these symptoms could be attributed to occult cancer, to her chemotherapy, and to her depression may be difficult to say. Nevertheless, I felt she should be considered to have a moderate major affective episode. She then indicated to me her resiliency and initiative by describing how she went to Alaska with her husband during one of his trips and, rather than sit around the motel all day, got herself a volunteer job. They thought she was great.

T: Why don't you tell me about your depression.
P: Well, like I said, I don't really know what makes me this way, but I do know that I got more depressed when my husband called the other night and said that he won't be home now until Tuesday, when I expected him home tonight. I was upset, and I get depressed every time they send him out of town for any period of time because my thoughts are that life is so short, you know, and I think I feel it more now that I know that my years are numbered* and I feel that we should be spending more time together. Because we haven't been married that long.
[She then described her first husband's affair, their divorce, his mistreatment of the children, and mentioned his remarriage.]
T: Do they have children?
P: No. His wife had a hysterectomy about eight years ago. She's quite a bit younger than I am, she's about 13 years younger than me. But I suppose I should probably tell you that after the divorce—we were divorced in March and I wasn't dating—I didn't know anybody. I'd been home with my three kids all these years and so I didn't know anybody. Then I finally went out with a friend to some of these singles dances and she introduced me to this fellow. I used to take the kids with me too. He had a place out on the water, so we used to go out there sometimes for dinner, for a barbecue or something. They would row around in the boat and it was really

---

*Only in reviewing these typed scripts did I recognize that this theme recurred in our later sessions in December 1984. One of her major beliefs at that time was that her husband withheld important information from her concerning decisions important to both of them.

*I thought this would be an important theme to develop.

just a calm relationship. There was really nothing to the relationship. He was just a nice man. That's all I remember him being. Well, anyhow, it was one night that we went out, he came and picked me up and, we were going to a barbecue back at his house. We had 80 people there and he wanted me to help him, so I said fine. So, anyhow, I came and by the time I got home it was about 3:00 A.M., and we just pulled inside the driveway and this car comes in from up the street and here is my ex-husband, jumping out of the car, with the engine running and the doors open, and he pulls the door open and starts beating this guy, and I had to holler at him to stop. Stop! The next thing I know, I hear this popping sound, and I thought what is that and then I see all this blood pouring from this guy. Well, he killed him. Right in the front seat of the car, in my driveway. And my oldest son was standing on the porch. And then I just got hysterical and jumped out of the car because my son kept saying, "Mom, get in the house." So, I tried, I ran around and just as I got to the side of my car, my ex-husband said, "Look," and I stopped dead in my tracks, and he said, "I'm going to shoot myself." And he did fire a shot, but he just grazed himself. Then he evidently walked away, because the police spent all night trying to find him. They had to take me and the kids out of the house because they were afraid he would come back to get me and [sigh] that's something I've had to put in the back of my mind. That was in August of '71 and then by December, when he was still in the King County Jail, he got married to this gal. And they've been married ever since.
[I was astounded.]
T: And where is he still, now?
P: He's living over in a condo by ———.
T: How'd he get out?
P: Oh, he was out in less than two years. Good behavior. Well, he, he never really was a bad man, and he never ever hit me or anything like that. He evidently had a complete breakdown or something. He couldn't cope with the fact that he was losing his kids. He was really obsessed with his kids.
T: And so he got out because it was called a psychiatric problem?
P: Well, he went into work release. He was released because he had been taking psychiatric treatment at [local prison], and I got a letter that I still have at home from, I can't remember now whether it was the person who was treating him or whether it was the parole officer, telling me what they were considering doing. They were considering letting him out on a work-release program, and he wanted to know my feelings. Well, when I got that letter, I was horrified. Because I thought, "Oh, my God." That's the only time I had felt safe was when he was locked up. 'Cause I just thought, well what's to stop him from coming back and getting me next time. So I wrote the letter back, and I have a copy of that at home too, that I told them exactly my fears. And the fact that he was so obsessed with the kids all the time, that if I was dating another man, at the time, I would be afraid of what he might do to that one. The kids were still living at home. And, I just let them know my fears, but next thing I know, within about four or five months, he was released. But they said that he would start paying child support again, 'cause I was going on two years or so without any child support and trying to raise the kids with $400 a month gross.
T: So, you've been able not to be so afraid of this, today?
P: I'm not afraid of him at all anymore. I found that when I was dating, and I was single for almost eight years, there were quite a few men that as soon as they would hear of this incident, I'd

never see them again. So, obviously it scared a lot of them. But my husband [Mr. G.] said, "He doesn't scare me."
T: What sort of treatment are you expecting from talking to a psychiatrist?

She tried Valium from a friend and liked it. She had asked the pharmacist for something for her nerves. Medications had helped her cancer. I thought she would be a strong placebo responder. She also found out that her insurance did not cover outpatient psychiatric treatment. This fact added to her motivation to change.

She fills out Beck Depression Inventory Scale and I summarize:

T: As you suspect, it indicates that you're very depressed.* There's two ways that I work with people who are depressed. One is medications. And medications might be of some assistance to you. Valium works on part of what people are depressed about, namely their anxiety. It does not usually help with peoples' depression. Anxiety and depression are two different things. Another way to work with people who are depressed is to begin to examine the thoughts they have that seem to make them depressed or irritable or anxious. When we first started talking today, we were talking about thoughts that made you upset, like you can't vacuum because then you'll wake up your son, but then you think, "I'm angry at him for being there and restricting what I want to do," and that makes you feel tense. Changing these thoughts, which, as you can see, can be changed. You don't have to think those thoughts and, therefore, you don't have to have those feelings. So what we could do, if you wanted to, is work on the thoughts you have, examine the thoughts that are in there. We call them automatic thoughts because they come on automatically and you don't think about them. We would think about them. I would point out to you, "Is this really true?" Just because you were taught not to vacuum, do you still have to behave that way? I ask you not to take your thought like something that's totally true but is open to question, and I would help you question some of your thoughts so that you could get a more realistic automatic thought in there and, as you can see, if you change some of your thoughts, you would feel better. [The tape ran out here. I reconstruct my last attempt to bring it all together: I suggested that with her husband's failure to return when expected, she was once again experiencing sudden abrupt changes. She had been returning from an outing when her man friend was killed by her ex-husband. Then he was released from jail. Years later she was expecting to die of metastatic cancer and she was suddenly declared in remission. Now she also had to adjust to dramatic switches of expectations again.] [I gave her the antidepressant trazodone, prescribing 50 milligrams at bedtime for the next five nights until our next appointment. This is a low dose of a medication known to have minimal side effects. I intended it to be an "active placebo" by which I meant that it had antidepressant properties but not in this dose range. It also could be called homeopathic treatment.]

*11/10/82*

I did not tape-record this session since the cognitive therapy seminar for which I had prepared the first session required only one tape. Mrs. G. reported that immediately after taking the first dose of the medication she felt better and had slept well each of the following nights. On the fourth day, she stopped the medication,

---
*I had yet to learn the Beck Depression Inventory Scale. In fact, it indicates moderate depression.

having taken it then for three nights. During the interview she was markedly calmer and more accepting of the fact that she had to adapt to her husband's repeated delays. She realized that she wanted more time with him, but sometimes it wasn't possible. She believed she did not need more psychotherapy. We terminated.

*Discussion of One-Session Psychotherapy*

A small body of literature confirms the efficacy of very brief and one-session psychotherapies. Rockwell and Pinkerton (1982) found three general sources of information confirming this notion: single case reports, reevaluation of early-treatment dropouts, and the Kaiser-Permanente studies.

Ever since Freud treated Katharina in a single session on an Austrian mountain top, therapists have reported single-case cures. Psychoanalysts, behaviorists, hypnotists, and others have proclaimed their own effectiveness through single-case examples. Others have reviewed early-treatment dropouts only to find that many of these patients originally thought to be treatment failures had actually terminated following satisfaction with a session or two. Malan et al. (1975) reported the results of a careful study of all patients seen at the Tavistock Clinic in London who had not seen a psychiatrist more than twice in their entire lives. Of 45 patients fitting this criterion, 23 (51%) were judged to be symptomatically improved upon follow-up. Malan et al. also included criteria for "dynamic" improvement for which 11 fit. Follow-up ranged from two to seven years. Using medical utilization as an outcome measure, Follette and Cummings (1976) found that one-interview patients as well as brief-therapy patients (two to eight sessions) had subsequent significant declines in medical outpatient visits and hospitalizations.

Rockwell and Pinkerton also described three general types of cases for which single sessions might be applicable. Some patients may need only the opportunity to review and receive approval for psychological work already done or require affirmation for a psychological decision already made. Other single-session responders may need only assurance of normality. Since the standards for normality are hardly clear, therapists may fear error and extend sessions with patients about whom they are uncertain. The most challenging group are those who appear capable of significant change in a short period of time. Such people are likely to respond to almost any approach. The challenge is to find quickly and comfortably a focus for change and promote it.

According to Rockwell and Pinkerton's analysis, a number of factors appear necessary in order for a single-interview change to take place. The patient must rapidly accept the therapist's authority, and the therapist must be able to help the client quickly to see him/herself differently. The therapist must be confident in his/her ability to conduct a proper therapy in general, must be willing to attempt therapy in the first session, and must be able positively and decisively to let the patient go. This latter element may be particularly difficult because of the uncertainties about what was left undone and whether or not the changes set in motion would proceed successfully without further therapist intervention (p. 38).

Mrs. D. G. was rapidly engaged because her trusted oncologist had recommended me and because she wanted to stop being depressed as rapidly as possible. She readily caught on to the style of therapy I was introducing since examining her own thoughts was something she appeared to have done frequently. She seemed to grasp the idea that talking about her thoughts might be useful. She also seemed to know what needed to be changed, rather than simply being in despair without having any idea about which direction to move.

As suggested by Prochaska and DiClemente (1984), the stage of change in which the patient presents is probably a powerful predictor of outcome. She did not like having to ask for help and seemed to believe that she should be able to help herself on her own. Not included in the transcript because the tape ran out was her belief that psychotherapy cost four times my actual fee, another powerful motivator for short-term help.

The factors that predisposed her to change, she brought with her to the therapeutic encounter. They demonstrate how much of the outcome is determined by factors outside the therapist's influence. Causes of change itself were multiple. She readily accepted the necessity for her to take responsibility for the problem. One could argue that she knew she would have to accept the uncertainty of her husband's returns. My comparison with previous unexpected events to which she had to adjust represented an attempt on my part to foster those previously effective coping mechanisms. I hoped to elicit those old emotions, place the current unexpected events in the same context, and thereby elicit similar tolerance. Aside from this specific technical maneuver, other more general factors were at work. The introduction of a medication could have stimulated her belief in the power of pharmacotherapy, which had already provided her with a "miracle cure" of metastatic cancer. She had not taken enough medication for a sufficient period of time to attribute the relief of her depression to active medication effects. The placebo response is a powerful healing force, which is hardly understood. My own view is that patients may be able to stimulate the production of desirable biochemical activity under favorable circumstances called placebo conditions.

One also cannot ignore the possibility that the depression may have remitted anyway. One can never tell in the individual case whether or not the apparent relief of symptoms was part of the natural course of the disorder. Since she had gone for four months with an increasingly severe depression, I judge that something about her encounter with me was ameliorative.

*Follow-Up Letter—August 17, 1984*

After accepting the invitation to contribute to the *Casebook,* I sent Mrs. G. a copy of the transcript of the November 5, 1982 meeting, requesting her views of what helped her to change. She was unable to specify the causes of her change.

Dear Dr. Beitman:
After reading the transcript of our meeting in 1982 I have come up with the following observations:
I found that I had very little reaction at all after reading the complete transcript except for Item 1.
1. I remember at the time resenting the fact that you asked me, "Are you *expecting* me to give you something [medication] today?" Although it was probably true, I was hoping, and at the time I felt that that was all I would need to get over the depression.
I think also that I expected to leave your office knowing exactly why I was so depressed and what to do to eliminate the problem. However, it is possible that had I had more sessions with you, this would never have been discussed. To answer your question, it is very difficult for me to tell that the one session I had did help me or whether the medication did the trick.
I'm sorry I can't be of more help with your survey but hope what little I have said will be of some help.
Sincerely,
Mrs. D. G.

Mrs. G.'s follow-up letter was interesting in that she was unable to ascribe her change to anything specific except possibly the medication. She therefore learned nothing specific from the single session about herself that she was able to articulate. As therapists, we often hope that patients will gain something constructive from the experience that they may apply in other circumstances. She herself appeared to be primarily responsible for this change. Somehow, I performed the ritual through which she could allow herself to make the changes she wished to make.

## PART 2

The patient called me in November 1984 saying she wanted an appointment because she felt very depressed. I was glad to hear from her, in part, because I had been criticized by some of the editorial consultants for the *Casebook* because my case was too short. Now I had the opportunity to illustrate the clinical reality that patients sometimes relapse and choose to return to therapy with the original therapist. Shortly after writing the follow-up letter to me, she had experienced a recurrence of cancer.

*11/26/84*

[BDI = 40—Done before talking part of interview.]

T: It seems that you're more depressed than you were the last time I saw you.

She had no energy and lacked interest in everything. It started after her vacation in September 1984. She rambled on in a jumbled, excited way. She reported that it all hit her after returning from vacation. During the summer she and her husband had decided to move to Alaska. The cancer had spread to her hip socket, where she had five separate lesions, and also to her vertebral column, where she had three separate lesions. Because these vertebral lesions caused her so much pain, Dr. A. prescribed 10 days of radiation therapy. She had known of the recurrence before her vacation but decided to go anyway. This time she received radiation in addition to medications. She interpreted this to mean her condition was worse. She suffered some painful radiation burns, but her husband went on a hunting trip anyway. They had decided to move to Alaska, and she worried whether her husband would give her the support she needed. She stated that she believed that once they got there, everything would be all right.

T: Are you sure of that?
P: Well, see, I don't know, I'm scared; but I don't have a choice. I either go with him or I stay here by myself. I would say every weekend for the last four or five weeks we've had a running battle and then he doesn't speak to me for three days.
[I want details of their arguments.]
T: What do you fight about?
P: About going to Alaska.
T: What's the general way the arguments go?
P: Well, it just seems that every one of these has been on a weekend. He'll be working downstairs in the basement and I'm sitting upstairs by myself again with nothing to do because I don't knit anymore. I start to get this horrible creeping feeling and then I start thinking: "I have, we have a beautiful house and I love it, I just love that house. And . . ."

She describes how her husband has "given up" on his three children because he gave them everything and then they walked away from him when he needed them. He has no contact with them. I wonder to myself whether she fears he will cut her off. He will not acknowledge the existence of one of her daughters because she did something to anger him.

T: Back to the weekend fights though, he's downstairs . . .
P: He's downstairs. I said, I've gotta talk. He says, okay, just talk, what do you

want to talk about? I said, I'm scared to go to Alaska. He says, well, what are you scared of?

She talked about her fear of leaving her three children and then described how her husband had gotten angry at her daughter, Chris, because she had left a mess in the house she rented. The patient and her husband, H., had to clean it up around Easter, 1984. H. had complained to his friend Rick that no matter how much you do for children they always want more. Then each time Rick and H. got together, they both complained about that "lazy Chris." Since Rick and his wife had gone on the September vacation with the patient and her husband, she felt her vacation was ruined by their snide remarks about Chris. Chris apologized to H. just before Thanksgiving.

P: I told H. after vacation, I said, I am never gonna get together with our friends again if you guys do not stop bugging me about Chris. And so, I even made a point of saying to him a couple of days before Thanksgiving, I said, "I want to make something perfectly clear and that is that there will not be any comments made about Chris to ruin our Thanksgiving." "Oh, I think that can be arranged," he said. So, anyhow, that is what has been depressing me and it ruined my vacation. . . .

I had a lot of trouble following this story of Chris, H., and Rick during the sessions even while going over the typed scripts. I moved to the details of the decision to go to Alaska.

T: Okay, well, let's leave that aside for a little bit and talk about some of the other things that are bothering you. Because these may all come together. When did your husband say you were going to move to Alaska?
P: We found out in June, when we were up there. The boss came up and took us out for dinner.
T: And told you then?
P: Uh-huh. But the thing is, ah, that it was pretty well discussed before I even knew; I mean it was a definite goal before I was even told.
T: All right. So that was just a formality, the boss took you out . . .
[I did not believe this entirely.]
P: Yeah, right.
T: Okay.
P: And I knew, I knew it was preplanned.
T: So, you were told in June?
P: Uh-huh.
T: Again, you were given a situation that you couldn't do anything about.
[I pick up again on the theme of helplessness.]
P: Right.
T: And that's hard for you. It was a little bit the way H. and Rick were interacting was a situation you couldn't do anything about. . . .
P: Uh-huh.
T: Otherwise they kept doing it.
P: Right.
T: The sense of helplessness you had starting at least with Easter and then with being told about the Alaska move and then you get a recurrence of the cancer.
P: Uh-huh.
T: And that you can't do anything about either and this radiation on top of it.
P: Uh-huh.
T: And then your son leaving the house . . .
P: Uh-huh.
T: You know it's a good thing for him to go, ah, but you're losing your baby, you're on your own again.
P: Uh-huh.
T: At least four things happened over the last six months or so, that are beyond your control, or relatively beyond your control, and that's been very frustrating for you.
P: Uh-huh.
T: And that's contributed to your depression.

P: Yeah, and you know, I really think that I would like to go. Well, we've bought a house, I've gotta go.
T: And you really think you would like to go, and that's what's so crazy about this.

We discuss her medical care plans. Her husband has been very active in helping with the arrangements for follow-up in Alaska. But he rarely takes her for treatment himself and that hurts her. She describes him as more affectionate in Alaska and then describes their Alaska friends in more detail.

P: I guess like I said to my husband: actually they're all your friends that we socialize with. They're all men that he has met through work and they all have their own airplanes, including my husband; he just got his pilot's license this summer up in Alaska and we bought an airplane. And these guys just sit around, and Tuesday night is boys night and they sit around and they all talk airplanes and I just sit there and knit; and I'm quite happy.*
[She then describes his kindness during a very uncomfortable Alaska trip.]
T: You wanted to tell me that he can be understanding, particularly up there.
P: Up there. See, I mean everything is yes dear, no dear. He would do anything for me up there. And then the Monday after we came back, a dozen red roses comes to the door. And it said, I love you very much and hope this makes up for the bad weekend, because everything went wrong, the flight and everything. This is how he tells me he loves me.

We discuss her ambivalence about going, the depth of her depression, and a friend who said, "What's the matter, D., do you feel you're going up to Alaska to die?" She agreed. She felt as if she was not fighting the cancer as she had before. She felt that she had no future. I sensed anger at her husband.

T: You sound like you're very angry with him. You're very angry with him. And it's almost as if you're going to just stop fighting the cancer and die because you're so mad at him because you don't want to die in Alaska.
[A way to pull ambivalence and depression together.]
P: Yeah.
T: You're just gonna die right here.
P: Uh-huh.
T: Period.
P: And, I, we both went to a counselor last week at the University together [at the outpatient oncology department]. We met with her for about an hour and a half. She just listens to you, and she turned to me and she said, "Well, it sounds to me that you don't have too many choices." I mean, my choices are I either go up there or I stay here, get myself a little apartment, and stay down here by myself and, of course, I wouldn't have anybody coming home for dinner at night. So, I'd be day and night by myself because I don't work and that is depressing, because I know I couldn't take much of that. So my only choice is . . .
[This is the central current conflict.]
T: To go.
P: Yeah.
T: But you hate the idea of going.
P: Yeah. Now that I've gotten myself in this hole—I call it a hole because I can't seem to get myself up and this is not me. I've always been bubbly and go, go, go.
T: You thought you were dying after you got cancer the last time. And then you told everybody you were dying. You all got used to it and then suddenly you were in remission again. And you had

---
*Airplanes are an important subject in her follow-up letter.

this very sudden horrible thing happen to you when your husband shot that guy you were dating. That was another death that was out of your control and horrible for you and your family. Just horrible.

P: Uh-huh.

T: Another hopeless circumstance for you to have to fight against.

P: Uh-huh.

T: And now you're being pushed into yet another situation where you have only one thing you can do. Actually you have two things. You can die. You have cancer. No one will ever know that you just let go. If you even tell them, they won't believe you. They'll say the cancer got to you. And you'll do that because you want to die in Seattle.

[I expand on this side of her ambivalence.]

P: Uh-huh.

T: You want to die at home. And you'll do it partly because you're so furious at your husband for abandoning you as he has. Even though the evidence is that he might not do it while you're up in Alaska.

P: Uh-huh.

T: You're still so furious at him now.

P: Yeah. Because, I guess the reason I'm so furious at him is because, he doesn't have to go. I mean, ah . . .

T: He doesn't have to go to Alaska?

P: I mean; he didn't have to agree to go; I mean, everything's cut and dried and the house is bought and . . .

T: And he didn't discuss it with you?

P: Not really. I mean, it was discussed with me when the decision . . .

T: Had been made.

P: Yeah. And I mean, I know it was all discussed before.

[Return to the theme of helplessness.]

T: So here was one thing in your life; the life of a woman who has had her husband shoot somebody; kill somebody; who has had cancer come back once after having had it before; things that seem like they were very much out of her control. Here was a situation where you could have had some control. Even if you would both have decided to go to Alaska. At least you would have been part of the decision. But he did it behind your back and that's hard enough for most people anyway. For you it's even harder because you have cancer, which is beyond your control and you would like to have some control in your life; some experience of that; and he took this away from you too.

P: Yeah. This is what I said to him. I said, I never ever get to make any decisions. They're always made for me, and, it's like I said, financially it's a big promotion, financially for him; plus a lot of extra benefits.

T: No matter what you tell me, he did not involve you in this decision. Now let me ask you about a decision I want you to be involved with. The last time I saw you I gave you some medication.

[I model a collaborative decision.]

P: Yes.

T: Now, are you looking for medication today?

P: Well, I . . . yes, to be perfectly honest. I don't know what it was that you prescribed but it was only one week's supply. And then when I came in the next week, I was driving in and I thought, "What am I going in there for? I don't need any help, I'm fine." But I was never in the shape I'm in now. I mean, I never was this low. And, it scares me, I mean, it's just frightening because I feel like I'm slowly dying.

T: You are.

P: And I've got to get out of it or I will die.

T: That's right.

[She describes in great detail how her husband refuses her the smallest kindness because he doesn't want to "pamper" her.]

T: Is it possible that your husband could come in next week; to see me?

[I want to see his side of this story.]

P: I don't see why not.
T: I would like you to ask him to come in. Try this. It is the same medication. I want you to take one tonight and one tomorrow night. And then if you feel all right, go up to two on Wednesday night and then two on Thursday night and then Friday night take three a night.

I gave her a higher dose than the last time. I was hedging toward the standard dose range. But therapeutic doses for this medication are usually twice this amount. I judged it to be a more active placebo than the last one.

P: Oh, now, that'll all be on the bottle will it?
T: Yes. Yes.
P: Okay, just in case I forget.
T: By the time I see you, I want you to be taking three.
[By the next appointment she had forgotten this instruction.]
P: Now is this the same?
T: Same stuff. Yeah.

She expresses surprise that her husband came for counseling but doubts he will take the advice of giving her a little TLC. We discuss dying again. I attempt to reframe her experience by calling her leaving Seattle a partial death.

T: You are really dying in regard to Seattle. Just like I am, I'm leaving Seattle too, permanently, so I understand that. [Therapist self-revelation to imply termination.]
And that's painful enough, but you've also got a bad disease, and you've got a husband who doesn't acknowledge it. And you're angry at him and you're gonna kinda kill yourself.
P: Just to get even.
[She seems to accept this notion.]
T: Just to get even.
P: It makes sense. Because I know, I'm just angry all the time. I don't like being this way.
T: You are angry; partly at him, but separate out what's him from what's Seattle. You're angry about having to leave Seattle and you're angry about having cancer.
P: Yeah. I mean . . .
T: And having it come back again after beating it.
P: And having a husband who doesn't acknowledge it. Like the time when it came back I went through days and days of tests and x rays and bone scans. He told me this one time, I'm not gonna pamper you. Dr. A. said that your problem is probably arthritis. I said, he doesn't know for sure. And he says, "Well, I'm not gonna pamper you." So, I thought, "Okay," then it really started hurting and I just went ahead and made my appointment with Dr. A. and I never even told him I was going in because I was mad.
T: You're still mad. This is our next appointment. December 5. It's a week from Wednesday.

*12/5/84*

Both husband and wife are present.

T: What is your understanding of the reason that I asked your wife to ask you to come?
H: Why, I think she wants me to hear both sides, I guess, and understand her problems. I don't think I have a problem.
T: Well, you have a problem.
H: Well, yeah, I mean personally, a problem.
T: Well, I think it affects you personally. I'm not saying I'm pointing at you, within you exactly, but . . .
H: Oh, I realize that, I understand that.
T: And, in part, the problem your wife has is the problem she perceives you have with her. Usually in cases like this it's both people contributing something,

and maybe that's true here and maybe it isn't. And that's one of the things to see. [Turning to patient.] I see that you are not feeling any better since I saw you last time. [BDI = 45.]

She has remained very depressed, feeling as if she had the flu. I was anxious because she had not responded dramatically as she had in Part 1. How much was due to her cancer or its treatment?

T: How do you understand your wife's depression? How do you understand the reasons for it?

Husband describes the possibility that she may be dying but counters that fear with the argument that she has not yet been declared terminal. He also states that the move is probably hard on her and that she fears a lack of support in Alaska. He counters that with the argument that people in Alaska are just like the people here. This statement strikes me as coming in part from the world view formed by his being a repairman—the interchangeable parts notion. But I am also impressed with his understanding of her concerns.

H: Well, I think she feels that if she goes up there and leaves all the support that she gets here that she'd give up. . . .
T: Well, the idea of her giving up is around.
H: That's right, it's been around and I've heard it, and I understand that part of it. But I don't think that she would. I just don't believe that she could give up that way because I've tested her. I can get her mad and she's ready to fight and she's gonna go, go, go.
T: What can you get her mad about?
H: Oh, I can make her mad over several things. And then I can see the inner part of her, that's her fighting.
P: Probably the easiest way he can get me mad is by not speaking to me.
H: But then she's ready to fight.

P: And I'll fight back.
H: And that fight's there. I mean, I think that the fighting is still in her, it's just that she's . . .
P: That's my anger.
T: Do you talk to him about your anger?
P: I just told him what you said, that I was angry.
T: Did you tell him what you are angry about?
P: No, that I was angry, that I was angry.
T: Well, here's the place to start talking about anger, and some of it is at you.
H: I'm sure that's right. And I probably have some for her, but I, I don't express my feelings, I keep them to myself. If I get angry at her I don't express it to her.
T: You still probably show it to her.
P: He shows it to me by not speaking, you know, I just get angry and I yell and holler and . . .
H: Well, I'm a believer this way. When you say something in anger, you don't mean it, but it still hurts and you can't ever retract that statement. And I don't like to hurt people that I really care about, I don't like saying something that will hurt them.
T: Well, you hurt her by *not* saying things too.
H: Maybe as . . .
P: And see, that hurts me more . . .
H: To me, no, I don't hurt her as much as saying something.
T: Okay, now this is where you (talking to H.) don't have a problem, but both of you have a problem.
H: Yeah.
T: Now, whose standards are you living up to? Your own, or what really hurts your wife?
H: Well, either way, I'm gonna hurt her.
T: Yeah, which way are you gonna hurt her least?
H: Well, that's her. I don't know. My opinion is if I say something that's gonna hurt her, it's gonna hurt.
T: But if you don't say anything?

H: It's still gonna hurt her.
T: Well, can't she pick her poison?
[I try to force him to see for whom he is making this decision.]
H: Well, that's true.
P: I don't think he would say anything to hurt me. If he said anything, he would just say, look, get off my back. If he just said something like that and then let it go. Sometimes he'll go for days without speaking and that gets me upset.
H: Well, that's not true. That's not true, because I know my temper.
T: And you really do get mad.
P: I've never seen his temper.
H: I can get mad, and I don't let myself get mad.
T: Have you hit anyone before?
H: Yes, one time.
T: And who was that?
H: That was my first wife.
T: Did you know about that?
P: No. I've never seen him angry.
H: I'm not an arguer. I will not argue. I've never argued.
[He is very categorical.]
T: How badly did you hurt your first wife?
H: Oh, I just smacked her in the mouth.
T: But that really bothered you?
H: Yes, it did.
T: You didn't like losing your control like that?
[I transit to the control issue.]
H: No, I don't lose my control.
T: Well, control is the other important subject for us to talk about because that's what Mrs. G. and I were talking about the last time too, control. Now, could you tell him about control, rather than me telling him about it; how you feel like you're losing it? And how he's been taking it away from you.
P: Oh, about not having any choices?
T: Yeah, tell him, not me.

Trying to encourage discussion. In fact they had discussed her sense of having no choices, especially about her not being involved in the decision to go to Alaska. But she would not confront him with the specifics without my encouragement. At first I thought she did not remember our discussion the previous week.

P: That's how I felt the night we went out to dinner, that it was kind of all decided then anyhow.
T: And when we talked last week, you didn't like that. It was another instance of not being included in important decisions.
P: Uh-huh.
T: He had done it by himself.
H: Well, I object to that a little bit, because it had been discussed. In my viewpoint of this thing, I have not excluded her in everything. I keep her informed. I don't think I held anything back.
P: Well, the first that I remember actually hearing about it being for real was the night he [Dave] took us out for dinner and you'd already taken care of all the business part.
H: That was the first time I had heard; basically other than the night that George said something. But, the night that you and I went out with Dave was the first time that he ever said, H., I want you to be the man. That was the first time that I was told personally by Dave, other than two years ago.
P: Well, I had the feeling from the way Dave was talking that he's planned this for quite some time. And I felt like I was . . .
H: Maybe Dave had, but not me.
P: I'm talking about the way Dave talked and it sounded like he had already been talking to you about it.
T: Well, do you believe what he just said?
P: Uh-huh. I believe him.
T: How does it make you feel to hear his side of the story?
P: Oh, I mean, it makes me feel better, yeah.
T: How does it make you feel better?

P: I always thought that somebody was pulling a fast one on me. That they always knew but didn't say anything.
H: No, no, it wasn't.
P: And that's what I felt, yeah. That is was done for my entertainment.
T: Here is a difference of opinion that has harbored a kind of resentment in her for many months.
H: Well, I can understand that situation, but it wasn't a situation that was opened up, bingo, right at that time. It had been discussed a couple of years before of saying, hey, we're gonna put a service department and we want you . . .
T: It was a little bit in the air, but for both of you it was a surprise. More for your wife than for you. You had a little more sniffings about it.

I then moved the discussion to her concern for his support. He states that he gives her all the support she needs *when she needs it*. He lists the many phone calls he has made, the driving and other plans he has carried out. But he does not mention phone calls to Dr. A., for example, because he figured "she could handle it." If she couldn't handle it, he would be there.

P: But he didn't support my depression because he didn't understand what I had to be depressed about. And I couldn't actually tell exactly why I was depressed. I didn't really know. I didn't want to move, I didn't want to do anything.

He changes the discussion to saying he is moving for her. If he was on his own, he could live on very little money. But she wants to talk about her depression and how he does not understand it. I am impressed with his innate psychological astuteness when he sides with her resistance to going by saying he would rather not go either. But it is their last chance at financial security.

H: But I'm not 20 years old. How many more years of physical productive work in my line of business do I have left? So, what I've got to do is look for both of our sides and analyze the situation. You see, I've got five more years I can produce and we can come out actually with money we can do what we want to. And we don't have to travel, we don't have to do things.
T: And you agree with that?
P: Uh-huh.
T: He doesn't want to move either, but he feels it's a good opportunity and it may be the last opportunity.

His self-sacrificing position neutralizes her calls for support during her depression. She starts to look to the recurrence of cancer, the pain of treatment as the causes. I shift her to her cognitions. We move to a discussion of her possibly dying in Alaska. He counters with the belief that he is more likely to die than she is. This position is not open to my argument.

H: But that's what I'm trying to portray in her mind of a positive thinking situation. And that's the reason I made the statement, I will not pamper you, because if I pamper you, I'll make an invalid out of you.
T: This woman, you're gonna make an invalid out of?
H: Not if we make her do her own thing, keep her strong.
T: She's pretty independent anyway.
H: I know that. But if we would. The kids and I talked about it. We said, we're gonna treat her just like we always have. We're not changing.
T: What do you want him to do a little differently in regard to your cancer, your physical situation?
P: Well, what it really boiled down to be-

fore when we went to the counselor, is just a little more TLC. When I don't get it, I get the impression that he doesn't care. And, ah . . .
T: Tell him.
P: I get the impression that you don't care.
H: But, we've discussed this one time. I'm not an emotional person. And she knows this. We've been married six years and I'm never an emotional person. I don't make; I'm not a person who shows . . .
T: Let me ask you this. I don't know all that much about air conditioners, so I'm going into your area of expertise. Let's see how this works. You've got an air conditioner, it looks like a standard model. You know how it's supposed to operate, but it's not working. You go in there and you find that there's something in there that's not the way you thought it would be. Has that ever happened to you?
[I try to appeal to his explanatory model.]
H: Yeah, quite often.
T: Okay. So you're not gonna try to fix it the way you had in your mind in the first place. You're gonna adjust to what you find.
H: Well, that's true.
T: Well, that's what I . . .
H: You're right, that's true.
T: You got an idea about how to handle your wife.
H: Uh-huh.
T: It ain't workin'. So, you've got some good ideas, just like you have with an air conditioner, but she's different from the concept you have about the way it's supposed to be.
H: It's worked up until this. Or at least she's given me the impression that it has.
T: I think it has. It looked to me like it is a good marriage too. It still looks like a good marriage to me. But there are some adjustments necessary now, because the air conditioner has changed a little bit and your wife is asking for a little more sense that you are worried about her, that you are concerned about her. And I will say it in a very specific way. Your idea about positive ways of looking at five years up there and then retiring and let's get through it, we can beat this cancer, is very important. And it's a great attitude to have. But let's have another one too. That isn't 100% certain. It's a good idea to have a positive attitude, but now, she also has some other realistic possibilities in her mind. Five years, she told me, looks like forever. And it's possible, we can't say it's impossible, it's possible, that what she's doing is leaving Seattle behind and going to Alaska and dying. It's possible.
H: That's true.
T: Well, she wants that accepted also.
H: I've accepted that.
T: Has he?
P: Well, when we've ever talked, I mean, I've talked about it . . .
H: I've accepted it.
P: Well, yeah.
T: Has he, do you feel he's accepted that?
P: No, I just have said I feel like I'm going to go up to Alaska and die. And that's when he said, Well, he says the problem with you is that you're afraid to die and I'm not. And I said, Well, yes, I'm not afraid to admit that I am afraid to die. [He will not hear her as she wishes to be heard.]
T: The fundamental question you are facing as a couple is that this move to you means the good life in five years and maybe not a bad life for the next five years either, but after five years easy street, good retirement. This is what it means to you.
H: Yeah, right. Well, not just for me.
T: To her, she would like it to mean that, but you have a sick wife. To her now, she's not functioning as she'd like to. She wants to function the way you want her to because she likes to function that way. But you have now a sick wife. We

don't know how much of it is depression itself, we don't know how much is due to the illness itself. It's very hard to determine that. But she's going up there sick, feeling like she's not gonna come back to Seattle; feeling like she's gonna die.

[I don't feel I am getting far with him.]

T: I'm gonna have to stop for a minute. Are you still taking this medication?

P: Well, I only went six days like you said, even though I had some left over.

T: When did you stop taking them?

P: Saturday. [Our session was on a Wednesday.]

T: Oh, oh, all right. Why did you stop? [I am frustrated.]

P: Because it said one . . .

T: But then you were supposed to continue at that dose level.

P: Oh, well, I didn't know and I decided, I thought well, why would he prescribe . . .

T: Then you were supposed to continue at that level; get up to three a day and then stay there.

P: Oh, okay, I, I stopped on Saturday.

T: Did you feel any effect from them?

P: The only thing that I can say that I've noticed is that I haven't been crying. But then I haven't brought the subject of Alaska up and neither have you, so we haven't even discussed it at home. And that's the only time I would cry was when that was the discussion.

T: Well, let's try this stuff again. Take three at night, keep taking it. You're supposed to get there and keep taking it.

I felt uneasy with the sense that her depression seemed so dense that nothing could change it. I tried to encourage more positive responses by her husband and tried to underline his substantial commitment to her general well-being. He emphasized how he had tried to make the move easier on her. They discussed how he had told her many of the details of the move including the selling of the house but that she had forgotten. She began to consider the possibility that rather than being left out, she instead had not been paying attention. Perhaps, I thought, her depression had contributed not only to her lack of concentration but also to her failure to see H.'s positive contributions. Then he added a contribution right out of Beck et al. (1979). I appreciated the suggestion since I was feeling demoralized too. I did not like the idea of writing up a failed case for this *Casebook*.

H: I think that by her staying home, not getting out and doing things, it adds to the depression.

He remarks that she never listens to him, but if a friend tells her, she'll do it. I take the hint and ask her to fill out a daily activities schedule. I invite him to return next week with the likelihood that I will see her first, then both together. The session had gone 10 minutes overtime because I was looking for some ray of hope.

Thereafter, *I* felt depressed, helpless. I felt that she was going to Alaska to die. I felt that the stress of the move might exacerbate her weakness. I was worried that it would kill her. I was also being traumatized by my own leaving of Seattle. I would be leaving the same time as she was to leave. I thought that her memory problem appeared excessive. I would need to do a mental status on her. Does she have metastasis to the brain?

Later that day, I called Dr. A. I argued that she was likely to have an organic basis for her depression either with metastasis to brain or due to chemotherapy. I repeated my belief that she was going to Alaska to die. He doubted the organic basis of her presenting problems.

*12/12/84*

BDI = 23, approximately the same as the first time she saw me. I felt relieved and believed that she would probably recover as quickly this time as she had two years ago. She felt that she was "out of the hole" and attributed it to the medication. She could look at the move to Alaska in a better light now. She had begun to think of all the things she had to do where before she could care less. She decided to push herself a little bit but did not acknowledge that her husband had suggested it. Two days after our last session, she had gone to a large shopping center for three or four hours and then cooked dinner. She has been that active ever since. I found it difficult to attribute this change solely to the medication since she had been on it only two days after having stopped it for four days. Her memory remained a problem for her. She had forgotten to fill out the daily activities schedule. I asked her for feedback from the last session to see what, if anything, from it had helped her.

T: Do you remember anything about our session last week? Anything that seemed useful to you, that stood out to you, or seemed not useful to you?
P: Yes, the one thing that stood out to me, that I never found out before was the reason my husband doesn't speak to me when he's angry. I often thought that he had done something at one time that he was sorry for and so now he refuses to fight back. He's never raised his voice; he just doesn't get angry. It's nothing unusual for him to go two and three days without speaking to me; and of course, that doesn't exactly help me. Just gets me deeper and deeper into depression. After talking to him last week he seemed to be a little bit more attentive and so I think it was good for him to come in. Like I said, I thought there was something in his past. We've been married for six years and he comes from Texas so I don't know anything about his past, other than what his mother has told me. He was always very close-mouthed about it and so I often wondered why he never got mad. It wasn't normal not to show anger.
T: Now that you have some idea about why he doesn't, what does that mean to you?
P: It makes me feel a lot better because he has learned to control his anger so that he doesn't strike out at me. But at the same time he's chosen to do it by not speaking. I think that bothers me more. I would rather him say, Look D., get off my back and leave me alone, if something is bothering him. Then maybe a half hour or hour or so later, start talking just like nothing had happened. But he doesn't say anything. He just clams right up. A lot of times I would never know what I even said.

She describes her concerns about his "clamming up" and relates an incident during which he had become angry at her but did not tell her until she pushed it out of him. She worried about going to Alaska because most of the people there were his friends. She mentioned that in the past week her son had moved out, leaving them alone. Perhaps this freedom to be alone in the house had helped their relationship, she thought. In fact, perhaps that was the reason they got along better in Alaska. She believed that he was a little more mellow around the house and that perhaps talking to me had helped even though I had said some of the same things she had said to him.

P: I think husbands have a tendency to turn a deaf ear to the wives just like kids to their mothers.

She then told many details of instances in which he had invited other people to stay with them without first discussing it with her. These incidents contributed to her feeling that she had little control over her life.

P: I said to him, we're not going to be a motel for your company. I mean, last night, the secretary from the Alaska office was down. We had dinner with her last night. She called us from her motel to thank us for taking her to dinner and then she wanted to talk to H. for a couple of minutes. He gets on the phone and they're coming back. She and her husband are coming back through Anchorage Friday to go down to Florida for Christmas and so H. says, "Well, gee, why don't you come and stay with us?" And I just sort of looked up from my newspaper and he said, "Oh, just a minute, is that all right?" And, so, see with her I don't mind, but . . .
T: You still want him to ask.
P: Just ask me.
T: And he should ask before he says anything to anybody.
P: He caught himself.
T: He caught himself.
[Was this an indication of a positive change?]
P: He just says, Oh, is that all right.
T: Okay. So, he is responsive to you. He does listen to what you want from him.

I may be excessively optimistic. I then find myself becoming bored as she describes her Christmas plans. I summarize the apparent interpersonal change between her and her husband and then predict that based on her previous recovery from depression at a BDI around 25 that she is likely to be much improved next week. I also suggest that next week is likely to be our last session. I then bring up the subject of medications.

P: Oh, yeah, yeah.
T: And we'll see how you are again next week. Now, you're taking three of those pills at night.
P: Ever since Wednesday, I was here last Wednesday.
T: What do they feel like to you?
P: I don't feel like I'm even taking anything. And even when I took them two years ago, I thought strange how I feel so good now, but I never even felt like I had taken anything.
T: Yeah.
P: I get no, no . . .
T: Side effects.
P: Side effects. There's no; I don't feel like; they don't relax me and put me to sleep.
T: They don't do anything.
P: They don't do anything.
T: It's like you hardly know you're taking them.
P: I might as well be taking, what do you call them, those placebos.
T: Placebos.

I laugh silently to myself since I was attempting to elicit a placebo response. I then invite her husband in. He thinks she is improving, that she is more responsive, more willing to be involved, more able to joke a little. She seemed to him to be coming out of a fog and seeing the whole picture more clearly. I encourage her to tell him how she thinks he has changed.

P: You have been more attentive. I think we both seem to be more relaxed and I don't know whether part of it is our session here last week or having the house to ourselves for a change. [Her son had just moved out.]
H: Well, I don't think that I've changed any, I think she's just seeing that the things that I was doing I'm still doing, and she's just more aware of it.
P: That could be, that could be.
T: That could be, but I think you [Mrs. G.] have some points there too. Argue with him a little bit, because you think he's changed a little bit too. I think you're both right.
P: Oh.
T: What's he doing that's maybe a little bit more attentive?
P: Gosh, I don't know.
H: I don't think I've done anything differ-

ent. I'm still the same, and I still react the same. I think that she notices. I think she was brought aware of the things that . . .
T: You're doing.
H: Doing, and she wasn't aware of them before.
T: Aware of them before. So that's where you think I was of some assistance?
H: Yeah. And I think I was doing it, but she wasn't observing it.
P: It's just that I can't think of anything different.
T: Yes you can. What about "Is that okay?"
P: Oh, we were discussing about inviting people to come and stay with us.
H: Oh.
P: And I said that we had had discussions about this last summer. And I said, remember I told you.
H: Yeah, I remember.
P: And I said that, remember that I told you if I moved to Alaska I didn't want us to be a hotel/motel for your company. Then last night when Kathy called and you said to her, "Why don't you come and stay with us?" Then you turned real quick and said, "Is that okay?"
H: Oh, I . . .
P: Yeah, but I'm just . . .
T: You never thought about that?
H: I probably wouldn't have before, no.
T: You wouldn't have before?
H: No, I probably would have said come on up.
T: Come on up. And not asked her?
H: Right.
P: But there are very few people that we know well enough to invite that I would say "no" to. But there are a few that I just don't feel like spending my days and my nights for weeks on end with them. I don't have anything in common with them. It drives me crazy.
T: Well, you've made that clear. I think H. has gotten that message.
[Again, as suggested by her follow-up letter, I may have been too optimistic.]

I encourage them to discuss their arguments. She admits that when she gets angry at him she sometimes becomes silent too. She again threatens to leave Alaska if they have more long silences. He offers no guarantees. She wants to simply discuss things with him, not just argue. But she cannot get him to engage in simple discussions. I then confront her with her inability to bring sensitive subjects up to him. She seems frightened of him.

H: I know she's more free with somebody else. I've observed that for seven years. But, you know, it doesn't bother me to the point of letting it bother me. That's fine. I figure if she can talk to somebody else. I don't, it doesn't bother me to the point that I'm gonna dwell on it.

She cannot get him to talk with her. She complains that he always has his eyes on the TV set and only half listens while watching. He counters that if a question comes up he can respond to it. He does give her fuller attention during commercials. Then he complains that she won't pay attention to him while she's knitting. She says she will after she has finished a row. I state that I think of these as lesser problems and bring the session to a close.

*12/19/84*

BDI = 13, within the normal range. She reports feeling much better and begins to talk about her mother-in-law who was now staying with her for Christmas. She feels guilty because her mother-in-law does housework she feels she herself should be doing. D. also believes she should get up early in the morning when the mother-in-law gets up to keep her company. I note that the mother-in-law wants to do housework and likes getting up early by herself.

P: Well, she lives alone and she seems to be quite happy.

T: Maybe she likes to help. Maybe she feels guilty for living in your house without paying you back.
[I offer an alternative view.]
P: I think she probably does feel guilty, because when I took her downstairs she said, "Well, we'll get down here next week and we'll get this basement fixed."
T: So, maybe you're doing her a favor by letting her clean the house so she doesn't have to feel so guilty.
P: You're probably right. I didn't look at it; I was thinking about me, how I feel. I wasn't really thinking about how she feels.

I suggest that this is the kind of thinking that may lead her to being depressed. She goes on to describe how fat she feels and that although her chemotherapy may be contributing, she is very bothered by it. She is now very active, always on the go and hopes that she may burn up some calories in this way. She wanted to continue taking the antidepressant but at two pills per day rather than three and only for a few more days. I asked her once again what she believed had helped her reduce her depression.

P: Well, I think it might be the medication, but at the same time, I can't tell any difference when I take it. I mean, it's not like taking a Valium or something that relaxes you so you feel better. But I don't feel anything when I take these pills. But I figure it must be the pills that's doing it. Because although I think coming in here and talking does help. Just like this last conversation about my mother-in-law feeling guilty. You brought up the fact that maybe she feels guilty because she doesn't do anything and I didn't look at it like that.
T: And the last time it may have helped to see that H. really was trying to inform you about things.
P: Yes, and so you see, he really is very close-mouthed about everything. He's Mr. Tough Guy. He doesn't let anything get to him, he says.
T: He doesn't let anything get to him and show it.
P: That's right. And, he's pretty thick-skinned.
T: Actually he looks thick-skinned, but he's a very sensitive and caring person. That was clear to me. Your presentation of him and the guy weren't exactly the same. One of the reasons that I asked him to come in is to check out what you were saying about him to see how true it was. And a little bit of it was true. We didn't ask him about going hunting when you had that sore on your side. I'm sure that happened. But a lot of the other things. He wasn't quite as malicious as he appeared. Now sometimes when people are depressed, they think negatively of people. But you were beginning to think negatively of him because he didn't really tell you things, because he was close-mouthed and you like to be informed. His lack of telling you things at least helped to make your depression deeper. We don't know where it started exactly, but you're looking a lot better and I suspect the same thing will happen as did last time, that you'll come out of it and be fine.
[Did I try too hard to put H. in a good light?]

I invite H. in once again. After some preliminary discussion in which he states that he believes she has improved, I ask her about her memory problem. She describes being forgetful but perhaps not as frequently. Then she remembers an incident between them in which her memory was once again challenged.

P: There was something that just happened this week that you told me that I totally forgot.
T: That's one of the problems. You may

tell her and she doesn't remember.
P: Yes. There were other times that when we were driving somewhere the other night, I said, "I know you didn't tell me that." Then he says, "Well, maybe I didn't, but you know I thought I did." So there are times like that where I think that makes me feel better, makes me feel like I'm not going crazy. But you know, it happens time after time. I thought, "What's the matter with me, I can't remember anything anymore." Then I get upset with myself because I can't remember things.
[I am encouraged that he is not so dogmatic and perhaps a little more flexible.]
T: Chances are you'll remember better. When people are depressed, they don't remember things as well.
H: I try to tell her everything, at least I call home and . . .
T: You've got to be perfect though.
P: [Laughs.]
H: Well, I never hide nothin' from her.
T: Your anger you hide from her don't you?
[I challenge another of his absolute statements.]
H: Well, I do that now; that's probably . . .
P: And I've still never seen him angry.
H: And I don't know if I could change that or not.
[I then begin my closing summary. I try to declare positive feelings between them.]
T: Okay, we know that now. Just to know that there are certain limitations on each other's expectations of each other, that he may not tell you everything, and anger may be part of it. You may tell her a lot of like important information, but she may not think she knows everything. And you two may not have the kind of conversation that each of you want to have. You [H.] could turn the TV set off a little more often and maybe you won't. And maybe this will be another tension that you'll have between you that you'll both try to resolve. But for the most part, I'm glad you came in because I got to see you for you instead of what D. was saying. There's a lot of nice feeling between the two of you and that doesn't happen to a lot of marriages.
[I feel like a minister reaffirming their marriage.]
P: The thing is that when I first came in I was so depressed that I couldn't see the bright side of anything, and I always saw the bad side of everything.
T: Especially him.
P: Yeah.
H: I'm sorry.
[An unnecessary apology.]
T: It's not your fault. It wasn't your fault.
[Why did I say this?]
P: Yeah, yeah. Remember you said to me once, you're getting so negative lately. Everything is so negative with you. Well, that's probably when I was starting into depression, and I could not see anything positive in anything.
T: That's right. D.'s had two of these depressions now. They come around for what seems to be good reasons, but still you've had them and you've had them at the same time of year.
P: Right.
T: After you come back after the big summer trip and come home again.
P: Both of them have been in November.
T: You start going down further in November. I saw her almost exactly two years ago. So you have to start watching out for those Alaska winters.
P: Right, that's another thing. I thought if I'm depressed like that here in my home with all my support and friends around, am I going to be twice as depressed up there?
T: You were quite depressed down here. The first time you weren't as depressed as this time. It took you longer to get over it.
P: Well, I know, I could tell it.
[I try to encourage prevention or quicker

seeking of help.]

T: But you know that there are a number of psychiatrists up there in case you need to see one. And you can get on it a little faster maybe. When she starts getting overly negative and more withdrawn and more critical of you. You can take it as some part of it is real. There are some things you should question about yourself. Also, she is starting to get depressed again. We've tried medication and we've tried talking. And we don't know which one works, maybe they both do.

P: A combination.

T: Maybe a combination works, I don't know. But you're better now. I'll be sending you a letter....

[They give me an address correction and we part on a nice note anticipating letter communication within six months.

*Follow-up Letter—June 4, 1985*

Dear Dr. Beitman:

In reply to your letter, I am doing okay, can't say great, but I am slowly adjusting to life in Alaska. Our late and long winter didn't help either, as we were still having snow into May. My children, ages 22 and 25, came up for a visit around Mother's Day, which I really enjoyed, but I did find that after they left I did get depressed. I especially missed my daughter, as we are almost like sisters. I found it was nice to have someone I could confide in. Up here, so far, I don't know anyone that well yet. I had two real bad bouts with the flu, each one lasting about a week. One of these weeks my husband was in Denver, and again I found myself getting really depressed with the long days by myself.

I was taking Desyrel, not trazodone [trazodone is the generic name], and still am taking it. I find that it helps me to get to sleep, although I have reduced the dosage from three tablets to two, as I was having difficulty waking up in the morning.

My husband is still trying to get me to go out in the daytime, but I do find that there are some things I would rather do with him, like picking out some plants for our yard. I just would rather go with him than by myself.

Just today I returned from the doctor's where I am still having pain with the cancer. I am scheduled for another bone scan next week. This will be the fourth scan since arriving here in February. If the results show that the disease is progressing, then I will have to start taking chemotherapy.

As far as activities are concerned, I have signed up to volunteer at ——— Hospital here every Thursday. Part of my problem is that I don't like to do anything where I have to get up early to do it. I don't know whether I am getting lazy or what, but I don't plan anything at all until around 11:00 A.M., and I usually feel guilty, but sleeping in is something I've always enjoyed doing.

Another thing that is depressing me right now is financial. The idea of moving to Alaska was to better ourselves financially. We purchased an airplane one year ago and now that we are up here and my husband is involved with all these young men that are pilots and have their own planes, he is now looking around for a bigger plane, which could run around $40,000, and he wants to put floats on it, which would be at least another $10,000. Seeing as I am the one that writes all the checks I have a hard time convincing my husband that we are going way out of our league. I feel that decisions like this should be discussed together, but the only way I hear about these things is when I overhear him talking to "the guys."

I might say that as of this writing I am giving serious thought to packing up my dog and returning to Seattle, but doubt that I could survive alone with the state of my health and not being employable. Again I feel trapped.

I hope this will give you something to work with in writing the chapter in your book.

Sincerely,
D. G.

## DISCUSSION

Although Mrs. D. G. left therapy in remission from her depression, the apparently good mood did not maintain itself after her move to Alaska. Unfortunately, she did not complete another Beck Depression Inventory, but the tone of her letter suggests an increase in unhappiness. What are some of the factors that may have operated to increase her unhappiness and possibly her depression?

She did not state that her metastatic cancer had gotten out of control. She points specifically to her husband's continued failure to consult her on important issues. Rather than sitting happily while her husband discussed things with the "boys," she overheard plans that bothered her. Was he going to squander the money they had come there to save on an airplane so he could feel part of the crowd? Was he going to withhold the information from her as he had apparently withheld the decision about moving, as he may have about the first recurrence of her cancer, as he did about inviting people to stay with them? Was his real reason to come to Alaska not to save money for their retirement? If not, what else did he have in mind? Since she had great difficulty engaging him in discussions about anything, her only resource was to threaten leaving him or perhaps to get depressed. I wondered if the antidepressant may have been preventing her from becoming seriously depressed again although she was taking a relatively low dose.

The expectation of long-term improvement in personal adjustment following the completion of psychotherapy remains a tacit and generally untested assumption (Steffen & Karoly, 1980). Except for the obvious evidence to the contrary from many returning patients, psychotherapists appear to believe that once a positive change has been initiated, it will endure. Evidence from psychotherapy research on change maintenance is fragmentary. Researchers have enough difficulty trying to agree on adequate measures of change from the beginning to the end of therapy. Except for the study of addictive behaviors, measurable, adequate definition of relapse appears elusive and compounds the already difficult problem of adequate posttreatment criteria. For example, a patient's return for therapy may be used as a marker for relapse, but it also may indicate a readiness for further changes. Other follow-up problems include (1) sample attrition, (2) use of different measure and/or criteria and/or raters at follow-up from those used at treatment termination, and (3) the confounding effects of the events and experiences following termination (Klein & Rabkin, 1984).

The limited evidence from behavioral therapy suggests a consistent trend toward reduction of treatment aftereffect as the length of follow-up increases (Mash & Terdal, 1980). Smith et al. (1980) and Andrews and Harvey (1981) also conclude that the effects of psychotherapy are not permanent and appear to decrease at a regular rate.

Although these conclusions are based on very limited sample sizes, they are indeed sobering. What are the critical variables influencing the durability of change and what can therapists do to increase the likelihood of change maintenance? To answer these questions, psychotherapists must conceptualize their clients devoid of therapeutic input by picturing them in their environments subject to outside influences buffered only by what they have learned about themselves through previous experience and through therapy.

The major maintenance variables include many of the forces that create problems in the first place. Biological variables may override any psychological ones especially in syndromes like Alzheimer's disease and manic-depressive illness. Time and development bring the necessity to keep changing since the only constant is change. Simply because a person has mastered one set of developmental difficulties does not necessarily imply that the next hurdle will also be passed. How effective is the imparted psychotherapeutic learning? Is it problem specific or is it a learning how to learn? How unstable and disruptive is the person's life-style? Are there psychotherapeutic relatives and friends who will assist in the growing and adaptional processes? These variables appear to be crucial determinants in the process of not only maintaining psychotherapeutic change but also building on it (Beitman, 1986 in press).

In the case of Mrs. D. G., her husband appeared to make changes in what seemed to be a desirable direction but, according to her letter, had simply resumed his standard behaviors. Perhaps futher couple's therapy may have made some inroads into their patterns and prevented her current unhappiness. Perhaps the medication was preventing a deeper sense of despair. Perhaps the placebo response had worn thin.

This case illustrates the value of follow-up data and the need for psychotherapists to be vigilant about the sustained effects of their efforts.

## REFERENCES

Andrews, G., & Harvey, R. (1981). Does psychotherapy benefit neurotic patients? *Archives of General Psychiatry, 38,* 1203–1208.

Beck, A. T., Rush, A. J., Shaw, B. F., & Emery, G. (1979). *Cognitive therapy of depression.* New York: Guilford Press.

Beitman, B. D. (1986, in press). *The structure of individual psychotherapy.* New York: Guilford Press.

Beutler, L. E. (1983). *Eclectic psychotherapy.* New York: Pergamon Press.

Erickson, M. H., Rossi, E. L., & Rossi, S. I. (1976). *Hypnotic realities.* New York: Wiley.

Follette, W., & Cummings, N. A. (1976). Psychiatric services and medical utilization in a prepaid health plan setting. *Medical Care, 5,* 25–30.

Kelly, G. A. (1955). *A Theory of personality.* New York: W. W. Norton.

Klein, D. F., & Rabkin, J. G. (1984). Specificity and strategy in psychotherapy. In J. B. Williams & R. L. Spitzer (Eds.), *Psychotherapy research: Where are we and where are we going?* New York: Guilford Press.

Malan, D. H., Heath, S., Bacal, H. A., & Balfour, F. H. G. (1975). Psychodynamic changes in untreated neurotic patients. II. Apparently genuine improvements. *Archives of General Psychiatry, 32,* 110–126.

Mash, E. S., & Terdal, L. J. (1980). Follow-up assessments in behavioral therapy. In P. Karoly & J. Steffen (Eds.), *Improving the long-term effects of psychotherapy.* New York: Gardner.

Prochaska, J. O., & DiClemente, C. C. (1984). *The transtheoretical approach.* Homewood, IL: Dorsey Professional Books.

Rockwell, W. J., & Pinkerton R. S. (1982). Single session psychotherapy. *American Journal of Psychotherapy, 36,* 32–40.

Smith, M. L., Glass, G. V., & Miller, T. (1980). *The benefits of psychotherapy.* Baltimore: Johns Hopkins University Press.

Steffen, J. J., & Karoly, P. (1980). Toward a psychology of therapeutic persistence. In P. Karoly & J. J. Steffen (Eds.), *Improving the long-term effects of psychotherapy.* New York: Gardner Press.

Strong, S. R. (1978). Social psychological approach to psychotherapy research. In S. L. Garfield & A. E. Bergin (Eds.), *Handbook of psychotherapy and behavior change.* New York: Wiley.

# Commentary: Producing a Temporary Change in the System

## Marvin R. Goldfried

*Upon receiving the clinical material sent to me for my comments, I had fully anticipated reading about a course of psychotherapy that reflected each of the four therapy stages described by Beitman, namely, engagement, pattern search, change, and termination. I was fortunate enough to read an early draft of Beitman's (1986, in press) book* The Structure of Individual Psychotherapy *and had hoped to see how this conceptualization was put into clinical practice. Although initially dis-*

appointed in not having these expectations fulfilled, I nonetheless found the submitted case to be of interest on other grounds, not the least of which is that the four stages of therapy are all combined within just a few sessions.

A useful way of conceptualizing the psychotherapeutic change process is that it involves the therapist assisting clients/patients in focusing their attention on aspects of their functioning that they heretofore may have been unaware of. As suggested by Raimy (1975), all therapies are alike in that they help individuals to change certain misconceptions they may have about themselves and others. A good deal of this work takes place during the pattern search phase of the intervention, in that patients/clients are encouraged to adopt a different perspective on themselves and their world. In a sense, it entails having them learn a new causal model by which to better comprehend the problematic aspects of their functioning. Although this is an ongoing process during the course of therapy, there are a number of places in the therapy transcript presented by Beitman where this is nicely illustrated.

The individual therapy sessions conducted with Mrs. G. were based primarily on a cognitive therapy model. Consequently, one of the therapeutic objectives was to help the patient/client focus her attention on possible links between her thoughts and feelings. These connections are reflected in such therapist utterances as: "So when you say to yourself, 'Why can't I do this myself,' what kind of feelings do you have?" and "But you hate the idea of going [to Alaska]." Thoughts are also tied to actions (e.g., "That's what you say to him, but there's more going on in your mind"), and thought-emotion-action links are also made (e.g., "[In this session I have been] trying to define and unearth the thoughts that you may not be quite aware of in your mind, but still influence the way you behave and the way you feel . . . ").

But the search for patterns goes beyond just the linking of thoughts and emotions to other aspects of the client's/patient's functioning. For example, there is a focus on the specifics of situations (e.g., "So you were told in June?"), connections between situations and thoughts (e.g., "Okay, when you see him coming to the kitchen to get his breakfast after you've cleaned up, what thoughts go on in your mind?"); situations and emotions (e.g., "[Let's] talk about some of the other things that are bothering you"); situations and actions (e.g., "You were given a situation that you couldn't do anything about"); and patterns that entail links between situations, thoughts, and emotions (e.g., "So when you see him come in, you say to yourself: 'I don't like having someone else intruding on my time, my privacy. I don't like this.' So you get mad at him, even though you shouldn't, for intruding on your privacy").

In addition to various other connections made by Beitman in the available transcripts (e.g., links between intentions and thoughts, intentions and actions, emotions and actions), he also focuses on various patterns in the client's/patient's life. These involve either a pattern of situations that is pointed out (e.g., "At least four things happened over the past six months or so") or patterns of thought (e.g., "You know it's a good thing for him [her son] to go, ah, but you're losing your baby, you're on your own again").

The connections that the therapist urges the patient/client to focus on are primarily intrapersonal *in nature. In session 3, however, when Mrs. G. returns after a two-year interval, Beitman points out an* interpersonal *pattern that seems to be relevant to her feeling of not having control over her life. Specifically, he juxtaposes the situation where her former husband shot the man with whom she had gone out, and her current husband having unilaterally made the decision to move to Alaska. I would certainly concur with the importance of helping the client/patient become more clearly aware of this particular pat-*

tern in her life, especially as it seems to be a relevant determinant—along with the recurrence of cancer—of her depressive episodes. Additional pattern searches may have been called for, as well, although the severely time-limited nature of the intervention may have precluded this from occurring. Ideally, I would have liked to have explored the possibility that some of these situations—at least those involving her relationships with men—may, in fact, have been the consequence of certain actions or inactions on her part. Is there anything about her behavior that causes her to be mistreated by men? Does it have anything to do with the type of man that she selects to begin with? Thus, in addition to helping the client/patient learn to cope more effectively with situations that afford her minimal control over events (e.g., how to handle a dangerous ex-spouse, what to do when her husband has decided to relocate), the knowledge of her role in bringing about such situations may help her to take steps to ultimately prevent them from occurring.

It is evident that during the time the intervention was taking place, significant clinical improvement occurred, even though it was not maintained over time. The question is, why did it occur and why did it not last? In addition to the various reasons offered by Beitman for this improvement, it is also possible that the therapist instigated a temporary therapeutic change in the behavior of Mrs. G.'s spouse. By involving Mrs. G.'s husband in the sessions, Beitman provided her with something she lacked—a more caring and concerned husband. Unfortunately, this involved only a temporary change in the marital system. Had the marital intervention lasted more than just three brief sessions, and had the husband not ended up in his own social system that encouraged large financial expenditures, it is possible that clinical improvement might have been maintained over time.

## REFERENCES

Beitman, B. D. (1986, in press). The structure of individual psychotherapy. *New York: Guilford Press.*
Raimy, V. (1975). Misunderstandings of the self. *San Francisco: Jossey-Bass.*

# Commentary: Making More Use of Our Models

## James O. Prochaska

There is increasing consensual and empirical validation for the assumption that stages of change are a critical dimension for understanding psychotherapy (Dryden, 1984; Egan, 1982; McConnaughy, Prochaska, & Velicer, 1983). Bernard Beitman has been one of the leaders in articulating a stage model for systematic eclecticism. In the present chapter he provides an overview of the sophisticated stage model he has been developing. Beitman also presents a challenging case of brief psychotherapy for recurring episodes of depression.

What is striking, however, is that Beitman makes all too little use of his model for understanding or intervening with his depressed patient. He does a nice job of combining cognitive, interpersonal, and biochemical interventions within a very brief therapeutic relationship. But his interventions were not as systematic and perhaps not as effective as they might have been had he made more use of his model.

Recognizing that being a Monday morning quarterback is much easier than being on the firing line, I shall nevertheless take the liberty of applying a systematic model of therapy to the case at hand. Since I obviously know my own model better than Beitman's, I will apply a transtheoretical approach to see what differences a model might make.

As with Beitman's approach, our model relies heavily on the stages of change dimension (Prochaska & DiClemente, 1984, 1986). Empirically, we have identified four stages of change: precontemplation, contemplation, action, and maintenance (McConnaughy, Prochaska, & Velicer, 1983). In the present case, Mr. G. appears to be a good example of a client in the precontemplation stage. First of all, clients in the precontemplation stage do not usually enter therapy freely. Often they are brought or sent to therapy by a spouse, parent, employer, teacher, or attorney. As with Mr. G., people in the precontemplation stage tend to deny any need to change their own behaviors. They may seek help to change others but not themselves. Mr. G. said, for example, "The kids and I talked about it. We said, we're gonna treat her just like we always have. We're not changing." Or in talking about his communication with his wife, Mr. G. said, "I know she's more free with somebody else. I've observed that for seven years. But, you know, it doesn't bother me to the point of letting it bother me. That's fine. I figure if she can talk to somebody else. I don't, it doesn't bother me to the point that I'm gonna dwell on it." His denial defends him against any need to contemplate making changes in his relationship with his wife.

Mrs. G., on the other hand, appeared to be in the contemplation stage at the beginning of therapy. She was having difficulty taking action on her own, in part because of her depression, and in part because it was not clear just what needed to be changed. As Beitman points out, "The objective of the pattern search [what we call contemplation] is the elucidation and specification of psychological patterns that, if changed, would bring desired relief and promote enduring change. The content of the pattern search is most variable because the major differences among the schools of therapy lie with their theories of psychopathology and theories of personality development."

What is the content that Mrs. G. should change? Her cognitions, environmental contingencies, interpersonal conflicts, extended family system, personality, and biochemistry could all be candidates for change. In the transtheoretical model, we use the dimension of levels of change to organize the content of psychotherapy. Psychological content is organized across five levels that are ordered from most conscious and contemporary to least conscious and most historical. These five levels are symptom/situational, maladaptive cognitions, interpersonal conflicts, family/system conflicts, and intrapersonal conflicts.

Again, what is the content that we should help Mrs. G. to change? In the transtheoretical approach we have three basic strategies for intervening across diverse levels of change. The first is the shifting-levels strategy, which begins at the highest level that clinical assessments can justify. If we can begin at the symptom and situational level, we expect changes to occur most quickly at this more conscious and contemporary level of problems. Determinants of problems at deeper levels are further removed from consciousness, go further back in time, and are likely to be more resistant to change.

If we are relying on very brief therapy, as was Beitman, then we may do well to use a shifting-levels strategy. Therapy would begin at the symptom and situational level with the hope that clients can efficiently and effectively progress through the stages of change. If therapy is not effective enough at this level, then we would shift to the level of maladaptive cognitions and progress or shift accordingly. Beitman did not specify his strategy, but he appeared to use a less systematic form of this approach, as he shifted from cognitive therapy for depressing cognitions, chemotherapy or placebo therapy for depressive symptoms, and conjoint sessions to address interpersonal conflicts. From a transtheoretical perspective, shifting across three levels in one or two sessions can be expecting too much from clients and therapists. Interventions at each level are likely to be too diluted and clients can become confused about what therapy is intended to accomplish.

From a transtheoretical approach, we would prefer to apply a key-level strategy. If the available evidence, both clinical and empirical, points to a key level of causality for a particular problem and if the client can be effectively engaged at that level, the therapist would work primarily at this key level. Retrospectively, at least, the key level for Mrs. B. appears to be the level of interpersonal conflicts. She seems to feel helpless to change her interpersonal patterns with her husband. Of course, as long as he is in the precontemplation stage, she is helpless. Mr. G. is likely to resist even contemplating changes let alone taking action to change his patterns of relating to his wife.

Even when improvement occurred between therapy sessions, Mr. G. denied having made any changes: "I don't think I've done anything different. I'm still the same, and I still react the same. I think that she notices, I think she was brought aware of the things that ... [I'm doing]." His wife needs to change, not him. A wife who is already having too many changes imposed on her—cancer, Alaska, corporate visitors, and expensive airplanes—has to make all the changes. As we have indicated elsewhere (Prochaska & DiClemente, 1984), one of the common precipitants of depression is imposed change.

If a therapist is trying to facilitate lasting interpersonal changes with spouses who are in two different stages, the therapist cannot expect to rely on very brief therapy. We have presented cases of substantial and lasting changes in couples with very brief therapy, but only when both partners were ready for action and both could work together at the same level of change (Prochaska & DiClemente, 1984). It is impressive that Beitman was able to facilitate significant reductions in depression in just a couple of sessions; it is not surprising that the changes were not maintained. In a review of the therapy literature on depression like Mrs. G.'s, Coyne, Kahn, and Gotlib (in press) found that the cases that did not relapse were those in which substantial and lasting changes were made in marital relationships.

Making more use of our model in the case of Mr. and Mrs. G., we would focus most of therapy on trying to facilitate changes at the key level of interpersonal relationships. We would slow down therapy somewhat in order to give Mr. G. a chance to catch up with Mrs. G. on the stages of change. We would have to help him become aware of his resistance to change before we could expect him to participate in interpersonal therapy. Without such help, Mr. G. would at best function as the therapist's assistant, as he attempts to find further ways of changing his wife. With therapy of longer duration, Mr. and Mrs. G. could be helped to take interpersonal actions that could maintain substantial improvements in the mood that depresses their marriage.

These comments are not intended to be critical of Beitman's work. They are intended to highlight the fact that in the area of systematic eclecticism, theory is rapidly outpacing practice. In my own clinical work it is taking years for my eclectic practice to become as systematic as my eclectic model. Why are changes in practice much more difficult to make than changes in theory? One possibility may be that changes in theory can be limited to changes at the contemplation stage. Relying on processes like consciousness raising and self-re-

*evaluation can lead to changes in how we think and feel about therapy. Changing how we practice therapy, however, requires taking action and maintaining such action lest we slip back into old habit patterns. Taking such concerted action is difficult work that requires considerable time and energy.*

*Judging from my own experience, however, such effort can pay off. As my practice has become more consistent with a systematic eclectic model of change, my effectiveness as a therapist has taken a quantum leap. I have been successfully terminating most cases within 10 to 20 sessions. Even my long-term cases that seemed more resistant to change have been able to finish effectively. I have gone back to work with some cases with whom I had previously failed and have had much more of an impact as a therapist. In the meantime, referrals have markedly increased. One of the challenging, yet gratifying, types of referrals involves more difficult cases from other therapists. After 15 years of a relatively successful practice, it is exciting to be experiencing considerably greater effectiveness as a therapist.*

*It is impossible, of course, to determine just what increased effectiveness may be due to. It could be increased enthusiasm; it could be that my clients are working harder; or it could be a temporary streak of good luck. It will take controlled outcome studies to rule out biased judgments on the part of the therapist and to rule in what really makes a difference. My clinical judgment is that relying much more on a systematic model of eclectic therapy can make a profound difference in enhancing effectiveness as a therapist. So just as I am encouraging Beitman to make more use of his excellent model, so, too, would I encourage other therapists to make more use of the excellent models that are being developed for a more systematic approach to eclectic therapy.*

## REFERENCES

Coyne, J., Kahn, J., & Gotlib, I. (In press). Depression. In T. Jacob (Ed.), Family interaction and psychopathology. *New York: Pergamon.*

Dryden, W. (1984). Individual therapy in Britain. *London: Harper & Row.*

Egan, G. (1982). The skilled helper: Models, skills, and methods for effective helping. *Monterey, CA: Brooks/Cole.*

McConnaughy, E., Prochaska, J., & Velicer, W. (1983). Stages of change in psychotherapy: Measurement and sample profiles. Psychotherapy: Theory, Research, and Practice, 20, 368–375.

Prochaska, J., & DiClemente, C. (1984). The transtheoretical approach: Crossing traditional boundaries of therapy. *Chicago, IL: Dow Jones/Irwin.*

Prochaska, J., & DiClemente, C. (1986). The transtheoretical approach. In J. C. Norcross (Ed.), Handbook of eclectic therapy. *New York: Brunner/Mazel.*

CHAPTER 3

# Systematic Eclectic Psychotherapy: Growing into Separation

## *Larry E. Beutler*

### BASIC TENETS

From one eclectic viewpoint, all psychotherapies are founded in common processes, and these commonalities are the most reliable and consistently important ingredients for facilitating positive change in patient condition. Another eclectic viewpoint emphasizes the value of theoretical amalgamation, and still another type of eclecticism expresses belief in the value of technical integration as a guide to therapeutic decision making. The systematic eclectic psychotherapy to be illustrated here represents the latter form of eclecticism and is based on the joint assumptions that: (1) every psychotherapy approach has fostered unique and effective technologies and (2) these technologies can be applied effectively independently of the theoretical and philosophical formulations that initially spawned them. Although nontechnical and so-called *common variables* are typically regarded as the most powerful contributors to positive therapeutic influence, the technical eclectic or integrative psychotherapist maintains that adding the unique contributions from more specific treatments increases the potential for positive therapeutic outcomes. By applying specific technologies derived from a variety of philosophies, within a general approach that emphasizes the importance of a stable and collaborative therapeutic relationship, it is anticipated that therapeutic gains will be enhanced. However, this will most likely be accomplished, from the standpoint of the systematic eclectic therapist, if the technology is applied in a planned fashion which attends to the particular needs presented by the patient.

From the foregoing perspective, three tasks face the therapist who is interested in applying a systematic eclectic approach to treatment (Beutler, 1983, 1986). The first task is to ensure that there is an optimal compatibility of background and beliefs between the patient and the therapist, so that a fruitful and collaborative relationship can evolve. The second task is to bring specific and relevant techniques to bear on the particular problems presented by the patient at hand. The third task is to modify the therapeutic environment and the treatment techniques as the patient changes and as the variables that indicate or contraindicate various procedures come into focus. In the service of these three objectives, five more specific sets of questions must be addressed as one develops and implements the treatment program. These questions sequentially proceed from the general concern with the suitability of psychotherapy for this patient, to more specific matters having to do with the selection and patterning of particular procedures. To be more specific, the questions addressed in the course of evaluation and treatment are as follows:

*1. Is This Patient a Suitable Candidate for Psychotherapy?*

This question evokes an evaluation process that is designed to determine (a) whether the patient's problem is amenable to change through psychological means, (b) whether the patient is motivated to undertake and maintain a relationship of sufficient duration to modify the problem, and (c) whether the patient has access to sufficient social support systems to provide stability and direction during the course of this relationship. Resolution of these issues usually can be found in the patient's report and history. Of specific importance is a prior history of durable relationships with significant others in which some degree of intimacy is experienced and emotional support is received. Beyond this, it is important to ensure that intellectual resources are available at a level that will allow the patient to experience some continuity between intherapy and extratherapy experiences. At this point, it is sufficient to know that the patient is able to understand that the psychotherapy relationship is in some ways similar to and designed to impact relationships and behaviors in the outside world.

*2. What Should the Focus of Treatment Be?*

This question extends the evaluation process to determine whether the patient's problem can best be perceived as a collection of isolated symptoms, each with their own unique genesis, or as a pattern of interrelated behaviors emanating from a common interpersonal and/or intrapsychic struggle with wants, wishes, impulses, and fears. The term *symptom complexity* is used to describe this range of symptom dynamics. If the symptoms presented are seen as isolated habits, developed and maintained by a consistent set of reinforcing contingencies, they are judged to have low complexity, and this form of systematic eclectic psychotherapy asserts that the focus should be on the symptoms themselves, with the goal of symptom removal. On the other hand, various problems and symptoms presented by many patients are an indirect expression of a common set of unresolved internal conflicts, including an array of unrealistic interpersonal fears whose intensities are inconsistent with the observed environmental probabilities of encountering dangerous events. In the latter cases, it is assumed that the therapy focus should concentrate on the dynamically active struggle and conflicts that give rise to the various complex patterning of symptoms rather than on the isolated symptoms themselves.

An index of symptom complexity is derived from a clinical judgment which evaluates: (1) the extent to which symptoms have generalized to impair the patient's interpersonal functioning (i.e., the number of areas of life impacted), (2) the degree to which current problem and symptom patterns reflect a learning history with similar contingencies as opposed to being a disturbance arising from idiosyncratic generalizations and perceptual distortions of contingencies that never were or are no longer realistically present, and (3) how adequately the patient deals with the resulting distress (i.e., the severity of disturbance). A balance of these three factors is used to make an initial determination of whether the presenting problem represents a simple adjustment to a specific environment (i.e., habit), or whether there is a dynamic conflict represented that supports and maintains the disturbance (i.e., neurotiform adjustment).

In the event that one determines that the presenting problem is a reflection of a consistent and linear reinforcement history, the focus of treatment becomes the isolated symptoms, and one need only identify and prioritize these at this point in the assessment process. If, on the other hand, the initial assessment suggests that the patient's presenting problems represent a dynamic struggle, represented as a life pattern of similar struggles, the therapist's task must be extended to define the central theme or focus which has characterized the patient's struggle and which is assumed to underlie the presenting problems. This target of treatment, defined as the *core theme,* involves the process of postulating the nature of the motivating struggle.

In developing a postulate of the patient's life theme, the systematic eclectic therapist relies on whatever theoretical or philosophical foundations are most comfortable and with which she or he is most familiar. Psychoanalytic formulations, interpersonal formulations, or formulations derived from object relations and social persuasion are all possible guiding constructs. Because of their simplicity and their probable relevance to the patient-therapist matching process to be discussed shortly, the formulation of conflicts along the dimension of dependence-independence developed by Millon (1969; Millon & Everly, 1985) has been of considerable help to this author.

Although the truth of the formulation ultimately selected is impossible to assess, it is important that: (1) the therapist believes that it accurately represents the patient, (2) it is sufficiently logical to make sense to the patient, and (3) it is capable of being taught within the probable time frame of the therapy. This postulated formulation becomes the guiding thread of psychotherapy and serves as the glue that holds together a variety of specific interventions. The specific nature of these latter interventions is defined by the answers derived from responding to the remaining central questions addressed by the therapist.

*3. How Tolerant Is the Patient of Directive Influence?*

Once the decision is made that psychotherapy is a relevant intervention and the focus of this therapy has been defined, the subsequent questions address how the therapist should approach the patient. Raising a question of patient tolerance for directive interventions is designed to remind the therapist that psychotherapy is an interpersonal influence process. This question will focus the therapist on the fact that his or her viewpoints will be transmitted to the patient and that the manner and force with which this is done can either motivate the patient toward improvement or mobilize resistance against change.

Inherent in the determination of the patient's susceptibility to influence is a need to evaluate *what* is being transmitted. This process involves assessing the amount of compatibility existing between patient and therapist belief systems and backgrounds. Research on attitude change in psychotherapy (Beutler, 1981; Beutler, Crago, & Arizmendi, in press) has quite consistently observed that certain demographic similarities between patient and therapist facilitate the patient's initial commitment to the treatment process, whereas optimal differences of viewpoint around cardinal therapeutic issues (core themes) may mobilize the patient to make changes. However, if viewpoints between therapist and patient are too discrepant, the patient may find the therapist's views to be intolerant and unacceptable (Beutler, 1981). Unless this factor can be offset by other variables, the development of a collaborative and therapeutic relationship may be impaired. Therefore, the effective eclectic psychotherapist must be aware of the interpersonal and attitudinal compatibility that exists between himself and a prospective patient and make a judgment as to whether or not there is sufficient background similarity to maintain a collaborative relationship and for the patient to find the therapist's viewpoint credible. At the same time, however, the therapist must make a judgment as to whether there is sufficient difference of opinion around those cardinal attitudes and values which maintain the patient's problem to stimulate change.

The second task of the therapist in assessing the approach to take is a determination of *how* the interventions should be delivered. This decision is reflected in variations in how directive the therapist is in conveying alternative viewpoints, in dealing with problems, and in implementing the techniques designed to resolve the patient's problem. Systematic eclectic psychotherapy has borrowed the term *reactance* (Brehm & Brehm, 1981) from social psychology to describe the degree to which the patient might resist interventions that are initiated by the therapist. An assessment of the patient's reactance level, therefore, predicts the degree that directive procedures will be tolerated when mobilizing the patient toward change. Without belaboring the point, the principle of reactance is based on considerable research both in clinical and in laboratory settings which suggests that the highly reactant patient may resist both the attitudes conveyed by the therapist and any directive procedures that may be used for implementing change. It has been suggested that deterioration in the patient's condition may occur if the therapist's level of directiveness is not geared to the patient's tolerance for directiveness. In contrast to highly reactant patients, those with low levels of reactance seem to be very tolerant and may even present an affinity for directiveness in the therapist's efforts to convey both adaptive attitudes and in implementing technical procedures (Beutler et al., in press).

## 4. What Specific Interventions Are Likely to Yield the Greatest Gain?

Once interpersonal compatibility and degree of tolerance for directiveness have been determined, the therapist is faced with the task of deriving a menu of interventions that are both suitably situated on the specter of directiveness to be accepted by the patient and appropriately focused on either the conflictual theme or the independent symptoms that serve as the guiding thread of treatment. In order to make such a determination, the therapist now focuses on defining the patterns of behavior and defense that the patient typically uses to cope with the inner conflicts and/or situational pressures. In the case of habitform conditions, represented as simple or monosymptomatic patterns, this determination represents simply an assessment of whether the patient's presenting symptoms exist because of a relative excess of certain kinds of behavior or an insufficiency of alternative behaviors in their repertoire. This knowledge then determines for the therapist whether the treatment will concentrate on skill development (for behavioral insufficiency), or on curtailment and extinction of those excessive behaviors which are defined as "symptoms."

The situation becomes more complex if the patient has been defined as having a neurotiform or "adjustment" difficulty. In this event, the therapist must determine whether the *principal* way the patient attempts to control anxiety deriving from the thematic conflict is through: (a) overcontrol of both emotions and behaviors, (b) undercontrol of both emotions and behaviors, or (c) a middle point, usually represented by emotional lability in the presence of excessive inhibition of impulses.

It is postulated that patterns of direct *anxiety avoidance* (undercontrol) are most amenable to interventions that take a behavioral focus. These individuals cope with driving conflicts by externalizing anxiety through acting-out and excessive behaviors, dictating that the interventions concentrate on controlling and stabilizing the behavioral manifestations of the conflict. In contrast, some patients present defensive styles designed for *anxiety containment*. These patients overcontrol and compartmentalize emotions and engage in behavioral and social withdrawal. Such defenses suggest that these individuals have constrained their emotional experiences and have placed corresponding constraints on behaviors that represent these needs. Therapeutic procedures that emphasize the escalation and magnification of arousal as well as the awareness of emotional needs are therefore applicable.

A third group of patients present a mixture of both anxiety-containing defenses (e.g., internalizing, overcontrol, and impulse constriction) and direct-avoidance defenses (e.g., externalizing, undercontrolled and exaggerated feelings). This pattern, referred to as *anxiety magnification*, is indexed by the presence of emotional lability and the absence of corresponding behavioral displays. These individuals may express a great deal of affectivity, primarily in the form of anxiety and agitation, but continue to compartmentalize emotions and to constrain impulses, even when acting out certain impulses would be appropriate. Depressiform patterns of cognition are often observed, as are patterns of hypersensitivity. The recommended therapeutic interventions emphasize management of the perceptual patterns and cognitive beliefs which prevent modulation of emotions and which serve to constrain even normal and appropriate behaviors.

By selecting interventions suitable to the patient's defensive style and at the same time suitable to the degree of symptom complexity presented by the patient and still adjusted for greater or lesser directiveness in the intervention process, a menu can be constructed of the most probable interventions for realizing therapeutic gains. To do so requires that the therapist know the demand characteristics of each intervention he or she uses.

In making a task analysis of interventions, it is helpful to distinguish between *evocative* and *directive* procedures. Evocative procedures are those which are totally under the control of the therapist and require little specific response on the part of the patient. The evocative intervention is designed to facilitate the patient's exploration but does not predetermine the nature, form, or outcome of his response. In contrast, directive interventions are designed to engage the patient in carrying out a particular experiment or task. Although the end point of this task and experiment may be unknown, the process of its execution is under the discretion or recommendation of the therapist. Generally, directives require the exertion of more control on the part of the therapist and compliance on the part of the patient than do evocative interventions. In addition to this general rule, specific interventions within each of the broader categories vary in: (1) the degree of control required on the part of the therapist for implementation (directiveness), (2) the degree to which the interventions are amenable to symptoms or underlying conflicts, and (3) the degree to which the intervention is compatible with the patient's defensive style, varying along the general dimension of internalizing/containing to externalizing/avoiding.

For want of space and time, the reader is referred to other written sources in which a task analysis of various interventions has been described in some detail (Beutler, 1983, in press). It bears emphasis here, however, that the three categories of defensive style described in the foregoing are roughly equivalent to the three realms of experience to which various interventions are addressed. Interventions can be seen as emphasizing either *behavioral, cognitive,* or *affective* experience. These are broad categories of experience and associated interventions, but they do embody a certain logic and consistency. This is not to say that many interventions cannot be used alternatively to address two or all of these levels of experience. As a general rule of thumb, nevertheless, it is postulated that behavioral interventions are most appropriate for individuals with externalizing defensive styles in which direct avoidance of anxiety is achieved through acting out, projection, and attention seeking. Concomitantly, cognitive change interventions are postulated to be most appropriate for those individuals whose anxiety magnifying/sensitizing defenses are manifest in behavioral constraint and emotional lability or depression. In contrast, the affective interventions, which are typically drawn from experiential and humanistic therapies, are postulated to be most useful among individuals who most severely constrain emotional experience and withdraw from sensory stimulation. These internalizing, anxiety-containing individuals are judged to be amenable to interventions that heighten affective arousal and draw their attention to emotional experiences and nuances.

Within the foregoing broad intervention categories, specific techniques and procedures can be even more precisely defined in terms of the amount of therapist control and suggestion required for their effective implementation. Among the evocative strategies, for example, reflections require little power or control on the part of the therapist and minimal compliance on the part of the patient. In contrast, dynamic interpretations require that the patient exert focused energy to give up defensively protected awarenesses in order effectively to accommodate the insight offered by the therapist. Questions and clarifications fall somewhere between these extremes of required therapist control.

Among directive procedures, task-oriented homework assignments and in-session experiments require a relatively large amount of therapist control and patient compliance. Imagery-based procedures, however, may require less in the way of external manifestation of patient compliance and are thus less likely to threaten the patient's sense of autonomy. Such procedures as dream analysis, relaxation training, and hypnosis require varying but lesser amounts of therapist control when compared to directives that insist on some behavioral manifestation either within the session or external to the session.

It is a tenet of systematic eclectic psychotherapy that once the various therapeutic procedures are analyzed for their task structure and demand characteristics, one can select a menu of appropriate strategies, adjusting these to: (1) correspond with the ability of the patient to tolerate directive interventions (i.e., reactance level), (2) maintain the selected focus on the patient's cognitive, behavioral, or emotional experiences, and (3) suitably address the complexity of the problem by emphasizing either targeted symptoms or broad-band dynamic conflicts.

Unfortunately, therapists can only select from among the procedures with which they are familiar, and therapists have varying abilities to adjust specific procedures along the dimensions of directiveness and focus. Therefore, it is advisable for therapists to become very familiar with a wide range of therapeutic procedures and to seek to acquire considerable flexibility in their application so that these procedures can be made to accommodate the patients' defensive style, reactance level, and need for symptomatic or conflictual focus. Moreover, the therapist must know when to shift therapeutic stance and modify the treatment menu.

## 5. How Should the Interventions Be Changed over the Course of Treatment?

Neither patients nor the problems they present are static qualities. When therapy is effective, it exerts its effect through a dynamic process in which the patient's reactance level, coping skills, and coping effectiveness change as treatment progresses. As an outgrowth of developing a compatible and collaborative therapeutic relationship, the patient's ability to tolerate directiveness within therapy may change even though this change may not rapidly transfer to the extratherapy environment. Hence, the effective eclectic therapist is constantly engaged in the activity of process diagnoses, evaluating changes in response, defense, and receptiveness over the course both of a single session and as one proceeds through broader phases of treatment. The menu of interventions fruitfully used to initiate treatment, therefore, must be altered as treatment progresses. The nature of this adjustment reflects a complex interplay between adjusting the directiveness of the intervention, on one hand, and gearing the intervention to match the patient's defensive style, on the other. Throughout, the focal objective remains constant, whether it be symptom removal or core conflict resolution. This latter continuity of focus provides the integrative force of treatment.

Because patient reactance, defensive style, and problem complexity are all subject to idiosyncratic patterns of change, numerous possible scenarios of treatment patterning may emerge. One scenario often observed among patients who exhibit strong internalizing, anxiety-containing defenses may proceed as follows: (1) The initial treatment menu may emphasize emotional awareness and escalation in the beginning phases of treatment; procedures from Gestalt therapy may be used to heighten here-and-now, sensory-emotional experiences. (2) As the patient becomes less emotionally constrained in the middle phases of treatment, cognitive interventions may be utilized both to help the patient develop a new perspective on his behavior and to reinforce his ability to control the impulses that may be activated by new emotional experiences. (3) In the later phases of treatment, behavioral retraining and assertive skill training may be employed to facilitate the patient's social roles and interpersonal relationships.

On the other hand, when treating an externalizing, anxiety-avoidant patient, the initial behaviorally tuned interventions may be followed by cognitive interventions as impulses become constrained and agitation increases. These cognitive interventions may be used to reinforce the strength of the behavioral controls that have been implemented. In this case, an emphasis on emotional experience and awareness may be reserved for the late stages of treatment and will be designed to tune the patient to the subtleties of interpersonal communication and intrapersonal needs.

The principles outlined in the foregoing discussion can be only partially illustrated in a single case example. Since the fundamental propositions emphasize patient-to-patient variations in therapist planning and approach, one cannot hope to capture a full picture of these differences in action without a large number of systematically different therapy-patient-therapist matches. Nonetheless, the following case example is offered as a sampling of how the reasoning behind this form of systematic eclecticism operates in practice.

## A CASE EXAMPLE

*Patient Selection/Evaluation*

The patient to be presented in the remainder of this chapter was the first psychotherapy candidate to contact the author for treatment after a commitment to contribute to this volume had been made. Moreover, she was the only patient seen for this purpose and from whom weekly audio recordings of therapy sessions were made. Although this case cannot be considered entirely representative of patients in the author's caseload, no attempt was made to preselect the patient. Many aspects of the patient and her treatment were typical, at least to the degree that any one treatment process is "typical" of another. Although several features of the patient's history and status will be altered in the following presentation, in the interest of anonymity, the essential features will be preserved.

The patient (R. T.) was originally referred to the writer from out of state. She was relocating close to her mother in order to begin her college career. She is female, 18 years of age, and indicated that her initial problem was residual anger at her parents and a desire to get rid of her tendency to "think, judge, and question myself."

The referrent for this patient was a psychiatrist who, along with a psychological counselor, had been treating the patient for nearly a year. The patient's psychiatric and medical history was considerably more extensive than would be indicated by this knowledge alone, however. For example, she presented a long history of a "seizure disorder" and had recently been diagnosed as having narcolepsy. Moreover, the patient's parents were both alcoholic and had divorced when she was eight years of age. The patient recalled a good deal of turmoil in the family both prior to and following the divorce but had no knowledge of the specific reasons for the marital breakup.

Following her parents' divorce, the patient initially stayed with her mother, but because of her mother's disrupted lifestyle, the patient subsequently moved in with her father and stepmother at the age of 13. The patient reported that her stepmother was aggressive and hostile and frequently had "emotionally" abused the patient. Interpersonal problems reached critical levels between the patient and her father because of her reactions to her stepmother, and these problems were complicated by the presence of a half-brother (aged four) who occupied a favored role with the parents. Her father's continued alcoholism further introduced conflicts between him and his wife, and the intensity of these frequently left the patient feeling isolated from all family members. She was often restricted to her room for long periods of time and prevented from seeing friends. Thus, she remembered few good friendships during early adolescence. In her early years, she recalls her father as being physically abusive. He had a history of periodic depressions (probably representing a bipolar disorder), and these episodes significantly exacerbated his pattern of explosiveness and withdrawal.

The patient reported that her medical problems began at approximately age seven. Originally she experienced "dizzy spells," but later these were accompanied by blackouts, loss of memory, and probable psychomotor seizures. By the time she went to live with her father at age 13, these spells were sufficiently pronounced that they were interfering with other life functions. She had been a competitive swimmer but, because of social fears, depression, and seizures, was forced to give up the pursuit of her parents' dream of Olympic stardom. When she began to experience sleep paralysis and sleep attacks, she was treated by a neurologist who prescribed several antiseizure medications with little effect.

By age 16 family difficulties had become sufficiently intense that the patient began experiencing severe bouts of depression with pronounced suicidal ideation. It was at that time that she first was taken to see a psychiatrist. In the initial few months of treatment, he prescribed response trials of from 12 to 15 different types of medication, most of which did not substantially help either her depression or her seizures. She was ultimately diagnosed as having narcolepsy, on the basis of a clinical symptom pattern, and placed on Dexedrine with some benefit. At the time the patient saw the author several months later, she was taking 15 milligrams of Dexedrine twice daily and maintained that this had been a lifesaving force for her because it had partially relieved the intensity of her depressive episodes. Nonetheless, she reported the continuing presence of periodic blackouts, triggered both by intense visual stimuli and by emotionally arousing situations. Moreover, she acknowledged being dependent on the medication.

Prior to the initial appointment, the patient was provided with a series of psychological assessment devices. These included the MMPI (Dahlstrom, Welsh, & Dahlstrom, 1972) to assess personality organization, with particular emphasis on defensive style and reactance level; the Shipley Institute of Living Scale (Paulson & Lin, 1970) to assess her cognitive functioning and conceptual ability; the SCL-90R (Derogatis, Rickels, & Rock, 1976) to evaluate the pervasiveness of her symptoms; and the FIRO-B (Schutz, 1958), which was used as a brief screening inventory to assess the interpersonal attachments from which a core theme might be constructed.

The patient was oriented in all three spheres, but acknowledged being hypersensitive to any threat of altering her medication or treatment regimen. In that context, she was very distressed at the neurologist who had also seen her on initial referral and who was managing her medications. This attitude remarkably contrasted with her feeling about her prior psychiatrist, whom she idolized. Her negative feeling toward the current neurologist was instigated when he suggested that he would like to withdraw her from medication in order to evaluate her narcolepsy.

Figure 1 presents the patient's MMPI profile at the time of intake. As noted, she was extremely suspicious and quite depressed. The extensive reliance on traditional feministic philosophies and attitudes (Mf) contrasted with the assertiveness represented in scales Pd and Pa. This pattern was interpreted as suggesting an individual who was suspicious, particularly of men, who tended to confuse dependency and aggressive feelings, who felt victimized by others, and who presented a high degree of interpersonal reactance to external control.

By the same token, an analysis of the personality profile suggested that the patient presented an anxiety-magnifying coping style. For example, the evidences of depressiform patterns (D) suggested the presence of intropunitive self-consciousness, which was further exemplified in her obsessiform ideations about religion and her sense of guilt (Pt). This point was underlined at the time of the initial interview when the patient reported preoccupation with supernatural forces and religious experiences. She reported that she considered herself to have supernatural powers but felt tremendously guilty at her inability to utilize these to benefit others. She expressed great feelings of guilt about religion and the sense that God either had deserted her or was helpless to assist her. In either case, He had been a disappointment to her and had be-

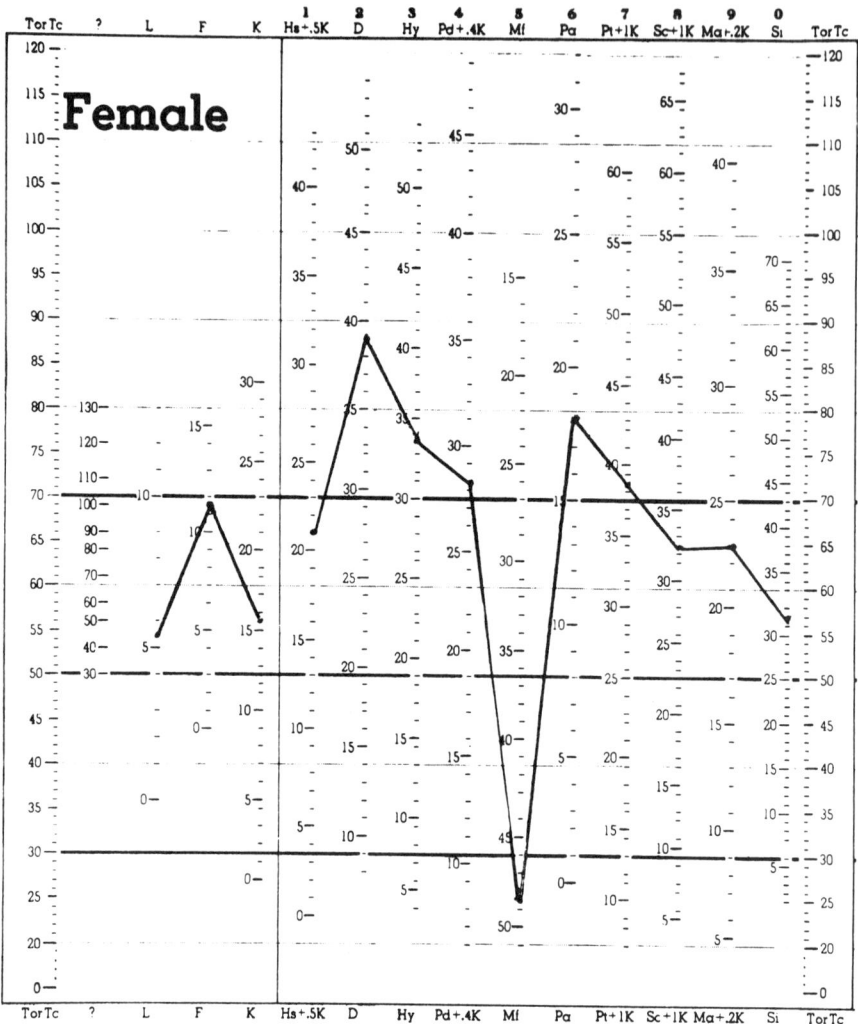

*Figure 1.* Pretherapy MMPI profile (corrected T scores).

come an object of her anger. Her primary social contacts had been with religious groups who maintained literal interpretations of scriptures and placed strong demands on the patient for compliance with certain religious codes and standards. Her failure to comply totally with these invoked considerable anger, guilt, and apprehension.

Prior to and during the first session, the patient's status was evaluated by addressing the five questions outlined in the earlier sections of this chapter.

## 1. Suitability for Treatment

The patient had a prior history of being able to benefit from a therapeutic relationship, both with a psychiatrist and with a counselor who had worked with her for approximately a year. She also exhibited hope for the pending therapeutic relationship. Moreover, she functioned within the superior range of intelligence and at a high level of cognitive efficiency, as assessed at the time of intake. These strengths suggested the ability to develop insight and to evaluate the significance and generality of intherapy behavior. Although she was overly involved and unable to step back and objectively assess her own behavior, her desire to do so and her cognitive resources suggested that she was a good candidate for individual psychotherapy.

## 2. Treatment Focus

The patient's difficulties had been going on for a long period of time, and at the time of initial evaluation she presented moderate to severe psychological disturbance as represented in formal psychological assessment devices (MMPI, SCL-90R). She had inordinate concerns with punishment, extensive guilt about minor matters, and extensive, self-imposed performance demands. These observations suggested compromised coping abilities and a broad-ranging psychological disturbance. The pattern of social withdrawal and ambivalence pervaded a variety of areas and had interfered with social relationships, religious activities, family relationships, and school. She had previously been a promising class A swimmer, for example, but had withdrawn in the midst of family crises and, for a period of time, had dropped virtually all social relationships. She reported evidence of periodically becoming fixated on one aspect of interpersonal functioning or another (e.g., religion, school, etc.), only to become frustrated with insoluble dilemmas, and had abandoned social activities in the midst of her depressions. This pattern suggested the complexity of the psychological disturbance and argued for a treatment approach focused on conflicts and conflict resolution.

A review of the patient's history, particularly those aspects suggesting abuse and abandonment, suggested that a primary focal theme in her interpersonal relationships may be in the counterbalancing desires for attachment and nurturance, on one hand, and distance and individuation, on the other (ambivalence; cf. Beutler, 1983; Millon, 1969). A review of both the patient's MMPI and her FIRO-B suggested intense needs for affection and dependency, counterbalanced by a striving for individuation and separation. In part, this struggle was age appropriate, but appeared to be exacerbated beyond the patient's years in the context of profound family struggles.

With the interpersonal focal theme defined as one of ambivalence, the therapeutic objective was designed to concomitantly assist the patient in selecting an attitudinal and behavioral pattern that would allow gratification of both her desires for nurturance and her desires for individuation. The patient's bipolar approach to this conflict was represented in a cyclical and disruptive fashion rather than in a pattern that modulated these two need systems as befit the situation. Developing the ability to modulate these competing forces was judged to be a critical treatment concern.

## 3. Approach to the Patient

The patient came from an upper-middle-class background, with traditional religious beliefs and a strong emphasis on social conformity. Interpersonal compatibility with the therapist was considered to be relatively similar in the dimensions of: religious background, socioeconomic background, and traditional values. In these demographic and background spheres, the patient's and therapist's similar history suggested compatibility (Beutler, 1983; Beutler et al., in press). However, compatibility also emphasizes the importance of differences of viewpoint, particularly around those critical issues of life reflecting needs for attachment and individuation. Here, the patient exhibited extreme views in both directions. My own views regarding attachment and separation issues are somewhat more moderate but place value on individuation and autonomy. Hence, this informal evaluation of patient-therapist value systems and the patient's developmental needs for individuation suggested a basis for a compatible and productive relationship. This basis was further explored in the first session by assessing and questioning the strength of contact and attachment that took place between the patient and therapist.

A second aspect of the approach to be used was determined by assessing the patient's reactance level. As noted, R. T.'s history suggested relatively high levels of interpersonal reactance and was supported by initial psychological evaluation which provided evidence that she was resistant to directives and sensitive to losing a sense of choice. These observations suggested that the patient would be most likely to benefit if the treatment interventions selected deemphasized directive control on the part of the therapist.

## 4. Specific Interventions

A menu of potentially useful interventions was selected initially from an assessment of the patient's defensive style. The MMPI profile presented in Figure 1 suggested that the patient presented a mixture of both internalizing, anxiety-containing (Pt, D) and externalizing, direct-avoidance (Pd, Pa, and Hy) patterns. The elevation in both externalizing and internalizing indices of coping style, coupled with the patient's history and affective presentation, suggested a pattern of anxiety magnification, expressiveness, and intropunitiveness. She had no history of impulsiveness or acting out, but clearly felt her emotions to be tenuous and exaggerated. This emotional undercontrol in the presence of behavioral constriction and inhibition suggested the probable value of procedures that were cognitively focused and emphasized perceptual change methodologies (Beutler, 1986).

Taking into account the patient's degree of reactance, the need for a theme-focused intervention, and her emotionally sensitized coping style, a menu of therapeutic procedures was outlined. This menu included the following types of interventions:

1. A relatively heavy reliance on low directive evocative interventions: reflection, questions, clarifications, and reframing
2. Lesser but selective reliance on patient-controlled, directed interventions: cognitive practice, role playing, fantasy/imagery, directed dialogue, evidence gathering, self-monitoring, and practice in alternative thinking

All these procedures were selected because an earlier task analysis (Beutler, 1983) suggested that they can be implemented with little therapist directiveness and would provide minimal threat to the patient's need for autonomy and freedom. The procedures also were selected to be applicable to assessing cognitive patterns and establishing cognitive control of emotional experience while still addressing underlying conflictual themes. The themes and schemas of relevance here were judged to be related to the patient's ambivalent attachment needs in family and interpersonal relationships.

## 5. Changing Therapeutic Interventions

The initial therapeutic menu was designed to focus on cognitive change and perceptual restructuring. A precise delineation of how the therapeutic procedures would need to change during treatment depends on how the patient responds to the initial interventions, how coping styles and reactance level are modified over the course of treatment, and what changes take place in the patient's defensive style. However, some prediction of the probable patterning of change can be based on clinical experience with the nature of change. In my own experience, for example, I observe that in effective relationships, high reactance levels are modified relatively early. Although, initially, a patient's reduced reaction propensity may not extend beyond the therapeutic environment, the establishment of a collaborative relationship allows a patient to benefit from increasingly directive, intherapy interventions.

Other changes are more difficult to predict at the outset, however. For example, a patient who approaches the world with a heightened sense of anxiety may, as one explores the expectations and beliefs that underlie this reaction, become increasingly emotionally constricted or occasionally manifest behavioral impulsiveness. The therapist must be prepared, therefore, to implement external, behavioral controls, in the latter event, or move increasingly toward an exploration of emotional issues, in the other.

As treatment progressed, this particular patient moved increasingly toward emotional control and overmodulation. Hence, with time, therapy became increasingly focused on differentiating among R. T.'s various feelings and sensitizing her to the meanings of these subtle nuances which differentiated emotional states. Only in the late stages of therapy did the focus turn to exploring the behavioral skills that she might directly implement in her relationship to other people. Thus, treatment was designed to initially impact cognitive patterns, including insight and understanding of the relationship between cognitions and feelings, and then progressed to an affective orientation and, finally, to a behavioral one. The therapist's stance, on the other hand, moved from very nondirected through a period of relative directiveness as the patient's reactance level decreased and then returned to a stance of relatively low directiveness in late treatment phases.

*Interventions*

The first session of contact was devoted to evaluations of the patient, problem, and environment and involved gathering information about the patient's background and providing her feedback about the results of the psychological assessment. At her request, her mother joined us in the latter moments of this session. During that time, I explained that the patient appeared to be quite depressed and anxious and that such individuals frequently felt like they were victimized in their relationship with other people. At that point, the patient confirmed this impression, and we made plans to begin an open-ended course of treatment the following week. It bears emphasizing that the distinction between the evaluation sessions and the treatment sessions is a very unclear and undefined one. My own view is that the evaluation session constitutes treatment and that each session includes an evaluation component, which we have called "process diagnosis." Nonetheless, treatment sessions are counted for the purposes of this presentation as those which followed the initial evaluation session.

The first treatment session (8/23) was not recorded. The patient was presented with the therapist's desire to make audio tape recordings during this initial session, and although apprehensive, she accepted the invitation after some thought and discussion. Beginning with session 2 the subsequent 27 sessions of treatment were audio-recorded. The following pages will present excerpts from various of these sessions, to illustrate both the patient's dynamics and the application, and, perhaps, the misapplication, of certain procedures. The second therapy session deserves special attention. It was in this session that we began to explore and clarify the patient's theme of ambivalent interpersonal relationships and a contract was initiated regarding the risk-taking activities that were deemed to be important if her treatment was to be successful. The patient's ambivalence was exemplified in her description of her father's behavior.

*Session 2 (8/30)*

T: What did you mean when you said that you felt "abused"?
P: Well, like when you showed her [mother] that test and told her that people like that, like feel that they've been abused, I remembered that three people have, what I call, abused me.
T: Can you explain that?
P: Well, the first was my father. I remember that when I was very young, like before he and my mother divorced, that he used to get drunk and slap me. Sometimes he'd hit me right here on the cheek or on my nose. All the time he'd be yelling at me and telling me that if I didn't like it, to run away. I tried to run away but I couldn't. I was afraid of being caught and hit harder.
T: How are you feeling when you describe that?
P: I'm afraid. I was afraid that he would, like, hurt me. It reminds me of one of my mother's boyfriends, after she and dad separated and he got remarried. She became very depressed and began doing really strange things. She started running around with younger men, getting drunk and staying out all night, like that. She had this one friend. D., who scared me a lot. He was drunk a lot and always made me afraid that he would, like, hurt me. One night I woke up and he was by my bed, touching my stomach. I was so afraid, I couldn't call out. I thought that maybe he had kissed me and I was afraid he was going to like touch me other places. When he finally got up and left, I went looking for my mother. I told her that he was really scaring me and touching me, and she only said, "Well he's not been very nice tonight to me either." She didn't, like, pay any attention to what I was trying to tell her and how frightened I was.
T: You had other times of being frightened too?
P: Yes, I was always afraid that mother would, like, die and not come back home when she was out late. She talked about killing herself, and I was always really afraid that something gory had happened to her.
T: Gory?
P: Yes, it wasn't as if she would die a healthy death. It was as if she would be hurt and like be destroyed and be bloody and everything. I remember one time I couldn't find her in the house and found an open window in our apartment on the sixteenth floor. I looked out and couldn't see her but then I saw her on a ledge and she began calling for me to come out and telling me that she could fly. She was drunk but I was scared that she was going to jump. I felt, like, I had lost my father; he was no longer interested in me. I was afraid that without her I wouldn't have anyone. I didn't want to see her die and began crying and pleading for her to come back in. She eventually came back in, but for weeks she laughed at me for being upset. She abused me too, you know, I mean, emotionally.

Later in the session, the patient was challenged with the possibility of taking some risks in her own behalf in order to overcome her fears and change her views of the world.

T: If I understand what you've said, it scares you when you start feeling better. It seems more comfortable and somehow, as if you're more "sensitive" if you stay kind of depressed.

P: That's right, I even get, like, afraid of being too happy. I think it's wrong to become so happy that you like lose sensitivity to what's happening around you.

T: You mean what's happening around you is depressing and you have to keep hold of that?

P: That's right.

T: Might it be just as dishonest to pay attention to the depressing things and ignore the happy ones?

P: Yeah, but if you get too happy, people will take it away from you—they'll leave you or something like that.

T: And if you stay unhappy?

P: Well, at least then you don't have, like, far to fall.

T: So, if you're unhappy you control what's going on, but if you're happy, other people can take it away from you and have control over you?

P: Yes, something like that.

T: I guess, a big risk for you would, then, be taking the chance that you could be happy and paying attention to all the happy things in your life. Would you be willing to take that kind of a risk?

P: Well, if you could, like, guarantee that people wouldn't disappoint me or leave me.

T: If I could make that guarantee, it wouldn't be a risk. Are you willing to take a *risk* in order to feel better?

P: I'm not sure. I guess I'm getting closer to the idea of doing that.

T: Maybe you'd find out that you could be happy and still be sensitive to the painful parts of life.

P: Yeah, maybe I would, but it sounds awfully scary to me.

The patient quickly developed an involvement in the treatment process. In subsequent sessions she began talking about her new role as student in a university environment and in session 3 described a nightmare she had of hell. The nightmare illustrated a pronounced tendency to think in dichotomous terms of "good" and "bad" and a similar tendency to apply this dichotomous thinking to other people, seeing them as either friends or enemies. Utilizing this nightmare, we began exploring the cognitive therapy concept of how her thoughts might change her feelings. At my suggestion she was able to reconstruct a sense of anxiety and depression and then to remove it by altering her thoughts about the nightmare itself. In session 4, the concept that R. T.'s depression could be altered by her conscious thoughts and images was developed further.

*Session 4 (9/11)*

T: Can we start, then, by me asking you a little bit about where your thoughts went after the last session?

P: Um, I don't think I thought so much. I mean I didn't analyze it or anything. I was just pretty happy you know. In the middle of the week I got a depressed feeling, but then I was able to get out of it within an hour, which is really good. I haven't had any more of these little depressions at all. I mean, things weren't too bad. It was pretty good because I kept thinking about the meetings that we had and how you just let me get out of depression. You know you got me to get into it and out of it when I wanted to. The depression came when I was with my mom, and as soon as I got back to the dorm with my roommates and everything I got smack, right out of it, like I totally forgot about it. And then the next day, I couldn't even believe I was mad about anything.

T: Mad and depression kind of go together?

P: Yeah, I guess so, yeah! Yeah, like it's really an injustice or something is unfair. Some of the past, sometimes, sneaks up on my mom and she started doing some things that bothered me a little bit. And . . .

T: I don't understand that. Can you remember a little bit of what went on last time you were with your mom, that might relate to being depressed?

P: Oh yeah, I know what it is, I know exactly what. See, my problem with her was that she likes that guy T., so it just bothered me a lot because she just gave up the mother role a lot. You know, saying she didn't want to be in that role, but yet she wanted me to always respect her; she wanted to have her cake and eat it too, and it really hurt. And then all this time with my father has been so bad, and when I talked to my mom over the last several months, before I came, she was very, very supportive of me. Extra-, extrasupportive; more than she'd ever been before. And I thought that she had changed. Right? She wasn't going to do this chasing guys any more. Right? And we didn't talk about the past or any of that and she didn't go to bars or anything. And then, I guess it was just three days ago, she said she went out to this really wild bar here, and I got kind of mad. She told me when I was in a great mood and I just got depressed. I just want a mom that doesn't do that. I'm tired of it. I guess there are two reasons why I'm angry. For one thing I get really jealous because, as much as the tests all say I fear men, it does not apply to this. I mean I like guys and it has always been this constant source of grief that I never get asked out. It just happens. Like, all my friends go out but I never get asked out; it's just the way it is. And it's been like this constant source of agony and grief and tears for me. I mean, it makes me so angry and I don't understand it and I get very depressed.

T: The tears and the anger kind of come together?

P: Oh, yes.

T: Depression and anger get all twisted up.

P: Yeah, anger turns to tears, cause, yeah, yeah!

T: So you get a little jealous of your mother, too?

P: Oh, it's extremely, it's not even a little bit.

T: She makes friends and I don't.

P: Um hmm. Yeah, that's one part of it. I get a little bit jealous of my friends but I get extremely jealous of my mother. Because I don't understand why me, as an 18-year-old, can't get asked out and she, as a 50-year-old, can. And she gets asked out by guys who are 23 and 24, and it makes me really mad because that's almost my territory at this point. I mean, it makes me mad that someone her age is trying to take away the males that are my age. They're like a couple years older than me, you know. I mean this is like, "It's our turn now, give us a chance." And yet she goes around and she's got them . . .

T: Give *"me"* a chance?

P: Yeah, right, give *me* a chance. It's not fair. It's like we're competing for the same aged guys.

T: *My* potential boyfriends.

P: Potential yeah, and it really makes me mad.

T: Help me understand the anger. What goes into it besides her competing for your boyfriends?

P: Okay, well that makes me angry but what also makes me angry is the fact that she doesn't want to play the mother role because as soon as she gets in these relationships, she's not "mother." Second of all, she's competing, like she's my enemy.

T: "She's my enemy." First, she's going with people who I want to go with or who I *could* go with and secondly, she is not taking care of me.

P: She's let me down. Right! They both go hand in hand. Right? I mean I've been let down and she's not . . .

T: It seems to me that those two thoughts

would cause very different feelings. One sounds like angry feeling and the other sounds like a feeling of loss.

P: Yes, exactly. Yeah, yeah! And one is much more like feeling like, I don't know. I guess they are both just as powerful, but they are different feelings. The one is jealousy really, and it makes me really mad. It's more explosive than the other and can end sooner, where the thing about her not being "mom" is gnawing there all the time, like a dull pain that doesn't go away.

T: That sounds like depression. It's always kind of there and then lying on top of that is the sharp pain of your anger or jealousy.

P: Right.

T: Then you *really* feel it.

P: Yeah, I do. I got really mad and then I went back to the dorm and I talked to my friend B. We've had some of the, you know, same things happen in the past and she understands. I mean, she understands where I'm coming from and she was saying that she understood about my mom not really wanting to be a mom. You know, I wanted to be able to sit down and talk to someone, but a lot of other friends started coming in and there was a lot of people congregating around our room and, you know when a lot of other people came in we stopped talking. We just had a good time, we all jumped around. It's like everyday . . . oh total, I forget about it and the next morning I wake up and it's, like, gnawing at me more than the fact that my mother is letting me down. I don't know why. I can't figure it out. Maybe one is worse than the other and I don't . . . I can't sort it out. I'd say right now, though, the one, the jealousy, is gnawing at me a lot.

T: If it's all right, let's follow those two things. Let me see if I understand because it seems like there's a chain of events that might be very important for us to focus on. One situation, mother going out with a guy, produces two different thoughts inside of you and hence, produces two different feelings, one angry and one depressed. But, one way you found to get away from those bad feelings is to distract yourself, get around your friends, and they make you think about other things and they make you pay attention to good things that are happening. Does that fit?

P: Yeah, except that I worry about that part because my friends are starting to go out now and it reminds me of mom and it gets to me, and then I get depressed 'cause I see in the future that I'll always feel the same way.

T: They start doing things that remind you of your mother. Then you start having the same kind of feelings you've had with your mother?

P: Yeah. Yeah. And it's hard not to get even a little bit jealous of them. I mean, I think it's that some of it just came from always feeling isolated in some way. Like, intellectually, because I was advanced in school; kids isolated me because I was good or isolated me because I was younger. I felt very isolated and then the whole thing with being isolated from guys. I mean. You know, I mean that's terribly painful. That's more painful than anything, almost, or at least to me.

T: Why is it painful?

P: Oh, it just makes me like, I . . . I mean if I can't have the feeling of being feminine, if that ever goes, that's just like the end of me. I mean, that's the end of me. . . .

T: Are you afraid it will go?

P: If I don't get a response from males to say that I am feminine . . . I mean it's hard to survive. . . .

[A little later.]

T: If I run down the chain of events maybe it'll help us understand it. Let's just take the situation of mother going with a guy.

P: Right. Except he's young so that makes a difference too.

T: Okay, a young guy. How much of a difference does it make if he's young or old?

P: Very big.

T: So, she goes with a young guy. The first thought that you're aware of seems to be "she's competing."

P: Um hmm, and winning.

T: Okay. "She's competing and she's beating me." Okay. And the second thought you seem to be aware of is "I'm going to lose my femininity."

P: Um hmm. I don't understand why she has more femininity at the age of 50 than I do at 17. It doesn't fit.

T: Maybe it's not a matter of losing it; you're afraid that you don't have it.

P: Um, yeah. I feel like, that it won't matter if I do or not cause it'll never be discovered. That's the whole thing of it.

T: And you see her as standing in your way of having it discovered.

P: Yeah, she stands in my way like 80% and my friends stand in my way maybe about 15%.

T: Okay, so about 80%. If pain is marked on a scale of 10 to 100 it gets up to about 80% when your mother goes out with a young guy and you have these thoughts.

P: Oh yeah, oh easy, yeah.

T: With your mother but only around 15 or so . . .

P: With my friends.

T: So it could be with your mother or it could be with friends. The pattern is the same except with your mother the pain is bigger.

P: Right.

T: Okay. And that pain is kind of a combination of the anger and depression.

P: Yeah, yeah, just like that, yeah, so far.

T: [writing] Let me see if this makes sense to you. You've described it really very well. I like to think that if we look at this as the *situation* A and this is C, your *feelings,* your feeling is not caused by the situation. It is caused by B, what goes on in your mind about this. How you interpret it.

P: Um hmm. Oh yeah, yeah.

T: You saw that a little bit last time; in fact you made a similar comment.

P: You can interpret things differently, oh yeah, yeah. But the thing is, to me it's almost like a basic obvious principle so that I think that if you're given 10 people, about some things you'd get 10 different views, but with this one I'd say maybe eight people view it the same and two different. I mean this thing is like, I'd say most people would feel this way.

T: You believe that most people would feel this badly in this situation.

P: Um, well I think I feel this badly because of the friend thing too, or maybe, I think the fact that all of this occurs simultaneously. I think that she becomes "not mother." I don't feel . . .

T: You begin interpreting her as "not mother."

P: Right. In fact, I guess I feel two things with my mother and a guy. I don't have a boyfriend so I don't feel protected, okay that's one thing, and my mother gets a boyfriend and believes she's protected, but I'm not protected by her as a mother.

T: You want her to secure you and protect you.

P: Right and I'm not protected by a male or anything.

T: So you don't have anyone.

P: Right, I guess maybe that's some of it.

T: So part of the feeling of real loss is your sense that you have no one.

P: Um hmm.

T: Okay, that's where we get the two different feelings it seems to me. We get the "angry" feeling and we get the "loss" feeling.

P: Yeah.

T: They both come down here to this pain.

But, what if your interpretation of that situation is wrong?
P: Well, how could it be wrong cause the pain is, like, immediate. And the pain happens first and then the thoughts for the pain follow.
T: Let me give you a perspective on that, a different way of thinking about it. Sometimes these thoughts or similar thoughts become what we call "automatic." That is, you've learned them over such a long period of time that they come so fast that you're not even aware of them being there. But if you change them, your pain wouldn't be there either.
P: Um hmm.
T: Now our job, as I would see it, is to look at those thoughts and see if there is another way of interpreting that situation.

Throughout this session, the patient appeared to be responsive to the therapist's intervention, with some struggle beginning to develop around the concept of the ABC's. The possibility of her reactance level getting in the way of her understanding the concepts and applying them in a systematic fashion became apparent. In the hope of exploring, more directly, the degree to which the patient's reactance level would prevent her from participating in directive intervention at this stage in therapy, a "reactance challenge" was initiated at the end of the session. The objective of such a challenge is to see how the patient manages a directed assignment, observing whether she will, in fact, comply (low reactance) or resist (high reactance). Utilizing this information, the therapist can then adjust the directiveness of the interventions, either being less directive to accommodate the patient or employing paradoxical interventions that capitalize on the presence of reactance by prescribing the opposite of that desired. The patient's response to this challenge was observed in session 5.

*Session 5 (9/18)*

P: I just have to say something. You know that form you gave me you wanted me to do. Right? Okay. Last time, like the next day I went to school and I was thinking of all these little things I was going to write down at the end of the day and I realized that I started focusing on all this mess. You know, what I was really afraid of. The more I focused on it, the worse I felt and the more afraid I got and the more I started getting this massive tension headache you know, and so the next day I didn't do anything with the paper. I left it. I was figuring out that this wasn't a really good thing cause it's not making me happy in my present life. I mean I'm trying to do something that might benefit our meeting a week from now, but right now I wasn't happy with this. So on Thursday I tried to do like you said. I started trying to notice everytime I have this thought and it made me so totally paranoid that, like, it ruined things so that what I did was I forgot about it. So I didn't do anything and then I felt a lot better and I wasn't afraid or anything. By focusing on it, it just makes me totally paranoid. I almost have the feeling that it puts fear in me that really wasn't there before. I mean, you know?
T: If I suggest to you to focus on something it makes it into a problem.
P: Uh huh. I think, for certain things. I don't think everything's that way.

This reaction, to become worse instead of better when complying with a home monitoring assignment, suggested that reactance level and sensitivity to interpersonal influence were still very high. Hence, the need to proceed cautiously and without a great deal of teaching-instructional activity was emphasized. The more typical and traditional cognitive therapy format, therefore, was modified to reduce the amount of formalized instruction.

In the next four sessions, the effort to identify and clarify the patient's theme of interpersonal ambivalence was intensified. Session 6 proceeded from a rather specific concern with achievement in her classes, to the more general theme of perfectionism and compliance.

*Session 6 (9/25)*

P: I feel as if I get really depressed because I'm coming nowhere near my ability. I know it. I often got that way when I was in swimming too. I got sometimes to where I swam a lot faster than girls I went to swim meets with and who beat me. You know? It happened time after time. It's just that every time I have to go faster or do more I'll think, "God, I can't do it." You know? It's like, why even do it?
T: You'll ultimately fail especially if you work hard at it.
P: Yeah. Exactly. And like the less I work, the better I do; the more I work, the worse I do.
T: Why do you do so much then?
P: Why?
T: Why spend 70% of your time working on . . .
P: I don't know. That's what I'm trying to figure out. I'm trying to figure out if I should. I mean it's so much easier to fail if you haven't studied and you can say, "Well, if I would study then I would do better." There's always that possibility of improvement. There's nothing worse than when you study and then you don't do well because then it's like a fact. You're *stupid*. Okay? And then at the same time, that can't be true so it's so much easier if you don't study, and you don't do well . . .
T: Then you don't have to call yourself "stupid."
P: Oh sure. I mean, only a stupid person gets a 60 on a Latin test.
T: They don't have any other kind of people getting a 60 in Latin?
P: Well, only those who don't have ability in that subject.
T: Any other kind?
P: No.
T: That's it?
P: Yes.
T: So if you do poorly, you're either stupid or you don't have that ability and that's it?
P: Yes.
T: No room in there for a person who's just anxious?
P: Yeah, but who cares then? I mean, at this point, if I can't take a test, I shouldn't be in college. You know? I mean, I don't want a series of D's or F's. I won't get a job from that.
T: It's interesting to me to kind of follow your thought process when you say that. It sounds almost designed to make you more anxious.
P: I don't feel anxious. I guess I am, but when I'm taking a test . . . I mean, I go in there and I don't feel nervous or anything.
T: You don't?
P: No. I know what it's like to feel nervous. I mean, I can't write anything if I'm nervous.
T: So it doesn't feel like anxiety.
P: No. I mean, it feels kind of like being a little depressed but not anxious.

There followed an exploration of her depression, particularly as it related to a demanding and accusing internal dialogue. A few moments later, this exploration took a turn when the patient began to explore why she had such a need for high grades.

T: If you don't get an A, you haven't done well?
P: Yes. Right, right, exactly and that's how I grew up. I mean, it's probably my fault that I took it on but I did it anyway. I don't know how to unload it. It's

like a pride thing, you know. I mean, if only people in my high school could have seen what my real ability was, you know. I mean, people kept talking about "how smart you are." And, I could swear that, I was smarter than just a lot. I mean, I don't think I was the smartest in school, but I think in some areas I was. I mean, I was in all the top classes always so I knew who was up, you know? And I'd get in a class, like English class, you know, and we had discussions about books, and I would find insight, after insight, after insight, then when I'd get to tests, I'd get a C+ on my written work on it. The teacher would say, "God, R., your ideas are A+ but your writing, it's terrible."

T: What makes anything less than A failure?

P: Um, I guess I have to tell you where it comes from, then. It's from having never felt good enough at anything. I guess it's like I have a negativism that I've always felt for myself. I'm the worst or I'm the best. And since I've always felt like the worst, then it becomes the best that I strive for. I have to be the best because I've always felt like the worst. There's no one worse than me. I've always been the worst. And so then I become, I *have to* become, the best.

T: You *have to* have something to counterbalance being "worst."

P: Yes.

T: But, you kind of see yourself as being at one extreme or the other.

P: Yeah.

T: You're either the worst or the best. What is similar about being the worst or the best that you have to be?

P: What is similar about them?

T: Yeah.

P: They're both extremes.

T: Does that mean you're noticeable in both positions?

P: Yeah.

T: Is it important to be noticeable?

P: Maybe that's it. I don't know. I've never thought about it before. I mean, if I'm the worst, it means the same thing as being the best. Why try to study for tests. Don't study and actually fail. Then it's easier to accept being the worst. I mean, there's nothing you can do.

T: If you try and fail anyway, you may have to confront the probability that you don't have what it takes.

P: Yeah.

There followed a discussion of the patient's need to succeed in all areas of academia and her anticipation that to fail at academia was to fail at life. Her dichotomous thinking was obvious, and some effort was made to explore the possibility that some middle ground might also represent truth. This led to a discussion of how she came to define the world in such extremes. She began with a description of her belief in God and her sense of inferiority which resulted from that belief.

P: I feel that this is why this religion thing is making me so irritated. I get so angry about my whole impression of "who" God is or "what" it is. The last three years, there's always this image that God is teasing me. He is being mean all the time to me. Like, He kind of sets things up for me and gives me hope and then makes me go and waste my time. I never really succeed. You know, it's like, I can never get what He promises. He gets me to waste my time on it and then purposely pulls it away so I can't get it. Like He has a big thing of gold or something, and I run and run and run to get the gold and He pulls it away.

T: God sounds a lot like your father. He makes a lot of demands and then won't let you have what you want.

P: Hmm, that's interesting. I never thought about it. That's true, I've never done anything my father gave me to do and heard him say, "God that was really good."

T: It sounds like you've made God into dad's image.
P: Yeah. Except that like . . . yeah I guess so. I mean, like, yeah, he's always been like that even like if . . . when I did get my 100 on the math test, it's like, "It's about time."
T: "It's about time you did what you're supposed to." It's not that you're bright. Instead it's, "Why didn't you do it before?" He kind of teases you like you think God teases you.
P: Yeah.
T: What if God's not like that at all?
P: Probably you're right, but He's so distant and everything and He irritates me anyway. I feel He's tricking mankind by not being in physical form and putting smut and stuff in the Bible and giving us, like, bad instincts and bad things that we have to always struggle against, you know. I think that's unfair and He's not down here to really show Himself or anything. Then on this little tiny bit of energy we have left, we have to try to figure out that He's really good and then He has all the stuff built into the Bible so that if we have any doubts that He is good, then we're going to go to hell for it. So it's really, I mean . . .
T: No way to win.
P: Oh no, no way. And then you work, like, on your own life and then He takes it away from you. I mean, my feeling is, "Don't give it to me in the first place."
T: Well, again it sounds like that's the same struggle you have with dad, maybe with mom too.
[Later.]
T: How did you learn to be so afraid?
P: I know, it's true. I mean, I know I'm afraid of a lot of things, and my dad, he's afraid really. I was five and six and he would go on at length about the Holocaust. And then when I was seven and eight, I remember him telling me about how the Christians were killed and everything. They said they believed in Christ, then they would get fed to lions and if they said . . . I was getting really scared when I was seven. I remember, I mean, I remember one day. I mean in my mind is, I swear, in my mind it's like it is today. I remember this heavy onset of emotions and I went to daddy about this same thing. I remember saying to my dad, "Well, aren't you scared?" You know, at the age of seven I was even more afraid.
T: By the age of seven, you've already learned that the world is going to get you if you're not really careful.
[Later.]
P: Oh yeah. He was very scary. I mean he used to . . . Oh God, he used to tease the hell out of me, he's just so mean. I don't know, like, he used to do stuff when I was little about . . . I don't know. By the age of three he used to hit me. He'd, you know, he'd bend down real low and hit me in the jaw and it like . . .
T: Did it hurt?
P: Yeah, it hurt. I would like cry.
T: What would he do?
P: He would laugh and he thought it was funny. So then I'd get really upset and I'd try to get away from him because he had a bad knee, and he couldn't run after me. He did this periodically, and then when I was like 14 or 15, it got really bad, you know. And then I couldn't take it anymore. I couldn't take the rejection so I just started laughing along with him like it was alright . . .
T: So you had it faked.
P: Yeah, I faked that it was all right. But that was when I got older. But when I was littler he'd hit me. That was the first; that was a physical fear. I remember . . . I remember I was three years old and we had a little complex we lived in. There was a little thing of flowers, and they were really pretty. I was out one day and I, you know, I loved to be outdoors. I always feared other kids because I was . . . I was always the youngest child around. It just happened

that way. And because of that, I always got hit or beat up on by older kids. I was always left out. Everyone would go over and leave me alone on the swings and they'd all whisper and start laughing and look over and come back at me and start pushing me off the swings. So, physically, I was afraid of the kids. So anyway, I'd be walking out of this complex, this was when I was three, and I'd be really scared that I was going to get hurt by one of the older kids so . . . and then I was looking around and I was feeling really down and I remember thinking, "I ought to give to somebody, I ought to give something." I remember I was sad. And I saw the flowers and I thought, "Oh, aren't they pretty." And thought, "Oh, I'm going to go pick one and give to dad and mom." You know? To make them happy because mom liked flowers. So I picked a flower. I went in and she was on the phone and my dad turned around and looked at me and goes, "What's that?" I said, "It's a flower." He says, "What did you pick that for?" And I said, "Well I was going to give it to Mom." And he said, "Do you know that you just killed that flower?" I was just like, you know, I'm like, "Oh my God." And he goes, "That flower's never going to live again because you've killed it." And I go, "Well is there any way to put it back?" "No, there's not," he said. "It's dead." And so I took the flower into my room and I remember it was my first really painful experience.

T: I can imagine that. What did you learn from that that translates to where you are now in your life?

P: Like, when I deal with someone, communication has been a problem. What I intended doesn't happen right.

T: The good thing that you try to give . . .

P: Turns to bad.

T: It's bad?

P: It's bad. It's evil! Only evil could have done it.

T: You murdered.

P: Yeah. I killed a flower and that was like really tragic for me.

T: Let me push you a little bit further on that. Imagine that you're in the room, as you are now, when that little girl comes in and tries to give the flower. What would you like to say to her or to your father.

P: I would say, "No, you didn't kill it," and "It's all right," and "It's a really pretty flower."

T: You would comfort the little girl.

P: Of course. Yeah.

T: What would you say to your father?

P: I'd say, "Why'd you do that?" or "Don't spread your ugliness to some child who can't protect himself."

T: Say it again.

P: I would say, "Don't spread your ugliness to someone who can't protect himself from it."

T: How does it seem to say that to your father.

P: I can't do it.

T: Don't do it, but imagine yourself doing it.

P: I'd be really scared that . . .

T: Of?

P: Of, of him totally falling to pieces and . . .

T: You'd be afraid of destroying him like you did the flower?

P: Yeah, but one was different. The flower was always good. The flower couldn't be destroyed, but he can.

T: Did you hear what you just said?

P: Yeah.

T: Are you afraid of destroying him?

P: Maybe that's why he always made me afraid.

T: Maybe you're right. Maybe what we're dealing with is that you're very angry at him. And you're afraid you have the power to hurt him.

P: Yeah. Oh yeah.

T: So what you do instead is destroy yourself.

P: Yeah. I let myself get hurt.

T: So you really have some kind of a choice somewhere in your mind. Are you going to let yourself live like a flower, or are you going to let him live? It sounds like you usually choose to let him decide.
P: Sure. Yeah, because the outcome is, if I let him live, and it was a bad choice, I'll be forgiven by God. And if I don't let him live, and that was a bad choice, then God's going to punish me, and I'm selfish having done that.
T: What if the choice isn't that? What if you don't have the power to destroy him?
P: Well, that would make the choice simple at that point.
T: Then what would it be?
P: Then it would be okay to choose me. I mean, if I couldn't destroy him.
T: Let's pretend for a moment that you can't destroy your father; only he can do that.
P: Though it might be different than what you are thinking because I have said some bad things to him before, and I felt that he'd go off and drink and quit his job or mess up. Then even if I'm not directly destroying him, I'm indirectly destroying him because I've triggered him on that. And if I hadn't done what I did, he wouldn't have . . .
T: So you are responsible?
P: Yes.
T: What if you're not? Where's his responsibility?
P: Oh wait. If you say I'm not, then I absolutely can't stand him.
T: Okay . . .
P: Okay. I mean, it's not . . . I don't want to say hate but it's close to it.
T: It's close to hate.
P: I mean, it's just, like to me, it's evil, I mean, *God*. It's just total hate.
T: How is it to think of him as an evil person?
P: Yeah, but it's like sometimes though, I know that he's loved me before. I mean, how can I hate . . . I cannot hate anything that's loved me, at any time. If they've ever loved me at any time I . . .
T: So the way to really get you is to love you once and then beat you. So you can never get back at me if I love you and then I treat you bad forever after?
P: Because there's always the hope that you might love me again.

The reader will note that during the course of this session, some exploration of cognitive pattern is combined with some tentative and preliminary initiation of imagined dialogue between the patient and her father. This denotes the shift in procedure from a strictly cognitive orientation to increasing emphasis on feeling awareness and impulse expression. This shift is initiated as the patient becomes somewhat less externalized in her expression of feelings and more introspective, thus revealing the inhibition of impulses that also characterizes her pattern.

Issues related to the patient's ambivalent restriction of certain feelings began emerging further in subsequent sessions, and these were frequently addressed in the context of her relation to me as her therapist. These connections were then extended to parental relationships, always with an eye to highlighting her conflicting attachment and autonomy needs. In session 7, for example, issues of trust were explored in regard to the treatment relationship itself. Then, these issues were applied to an imagined dialogue exercise in which the patient attempted to engage her stepmother.

*Session 7 (10/2)*

P: I used to talk a lot to teachers, during that time, and I felt very equal but I usually feel small and inmature, around other people . . . adults mostly.
T: How do you feel with me?
P: I don't know. I don't feel . . . I feel equal for some reason.

T: Because, I was just aware that you were standing up to me a moment ago in telling me "no." Did you feel guilty about that?
P: No.
T: Good!
P: I don't know why.
T: Did you lose respect for me, like you have with other people?
P: No. Mostly I feel, I guess, it's the difference between a healthy relationship and one that isn't healthy. I mean, I feel that if my relationship is good with someone . . . and yet, I trust you not to go back on me or something. I trust you. I'm not afraid. I am not afraid to, like maybe, disagree with you. I'm not afraid to take advice from you.
T: Why is that?
P: Because I trust you, because you've done lots of things that have worked out for me. Like some teachers, you know?
T: Yes.
P: But people that I feel I have unhealthy relationships with, I'm afraid they'll turn around and really hurt me.
T: But in a way, maybe it *makes* the relationship unhealthy because you don't stand up to them.
P: Well, I have. You see, that's the whole thing. Like there have been times when I've tried to, and they got . . . Like, once my parents, we got into the most hideous, ugly, gruesome four-hour argument. I mean, it was just screaming and it was like them against me.
T: They had to defeat you.
P: Oh God, they were *going* to.
T: So you finally . . . ?
P: I was just there crying and crying and they just did it even after I gave up. I mean, I didn't have the words to say it anymore. They would stay at me. I'd cry and she—my stepmother—would just keep at me. They wouldn't even stop if I was crying or sick.
T: It sounds like a vicious cycle. If you stand up for yourself, then they attack you and you finally have to give up.
P: Well, the reason—the thing is, it's always the two of them against the one of me.
T: That would overwhelm you?
P: Always. And if I ever tried to argue with one of them, like my dad you know, I could argue with him, but then his little punishment was not to talk to me for the next week.
T: So you're going to be punished.
P: Oh yes, you know . . .
T: If you win, you lose.
P: Yeah, exactly. And M. [stepmother], her thing with me is that if I started to argue, she would stomp upstairs. She'd . . . we'd be eating dinner or something and she'd throw her neck around and she'd stomp upstairs and slam her door. And then she wouldn't talk to me.
T: So you've lost.
P: Yeah, yeah, I mean . . .
T: You can't fight that.
P: There's no way. No, she'd just, like, leave and then she'd call me. She set so many rules down and things when I was really young and they really set in before I could say that wasn't right. You know? Like this swimming thing. When I came back I was 13 and I hadn't been swimming for a lot of years, you know. I was like seven or eight when I was out here and did really well and then I quit, okay? When I was 11, I came back east and that's how I decided to start swimming again. And mom goes, "You're a housebreaker," and so they decided to take me to the swim club at the YMCA, so they paid some money to have me join the YMCA and then join the team. And my father would see the coach and he told the coach that I might want to do double workouts, you know. More workouts! That's the reason I quit before. And I did really well in practice and my times were really fast, and they were really close to state records and things. And

this was just like in the first week's practice. And he got all bent out of shape about that and told me I must come to double practice, saying I would really mess the team up if I didn't. He was, like a really nasty guy. And one night on the phone I was just trying to talk to him and telling him what happened because I wanted him to know my reaction. I couldn't do anything. I mean, he was like . . . He was wrong. My dad was sitting there; I just felt depressed. I felt bad because of the money, you know. You know, dad tried to understand it and M. couldn't, she just got mad and said, "You're just a quitter." She said, "You run away from everything." Maybe that's the first time I had ever really been hurt by M. She called me a "quitter" and, and what was so painful was . . . like swimming was a really, really emotional thing to me. Because all my energy was tied up in ths incredible emotion . . . My own, and, of course, my mother's. She was always like pushing me, you know. And this was for a long time in my life. The swimming was my territory and they had the nerve to sit there and say, "Oh you quitter." I mean I always felt sort of guilty about quitting swimming but I always felt it was, I couldn't have done anymore, it . . .

T: It was another one of those instances where you couldn't win. If you'd gone, you had to face him, the coach . . .

P: Yeah, and I couldn't do that and then my . . .

T: And if you stood up to M., she'd beat you down. And if you left, you were quitting.

P: Yeah, I wasn't expecting her to do that to me though. She'd called me things before. You know, like, "you run away from anything." I mean, it was always like that. I'd just turned 13 and I can tell you at that time I wasn't quitting. I think back and I feel so sad at myself and so angry at her.

T: Those two feelings come together, feeling really sorry for yourself and very angry at her.

P: Yes, she is just mean. I don't feel sorrow for her.

T: I want to give you a sentence.

P: Okay.

T: I want you just to imagine that you say this sentence to her. Just once.

P: Okay.

T: "I have a right to live too." Try that on. Say it.

P: "I have a right to live too."

T: How does that feel?

P: Oh, it feels right. It feels . . . it definitely accomplishes a lot of things. But I can imagine her reaction. You know . . . she'll say, "I don't know what you are talking about," and she'll get up and leave.

T: She'd leave, she'd quit.

P: Oh yes, yes, that's the thing. She'd always quit, that's why I was the quitter, you know?

[Later.]

T: My head's going in two different directions. One is, it really sounds like you were so hurt and wanted to get close so much. And I'm aware of how empty it must make you feel.

P: Yeah.

T: The other side of me tunes in to how, in some ways, you and M. are kind of alike. That is, that she may be very scared too. And very empty.

P: Yeah.

T: What if we tried something. I'd like to be you for a minute, and I'd like you to be M. I would like to try on what I think you might feel sometimes. I don't know if I'll be right, and that doesn't really matter so much as seeing how you feel being M.

P: Okay.

T: "M., you really make me mad at you. You're always trying to control me."

P: "I don't know what you mean."

T: "I mean, you're always on me trying to tell me that I'm wrong; I'm bad, I'm a

failure; something's always wrong with me; and I get so tired of you always telling me that something's wrong with me."
P: That is, like, hard to do because my tendency is to cry and like agree with you. I mean I can't get into her personality that easily.
T: Maybe she'd feel that way, too. I don't know. What was that feeling like as we were just doing it.
P: I couldn't keep hold of both those characters.
T: Oh.
P: I can't. I mean I just, I sit there and, like, if I think of you as a child, you are helpless, you know? I mean, like I can't . . . I can't do it.
T: Ah. If you feel sorry for me, you'd then agree with me.
P: Yes.
T: Be you for a minute, let me be her.
P: Okay.
T: "You're a quitter, you never stick with anything. I'm not going to sit here and live in this house with you always quitting and never following through with anything. Talk to me."
P: She wouldn't say that, she'd leave. Um . . . well, "What do you mean by quitting?"
T: "Well, you quit the swim team, because they won't do what you want them to do. You want to run away and go to college and live with your mother because we won't be the kind of people you want us to be. If the people around you aren't the kind of people you want them to be, you want to run off and quit."
P: "Yeah. I mean . . . well, yes I wouldn't call it quitting but yet . . . "
T: "What would you call it?"
P: "I don't know. I just, I just don't think it's quitting."
T: "Well it certainly looks like quitting. You never stand up for yourself, you never take charge of anything, you never follow through with anything, you don't take care of anything, you always just quit."
P: "Yeah . . . "
T: Ah. You gave up.
P: I can't fight that.
T: What was your experience as we were doing that?
P: It just sounds exactly like her. I mean, she is . . . except she wouldn't have even provided the alternative of staying here, you know. She wouldn't even act it, she'd just say it. And then she'd go, "Yeah, go off with your mother."
T: Yeah, "Get."
P: Yeah.
T: "Go." "Quit."
P: Yeah.
T: "That's what you're going to do anyway, go, quit."
P: I can't, you see, I can't argue at all. I can't. I don't know, I can't argue with that at all.
T: Do you want to?
P: Not really. I don't know.
T: How do you feel, little or big?
P: I feel little but right.
T: Justified completely?
P: Yeah.
T: What would it take for you to feel big *and* right.
P: I can't imagine the two going together.
T: That's what I hear. "Right" means "small" to you.
P: Yeah. That's always been that way. If I think I'm really being good, it's wrong.
T: If you feel big you're wrong.
P: You know why I do that? Because she's so close to my father and I don't want to lose him. I think that's . . . because he *always* sides with her.
T: What you're really afraid of, is losing your father?
P: Yeah, I mean it's always a choice he makes, to see her again. I'll never go back to her, but my father will.

The ambivalence theme seen in this interchange became even clearer in the next sessions as we unraveled her fears of abandonment. They dynamic of ambivalence was particularly observed as she began talking about fears that occurred when she anticipated seeing a medical doctor. This ambivalent attachment to people was most prominent in her anticipation of being asked to give blood during a physical examination.

*Session 9 (9/23)*

P: I am not scared at all. You know, maybe I feel that you care. I feel that you're familiar with things. It's just that I don't like it when someone comes in and they're doing the stuff . . . It just seems so cold . . . they don't care. They forget it's a human being there and they're just like, "Oh, stick the needle in here." You know, they're hurting you and they don't even care, I mean, you know . . .
T: I can understand your concern. That's one that a lot of people share with you, but you seem to have a stronger concern with this "coldness" than many people do. I wonder why that is.
P: Um, I don't know, maybe my past? When my dad hit me sometimes.
T: What would happen in your worst fantasy if they didn't care while taking your blood or whatever?
P: Well, that would be that . . . Um, well I don't even know, um, maybe they'd leave me alone and forget me.
T: Oh?
P: That's what's scary.
T: Has that ever happened to you?
P: No.
T: Have you ever been locked in anywhere and abandoned?
P: I don't know, well, maybe, so to speak . . .
T: How?
P: Uh, like when I was with my mom and we lived alone and she'd leave to get out. She'd leave me alone and I'd be so scared . . .
T: You'd feel trapped?
P: Yeah. I feel trapped a lot. She's always saying, "I feel trapped in this house."
She said that today. "I feel trapped in this house." So did I, because I was 11 and I didn't have anywhere to go. I just felt all this pain, emotional pain, no one was there.
T: So it would be like being locked up and abandoned.
P: Yes.
T: That seems to be the emotional quality that comes through in a lot of these things that frighten you.
P: Yeah, that was like pain . . . emotional pain, and then she'd leave me there with the pain.
T: So, like if people don't care, there's a likelihood that they will ignore you and leave.
P: Yeah, yeah.
T: The real thing that seems to be bothering you through a lot of things is you are worried that people are going to abandon you.
P: Yeah, yeah, yeah. But, yeah! That's it. That *is* it. That's exactly it.
T: It's like you look at everybody through these big magnifying glasses and look for some possibility that they'll leave.
P: Yeah. Yeah, I don't know why except 'cause like they abandoned me. That's what my dad really did, and I don't trust my dad.
T: You don't trust anybody?
P: Like my dad would be the last person in the world that I would allow to give me a blood test. I know he would leave. I know he would do it wrong. I know he wouldn't care.

Later in the session this issue of trust was explored further by inquiring about how one moved from one level of trust to another. This was approached by drawing a series of concentric circles and trying to identify how the patient allowed people to move from one circle to the other as they became increasingly close to her.

T: Can I show you how I see you?
P: Sure.

T: It's kind of, like, this is you right inside here [draws].
P: Yeah.
T: And these are various layers here. You let some people get this close to you and some people get this close. Some people are clear up here. Some people may even be up further. But here, you don't let anybody get in here. You may let me get in *here* a little bit, but nobody is in *here* [indicating different circles].
P: Yeah.
T: I wonder how a person gets from one circle, here to the next.
P: Well, I'm the only one who can do it. I have to be in the mood and let them get by.
T: How do you get yourself in the mood?
P: I just feel that way some days.
T: I guess it's awfully lonely inside those circles if you don't let anybody in.
P: Well yeah, yeah, um, I mean, uh huh.
T: It's interesting to me that you've let Dr. L. [previous doctor] and me in. We're kind of people who . . .
P: It's cause you're smart enough to. You're the only two people I know that when I say something can either . . . I don't expect anyone else to understand. Like, my other counselor, when I told him something he'd say, "Wow" . . . like he's surprised. I mean, at least you guys are smarter than me so you understand what I'm saying and no one else knows what I'm saying.
T: When he says "wow" what does he . . .
P: Well, it made me happy because it made him understand, but I mean, like, "Oh boy," but I thought, "He's never going to fix all the things because he's never going to understand all of me if it surprises him so."
T: You lost confidence in what he was saying.
P: Yeah, yeah. I mean, I took the solution of my problems faster than he would. I'd come up with what was wrong with me, before he did. And he's a really good guy. I think he's a little slower than you and Dr. L. and you two are the only ones who can, um . . . who can keep up with it.
T: So that's an important element. You don't let people in if they seem like they can't keep up with you and can't give you some answers before you come up with them.
P: Yeah, yeah, and like you understand me and it's security to me. I don't like the way that I am but I can't help it either. If someone can't keep up with me, it's like something that's always going to be surprising to them, you know? No one's going to catch it and you don't know what it's about so, even though I don't like it, no one else even sees it. I guess it's like making friends. I don't have any boyfriends because I'm so scared about being abandoned by them that I want to abandon them first, you know? I mean, I'm really scared. It's supposed to make you really happy, but I get really bummed out because everyone is going out and here I am. It's late at night and I'm sitting here reading a book or drawing. It's so depressing to me and I go, "Well, God! Why don't I have a boyfriend? What's the problem here. Why is it only me?"
T: Because you're so afraid of being rejected that . . .
P: Yeah. I'm so afraid that the relationship will just go so sour and then I look around and I say, "Yeah, but other people have relationships that go sour and they make it," and I think that I'm a lot more evil and worse than they are.
T: There you go . . . so you talked yourself right back into keeping them out of your circle.
P: Yeah! But then I'm still really depressed because I don't fit in.
T: You talked yourself into keeping the guard up and into being depressed.
P: Yeah!

As treatment progressed, the patient began experiencing a heightened sense of her own identity. Her reactance levels lowered remarkably, and over the Christmas holiday she was able to make a successful trip to visit her father and stepmother. During the trip, she was able to disengage from the frightening thoughts that had been associated with her anxiety and depression in the past. In session 17 the patient reflected on these changes and how she was able to "anchor" herself by utilizing more favorable images. The interventions at this stage began to reinforce and support these behavior and cognitive changes.

*Session 17 (1/8)*

P: Well, let's see, um. It really was nice. Very enjoyable. I went out there thinking that it would probably be really awful and, like, I was really focusing on trying to keep in touch with myself and not be distracted by other people's emotions, and so when I ran into my dad he was really cranky and M. would hardly say "hello" to me, and was really mean and everything. I thought, you know, I thought, "It has no reflection on me." I just saw two unhappy people. I was able to be really happy and nice this time, right? So I was real happy with myself and then the more I said things to myself like that, the happier I got. It's kind of a cycle. So really it took to the fourth day before M. started really sticking it to me. It didn't bother me at all that she was like this, you know.

T: You were able, it sounds like, to reinterpret what had happened. Instead of taking it personally, you started attributing it to them. "It's their problem not my problem."

P: Yeah, I could really notice that, and then as vacation went along, you know, and I was really nice to her she got nicer. She was actually nice for two or three days there when I was willing to be nice and stuff. I don't know, I just suppose that people who appear strong to her or something, she'll be nice to, but if she senses a weakness in someone, she gets scared and cranky.

T: So your strength helped.

P: Um hmm. It did. I could tell. Because she doesn't want anyone resting on her. Leaning on her. Also, I got out a lot with friends. It was just really nice to see my friends and also to get out for a while.

T: So all that struggle you went through about whether or not to go, turned out okay?

P: Oh yeah, I was surprised.

T: You're pleased with yourself?

P: Really. Yeah, it really, made me feel pretty good. If I go back again, I feel like I can pick up from where I left now, not where I left off last year when everyone was mad.

As in most therapy experiences, periodic crises arose for this patient, which reinstituted central conflicts that seemed to be resolving. These reverberations during later therapy stages are usually short lived but provide important arenas for reviewing and practicing newly acquired coping skills. For example, session 23 began with the patient reporting that her father had sounded drunk during a recent telephone conversation. This event was clearly upsetting and reinstigated many of her rescue fantasies and anger, which characterized her core theme of interpersonal ambivalence. The following segment illustrates her effort to disengage from the competing desires to protect her father, on one hand, and reject him, on the other.

*Session 23 (3/28)*

P: My dad didn't call Sunday. He calls every Sunday night and in a letter I wrote, I said, "I'll call you back Saturday morning or you can call me Sunday morning." But he never called. I didn't think much about it because he's done that before, but he usually will *definitely* call back Monday. By Tuesday he hadn't called, and when I came home Wednesday, my mom said, "You better call your father because something could be wrong that he hasn't called you." So I said, "Wow! Are you sure?" And she said, "Yeah, just call and make sure he's all right." Well I called him and he definitely was drunk on the phone. I could tell it and he was really, really just . . .

T: What was your reaction?

P: Well I don't know what I thought. He was in really bad shape. When the girl answered the phone, I was talking to her, and I could hear him whistling in the background, you know? So when he got on the phone I told him, "You were whistling," and he goes, "No." He always lies when he's drunk; I mean always. I tried to talk to him and he didn't say anything. It was just silence, and I said, "Well, call me next Sunday." He didn't answer; he goes, "huh?" He was really . . . I mean it's just the tone of his voice. I can tell when he's drunk.

T: Does it offend you?

P: Well, it was weird because I got off the phone and I didn't feel much about it. I thought that it was too bad but I didn't feel anything. Then, later on in the evening, something else happened, a little small thing with one of my roommates. It was something she did that kind of ticked me off. She went back on her word or something that wouldn't normally bother me, but all of a sudden I almost wanted to cry. I was thinking, "Now wait! It's not because of this little thing." And then I realized that it was because of my dad.

T: It bothered you more than you realized?

P: Yeah! I mean it just hit me like, "Oh, isn't this something?" I felt really badly. And then I talked to a few people about it and I've been thinking about things since. It's been weighing me down a little bit.

T: Tell me what your thoughts tell you.

P: Well, how do you mean?

T: What kind of worries do you have?

P: About him? Well, it's not related, but I worry about why he's drunk. Something really had happened to him at work, which was really unfortunate. He had formed a little partnership within his company with two other guys. One of them was his boss and they were going to try to earn . . . I mean, they could earn lots of money over several years. About a month ago the company asked for a good amount of money to be given to them and my dad had talked to the partners about what they were going to ask for and what it was going to be used for. But my dad found about two, three weeks ago that they lied to him. Not only did they lie, they got in trouble with the company and they blamed it on my father, which was really rotten because one of them is his boss and he can't get back at him. So anyway, it's been really unfortunate and now people are giving him really bad looks in the office. It's been so unfair because he's innocent. He didn't do anything wrong.

T: They did something they weren't supposed to do?

P: Yeah. And then they lied to him and blamed him for doing something he didn't do. And it was unfortunate because he had done all the work for them. So much work that in terms of his own health it was bad for him.

T: You're worried about his health and about how he's doing at work and whether his drinking means things are getting to him and he's depressed?

P: Yeah. It just bothers me that he fails at everything he does. It's just like nothing works out. And in this kind of situation you almost think, "Why didn't this thing work out?" And it just didn't.

T: You have worries about his depression?

P: I don't know. I mean, it makes me upset.

I just worry that M. will divorce him and he won't have anybody. I just worry that he's gonna be a drain on her, and I worry that M. will get a divorce and he won't have anybody. I will feel obliged to go help him.

T: So the worry is that you might have to step in and take care of him?

P: Well, I guess I don't have to, but I would choose to. That would make him feel better. It just bothers me because he's so talented and it's all going to waste; I mean, he's incredibly smart.

T: There seem to be two sides to your worry about his drinking. One is that it's a waste for him and the other is that it threatens you.

P: Well, I think they're the same in a way. I mean worrying about him and being scared for me.

T: Worry is like being threatened?

P: Yeah, I guess so. So I don't know how to feel. I mean, I can't help but feel, like, sorry about it.

T: Yeah, I can understand that. Is there some belief that he's not going to be able to get where you would like him to be without you?

P: Well, I just pretty much think of it as "he seems to be happy but he's not." And I don't know how he can feel better because he doesn't go for help. He goes through phases, you know. On the phone the week before, he was real happy and he seemed okay.

T: In the past, how depressed has he gotten?

P: Nothing good. I mean everyone gets down but . . .

T: Does he come back up?

P: I would say that during the year there is about 20 days that he's happy. So if he comes out of his depression it's, like, a month later and then he's down again and it goes on and on and on.

T: So I wonder if it really makes any difference whether he's drinking or not or whether things are bad at work. He's kind of unhappy anyway.

P: If this hadn't fallen through, he wouldn't be so upset.

T: What role do you think he played in all this?

P: In what?

T: In making himself depressed or drinking.

P: Well, I think that when he joined the company, he was anxious about the job and he had a feeling that people were a little dishonest. He needed the money and the income at the time. He knew the deal would fall through, but he just didn't know when. He knew that there would be something going wrong. And it was a little bit risky to do this partnership.

T: He knew it was risky?

P: Yeah, but I don't think that he deserved it, you know, but he *did* know. So his whole world is really going to collapse and then there's really no place to go.

T: Are you worried about him committing suicide?

P: Yes . . . no, he'll drain other people before he does.

T: In a way, he is a survivor. He survives through a lot of ups and downs.

P: Well, it seems like his whole life has been that.

T: So any guess that he'll survive through this?

P: Yes, if you mean physically breathing, yeah. I mean it; he has incredibly bad luck all the time.

T: I wonder. Maybe if his luck is that bad so much of the time, it may not be luck.

P: What do you mean? The bad luck is intentional . . .

T: The bad luck he kind of . . .

P: Created? Well yeah! I mean, I think. But, of course, in this situation it's hard to say. It's bad luck but, yes, he needed to take the job and he was taking the risk, but I can say that I didn't feel the way that I perceive him to feel. It's okay to think that he made it happen, but I'm not him. I don't know.

T: What part do you think he plays in his

unhappiness?
P: It's his fault that he doesn't go to a psychiatrist or talk to somebody because . . . I mean, I was pretty messed up before I came to talk to you. I think I've gotten a little better and it's just . . . It's a macho thing with him, you know? He's not going to be talking to anybody; he's not going to take any medicine for it.
T: He doesn't take care of himself. He contributes to his own downfall? So, how realistic is it to be upset . . . *responsible* for him being depressed?
P: Well, I mean, it's just sad that that's the way he is.
T: I hear two things. One is, of course, it's sad, just like it's sad anytime somebody destroys himself. It's especially sad and hurtful if it's somebody you care about in the way that you care about him. So you're sad and it's kind of a reminder that you *do* care. So there's a nice side of it.
P: Well, yeah.
T: But there's another side. The other side of it is that it kind of scares you that it would then seem like you had to take care of him.
P: I don't know. It depends on how I take it. I mean, I don't know that it's unrealistic that my stepmother might divorce him.
T: That may be. What would that mean for you?
P: Then, he'd be alone. I don't know. I don't know. I'd just have to treat it like he was alone. What if he drank? He could fall and hurt himself and there wouldn't be anyone there because he has no one then but me.
T: There's some kind of belief in there that you should be there if nobody else is?
P: Yeah. I don't know.
T: Because he's taken such good care of you?
P: No! No, I don't know why.
T: Because you're his *daughter* and that makes it a requirement, so you just have to be there.
P: Yeah, I guess that's it.
T: Do you have a belief in labels . . . "daughter," "father"?
P: Yes. That's so weird.
T: It's understandable. My guess, though, is that it's not very realistic to think you "have to." If he goes under, you could decide whether or not you go and take care of him. It's not that you would "have to." It's the "have to" that may catch you. Somehow there's an obligation you feel because he's your *father*. Maybe one way to think about it is to step back a moment and think of how your relationship would be if he was "L. J.," not "Dad."
P: Well, I wouldn't have anything to do with him.
T: Yeah. So, why should you if you call him "Dad"?
P: Well because he's not L. J.
T: He is to everybody else in the world.
P: Except me because I'm his daughter.
T: What role did you play in that?
P: I don't know.
T: Is that something you believe you chose?
P: No.
T: It's something you had control over?
P: No. But it's the same way that a parent might protect a child if their child got into trouble.
T: But, parents have had control over whether or not they have a child.
P: So they're responsible for it!
T: They decided to have a child. The child didn't decide to have a parent. All of a sudden you reverse roles. You act like because you have the label "daughter," something you didn't choose to have; you didn't pick your parent; because you happen to have a parent who is alcoholic and has other difficulties, somehow you should always be responsible for him and take care of him when he can take care of himself. I think that's really very noble of you, but I question whether you "have to."

P: I don't know if I would *have to*.
T: Do you know where that sense of obligation comes from?
P: Maybe it's not realistic. I guess that if I couldn't go see him, I would feel badly about it. I feel badly about the reality of the situation.
T: You're a caring person and you'd feel badly about anybody in that spot. But, being a caring person is one thing; being obligated because he carries a label around and you are the only one in the world to use it, as his daughter, that obligates you for life?
P: I don't know. I mean, I guess it's not realistic when you think of it that way.
T: What would you think about him as L. J.?
P: I would be irritated with him, for not getting himself calm again.
T: Why should it be any different when he wears the label "Dad"? The behavior is the same.
P: Well, because as L. J. I wouldn't have any feelings for him and I could make that judgment on him without feeling anything about it. My major feeling would be one of anger or disgust for him.
T: That sounds like you love the label; you don't like the guy. What would your reaction be to the person, L. J., not filtered through a label?
P: Probably irritated. I get miffed because he had nice things going . . . I mean, it's irritating.
T: What would you want to say to him?
P: "Go see a psychiatrist!"
T: If you look at him as L. J. what you want to do is tell him to go get himself taken care of and to take care of himself. If you look at him as "daddy" or "dad," part of you wants to take care of him, whether he gets help himself or not?
P: Yeah.
T: If he is just L. J., where do your responsibilities end? How much do you owe him?

P: I feel sorry for him, but not that sorry. I mean, I can't.
T: Well, if he says, "I'm not going to go get help. I don't need help," and he's just L. J.?
P: Yeah. Well see I can't forget him, because I talk to him every Sunday.
T: I know you can't forget him, but how would you deal with it if it was just L. J. that calls?
P: Well, it depends on how much he says to me.
T: What do you think your debt is to him?
P: On a scale of 1 to 10, right?
T: Okay, on a scale of 1 to 10, how big a debt do you have?
P: Three or up.
T: Is that a big debt?
P: No.
T: What is your debt to him if you call him "Father?"
P: You know it's going to change [laughs]. Um, well, actually as I think now, it's only about a three or a four. It's about the same I guess.
T: So, do you need to take care of him?
P: No. I'm starting to see. Yeah, I understand. He's got to take care of himself.
T: Maybe the best thing you can do for him is to not take care of him.
P: Yeah. I guess he's just by himself or something cause he's always so mean to people who try to help. It's like the meaner you are to him sometimes, the more he's nice to you. It's really weird, people like that.
T: And the opposite works too? The nicer you are to him, the meaner he is to you?
P: Yeah, usually.
T: If you were to go back and take care of him, then, how would you expect him to be?
P: Mean. Like, he'd make fun of me for it.
T: Is that what you want?
P: No.
T: Maybe you could explore what you really owe, versus what you *want* to give. Maybe the "want to" is closer to realistic than the "need to."

P: Yeah, I see.
[Later.]
T: We've seen how you filter your feelings through the label of "father." Do you do it with your mother too?
P: No, not at all. She hardly has any motherly ways.
T: Do you miss "mother?"
P: Yeah, I guess. Well, I think of her as a "real good friend."
T: Yeah, as you talk about it it sounds like you're friends.
P: She's really nice, but it's just that . . . I don't know. It's just, my friends have a different relationship with their mothers. There's always a little bit of a gap between them. It's not bad, but it's just the way it is; there's not a little gap between us. You know?
T: It's like you're the same age?
P: Yes.
T: But you're not her age, she's your age?
P: Right. Only sometimes when I'm depressed, I feel like I'm her age.
T: When you're down you're the same age, but you're her age. When you're up you're the same age, but she's your age?
P: She seems older, though. She does seem older than I am, but not a whole lot. She just never does mother-daughter things. She never could, you know. There's not any labels on this. She never did act like a mother.
T: It sounds like neither one of your parents acts like your idea of what parents should be but, if I understand right, the idea of "father" has a whole lot clearer meaning to you than the idea of "mother" does.
P: I think it's because my parents are divorced and I lived with my mom and I missed him really really, really badly when I was little. I mean, I really wanted a father. And he was always very, very nice when I visited him.
T: He seemed bigger than real?
P: Oh yeah. He was everything. And then I went back and he just crumbled my image. And my mom was out here, but of course I was visiting. On the last visit she started to become more protective.
T: He was a real nice thing to think about when he was gone. It sounds like he disappointed you. You're not so disappointed that she doesn't act like a mother?
P: She never was a mother to me because she could be really mean to me. She'd yell and yell at me for not doing things.
T: So. She didn't use to be even like a friend?
P: No.
T: So she's gotten better by being like a friend?
P: Yeah.
T: Your father's gotten worse by being less like a father. What is your sense of that?
P: Of having a "mother?" I don't know. I don't know how to explain it. I love my mother, but I don't have any respect for her.
T: What would give you respect for someone?
P: I don't know what it is that makes respect.
T: Do you find it in anybody? In your friend's mothers?
P: Yeah, I guess it's a person that actually puts some limits on me that I can't go past. They take a little bit of my life into their hands and a little bit of . . .
T: A little control?
P: Yeah, just a little. Just to help me. I don't know. It's just a sign of protection.
T: A good mother in your mind is protection; she gives structure and she puts limits on you.
P: Yeah, I guess that's what I needed because sometimes I wish I had someone to say, "No.'
T: Because not saying that lets you feel like you weren't being protected? That it didn't matter?
P: I never really thought of how they thought of it. I just thought my reaction to it was . . . I mean, it's like I wanted someone to put a limit there so I could

kind of go, "Oh, what a pain," but on the other hand, I'd feel protected.

T: It sounds like a limit is like an arm around the shoulder. Somebody saying, "Here I'll take care of you."

P: It's fun, sometimes, having someone take care of me. But, it's something that I miss; that I didn't have. It probably isn't appropriate now that I'm in college, but it's something that is missing.

T: What's the closest you ever had to that?

P: Probably my Aunt A. Definitely. She would be my ideal mother. My mom just hates things that mothers do. I mean, she hates cooking; she hates station wagons; she hates families.

T: All of the things that mothers do?

P: Yeah. She hates house cleaning and all the kids and the groceries, and she's always complaining about those things. Everytime she has to do mother things, she gets irritated.

T: It would be nice if father could be a little less "father" and a little more "L. J." And it would be nice if your mother could be a little less "C." and a little more "mother."

P: Yeah.

## Termination

Through the final sessions of therapy, the patient continued to struggle with her unmet need to feel close to other people. She focused most of her frustration on her mother's unwillingness to stay in a maternal role, but also expressed awareness of her own developmental need for separation. In the final stages of therapy she began experiencing more comfort with the idea of independence and seemed to give up her struggle to create a mother-daughter relationship.

After the twenty-fifth session, therapy tapered off to less frequent visits, and we did not have another session for four weeks. At that time, she reiterated her continuing progress, particularly referencing a trip that she had taken home during spring break. She had a successful encounter with her father and stepmother and was able to "let go" of the criticism they offered of her. At the end of this session we decided to meet again approximately a month later. She canceled that appointment and rescheduled for three weeks later. By mutual agreement, this session was the last regularly scheduled appointment. At this time, her progress was reviewed and plans were made for the future.

*Session 27 (7/16)*

P: That's funny. It's funny looking back at both my parents, how I felt removed from both of them. I mean I have a lot of love for my mother, but I still don't think I have for my dad. But, I feel a lot more like my own person; a lot more relaxed. You know?

T: This is a good time for you.

P: Yes! In school, too. I don't know what I got on the final, but I was kind of excited about how I was going to do in math, and it was a brand new subject. At first I got an 83 so I was pleased, but on the second test I got a 98; it just blew me away. I haven't had a grade like that since Latin and it just made me so happy because I had so much trouble with math before. I failed so long at it. I think I may get an A in the course. I would be very happy. So, that's something that really made me happy, you know, that math ability coming back, and being with my mom a little bit and then getting a job. It's real interesting.

T: What about your relationship with guys? Has that changed?

P: Well, I feel like I flirt a lot more; I talk or laugh and joke. I enjoy their company an awful lot and I think I used to be kind of scared of them. Now, I actually enjoy being with them; it's a lot of fun. I'm a lot . . . I'm very relaxed around them ever since I got rid of the idea that the guy does not have to look this certain way. Then, you know, I'm attracted to a lot of guys; it's probably my age, too, but it's nice. It's nice to have that freedom.

T: And the freedom is, getting rid of that idea that there's only one kind of guy that counts?

P: Yeah, yeah. It's nice, especially being able to talk to my friend B. Though I think she's a little too forward . . . she goes out all the time; she's really, really crazy [laughs].

T: You're dating?

P: No, not yet, but I think I probably will next year. At least right now, I don't think I have to go out. I just enjoy being with guys; you know, talking to them and joking. They'll come into the store and they're nice, you know?

T: That's nicer than going out and being worried about how you're coming across; you're more relaxed.

P: Things are getting better and, just different. I think it's changing. I'm also thinking of getting a computer degree. There's this thing called a "computer auditor" and I think it's something I can . . . want to do. I'd like to see about that. And also, my mom found out about this program where you can go work for an accountant for a semester and move to another city. I think that it would be really neat to go for a semester and be away from mom and dad . . . on my own and working and doing what I'm gonna be doing after I get out of school. So, I'm really very interested in that.

T: I hear a little excitement.

P: Yeah, yeah. I'm excited about it.

T: How can I help you in all of that? Where are we?

P: Uh, I don't know; it's hard to say. I feel happy; I feel very confident about my life at this time. I don't feel that there are any snags coming up that I can't get over. I'm able to get over the things that arise in life right now.

T: You've not come in for some time and that says to me either that you're unhappy at what went on here or that you don't need what's going on here, at least not with the frequency that you did earlier.

P: I enjoy talking to you a lot, but I don't need it. You know, I feel straightened away. I feel that way! It could change and I might come back some day, too. I don't know.

T: Well the door doesn't close. The door stays open. I'd like to hear from you, though, and it sounds like you want to kind of let this go and if you need it, to call back.

P: Yeah. That would be neat. I feel good right now.

*Patient Reaction*

Approximately one month after the patient's terminating session, she was seen in the Sleep Disorders Center for evaluation of her narcolepsy and seizure disorder. By that time she had been completely withdrawn from all medications for two months and reported functioning well.

Two nights of polysomnographic monitoring and a series of multiple sleep latency tests confirmed the presence of a seizure disorder. During the course of the sleep studies, the patient experienced two seizures, one of which occurred during a period of wakefulness. A definitive diagnosis of narcolepsy could not be rendered, however. These findings are interesting in two respects. First, the patient's initial assertion early in the therapy process was that she would never be able to go off her medications because she experienced such great fear any time seizures seemed to be imminent. Hence, the fact that she voluntarily withdrew from all medication and desired to stay medication-free in spite of continuing seizures directly attests to her lowered fear levels. Second, seizures had been initially linked to her fear of death and, more dynamically, to her fear of loss. Just prior to the sleep studies, the patient was reporting no more than one seizure auora per week, which contrasted to several of these per day at the time she was initially placed on the medication at the beginning of treatment. The observation that seizure frequency had reduced substantially even when she was no longer medicated is testament to resolving conflict patterns.

One month after the last psychotherapy appointment, R. T. was contacted and asked to respond to three questions. First, she was asked to describe the aspect of the therapy process and activity that was most helpful to her. In response to this question she provided the following:

I feel the most helpful part of my therapy was the honesty expressed by Dr. Beutler. I believe that a lot of my problems were a result of poor communication—i.e., people not showing me their real feelings, which caused me to misjudge the relationship. Because Dr. Beutler said what he felt about me, I was able to come out of my shell and express, at times, how I felt about him. Being able to confront a person who I believe to be honest, rid me of the fear I had of doing that with others. And it seemed, that once I was able to conquer my fear on that front, fear of other things in my life disappeared. I was able to confront them too.

Second, the patient was asked to describe those things about the psychotherapy relationship which she did not find to be particularly helpful. Her response was as follows:

It is hard for me to say what, if anything, got in the way of my therapy. I feel that every session really helped and I felt that each session cleared up some confusion in my mind. Maybe because I put a lot of effort into learning from Dr. Beutler, I am prejudiced and unable to find fault with his teaching, or my learning.

Finally, the patient was asked to assess her progress, to which she responded:

I feel that the program was very helpful because I am able to understand how far I've come. Though I realize that it worked because I put forth effort, I know that the program would not have been complete without Dr. Beutler's help. He is a sincere person who, I sense, has a lot of faith in himself and in others. It is this drive to succeed that I would truly like to thank him for teaching me.

## REFERENCES

Beutler, L. E. (1981). Convergence in counseling and psychotherapy: A current look. *Clinical Psychology Review, 1,* 79–101.

Beutler, L. E. (1983). *Eclectic psychotherapy: A systematic approach.* New York: Pergamon Press.

Beutler, L. E. (1986). Systematic eclectic psychotherapy. In J. C. Norcross (Ed.), *Handbook of eclectic psychotherapy.* New York: Brunner/Mazel.

Beutler, L. E., Crago, M., & Arizmendi, T. G. (In press). Therapist variables in psychotherapy process and outcome. In S. L. Garfield & A. E. Bergin (Eds.), *Handbook of psychotherapy and behavior change* (3rd ed.). New York: John Wiley & Sons.

Brehm, S. S., & Brehm, J. W. (1981). *Psychological reactance: A theory of freedom and control.* New York: Academic Press.

Dahlstrom, W. G., Welsh, G. S., & Dahlstrom, L. E. (1972). *An MMPI handbook: Volume I: Clinical interpretation.* Minneapolis: University of Minnesota Press.

Derogatis, L. R., Rickels, K., & Rock, A. F. (1976). The SCL-90 and the MMPI: A step in the validation of a new self-report scale. *British Journal of Psychiatry, 128,* 280–289.

Millon, T. (1969). *Modern psychotherapy.* Philadelphia: W. B. Saunders.

Millon, T., & Everly, J. (1985). *Personality and its disorders: A biosocial learning approach.* New York: John Wiley & Sons.

Paulson, M. J., & Lin, T. T. (1970). Predicting WAIS IQ from Shipley-Hartford scores. *Journal of Clinical Psychology, 26,* 453–461.

Schutz, W. C. (1958). *FIRO: A three dimensional theory of interpersonal behavior.* New York: Holt, Rinehart and Winston.

# Commentary: Growing into Separation

## Windy Dryden

*Commenting on a colleague's work with a patient in the format of this* Casebook *is a risky enterprise. Even though Dr. Beutler has provided extensive verbatim transcripts of his therapy sessions, my task is akin to giving an adequate critique of the Mona Lisa when one is color blind and can only see the painting through a grille, under conditions where one's line of vision is obscured by the heads of other art aficionados. However, let me state that Beutler has amply demonstrated in action some of the major ingredients of his systematic eclectic psychotherapy. He has shown how his therapeutic stance changed over time, what factors influenced some of his therapeutic decisions, and that he is a caring individual whose honesty and competence were appreciated by his patient. His clarifying style of practicing therapy in this case comes over clearly, and he presents a convincing rationale for this style of therapeutic participation.*

*Let me, however, make a few points that struck me on reading Beutler's chapter.*

*1. Beutler's opening succinct account of his approach is a masterful exposition of his brand of eclecticism, possibly the best I have read on his model. However, the complexity of his ideas is not matched by his chosen case. For example, the sophistication of his idea of formulating complex therapeutic menus does not come across in his work with this patient. This may, of course, be a function of the case he has selected to present.*

*2. I am not exactly clear how Beutler conceptualizes his client's psychological problems. Specifically, he does not present a clear model of emotional disturbance. He relies too much, in my opinion, on the concepts of "core theme" and "conflicts"—terms that do not seem to adequately account for the diversity of emotional reactions that may accompany such themes and conflicts.*

*3. In several instances, his cognitive interventions are not clearly designed. Thus, in the examples he provides he fails to give a credible account of the ABC theory of disturbance, fails to show his client clearly how "wants" differ from "have to's" and how these different philosophies may have far-reaching differential effects on her emotional responses. He attributes his client's failure to successfully execute a self-monitoring procedure designed to help her see the impact of her thoughts on her feelings to her high level of reactance, whereas other explanations may be more parsimonious. Thus, clients often have initial difficulty with such assignments because they do not clearly understand the ABC model (there is a case for arguing that this is so for Beutler's patient). Also, many clients have secondary problems of anxiety that accompany such tasks, which do interfere with the successful initial execution of these tasks. In my opinion, Beutler is too quick to confirm his own reactance hypothesis in this case. All this raises the interesting issue concerning how skillful eclectic therapists must be in executing various interventions in order to practice effective eclectic therapy.*

*4. My own thoughts about the patient are that her major anxiety centers on being abandoned. Gilbert (1984) has argued that such anxieties often underlie many depressive episodes, and the response of Beutler's patient when he hypothesizes its importance in her problems is marked. "P: 'Yeah, yeah, yeah. But, yeah! That's it. That is it. That's exactly it.'" And yet Beutler does not seem to keep it as a central focus. Taking this further, Beutler's work* occasionally seems unfocused to me, as if he is more ready to follow his client's lead than to keep the work focused on core themes that he himself hypothesizes to be central.

5. It is unclear what accounted for the client's improvement. Has she overcome her anxiety of being abandoned? In this respect, does she view abandonment as less likely to occur than formerly or can she cope with it better if and when it occurs? I would like to have seen Beutler help his client (and himself) to understand better the reasons for her improvement.

6. Finally, I was disappointed with the client's own comments about her therapy. They tell us relatively little. Has she idealized Beutler in a similar way as she idealized her former psychiatrist? If so, what are the implications of this for her sustained improvement?

These, then, are some of the points that occurred to me on reading Beutler's chapter. They need, of course, to be put in the context discussed at the beginning of this commentary. As I have argued elsewhere (Dryden, 1986), I like and admire Beutler's work. Most important his conceptual schema does succeed in explicating criteria that help therapists to make important clinical decisions. It is difficult to demonstrate one's approach to eclectic therapy through disembodied case material, and I am quite prepared to attribute some of my criticisms to the present format rather than to flaws in Beutler's actual clinical work with this patient.

## REFERENCES

Dryden, W. (1986). Eclectic psychotherapies: A critique of leading approaches. In J. C. Norcross (Ed.), Handbook of eclectic psychotherapy. New York: Brunner/Mazel.

Gilbert, P. (1984). Depression: From psychology to brain state. Hillsdale, NJ: Lawrence Erlbaum Associates.

# Commentary: An Explicit, Selective, and Consistent Eclecticism

## Stephen C. Paul, Addie Fuhriman, and Gary M. Burlingame

Beutler's systematic eclectic psychotherapy definitely warrants the name. His chapter presents a substantially abbreviated and yet tightly comprehensible explanation and example of his thoroughly thought-out model of eclectic therapy. The years of consideration, research, and applied validation that undergird the approach are clearly visible. Beutler's claim that he has designed a systematized approach to the integration of intervention techniques is backed with an uncanny consistency of concept development, operationalization, and actual application which defied our search for discrepancies.

The clear strength of Beutler's model lies in the extraordinary extent to which relevant issues are identified in ways that lead to the selection of specific, suited interventions. As Beutler noted, this is an approach to an integration of techniques from any number of theoretical perspectives which attempts to planfully match the techniques employed to patient need. As such, especially if one adopts his conceptual terms, the model offers the eclectic therapist at *least one clear road map for practice.*

The five questions Beutler asked at the beginning of therapy with the prospective client seemed remarkably straightforward and simplistic, given the otherwise tangled web of psychotherapy literature. Those five simple questions veiled a well-conceived complexity, removing much of the impressionistic or nonspecific from the art of psychotherapy. They addressed head on client suitability and client/therapist relationship factors that have been recognized as critical to successful treatment (cf., Bergin & Lambert, 1978; Parloff, Waskow, & Wolfe, 1978). In addition, they directly attended to Gordon Paul's well-worn question (1967, p. 111), "What treatment, by whom, is most effective for this individual with that specific problem, and under which set of circumstances?" The resulting complex of information about the client's symptom complexity defenses and reactance formed almost an equation that could be computed to guide technique selection.

The illustration of the therapeutic proceedings in the case material shows the consistency promised by the model. Clearly, the assessment gleaned in the pretreatment phase largely determined the course of therapy that followed. Once the attachment-individuation theme of the symptom picture was drawn from the client's history, that theme was pursued tenaciously throughout subsequent sessions. An appraisal of client history suggested a tendency toward reactance that was tested later in therapy and confirmed. Likewise, the conclusion that the client presented an emotionally undercontrolled and behaviorally controlled defense system was arrived at very early from testing data. These combined conditions suggested a minimally directive cognitive approach in light of Beutler's previous analysis of the available intervention approaches. He began with and stuck with cognitive approaches including reflections, questions, interpretations, and reframing throughout the sessions. Later in therapy, he expanded into what he considers mildly directive techniques (fantasy, role play, alternate thinking) just as he had forecasted he might when he deemed the client receptive. He said what he would do and then proceeded to do just what he had said.

The deliberateness of the systematic eclectic psychotherapy model seems to be a two-edged sword. On the one hand, its explicitness and precision can be thought to provide well-reasoned direction for the practitioner. If we are amenable to his specific formulation (e.g., reactance, dependence), Beutler has almost done our thinking for us. It is imaginable that the whole system could be converted into an extended decision tree like those presented in the third edition of the Diagnostic and Statistical Manual of Mental Disorders (American Psychiatric Association, 1980). Such a tool, even in its current form, is a real boon for those therapists, particularly therapists-in-training, looking for a source of order in the midst of chaos. This is particularly attractive for the eclectic practitioner, who has had few clear theoretical guidelines for practice.

On the other hand, if the practitioner had difficulty with the overall structure or any of the basic concepts that Beutler has adopted in formulating his model, its simple straightforwardness of the model could be jeopardized. Basic assumptions that underline the five critical questions in the model may not match the assumptions held by many eclectic therapists. The very existence of a distinction between simple and complex (neurotoform) problems accepted by Beutler has been debated in the literature for years (cf., Ullman & Krasner, 1969). Interpersonal reactance, one of the core dimensions, may or may not be conceptually congruent with a therapist's formulation of critical elements in the patient-therapist relationship. Likewise, the analysis that each individual therapist would make, if other therapists were energetic enough to do so, of the array of available treatment techniques may differ considerably from what Beutler arrived at due to differences in theoretical interpretations. Beutler acknowledges the possibility and value of other therapists substituting their own concepts and techniques, yet the very process of doing so requires the therapist to construct a parallel formulation with corresponding alternative concepts, questions, and procedures. In a sense, he or she would have to recreate an equally detailed and complex system that would require its own period of conceptualization, research, and application. Despite Beutler's openness to the mixing of new ingredients into his general recipe, what would seem to necessarily result would be an entirely new meal.

A second extension of this idea concerns therapist match with the model. We often talk of matching client and treatment model, but talk much less of matching therapist and model of treatment. Even though Beutler's model is eclectic in nature, it still has certain characteristics that would be present even if internal elements were modified. The strength found in the structured, objectified nature of the model mentioned earlier suits it particularly well to the structured, deliberate therapist or new therapist in search of structure. However, many therapists, eclectic therapists in particular, tend to be somewhat pragmatic or even iconoclastic (Garfield & Kurtz, 1977). Whether you choose to classify these therapists as nonsystematic, intuitive, or by some other term, they represent a large segment of practitioners. Although many of them simply may be looking for the right structure to integrate the elements of their practice, others actually may prefer to operate in less linear ways. In fact, they might take pride in their unstructured approach to therapy. Such practitioners would no doubt find the Beutler model to be too structured and restrictive. Modifications of elements inside the systematic model would not change the fact that the systematic nature of the model is inherently unacceptable.

To give him due credit, Beutler notes at the beginning of his chapter that his model is meant to be applied to suitable clients within "a stable and collaborative therapeutic relationship." He spells out the importance of examining the compatibility between client and therapist belief systems and backgrounds to ensure that the discrepancy is not too great, but adequate to promote optimal change. He further pays particular attention to the role of client reactance in the therapy process and includes this element in his decisions about appropriate technique selection. Nevertheless, his major emphasis seems to remain with the particular technique selection which then constitutes therapy.

Unfortunately, Beutler provided few of his own observations or reflections throughout or at the end of the transcript material. It would have been interesting to compare his comments with those reportedly made by the client at the close of therapy. The client indicated that she felt the most helpful part of her therapy was Dr. Beutler's honesty because he said what he felt about her, allowing her to interact with such an honest person instead of the types she had dealt with in the past. She further commented that her own effort and Dr. Beutler's sincerity and faith in himself and others were important factors. Although she made no reference to specific techniques or procedures, she did mention that she was grateful for Dr. Beutler's teaching, which facilitated her learning. This global assessment was strikingly similar to the results of outcome research findings that suggest the far greater importance of client characteristics, therapist, and client/therapist relationship relative to technique application in therapy (Lambert, 1983; Prochaska & Norcross, 1982; Smith, Glass, & Miller, 1980).

Would Dr. Beutler have interpreted the positive results of the sessions in the same fashion given the nature of his technique-centered work? It appears that he would have to experience some cognitive disso-

*nance if his own conclusions corresponded with those of his client. Would he ignore the role and importance of the specifically selected techniques and the skillful unfolding of their delivery as she did in his discussion?*

*There have been those over the years (e.g., Frank, 1982; Wachtel, 1977) who have argued that it is the common elements of therapies that account for their effects and that the specifics of therapy tend to be less significant. Beutler may even agree with that reasoning to some extent. However, content is part of each session, even if that content is simply the background for the actual, less explicit curative process. Beutler has provided a systematic approach to eclectic therapy that acknowledges and incorporates many of the important common components of therapy as well as addressing the issue of technique selection and utilization. His model represents a remarkable and useful piece of work.*

*It was a very pleasant experience to watch the model unfold in an actual case. At the same time, we got a glimpse of Dr. Beutler's skill and persona as a therapist. We thank him for the generosity that offered both his extraordinary model and the vivid sample of its application. The* Casebook *forum displays theory, practice, and reactions, thus providing an unfolding of the complex, creative therapy process. Hopefully, the* Casebook *will stimulate additional glimpses at the way clinical theory is translated into practice. The synthesis of case study and normative approaches to therapy research provides a much richer depiction of the therapy process which will allow a closer, more adequate scrutiny and, at the same time, stimulate it to flourish.*

## REFERENCES

American Psychiatric Association (1980). Diagnostic and statistical manual of mental disorders *(3rd ed.)*. Washington, DC: American Psychiatric Association.

Bergin, A. E., & Lambert, M. J. (1978). The evaluation of therapeutic outcomes. In S. Garfield and A. Bergin (Eds.), Handbook of psychotherapy and behavior change. *New York: Wiley.*

Frank, J. D. (1982). Therapeutic components shared by all psychotherapies. In J. H. Harvey & M. M. Parks (Eds.), The master lecture series *(Vol. 1)*. Washington, DC: American Psychological Association.

Garfield, S. L., & Kurtz, R. (1977). A study of eclectic views. Journal of Consulting and Clinical Psychology, 45, 78-83.

Lambert, M. (1983). Psychotherapy and patient relationships. Homewood, IL: Dow Jones-Irwin.

Parloff, M. B., Waskow, I. E., & Wolfe, B. E. (1978). Research on therapist variables in relation to process and outcome. In S. Garfield and A. Bergin (Eds.), Handbook of psychotherapy and behavior change. *New York: Wiley.*

Paul, G. L. (1967). Strategy of outcome research in psychotherapy. Journal of Consulting Psychology, 31, 109–118.

Prochaska, J. O., & Norcross, J. C. (1982). The future of psychotherapy: A Delphi poll. Professional Psychology, 13, 620–627.

Smith, M. L., Glass, G. V., & Miller, T. J. (1980). The benefits of psychotherapy. Baltimore, MD: Johns Hopkins University Press.

Ullman, L. P., & Krasner, L. (1969). A psychological approach to abnormal behavior. Englewood Cliffs, NJ: Prentice-Hall.

Wachtel, P. L. (1977). Psychoanalysis and behavior therapy: Toward an integration. New York: Basic Books.

CHAPTER 4

# The Case of Julie: An Eclectic Time-Limited Therapy Perspective

*Gary M. Burlingame, Addie Fuhriman, and Stephen C. Paul*

This chapter presents a case in which the therapist followed a model of eclectic time-limited therapy (ETLT) developed at the University of Utah Counseling Center. In the first section of the chapter the approach is placed in the larger context of general time-limited or brief therapy, and the process stages and basic elements on which the model is based are introduced. The majority of the chapter presents actual case transcript material with elaborating comments added by the client, therapist, and model authors. At the end of the chapter, we have added a short description of a second case for comparative purposes, highlighting the potential for differing applications of the model. Hopefully, the chapter will serve as a good illustration of how the approach can be flexibly adapted to incorporate various theoretical concepts and intervention tactics.

## SHORT-TERM PSYCHOTHERAPY

Several factors have contributed to the increasing interest in the development and use of brief approaches to treatment. In their recent book, Gelso and Johnson (1983) suggested that some of those factors include: (a) an increasing demand for services, which taxes agency resources and results in long wait lists; (b) an increased awareness of the role of psychological factors on the part of the public; (c) an extension of services to groups other than the typically served verbal, middle-class group; and (d) an increased demand on insurance companies to pay for services.

These motivating factors are supplemented by empirical evidence regarding the consumer's experience and treatment outcome. For example, collected findings suggest that clients often hold expectations that they will improve within five to six sessions and recover entirely within 10 sessions (Coleman, 1962; Garfield, 1978; Garfield & Wolpin, 1963). Another area of study has indicated that patients who have been in treatment nationwide report an average of only five or six therapy contacts (Lorion, 1974), suggesting than many treatments are brief by nature. In addition, these findings can be considered in light of evidence accumulating from treatment comparison studies where it has been suggested that time-limited approaches are equal to, or occasionally, even superior to time-unlimited varieties of therapy (Bloom, 1980; Gelso & Johnson, 1983; Luborsky, Singer, & Luborsky, 1975). As a result of these and other factors, and the supportive empirical findings, attention to brief therapies has greatly increased in recent years, and a number of therapy models based on widely differing theoretical perspectives have resulted (Budman, 1981; Butcher & Koss, 1978).

## SYNOPSIS OF ETLT

The particular model of ETLT presented in this chapter was generated out of a set of pragmatic and theoretical considerations. Development of the model was stimulated by staff reactions to a relentless wait list. Discussions of the problem led to the conclusion that a brief treatment procedure should be considered as a possible remedy to the wait-list problem; so a small group of staff members, which included the authors, set out to examine options. Because of the interdisciplinary (counseling and clinical psychologists, social workers, psychiatrists) and multitheoretical (dynamic, social learning, existential-humanistic, eclectic) nature of the staff, we were looking for a model that could easily assimilate divergent perspectives. We thought that such a model would improve the likelihood that the approach would be adopted, especially if the staff members were not forced into a totally alien orientation or set of practices.

An exploration of the existing literature uncovered a number of well-developed models (cf., Malan, 1976; Mann, 1973; Mann & Goldman, 1982; Reid, 1978; Sifneos, 1979). However, we found that the models we encountered were organized around the tenets of particular theoretical orientations. As Butcher and Koss (1978) noted in their extensive review of brief treatment, there are no broad-based models of brief therapy in existence that can accommodate divergent theoretical orientations. Therefore, we returned from our search without having found the hoped-for eclectic model and faced with the prospect of having to construct our own.

What we did find through the course of our exploration of the literature was a set of theoretical and/or empirically recommended elements of brief treatment that tended to recur across the orientations and models we examined (Budman, 1981; Butcher & Koss, 1978). A compilation of those elements resulted in a list that included: (a) client selection, (b) time limitation, (c) therapeutic focusing, (d) client expectations, (e) therapeutic relationship, (f) therapist activity, (g) emotional ventilation, (h) goal orientation, and (i) specific techniques. These elements appeared to be critical, common ingredients in the brief therapy process. Five of these regularly noted elements were selected to form the core of the eclectic time-limited model.

### Time Limitation

The first element, time limitation, is by definition a central focus in any brief or time-limited model. The time limit not only serves as a demarcation of the end of treatment, but also provides an impetus for the work. There is some evidence (Young, 1977) that establishing a time limit increases the expectation of therapeutic gain and that this heightened expectation subsequently leads to improved treatment outcome. However, depending on the purpose of treatment and theoretical orientation, the time limits established by practitioners in the literature range from 1 to more than 40 sessions (Bloom, 1980; Wolberg, 1980). In our particular setting, a 10-session format, including an intake session at the beginning and a follow-up session after the close of treatment, seemed more appropriate given the nature of agency resources and commonly presented client problems. This time-limit matched our particular agency's staff and clientele, and perhaps should be adjusted to match other settings and clientele.

*Expectation*

Attention to expectation sharing between the client and therapist in the model is based on the underlying assumption that explicitness increases the rate of progress within the restraint of an imposed time limit. Such explicitness is particularly well suited to the type of generally well-functioning client selected for ETLT. In addition, expectation sharing may serve to increase the client's sense of independence and responsibility, which is critical in maintaining and perpetuating change after the termination of treatment. Two specific types of expectations are attended to directly in the model: expectations about the course of treatment outcome (e.g., "Because of your characteristics and the nature of your problem, time-limited therapy seems to be the treatment of choice for you"; "We will meet weekly for eight weeks") and expectations about the roles that client and therapist will assume during the course of the treatment (e.g., "I expect that we will both be quite active in the sessions to come").

*Therapeutic Relationship*

The emphasis on the therapeutic relationship in the model arises from a recognition that the client-therapist relationship plays a significant role in any brand of therapy (Bergin & Lambert, 1978). A solid therapeutic relationship may hold the client in therapy long enough to accomplish desired treatment aims (Heitler, 1976). The model assumes a collaborative relationship posture between the client and therapist which encourages greater involvement and activity on the part of both participants. This, again, is expected to heighten the client's sense of personal responsibility.

*Therapeutic Focusing*

Accumulating evidence suggests that developing a treatment focus early in therapy can lead to better treatment outcomes (Malan, 1976; Burlingame, 1983). Two major types of focusing are addressed in the ETLT model. The first type is concerned with the therapist's efforts to identify the focal aim or a conceptualization of the client's presenting complaint. In the ETLT model, the focal aim is likely to be interpreted in ways that are consistent with the therapist's theoretical orientation. The second type of focusing applied in the model is called "focality," which is described by Malan (1976) to be the ability to concentrate the majority of the treatment activities around the identified focal aim. Focality is achieved through attempts to encourage the client to move from more general to more specific aspects of the presenting problem and by fostering directness and explicitness between the client and the therapist. This is done not only with respect to the content of interventions, but also with respect to the actual process of therapy. The focusing efforts of the ETLT therapist are intended to accelerate progress within the compressed time frame by concentrating both therapist and client attention on the purpose and process of treatment.

*Client Selection*

The client selection element takes on particular importance because of the level of participation required of the client in the model. All the preceding elements assume the client to be capable of operating collaboratively and actively with the therapist. In the ETLT model, client selection factors are considered during the intake session and the first treatment session. Both selection inclusion and exclusion criteria are considered. The inclusion criteria include: (a) at least one satisfactory past relationship, (b) a good premorbid adjustment, (c) the ability to form a relationship with the therapist, (d) the ability to establish mutual expectations with the therapist, and (e) a relatively circumscribed problem. Clients are excluded from ETLT if they: (a) are severely depressed; (b) present anger as their main affect; (c) are currently or have recently been psychotic; (d) show signs of organicity; or (e) are presently medicated. These inclusion and exclusion criteria are meant to serve as a set of minimal entry conditions, which, if met, help to ensure that the client can take full advantage of the approach.

Rather than recombine these brief elements into a new theoretical formulation, which would have defeated our pragmatic purposes, we decided to provide a flexible, skeletal therapeutic structure upon which the elements could be overlaid, depending on the unique theoretical orientation of the practitioner. We drew the skeletal framework from the atheoretical therapy process model of Gerard Egan (1982). Egan proposed that, in general, successful therapy follows a progression beginning with a period of client self-exploration, moving to a mutual integrative understanding of the client's issues, passing through a series of problem resolving actions, and culminating in a final termination phase. Drawing on the common elements in the short-term therapy literature and Egan's work, the final model of ETLT proposed was based on a set of background process stages and process elements upon which the individual therapist could overlay his or her own foreground of theoretical understanding and technique. The content and sequencing of the five stages and the elements of the ETLT model are represented in Table 1.

## CASE DESCRIPTION

The following case[1] was selected to illustrate the four therapeutic stages of ETLT as well as the mechanisms of change of focusing, collaboration, and expectations. The therapist in the present case was a psychologist with approximately eight years of postdoctoral clinical experience who had been trained in ETLT by one of the authors. Her preferred therapeutic orientation is psychodynamic, although she was clearly eclectic in her approach to the present case. More specifically, therapeutic interventions in the present case included dynamic linkage between an early childhood incestual experience and current interpersonal difficulties, behavioral rehearsal, homework assignments, and a modified bibliotherapeutic approach.

In addition to the eclectic nature of the interventions, the case was also selected because it involved a therapist who was relatively new to the ETLT approach. In contrast to demonstrating the "ideal" way the model might be applied, we thought selecting such a therapist might provide more insight into how one might integrate the ETLT approach within a well-established therapeutic style. Beyond asking the therapist to practice ETLT, both therapist and client agreed to videotape all sessions and provide us with a brief-session key-event summary report at the end of each therapy hour. This information enabled us, in a two-month follow-up interview, to have both therapist and client view and respond to videotape segments of therapy that corresponded to specific aspects of ETLT and to key events they had identified during the course of therapy.

Separate and conjoint debriefing in-

TABLE 1
Brief Psychotherapy Program

| Intake | Therapeutic stages | | | |
|---|---|---|---|---|
| | Stage I | Stage II | Stage III | Stage IV |
| 1st Session
Exploration and assessment | 2nd Session
Role description, rapport building, and problem specification ---→ | 3rd Session
Enhanced self-understanding and anticipated action ---→ | 5th Session
Active coping
→ 6th Session
Active coping ---→ | 8th Session
Pretermination
→ 9th Session
Termination |
| | | 4th Session
Action planning | 7th Session
Active coping | 10th Session
Follow-up |

terviews were conducted with the client and therapist. The conjoint interviews allowed us to ask questions of both client and therapist regarding: (a) rationale for a specific interventions, (b) the immediate, and (c) long-term impact of particular interventions on the client. The separate interviews provided their independent perspectives regarding: (a) the major events in the therapeutic experience, (b) thoughts regarding the change process (or lack of change) in ETLT, and (c) perceptions regarding the developmental phases of the therapeutic alliance in ETLT.

In the pages that follow we will elaborate on one or more of the mechanisms of change from each stage of ETLT. In doing so, we will draw heavily from transcripts of the debriefing interviews and actual therapy sessions. In addition to these verbatim accounts, a short commentary will be provided to integrate the therapeutic events and concomitant interventions with the mechanisms of change in ETLT.

## Identifying Information

Julie was a 26-year-old Caucasian female, employed as a physical therapist in a local hospital. At the time of treatment she was living in a one-bedroom apartment on a large university campus (married student housing) with her husband of 2 ½ years and a nine-month-old daughter. She was in her first year of employment after recently finishing her master's degree. Her husband was in his last year of work on a master's degree in computer science.

## Family History

Julie was born and raised in a conservative Protestant home in the Midwest. She was the youngest of five children, with three older brothers and one older sister (eight, seven, two, and five years older, respectively). Her father, a traveling salesman, was absent from the home for long periods of time while she was growing up, resulting in a family constellation similar to that of a single-parent home.

Julie reported that her mother went through a number of severe manic-depressive episodes during Julie's late-childhood and early-adolescent years (9 to 14 years old), some of which required hospitalization. During this time, Julie reported her mother having mood-congruent hallucinations at home (e.g., messages received through the television and/or radio), which frightened Julie a great deal. During the times when her mother was incapacitated, Julie's older brothers and sister managed the home.

In addition to her mother's mental disorder, Julie's maternal grandfather purportedly suffered from an agitated depression resulting in abusive behavior toward her and her siblings. The only sibling who appeared to have any similar problems was Julie's brother John, who was nearest to her in age. He was consistently truant during the time of his mother's illness (late elementary and high school), accumulating a lengthy police record (e.g., aggravated assault, larceny, and public intoxication). John's violence at home was manifested in a variety of ways such as smashing the TV, tearing the phone off the wall, or striking his mother. At the time of treatment, he was incarcerated in the state penitentiary. On the other hand, Julie's other brothers and sister had all obtained higher-education degrees and were productively functioning either at work or at home.

## Psychiatric/Medical History

At age five, Julie took a deliberate overdose of an unknown number of pills from her mother's medicine chest. In recalling the incident she reported wanting to get sick so she could get her father's attention on a Saturday morning. Her memory of the incident, although vague, included an image of her stomach being pumped.

Prior to treatment, the client's only other formal contact with the mental health community was when she was 12 years old and had three or four visits with her mother's therapist. She remembers her mother's therapist as "loud, kinda young, who smoked and swore a lot." Her mother suggested that she go to talk over her feelings about her brother's violent behavior in the home and fears that she might have regarding being hurt by him. Julie's account of this experience is that she basically did not talk with the therapist because she did not seem very understanding or kind. Examination of the client's medical history produced an uneventful profile with the exception of a mild premenstrual syndrome in late adolescence.

*Case Overview*

The client's presenting complaint revolved around interpersonal difficulties with two "older" male colleagues in the facility where she was employed. She was referred by a co-worker who felt that there was "more to her problems than just interpersonal differences." The therapist to whom she was referred conducted a standard ETLT initial assessment interview. During the interview, the client discussed her problems at work, anxiety, and interpersonal distrust as well as the fact that she had been an incest victim. After assessing the client's appropriateness on the ETLT selection criteria, the therapist introduced the idea of time-limited therapy and the opportunity to participate in a treatment evaluation project, to which the client agreed.

During the course of ETLT, three primary issues were consecutively examined: (a) a four-year incestual relationship with her delinquent brother, (b) obsessional thoughts of being and/or going crazy, and (c) the impact of her dependent or "victim" stance in current interpersonal relationships. At the two-month followup the client reported that her interpersonal relationships had significantly improved and that she was generally less anxious. This self-report improvement was also supported psychometrically by pre-to-post changes on complementary MMPI clinical scales (T-score reductions of 17 on Pa, 11 on Si, and 12 on Pt and A), suggesting that the client perceived relief and demonstrated change psychometrically.

The following case will be examined within the stages of the ETLT model. In reviewing the case, four types of transcripts will be examined. The first will be drawn from actual therapy sessions. These transcripts reflect interactions from actual therapy sessions that were videotaped and then viewed conjointly by both therapist and client at follow-up. The second set of transcripts reflects the therapist, client, and an interviewer[2] discussion of these videotape segments. These transcripts essentially represent retrospective comments from the client and therapist regarding what was going on "in their heads" during a particular part of a session. The videotape segments were selected primarily from therapist and client comments regarding key events during the therapeutic enterprise. The third and fourth set of transcripts represent separate interviews conducted with both client and therapist. These interviews were conducted two months after the termination of treatment in an attempt to get independent perspectives regarding the course of events during therapy. The various types of transcripts will be designated parenthetically or in the text.

## ANALYSIS OF CASE

### Intake and Assessment Stage

The primary therapeutic objective of this stage is to assess the appropriateness of the client for ETLT on the aforementioned selection criteria. The first task pursued by the ETLT therapist in the present case was to ascertain whether any severe psychopathology was present. This was especially pertinent given the family's psychiatric history. The absence of any severe psychopathology was assessed in two ways: MMPI profile and psychiatric interview. The conclusion from the data generated from both sources was that no severe psychopathology appeared to be present.

The next task in this stage is to assess the presence of the five inclusion criteria. To a great extent, the five inclusion criteria parallel the three mechanisms for change emphasized in the ETLT model: focus, collaboration, and expectations. Thus, the review of the intake session will be structured according to these three components.

### Focus

The ETLT therapist is encouraged to "let the client tell his/her story" completely enough so that a determination can be made regarding whether one can arrive at a circumscribed focal aim for treatment. More specifically, the focal aim can be thought of as the therapist's reformulation of the client's presenting complaint into a treatment plan. This presenting complaint often includes a variety of symptoms, a precipitating event, and related past events. Based on theoretical orientation, the ETLT therapist then develops a focal aim which includes probable etiological factors and the necessary therapeutic steps required to remediate the problem behavior (cf., Fuhriman, Paul, & Burlingame, 1985).

After arriving at a tentative focal aim, the therapist determines whether it is circumscribed enough to work on in ETLT based on four criteria: (a) pervasiveness of disruption in client's life, (b) acuteness of onset, (c) client ability to engage in disturbing material that is central to focal aim, and (d) feasibility of creating a treatment plan to address the focus.

In addressing the development of focal aim in the present case we will begin with the client's pretreatment focus. The importance of taking into consideration the client's pretreatment focus in ETLT is twofold. First, there is evidence that many early treatment terminations are linked to a client belief that the therapist is not responding to the primary concern (Epperson, Bushway, & Warman, 1983). Hence, clients give up on therapy before it begins. Second, given extant models that delineate the process of focal aim development (cf., Burlingame, 1983; Malan, 1976), the client's pretreatment focus is invariably the first piece of information to be carefully considered. The client described her pretreatment focus in the separate debriefing interview[3] as follows:

C: Basically what I wanted in a therapy experience was to stop feeling lousy, angry, and depressed. I was also running from the issue of whether I was crazy primarily because my mother and some other members of my family have a history of hysteria and manic-depressive disorders, so I was really scared that I was crazy too, and that someone was going to find out that I really needed to be helped.... The incident that led to this therapy experience was starting a new job as a real professional. I finally had to face my colleagues and count myself as an equal.

It is important to note that although the

client's childhood incest experience was an important part of therapy, this was initially not part of her original presenting complaint, nor was the fear of being "crazy" verbalized in the first session. Rather, the client's presenting complaints revolved around relief from her disruptive feelings and interpersonal difficulties at work. She explained it as follows:

C: I really hadn't planned on talking about my incest experience primarily because I was not reliving it or facing each day. [At the time], I didn't remember the experience as something that really bothered me.... However, [looking at it now] I think it was a very big issue in my life and I was just fighting to keep it suppressed... I guess I wasn't in touch with what was making me angry and depressed. I was tired of having the feelings and wanted to get rid of them. I realized that some of my colleagues had the power to bring that stuff out of me.... But, I didn't understand where they [the feelings] were coming from.

In later interviews the client more clearly articulated that, rather than being "tired of having the feelings," she thought that these feelings might be the first signal that she was going crazy and that this frightened her a great deal. It is important to note that this fear of going crazy was the first issue addressed after intake. A second point to note from the client's perspective during the intake stage was her change in expectations regarding the focus of therapy. After discussing her incestual childhood experience during intake, she stated in her session summary report:

C: Today, I was able to admit that I was a victim of incest. [My therapist] asked me what I planned to gain from these sessions and I said I wanted to feel that everything would be all right. She immediately picked up a lot of emotion and pain and said "you sound like a victim of incest." Her facial expression, the way she leaned toward me and held me on the arm showed me that she understood and that it was okay to tell her. What made me able to let out an awful rotten secret was also her frankness which left me with no response other than "yes" or "no."

The therapist's goal in the intake interview was to develop a tentative focal aim and determine whether it was sufficiently circumscribed to warrant a time-limited contract. In developing the focal aim, the presenting material that she had to work with was a role transition with the apparent precipitating event being a difficult move from the role of student to professional. This precipitating event was coupled with symptoms of depression and anger toward her co-workers. In an attempt to understand related events, the therapist probed for more detail regarding the interpersonal disruption the client experienced with her colleagues. What unfolded was a consistent nonassertive interpersonal stance toward two male co-workers. On closer examination, the therapist discovered that the client not only responded seductively toward these men but also had sexually laden dreams about them. Another important fact was that, from the client perspective, these male colleagues had legitimate authority over her work activities.

After listening to the client talk about her sexual feelings toward these "authority figures" and the passive-dependent interpersonal stance, the therapist stated to the client that her interpersonal stance was very similar to that of victims of incest. She then pointedly asked the client whether she had been a victim of incest. This intervention appeared to be a critical high-affect event in the intake interview. The client then told the therapist about a four-year incestual relationship that she had had with her older brother during the time of her mother's breakdown. Shortly thereafter, the therapist ended the assessment session with a time-limited therapeutic contract being offered. The therapist's focal aim in the intake session is better understood after considering her comments about the case, which also provide insight into why she considered the incest experience circumscribed enough for ETLT.

T: As I listened to Julie, and the interpersonal stance she took with male colleagues, it became apparent that she had some unresolved issues with authority and dependency. Her interpersonal stance was one that I had seen with several adults who had been sexually abused as children, you know, where they are quiet and just take anything that comes at them. That's where the question about sexual abuse came from. After finding out that she was a victim of incest, I began to think that the difficulties at work probably stemmed from unresolved issues with men. For instance, her dependent and seductive stance with men who were authority figures....

My strategy in dealing with her was very similar to my typical approach with incest victims. First the client has to acknowledge the affect attached to the incestual experience. However, most incest victims have blunted the affect attached to the incestual experience. Because of this, I generally take a less direct approach to uncovering the emotions attached to the incest experience. In Julie's case I did this by immediately assigning a book for her to read, *Sexual Addictions*, which is generally a nonthreatening, third-party way of approaching the subject. After the experience is acknowledged and the affect owned, I then move to the present in an attempt to identify symbols of the incest experience. With Julie, the symbols initially appeared to be her relationship with two male colleagues. After the symbols have been identified, I attempt to desensitize the client to the symbol by explaining its relationship with past events....

Julie did not report any similar past or present problem, and it seemed that her problem had a definable precipitating event, that is, her new job as a "professional." I was quite surprised that she could so easily engage in material that was obviously painful, which was a good sign for time-limited therapy, given my understanding of the model. Finally, I have worked with a number of incest victims and felt quite comfortable in understanding the steps needed to go through in resolving this traumatic experience....

*Collaboration*

A collaborative therapeutic relationship is seen as a key mechanism of change in the ETLT approach. The potential for such a relationship is represented in three of the client selection inclusion criteria. The first criterion is an early and positive relationship with the therapist, which not only is considered a good prognostic sign for a collaborative relationship, but also enables the therapist to see how the client responds to the therapist's "work style." The second is the existence of at least one satisfactory relationship in the client's past or present, which suggests that the client is capable of the level of self-disclosure and intimacy required in ETLT therapy. The third criterion, good premorbid adjustment, not only portends the likely end point of therapy (i.e., return to premorbid adjustment level), but also suggests that ETLT clients walk into the therapeutic encounter with enough resources that they can engage collaboratively with the therapist. An ETLT therapist should not expect a client to call on resources in therapy that have not been present before. If the client reports a history of inadequate coping skills, then it is likely that the client does not have the resources (good premorbid adjustment) to enter a collaborative therapeutic relationship and should be considered for an alternate treatment.

More specifically, the collaborative relationship in ETLT can be thought of as a horizontal relationship, which is in contrast to a top-down or vertical relationship. Vertical relationships typically define the therapist as a protagonist for change, whereas horizontal relationships emphasize cooperation and mutuality (Papp, 1983). ETLT is considered a catalytic rather than a curative treatment, with continued work expected on the client's part after therapy is terminated. Hence, the ETLT therapist is expected to inculcate an attitude of mutual responsibility for change, which is thought to encourage attributions of change to the client. This is in contrast to the therapist being seen the primary change agent (cf., Fuhriman et al., 1985).

Given these criteria, and the definition of the type of therapeutic relationship desired in ETLT, we turn to the therapist to better understand how she saw the above criteria fitting the present case and, more important, what potential she saw for a collaborative relationship with the client.

T: Julie struck me not only as someone who was ready to work, but also as someone who had a fair amount of inner strength. I experienced her as having more ego strength than her MMPI profile indicated [T score of 52]. Her support system seemed adequate with an especially solid relationship with her husband. She reported relationships in the past where she had been able to share herself with others in a fairly intimate way, which made me think she had the necessary strength to successfully deal with the emotionally laden material that would be looked at in therapy. I guess another point along this line is that my first contact with Julie ended in me liking her. I could positively respond to being able to work collaboratively with her as a client.

*Expectations*

The setting of expectancies within ETLT is done in two primary areas: expectations about treatment itself (i.e., time and reasonable goals) and expectations regarding the roles of therapist and client. One way expectations are addressed in the intake session is the client's ability to arrive at a mutual set of therapeutic expectations with the therapist. An example of this in the present case is seen in the above transcript where there was an apparent shift in the client expectations from "getting her lousy feelings under control" to her examining the incest experience as part of therapy. After the therapist heard about the incest experience and began to tentatively link this with the client's current interpersonal difficulties, she immediately suggested that the client read the book *Sexual Addiction*. This essentially provided an early test of the client's willingness to address what the therapist saw as important as well as her goals (expectations) for therapy.

This assignment in the intake session was not only important with respect to the goals of therapy, but also had implications for the respective roles of the client and therapist in ETLT. The therapist began to behaviorally address expectations regarding client and therapist roles in the first session. More specifically, the client entered the intake session and left with a book to be purchased and read outside of the therapy hour, suggesting she was to take responsibility for her own therapy.

*Commentary*

As we examined the entire intake session, we noted some variations from the original protocol that seemed important. First, with respect to therapeutic focusing in assessment, the client entered therapy primarily wanting relief from emotional disequilibrium (depression and anger). However, this request is clearly not circumscribed enough to make a decision regarding appropriateness for time-limited therapy. Therefore, the therapist moved to a greater level of specificity and uncovered the prior incest experience and the similarity it had with the client's present interpersonal stance and introduced this as the focal aim for therapy.

When we first examined this focal aim, we felt that resolution of a past incest experience might be an inappropriate focal aim for ETLT, i.e., too involved and not circumscribed enough. However, as will become evident, the therapist had a more specific focal aim. She was not striving for resolution of the myriad of problems often associated with an incest experience. Rather, she wanted the client to understand the typical interpersonal problems facing incest victims and how these might relate to the client's current life experience. Given the existence of particular client characteristics, the therapist was essentially operating on the assumption that ETLT is a catalytic rather than a curative experience and that therapy would be a beginning rather than ending point for the client to deal with her traumatic early life experience.

The case clearly meets the model's expectations regarding collaboration as demonstrated by the high degree of client self-disclosure in the first session. This level of disclosure often portends an early and positive therapeutic relationship. With respect to expectations, the therapist again provides a unique deviation from the model. ETLT therapists are typically advised to describe the anticipated client and therapist roles. However, this therapist went beyond an oral discussion and behaviorally defined the roles from the onset of therapy. By assigning the client independent work in the first session, the client was given a clear message that she was as much responsible for change as the therapist. This may have strengthened the therapist's stance, thus enabling her to push the client in later sessions.

## STAGE I: PROBLEM SPECIFICATION, RAPPORT, AND ROLE DESCRIPTION

The three tasks of this stage also parallel the three primary mechanisms of change in ETLT: focusing, collaborating, and expectation setting. In stage I the therapist is instructed to: (a) return to the tentative focal aim of the assessment session in order to assess its accuracy and feasibility for a time-limited contract, (b) reinforce the collaborative relationship begun in the first session, and (c) attend to client expectations about the therapeutic goals and behaviors.

### Focus

The following transcript begins with the client returning to the topic of incest discussed in the previous session. In essence, this interaction illustrates the client, rather than the therapist, directing therapeutic attention onto the tentative focal aim identified in the previous session. What is also evident in this interaction is the therapist's "on-task" behavior and directiveness with respect to the tentative focal aim. Apropos to her treatment strategy, she attempts to have the client begin to "own" the incest experience by first labeling it as such rather than thinking of it as "something that happened with my brother." A portion of the interaction is transcribed below followed by elaborating client and therapist remarks concerning the client's primary and secondary response to therapist interventions and the therapist's strategy for using these particular interventions.

C: After I left your office last Tuesday night I went home and I was kinda okay, but I had never really come to grips with the things that had happened to me in my childhood. I can't even say it.

T: Do you have a name for it?

C: If I were going to call it anything, I would call it "what happened with my brother."

T: Would you call it incest?

C: I don't want to call it incest. I hate incest, it's gross. But if that is what I'm supposed to call it and if that is what I need to face then. . . .

T: Technically that's what it really is.

C: Yeah, but that is the worst, most gross thing socially that I ever thought anybody could do. I think it is really gross. . . .

T: Bad?

C: Yeah, bad. Real bad! It is one of those really bad things that happens to other people, and not you.

The remaining portion of the interaction involved the client describing the incest experience in great detail with the therapist primarily responding reflectively. This was followed by the therapist introducing general information regarding childhood incest (e.g., incidence rates, typical settings, etc.). We discussed the entire interaction with the client and therapist to better understand the impact of the directive therapist interventions aimed at having the client reexperience a traumatic event. The client described the impact of this interaction as follows:

C: The biggest impact [this interaction had on me] was that I could really relate to what was going on inside myself then. I was really being tortured inside but on the outside . . . I thought of two words that described what was going on inside. The first thing was that I was really angry. I was angry that I had to face this, I was angry that I had to talk about it, I was angry that it happened. The second thing I was angry about was that I was being so contrived and controlled in this session like "Guess what happened to me on the way to the store?"

T: Were you angry at me?

C: Yeah, but I was just angry at everybody then. Anybody I could blame it on. As I started to talk about it, finally, I think it helped me to begin to resolve it. I wasn't going to allow myself all the emotion in this session, but at least the talking was helpful in putting my experience into perspective. . . . I mean, that the experience is mine, this is what happened to me and it's not the end of the world. I haven't died. I admitted it. . . . I guess I started realizing all this when I began to say the word, incest. And what I felt the first time I said it was "Oh, I said it, now that's out." And then by the end of that interaction I started to say to myself, "This is getting better, it's better to face this now. I don't have to cover anything up anymore." But I also was really insecure about it . . . what am I going to think of myself from now on? And what if my husband really, really doesn't hang in there. . . .

The therapist is clearly working from the tentative focal aim of incest. This is illustrated by the therapist's description regarding the intent of the above set of interventions. The client elaborates more specifically on the impact of the therapist setting her incest experience within a larger framework.

T: The biggest thing that I wanted to have happen in the above interaction was for Julie to name it, acknowledge it, and be able to say, "Yeah, it was incest." I think this is the first and most important thing for an incest victim to do. I wanted to intensify Julie's affect around that, and then I wanted to deintensify it a little bit so that it didn't seem so overwhelming. This is why I moved to providing the statistics... but I also wanted her to know I recognized her pain.

I: [turning to client] How did providing information in this interaction impact you?

C: I didn't feel as alone as I had, and I didn't feel as bad. Like it was my fault. All I knew was that I had done it with my own brother.... I also got a great deal of empathy from [therapist] which helped a lot.

*Collaboration*

The strength of the collaborative relationship in this stage is demonstrated in the above interaction by the client's willingness to immediately begin working on emotionally volatile material. It is also important to note that the client is initiating work very early in treatment, i.e., at the beginning of the second session. The client's perception of the collaborative relationship and what it represented for her in this stage is illustrated in the following comments:

C: I was looking at [therapist] body language and facial expressions and I could feel she was very supportive, so I guess that I didn't need to hear her say, "You're not bad." I also appreciated the way that [therapist] made me not depend on her in this session and let me be a separate individual... so that I was doing the work.

*Expectations*

The primary expectations to be addressed in this stage relate to the roles of both client and therapist (e.g., collaboration) and those that center around treatment procedures (e.g., length, objectives). As will be discussed later, the therapist in this case did not explicitly discuss the role expectations in as great a detail as the model suggests. However, she did attend to expectations regarding treatment length and the goals of therapy. The impact of the time expectancies is shown in the following client statements regarding how time limit affected her behavior in this stage of therapy.

C: Well, I guess the biggest thing I thought about [regarding the time limit] was that we had to really get busy, so I just got down to it. I would have been really frustrated if I had to go on for months trying to figure out each and every part of my life as it related to the incest experience. I really appreciated the fact that [therapist] pushed me to look at things in therapy quickly.

*Commentary*

ETLT therapists are advised to begin each session by reconnecting with the content of the previous session. The process of reconnecting session content is termed *therapist focality*. Focality often enables the therapist to move toward greater levels of specificity in targeted areas of the client's life. The resulting therapist directiveness and specificity push the client to consistently deal with material related to the focal aim of treatment, which, in turn, can lead to emotional ventilation.

In the present case, the client begins the session by addressing the incest content discussed in the prior session. The client's direct attention to this not only suggests the accuracy of the tentative focal aim identified in the first session (cf., Fuhriman et al., 1985), but also gives the therapist more license to push onto the next step in her treatment plan: an overt acknowledgment and description of the incest experience. The client responds to this invitation by describing the events during the four years that she had intercourse with her brother.

However, she also experienced two additional responses that are difficult to detect in the transcripted material. First, she experienced anger directed toward the therapist for reminding her of the incest. This anger may be partly explained by the directiveness of the therapist in asking her to quickly reconnect with the incest experience. This anger was not expressed in this session, due primarily to her second response, which was the avoidance of an overt expression of the affect. This avoidance response, as will be seen in later transcripts, is of great importance and determines the flow of therapeutic events for the next few sessions.

The client's perception of the collaborative relationship is reflected in her statement regarding the therapist's attempt to keep her independent and working on her own. In other words, the client perceived the responsibility and independence the therapist was attempting to foster, which, in part, describes the definition of the horizontal relationship in ETLT. It is also important to note that the independence fostered by the collaborative relationship did not result in the client experiencing a lack of empathy during this session. In fact, she comments on how much caring and warmth she felt from the therapist.

In response to the client/therapist role expectations to be addressed in this stage, the therapist modeled the roles and behavior expected rather than explicitly discussing them with the client. This strategy, although powerful, may not be as potent as the oral discussion coupled with modeling suggested in the ETLT model. As will be seen in the next stage, the therapist and client get into a competitive relationship with respect to focus that might have been avoided, in part, if there were more explicitness with respect to "how we work in here." The exception to this modeling approach is the explicit discussion about length of therapy, i.e., expectations about treatment. For example, in the above debriefing interview the client clearly states her awareness regarding the explicit time limit. The result of this time limit, as predicted by the model, is a client perception that she had better get down to work because "there was not a whole lot of time to waste," which is essentially maintained throughout the course of treatment. Perhaps if there had been as much explicitness regarding the other ETLT expectations, some of the conflict between the client and therapist considered in the next session could have been avoided.

## STAGE II: ENHANCED SELF-UNDERSTANDING AND ACTION PLANNING

The primary objective of the second stage of ETLT is to provide a context within which the client can better understand the focal aim identified in the previous sessions. The principle governing this stage is that the interventions should result in an increased understanding of the intrapersonal and interpersonal issues surrounding the focal aim. This increased understanding is important in moving the therapist and client toward a clearer shared conception of regarding the work of therapy. In addition, the therapist is instructed to foster key aspects of the collaborative relationship (e.g., interdependence, increased responsibility, etc.) and maintain the expectations set in earlier sessions. In this stage, we will primarily examine an obstacle that developed in the present case with respect to the focus of therapy and how it affected the collaborative relationship and client/therapist expectations.

*Focus*

The model proposes that the three mechanisms of change act in a synergistic manner (cf., Fuhriman et al., 1985), and, that if an obstacle exists for one mechanism of change, it will create problems for the other two. This principle is clearly illustrated in the following interaction drawn from a stage II session. The collaborative relationship and expectations regarding therapy were clearly effected as the client and therapist essentially miss each other with respect to the focus of therapy. A retrospective examination of the second session (stage 1) revealed that the client experienced a great deal of affect but also recognized that she was controlling it by presenting a "really contrived personality." It is clear from her comments that she had connected this observation with her fear of going crazy, and that she returned to the third session (stage II) wanting to do things differently than they had been done in the last session. However, the therapist returned to the session with an agenda dictated by the model (i.e., increasing client understanding around past incest experience) and a desire to move onto the next aspect of her focal aim, i.e., identifying here-and-now symbols associated with the incest experience. The following is the interaction that developed immediately when the two agenda collided.

C: I'm feeling real scared about last week. It feels like we went up to the edge of a cliff and then you walked away and just left me there, or I went to the edge of it and said, "Yeah, I could jump," and then walked away . . . you know, I was at the verge of something that really scared me, . . . you know, that I could go crazy. That's really scary to me, [pause] that's so scary to me.
T: Yeah.
C: I left thinking. . . . I caught myself comparing our relationship to the relationship that I have with my clients [at work]. You know, when a trauma victim comes in and they have brain damage and I'm there as the therapist. I know they have a problem, but they don't know if they've got a problem. Do you know what I mean. That's scary to me. I just sat there with you last week, and I didn't know what you were thinking . . . probably it was, "she has a problem but she doesn't know she's got a problem." You know, there's always a chance that I've got a problem.
T: A problem like?
C: Well, like I am crazy or that emotionally something is wrong with me and that you are treating me and know what it is. Does this all sound weird?
T: No, it doesn't. [Therapist gives two-minute discourse on the difference between problems in living and people who have mental disorders or are crazy using example of thought disorders. She ends this discourse with the following statement to client.] I don't think you're crazy.
C: I guess I needed to hear you say that.
T: Maybe I should have said it last week . . . but I wanted you to sit with your feelings.
C: I think I'm going to cry, because, you know, I think I'm aware of relating to you and I think you know the weak spots that I have. Who knows, I could be totally tetched, you know, really nutty.
T: What does real nutty mean to you?
C: I guess emotionally not being able to cope. I guess losing track of reality. Doing weird things that scare other people. . . . [Client gives example of misplacing her books in the library when she was pregnant and was unable to find them for two hours. She ends this with a statement that that's an example of crazy behavior.]
T: Okay, but losing your books is not crazy or psychotic.
C: No just weird. I guess that's a problem, you know, I just. . . . [Client goes on to give two more examples where she lost her temper and went out of control at home and then describes some of the

similarity between this behavior and what she remembers as a child about her mother's behavior right before she was hospitalized.]

T: .... So, the crazy part is that you say to yourself, "I have a lot of crazy stuff underneath?" just like my relatives?

C: Yeah, I guess the crazy part is a feeling of losing control.

T: So, you feel like you're losing your emotional control?

C: Yeah....

T: So if I pushed you hard enough you might....

C: Right now I feel like I could cry. [Begins to cry.]

T: Okay, so the scary part in you is "Gee if I let go of my emotions in here, then they will make me go out of control and then I'll be crazy outside of here too."

C: Yeah, it seems crazy to laugh and cry at the same time or to be giggling when I really feel like I need to be crying and sobbing ... to me that's crazy ... [Client then goes on for several more minutes and discusses several examples of when she had a highly emotional experience and tried to not show her emotions because she was afraid of them. Each time the therapist responds by stating that expressing strong emotions does not mean that you are crazy.]

*Commentary*

Up to this point, the case had gone almost letter perfect with respect to the ETLT model. The client had: (a) met the exclusion and inclusion criteria; (b) begun to work collaboratively from the beginning of therapy; (c) accepted the expectations of ETLT regarding therapist/client roles and the treatment contract; and (d) presented with what the therapist thought was a circumscribed focal aim. In this session, the client is moving in an entirely different direction from that of the therapist. In terms of ETLT nomenclature, the client was raising new and seemingly pertinent information with respect to the focal aim. However, the therapist is essentially missing the client's cue that what she is talking about is important. The client describes the impact of this interaction as follows:

C: At the beginning of this session I was thinking: "What did you [therapist] think you were doing to me letting me walk out last week with all those feelings." I was really mad because ... she had left me in a lot of pain. I was also angry because I wanted her to tell me whether I was crazy or not. At that point she said something like, "Do you want to know what I think?" I thought, "Hallelujah, yes, I want to know" ... I was really pushing her by saying, "Are you sure you don't think I'm crazy?" I was saying that with every question. And then when I was talking about all the stuff that made me think I was crazy, I just got more mad ... I was overwhelmed by everything I'd shoved inside and I didn't know how I was going to deal with it ... I think that I was trying to say, "So, you don't really think I'm crazy even after I told you all this crazy stuff." And then at the end I asked her again if she thought I was crazy even after I had told her all that stuff ... I don't know what effect it would have had if she'd said, "Well what are you like when you're really crazy?" I think you could really tell how desperate I felt about reassurance. Maybe it would have been a relief if I'd understood but I kept asking.

Retrospectively, it is easy to see the intense impact of the client not being attending to in the session. Julie had immediately begun to work on emotionally volatile material (incest), which, in turn, allowed her therapist to quickly identify a focal aim for treatment and begin to work on it. However, as the client began to relive the incest experience, the affect associated with it raised an underlying fear that she had about herself. Namely, when she experienced strong emotions she associated this with insanity, i.e., represented by her early life experiences with mother, brother, and grandfather. In addition, these fears were further fueled by the incongruity she was experiencing between what she felt like on the inside and what she was expressing on the outside.

The unresolved fear essentially made it very difficult for her to work any further on the incest; however, what her therapist saw was Julie resisting the agenda of focusing on the incest experience. A frequent problem with new ETLT therapists, which is exemplified in the above interaction, is that the structure of the stages, and moving the client through these stages, begin to take importance over client concerns. The potency of the structure is evident in the following therapist's comments regarding the above interaction.

T: Well, as I watch it now, I'm real surprised that I didn't go after her affect in that interaction. . . . I had about five or six choice points where I could have said, "Tell me more about that," or "What are you feeling?" I think what happened here is not at all like me. I don't know if I was pressed by the time limit or what . . . I guess I was impatient in this session.

It is apparent from the therapist's initial interventions that the direction the client was going was not in her "therapeutic game plan." She first responded with a few reflective interventions (e.g., "yeah," "a problem like") and then quickly moved to cognitive interventions in an attempt to allay the client fears regarding her being crazy so that she could get back on track, i.e., deal with the incest. The therapist's strategy appears to have been a simple and directive message: "You are not crazy, so let's get on with the rest of therapy."

ETLT therapists are counseled to use selective attention in guiding their interventions (focality) across the course of therapy. However, they are also instructed to use three principles identified by Luborsky (1984) to refine the initial focal aim through stage II of treatment. Two of these principles would have assisted the therapist in responding differently to the client in the above interaction: redundancy of themes and contiguity of content (cf., Fuhriman et al., 1985; Luborsky, 1984). In each of the prior sessions one can find interactions regarding the incest experience that were immediately followed by comments regarding the client's family "craziness." Clearly, this interaction might have evolved differently if the therapist had taken note of the redundancy and contiguity of content associated with the client's fear of being crazy. Given our experience in training and investigating this mode of therapy, the interaction illustrated above represents a frequent mistake and consistent danger in the ETLT model, i.e., therapist inattention to content and issues that are important and relevant for the focal aim of treatment.

Nevertheless, the therapist's shift in intervention emphasis in the latter part of the transcript demonstrates her recognition of the client's need to deal with her strong affect and the need to refine the focal aim of treatment. This is demonstrated not only in her summary reflection regarding the client's experience of strong emotion, but also in the majority of her interventions in the remainder of the session.

It is clear from both client and therapist remarks that the level of "we-ness" that characterizes the collaborative relationship was absent in the early part of this session. This was probably a function of the therapist and client having different agendas and the resulting collision of these two. It also underscores an issue raised by the authors of the model concerning the synergistic manner in which the three mechanisms for change work together.

More specifically, the focus of this session differed for client and therapist (e.g., fear of going crazy versus incest), which, in turn, violated some of the expectancies set earlier in the treatment contract (e.g., cooperative client/therapist roles, single focus, etc.), which, in turn, made the therapeutic relationship competitive rather than cooperative (e.g., vertical rather than horizontal relationship). Nevertheless, the dissonance created by the collision of agenda was productive, as will be seen below, in modifying and refining the focal aim of treatment as well as redefining how the therapist and client would work together in the remaining portion of the therapy experience.

## STAGE III:
## ACTIVE COPING OR WORK STAGE OF THERAPY

The objective of the third stage (sessions 5 to 7) of ETLT is characterized by "doing and reviewing." The working assumption in this stage is that the focal aim of treatment has already been collaboratively refined and modified in previous sessions. This process was illustrated in the above interaction in a less than ideal manner. The primary therapeutic task identified in stage III is for the therapist to maintain a high level of focality. More specifically, this means that the therapist's interventions should be consistently targeted on the focal aim rather than exploring "new material," which often characterizes time-unlimited approaches (cf., Fuhriman et al., 1985).

This stage provides the therapist with the least amount of guidance with respect to specific therapeutic tasks, which results in stage III being the point where the therapist's unique style and orientation becomes evident. Therefore, the unique style and orientation of the therapist in the present case will be highlighted, with the three mechanisms of change essentially providing a backdrop for this discussion.

From a process perspective, the client and therapist in the present case were moving into stage III during the fourth session. This early movement was probably stimulated by the interaction just examined, which appears to have resulted in a clearer identification by both the client and therapist regarding the work of therapy. More specifically, the therapeutic work now included the client's fear that she was going crazy when she experienced strong emotions. This shift can be seen in the client's end-of-session report for session 3.

C: In this session, I was able to identify my fear of being crazy or someday losing my mind by discussing my mother's and family's mental and emotional problems and behavior which I thought was "nutty." Then I was able to identify my behavior which I thought was "nutty" and analyze how I was perceiving myself.

This insight is important because it not only opened the way for increased understanding regarding the incest experience, but it also enabled the client and therapist to more freely examine how this event might be linked to the passivity and dependency noted in her current interpersonal relationships. In fact, the client understood this insight well enough at the end of the third session (stage II) to act on it in an interaction with both her father and husband during the week. The fact that the client was doing work outside of therapy further underscores the degree to which she took the collaborative relationship seriously.

Although it would be impossible to fully represent the work of the next four therapy sessions, we have selected two excerpts from two different therapy sessions that highlight the therapist's unique style and orientation. In these excerpts, the client's dependent interpersonal stance was manifested and discussed in two ways: (a) dependency within the therapeutic session, and (b) etiology of the dependent stance, which led back not only to memories of the incest but also to memories of child neglect experienced during the time that her mother was hospitalized and her father was absent from the home.

The therapeutic style and typical interventions evident in these interactions included: (a) a here-and-now or present oriented interpersonal stance on the part of the therapist; (b) a moderate amount of interpretation and labeling of events for the client, and (c) a directive and active stance that often looks didactic and problem solving in intent. The therapeutic orientation or, more specifically, the principles of change that the therapist appears to be operating from were mixed and included: (a) a belief in the psychodynamic principle that early conflict (incest) helps explain present dysfunctions and that insight into this conflict is an important aspect in change; (b) a belief that information or changing one's beliefs and cognitions regarding an event (incest) helps; and (c) a belief that immediacy with self and client, or an interactional approach, will lead to catharsis, which, in turn, becomes an important part of the change process.

Beyond using interventions tied to the above principles of change, the therapist incorporated a modified bibliotherapy approach with the client as well as using role rehearsal techniques to help the client begin to behave in a more assertive manner in interpersonal relationships. The client practiced these new skills and roles both during the session and through parallel homework assignments. The impact of these techniques is seen from the client's perspective through a review of end-of-session client reports and the debriefing interview. Although the model does not espouse the use of any particular interventions, it does encourage the therapist to use a variety of techniques in addressing the focal aim of treatment, which is clearly seen in the transcripts that follow.

The first excerpt, taken from session 4, illustrates the interpretive style of the therapist where links are made between in-session dependency and events in the past. In addition, the here-and-now style of the therapist is seen in the following excerpt, with attention being paid to interactional events as they occur in the session ("Are you mad at me?"). The content that preceded this excerpt was a highly cathartic memory of childhood neglect during the period when Julie's mother was in and out of the hospital. The interaction that follows quickly moves from remembering these unmet needs as a child to expecting the therapist to anticipate, acknowledge, and meet her needs during the therapy hour.

C: Am I supposed to feel it some more? I don't want to.
T: I know it's painful but it's not going to just go away.
C: We really do need tissues here.
T: Do you have some in your purse? I'll be sure to bring some next time.
C: I'm all right. . . . [crying some more and then wiping her nose on her hand]. . . we are really going to have a problem this time.
T: Do you want me to get some?
C: Where's the clock? [locates clock] Oh, we only have 20 more minutes.
T: I would but I need you to ask me more directly. If you don't ask me for what you need, you won't get it, because I don't read minds very well. [pause] My guess is that what we're doing right now represents one of your issues in the present. If you don't get what you need when you want it, then you think it's because people are just unwilling to

give it. Julie, they may not know what you need.
C: Well, it's pretty obvious that I need a tissue. [delivered angrily]
T: So if something is obvious, you can't ask for it?
C: Well, I don't even know if I want it now. Does that make sense? [pouting]
T: No, I want you to follow that.
C: A lot of times I'm not very direct.... It is hard for me to decide if it is worth it or not for you to go get tissues.... My direct request would have been, maybe you need to go get tissues. That is as direct as I could be.
T: Is it hard to say, "I need some tissues. Will you go get some?"
C: Yeah, I don't know why that is hard.
T: We could probably guess, maybe when you were growing up every time you asked for something, you didn't get it.
C: I really don't want tissues now, I'm fine. I guess what sent me into a trauma was that *you* thought I needed a tissue.
T: So it's not your need, it was what I think you need that's important. Heck, that can get you into a lot of trouble because I don't know what your needs are. But you apparently assumed I thought you needed something.
C: Yeah. I'm trying to think whether this happens a lot, you know, not just in therapy, but in other places too.
[Client then goes over a few outside situations, e.g., with child care, where she expects other people to just know what her needs are without telling them. This is then followed by about one minute of silence, which is broken by the following client comment.]
C: I'm waiting, trying to figure out what's going on, what to do next....
T: What's going on inside right now?
C: I'm feeling depressed right now. I'm feeling really lost. I'm getting really mad at the core of this whole thing. I want someone to understand what I'm feeling and where I'm coming from and what has happened in the past. I guess I expected you to understand my feelings. You know, if you can't understand them, then I can't either.
T: Are you mad at you or me?
[Client says she is mad at therapist. Therapist then moves to increase client's anger at her and later points out that she not only experienced anger at therapist without going crazy but that the relationship did not suffer as a result.]

The therapist's interventions in the above interaction are clearly aimed at having the client recognize her dependency assumptions in relationships, part of her original presenting complaint. One result is that the client, once again, experiences strong emotions toward her therapist. However, as the client elaborates on this interaction below, we see other results including a desensitizing of the client to strong emotions, as well as the intended result of increasing awareness about her dependent stance in relationships. The client explains the impact of this interaction as follows:

C: I guess I wasn't going to deal with my feelings here... I just wanted to pass it on to somebody else. I'm realizing in this session that I just can't do that and it's just really painful... I have to take responsibility for and it makes me feel alone. I think in this session I saw for the first time how I was trying to shovel out my needs to somewhere where I didn't have to deal with them, and for a while it was on my therapist. I was kinda saying, "Here, you take care of this, you wade through it. You explain it to me...." Another thing that I was thinking with the tissues thing was "Why are you picking on me, I'm so mad, can't you just get me the damn tissues? You're pushing me, I want you to fix my problems for me and tell me what to do next, but you directed me back into myself. I guess I'm getting the message that I'm really out of touch with myself and I guess it's time to get back in touch."

The collaborative relationship in the above interaction is evident in the manner in which the therapist interacts with the client. More specifically, the therapist took a peerlike interpersonal stance with Julie in this session by essentially saying, "Heck, thinking that I can read your mind regarding your needs can get you in a lot of trouble because I'm mortal just like everyone else in your life." By being spontaneous and admitting that she was just an "everyday person," the therapist essentially shed the therapeutic mantle. The intentional use of immediacy in the therapeutic hour, coupled with "therapistlike" roles at other times (e.g., interpretations) continually turned the client inward, which was part of the focal aim stated at the beginning of treatment. From the client's perspective, this led to the increase in self-reliance which she describes as follows:

C: Well, I was certainly more self-reliant after that session. I had no choice but to face my own feelings and work through everything myself. . . . I think if I would have had six months I would have given up. I would have gotten confused and frustrated. It seems like the eight weeks kept me centered. I also think that . . . my therapist was task-centered and focused, and I realized that I had to make a go of it in the eight sessions.

Another point to note in the above client perspective is the strength of the time expectancy and its continued impact. The client once again reiterates that the eight sessions kept her centered on resolving the issues that brought her into therapy. Interestingly enough, she also describes the therapist as task-centered and focused, which provides a validation from the client perspective of the presence of therapist focality.

In stage III, the therapist not only identified current symbols of dependency, but also tried to identify past incidents that reflected a dependent style. This, in essence, reflects the psychodynamic principles of change from which the therapist at times seemed to operate. In the second therapy excerpt below (session 5), the therapist pushes for more insight by interpreting past symbols of dependency (driving a car), while also moving the client to experience more affect in the session. The intent in increasing affect seems to be to underscore her beginning disassociation between experiencing strong emotion and going crazy. This separation is evident in the client's end-of-session report from the prior session:

C: In this session I told [therapist] about something significant that happened during the week. I was able to stand up to my father on the phone and tell him my honest opinion about the sob stories he always gives me about how hard his life has been. During the week I was also able to pinpoint with my husband why I was feeling angry about something rather insignificant that had happened. We found that what seemed to be an irrational response was based on some things that I had done in earlier years. I was able to verbalize to him [husband] that I was not feeling crazy, and that I had been afraid of being crazy like my mom for a long time. The fact that I had resolved the long-standing issue of craziness was rewarding because I knew I had begun to make some progress and the hard work had paid off.

The therapist enters this session with apparent confidence that the client could now experience higher levels of affect. This is illustrated by the fact that the therapist essentially goads the client with a rather sarcastic comment, "Here we go again, come on now, give me a break," when she talks about being tired of feeling and talking about painful events in the past. The result is an increase in affect coupled with more vivid memories regarding painful past events.

In addition, the following transcript reflects the aforementioned therapist belief that immediacy (statements like "I'm tired of this") leads to catharsis. Finally, the interaction ends with the therapist essentially encouraging and rewarding the client for the hard work she is doing or reinforcing the process being used for self-discovery and catharsis.

C: When I was 19 and 20 years old I would say things like this is where we are and this is where we need to go, and remember where we were going.... I used to have to be behind the wheel and drive it 10 times before I could find my way down to the corner store.
T: Do you think that's another symbol of trying to ... get someone to shelter you?
C: It protected me from making a mistake....
T: Do you understand why you're that way?
C: Well, kind of ... [shakes her head no]....
T: Not really?
C: I'm not feeling it. I know I could dig it out and say, Hey, ... but it's probably the things that happened to me in my childhood, but I'm not feeling it....
T: That is about the fourth time that you've said you're tired of feeling.... [sarcastically] come on give me a break.
C: I'm tired of thinking about it.
T: Is that why you don't want to talk about it?
C: Uh huh. [cries] [Client then talks with a lot of catharsis about what it was like to be neglected as a child and not feel loved. She describes in great detail incidents where she would ask her father for affection and he would tell her that she needed to stand on her own two feet or he would sexualize her request. The therapist reflectively responds to this for about 15 minutes and then responds in the following manner.]
T: It's really painful to hear about this....
C: I didn't use to remember any of this.
T: I guess it's like you have opened a door to the past and a bunch of dominoes have started to fall into place?
C: Yeah.... It was just so strange; when I was a teen-ager I always thought my daddy was my closest friend. I used to think that he loved me so much, I really don't think he loved me now though.
T: He couldn't, or wouldn't?
C: I don't think he knew how, I mean they [parents] just didn't know how to take care of me. It makes me so angry. It's so stupid. [cries] What am I supposed to do with all of this?
T: Keep on doing what you're doing.

The potency of the client reexperiencing these painful past events is illustrated by this interaction being selected as a "key event" in the client's end-of-session report. This report reads as follows:

C: In this session, I was able to admit that I had been neglected as a child and to acknowledge and verbalize the loneliness I felt as a child. The events that led to this realization happened during the week as I thought over what I had discovered in last week's session. I felt that [my therapist] was empathizing with what I was saying and knew what my feelings were. Maybe even felt them before herself. She cried several times while I was telling her about my pain, which made me feel like she was with me and my pain.

An important point, found in this report

with respect to the above interaction, is the client's perception regarding therapist empathy. Even though the therapist was pushing the client rather hard, illustrated by Julie's report that her therapist was "task-centered and focused" she also reported experiencing a great deal of empathy. The latter perception is probably due to the long periods when the therapist primarily responded with reflective interventions when the client was experiencing a high level of emotion, as well as the noticeable impact that the client's experiences had on the therapist.

Both the above excerpts illustrate some of the major interventions used by the therapist to address the dependent interpersonal stance of the client. More specifically, these interventions were targeted at the primary presenting complaint of the client, i.e., interpersonal conflict with men at work.

Another therapeutic strategy used in this case, a modified bibliotherapeutic approach, was directed more specifically at the client's incestual experience with her brother (initial focal aim). In summary, beyond the early session where the therapist specifically dealt with the client's early incestual experience, the remaining in-session interventions essentially revolved around the client returning to therapy with questions about the assigned reading material on incest. The therapist responded by helping the client understand how her past experience matched, or didn't match, the specific content of the book.

In addition, she occasionally made links with this material and the dependent interpersonal stance that they were working on in therapy. As the client's fear of expressing emotion decreased, she began to reconnect with some of the affect associated with the incest experience in later sessions. The client elaborated on the impact of the literature assignment strategy as follows:

C: Reading the book was helpful. It brought up a lot of issues that were very fearful to face. It helped me put a lot into perspective like where my sexual impulses came from and what I could do to stay up on them. It also helped me to look at my childhood and be real frank about the things that had happened to me. . . . It helped me to face the hard times and rough times I had as a child, like being left alone. I was able to see how people can get out of control, and just do impossible things that they wouldn't ever think of doing just because they're lonely and because of what happened to them when they were little.

It also made me realize that sexuality is a part of us and it's not something that's bad. It's just a part of our being. Bad things can happen to a person and screw them up, but that person is not a bad person and it's not their fault. It helped me to understand my impulsivity a little bit better. Although mine was not out of control, at times I was impulsive, and it taught me to see where that was coming from. I got the message from the book that impulsivity is often created from loneliness and empty feelings and a fear of dealing with core issues in your life. So I guess it helped me better face the real pain.

After modifying the focal aim to include the client's fear of experiencing strong emotion, the therapist essentially dealt with the incest experience as just one more place that she had learned to take a dependent stance in relationships and keep powerful emotions inside. From the above client perspective, it appears that she made some progress on issues relating to her incestual experience. However, as will be seen below, the primary unfinished business that was discussed at the end of therapy were issues regarding her dissatisfaction with her current sexual behavior.

The final set of interventions used by the therapist in the present case involved in-session role rehearsal and homework assignments regarding assertiveness in interpersonal relationships. Rather than report on a fairly standard behavioral intervention, we have noted the client's progress notes outside of therapy by including her end-of-session reports for the seventh and eighth therapy sessions. These illustrate her not only being more assertive, but also being more aware of her emotional state and being proactive with respect to strong emotions experienced during the week.

C: During the week I was able to identify a concrete example of my new-found ability to experience and be aware of my feelings, face the issues that were causing my anger, and then actively change or deal with the situation at hand. I feel that the actions which enable me to do this were based on things I had better understood in the past few therapy sessions.

I was able to identify, by myself, why I had been feeling angry and overwhelmed during the week. I named all the issues, worries and events that were precipitating my feelings of panic and I realized the many demands which were being placed on my time and energy. From this point, I was able to deal with these stresses and put my feelings into perspective. I think the setting [therapy] and the fact that I was consciously trying to pinpoint my feelings were what enabled me to do this. I also verbalized that the relationship I have sexually with my husband is separate from things that happened in my childhood.

The last session report alludes to the unfinished business of her sexuality. In essence, the client is anticipating future work, which is the primary objective of the final stage of the ETLT model.

## STAGE IV: PRETERMINATION, TERMINATION, AND FOLLOW-UP

This stage marks the end of treatment and often the beginning point of testing the self-reliant attributions that have hopefully been inculcated in the client's attributional system over the course of treatment (cf. Burlingame, 1985). More specifically, the objectives of this stage are to provide closure, review the therapeutic goals and progress, and relate them to the client's future functioning. By reviewing the progress to date, the client recognizes there is still work to be done, anticipates potential stresses, and determines strategies for dealing with increased independence. During the follow-up session, which in the present case represents the debriefing interviews, the client and therapist review the goals of therapy and what has occurred since termination (cf., Fuhriman et al., 1985).

In the present case, the client left the therapeutic experience having changed her belief that experiencing strong emotions was comparable to going crazy like her family members. This insight enabled her to better recognize her emotional states and handle them in a more productive manner. In addition to recognizing when she behaved in a dependent, non-assertive manner, she also gained insight into why dependency had been part of her interpersonal style for so long, primarily generated from the dynamic perspective painted by the therapist. These insights also helped her to examine more seriously her sexual behavior in the present and the past.

As can be seen from the client's comments during the follow-up interview below, she had initially identified two areas as "unfinished business." The first area was learning to establish a normal adult relationship with her parents. The second revolved around her sexuality and being able to disassociate her incestual relationship with her brother from her current sexual relationship with her husband. These transcripts also indicate some of the successes of therapy and how she was behaving differently around the original presenting complaint, difficulties with older men at work. Finally, they illustrate proactive behavior around her second area of unfinished business, sexuality.

C: As I was coming to therapy—maybe about a month in—I started to deal real directly with my colleagues at work, I just went right for them, verbally and nonverbally, and just decided it wasn't going to happen any more. A couple of weeks after that, I started to work more professionally with these people—like a colleague, like I actually had a professional relationship and was respected and if I developed a new theory they would listen to me. It's getting quite positive at work....

I: Are there one or two events in your therapy that are extraimportant to you?

C: I think being able to face the issue that I was going crazy was real important .... Facing that and analyzing it and realizing that I wasn't crazy and being able to say that I am not crazy ... made a real big difference. It took several sessions to come to that.... I think a lot of it came from growing up with my mother.... I watched her just lose control and lose track of things. At one point, she was out of control for years and years, having hallucinations, making statements that were not in touch with reality, and I thought, gee, I'm her daughter and I could be that way and I probably will be that way because I am her daughter....

I: Do you think that you have begun to put some of the trauma with the incest to rest?

C: After a certain point in therapy, I got to feeling like I could actually go up to a man and really try to get to know him. I have seen a change now. I am more interested in the other person and ... and I don't mind letting them get to know me. I'm more open now and interested in making friends with them.... The fact that I was able to tell my husband about the incest, you know, and get everything out in the open means I'll never have to worry about it again. Now I can be close to him and in a number of ways I was not allowing myself to be—just in case he found out.

The fact that I understand where part of my craziness comes from was important.... I still have strong emotions but now I'm able to identify them more and understand where they are coming from and what's causing them and to deal with the issues before they get big. That's priceless. My life is a lot more turbulent. There is a lot more anger in my life right now and frustration and pain and those kinds of things, but somehow I feel more in control and more safe. I mean I can handle it. I think it was really beneficial....

One thing that really helped me deal better with things now, and that made me frustrated before, is that I had not been dealing with my emotions for at least 20 years. So I feel like now I'm beginning to catch up in those 20 years. The good things that help are to look at them and analyze them now.... In here [pointing to heart] is something that's okay to look at now.... I'm not going to go crazy if I look at my emotions. As I begin to find out what happened to me and get it out, then I feel better.

I: Are there things that are still unfinished with respect to what you worked on in your therapy?

C: One of the big things that was unfinished when I left therapy was the relationship that I had with my parents. I am now beginning to say that they tried as hard as they could, but they just didn't know how. I am not going to continue to personalize that. I find that there are other people that had the experience that I did. The thing with my parents is getting more and more resolved now as I begin to think that they probably did love me. I am also beginning to stay more current with the stuff I am doing with my parents.

Another thing that was unfinished was my sex life. Since therapy ended, I have been to my gynecologist. I think part of the explanation for lack of enjoyment is that I have the symptoms of PMS. I'm beginning to explore that more with my physician. Although I am sure that the stuff that happened with my brother is also part of the explanation for why I was unable to enjoy sex with my husband, I am getting to the point where I don't think about my brother when I'm making love with my husband. One important thing that happened one night toward the end of therapy was when my husband just broke down and said:

I can't stand making love to you when you are being angry about your brother. If he were here I would probably kill him, but he is not. I can understand that you are angry with your brother but all I feel from you is anger when I make love with you. I just can't make love with you when you're feeling angry. I'm feeling guilty for wanting to have pleasure with you and I am wondering if I should be doing this when it is just agony for you. I just hate feeling your hesitation. I just feel like he is there in our bedroom and that you are reliving it each time. I just don't understand why you can't relax and know that I love you and just share our love instead of thinking about your brother and realizing that it is just the two of us together now. What we are doing is because we love each other and it has nothing to do with your brother.

You know, when he said that, it really helped me to see what I was doing to him. Right after that, we made love and it was us together . . . it was very good. Once I had that experience it's been very good. I have been able to have that experience and move closer to him each time.

*Commentary*

A number of things can be noted from the follow-up interview. The most prominent involves the catalytic assumption regarding ETLT. More specifically, given the type of client selected, it is assumed that ETLT provides a stimulus for change rather than moving the client to the end point of change. In the present case, the client ended treatment being able to more fully face two emotionally laden troublesome areas in her life: her relationship with her parents and her sexuality. In fact, she describes her ability to live with her emotions as the most important result of therapy. The proactive movement seen in both these areas (relationship with parents and sexuality) at the two-month follow-up not only supports the catalytic principle of ETLT, but further validates the early shift in focal aim, the fear of going crazy with strong emotion.

The client clearly shows a change in perspective regarding her relationship with her parents. She has recognized that what happened as a child was unfortunate and unfair, but appears to be moving past her anger toward her parents. The fact that she dealt with some of this anger in the latter portion of therapy and is now attempting to establish an adult-to-adult relationship with her parents is seen as a prognostically good sign. The client also demonstrates proactive movement with regard to her sexuality. She initiated work with a gynecologist in an attempt to separate the biological problems associated with her sexuality from the psychological problems. In addition, the follow-up interview was the first time that the client talked about the interaction recorded above with her husband, which can also be seen as proactive movement. The fact that she productively dealt with her husband's anger not only demonstrates the movement she made in dealing with emotions, but also portends a successful end point for their future sexual relationship.

Another promising aspect from the above transcript is the client rapprochement with men in general. She clearly states that she is not only trying to get to know men from a different perspective, but is also being more open to letting men know her as a person. During this session, the client provided several behavioral examples to support these statements, thereby making it difficult to dismiss her report as a halo effect. Finally, we see the client's report of her life being more turbulent as positive. This turbulence was better understood by further questioning. Given her prior interpersonal stance, her more assertive posture at work and home essentially resulted in more turbulence in interpersonal relationships, primarily because she would no longer let people "take advantage of her."

## A CASE COMPARISON

One of the features of the ETLT approach is its applicability to a variety of theoretical orientations. Because of the limited amount of precise structure that is placed on the therapist and the broad, general principles that are suggested, it becomes important to identify how therapists of differing persuasions apply the model. For this reason, we examined two cases, the first being more explicitly presented and the second, more comparatively.

In the case of Julie, the therapist was described as having a therapeutic style that was directive, active, interpretive, and that exhibited a high degree of therapist presence. The therapist conceptualized the case in psychodynamic terms but utilized therapeutic techniques that ranged across a variety of orientations. The therapist gave interpretations, provided information and opinions, elicited catharsis, and focused not only on the then-and-there, but also on the here-and-now experiences of the client and, to some extent, of the therapist.

In the comparative case, the therapist style was active, patient, reflective, speculative, and also displayed a high degree of therapist presence. The therapist conceptualized the case from a client-centered orientation but also used a variety of techniques representative of other therapeutic models. The therapist reflected client intentions, ideas, and feelings, probed, presented metaphors, shared insights, and confronted the client's incongruent messages.

In examining the application of the ETLT approach to these two cases, the comparative-case therapist adhered more explicitly to some of the specific instructions such as reviewing the process at the beginning of the sessions and commenting on the amount of time remaining in therapy. In a sense, regarding the application of the model, Julie's therapist used the approach in a more fluid and general manner, whereas the comparative-case therapist implemented the approach in a more consistent and specific manner. The variability in application may, in part, have been due to the perceived differences in client characteristics and diagnosis. The following is a brief description of the comparative client:

The client was a 24-year-old, Causasian female who was employed as an accountant. Her presenting complaint was an agitated depression precipitated by her husband asking her to leave his house after two years of marriage. At the time of treatment, the client was in the process of divorce proceedings.

We tend to believe that the two styles are

more representative of the therapists' typical therapeutic style with some adaptation relating to client characteristics.

A clearer comparison of the therapeutic process in these two cases is best described by examining how the elements of the ETLT approach were implemented. The differences between these two therapists become more distinctive when the interaction is analyzed through the elements of focus, collaboration, and sharing of expectations. This distinctiveness illustrates how the model can be applied in principle while using differing techniques to complement and enact the principles.

## Focus

Both therapists directed and emphasized focusing throughout the therapeutic process. The two were similar in their emphasis on staying on task, the task being the focal aim as determined by the client and therapist. Julie's therapist directed the interaction by introducing and making more explicit the topics of incest, relationship with co-workers, and fear of going crazy. The comparative therapist provided focus by reflecting and by extending the direction of the interaction through questions that required logical and linear responses. Two differences in the therapists' focusing were evident: the focal aim was narrower in the comparative case, and in the later sessions, the comparative therapist centered the discussion more often and more specifically on the target complaint. These resulted in more interventions by the comparative therapist directed toward focality.

A difference in client characteristics and diagnosis may also have accounted for the need for or display of focusing by the therapist. Julie was task oriented and concomitantly more focus oriented herself, thus alleviating the need of more therapist focus. The comparative client's diagnosis was acute rather than chronic with the presenting problem less connected to long-standing issues, thus lending itself to a more specific response from the therapist. These two cases illustrate strikingly different ways and means for the therapist to accomplish the task of focusing.

## Collaboration

In the application of the element of collaboration, there is also quite a distinct difference between the two therapists. Julie's therapist presented both behaviorally and attitudinally more of a presence of collaboration than did the comparative therapist. The point of view of Julie's therapist was egalitarian; the style was spontaneous and matter of fact. The therapist conveyed this view by sharing opinions, experiences, and values and displaying somewhat casual, nonverbal behavior. The attitude and personal style of the therapist conveyed the collaborative element in a predominant manner that overrode the impact of the authoritarian techniques of interpretation, homework assignments, and directiveness.

The comparative therapist's personal style was more formal, and perhaps more traditional. The therapist did not take off the "therapeutic mantle" and thus presented a less collaborative style. On the other hand, this therapist adhered to the directions of the ETLT approach and involved the client in explicit discussions of where they were, what they were doing, and where they wanted to go. Thus, the collaboration, as conveyed through dialogue, was more explicit and more frequent in the comparative case. An interesting pattern begins to develop between these two cases. Once again, the model is implemented by Julie's therapist through attitude and presence, whereas the comparative therapist implements through specific techniques and dialogue.

## Expectations

The two therapists are more distinctive in their implementation of the element of expectation sharing. Julie's therapist almost exclusively shared and elicited expectations regarding diagnosis, hope, and impact of information; in addition, there is more evidence of the therapist's expectations being shared than the client's. The comparative therapist specifically raised the issues of the time limit, the process of therapy, and the client's involvement in therapy. This therapist not only shared self-expectations regarding these issues but elicited more sharing of client expectation. The comparative therapist was also more explicit in focusing on what was unfinished and what was helpful in therapy. The sharing of expectations on these two topics also demonstrates collaboration and exemplifies the catalytic nature of the approach.

The main focus in this comparison has been on therapist differences in implementing the eclectic approach, but there are a number of similarities that existed between the two. Probably the most striking similarity is the therapists' value or belief that client insight is an important component of healing, and that one reaches insight through cognitions and catharsis. Although the two therapists held the same value, each worked to generate insight in their clients through differing methods and techniques. Both therapists valued the here-and-now focus in therapy, but the here-and-now value also was demonstrated in different ways. One therapist confronted the client with the effect of the therapist on the client, whereas the other therapist confronted the client with her in-session incongruities.

In comparing these two therapists on their application of the ETLT approach and their methods of implementing the elements, it becomes apparent that differing theoretical orientations and styles can be accommodated within the model. Therapists in these orientations can also be successful in both model implementation and client outcome. The two cases also illustrate how client characteristics and diagnoses can affect how the therapist creates the elements of focus, collaboration, and expectation sharing through style and technique.

## IN RETROSPECT

Analyzing the interaction of these two cases has been instructive regarding the application of the ETLT approach. In addition, insight was gained into some dynamics of the therapeutic process. As both therapists applied the model, some strengths of the approach were highlighted. For example, both therapists seemed to apply the model with relative ease. Also, one of the intents in designing the ETLT approach was to make it applicable across varying theoretical orientations; these two cases illustrate some accomplishment of that intent. It also became apparent that therapist style can compensate for the absence of techniques specified in the model.

Insight gained by the examination of these two cases may relate not only to brief therapy, but to therapeutic interactions in general. It became obvious that if a therapist has broad, general principles to guide him or her, these principles, in turn, can be fulfilled using a variety of therapeutic techniques. This may represent a means of linking theories and discovering core themes across them. Finally, client selection is deemed important in ETLT, in part owing to the collaboration that is required and the specificity of diagnosis necessary for focusing. However, in these two cases, the client characteristics illustrated the importance of what the client contributes to the therapeutic enterprise, and how the therapist can adjust style and technique to client need and contribution.

## NOTES

[1] As per typical case study protocol, client identity has been protected not only by using a pseudonym, but also by changing pertinent identifying information, i.e., occupation, husband's occupation, etc.

[2] The interviewer who debriefed the therapist and client separately and conjointly was the first author.

[3] Unfortunately, because of technician error, videotapes from the original intake interview were lost. Therefore, content from this session is based on therapist and client account in the debriefing interview.

## REFERENCES

Bergin, A., & Lambert, M. (1978). The evaluation of therapeutic outcome. In S. Garfield and A. Bergin (Eds.), *Handbook of psychotherapy and behavior change*. New York: Wiley.

Bloom, B. (1980). Social and community interventions. *Annual Review of Psychology, 31,* 111–142.

Budman, S. (1981). *Forms of brief therapy*. New York: Guilford.

Burlingame, G. (1983). Therapist content focus and specificity in brief therapy. Unpublished dissertation, University of Utah.

Burlingame, G. (1985). Self-reliance in short-term therapy: Client attribute or therapeutic goal. Paper presented at the annual convention of the American Psychological Association.

Butcher, J., & Koss, M. (1978). Research on brief and crisis-oriented therapies. In S. Garfield & A. Bergin (Eds.), *Handbook of psychotherapy and behavior change*. New York: Wiley.

Coleman, J. (1962). Banter as psychotherapeutic intervention. *American Journal of Psychoanalysis, 22,* 69–74.

Egan, G. (1982). *The skilled helper: A model for systematic helping and interpersonal relations*. Monterey, CA: Brooks Cole Publishing Co.

Epperson, D., Bushway, D., & Warman, R. (1983). Client self-terminations after one counseling session: Effects of problem recognition, counselor gender, and counselor experience. *Journal of Counseling Psychology, 30* (3), 307–315.

Fuhriman, A., Paul, S., & Burlingame, G. (1985). Eclectic time-limited therapy. In J. Norcross (Ed.), *Handbook of eclectic psychotherapy*. New York: Brunner/Mazel.

Garfield, S. (1978). Research on client variables in psychotherapy. In S. Garfield and A. Bergin (Eds.), *Handbook of psychotherapy and behavior change* (2nd ed.). New York: Wiley.

Garfield, S., & Wolpin, M. (1963). Expectations regarding psychotherapy. *Journal of Nervous and Mental Diseases, 137,* 353–362.

Gelso, C., & Johnson, D. (1983). *Explorations in time-limited counseling and psychotherapy*. New York: Teachers College, Columbia University.

Heitler, J. (1976). Preparatory techniques in initiating expressive psychotherapy in lower-class unsophisticated patients. *Psychological Bulletin, 83,* 339–352.

Lorion, R. (1974). Patient and therapist variables in the treatment of low income patients. *Psychological Bulletin, 81,* 344–354.

Luborsky, L. (1984). *Principles of psychoanalytic psychotherapy*. New York: Basic Books.

Luborsky, L., Singer, B., & Luborsky, L. (1975). Comparative studies of psychotherapies: Is it true that everyone has won and all must have prize? *Archives of General Psychiatry, 32,* 995–1008.

Malan, D. (1976). *The frontier of brief psychotherapy*. New York: Plenum.

Mann, J. (1973). *Time-limited psychotherapy*. Cambridge, MA: Harvard University Press.

Mann, J., & Goldman, R. (1982). *A casebook in time-limited psychotherapy*. New York: McGraw-Hill.

Papp, P. (1983). *The process of change*. New York: Guilford Press.

Reid, W. (1978). *The task-centered system*. New York: Columbia University Press.

Sifneos, P. (1979). *Short-term psychotherapy and emotional crisis*. Cambridge, MA: Harvard University Press.

Wolberg, L. (1980). *Handbook of short-term psychotherapy*. New York: Thieme-Stratton, 1st ed. 1965.

Young, D. (1977). Time-limited psychotherapy: The effect of the time factor on patient expectations. *Dissertation Abstracts, 37,* 7B, 3639–3640.

# Commentary: Time-Limited Therapy and the Stages of Change

### Carlo C. DiClemente

Short-term and time-limited psychotherapy are not identical. As the authors of "The Case of Julie" point out, many therapy encounters are short-term in nature with an average of 5 to 10 sessions. Most often brevity is a result of premature *termination rather than design. A multitude of reasons for the brevity have been proposed. Frequently, the cause is assumed to be a mismatch between client and therapist along particular dimensions of personality, expectations, relationship, or interventions. In some way what the client and therapist are doing during the session is incompatible. As a result, the client actively or passively terminates therapy. A second reason for brevity may be the nature of the problem. Psychotherapy makes demands on the client to be analytical or engage in cognitive or behavioral activities. If the problem is so incapacitating or the person so limited as to be unable to perform these activities, the therapy will be truncated. Client motivation is a third often-cited cause for brief therapy. Clients may lack sufficient desire to acknowledge or take action with their problem, want to solve the wrong problem, or are too oppositional. In any case, developing a working relationship is problematic, and the course of therapy is sporadic or very brief. A final cause of the brevity of therapy would be that the problem is resolved rather quickly or the brief assistance given by the therapist is considered sufficient for the client to go on his/her way with little thought of any long-term contact with the therapist.*

*The case of Julie provides an instructive example for a discussion of short-term therapy in general and the eclectic time-limited therapy (ETLT) model in particular. Strengths and weaknesses of the ETLT model are interrelated and will be discussed from the more general transtheoretical eclectic approach presented in Chapter 4 of this* Casebook *and elsewhere (Prochaska & DiClemente, 1984, 1986). The ETLT model provides a framework for a consciously designed, time-limited intervention and offers some basic concepts to assist the therapist in structuring the therapy. It accomplishes this by concentrating on the common elements or preconditions for therapy of expectation and relationship (Prochaska, 1984) and by patient selection.*

*Focusing, collaboration, and congruent expectations are assumed to be the common mechanisms of change which are intensified by the short-term nature of the therapeutic contract. These key elements seem to be clearly illustrated in the case of Julie.*

*Although the authors clearly illustrate the four stages of brief therapy, I would like to discuss their work in terms of the stages of change: precontemplation, contemplation, action, and maintenance. In its emphasis on patient selection and on swift movement to action planning and active coping, the ETLT model concentrates almost exclusively on the action stage of change. As the authors acknowledge, Julie comes to therapy rather fully prepared to take action. She had already accomplished on her own many of the tasks of the precontemplation and contemplation stages of change prior to entering therapy, at least with respect to difficulties with her male colleagues. Julie appears to be a capable, resourceful woman seriously engaged in the process of change even prior to therapy. The assumption of the model and the assessment of the therapist were in agreement. Julie would be open to action strategies of reevaluating current and past experiences and becoming more assertive.*

*Client selection ensures motivation and capability as well as increasing the probability of a good match between therapist and client. In this way the ETLT model avoids many of the problems that lead to premature termination. Matching action strategies with a person in the action stage of change offers the best chance for successful short-term intervention. This perspective may also explain the rather intense anger Julie experienced in the therapy. While in action around some issues, it seems that Julie wanted to spend more time in contemplation for the incest problem. She seemed to want more support and a more thorough cognitive exploration of the issue. The action orientation of the time-limited therapy seemed to short-circuit this exploration, creating frustration* and anger. Julie was open and resourceful enough and the therapist sensitive enough to address that issue in the therapy and move ahead.

While concentrating almost exclusively on action strategies (stages II and III) the ETLT model does give some consideration to the issue of maintenance. The work of stage IV of the ETLT approach essentially promotes maintenance of changes made during stage III. The time-limited nature of the therapy leaves much of the work of maintaining change to the client. In this case Julie seems to be doing a good job of both maintaining changes and generalizing them to other areas of her life. Thus, the ETLT model relies on self-change for the movement from precontemplation to contemplation, assists in the final movement from contemplation to action, intervenes in the action stage, and assists in maintenance relying again on self-change.

In many ways Julie does not appear to be a "good" or typical short-term therapy client. Her current problems with work relationships are integrally connected to an early traumatic incestuous experience which impacts self-concept, relations with all men including her husband, and her role as a woman. The combination of a sensitive, well-trained therapist and a client who is a resourceful self-changer in or very close to the action stage of change makes the ETLT model work well in the case of Julie. The perspective of the therapist and the interventions or processes of change she employed provide the eclecticism. The model provides the structure for a time-limited, action-oriented therapy approach. The authors could profitably explore whether the model could be used for promoting change at any of the other stages of change and how a less well-trained therapist would do with the model since the model relies on the therapist for the active coping interventions.

Time-limited therapy, because of its brevity and its focus, could easily lend itself to a rather rigid, locked-step, single-system approach to psychotherapy. To their credit, the authors of the ETLT model have resisted the more dogmatically defined approach in favor of an eclectic one. The case of Julie and the comparison case at the end of the chapter demonstrate the ability of the ETLT model to discuss in detail the common structure of time-limited therapy while allowing for an eclecticism in problem definition and process interventions. Adding a stage of change perspective could help in the definition and development of the ETLT perspective.

## REFERENCES

Prochaska, J. O. (1984). Systems of psychotherapy: A transtheoretical analysis. Homewood, IL: Dorsey Press.

Prochaska, J. O., & DiClemente, C. C. (1984). The transtheoretical approach: Crossing traditional boundaries of therapy. Homewood, IL: Dow Jones-Irwin.

Prochaska, J. O., & DiClemente, C. C. (1986). The transtheoretical approach: Toward a systematic eclectic framework. In J. C. Norcross (Ed.), Handbook of eclectic psychotherapy. New York: Brunner/Mazel.

# Commentary: Advantages and Drawbacks of Generic Eclecticism

## Stanley B. Messer

There are at least three different ways in which the term eclecticism is applied in the field of psychotherapy. In what I have referred to in this book's companion volume as selective eclecticism (Messer, 1986), the therapist is prepared to call on one of several distinct therapeutic approaches from his or her repertoire that seems best suited to the client or problem at hand. Integrative eclecticism, by contrast, attempts to wed one kind of therapy to another. We may have, for example, combinations of psychoanalytic and behavior therapy (e.g., Wachtel, 1984) or individual and family therapy (Pinsof, 1983). In a third approach, the common elements eclectic model, those ingredients that seem to be shared by many psychotherapies are extracted and sculpted into a single approach (e.g., Prochaska & DiClemente, 1984). In one variant of this model, the focus is on therapeutic techniques that are held in common by the various therapies and that are considered to be the most efficacious. In the other variant, a generic model or general scaffold is constructed to encompass a variety of therapeutic approaches. It is the latter model that is employed by Burlingame, Fuhriman, and Paul in their version of short-term therapy, which they call eclectic time-limited therapy (ETLT). They developed it out of a pragmatic need to encompass the varied theoretical predilections of a particular clinical staff. "We thought that such a model would improve the likelihood that the approach would be adopted, especially if the staff members were not forced into a totally alien orientation or set of practices" (p. 97).

Given this particular aim, the authors have succeeded very well in constructing a system that is straightforward, beguilingly simple, and reasonably neutral theoretically. It can be employed by a broad range of mental health practitioners without the necessity for much further training, which is an advantage of a generic-eclectic model. In addition, they have extracted some major elements of short-term therapy that most experts would agree are critical aspects of that enterprise. We have been treated to a fascinating case which illustrates how much can be accomplished in a planned short-term therapy with a well-selected client. For their second case, however, I would have preferred the application of ETLT within a strongly differing theoretical orientation in order to illustrate the broad applicability of the model.

The advantages of genericism notwithstanding, it is important to consider whether something is not lost by adopting a generic model alone. Such models, and ETLT is no exception, must of necessity be general or else they fail to be generic. But, being generic, they lose the kind of specificity in theory and technique that makes the noneclectic, nongeneric models so useful. To illustrate this, I will examine the case presented and try to show how the application of an informed short-term psychodynamic therapy framework could complement the generic model employed.

The focus as conceptualized by ETLT in the case of Julie is incest. ("The therapist is clearly working from the tentative focal aim of incest," p. 108). As a very general statement of focus, this may be acceptable, but as a psychodynamic focus, it is much too general and cannot serve as a useful *guide. How would brief psychodynamic therapists proceed? They would note the following: Julie's presenting complaint of interpersonal difficulties with two "older" male colleagues, which involved her responding seductively toward them and having sexually laden dreams about them; her incestuous experience with her brother during the time of her mother's breakdown; and her fears of going crazy when some related feelings recurred in connection with her male colleagues. From her early history it would be noted that she took an overdose of pills when she was five in an effort to gain her father's attention; that her father was often absent from the home; that her grandfather was abusive; and that her mother went through a number of severe manic-depressive episodes for which she was hospitalized during Julie's late childhood and early adolescence.*

*How can this material be woven into a narrative that makes psychodynamic sense and that can serve as a focus for therapeutic interventions? Starting with the developmental information, we can say with some assurance that Julie was a deprived and abused child who had so desperate a need for parental attention that she even resorted to taking an overdose of pills. Her father was rarely available, so when her mother was hospitalized she was left bereft, making her an easy and willing victim of her brother's sexual advances. In other words, she acted out her unfulfilled dependency needs in this deviant way. That she recently started having sexual fantasies about older male colleagues and that she confuses husband and brother in lovemaking point to the continued existence of conflictual feelings about these earlier events and her need to reenact them. Given the strangeness to her of her feelings in the current context, and the background of having a "crazy" mother, we can well understand her fear that she, too, is going crazy.*

*Some version of this dynamic focus seems to have been implicit in the therapist's work, but formulating it in this way helps keep the therapy focused and sensitizes the therapist to the context for the client's associations. It also helps to alert the therapist to the connections between relationships from the past (e.g., to father, mother, grandfather, brother) and current relationships (older male colleagues, husband), and to the developing relationship to the therapist (transference). Malan (1976) has demonstrated empirically a positive correlation between the number of transference-parent links and the outcome of brief, dynamic therapy. By spelling out the nature of the interconnections of past, present, and transferential relations, the focus, as presented above, aids the therapist in making such links in a considered and informed way. Thus, the incest experience was not "just one more place that she learned to take a dependent stance in relationships...." (p. 119), but rather it was a way in which Julie expressed her very strong need to be close to and loved by a close family member.*

*Although the dependency needs were brought to light in Julie's therapy, they were not emphasized as much as the above psychodynamic focus and linking technique would require. This may be why Julie left therapy feeling that the issue of the relationship to her parents was quite unfinished.*

*Besides focusing and drawing the transference-parent (and transference-current relationship and parent-current relationship) links a short-term psychodynamic therapy stresses the importance of the termination phase of the therapy much more so than ETLT. In his version of brief dynamic therapy known as time-limited psychotherapy, Mann (1973; see also Mann & Goldman, 1982) capitalizes on the universal problem of separating from important people in our lives by emphasizing the termination date and listening for the themes that it elicits, especially in the last few sessions. In a therapeutic relationship as intense as Julie's, and in a client who* suffered repeated separations from her father and her mother, we would expect the issues of separation and dependency to be particularly acute at termination. Yet the case presentation hardly mentions these issues as central during the final sessions. The termination phase would have provided an excellent opportunity to focus on the dependency feelings as they were manifested in the transference and then to link them to past events.

The point is not to pick out flaws in this particular case presentation (which one can always do no matter how brilliant the work), but to demonstrate that a specific theoretically based *model has certain advantages over a generic model in formulating a game plan for therapy. Is there some way of combining the advantages of a generic model and specific, theoretically based models? I believe there is. The generic model, like ETLT, can be useful in orienting a heterogeneous staff to short-term therapy, particularly if it extracts successfully, as does ETLT, common elements from among those orientations adhered to by the staff. It is also a useful way of illustrating the overlap of the different approaches, at least in broad strokes. This is conceptually interesting and can also improve staff appreciation for the models adhered to by others. It can even influence their own work in therapy. But within the broad ETLT frame, therapists, in my view, should learn in greater depth a short-term therapy model that will allow them to employ most usefully the theory and skills they already possess. This is what I have tried to illustrate in my commentary on Julie's therapy.*

*Burlingame et al. could argue that theirs is an eclectic model, not only in the generic form, described at the outset, but also in the "integrative" sense. They, presumably, would not want therapists to follow one theoretical orientation too closely. ". . . the model . . . does encourage the therapist to use a variety of techniques in addressing the focal aim of treatment, which is clearly seen in the transcripts that follow" (p. 115). Thus, we have the therapist engaging in nonanalytical techniques such as assigning a book, in-session role rehearsal, and giving homework assignments regarding assertiveness in interpersonal relationships. How, then, does this mesh with the dynamic focus as outlined above? One could view these importations from other therapeutic approaches as dependency gratifications which could make the dependency needs that much harder to analyze. (Of course, one could also view them as cementing the therapeutic alliance or as supplementing the verbal insight achieved.) But in either case, there is a need for the ETLT model to spell out the nature of its integrative eclecticism lest it deteriorate into an "anything goes" attitude.*

*Finally, the authors are to be congratulated for encouraging end-of-session reports by both client and therapist and conducting follow-up interviews in order to "unpack" the text of the therapy. This is rarely done and gives the reader a particularly rich view of this instructive psychotherapy and the model on which it is based.*

## REFERENCES

Malan, D. H. (1976). The frontier of brief psychotherapy. New York: Plenum.

Mann, J. (1973). Time-limited psychotherapy. Cambridge, MA: Harvard University Press.

Mann, J., & Goldman, R. (1982). A casebook in time-limited psychotherapy. New York: McGraw-Hill.

Messer, S. B. (1986). Eclecticism in psychotherapy: Underlying assumptions, problems and tradeoffs. In J. C. Norcross (Ed.), Handbook of eclectic psychotherapy. New York: Brunner/Mazel.

Pinsof, W. M. (1983). Integrative problem-centered therapy: Toward the synthesis of family and individual psychotherapies. Journal of Marital and Family Therapy, 9, 19–35.

Prochaska, J. O., & DiClemente, C. C. (1984). The transtheoretical approach: Crossing the traditional boundaries of therapy. Homewood, IL: Dow Jones-Irwin.

Wachtel, P. L. (1984). On theory, practice and the nature of integration. In H. Arkowitz & S. B. Messer (Eds.), Psychoanalytic therapy and behavior therapy: Is integration possible? New York: Plenum.

CHAPTER 5

# Differential Therapeutics: A Case Illustration

*John F. Clarkin and Phillida B. Rosnick*

## INTRODUCTION

Differential therapeutics is the science and often the art of selecting the most effective treatment or array of treatments for patients with unique combinations of assets and psychological difficulties. This decision-making process is concentrated during the initial assessment of the patient. In addition, as treatment progresses, clinicians must gauge the progress of treatment and assess the need for therapeutic changes. The body of knowledge useful to a clinician involved in this process comes from psychotherapy process and outcome studies, studies of psychopharmacological effectiveness, and (since the research base is not totally extensive or exhaustive) the accumulation of clinical wisdom.

There are many ways to structure the growing body of available information for clinical decision making (e.g., Beutler, 1983) and our own involves the organization of data around five axes of treatment planning: treatment setting (inpatient, day hospital, outpatient), format (individual, family, group), duration and frequency (brief therapy, long-term therapy, total number of sessions), strategies and techniques, and appropriate use of medication (Frances, Clarkin, & Perry, 1984). This system is extensive enough to provide guidelines for treatment of patients along the entire spectrum of severity. This system is not focused exclusively on the axis of treatment technique as some other systems, as decisions on the other axes must be made, and treatment technique alone seems to result in little differential effectiveness. This system is eclectic in its selection of interventions across therapeutic schools of thought (e.g., psychodynamic, behavioral, systems, etc.), modes of intervention (psychosocial and pharmacological), and different treatment environments to arrive at a treatment plan tailored to the uniqueness of the individual patient. The intent of this system is to provide the clinician with operating guidelines, formulated in terms of indications, contraindications, and patient enabling factors, for interventions on the different axes of treatment planning.

In this chapter, we will illustrate the process of differential treatment planning by discussing an actual case assessed and treated by one of the authors (PBR). Because of the need for detailed transcripts of the treatment, and also the need for a patient stable and cooperative enough to provide follow-up and reactions to the treatment, we selected an outpatient with considerable assets and a somewhat focal problem suitable for time-limited intervention. Thus, this particular case is better suited for following the intricacies of the therapy process than for following the complications in differential treatment planning. For the application of differential therapeutics across diagnostic categories, see Perry, Frances, and Clarkin (1985).

## INITIAL ASSESSMENT: A DECISION TREE

The patient is a 21-year-old, female college senior who presented at an outpatient clinic complaining of "family tensions" which were beginning to disturb her sleep and preoccupy all her waking thoughts. She had eloped six months before with her boyfriend of some four years' duration, but had never told anyone, including her parents. Her husband thought that her parents knew, but because he was out of state in military training, he did not know anything was amiss.

The patient's parents, especially her father, had actively opposed her relationship with this young man when it became clear that it was sexual. The young couple became openly engaged a year ago, prior to their living together during the summer. When informed of their cohabitation, the father went into a tirade. Ostensibly fearing another such attack, the patient eloped three months later.

The patient is doing well in her courses, has several close friends, and is employed on campus, a job in which she uses her considerable poise and social skills. With the end of college approaching, and her husband due to return to the area at any moment, the patient was eager, if not desperate, for help. The admission DSM-III diagnosis was as follows: Axis I, Adjustment Disorder with Depressed Mood; Axis II, No Personality Diagnosis, but some dependent Personality Features; Axis IV, Moderate Stress due to the recent elopement; Axis V, 2, Very Good. This patient has functioned above average in both school and work, and her interpersonal relations are mature, if at times too dependent.

### Treatment Setting

The patient has a stable living situation and does not present with a major Axis I disorder so there is little doubt that outpatient treatment is indicated.

### Format

With this particular patient and focal problem, one could make an argument for each of the major treatment formats—individual, family, or group. A heterogeneous group of patients with various interpersonal problems could help by providing feedback to this patient on her specific situation. However, group format could not *focus* exclusively on her specific issues and would take longer to give her some directed assistance.

Because of her particular chief complaint—a crucial secret between her and her parents—one might recommend family/marital format with patient and parents; patient, husband, and parents; or patient and husband. The family/marital format could be used exclusively or in conjunction with individual sessions for the patient. This combination of individual and family/marital formats would allow for more intimate exploration in individual sessions, and then the actual disclosure and subsequent working through of the conflict in the presence of the people involved. However, this particular patient was not ready for such a meeting, describing her parents as opposed to any kind of psychological counseling. If the parents would, indeed, be adversarial, then this treatment format must be excluded on the grounds of expediency and efficacy. In addition, this patient refused to let her parents know she herself was seeking help. The patient could not be seen with her husband as he was residing some distance away.

## Medication

Although the patient presents in an acute upset with both anxiety and depression, these symptoms are not severe enough to warrant medication.

## Duration and Frequency

In cases where the severity of pathology is moderate to mild and premorbid functioning is good, planned brief as opposed to long-term or open-ended intervention should be immediately considered. This represents a conservative attitude toward intervention, namely, that one starts with the treatment with fewer risks and less ambitious goals. If that fails, one can intervene more aggressively with a treatment that is more invasive and ambitious.

This patient meets simultaneously the indications and suitability requirements for several brief therapy models. There is a clearly defined focus with a precipitating event, the patient's goals are limited, she seems able to separate from treatment, and her usual level of functioning is adequate. She does not manifest some of the major contraindications for brief therapy such as chronic and pervasive Axis I conditions, a lack of motivation, etc. (Clarkin & Frances, 1982). And finally, as the patient was leaving the area when she graduated, the treatment was, of necessity, time-limited.

Thus, the patient was scheduled for two sessions a week for seven weeks. She was seen for 10 of the 14 scheduled appointments, in addition to one follow-up session, in the outpatient department of a large psychiatric facility.

## Strategies and Techniques

The field of psychotherapy has devoted a great deal, if not an inordinate, amount of time and effort in debating the relative merits of different treatment strategies and techniques. This attention continues despite the evidence that most variance in outcome is accounted for by patient and therapist characteristics and very little by strategies and techniques (e.g., Orlinsky & Howard, 1978; Smith, Glass, & Miller, 1980).

Focal psychodynamic techniques (Malan, 1976; Davanloo, 1978; Luborsky, 1984) were chosen for this particular patient because of the delimited problem area involving interpersonal conflict (Clarkin & Frances, 1982; Perry, Frances, Klar, & Clarkin, 1983). In addition, focal dynamic therapy calls for rather stringent patient enabling factors which this young woman meets, such as a capacity to focus on central issues, a capacity for self-object differentiation and reality testing, a tolerance for anxiety frustration and ambiguity, a capacity for introspection, an ability to form emotionally meaningful and reciprocal relationships, and intelligence and an ability to abstract.

Alternative techniques that were considered included interpersonal psychotherapy (Klerman, Weissman, Rounsaville, & Chevron, 1984) and assorted behavioral techniques. As results of the Sloane et al. (1975) study suggest, it is quite possible that specific behavioral approaches would have done equally well with this case. However, she seemed more inner directed

(Beutler, 1983) and needed more autonomy to generate her own plan, a level of freedom that would be fostered with dynamic techniques.

For the most powerful effect in brief psychodynamically-oriented therapy, the patient's presenting problem, transference responses, and infantile neurosis should overlap (Clarkin & Frances, 1982). Whether one uses conceptualizations such as Luborsky's "core conflictual relationship" (Luborsky, 1984) or Malan's "current" and "nuclear" conflict (Malan, 1976), the distinguishing feature of this therapy is the interpretation of unconscious wishes, fears, and defenses within the arenas of the transference relationship, the current conflict, and the infantile neurosis to bring about conflict resolution.

It should be emphasized that although focal psychodynamic techniques were chosen for this case, we also placed heavy reliance on the "nonspecific" techniques that are common to all the schools of psychotherapy. These nonspecific factors may potentiate almost equal outcome across the schools of therapy in patients such as this one who have relatively good adjustment and seem motivated and primed for therapy (Gomes-Schwartz, 1978; Strupp, 1980). These common strategies and techniques include the hope engendered in the patient by seeing an expert, the generation of treatment goals with the expectation of some change, the structure of specific times for the therapy meetings, and the provision of a therapeutic atmosphere and alliance which includes warmth, empathy, and nonjudgmental respect from a therapist.

The patient, whose treatment we are following, is a quietly and unconsciously angry young woman attempting to bypass the adolescent passage and its consequent depressions by marriage. Overriding in her choice of marital partner was the perpetuation of her childhood with in-laws who were quite ready to reciprocate. Disappointed with and resentful of her own parents' aloof treatment (which by her account was not a recent development), she was sullenly aloof in return and had angrily eloped in revenge. She was managing to stay just a step ahead of a depression comprised of guilt over what she had done and, more important, the emptiness and apathy that is part of loosening the parental ties in preparation for seeking new investments. This important developmental step had been stalemated with potentially serious consequences for her character and identity development. The mediating goals of this dynamic treatment were to focus on and make explicit the patient's conflict and ambivalence in separating from her own parents, inappropriate overinvolvement with her mother-in-law, and intense ambivalence about moving on to a reciprocal and peer relationship with a marital partner. A behavioral mediating goal would ideally be some honest communication with parents and husband about her ambivalence. The final goals of the brief treatment would not be total resolution of these issues as they are significant developmental ones that take more time. A more realistic final goal is some diminution of the intense anxiety about her conflicts, some more honest and open communication with her husband about their relationship, and a diminution of the overinvolvement with her in-laws.

There is general agreement (e.g., Beutler, 1983; Orlinksy & Howard, 1978) that the patient-therapist match is extremely important although the research literature is not totally conclusive about the important variables in this match. In this case a young adult, white, middle-class female patient with a college education and above-average intelligence was matched with a white, female psychologist. There was every indication during the initial evaluation phase that the patient and therapist would share certain key values and beliefs: a need to introspect and understand one's feelings and emotions, and a high priority on interpersonal closeness, loyalty, and family relatedness. It seemed therapeutically propitious that this young person having difficulties making a transition from her family of origin to a married state be treated by a somewhat older person who had successfully completed those milestones. The fact that both patient and therapist were female was not considered extremely important for this brief therapy.

*Course of Treatment*

As Goldfried (1980) has indicated, there are probably basic therapeutic change principles or strategies that cut across all therapies regardless of the school of thought. We will focus the presentation of this case around a small number of central strategies: (1) structuring the treatment, (2) focusing the treatment, (3) dealing with the relationship between therapist and patient, and (4) terminating treatment.

*Structuring the treatment.* There were two principal components in structuring this treatment: first, the delineation of the patient's responsibility and expected role behaviors in the treatment mirrored by expected behavior on the part of the therapist, and second, setting the time limits to the treatment.

At the beginning of session 2, the therapist enunciates the expected behaviors of the patient.

T: The last time we met, I asked you a lot of questions and you answered them and at this point I think it would make more sense if we shifted the burden of that and you would be more responsible for telling me all the thoughts that you've had and when we're here to tell me anything that comes into your mind. Anything you think of while you're here: thoughts, feelings, even bodily sensations that occur while you're here so that I'll be able to respond to what you're coming here for. For you to, you know, start telling me as much as you can about why you're here and what's been on your mind and even just if a stray thought crosses your mind, I'd want to know that.

This is a standard structuring statement in a dynamically oriented therapy to which every patient responds idiosyncratically. In this case, there is a special irony to the structuring, as the patient is asked to relate everything that comes to her mind to an older female therapist figure, while the chief complaint is that she cannot tell everything to her mother. The patient's response to the structuring is often predictive of the shape and intensity of future resistances in the therapy.

P: Okay. I was thinking a lot about what you said at the end last time about keeping secrets from you or anything like that and I want to do this so that there is someone that I don't *have* to keep secrets from. I mean it's kind of pointless if I don't tell you things. I mean, that's the whole problem, I'm not telling anyone things and that's why the whole thing is just getting to be kind of a burden and making me very anxious sort of . . . I felt like last time and then I told you a lot of things but then there are also things that I'm sure I left out. I mean the whole history of my boyfriend and I, well, my husband, my relationship and things that have happened in the past with my parents. . .

After the therapist has begun to delineate the expected behavior of the patient, the patient begins to question what she wants from the treatment and more directly what she expects from the therapist.

P: Well maybe I didn't come here to ask for help in telling my parents. I mean maybe I came here just kind of to ask for help in how I'm going to deal with telling my parents, but not necessarily. . . .

T: Telling them?

P: Well, not necessarily telling them while I'm here. I mean nothing . . . I don't think that anything here is gonna help me when I tell them except for preparing me to deal with whatever is gonna happen. I don't think it's gonna make it any easier for me to tell them. . . . How do you think being here is gonna help me if I were to tell them now?

T: Well, presumably you came here for help with *that,* I mean that is what you said and so I would expect that that would be something we would be working on together unless I was mistaken. And I think that you know you've told me about the ways in which you don't want to face what you have to face and that you've been putting off doing something about it in ways that are rationalized in various kinds of ways. "Well, if I wait until after graduation, then I won't have to worry about school." But meanwhile you're very preoccupied with this. So that I think it's a fiction that it's gonna be easier for you after graduation. Things are not easy for you now. And you know it.

P: Huh, uh. [sighs] Well, how . . . I mean how am I gonna do this now?

T: And you're asking me?

P: Yeah. I mean if I knew then I would do it.

The therapist makes explicit what the patient is asking for and the therapist chooses to counter not with advice or role playing of possible ways to tell the parents but by putting the responsibility on the patient who is struggling for autonomy.

T: One of them is that you'd like me to tell you how to do it.

P: Well, I'm not, I don't think that you really can tell me how to do it.

T: I agree.

A few minutes later in the same session the therapist makes a second and key structuring move by letting the patient know that she expects the treatment not to be a mere discussion of the problem but a period of positive action. This interpretive work is aimed at the patient's denial of the hostile and vengeful aspects of her elopement and of the continued secret. To undercut her by now rather exaggerated delaying tactics, the therapist requested she tell her parents during the time of the brief treatment.

T: And whether you feel differently now, or in three weeks I would assume, I think we'd both agree then that you're not gonna feel much different in three weeks about telling them.

P: No.

T: You may know a little bit more about why it was you needed to keep it a secret more than you know now, but at some point it's got to be done and waiting doesn't seem to me to be helpful to you. It's just a wish to put off facing it. And if you were to tell them while you were still seeing me, then I would be here. Otherwise, we have a kind of academic treatment. You know what I mean. Sort of, we'll just talk about a lot but nothing happens.

P: Huh, huh. So, I mean what you're saying is that you really think I should tell them and then we should just deal with whatever happens afterward. Which could be one of [laughs] various things.

T: Like what?

P: Well, I mean I don't know exactly how, I know it's gonna be a very big deal, I know it's gonna be a very big scene, I don't know if my father is gonna get violent. I don't know . . . I mean, I don't know.

Once the structure of the therapy is communicated to the patient, in terms of what is expected of the patient and what the patient can and cannot expect from the therapist, the patient's reactions to the structure of the treatment become manifest and the therapist interprets that reaction.

P: No, I mean I'll eventually tell, naturally I'll eventually tell them, but I'm saying I don't know what's gonna make me tell them now. I mean what you're telling me is that I have to tell them, right? But I already know that.
T: So I'm not telling you anything you didn't already know.
P: Right.
T: But you're reacting to it as if I'm forcing you. And then you say, "Well, maybe I just won't tell them at all."
P: No, not at *all*.
T: Or maybe I won't tell them.
P: I'm saying maybe I won't tell them now.

*Focusing the treatment.* The therapist then points out how the struggle between patient and therapist over the structure of the treatment mirrors the patient's struggle with her parents currently, a struggle that is the focus of the patient's problem.

T: You know one thing I noticed when we were having that interchange about when you would be telling your parents, and if you would, that as I pressed you to consider telling them while we were still together you seemed to get firmer about not telling them.
P: Well, because I'm afraid.
T: I had a different take on it.
P: What is that?
T: Which was, it felt to me as if you didn't like being told what to do.
P: I never like being told what to do. [laughs]
T: Just like your parents told you not to be involved with your husband.
P: Huh, uhm.

Predictably and optimistically, the resistances just pointed out became more exaggerated over the next several sessions permitting greater ease of interpretation. The patient canceled two sessions in a row (4 and 5) and requested to change the time of a third (7).

P: Well, I have to go to this thing so...
T: You would cancel out?
P: Yeah, I would have to.
T: And that would be three cancellations.
P: I know.
T: Cause we didn't meet on a week from today. . . .
P: Yeah.
T: Or on last Tuesday.
P: Let's see if they could do it Monday [reschedule the audio-visual room].
T: Uh hum.
P: I hope so.
T: I think the chances are going to be slim.
P: Really?
T: Yeah, but I don't know for certain.
P: All right, we'll see. How do you want me to start?
T: We've already started.
P: Oh, we had already started, but I mean, you know. . . .
T: I think this is part of it, that one of the things that's going on right now is, uhm, we started to meet, uhm, and you became, I put some pressure on you to start to deal with this, you became depressed. And then you canceled two meetings and we're meeting now, and there's a third cancellation coming up.
P: Well, the third cancellation has nothing to do with me being sick. [One cancellation was due to patient illness.] So, you know, I don't know what to tell you about that. I did become depressed, that's true. I am depressed. I suppose, uhm, I know I'm, I don't know how to get out of the depression. I don't know how to relieve various pressures. I don't, I mean, I feel kind of lost and

isolated and, uhm, depressed. I guess part of it is that I've always considered myself fun, strong, and knew how to deal with whatever it is that I needed to deal with and go on with what I have to do. But it's getting, it's just getting to be a lot. I think I've always put certain amounts of pressure on myself but I'm starting to feel, like, nervous about a lot of things which I didn't, which didn't, you know, use to make me nervous. And sometimes I feel nervous about coming here and, uhm. . .

T: When did you feel nervous about coming here?

P: Well, I always feel nervous about coming here.

T: But more than usual?

P: Yeah.

T: When?

P: Well, before I come.

T: You said "I started to feel nervous about coming here," making it sound like there was some change.

P: No, I always feel somewhat nervous about coming here. I mean, I didn't feel nervous when I'm coming for, like, evaluations and stuff like that. Being here, I feel kind of nervous. And, uhm, I don't think I should feel that way about coming here. I guess I'm not sure.

T: Why not?

P: Why shouldn't I?

T: Yeah.

P: Well, I think that I should kind of have a different outlook that this is something that is, that I felt that I was doing for myself to kind of help me out or relieve some of the nervousness or relieve some of the tension. But. . . .

T: Well, but you weren't feeling nervous before. And you had every reason to feel nervous and upset and depressed. And you weren't feeling that. And so we've been working on your not avoiding now what you have been avoiding for a very long time. And it's not going to feel good. Although you are doing what you can now to avoid here.

P: [sighs] Well, I guess I'm also not really sure, I mean, I guess it makes me think about why I react the way I do to certain things and why I, I kind of take on a lot of things. And why I avoid a lot of things. And I'm not, I'm not really sure why that happens. I mean, I guess I should feel nervous coming here, apprehensive, or whatever. But it also makes me feel more nervous and apprehensive while not here. Which isn't really a good thing and I guess that I thought that coming here would be a good thing.

T: You did hope, it sounds like you did hope that somehow, magically, you wouldn't have to feel anything about the situation you're in.

Another aspect for focusing the treatment is the order in which interpretations are made and in which themes are taken up. This young woman had made a slip of the tongue in the second session, saying, "I'm married and I don't want to," adding to the therapist's impression that such a wish was a powerful motivating factor in her elopement and continued secret marriage. She could believe she wasn't married, and in all important objective ways, she wasn't. But the therapist let the slip go by without a remark, deciding that to take it up that early in the treatment would be premature. Only after she could admit her hostility and vengefulness, and begin to experience some of the sadness and apathy associated with losing fantasied parents and their surrogates (her in-laws), could she consciously contemplate the relationship with her husband.

P: I find myself doing things, I find myself not, kind of changing, when you get married you change, I think the ways in which you do certain things. And a lot of your dependencies on parents or whoever and I find myself not changing those things. I'm not saying, you know,

I'm married, I can't, I don't. The only thing that I don't do because I'm married is go out with other men. I mean that's the only thing, and that's fine because I didn't do that that much in the past either.

T: So it really hasn't meant anything different for you.

P: I guess I just kind of felt that it couldn't really mean anything different until we were together. 'Cause I'm not exactly sure how I'm supposed to be different. I live with people, I'm surrounded by people all day, everyday, who are not married, so, but who are in the same, who are just like me in every other way. So, I'm just kind of, I just, I really did keep my same life-style.

T: And that's the idea.

P: The idea....

T: You weren't ready for whatever reasons to accept the idea that you're a married woman so by keeping it a secret, you could keep on going as if you weren't married and keep everything the same. And buy time that way.

P: So if that's true, then the conflict is really not with my parents, and my parents' approval or disapproval of the marriage. It's with myself and accepting the fact and everything else that goes along with it that I'm married.

T: Did you know that already?

P: Not well enough to say [laughs]. And I guess I would start to think about what I shouldn't be doing as someone who's married. And I couldn't even begin, I don't know what those things are. I feel like, in a way, I feel like I was trying to get in, like the last months that I could have been someone's daughter, and...

T: Uh hum. And it didn't work the way you had hoped.

P: Uh, huh. And I guess also, because it didn't work the way I had hoped, I decided to be my mother and father-in-law's daughter, because that worked, really easily.

By the sixth session her ambivalence about her dependency on her in-laws has come under scrutiny.

P: I mean they [her in-laws] treat me like I'm a married woman by acknowledging the fact that I'm married, but they really treat me like another one of their children, not like an adult friend. And I've also been looking at, you know, but yet I depend on that treatment.

T: That you may in fact like it.

P: I don't think that—that's not a good thing. You know, I mean, you know, in a lot of ways, you know of instances, they put me not in the same category, but sometimes they treat me in the same way like they would treat their daughter, but their daughter is 14. And, you know...

T: That doesn't fit so easily with you any more?

P: Well, it did, it did. It makes it...

T: You probably enjoyed it for a long time.

P: Yeah, I've enjoyed it for a really long time, but it's not what should be happening. You know, I was looking at the fact that for Easter, uhm, my husband's father has always given me some kind of stuffed animal, and you know, he did it again this year, and like, the same kind of thing that he gave to his daughter, and it means a lot to me, but I don't think that it should, you know, that it should make me that happy, that it should make me that excited. I don't, you know, I shouldn't be expecting Easter presents any more, or especially of that sort.

T: You sound today a little bit more like you'd like to grow up. You know, it doesn't, it's like a suit of clothes that doesn't fit any more.

P: Well, I think that it's really important that I do, you know, I look at all the things that I get angry or frustrated with my parents for not doing, you know, that his parents do do. Like when I went to . . .

T: Neither one and you're not happy with either?
P: Right. When, you know, the morning of the funeral, I, uhm, I was really hungry. And I hadn't slept at home, but one of the ladies, one of my grandmother's friends that was there, you know, said to my mother, "Why didn't you feed your daughter this morning? Why didn't you give her breakfast?" She said, "My daughter is going to be 22 years old this week, you know, she wants breakfast, let her get breakfast" [laughs]. But where, as I was thinking, you know, if I were to be at my husband's house, I would walk downstairs and breakfast would be on the table. And I wouldn't have, you know, I don't have to think about those little things. And they ask me things like, "When are you going to do your homework? Have you done your schoolwork?" Why should they be asking me that? You know, these are all things that I should be able to take care of without having people tell me. And I've made such a big. . . I always bring my clothes home to wash them, you know, and I always did it myself, and one time this year I asked my mother to do them, to do it 'cause I had a lot of other things to do, and I never really ask her, and she really did, this sounds so ridiculous, but she really did a terrible job, and she didn't take care of my clothes like she used to. And then a couple of weeks ago, I had . . . I brought them all to my husband's grandmother's house 'cause I wanted to spend the time there, and they only have a washer, so I couldn't really dry them, so my mother-in-law took them all home and did them, and, you know, folded them, and I didn't have to do anything, but these should be all, you know, all these little things I should be perfectly, you know, I should just feel, I should never feel that I want to ask anyone else to do these kinds of things for me, you know, I shouldn't, I get so frustrated when I go home that my mother isn't making meals anymore.
T: And you feel ashamed about that?
P: Yeah, it's kind of, it's ridiculous that I expect these things of her. . . .
T: But you do.

The therapist underscores her nascent changes, all the more convincing for the wistful confessional tone in admitting to the old pleasures. At the same time, as she nourishes these new beginnings, the therapist is attentive for more opportunities to continue the focused line of interpretation. Soon the opportunity arises.

P: Like half the time I take on responsibilities that are supposed to be adult responsibilities, like, you know, dealing with his grandmother and taking care of her. . . .
T: And the other half?
P: It's not consistent. And I think that it really needs to be consistent.
[More unrealistic thinking.]
T: But it will be consistent in time. It's just you have to go through a transition right now, and it sounds like what you're doing. It's going to be a bit uneven, more than a little bit uneven. It's going to be uncomfortably uneven for a long time.

The patient continues, showing a greater acuity now in her reality testing as a result of the line of interpretations, and she adds an important piece of historical information, the psychological meaning of which is just beginning to dawn on her.

P: [sighs] And I was also looking at, uhm, like the relationships between my mother and father, and the relationship between like my mother- and father-in-law, and when my mother- and father-in-law don't have a very stable marriage, and part of that is because, you know, throughout their whole marriage, my father-in-law treated my mother-in-law like a child. She was really dependent on him for everything. And then, when he couldn't, you know, didn't really fulfill that need anymore, and she was expected to do a lot of things on her own, she became really bitter and resentful. And the incredible depression that she's going through over the loss of her mother is because she really has to become, she never became independent of her at all. Like in any aspect. Whereas my mother didn't even live with her mother till she was 17 and was completely independent of her.

T: Your mother didn't live with her mother until she was 17? Who did she live with?

P: Uhm, her father, her father's mother, and her aunt. Her parents were divorced when she was three years old. So, when she came to go to school in New York, she lived with her mother.

T: So you've got two different models of married women now to look at, too. And you're not sure which one you want to be.

P: Well, I want, I know that I want to be independent of everyone [laughs], but, uhm, it's really hard, and, I guess, you know, part of coming here has made me realize how dependent I am on everyone.

*Relationship between therapist and patient.* The patient's magical and childish expectations of the therapeutic relationship are now becoming more overt and open for her inspection. While they work on these aspects of the relationship between therapist and patient, using the structure of the treatment to highlight her idiosyncratic wishes and fantasies, the focus of the secrets between patient and mother became sharper.

T: Listening today, I could reconstruct how you were thinking last fall. "If you, my parents, are going to act this way when I try to discuss something with you, there's no point in discussing it, so I'm going to elope without your knowing it and never tell you, and not tell you." Uhm ... as a way of both protecting yourself from getting hit again and also as revenge for their having hit you before.

P: Huh, uh. Yeah, I guess so. And I think, I think there are a lot of things that I just decide not to tell them because I don't feel that I could discuss it with them. . . . I learned in the year, I was really sick and, uhm, doctors had first thought that I had a tubal pregnancy and I had to go see a lot of different doctors before they figured out that I had a cyst and, uhm, and in the beginning I was really scared and it was right after my husband had left and people were saying, "Now why don't you tell your mother?" And I just, I never told her. I just didn't want to tell her. In fact, I've never discussed anything, uhm, that had to do with gynecology or, or, me with her. And I guess I also resent her for not asking me . . . I resent her for not asking me about things like birth control and where she knows that I must see a doctor or where I see a doctor, or anything like that. She did know one time when I went to her gynecologist once, last year, and I told her that I wanted to go. I wanted to go before I went to California and he gave me a prescription for the Pill and I told her that and she just kind of made herself feel comfortable with it by saying that it was really for cramps.

The psychotherapist then proceeds to do what the patient has always wanted (and not wanted) the mother to do, to ask about sexual matters.

T: What are you using for birth control now?

P: Well, I got off the Pill and my husband left so I guess I'll have to go back to

using a diaphragm when I see him again. Because the Pill wasn't good for me.
T: Do you have a diaphragm?
P: Yeah. Which also I know that she knows about because it was, I didn't take it with me to California over the summer, I left it in the drawer in my room and when I came back it was thrown in my closet...

The psychotherapist makes a "prophylactic" interpretation designed to prevent any further acting out in a situation rife with acting out. Although it is predictably denied by the patient, the patient will, nonetheless, be less likely to act on this impulse.

T: The two of you are at a standoff, and there's a vengeful component to your, at this point, being married and keeping it a secret. The part of it that motivated it is to get back at her for not acknowledging that you are a sexual person. You might even be tempted to get pregnant to...
P: I seriously doubt that... I don't think that. I have no desire to be pregnant now. I really don't.

By this point the patient was visibly depressed, and again, unlike the patient's mother, the therapist commented on it.

T: You look different today. You look depressed today. Are you feeling kind of low?
P: Well, one of the main reasons I look different today has been because I guess I didn't get a lot of sleep last night. I got up this morning and went swimming and, yeah, I guess I'm also a little bit depressed.
T: What's the content of your depression? Are you aware of it at all?
P: Well, I'm just depressed about facing this whole situation. And maybe I was also a little depressed coming here and knowing that I was going to have to really face it again. So you know [sighs]... I'll probably go home one day this week... 'cause usually when I go home I don't stay around them very long, you know, I do what I have to do and I take the car to go to do what I need to do... so, Sunday I stayed home all day, which I hadn't done in a long time. I guess maybe inside I expected something miraculous to happen [laughs] but, uhm, it didn't.
T: It never does.
P: No, it doesn't. But I guess sometimes I expect them to just maybe come to me and say, "What is the matter?" You know, "What's going on?" You can look at me and say, "You look depressed." They can certainly look at me and say that I look depressed or think that I look depressed. I certainly don't walk around the house smiling and happy.
T: You don't?
P: No, and I suppose that at certain points, maybe I even, uhm, consciously don't do that. So that maybe they'll say, "What's wrong?" but they never do [laughs].

Increasingly and repetitively, this patient's sullen, passively hostile, and avoidant attitude toward her parents is taken up alongside her passive and magical wishes for the treatment. As a result of this, the patient becomes more direct about and responsible for her anger. In the fifth meeting, she was able to say the following:

P: Uh hm. I am really angry with them.
T: Yeah, you are. I think you alternate between being very angry about it and very depressed about it. You know, feeling hurt and rejected. And I think it was from that that you made the decision to marry your husband when you did and how you did—keeping it a secret was a way of getting back at them. You felt that they were keeping secrets

from you. That they had really excluded you, and so you were going to exclude them to get back to them. And I also think that you're trying to cope with a big transition in your life from being someone else's daughter to being someone else's wife. And that you somehow, as you said to me at the beginning of the hour, you said, "I just don't want to feel this way. I don't want to feel this." That you had hoped that you could get through this without feeling any of it. Without feeling depressed, without feeling angry.

P: But I think a big part of it is that I really [sighs] I really want them to be part of it, and I also think that I really, I need them more than I ever thought that I did. I, I really need the help now. And I've needed their help for a long time but I really need it now . . . everytime, they hurt me I would always come out of it deciding, well, you know, if they're going to do this then I don't need them. But I really do. Yeah, before I went to California I remember telling you that, uhm, you know, she said "to go and do what I had to do" and that she would be there for me when I came back and she wasn't. And that really probably has hurt the most out of all of it. And I thought that in the beginning of the year I did, you know, I did make an effort, I asked her to come up to school and took her out to dinner. And we talked, we had a serious talk, and I thought that that would maybe be like the first gesture in a long line of, I mean my mother does not live that far away from me and she sees me and it's not that much for her to get in the car and come up and go out to dinner with me or just come over to my house once in a while. And I thought, I really thought that she would take this opportunity to do that but instead I feel like she's just kind of tending to what my father needs.

T: Had she ever done that before, though? Just get in the car and come up and see you?

P: No.

T: So you were expecting something more from her now, and back then, you know, last fall. You were expecting more from her than she'd ever given you.

By focusing on her increased and unrealistic expectations of her mother and the ambiguous and ambivalent move into marriage, the patient can begin to experience affects she has been suppressing and repressing. Just a few moments later:

P: I should be prepared for that to happen, instead of, uhm, wanting to have kind of a closer relationship. Well, also, I mean, a part of it is, I felt that we never really had that very close relationship. And I, part of the reason that I wanted to come back was maybe to try to have that kind of relationship. But, it's not, it wasn't going to happen [sighs].

T: What was that sigh?

P: Well, that doesn't . . . you begin realizing that doesn't stop me from wanting it to happen.

T: And feeling hurt. I had the impression you're feeling quite sad now.

P: Uh hum. I mean, I also, I think that I need [sighs] . . . I needed to have that kind of relationship for awhile. And I didn't, and I wasn't finding it in my mother and in a lot of ways I found it in my mother-in-law which has led to a kind of dependence on my part and on her part but concentrating on my part, uhm, that maybe isn't necessarily a good thing, either.

*Terminating Treatment*

As the end of treatment approached, a number of hazards, common in brief psychotherapy, became apparent. Chief among them is the patient's attempt to leave in despair, recapitulating in an almost perverse fashion the old behaviors that brought them to treatment. The progress and momentum of the earlier part of treatment are called to a halt, and attention must be paid again to the relationship with the therapist with special attention to the meanings of the imminent separation. To counter the centrifugal pull to undo all the work accomplished so far, therapist and patient alike must review the achievements realistically. Not surprisingly, the harbinger of the termination phase was a broken appointment. All previously missed sessions had been cancelled. Her husband's grandmother had died and the funeral was scheduled during the appointment. At the next meeting, the patient was distant and unable to account for her not calling the therapist. Her husband had flown in for the funeral and stayed with her over the next week. Resistances were intensified. She had devoted herself to her in-laws with a vengeance, using the funeral as the rationalization. With three more sessions left, she had not told her parents about her husband and appeared to be repetitiously engaged in the same behaviors that brought her to treatment. She complained to the therapist:

P: I just wait, and wait, and wait, and sometimes they get done, and sometimes they don't, depending on, I guess, the importance of the situation. And then, at the same time, I also always take on a tremendous amount of, you know, extra activities, extra responsibilities, and I end up rushing to get them all done, so, it's not always at the most opportune time, so. . .

She is telling the therapist that she will end treatment the same way she came in, procrastinating and feeling fragmented. The ending is near, but she is not fully aware of her reaction. The therapist used this opportunity to reorient and focus the patient on her initial complaint and did not get interested in the broader characterological issues.

T: Well, that may be, from your description, sounds like it's a broader issue than what you brought here. That it's an issue that has to do with your character in some ways, but I have a feeling, at this point, it may be, you may be using it to try to diffuse our focus on just the specifics of your delay in beginning to rearrange your relationship with your parents.
P: And to accept the fact that I'm married.

Now that her husband had joined her, one hindrance to the evolution of her ambivalence was momentarily remedied. Her husband was keenly aware of her unfinished business:

P: My husband keeps saying to me now at the basis of every argument is the fact that he feels that I'm not, that he's not like my first priority and that I think I told you that he thinks his parents are but that's not really what it is. [Long pause.] It's scary to say it but I guess after my parents, you know, after I've finished everything I need to with my parents, that's when I'm going to be able to really look at my relationship, I guess.
T: What was scary about saying that?
P: But if that's the point, that I'm going to be able to look at it then there's still a possibility that it's—that I'm not going to want it. I guess it's also kind of a question of do I need or do I want a husband or as far as like fulfilling my part of being a wife or do I need a mother, and, you know, then fulfilling my part as being a child. My husband made a comment to me that he thinks his mother and I have what could be considered a marriage, that kind of relationship [laughs]. I mean I thought that was really ridiculous, but he, that's not it at all; it's that we have what could

be considered a mother-daughter relationship.

She and her husband had talked about ending the marriage. The patient reported this in a cursory fashion initially, as if admitting to failure, not aware of how long overdue such a talk was.

P: Uhm, he said, well, maybe we just, you know, aren't the right people for each other and, you know, maybe you need something different, maybe I need something different. And I wasn't happy with that and then afterward he said that that wasn't really what he wanted, he wanted for things to work between us but he wanted, you know, needed to be able to understand more of what he needed and, you know, he said that he compared it to when I was in California and that he was working really hard and he was working a lot of hours but he always took out time for me but then again he didn't have anything else there, you know. My classes end, I'm like . . . when day ends my school work is hardly over. So I have, I'm thinking about other things. But, you know, he felt that I was thinking about his family too much. So, but we, I mean, that's how the thing about marriage ending came up but then he said that isn't what he wanted. So we kind of dropped that idea but it was just sort of startling to have it even come up. You know, that we shouldn't be together.
T: I don't know how startling it is. You certainly have begun to wonder yourself with me how much you wanted to be married.
P: Yeah, but I did, I have, you know, I definitely wondered about that but I think that wondering if I want to be married or not is like sort of the same things wondering if I want to break away from being, uhm, a child, or you know, having that security.

At the last session, the patient's affect was stoically depressed. Together, therapist and patient go over what has been accomplished. Of her marriage she says:

P: I think I realized that I wasn't really as ready for it as I thought that I was. But, all in all, it exists and it's not something I want to end so I just have to live up to my part of it. And my parents being included in it isn't really, you know, that's not really where the problem lies whether they're part of it or not. It's completely my own thing, my own doing and they shouldn't really be making it any better or any worse for me. You know, it's kind of looking for them to be able to make it easier for me. And that's not really their, it's not their job.
T: Yeah, well, they're not able to do that.
P: Right. So it's also not fair for me to have those kinds of expectations of them, I guess.
T: You can wish to, but when it's as clear as it is that they cannot be more helpful to you now, then it's a problem if you can't recognize that and do what you have to do.
P: Right.
T: And that was the position you were in when you came. And I think you've changed in that regard.

The psychotherapist picked up on her stoic affect.

T: This all sounds right but I'm wondering about a certain flatness in the way you talk about it or I don't know whether you're mildly depressed today?
P: Well, I kind of feel like shit anyway so I'm sure that doesn't help, it doesn't help at all so—yesterday I stayed in bed all day, which is something I haven't done in a really long time and I really didn't feel well [a cold]. And I think it's also kind of everything coming, you

know, the last couple of weeks just kind of came down on me I guess. The weather and all that doesn't help. But I also know that, now I can take care of my responsibilities and I can do what I have to do, just sort of let everyone else do what they have to do also.

T: Part of the things that are coming down on you is our ending.

P: Yeah, that's part of it. School's ending. Lots of things are ending. My husband is back, you know, doing what he has to do, so I have to pick up my end. That's it. [Pause] I don't think there's a lot more to say. [Long pause] I think I've said just about everything there is to say about it.

T: What's the mood you have about all of this?

P: About all, everything that's happened? Uhm, I could let it be really depressing if I chose to but, uhm, so, in a sense maybe, you know, maybe I am trying to ignore it but, you know, that's just kind of the only way I feel like I can get things done. I also don't feel like it's that severe a depression 'cause, you know, whatever I would be depressed about I more or less know how I have to handle, so. It's not like a hopeless depression.

She ended seeing her mother-in-law with a clearer eye, aware of the gaps in her relationship with her mother. She saw how it had happened. She ended with apprehension for her future with her husband. She ended sadder but possibly wiser.

## FOLLOW-UP INTERVIEW

For the patient's reaction to the treatment, she was invited for a follow-up interview with the therapist four months after termination. The patient continued to live apart from her husband, with her paternal grandmother or with her parents a couple of nights a week. She was working, saving money, and planning to move to the West Coast in two months when she and her husband would be provided housing by the military. She had not told her parents of her marriage, but she had told her paternal grandmother, hoping, perhaps, that she would tell for her. She had spoken to the therapist two months earlier asking for the name of a psychiatrist for her mother-in-law. She specified a psychiatrist because she felt her mother-in-law might need medication. This represented a consolidation of her new attitude toward her mother-in-law and a clear behavioral change.

P: ... I don't have the power to make everything better for them. I don't have the power to change them. I can't let their problems consume my life and my thoughts because that can only be done by them.... And I have to keep in mind a distinction between her relationship with her children and her relationship with me. I can't go around seeing her as a mother figure. The whole thing about blood is thicker than water. Well [laughs], it's really true. I have to keep in mind whose mother she really is.

She saw her mother-in-law much less frequently than before, even though she lived even closer to her after graduation.

Symptomatically, the patient was no longer depressed or in crisis. On follow-up, her mood was bright and she had no complaints of disturbed sleep or appetite. She was working as a receptionist for the mail order department of a nationally known department store. She looked poised, and as if she was enjoying her first job.

During this meeting the therapist read several key transactions and asked her to say what she was thinking at the time and what she thought about it now. The first interchange used was from the second session.

T: You may know a little bit more about why it was you needed to keep it a secret more than what you know now, but at some point it's got to be done and waiting doesn't seem to me to be helpful to you. It's just a wish to put off facing it. And if you were to tell them while you were still seeing me then I would be here. Otherwise, we have a kind of academic treatment. You know what I mean. Sort of we'll just talk a lot but nothing happens.

Four months later, the patient replies:

P: I think maybe at the time I was telling you that because I knew that's, that's really what, it was only the second time we met, and, uhm, I don't think that I ever really thought while we were meeting that I was going to go home and tell my parents. I mean, I think that I thought *about* it, but I don't think that I ever really, inside, felt that that's what I was going to do.
T: And you never told me that. That you knew in your heart of hearts you would never tell them while you were seeing me. Why do you think you never told me?
P: Why didn't I ever tell them?
T: No, told me.
P: Well, because, number one, maybe, somewhere I hoped that I would. I hoped that something would happen in our sessions that would make it possible, easier, whatever. I had no idea what that would be, and also I thought that maybe we wouldn't be able to have treatments if I said that I wasn't going to do it. So, I mean, I guess I felt like that was really the point why I was there, or that you thought that's why I was there.
T: And that I would kick you out.
P: And also, well, yeah. And also, we also were doing, I mean this wasn't like normal treatment, I mean, you were doing it for a reason, and you were. . . .

T: What do you mean?

The patient repeated with the therapist the same expectation—passively hostile deception, fear of expulsion, and hope for the magical solution in relation to the therapist's injunction as she had with her parents. She adds, to drive the point home:

P: You were doing it . . . I also had in mind that you were doing it for educational purposes. So, and that if I guess, maybe, if I were to tell my parents while we were in treatment, then that would have gone along very nicely with what you were doing. So maybe if you believed that that was, that I was going to do that, then we would be able to keep having treatment.

While the therapist's injunction is a "nonneutral" intervention and controversial in its usefulness, several things could be said about it. Certainly, the patient would bring to bear on this injunction all salient aspects of her personality; namely, she would react within the confines of her transference to the therapist. This is to be expected. The treatment was not successful in bringing to light and working through all these aspects in the therapeutic relationship. And there is reason to believe that in the limited time available one could not have accomplished it, although ideally if one uses such a parameter, one should be prepared to take up and analyze in the therapeutic relationship her reaction. However, in this particular case, the injunction served another purpose, which the therapist had intended. It is best expressed by the patient during her follow-up interview.

P: I think that what really came out of our sessions for me is, was, *not* that I absolutely had to tell my parents that I was married but *why* I wasn't telling them. But a lot of it had to do with my maybe not being able to make the transition to really independent living and maybe my being so ambiguous about my husband and things like that. And also looking at my dependence on his family.

T: Was it helpful for me to have insisted that you tell them?

P: Well, it made me look at the whole idea of telling them in a way I hadn't before. It was also kind of frightening. No, it wasn't even frightening. I'm not sure, not sure of the word to use to describe it. It made me very, uhm, kind of uneasy, but it also made me look at the situation differently.

She confirms our impression that the early structure of the treatment served as an "anxiety-provoking" device to move and focus the treatment.

The next quote was the slip of the tongue, "I think sometimes about what things would be like if I didn't get married," from the fifth session.

P: Well, then, when I said it, I really did think it was a slip or a grammatical error, however you want to put it. But I remember that very, very clearly. Probably it was the first time that I really thought about the whole idea of not wanting to be married. That was *another* part of why I didn't tell my parents. That's, I really didn't want it to be true. Then I began to think about how many other instances there were that I was acting like I was not married. I remember telling you the only way I felt like I was married was either when I was around his family, or when I was approached by other men. Now, that's really not that different. I don't feel—I mean—I feel tied. I don't feel married. I feel, uhm, like I don't have the freedom to direct my own life in courses I would choose to take after I graduate because there are certain things that I have to do. That's basically it.

But she goes on to say she did not know, when she came for treatment, that she was ambivalent about her husband. The work of treatment was making her conscious of that. On follow-up, she was still aware of it and still seeking compromise positions. She was married, living on the other side of the country from her husband, and planning to live with him in several months. She led the life of a single woman but was married, without a husband.

On follow-up, she had accomplished some of the mediating goals of the treatment. She had accomplished more honest and open communication with her husband that included awareness of her ambivalence. She had greatly diminished her overinvolvement with her in-laws. She now saw her mother-in-law as someone who was depressed and in need of treatment—including somatic treatments. And she was no longer tempted to go to any lengths to get her the help. She decided in the face of her mother-in-law's reluctance to make an appointment, that she had done enough in finding a referral. Her mother-in-law would have to do the rest.

She didn't accomplish the same improvement in her relationship with her parents, nor did she take any major steps toward normalizing her role as a married woman. Was the treatment not long enough? On follow-up she voiced that opinion. She declined the offer of a referral to a therapist in her area, and she did not want to renew treatment with the same therapist because of the difficulty in arrangements. Her priority was her job and saving money to move to be with her husband.

Another factor in not making more gains in the area of marriage was that of her living arrangements. As she and her husband resided on opposite coasts, there was no environmental pressure to announce to her family that she was married, nor to account to her husband for the discrepancy. There was an arbitrary limit on how much she could elaborate and expand on her ambivalence and no opportunity to test out and work through behaviorally (and otherwise) the problems with her husband. The course of the treatment conceivably might have been quite different had her husband lived in the area.

This case, then, demonstrates the possibilities and limitations of brief psychodynamic psychotherapy. The nature and extent of this patient's conflicts are more readily apparent, as well as her response to treatment. Three future treatment possibilities seem immediately apparent. The first would be no further treatment to assess her capacity to understand and work through issues on her own, combined with a now less conflicted developmental push. Results from another follow-up in several months would provide the needed information.

The next two possibilities involve further treatment, the format, length, and setting depending on variables such as motivation and timing. Perhaps in the future this young woman will seek continued therapy on her now troublesome ambivalence and paralysis with regard to her husband. The format could once again be individual, but perhaps a marital format would now be more efficient in fostering a more direct exploration of her conflictual relationship with the mate she denies.

## REFERENCES

Beutler, L. (1983). *Eclectic psychotherapy: A systematic approach.* New York: Pergamon.

Clarkin, J. F., & Frances, A. (1982). Selection criteria for the brief psychotherapies. *American Journal of Psychotherapy, 36*(2), 166–180.

Davanloo, H. (1978). *Basic principles and techniques in short-term dynamic psychotherapy.* New York: Spectrum Books.

Frances, A., Clarkin, J. F., & Perry, S. (1984). *Differential therapeutics: A guide to the art and science of treatment planning in psychiatry.* New York: Brunner/Mazel.

Goldfried, M. R. (1980). Toward the delineation of therapeutic change principles. *American Psychologist, 35*, 991–999.

Gomes-Schwartz, B. (1978). Effective ingredients in psychotherapy: Prediction of outcome from process variables. *Journal of Consulting and Clinical Psychology, 46*, 1023–1035.

Klerman, G. L., Weissman, M. M., Rounsaville, B. J., & Chevron, E. S. (1984). *Interpersonal psychotherapy of depression.* New York: Basic Books.

Luborsky, L. (1984). *Principles of psychoanalytic psychotherapy: A manual for supportive-expressive treatment.* New York: Basic Books.

Malan, D. H. (1976). *The frontier of brief psychotherapy.* New York: Plenum.

Orlinsky, D. E., & Howard, K. I. (1978). The relation of process to outcome in psychotherapy. In S. L. Garfield & A. E. Bergin (Eds.), *Handbook of psychotherapy and behavior change: An empirical analysis* (pp. 283–329). New York: Wiley.

Perry, S., Frances, A., & Clarkin, J. (1985). *A DSM-III casebook of differential therapeutics: A clinical guide to treatment selection.* New York: Brunner/Mazel.

Perry, S., Frances, A., Klar, H., & Clarkin, J. (1983). Selection criteria for individual dynamic psychotherapies. *Psychiatric Quarterly, 55*(1), 3–16.

Sloane, R. B., Staples, F. R., Cristol, A. H., Yorkston, N. J., & Whipple, K. (1975). *Short-term analytically-oriented psychotherapy versus behavior therapy.* Cambridge, MA: Harvard University Press.

Smith, M. L., Glass, G. V., & Miller, T. I. (1980). *The benefits of psychotherapy.* Baltimore: Johns Hopkins University Press.

Strupp, H. H. (1980). Success and failure in time-limited psychotherapy. *Archives of General Psychiatry, 37*, 947–954.

# Commentary: Common versus Specific Ingredients in Differential Therapeutics and Psychotherapy

*Larry E. Beutler*

*Differential therapeutics as outlined by Frances, Clarkin, and Perry (1984) employs a decision tree procedure for assessing the appropriateness of treatments. The procedure represents a grand step forward in applying clinical wisdom systematically to the task of selecting among broad categories of treatments, of which individual psychotherapy is one. The broad-ranging objective of this approach is one to which few other eclectic models have been applied. Most models seek only to address variations in the application of group, individual, or family therapy. As noted by Clarkin and Rosnick, the decisional procedure of differential therapeutics was neither designed for nor is it well suited to predicting the application of specific technical procedures within the context of a program of psychotherapy. For this reason, the exploration of differential therapeutics within the context of a single treatment case loses the most unique and powerful elements of the approach.*

*Differential therapeutics has taken the position that once the format, duration, and frequency of psychotherapy are set, the outcome of psychotherapy relies on the healing qualities which cut across therapeutic procedures—the "common" rather than the "specific" ingredients. If one accepts this assumption, little can be said about the particular psychotherapy approach illustrated in the case presented by Clarkin and Rosnick except as reflected in the "common" ingredients such as caring, understanding, and empathy. For the sake of discussion, however, let us propose that Clarkin and Rosnick are in error when they conclude that because research has failed to demonstrate differential effects of psychotherapy, no differential effects occur. The research to which Clarkin and Rosnick, as well as others who reject the value of technical specificity, allude is based on competitive assessments of different psychotherapies applied to single, heterogeneous patient samples. Relatively little research has been directed to assessing the differential effects of different psychotherapies when applied to contrasting patient samples. Although the average effects of psychotherapies may be indistinguishable, their efficacy with specific patient populations may be quite different. Clarkin and Rosnick are quite right in suggesting that strong evidence for this assumption is not yet available, but it may be unfair to reject such a persuasive clinical hypothesis because it has not yet been empirically tested.*

## AN ALTERNATIVE VIEW

*Differential therapeutics allows selection among global treatments or settings. The application of the decisional model allows the selection of nonpsychotherapy as well as psychotherapy alternatives. When psychotherapy is selected, it encourages and directs choices among various treatment formats (individual, family, and group therapies), various levels of frequency, and variations in length of treatment. Unfortunately, application of the decision rules often does not result in a narrow listing of treatment alternatives. As observed in the case described by Clarkin and Rosnick, many patients can fit a number of different decisional criteria. The patient described, for example, was a suitable candidate for either individual, family, or group therapy, and the ultimate selection of the format, the frequency, and the duration of therapy was made more on the basis of external convenience than with specific patient determiners. It may be interesting, therefore, to see where a more specific psychotherapy model might take us in treating this patient. Once we assume that the patient has already been found to be appropriate for psychotherapy and attempt to select among specific therapeutic processes and procedures, the first and most persistent thing we observe is that the information provided by Clarkin and Rosnick is insufficient to make a determination of the available array of therapeutic procedures to be used. Let's illustrate this point with a view to my own decisional model of eclectic psychotherapy.*

## Systematic Eclectic Psychotherapy

*In my model of systematic integrationism (Beutler, 1983), it is assumed that the decision to initiate individual psychotherapy has already been made. The focus of the model, therefore, is on providing the therapist with information about how to define the patient's problem, how to establish a compatible and fruitful therapeutic relationship, and how to provide interventions that will accommodate the changes observed across the span of treatment. In this process, issues of patient and therapist compatibility, breadth and severity of symptoms,* defensive style, *and patient interpersonal resistance or* reactance level *(Brehm & Brehm, 1981) are assessed. It is difficult to apply this approach to the case described by Clarkin and Rosnick for want of information about these variables.*

*1. A compatible and potentially fruitful therapeutic match is based in part on the demographic and attitudinal similarities/differences between patient and therapist. Clarkin and Rosnick address this issue in a general way, but the systematic eclectic psychotherapy approach emphasizes the need for greater specificity. Ideally, patient and therapist should be matched in terms of similar demographic backgrounds but dissimilar evaluative beliefs with regard to the dynamic, interpersonal needs expressed in the focal conflict.*

*2. The next question posed by systematic eclectic psychotherapy concerns the symptom complexity and severity presented by the patient. In the case described by Clarkin and Rosnick, it is uncertain whether the problem represents a situational adjustment difficulty or a broad-band, personality disturbance. It appears, however, that the therapist initially approached the matter as if it were a situational disturbance and accordingly adopted very focal objectives. Without systematic assessment of this dimension, however, it is possible that therapists may be misled by their own particular preferences for symptomatically focused or conflictually focused treatments. At the conclusion of this treatment case, for example, the therapist suggested to the patient that the problem may have been more characterological than originally thought, suggesting that the symptomatic focus of the treatment may have been somewhat less than ideal.*

*3. Clarkin and Rosnick suggest that the patient's defensive style is more internalized than externalized. However, they also discuss the patient as "acting out" against parents. This contradiction suggests that the patient either presents some disconti-*

*nuity between the two very different defensive strategies, changed her defensive strategy over the course of therapy, or exhibits one defensive style within therapy and another outside of therapy. This matter is left unclear in the assessment process and, yet, may be important for determining whether the intervention should be focused on behavior change, insight, or emotional awareness. The treatment itself seemed to move from a behavioral (e.g., the early objective was for the patient to tell her parents of her marriage) to an insight focus (e.g., at the conclusion of therapy the treatment goals are judged to have been met because the patient has more awareness of the conflict even though she did not change her behavior).*

*If a careful evaluation were to determine that the patient's symptom of inhibition was circumscribed to a setting or relationship and that her most disruptive defenses entailed "acting out" against her parents, behavior change in the form of reduced acting out and increased self-assertion would be the principal focus of the systematic, eclectic therapist. If, on the other hand, the patient was found to have generalized (i.e., characterological) symptoms, the quest then would be to define the underlying conflict in some theoretically specific way. If the patient's accompanying defenses were found to emphasize internalization of anxiety, as initially suggested by Clarkin and Rosnick, the subsequent focus of treatment would be to focus either on enhancing affective awareness, if the particular defenses emphasize overcontrol of affect, or on cognitive control, if emotional intensity and lability is high.*

*4. The patient's interpersonal reactance level is a particular area of concern in the current case presentation. The therapist's initial injunction for the patient to tell her parents about her marriage clearly escalated her resistance. This resistance, subsequently, was quite rightly observed and addressed by the therapist, but never changed. The therapist pointed out, for example, that the patient reentrenched herself and asserted more strongly that she would not tell her parents after the therapist had made the intervention. If initial assessment had revealed the patient to be highly reactant, such a directive intervention as that given in this case would not be considered appropriate unless the therapist had wanted the patient to do exactly as she did, reaffirm her boundaries and resist telling her parents. If symptomatic change was considered desirable by the therapist, a reactance challenge may have been a suitable test, if it had been constructed around an activity that was not so central to the patient's symptoms. Such a test could include assessing her response to homework assignments or to an insight-oriented interpretation. Observing the high reactance of this patient, the systematic eclectic psychotherapist would have ordinarily responded either with less directive interventions than manifest by the therapist in this example, or by relying on paradoxical interventions which would capitalize on the patient's reactance tendency (e.g., prescribe the rebellious activity/symptom).*

## SUMMARY

*Collectively, the differential therapeutics model proposed by Frances, Clarkin, and Perry (1984) lends a considerable amount of clinical wisdom to the process of treatment selection. Certainly, more than any other eclectic approach to treatment, it addresses the broad-band issues of selecting treatments from a variety of modalities other than individual psychotherapy. Its most valued contribution may well be in the definition of the treatment format, the setting, and the relationship of the primary treatment to adjunctive interventions.*

*The model is less specific in prescribing the most desirable and specific processes and technologies to be emphasized in psychotherapy. Its reliance on an assumption of therapy equivalence, although possibly correct, does relatively little to assist in the definition of specific treatments for specific patients at a microanalytical level. In this context, it might be suitably applied along with a variety of more specific eclectic orientations that are better suited to the prescription of differential psychotherapeutics. Certainly, the "nonspecific" emphasis of differential therapeutics takes a more conservative approach than those who emphasize specific models of psychotherapeutic change. As such, the treatment outlined is rational, sensible, and of immense potential value to both clinical practitioners and clinical researchers.*

## REFERENCES

Beutler, L. E. (1983). Eclectic psychotherapy: A systematic approach. New York: Pergamon Press.

Brehm, S. S., & Brehm, J. W. (1981). Psychological reactance: A theory of freedom and control. New York: Academic Press.

Frances, A., Clarkin, J. F., & Perry, S. (1984). Differential therapeutics: A guide to the art and science of treatment planning in psychiatry. New York: Brunner/Mazel.

# Commentary: Eclecticism Should Provide Versatility

## Richard H. Driscoll

*Organizing and integrating competing approaches allows and even requires comparison of alternative case formulations and interventions. It invites us to be both practitioners and at the same time investigators, selecting and acting on what seems appropriate in our sessions, and then critiquing our procedures, generating alternatives from other approaches, judging between them, and so broadening our perspectives and expanding our competencies. The advantage of eclecticism is its potential versatility.*

*The focus of the differential therapeutics method is on several pretreatment considerations which may be made implicitly in other approaches. Clarkin and Rosnick seek to specify the ways to match clients to treatment modalities. The client/patient in this case is surely suitable for outpatient treatment, and seeing her more intensively (twice a week) is a nice solution to the time limitations imposed by her graduation. The individual sessions seem appropriate initially, although one might have left open the possibility of seeing her later with her husband when he could get leave, or perhaps with her in-laws.*

*The choice of a transference-focused brief psychodynamic therapy as the approach for this woman sets the parameters for the rest of the treatment. Integration can be by the selection of a single orientation matched to the client, as was done here, or by the use of many orientations as they apply to a case, which is the more usual method. The advantage of a single matched orientation is that it maintains the coherence and integrity of the single method, hopefully well suited to the particular client. The advantage of integration of orientations is that it provides a versatility of options within each case which is not found in any single orientation.*

*In the single matched approach, the choice of the matching is especially important. Although a reasonable case was made for brief psychodynamic therapy, several alternatives could have been equally plausible. This woman may have done well* with the support and gentle exploration of client-centered or humanistic therapy, the assertiveness practices of behavioral therapy, the confidence building of cognitive approaches, or aspects of other methods.

The authors mention that one should start with the treatment with fewer risks and less ambitious goals and then become more invasive and ambitious if the initial interventions are unsuccessful. It is a good point and possibly critical here, for it would argue against the method selected. The method as initially proposed and as actually used in the case relies on ambiguity, anxiety, frustration, and the generation of a rather prominent transference reaction, all of which are quite unsettling to the client and would have higher risks than the more supportive methods from other approaches.

Aside from the initial method selection, the case itself is presented as a brief focal psychodynamic therapy treatment by a particular practitioner and not an illustration of differential therapeutics. My remaining commentary on the case itself introduces alternative perspectives for comparisons and suggest that some of the principles that can be used in organizing eclecticism can also assist here in clarifying the case and adding versatility to the treatment approach.

Each orientation has its own ways of conceptualizing things, and one of the problems in integration is in getting competing approaches to agree on any account of the principal phenomena. What one sees as a reliable observation strikes another as unfounded interpretation, and each approach uses concepts and terminologies that are foreign to the others. I see these same sorts of problems as I try to understand what went on in this case. Although some subjectivity is inherent, it behooves us to take precautions to improve the objectivity and reliability of the clinical observations we report. Specifics are usually more reliable than generalities, and ample case transcript material allows the readers to see it for themselves. Comments that are more interpretative might be presented as possibilities rather than givens, placed alongside the viable alternatives, or backed up with supporting specifics. And some respect for our ordinary language concepts and conventions can help tune in a clearer picture.

Clarkin and Rosnick mention the importance of the therapeutic relationship, as do writers from various orientations, and a focus on the nature of the relationship established seems a good place to begin in understanding the case. The authors mention that therapist factors such as warmth, empathy, and nonjudgmental respect serve to create a therapeutic atmosphere and to establish an alliance with the client. These are usually termed nonspecific factors, in that they are common to various schools of therapy, but the choice of the term may be somewhat misleading. It is often possible to be quite specific about the sorts of interventions that contribute to these relationship factors or undermine them. We can often gauge which interventions would come across as empathic or respectful and which would not, and which interventions would appear supportive, and so cast us as allies to our clients, and which appear unsupportive or contentious, and so undermine the therapeutic alliance. Attending to the appropriate nuances, we should try to choose interventions which establish and maintain an alliance and avoid those which undermine it.

Rosnick uses the central issue of the client telling her parents to structure the treatment, and in so doing she sets the tone of the therapeutic relationship. She specifically rejects using methods that might assist the client in this difficult task, such as advice or role playing, but attempts to pressure the client simply to do it on her own. Intervention tactics such as this could easily leave someone feeling both unsupported and forced, and the client responds not too surprisingly by digging in her heels and resisting the prescription.

*The unsupportiveness and pressure are intended to create a transference reaction, which is to say to recreate in this client the same sort of attitudes and reactions toward the therapist as she has toward her own parents. The interventions are successful in doing just that: The client becomes ambivalent about her therapist but clearly mistrustful, is uncomfortable with the sessions with her, plays hooky from several of them, conceals information for fear of the consequences, and in other ways resists the therapist whenever possible. Rosnick then interprets these reactions not as situational reactions but as general characteristics of the client. Other sessions seem to continue in the same vein, with the therapist trying to force various viewpoints on the client and then interpreting her uncomfortableness and resistance to the interpretations and to the process of therapy itself.*

*A transference approach is necessarily a gambit, in that it sacrifices the immediate assets of the therapeutic alliance in the expectation of later gains from the interpretation of the transference reaction which it generates. A gambit is usually a losing game, unfortunately, for anything unplanned can foil the expected advantage so that the loss at the outset translates into a loss at the conclusion.*

*Although the importance of a working alliance is acknowledged by advocates of transference cures, the extent to which the alliance is sacrificed by the transference is too readily overlooked. In this case the attitude the therapist created by being unsupportive and controlling overshadows an alternative view of her as an ally, and therapy proceeds without the benefits of a working therapeutic alliance.*

*The point of an eclectic integration is to pull the best from competing orientations. Where the various orientations are going the same way we look for general principles that underlie the practices, and where orientations are complementary we seek ways to combine them. But where the principles in one orientation are in direct conflict with principles from other orientations, we must compare and make hard choices on what to accept and what to reject. Some orientations emphasize the alliance for the direct benefits it has for clients, whereas others see it as a condition for adequate persuasive influence by the therapist. Either way, most agree that it is important to maintain an alliance. And to do that it seems clear that we must not willfully generate negative transference, but instead might challenge and counter transference reactions when they do occur.*

*How might a therapist have drawn from a broader array of therapeutic principles in conducting this case? Several intervention objectives are suggested here as alternatives to consider.*

*It would be good to be more supportive with this client. Having been raised by parents who were apparently aloof and at times controlling, this client is nonetheless quite open to others and appreciative of the support she receives. In entering therapy, it is a reasonable guess that she was seeking support and nurturance, and she did mention that she wanted a confidante from whom she did not have to keep secrets. Although looking to others does have its risks, it is neither wrong nor inherently pathological. Some of the strongest and best adjusted people are those who have established positive bonds with friends and family, and who rely on those relationships for support and meaning in their lives. So rather than trying to break this woman of her reliance on others, one could explore with her the advantages and the pitfalls and so try to guide her toward more balanced social relationships.*

*Clients often see themselves as unacceptable and weak, and it is good to identify and credit the positives and strengths they do have and to build from there. With this client the task would be an easy one. She sees herself as fun, strong, and generally able to deal with things—a view gen-*

erally supported by her school record and her interpersonal relationships. Some of her transcript comments were insightful, and her laughter suggested an appreciation of irony and a solid sense of humor.

In several instances I felt that she deserved more benefit of the doubt than was given, and that insufficient notice was taken of situational factors in accounting for her actions. Her marriage was interpreted as a hostile and vengeful act against her parents, which seems unnecessarily pejorative and which she never quite accepted. One might portray getting married as a reasonable action under the circumstances, and her parents' contentious objections made a quiet civil wedding without them the preferred option. She herself was interpreted as unconsciously hostile, but she does not seem hostile in her comments and surely not as hostile as someone else might be in her situation. The use of more positive interpretations would be supported by perhaps the majority of therapeutic orientations.

Steps might have been taken to make suggestions and interpretations more acceptable, and thereby maintain the alliance and avoid generating resistances. In suggesting that she tell her parents, one might portray the benefits and then deal seriously with her objections, so that she can weigh gains against risks and make up her own mind. When she sees that the benefits outweigh the risks, she would be inclined to tell them on her own and would not have to be forced. Perhaps she might try talking more with her close friends about her marriage, to gain some confidence and perhaps a new angle before telling her parents.

In focusing on her marriage one could mention that anyone might have second thoughts, especially when she and her husband are separated and have had to maintain a long-distance relationship. A comment such as this is supportive and would be easily accepted. The issue from there is not whether she has ever had second thoughts, but whether she wants to make the marriage work and how to go about it. It is a relationship issue, and a relationship-oriented approach should be used in dealing with it. Situations and relationships are emphasized in behavioral and family approaches, but are too often overlooked in analytical and psychodynamic orientations.

The outcome of the treatment this woman received was mixed. Major issues remained unresolved, and the client was apparently more apprehensive later in the sessions than when she began. Some of the added turmoil was apparently an iatrogenic consequence of the treatment approach itself, which should be a matter of more concern than was given to it in the case writeup.

The client did recognize that she tends to take responsibility for others, and took steps to curtail that tendency. This could be of considerable benefit in avoiding being used and worn out in various social relationships. She was feeling better several months after therapy, which could have to do with any of a number of factors. My guess is that she was benefiting from the greater responsibility and less forced reliance on her parents which comes from being out of school and having a job.

The authors recognize that some of the intervention was controversial in its usefulness and that the outcome was not particularly impressive. We can only "guestimate" the tenacity of the problems, but it would seem that a woman with as many strengths as this one might have benefited, and perhaps quite readily, from other therapeutic methods involving support, collaboration, and guidance. One of the strengths of eclecticism is its willingness to consider alternatives, and I would have wanted to see the authors provide their own views on what might have worked out better with this case.

# CHAPTER 6

# Antonio—More Than Anxiety: A Transtheoretical Approach

## Carlo C. DiClemente

### INTRODUCTION

The proliferation of psychotherapy systems reflects the complex, interactive nature of psychotherapy, which involves the varied dimensions of client, therapist, relationship, problem, and interventions. The daily dilemma facing the clinician is what to do, when, with whom, in what way, with which problem. Both the research literature and the experience of many clinicians seem to indicate that no single system of therapy addresses adequately all these questions. The practical solution for many therapists is an amalgam of two or more favorite systems.

Integration, collaboration, and rapprochement represent the promise of eclecticism. Bringing to bear the insights and approaches of a variety of therapy systems could provide some practical answers to the questions faced by clinicians. However, only a systematic integration offers some hope of fulfilling the promise of eclecticism. What is required for a systematic eclecticism is a structure or set of principles comprehensive enough to include the critical dimensions of psychotherapy and adequately flexible to promote collaboration.

The transtheoretical approach to psychotherapy is an integrative eclectic perspective which views therapy as a process of change engaged in by the client with the assistance of therapists' interventions. The core dimensions of this approach are the processes, stages, and levels of change (Proschaska & DiClemente, 1984). From this perspective the client is helped to move through specified stages of change at one or more levels of change by engaging in specific, appropriate processes of change. Both clients' efforts at self-change as well as the various systems of psychotherapy can be viewed from this perspective.

Analysis of the 24 most popular theories of psychotherapy (Prochaska, 1984) yielded the first of the three basic elements of the transtheoretical approach—the processes of change. Transtheoretical therapy began with the assumption that integration across a diversity of therapy systems most likely could occur at an analytical level between theory and technique, the level of processes of change. Interestingly, Goldfried (1980, 1982), in his well-known call for a rapprochement, independently suggested that the principles or processes of change were the appropriate theoretical starting point at which rapprochement could begin.

The processes of change, then, represent a middle level of abstraction between a complete system of psychotherapy and the techniques proposed by the theory. Basic coping activities that the individual engages in to modify a particular problem could be categorized as representing defined processes of change. Thus, a process of change represents a type of activity that is undertaken or experienced by an individual in modifying thinking, behavior, or affect related to a particular problem. Although there are a large number of coping activities, there is a finite set of processes that could categorize these activities. In a similar manner, techniques of therapy can be analyzed to see which type of process they would engage or promote (Proschaska, 1984). Thus, confrontation by the therapist would provide new information, challenge current thinking about the problem, and offer feedback. All these therapist activities would enable the individual to engage in more accurate information processing. From our perspective these activities represent the process of change named consciousness raising. Subsequent modifications of the original formulation through research on self-change and therapist surveys yielded 10 separate and distinct processes of change (Table 1). Our studies indicate that people in the natural environment generally use these 10 different processes of change to modify problem behaviors (DiClemente & Prochaska, 1982, 1985). Most major systems of therapy, however, theoretically employ only two or three processes (Prochaska, 1984). One of the assumptions of the transtheoretical approach is that therapists should be at least as cognitively complex

TABLE 1
The Processes of Change

1. Consciousness raising
2. Self-reevaluation
3. Social reevaluation
4. Self-liberation
5. Social liberation
6. Counterconditioning
7. Stimulus control
8. Contingency management
9. Dramatic relief
10. Helping relationship

as their clients. They should be able to think in terms of a more comprehensive set of processes and be able to apply techniques to engage each process when appropriate.

A second basic element in the transtheoretical approach is the stages of change. The stages reflect the temporal and motivational aspects of change. Early in our research on the processes of change it became evident that the utilization of the processes varied according to where an individual was in the cycle of change. Therapists have often talked about clients' motivation, defenses, and readiness to change. Especially with addictive behaviors, clinicians discuss maintenance or relapse. However, theories of therapy have not proposed a sophisticated framework to deal with this phenomenon. Intentional change is not at all-or-none phenomenon but a gradual movement through specific stages of change. Lack of awareness of this staging phenomenon has contributed both to inadequate theorizing and inappropriate assumptions about the homogeneity of any group of individuals who came to therapy. Studies of various outpatient populations (McConnaughy et al., 1983; McConnaughy, 1984; DiClemente & Hughes, in preparation) have found a variety of profiles on a stages of change scale. All individuals who come to therapy are not at the same stage of change. We have been able to isolate four basic stages of change: precontemplation, contemplation, action, and maintenance. A decision-making stage between contemplation and action has been difficult to isolate. Decision-making may represent simply a mechanism for movement from contemplation to action or may ultimately be considered a separate stage of change. Figure 1 illustrates the four stages and describes some characteristics we have found about these stages.

The concept of stages is extremely important in understanding change. In the dictionary definition a stage is a "period, level, or degree in a process of development, growth, or change." In our conceptualization, a stage of change represents both a period of time as well as a set of tasks needed for movement to the next stage. Although the time an individual spends in each stage may be variable, the tasks to be accomplished in order to achieve successful movement to the next stage are invariant. In the move from precontemplation to contemplation an individual must become aware of the problem, make some admission or take ownership of the problem, confront defenses and habit aspects of the problem that make it difficult to control, and begin to see some of the negative aspects of the problem in order to accomplish the move to the next stage of seriously thinking about change.

Since the stages require that certain tasks be accomplished, it follows that certain processes of change are more important at certain stages of change. Although it may appear overly obvious at this point that the process of counterconditioning or stimulus control is inappropriate for an individual in the precontemplation or contemplation stage of change, some of our clinical and research strategies in effect have proposed just that kind of mismatch. Appropriate use of the various processes at the different stages of change represents the basic integrative framework of the transtheoretical approach.

At this point in our analysis it appears that we are discussing only how to approach a single, well-defined problem. However, as all of us realize from clinical practice and knowledge of psychopathology, reality is not so accommodating and human behavior change is not so simple a process. Although we can identify and isolate certain symptoms and syndromes, these occur in the context of complex, interrelated levels of human functioning. The third basic element of the transtheoretical approach addresses this issue. The levels of change represent a hierarchical organization of five distinct, but interrelated, levels of psychological problems that are addressed in psychotherapy. These levels are as follows:

1. Symptom/situational
2. Maladaptive cognitions
3. Current interpersonal conflicts
4. Family/systems conflicts
5. Intrapersonal conflicts.

Historically, systems of psychotherapy have primarily attributed psychological

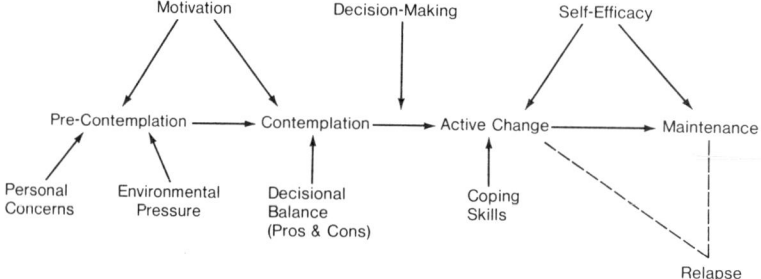

*Figure 1.* The stages of change.

focused ese lev- on the ninants; ive cog- family erapists appears change agree- ute the els they as they havior. nt that an ap- r levels o prog-

ach we symp- e tends re con- scious and contemporary level of problems and because this level often represents the primary reason for which the individual entered therapy. The further down the hierarchy we focus, the further removed from awareness are the determinants of the problem likely to be. Moreover, as we progress down the levels, the further back in history are the determinants of the problem and the more integrated the problem is with the sense of self. Thus, we predict that the more complex the level that needs to be changed, the longer and more complex therapy is likely to be and the greater the resistance of the client (Prochaska & DiClemente, 1984). In addition, these levels are not completely separated from one another. Change at any one level is likely to produce change at other levels. Symptoms often involve intrapersonal conflicts; maladaptive cognitions often reflect family/system conflicts. In the transtheoretical approach, the complete therapist is prepared to intervene at any of the five levels of change, though the preference is to begin at the highest level that clinical assessment and judgment can justify.

In summary, the transtheoretical approach sees eclectic psychotherapy as the differential application of the processes of change at the four stages of change according to the problem level being addressed. Three basic strategies can be employed in this context.

The first is a *shifting-levels* strategy. Therapy would typically focus first on the client's symptoms and the situations supporting the symptoms. If the processes could be applied effectively at the first level and the client could progress through each stage of change, therapy could be completed without shifting to a more complex level of analysis. If this approach were not effective, therapy would necessarily shift to other levels in sequence in order to achieve the desired change.

The second is the *key-level* strategy. If the available evidence points to one key level of causality of a problem and the client can be effectively engaged at that level, the therapist would work almost exclusively at this key level.

The third alternative is the *maximum-impact* strategy. With complex clinical cases, it is evident that multiple levels are involved as a cause, an effect, or a maintainer of the client's problems. In this case interventions can be created that attempt to affect clients at multiple levels of change in order to establish a maximum impact for change in a synergistic rather than a sequential manner.

## CLIENT DATA AND ASSESSMENT

Antonio is a 28-year-old Mexican-American male who is married and has a two-year-old son. He and his wife met while living in Mexico about six years ago. After completing his master's degree in engineering, Antonio was recruited by a prestigious engineering firm and came to Houston to work on oil-related projects.

He and his wife have been in Houston for five years.

In the initial phone contact, Antonio stated that he was having trouble at work with anxiety and difficulty dealing with authority. An evaluation appointment was made for the next day. When asked to list three problems that he would like to deal with in therapy, Antonio wrote the following:

1. Control anxiety
2. Become more assertive
3. Be less nervous in public situations

He began the intake session stating that he worries a lot and needs relaxation. Describing an anxiety attack yesterday, Antonio talked of being extremely anxious at a company meeting. He felt that since he was new he could not say much and that he was shy. When he returned home from work, he was anxious and worked up. He attributed some of the heightened anxiety to the fact that he had not been able to exercise at noon. In his conversation with his wife, what began as anxiety quickly turned into anger. In the discussion with his wife, he became hostile and sullen, ending the conversation with his anger.

The reference to his anger with his wife triggered a spontaneous discussion of Antonio's father. It seems that when his father came home from work, he would come in complaining and screaming. Like Antonio, his father could not express feelings in a calm manner but seemed pressured and frantic as if everything was an emergency. Relating a memory of adolescence, Antonio realized that he always felt like he was hiding and isolated. His best friend was a first cousin, but he had to conceal the friendship because their fathers were angry and fought with one another. This pattern of hiding and becoming withdrawn instead of dealing with emotional problems began early in his life.

With little probing Antonio revealed that he believed that his parents thought he was dumb or retarded. In high school he achieved good grades but was shy and worried a lot about how he looked. Sexual identity concerns were also present. Antonio thought he was gay because he was weak, so he decided to get involved in sports and tried to become more aggressive.

Interpersonally, Antonio has remained rather isolated. He has few friends and none he feels he really can talk with except for one male friend who moved. He feels the cultural differences contribute to his isolation. He is closest to his wife of 5 ½ years, yet he stated that they have had troubles and "lows" from early in their marriage. They can easily get into conflict and arguments. His angry reaction is especially strong when his wife is critical of him or compares Antonio to his father.

Antonio feels like a child with authority figures and is always looking for approval. At work when others are talking, he feels left out because he is not talking, so he will push himself to speak out to get attention. Again he related this to his father's demand for the children to be experts. It appears that at work or with others socially, Antonio experiences a great deal of anxiety and is on emergency alert all the time, scanning for insults to self-esteem or opportunities to meet what he perceives as others' expectations.

The above description is a rather unedited presentation of the basic areas covered during the intake session. Antonio appeared moderately anxious and excitable during the interview. He was open to questions and feedback and seemed eager for a solution to his dilemma of anxiety, anger, and difficulties at work. He was intelligent and appeared to have some insight into the intrapersonal and family issues related to the anxiety problem. However, the presentation was somewhat scattered and unorganized. There was somewhat of a paranoid flavor to his concerns about others watching him and his anticipation of others' expectations. Nevertheless, reality testing was intact and there were no signs of psychotic thinking. His descriptions of his anxiety attacks did not appear to meet the criteria for panic attacks but seemed more of an exacerbation of a rather constant state of high anxiety. Antonio described heart palpitations, flushing and sweating, tremulousness, and difficulty breathing. At the end of the first evaluation session, Antonio was diagnosed as an atypical anxiety disorder (DSM-III 300.00).

My impressions at the end of the first session were that Antonio is an anxious, driven person who has a great deal of anger and resentment regarding his struggle to prove himself. He seems to place a great many demands on himself and his world to be a certain way and seems to have learned this from his father. I made two suggestions at the end of the session both as interventions and as diagnostic probes to assess further the problem and coping mechanisms.

Antonio presents a rather typical problem often seen by general practitioners or in programs that focus on anxiety problems. Since I was beginning to work on this project when he arrived for therapy, I asked if he would consent to having sessions tape-recorded. He consented and agreed to have material from his therapy presented for educational purposes. This is an actual case, but details have been changed to provide anonymity. Antonio was the only client asked to participate in the project. The case is not chosen to be a particularly good example of the transtheoretical approach but rather is representative of my current therapy practice. However, in retrospect, therapy with Antonio proved to be quite a challenge to me personally and to the eclectic transtheoretical framework I was employing.

To begin with, we need to examine the problem that Antonio brings to therapy in terms of the levels of changes. At the symptomatic/situational level, Antonio complains of uncontrolled anxiety at work, which seems to spill over at home. This anxiety seems to interfere with his job performance, making him either reluctant to speak or being inappropriately aggressive or distracting. Anxiety also interferes with his ability to concentrate on the task at hand. At the level of maladaptive cognitions, it appears that Antonio makes a lot of negative self-statements and is constantly evaluating his performance. He has constant thoughts about how to impress his peers and superiors. Although it is unclear how the cognitions operate and interact, Antonio brings with him many parental messages that influence his performance, serve as self-recriminations, and increase his anxiety. There are significant and multiple problems at the symptomatic and maladaptive cognition levels.

On the interpersonal level Antonio reports problems in communication with his wife and few satisfying interpersonal relationships or friendships. Difficulties with supervisors are serious interpersonal problems since he "feels like a child with authority figures, always looking for approval." There are marked problems at this level, which relate to family/system conflicts. Although Antonio married and moved away from home, he appears to continue to have serious conflicts with his own family of origin that affect his attempts to create a nuclear family with his wife and child. Both he and his wife seem to have issues with their parents that cause conflicts in the marriage. These conflicts are only touched on briefly in the first evaluation session. However, it seems that family problems may be contributing to Antonio's anxiety. At the very least, his anxiety problems at work are causing serious problems at home.

The family/system level is not limited to current family or family of origin. Clearly, the work/employment system is conflicted. Antonio is unsure of himself at work. He has been moved to a new section and feels he needs to prove himself. It is unclear whether this is an accurate assessment or a reflection of his insecurity and anxiety. There appear to be no conflicts or problems with the legal system or Antonio's limited social network.

In an initial session it is often difficult to evaluate conflicts at the intrapersonal level. However, with Antonio there are several indications of problems at this level. He experiences rather low self-esteem and focuses on parental comments that he was dumb or retarded. Low self-esteem seems compounded by early sexual identity conflicts, which appear never to have been completely resolved. There were also traces of what could be some paranoid ideation. Table 2 illustrates the major problems at each level.

As with many clients, there are specific symptomatic complaints that bring the person to therapy. However, problems at other levels are also obvious and interrelated. Anxiety problems and lack of assertiveness coexist and interact with problems at the interpersonal, systems, and intrapersonal levels and seem closely connected to the maladaptive cognitions identified. Antonio presents a complex picture of problems at different levels of change. The first question is how and where to intervene.

Prior to intervention, I assessed the stages of change. Antonio appears to be motivated to participate in therapy. It was a big step for him to ask for help. Latin males often have difficulty turning to therapy, so his presence required a substantial amount of motivation. He appears to be in a great deal of pain. The anxiety has become quite troublesome, and Antonio has thought about his problems a great deal. He has made some connections with his familial history (being like his father) and has been thinking about coming to see a therapist for some time. The contemplation phase and the decision to take action seem to have been negotiated with regard to anxiety problems. Antonio wants to control his anxiety and seems open to take some action to achieve this. It is not clear whether Antonio is ready to take action at other levels

TABLE 2
Levels of Change Analysis for Antonio

I. Symptom/situational—Anxiety especially at work
   —General nervousness in public situations
   —Lack of assertiveness

II. Maladaptive cognitions—Obsessional worry
   —I must prove myself in every situation
   —I am dumb and retarded
   —If something goes wrong it is an emergency
   —I must meet the expectations of others

III. Interpersonal conflicts—Angry outburst at wife
   —Communication problems
   —Conflicts with supervisors and authority figures

IV. Family/systems—Issues with his father and being like his father
   —Problems with in-laws
   —Employment system problems

V. Intrapersonal conflicts—Sexual identity problems
   —Low self-esteem

of change. Although he identified problems with his wife, issues with his father, and wanting approval from his supervisors, Antonio did not appear as ready or invested in taking action at these levels. However, readiness to change at these other levels would need further assessment. Most clients are eager to change the symptomatic problems that bring them to therapy if they are not coerced to come to therapy. The true test of the client's ability and willingness to take action is in the doing.

Although the first session was devoted largely to history taking and evaluation, intervention can and often should begin during the first session. Establishing some rapport in order to increase the process of helping relationship is the first step. With Antonio rapport building began with a rather low-key approach to the initial interview. Since he was anxious and pressured to tell me all his problems and make me understand, a calm and not overly nonintrusive or authoritative position was taken. In my initial assessment, I felt it was important to make some concrete interventions around the anxiety problem. During the interview it seemed that Antonio was overusing the processes of self-liberation and self-reevaluation to control the work situation. He was constantly evaluating himself and his performance. This led to a constant questioning of himself and increased anxiety. He was committed to making sure he was noticed by superiors. This commitment to take action, in actuality, often backfired and created more anxiety. In addition his self-statements about needing to take action and how others viewed him were creating a positively accelerating curve to his anxiety, which quickly escalated beyond his control.

Antonio was given two homework exercises to do during the week before his next appointment. The first was geared to alleviating some problems at home, helping him gain some control and creating some space for Antonio to relax. He was told to give himself 15 to 30 minutes when he comes home from work to worry about the day and what he did wrong. He should find a quiet place and advise his wife that he needed this time. However, when the time allotted was over, Antonio was to shut out all worry and tell himself that he already had taken care of the worrying. This technique would engage the stimulus control process. A second suggestion was concerned more directly with work. During the day whenever Antonio noticed that his mind was racing or he was obsessing, he was told to tell himself to calm down, to take it easy. Antonio was given some deep-breathing and tensing-relaxing instructions to help him calm down. This counterconditioning intervention was geared to slowing or stopping the emergency reactions that Antonio experienced. A pause and some deep breathing as well as more constructive self-statements could be helpful at least as interference and actually create greater control over the anxiety. The initial intervention also served as a test to see whether he would be able to take appropriate action at the symptomatic level which would represent the use of the self-liberation process.

## THE COURSE OF THERAPY

Therapy with Antonio and his various problems consisted of 13 regularly scheduled sessions over a five-to-six-month period. There was no formal termination since Antonio wanted the option of returning to therapy on an as-needed basis after canceling the fourteenth session. After six weeks, the therapist reinitiated contact with Antonio and asked him to come in for one or two evaluation sessions for the purpose of getting his feedback on the therapy experience. He readily agreed and eagerly attended. It should be noted that for the regularly scheduled sessions Antonio was being charged $75 an hour.

However, several later sessions were charged at $50 for 45 minutes because he was very concerned about finances. The final evaluation sessions were not charged since they were initiated by the therapist. Antonio seemed to feel honored and special to be asked to return to give feedback, and he was eager to discuss his problems further.

It is entirely possible and even likely that Antonio would have contacted the therapist again. In fact, the posttherapy evaluation extended to three sessions since there were some serious environmental crises at the time and the therapist felt a commitment to see Antonio through these as well as obtain additional information about the course of therapy. At the time of this writing, the three evaluation sessions have been completed for two weeks and Antonio's wife has called to make an appointment to see the therapist.

Antonio's wife's request for a session was not a new occurrence in the therapy. The 13 regular sessions of therapy consisted of eight individual sessions with Antonio, three conjoint sessions with Antonio and his wife, one individual session with Antonio's wife, and one family-of-origin session, which included Antonio's wife and her mother. This description of the types of sessions may be confusing to the reader and gets ahead of our story.

## THE THERAPY SESSIONS

The initial intake and evaluation session has been described in great detail above. What follows is a description of each of the subsequent 13 sessions with a discussion of what went on from the therapist's perspective. An evaluation of the therapy from the client's perspective will follow this presentation.

The second session was an individual session with Antonio approximately one week after the intake session. Two critical incidents were immediately brought up by Antonio at this time. While away on a business trip not far from the city, Antonio became lonely and asked his wife to come up to stay and be with him in the evenings since it would not cost any more for her to be with him and she could use a break in her routine. However, when she arrived, Antonio was uneasy. He tried to conceal his wife's presence from a colleague out of anxiety about what the colleague would think and what he might say back at the office. He worried and obsessed about this the whole time Ann, his wife, was there and effectively negated much of the comfort she would provide.

The second incident had more to do with his desire to achieve and prove himself. In order to help control his anxiety about achieving and his depression about his work situation, Antonio had enrolled in an MBA program and was trying to take two courses a semester. During the week he took an examination in one of his courses and felt he did poorly. He reported that he spent a great deal of time thinking about his mistakes on the examination. This led to a lengthy discussion of criticism. Antonio tends to criticize himself in order to anticipate and avoid the criticism of others. He stated that he "used to think of himself as being something special" and that often or rather almost always his achievements fall short of these fantasies of specialness. So he tries to build his confidence all the time trying to achieve and impress. If he did not do this, he felt that he would be very depressed and feel bad about himself. The fantasy of greatness, the self-criticism, and his unwillingness to let others see any vulnerability or weakness appear to be central or core beliefs and self-statements that direct most of Antonio's actions.

The intervention for this session focused on the maladaptive cognitions. Since Antonio reported using both the strategies suggested after the first session and that he felt more relaxed overall despite the problems he discussed in this session, additional interventions were suggested for the next week. During the session Antonio's avoidance of criticism was compared to being phobic—elevator phobic. So he was advised to use a desensitization procedure with criticism as is often done with people who are afraid to get on an elevator. He should approach criticism carefully and slowly but approach rather than avoid. Maybe he could solicit feedback about some minor incident he was concerned about. Second, he was advised to allow himself to be depressed if he felt this and that it was appropriate to be depressed if he was disappointed. Finally, he was again encouraged to worry for a specified time after returning home from work. Antonio was also given the Millon Clinical Multiaxial Inventory (MCMI) to take home with him and complete. The MCMI was used to get some sense of both symptomatic complaints and personality dimensions in relation to other clinical populations.

The third session followed a week later. Antonio called prior to the session asking if his wife could come to the session since they were having numerous conflicts that were upsetting them both. The anxiety Antonio experiences at work seems to create additional pressure on the marital relationship, which has been problematic in its own right. When Antonio returns from work, he looks around at the small condominium they live in and he gets frustrated. He complains that there is little room for the couple and their son and that he has no place to relax. This seems to get translated into his being a failure and working for nothing. Often he takes his frustration out on Ann, blaming her for little things that go wrong around the house, accusing her of not paying attention to him and, at times, being jealous of the attention she gives to their son.

Currently, Antonio has become preoccupied with selling the condominium and buying some land around a lake north of town. He has some idea about building a home or buying one already constructed.

As he talked about the new home, he fantasized about how wonderful the move would be for his son and seemed to see getting rid of the condominium as the solution of all his problems. When challenged about why he was so preoccupied and had to have it right now, Antonio responded: "Oh, I'm just desperate—I mean that's my personality. I always like to get things done now."

Ann agreed with Antonio that the space problem was an important one but resisted seeing it as the solution to their problems. She complained of their communication and that Antonio was demanding, pouting, and difficult to talk with. She felt he needed to be right and would put her down in their conversations. She has a lot of resentments from their past arguments and complained that Antonio projected blame on her when things were not going well. Antonio was visibly uncomfortable while his wife described her feelings and several times interrupted her trying to justify what he was doing. However, he also seemed able to agree with her and laugh at himself at times.

The couple were able to talk about their families of origin openly and with more agreement. Ann had a very domineering mother but also saw her father as an authority and in charge of the family. Although they did not discuss it in detail, both Antonio and Ann referred to some sexual abuse on the part of Ann's father that both realized had an impact on their relationship. Antonio does not like Ann's parents. He is angry at her father because of the abuse and at her mother because she is intimidating and bossy. Moreover, her family visits them often, imposing on the couple for weeks at a time. Both feel helpless or unwilling to limit this behavior. These visits make the already cramped condominium feel intolerable. Antonio discussed his domineering father, and both Antonio and Ann agreed that he kept a greater distance from his family.

The couple was encouraged to explore how their families of origin were affecting their current communication patterns. They were asked to discuss how they wanted to set up their own family rules and how these would follow or deviate from their respective families of origin. Both of them appeared to have genuine feelings of concern for one another and for their child, who was brought to the session. They were encouraged to find ways to support one another in the difficult times and the conflicts rather than argue. Both seemed to want understanding at the same time, which created the conflict. Ways of taking turns or recognizing who was most upset were discussed.

*Discussion*

It becomes even clearer from the first three sessions that Antonio presents more than a case of anxiety. As previously noted, there are problems at many levels. Antonio follows the suggestions of the first session. He appears to be genuinely invested in taking action and relieving his anxiety. The suggestions to calm himself down and set aside time for worry seemed to have helped lower his anxiety level at work and at home. However, it becomes clear during the second session that his self-esteem is very weak and threatened by any criticism. Apparently, Antonio compensates for this low self-esteem by fantasies of specialness and avoiding criticism.

Although I typically do not employ standard psychological testing in therapy, I have found that the MCMI can be helpful for exploring intrapersonal conflicts and personality patterns as well as giving information that would help assess the interpersonal and symptomatic problems. Antonio took the MCMI home to complete and returned it at the second session. His obsessional manner was readily apparent as he returned the test. He expressed concern about one of his answers and wanted to change it after reviewing it in the waiting room. The profile of score on the MCMI is included in Table 3.

The MCMI profile was helpful in identifying some personality dimensions that were not completely apparent in the first two interviews. The clinical syndrome subscales confirm the presence of anxiety and dysphoria. On the personality scales Antonio endorsed a high level of avoidant, passive-aggressive, and schizoid personality traits. The description of the personality patterns in the report that accompanied the profile seemed to accurately capture certain aspects of Antonio's style.

The behavior of this man is characterized by a pervasive apprehensiveness and the expectancy that people will be rejecting and disparaging. Despite a long-suppressed desire to relate and be accepted by others, he feels it is best to maintain a safe distance. Recurrent anxieties and a pervasive mood disharmony typify his emotional life. A surface apathy may be exhibited in his effort to damp-down or conceal his excess sensitivity. Behind this front of restraint are intense contrary feelings that occasionally break through in the form of angry resentment toward those who he feels have been critical and disapproving. The peace and security that he needs, however, are threatened when these resentments are expressed. To constrain his anger and thereby protect against further rejection, he attempts, albeit unsuccessfully, to conceal these oppositional urges.

It is most notable that this man will frequently display an edgy irritability and negativism. Innumerable wrangles and disappointments with others occur as he will vacillate among being agreeable, sullenly passive, and explosively angry. These moods are frequently interspersed with expressions of guilt and contrition. He feels misunderstood, unappreciated, and demeaned by others and is characteristically pessimistic and disillusioned about life. His resulting low self-esteem is further compounded by his tendency toward extreme introspection and self-derogation. The alienation that he feels from others is paralleled by a feeling of alienation from himself. Of course, he hesitates to express this self-contempt publicly, lest it invite a chorus of further derision from others.

Not only is he hypersensitive and apprehensively ill at ease, but, in addition, he experiences a constant and confusing undercurrent of tension, sadness, and anger. Moreover, he frequently turns against himself, feeling remorseful and self-condemnatory. Vacillation is exhibited among his desires for acceptance, his fears, and a general almost numbness of feeling.

TABLE 3
Millon Clinical Multiaxial Inventory for Antonio

```
NAME =                          VALID REPORT  WT. FAC. = -3  27-MAR-85
CODE = 8 2 **1 * 6 4 + 3 5 7 " - //- //- **D A * //- //
                                                                680 0091
**********************************************************************
   SCALES        * SCORE *         PROFILE OF BR SCORES      * DSM-III (MILLON)
                 *RAW  BR*    35    60      75      85    100  PARALLELS
******************------+---+---+----------+---------+---------+*****************
            [1 [ 18[ 82[XXXXXXXXXXXXXXXXXXXXXXXXXX            | SCHIZOID (ASOCIAL)
            +--+---+---+------+---+----------+---------+---------+-----------------
            [2 [ 23[ 94[XXXXXXXXXXXXXXXXXXXXXXXXXXXXXXXX      | AVOIDANT
            +--+---+---+------+---+----------+---------+---------+-----------------
    BASIC   [3 [ 11[ 47[XXXXXXX    |         |         |       | DEPENDENT (SUBMIS)
            +--+---+---+------+---+----------+---------+---------+-----------------
  PERSNLTY  [4 [ 14[ 61[XXXXXXXXXX |         |         |       | HISTRONIC (GREGAR)
            +--+---+---+------+---+----------+---------+---------+-----------------
   PATTERN  [5 [ 17[ 42[XXXXXXX    |         |         |       | NARCISSISTIC
            +--+---+---+------+---+----------+---------+---------+-----------------
            [6 [ 18[ 73[XXXXXXXXXXXXXXXXX    |         |       | ANTISOCIAL (AGGRS)
            +--+---+---+------+---+----------+---------+---------+-----------------
            [7 [ 19[ 37[XXXXXX     |         |         |       | COMPULSIVE (CONFO)
            +--+---+---+------+---+----------+---------+---------+-----------------
            [8 [ 21[ 96[XXXXXXXXXXXXXXXXXXXXXXXXXXXXXXXXXXXX  | P.AGGRESS (NEGAT)
  ********+**+***+***+-------+---+----------+---------+---------+*****************
  PATHLGCL [S [ 23[ 68[XXXXXXXXXXXXXXX       |         |       | SCHIZOTYPAL (SCHIZ)
            +--+---+---+------+---+----------+---------+---------+-----------------
  PERSNLTY [C [ 17[ 54[XXXXXXXXX|           |         |       | BORDERLINE (CYCL)
            +--+---+---+------+---+----------+---------+---------+-----------------
  DISORDER [P [ 13[ 52[XXXXXXXX  |           |         |       | PARANOID
  *********+**+***+***+-------+---+----------+---------+---------+*****************
            [A [ 13[ 76[XXXXXXXXXXXXXXXXXXXX |         |       | ANXIETY
            +--+---+---+------+---+----------+---------+---------+-----------------
            [H [ 19[ 64[XXXXXXXXXXXX         |         |       | SOMATOFORM
            +--+---+---+------+---+----------+---------+---------+-----------------
            [N [ 24[ 65[XXXXXXXXXXXXX        |         |       | HYPOMANIA
            +--+---+---+------+---+----------+---------+---------+-----------------
  CLINICAL [D [ 15[ 78[XXXXXXXXXXXXXXXXXXXXXX|         |       | DYSTHYMIA
            +--+---+---+------+---+----------+---------+---------+-----------------
  SYNDROME [B [  9[ 52[XXXXXXXX   |          |         |       | ALCOHOL ABUSE
            +--+---+---+------+---+----------+---------+---------+-----------------
            [T [ 16[ 61[XXXXXXXXXX |          |         |       | DRUG ABUSE
            +--+---+---+------+---+----------+---------+---------+-----------------
            [SS[ 15[ 68[XXXXXXXXXXXXXX       |         |       | PSYCHOTIC THINK.
            +--+---+---+------+---+----------+---------+---------+-----------------
            [CC[ 13[ 64[XXXXXXXXXXXX         |         |       | PSYCHOT. DEPRESS.
            +--+---+---+------+---+----------+---------+---------+-----------------
            [PP[  5[ 54[XXXXXXXX| |          |         |       | PSYCHOT. DELUSION
```

He has learned to be on guard against anticipated ridicule and contempt. Detecting the most minute traces of annoyance expressed by others, he makes the molehill of a minor slight into a mountain of personal derision and condemnation. Moreover, he has learned that good things do not last and that support and friendship end with disappointment and rejection. Anticipating disillusionment, he often jumps the gun with impulsive hostility. A cyclical variation may be observed in his behaviors as constraint is followed by angry outbursts, which are followed in turn by remorse and regret. These erratic emotions are not only intrinsically distressing, but upset his capacity to cope effectively with his everyday life.

The MCMI confirmed the presence of serious problems at the inter- and intrapersonal levels. With such a character makeup, how much change can we expect from Antonio? Clearly, in any brief intervention we are not going to change his personality style. My approach was to continue to offer interventions at the symptomatic and maladaptive cognitions levels. Even with problems at the intrapersonal level, individuals can modify behaviors that create problems without first changing their character structure. Antonio is actually a good example of this. He is gaining some relief and carrying out the exercises despite his passive-aggressive and negativistic style. However, we must keep in mind the problems at the intrapersonal level since they can impact the therapy process at any time.

The eclectic nature of the transtheoretical approach includes the possibility of more than one modality of treatment as well as multiple levels of problems. Since much of Antonio's work anxiety seems to be played out at home, the couple's session was seen as an appropriate way to assess problems at this level, relieve some pressure, and get a perspective on Antonio's interactions with others. Moreover, it might be possible to get more positive interaction and support at home, which could alleviate some of Antonio's anxiety and depression.

With the transtheoretical approach we generally begin with a shifting or key-level intervention strategy. In this case I have identified several key levels and during the first two sessions focus on the symptom/situational and the maladaptive cognitions levels. In the third session the therapy shifts to the interpersonal level and an assessment of the involvement of family system conflicts.

Both Antonio and his spouse seem to be at the contemplation stage of change with respect to interpersonal and family system problems. Both consciousness raising and self-reevaluation processes are encouraged to assist them in exploring their problems and deciding whether and how to take action. The helping relationship on the part of the spouses as well as the therapist is also utilized.

## THERAPY SESSIONS

In the fourth through the seventh sessions Antonio was seen individually, and the focus returned to his anxiety and depression on the job. These sessions would prove to be the most sustained period of therapy for Antonio alone. Antonio described his new supervisor as pushy and somewhat of a dictator. This behavior was intimidating to Antonio, and he expressed feelings of anger and rebelliousness. Once again Antonio returned to a discussion of his relationship with his father. Antonio felt that his father was angry with him and constantly pushed him away from his mother challenging him to become a man.

By the fifth session Antonio reported that he was feeling calmer and was able to stay on task at work. My suggestion during the previous session to be quiet and not try so hard to impress his supervisor and fellow workers seemed to work well. He discovered that if he was quiet, others came to him and asked him questions.

This was a marked change from his efforts to anticipate and impress others.

During these sessions Antonio also focused on his sensitivity about being a man. He felt that he was too sensitive and gentle and that these qualities were not accepted in his home. Both his father and his brother seemed to make fun of him about his lack of sexual prowess and his sensitivity. As a result, Antonio was very self-conscious. He did not date till he was 17 or 18 years old and saw his "gentleness" as a sign of homosexuality. However, he could get angry and assertive with his father. He related an incident when his father became violent with his mother and actually had a gun threatening his mother. Antonio intervened and took the gun away. This incident was used to help him reevaluate his assessment of himself as being weak.

Once again Antonio talked about his concerns about being stupid or looking foolish. His self-esteem appears to be very conditional. If he actually lives up to his "shoulds" and does a task "right," he is all right. However if he sees himself as falling short, he becomes extremely self-critical. Thus, every task becomes a test, and Antonio is always rather anxious.

A particular interchange during one of the sessions illustrates well the pattern and the therapist's efforts to challenge his thinking.

P: The problem is that I feel I am lazy. If I don't push myself, I just won't do it. Like two days ago I wrote a memo that I was working on for two weeks. I kept saying this is not good. You know it. This is not good. But when I did it, it came out perfect. But a lot of times I have to put that pressure on myself. Otherwise I am just going to relax. That's how I turned out to be a good student at the University. I had to learn. I had to put pressure on myself. Actually, probably the pressure comes from Dad. But I'm glad there is some pressure there.

T: Well, yeah, you wouldn't do it if it didn't work. See, some pressure works. But the fanatical way you put pressure on and, I do think it is fanatical, at times, is because you basically believe that you are lazy. How in the hell can a lazy guy accomplish the things that you have accomplished? I don't understand it.

P: Yeah, but again, I push myself.

T: Okay, so that is what your belief system is. Your belief is that I really got a lazy guy here. If I don't keep pushing him all the time, he is going to go to sleep. He is going to sit there with a big sombrero on his head and he's going to tilt the sombrero down and fall asleep. Like the old stereotype of the Mexican sitting in the village, just kind of sitting there saying, Mañana, mañana."

P: I am like that I think. I mean that is the way I was, I would just go home and sit in front of the TV instead of getting going and doing the yard work. My Dad pushed me. I think that I learned that was the only way.

During these sessions, Antonio was encouraged to be easier on himself and to challenge the "shoulds" that he uses to make demands on himself. He was encouraged to see that it was acceptable not to be perfect and that all men had areas of sensitivity and vulnerability. Normalizing some of his fears appeared to bring him some relief from his anxiety.

*Discussion*

During these sessions the focus of therapy shifted from his anxiety on the job to cognitive self-statements related to his family of origin. He continued to take action regarding his behavior on the job, and these actions seemed to increase his ability to concentrate as well as his productivity. In turn, he began to get more appropriate attention, which was rewarding. At the same time Antonio was able to develop greater insight into problems at the family systems level and to shift some self-statements at the cognition level that related to his family system. Self-reevaluation, social reevaluation, stimulus control and reinforcement management processes all appear to be actively engaged in these sessions.

**THERAPY SESSIONS**

In the eighth session Ann came in alone to discuss her relationship with her family. Both she and Antonio felt that he had made progress and was less anxious. At this point she felt that she needed to get some help with her anger at her father and her feelings that she could not trust men. Ann described her role in the family as "miss-in-between." She felt that her mother betrayed her since Ann had told her mother some of what her father did but her mother played it down and did not take any action. These negative feelings about her parents were accompanied by an intense loyalty to the family, which created ambivalence and conflict for her. These issues were more salient at present because her mother was coming to visit soon. Ann feels that her mother takes over when she comes to visit, and they inevitably get into conflicts. Antonio becomes distant when Ann's mother is around, and Ann often feels pulled between the two.

In the session with Ann, she was encouraged to express her feelings about the sexual abuse. She had discussed this with Antonio, but she had been reluctant to fully express her feelings because he became so upset with her father. Ann was the most rebellious and openly angry of the three sisters. She felt that they had somehow denied the impact of their experiences, and she felt different and more disturbed by the abuse. A discussion of how incest and sexual abuse were being acknowledged more by many women and that her anger and other feelings were justified seemed to provide Ann a great deal of comfort.

The next two sessions were conjoint and focused on Ann's mother's visit. Mother's visits often heightened the conflict between Antonio and Ann. We discussed many of the family system issues and explored strategies for the couple to set boundaries, to pull together, and to support one another as mother arrived. After 10 days of visiting by her mother and grandparents and a good deal of conflict, Ann got up enough courage to ask them to move to a boarding house while they awaited some medical test results on her grandfather. Even before she took this action, however, both Antonio and Ann agreed that they were doing better as a couple since our sessions together and were being more supportive of one another. Although they did feel some guilt about the stand they took with her family, they were united and not engaging in blaming one another. Antonio was able to be sympathetic while giving Ann enough space to handle her mother without a lot of interference.

*Discussion*

Clearly the focus has shifted to problems that Ann is having with her family. Since these problems are connected to the anxiety and depression presented by Antonio and create problems for the couple's relationship, a shift to working at the family systems level could be considered still a part of Antonio's therapy. However, we are also beginning to get into Ann's individual issues, which could be considered a separate therapy. The return to couples sessions after the individual session seems to put the session back into the context of the individual and couples therapy that preceded it.

The couple was responsive to contemplation strategies of consciousness raising and self-reevaluation. The transactional analysis construct of parent-adult-child and the interactions between people from these ego states were used to give the couple a framework with which to deal with interactions between each other and with her mother. This information seemed to assist the couple to discuss how they hooked each other at parental or child levels and how they responded to the demanding maternal parent figure. They seemed to appreciate the value of adult-to-adult interactions and were able to identify these patterns in their communications within the session and after they went home.

The contemplation activity helped them to make a decision to take action about her mother's stay with them. They made a commitment to set limits and were told about reinforcement management principles. If they continued to accede to mother's demands, they were actually encouraging her to interfere in their lives. They planned the action of asking her to move to a boarding house during the session but did not set a time to implement the plan. Several days after the second session Ann called to report that she had told her mother that she would have to move to a boarding house nearby because of the cramped conditions. Reluctantly, her mother agreed to move. Ann wavered several times in the process of moving, but she and Antonio supported one another (helping relationship) and reinforced one another through the difficult move. The couple moved to action together and struggled to sustain this change in dealing with her mother. The work at the family system level certainly made an impact on other levels. Interactions between the couple improved, and each was feeling more in charge of their lives. For Antonio, he felt that Ann was really putting him and their family first and was much less anxious around her mother. The presenting symptomatic problem of anxiety on the job recedes into the background, first because there was significant improvement and second because the family system issues were triggered by the mother's visit. Environmental events often change the course of therapy. In some therapy systems this would be seen as a distraction. However, Antonio clearly was not using this as a diversion tactic. Ann's mother's visit posed serious problems for him, and both he and his wife were open to take action at the systems level.

At this point it is interesting to note that significant action has been taken at almost all the levels of change. Symptomatically, Antonio is more in control of his anxiety and work situation. Self-statements have been shifted somewhat. Interpersonal communications between the spouses has begun to be modified and the issue of boundaries addressed at the family system level. Although the impact at the intrapersonal level is minimal because these are long-standing types of conflicts, Antonio does appear to be feeling better about himself with a slight increase in self-esteem. However, maintenance of many of these changes continues to be questionable. The hope is that the changes at the various levels would be self-reinforcing for Antonio. In light of the intrapersonal conflicts, these changes may not be able to be sustained.

## THERAPY SESSIONS

The next session expanded even more the family-of-origin work begun with Ann. It seems that the request for her mother to move into the boarding house triggered a frank discussion of the mother-daughter relationship. Ann revealed to her mother the full extent of the sexual abuse to her and her sisters by their father. Ann's mother became upset and did not know what to do. Ann requested a session with her and her mother.

Ann's mother was upset and frantic that others in their hometown would find out about the abuse. Although she still tended to minimize and justify her own actions, stating she talked to Ann's father about the problem and was reassured that it would never happen again, Ann's mother seemed to have absorbed some of the enormity of the impact this had on Ann. On the other hand, Ann seemed to have expressed her anger and was feeling on better terms with her mother. The possibility of divorce was raised by Ann's mother, but after a short discussion it was clear that she did not want to do this. Since the mother had been experienced as rather intrusive in Ann's life and even during the session appeared controlling, the mother was encouraged to take care of herself. In a paradoxical manner I explained that she had been giving and had focused for too long on husband and daughters and that she needed to really take care of herself and get involved in activities for herself. At the end of the session it was still unclear how the mother was going to handle any confrontation with Ann's father. However, both she and Ann appeared to be more relaxed and able to discuss their feelings more openly. Ann stated that she did not necessarily want her mother to divorce her father but that was an issue her mother would have to decide for herself. During the session Ann handled boundary issues well and was rather successful in extricating herself from being "miss-in-between."

The two final therapy sessions prior to the evaluation visits returned to an individual format with Antonio alone. The first occurred about three weeks after the session with Ann and her mother and the second session about one month following. Several phone calls and a canceled session also occurred during this two-month period. Antonio gave several reasons for the more infrequent sessions. First, he felt he was doing better at work and that he and Ann were getting along. Then, there was his concern about money and the expense of the therapy. Finally, he wanted to try to do things more on his own.

The first of the final two sessions was rather upbeat. Antonio reported on his progress and lack thereof in different areas. He was learning a lot about himself in his interactions at work. He realized he still has a tendency to go to his boss for problem solving that he should be doing. He again talked of how he turns his bosses into father figures who are critical of him. With my help, this time he realized that his father never offered any constructive alternatives so he either guesses at what would get approval or tries to get others to tell him what to do. Antonio also reported that he and Ann were trying to be more social. Ann's mother returned home, and the situation with her family seems calmer.

Since he was feeling better, Antonio suggested that he see me on a more infrequent basis, and an appointment was scheduled for three weeks later, which was canceled. Approximately one week later Antonio requested an appointment because of a crisis at work. He received a letter from management stating that his performance was not up to par and that he was being put on probation for the next two months and would be reevaluated at that time to decide whether to continue employment. It seemed clear that this was a not-so-gentle way to give him the message that he should look for other employment and resign rather than be fired.

Antonio was anxious about the news and rather confused about what to do. However, he was not falling apart. He had made some inquiries about other jobs and had been thinking about whether to resign right away or stay as long as he could. Because of his concerns about the family and the recession job market, he decided to stick it out and try to fulfill the expectations of probation while seriously looking for alternative employment in his field or some related field. Since he chose this option, we did some problem solving around how he could get the supervisors to be specific about what he needs to do, keeping a weekly log of his activities and clarifying options of severance pay and insurance coverage if he left at different times during the probation period or if he was dismissed.

Concerns about money became even more predominant, and Antonio did not want to continue therapy on any regular basis. He was advised that he could call and consult with me by phone and could schedule a session when he really needed one.

With the exception of one phone call, there was no further contact with Antonio or Ann for about six or seven weeks at which time I called him offering a couple of evaluation visits to get feedback on how the therapy went. He eagerly agreed to come in when I told him there would be no charge for these sessions and that we could talk about his plans.

*Discussion*

After a period of rather regular sessions with shifting problem levels, the therapy slowed dramatically and ended on an as-needed consultation basis. It was certainly not a planned spaced termination as I am want to do with my clients to ensure maintenance of behavior change. Antonio seemed to want to do things on his own and both reported and appeared to be doing better. Possibly I should have recognized this earlier and developed a termination plan. However, I believed that he needed to continue to work at the various levels of change to maintain his progress. The issues with his father and his own identity and role as a man also were unresolved. Antonio could verbalize a great deal about his father, but affective expression was notably absent and he was having difficulty changing his way of relating to supervisors. The lack of affective connections would continue to make change difficult from my perspective. Thus I was more invested in seeing him continue than he was.

In retrospect, I believe several things were happening. Significant changes had occurred, and Antonio no longer was in crisis or severe pain. As often happens, motivation to change other problem areas, especially intrapersonal level conflicts, is not as great once the symptomatic problems are relieved. This is not necessarily either bad or good. Intrapersonal changes will probably occur slowly and often will be a by-product of changes at other levels. However, intrapersonal conflict can be problematic for successful long-term change at other levels. The task of the therapist is to engage the client at least in making a decision about whether or not to work at other levels. Frankly, I saw Antonio as really backing off and unwilling to challenge basic personality patterns. Moreover, the patterns were also operating in the therapy. Once he had received help over the crisis, Antonio became more reserved as would be expected from his avoidant personality characteristics. Thus, he was more comfortable with a consultant role where he could define the limits of our relationship. It was very difficult to engage Antonio in a more intensive and extensive therapy experience.

## EVALUATION AND OUTCOME

The case presented here is neither usual nor uncommon. The twists and turns of the therapy across the levels of change with a mixture of modalities are eclectic in both substance and intervention. The pattern of the therapy was dictated largely by the events and initiatives of the client. However, the therapist set the stage by allowing the process and the problems a rather ecumenical scope and encouraging the client to explore the various problem levels.

In the case of Antonio it was apparent early in treatment that the presenting problem was more than a symptomatic case of anxiety. In fact, few clients present with simply symptomatic anxiety. The involvement of other levels of conflict and problems in Antonio's case, however, is quite extensive. Nevertheless, the anxiety problems were not viewed as simply the ticket for entry into therapy to deal with other issues nor the sole issue to be addressed. Anxiety and the obsessive, ruminative, and dysphoric cognitions that both accompany and instigate the anxiety became the central focus of the initial therapy sessions and, for the most part, remained the key levels of intervention. The conflicts at the interpersonal, family/employment systems, and intrapersonal levels were assessed and periodically addressed throughout the therapy. Therapists with different orientations could have chosen to concentrate at each of these levels primarily or exclusively. However, in my estimation, it was at the symptomatic and cognition level that I had the most leverage for change.

The stages of change provided some of the rationale for the choice of levels. At the intrapersonal level Antonio had developed a rather stable defensive style. His fear and ambivalence about dependency made it difficult for him to engage in the intensive, long-term therapy that would be necessary to address the characterological issues adequately. However, he did appear to engage in contemplation and action processes with respect to the anxiety problems at work and at home. Although his desire to quickly solve problems would work against a more extensive therapy, he could be engaged with some cognitive–behavioral action techniques. In fact, both Antonio and Ann were eager and amenable to follow some of the suggestions given by the therapist. Even Ann's mother, who was quite reluctant to take any action with respect to her marriage in light of her husband's sexual abuse of their daughters, was open to some consideration of the issues and a discussion of alternatives.

During the therapy there was significant movement from precontemplation to contemplation and from contemplation to action. The critical issue is whether Antonio and Ann will be able to maintain changes that they made. Will Antonio be able to sustain his more productive work behaviors and attitudes and the initial shifts in his self-statements? This is quite difficult to predict. Relapse is a real danger for them. Since many of Antonio's attitudes and behaviors are related to the rather ingrained, problematic character difficulties, one can imagine that he would find it very difficult to sustain change. On the other hand, he was able to maintain some gains over the six months of therapy even though he experienced severe stress and often slipped back in former ways of thinking and behaving. During many of the sessions Antonio was reminded of the changes he made and the difficulty of sustaining these changes in an effort to both reinforce them and reactivate his commitment to continue to take action.

As is often the case, much of the work of therapy is accomplished outside the therapy sessions. In fact, during the evaluation sessions Antonio gave as a rationale for not coming in too often the following: "I think it is good to keep distance between sessions because I had a chance to experiment more with some of the things I learned in the session." He seemed to use the therapist as a consultant or coach to teach skills and suggest strategies that could be employed. This strategy is quite compatible with the transtheoretical approach to therapy. Self-change and therapy-assisted change are complementary not competitive.

Was the therapy a success? If we measure success by the elimination of anxiety problems or a significant shift in character style, then therapy could be considered a partial success or a failure. During the first evaluation session Antonio reported that the anxiety problems were still "pretty bad" and that he still gets "very nervous when the supervisor comes by and asks him for something." He also reported that he and his wife were still having problems and conflicts. It must be kept in mind that at this time he was on probation at work. He was actively searching for a new job and was feeling pressured by his wife to return to Mexico to be closer to family. However, Antonio was able to see that he has profited some from therapy:

P: I am telling you that I am concerned about when I will be able to solve this [anxiety and other difficulties], but it is not like before. Before I would have concern that I would really drive myself crazy. I have to solve it. I have to solve it. It is not that way any more. It's better. Maybe I want to solve too much. . . . The problem is I am asking for a quick solution, maybe it takes time. I put a lot of pressure on myself.

In the therapy Antonio has been able to recognize his expectations and the role they play for him both in his therapy and in his life. He was also able to express his disappointment in the therapy as well as his achievements.

P: Maybe I expected more. I thought that after five or six sessions I would be cured or I would be able to handle anxiety a lot better. Again I might be asking for too much like I am asking about myself. . . . There is a lot I have been able to get out of it. I think my adult is maybe a little bit bigger and stronger than before. I have grown in that area. I don't think that last year I would have been able to go through this [probation] the way I was. No way, Carlo, no way. Cause I would not have been able to segregate my Dad from my own, from myself. I would not have been able to segregate the fact that I am on proba-

tion because I did a poorer job last year with the fact that maybe you are a failure. I would not have been able to segregate those two.

The therapy has helped Antonio to cope with stress and be more realistic about himself and his behaviors but clearly fell short of his expectations.

Antonio was also able to see some changes in his relationship with his supervisors. Although he was still scared, he was able to modulate that fear somewhat. He also reported a phone conversation with his father where Antonio noted that his Dad was "a lot more respectful, he was treating me more like a man." The issue of his confusion and conflicted feelings related to seeing his supervisors as father figures was a central focus of therapy that did seem to have an impact. As Antonio puts it:

P: I don't know if it was facing the supervisor that allowed me to face my Dad or facing my Dad that allowed me to face my supervisor. It was funny.

In two of the evaluation sessions Antonio was asked about his reluctance and ambivalence to engage in the therapy. When asked why he stopped coming to therapy, he responded:

P: I stopped coming partly because of finances, I thought it was better to save money. Also because of confusion. I said if I go to Carlo now [after probation] I might not agree with certain things you might tell me and I would have that extra pressure saying, "Well, Carlo told me to do this and I don't agree with it," so I said maybe I should go and do it myself.

At another point when he was asked about the increasing distance between sessions in the latter half of the therapy, Antonio was able to go into more detail about how the therapy process threatened him.

P: I felt like I was depending too much on you. It's not going to help me. It was better to come now and then and get some feedback, some ideas from you but not to come all the time.... I don't know ... I felt confused, perhaps down on myself ... perhaps the criticism I would get from you, maybe positive, but I would internalize it and that would make me feel down perhaps ... like saying I can handle some of these problems myself. I don't need to be seeing Carlo all the time.

Although there was a great deal of ambivalence about the therapy, Antonio was able to maintain some shifts in his thinking that he learned in therapy. The consciousness raising and self-reevaluation interventions aimed at the self-statements, while being perceived as criticisms at times, were successful in shifting them. Although it could be argued that a more empathic and less cognitively confronting therapy relationship might have been less threatening, it is clear that Antonio was engaging in the therapy process and reported several important new realizations at the evaluation.

P: I think I am doing a lot better. I still have hangups, I get down but I realize that is something that is normal. I don't feel bad anymore—well, I still feel bad. I don't feel completely lost like I used to. I am more realistic with life....

P: When I first started coming, I felt that, golly, I really thought the right position was somewhere and I had to get it. That is not the way it is anymore....

P: As long as I can do better than average I am okay now. In the past I needed to feel that I was number one. Now I don't have to be number one....

Antonio tended to devalue his therapy as he did himself and his accomplishments. His expectations about the process of change were unrealistic. During therapy and in the final evaluation I had to resist Antonio's efforts to negate any achievements. Many significant changes had been made at various levels. Antonio was performing better at work. The decision to put him on probation had already been in the works when Antonio came to therapy, so no amount of change would have impacted this decision. The couple was more supportive of one another and significant changes occurred with respect to the families of origin. Perhaps the greatest change occurred at the level of maladaptive cognitions with shifts in some basic beliefs and self-statements. It is these changes in cognitions that continue to help Antonio move toward change in other areas. The 13 therapy sessions actually were quite productive in a rather extensive manner.

From my perspective the therapy has been rather successful in a modest way. Although Antonio has discontinued therapy for all intents and purposes, he has continued to make significant efforts to gain control of his anxiety. In lieu of long-term therapy, he will rely on self-change using processes he learned in therapy to continue to make an impact on his life. Often with deeply ingrained personality styles that are dysfunctional, the most a short-term therapy can do is provide some relief from the current crisis by stabilizing the defenses. This therapy did more than that by creating movement at certain levels which continues. Hopefully, Antonio's experience of therapy will be positive enough to enable him to return if things get out of control or if he needs help when he is ready to take action with the more deeply rooted intrapersonal problems.

## CONCLUDING COMMENTS

In the case of Antonio the constructs of the transtheoretical approach—stages, levels, and processes of change—provided a framework for conceptualizing and guiding the therapy process. The levels of change assisted in clarifying the myriad of problems that Antonio presented during the course of therapy and in keeping track of progress and obstacles. The stages of change offered some insight into the possible avenues that the therapy could follow. Readiness for action and openness to contemplation at each of the levels was a key determinant for the course of therapy. Focusing on the change process activity that was the goal of the interventions gave them a more integrated rationale. These constructs certainly helped to determine and track the process of therapy in what turned out to be a complex and complicated case of anxiety.

Although no particularly new intervention techniques are described in the therapy, there is a broad representation of behavioral, cognitive, family-system, interpersonal, and insight-oriented techniques employed during the sessions. These techniques come from my own training in cognitive-behavioral approaches (Meichenbaum, Mahoney), rational emotive therapy (Ellis), system and paradoxical interventions (Haley, Watzlawick, Weakland), behavior therapy (Rimm & Masters) as well as readings in the areas of couples therapy, sexual role development, and sexual abuse. The transtheoretical approach does not propose a new set of intervention techniques. It offers a model for integration of various approaches and the coordination of these in a systematic, eclectic fashion. This case certainly demonstrates an eclectic use of interventions derived from several therapy systems. Categorizing the interventions in terms of the processes and stages of change helps to present a more coherent explanation of the process of therapy with Antonio and to see how therapy and self-change blend together.

The transtheoretical approach is broad enough to encompass an eclecticism of theories, techniques as well as modalities. In this case a combination of individual, couples, and family therapy sessions was utilized. In terms of modalities the therapy could be seen as a brief eight-session intervention with Antonio, a couples therapy with some individual spouse work, and a family-of-origin therapy. These three different types of interventions can be integrated nicely in the perspective of the shifting levels of change used with Antonio and his family. This breadth of intervention modalities is not uncommon in other cases presented from the transtheoretical perspective (Prochaska & DiClemente, 1984; Prochaska & DiClemente, 1986).

In the case of Antonio the brief therapy was not able to produce complete change at any of the levels of change. However, on almost every level there was significant movement within and across the stages of change. The constructs of the transtheoretical perspective helped to track the process of therapy with Antonio and to better understand that process in an integrated eclectic manner.

## POSTSCRIPT

Several months after the evaluation sessions Antonio invited me to lunch with his wife and child to celebrate his new job in a distant city with a substantial salary increase. He requested and was given several names of therapists in that city so he could continue working on his problems.

## REFERENCES

DiClemente, C. C., & Hughes, S. (In preparation). Stages of change in alcoholism treatment: Profiles and comparisons. Manuscript, University of Texas Mental Sciences Institute.

DiClemente, C. C., & Prochaska, J. O. (1985). Processes and stages of self-change: Coping and competence in smoking behavior change. In S. Shiffman & T. A. Wills (Eds.), *Coping and substance use.* New York: Academic Press.

DiClemente, C. C., & Prochaska, J. O. (1982). Self-change and therapy change of smoking behavior: A comparison of processes of change in cessation and maintenance. *Addictive Behaviors, 7,* 133–144.

Goldfried, M. R. (1980). Toward the delineation of therapeutic change principles. *American Psychologist, 35,* 991–999.

Goldfried, M. R. (Ed.). (1982). *Converging themes in psychotherapy: Trends in psychodynamic, humanistic, and behavioral practice.* New York: Springer.

McConnaughy, E. A. (1984). Relationships among stages of change, types of psychotherapy and psychotherapy outcome. Doctoral dissertation, University of Rhode Island.

McConnaughy, E., Prochaska, J., & Velicer, W. (1983). Stages of change in psychotherapy: Measurement and sample profiles. *Psychotherapy: Theory, Research and Practice, 20,* 368–375.

Prochaska, J. O. (1984). *Systems of psychotherapy: A transtheoretical analysis.* Homewood, Il: Dorsey Press.

Prochaska, J. O., & DiClemente, C. C. (1984). *The transtheoretical approach: Crossing traditional boundaries of therapy.* Homewood, IL: Dow Jones-Irwin.

Prochaska, J. O., & DiClemente, C. C. (1986). The transtheoretical approach: Toward a systematic eclectic framework. In J. Norcross (Ed.), *Handbook of eclectic psychotherapy.* New York: Brunner/Mazel.

# Commentary: A Systems Model for a Case of Eclectic Therapy

## Edward J. Murray

*The purpose of this commentary is not to evaluate the clinical effectiveness of the therapy in this particular case but to try to understand how an eclectic approach works in action. Clearly something meaningful occurred, and if Antonio's problems were not fully resolved, both he and his wife gained some benefit from the relatively brief treatment. The real questions are why particular techniques were used when they were and whether the use of several techniques was more appropriate than the use of a single, systematic approach.*

*According to the transtheoretical approach, the client is supposed to progress through certain stages of change: precontemplation, contemplation, action, and maintenance. Different techniques are supposed to be appropriate at different stages. Thus, for example, counterconditioning and stimulus control are most appropriate in the later stages of action and maintenance. It was a little surprising, then, to learn that in the first session, Antonio was given two homework assignments involving counterconditioning and stimulus control. He was instructed to give himself 15 minutes or so each day when he came home to worry and get relaxed. During the day, he was told to do deep-breathing and relaxation procedures to combat his anxiety relaxations. Why were these later-stage interventions used in the initial interview?*

*DiClemente acknowledges that counterconditioning and stimulus control techniques appear inappropriate at the initial stages of therapy, but argues that such a "mismatch" is justified by experience. He states that such interventions are appropriate at the symptom-situational level before moving to cognitive, interpersonal, and family levels. My own clinical experience corroborates this strategy. I have found it very useful to teach deep-breathing and relaxation techniques to anxious clients early in therapy. With depressed clients, I use methods such as monitoring activities, scheduling pleasant events, and, even, physical exercise. But what is the rationale for the use of these methods?*

*In my view of it, these active interventions aid in what Frank calls the "resto-*

ration of morale." Just suggesting such techniques communicates the message that the therapist does not consider the situation or symptom beyond the client's ability to cope. It is also useful to discuss these techniques in terms of self-efficacy. The important idea here is that these techniques seem particularly helpful in the initial stages of therapy.

What, then, happens to the idea of stages of change? The stages do not seem appropriate to symptoms such as anxiety and depression. People who come in with problems such as these are not in need of consciousness raising about them. However, they do need, as Antonio needed, consciousness raising about the connection between their emotional stages and their cognitive and interpersonal problems. The transtheoretical approach needs some clarification about this issue.

The counterconditioning and stimulus control techniques are classified as behavioral. Yet, are these techniques simply behavioral, in the sense of dealing with the isolated symptoms? In addition to raising morale and the sense of efficacy, mentioned above, these techniques can be seen also as the forerunners of the interpersonal and family intervention used later. The breathing and relaxation techniques used in the workplace may be viewed as providing alternatives to the maladaptive patterns that Antonio engaged in with supervisors and fellow workers. The stimulus control method used when he got home appears to have helped break up Antonio's pattern of dumping on his wife. DiClemente does talk about how these various levels do interact, but perhaps it should be stressed that all of the interventions might be viewed as attempts to alter the interpersonal systems that Antonio was involved in. In fact, an interpersonal systems model may be the most useful way of organizing the interventions used with Antonio.

Much use was made of cognitive techniques with Antonio. These included dealing with conceptions of the self as dumb and too gentle, beliefs about meeting the expectations of others and perfectionism, and the generalization of attitudes from the father to bosses. However, it should be noted that most of these cognitions dealt with interpersonal issues, particularly in the workplace. Cognitive therapists are becoming increasingly aware of the intertwining of belief systems and interpersonal systems. The cognitive work was followed by attempts at behavioral change such as approaching criticism, taking more responsibility for problem solving at work, and reducing his dependency on his boss. Some of the cognitive work has a dynamic flavor, such as his growing insight into his tendency to turn bosses into critical father figures—one of the classical vicious circles of interpersonal dynamic theory.

The problems in the workplace were clearly related to the problems Antonio had with his family of origin. On the cognitive level, the father and brother appear to have fostered a belief that male behavior is dichotomized into macho and homosexual categories. Some work was done on this, although DiClemente would have liked to do more. The vicious circle that Antonio showed with his boss was related to the pattern with the father. Antonio, himself, saw that changes in his attitudes toward his boss and his father went hand in hand. He must have altered his behavior with his father because the father seems to have treated him with more respect at the end of treatment.

The other major interpersonal system that was dealt with in the therapy was the marital relationship. The wife was concerned about Antonio's dumping his work problems on her. The marital relationship also suffered from the residues of both families of origin. The marital relationship problems were aided by the techniques of encouraging open communication and appropriate assertiveness toward the demands of parents. Possibly one of the most important changes in the entire treatment was getting the couple to work together to deal with the family and work pressures.

The timing of the marital and family interventions is of interest in understanding an eclectic approach. The shift from individual therapy with Antonio to couple therapy, then back to individual therapy, followed by an individual session with the wife, several couple sessions, a session with the wife and her mother, and, finally, some individual sessions with Antonio appears at first blush to be capricious. Yet, there is a logic if you think of this therapy in systems terms. First, the instigation for the marital and family sessions came from the clients, not from the therapist. Is this good or bad? Some therapists would take a more active role than DiClemente did. However, DiClemente was actually dealing with the systems from the first interview. The first couple interview came when the marital situation reached a crisis point, and the interventions with the wife and her family of origin were precipitated by a visit by the mother. These were hot times, and there is reason to believe that interventions are most effective at hot points. Did the time spent with the wife's family-of-origin problems detract from Antonio's treatment? Possibly, but on balance it strengthened the couple's relationship and may even have served as a model for Antonio's dealing with the boundary problems with his own family of origin. The principle here seems to be to deal with the problem of greatest urgency.

At the end of treatment, DiClemente seems to be concerned that he had not dealt sufficiently with intrapsychic problems such as identity conflict and basic personality structure. There seems to be an assumption here that purely intrapsychic problems do indeed exist. Perhaps they exist only in the abstract. Antonio's identity problems are clearly tied to interaction problems in his family and the cognitive residues from them. Further work here might be useful, but it is really not of a different order than what has been done. As for changing basic personality structure, I have my doubts that any psychotherapy changes anything but patterns of thinking and interpersonal behavior.

Could DiClemente have done anything different? I think he could have dealt more directly with what dynamic therapists call transference. Toward the end, the same pattern of dependency-control came up in the therapeutic relationship to the boss and the father. Intervention in this area might have extended therapy and provided the full affective experience that DiClemente wanted.

Would the therapy have been more effective if DiClemente had used one technique consistently rather than an eclectic approach? The answer to this must be speculative. He could have used a dynamic approach focusing on the transference and its problems in the relationships with the boss and the father. As I indicated above, some of this might have been useful. However, an exclusive reliance on this method would have not dealt with the problems in the marital relationship sufficiently. In addition, the very positive effect of getting the couple to work together in establishing boundaries with their families would not have been achieved.

So, too, the entire therapy might have focused on the marital relationship. Although such an approach would have been of some use, the work done on the father and boss problems would not have been advanced. In view of the fact that Antonio entered therapy with the primary problem of anxiety in the workplace, he would probably have resisted such an approach.

A purely cognitive-behavioral approach would have dealt directly with all of the interpersonal and family problems. However, the actual involvement of the spouse and family probably adds a great deal to the vividness of the treatment process. As mentioned above, the strategy of dealing with the emotionally hot area with whatever family member was available may have been the strongest aspect of this case.

In trying to understand what went on in

this case and trying to rationalize the eclectic strategies used, I have used a systems model. I am not committed to a systems approach exclusively and in fact I use other models in my thinking. However, this case seemed to me to fit a systems model best. Antonio came to therapy with an anxiety problem, but it was soon apparent that this anxiety problem was embedded in and infringed on a whole set of interpersonal relationships. Antonio was in a problematic marital relationship, he was still enmeshed with his own family, and his wife with hers. Perhaps this was clearer because of the Hispanic culture. In any case, when DiClemente took on Antonio as a client he also got a wife and her mother as clients. I have a suspicion that if Antonio's parents had lived closer, he would have had them as clients also.

The various techniques used become understandable if one thinks about their impact on the interpersonal relationships of Antonio. The initial behavioral techniques broke up maladaptive patterns with the boss and the wife. The cognitive work led to changes in the vicious circles with the father and the boss. The marital therapy helped strengthen the working relationship between Antonio and his wife. In turn, they were both able to establish better relationships with their parents. Each of the interpersonal systems affected the others. The interventions were aimed at the target of opportunity in the constantly changing social field.

On the other hand, I did not find the transtheoretical model satisfactory as a guide for understanding what went on. I saw very little evidence for an orderly flow across stages of change. Techniques did not seem to be geared to these changes. So, too, the levels-of-change analysis seemed to do little more than label parts of the system. Symptomatic treatment seemed to involve cognitive and social changes. Cognitive techniques seemed to be important only to the extent that they changed interpersonal behavior. This is not to say that the change model is without its use, but it did not provide me with as coherent picture of what went on in this case as did the systems model.

# Commentary: Approach to Psychotherapy or Theory of Change?

## Martin R. Textor

Before I comment on Dr. DiClemente's approach to psychotherapy I would like to congratulate him for his courage in presenting a case that is not a total success story. Moreover, he has chosen a complex and extremely difficult one with which any therapist would struggle. DiClemente's case, however, represents the harsh and often frustrating reality all of us are fighting with—a reality of clients dropping out after one or two sessions, of unsuccessful cases, of goals only partly reached.

Another preliminary remark I have to make is that I come from a family systems orientation (Textor, 1985)—and, in my commentary I will not be able to hide it. Equally important, I have a different concept of therapeutic integration (Textor, 1983). Both these factors tend to make me critical of DiClemente's approach, especially when I leave the context of the transtheoretical approach and look at it from the outside. This does not mean, however, that I do not value it and did not learn from it—in fact it made very stimulating reading.

While reading DiClemente's case, I had problems relating to his concept of levels of change. On the one hand, I cannot discern why DiClemente uses the five levels as diagnostic categories. For me change is a process, something moving, being in flux, whereas diagnosis tries to describe and categorize a state at a given moment of time. On the other hand, I had difficulty in differentiating between the five levels of change—and in judging DiClemente's examination of Antonio's problem in terms of the levels of change (Chapter 6, Table 2), I got the impression that DiClemente also had similar difficulties. There is much overlap; e.g., Antonio's problems with his superiors are mentioned on the first, third, and fourth levels, messages of his parents are listed on the second and fifth levels, and his looking for approval is classified on the second, third, and fourth levels. I experienced great difficulty in trying to distinguish between the levels of maladaptive cognitions and intrapersonal conflicts and between interpersonal conflicts and family/systems. Differentiating between intrapersonal (which would encompass Antonio's obsessional worry, low self-esteem, and sexual identity problems), family (incorporating Antonio's conflicts with his spouse, father, and in-laws), and employment system (his problems with supervisors) would make more sense to me.

In general, I see DiClemente's five (hierarchical) levels of change as a step back because he does not consider systems theory (or cybernetics). With the help of this theory he could differentiate in a more evident way between systems (e.g., individual, dyad, family, network) and subsystems (e.g., personality, engineers-supervisors-subsystem). Concepts like feedback would also serve as a better substitution for expressions like "Change at any one level is likely to produce change at other levels" (p. 161). Moreover, using systems theory would lead to a less individual-oriented diagnosis ("atypical anxiety disorder") in examination of Antonio's problem (p. 163, Tables 2 and 3). This, in turn, might have made the therapist involve significant others in therapy—in DiClemente's case this was left to chance, e.g., Antonio asked whether he could bring his wife, and Ann volunteered to bring in her mother and called to make an appointment two weeks after the last evaluation session. Realization of the extremely negative impact of Antonio's father and of Ann's parents (see the many references to them) should have led to a more pronounced effort to get them involved in therapy. It certainly was an experience of great success when Antonio and Ann had Ann's mother move out. However, DiClemente left the latter alone when she had to confront her husband. It also might have been beneficial if Ann had told her mother in the presence of the therapist about the sexual abuse she had suffered.

With my last remarks I left the context of the transtheoretical approach and argued from my family systems orientation. Moving back to DiClemente's stages of change, I would like to draw attention to the fact they were first derived from smokers who successfully stopped smoking (Prochaska & DiClemente, 1982)—and I believe that they may be limited to such well-circumscribed problems and goals. Saying that Antonio was at the precontemplation stage at the intrapersonal level suggests that the therapist will not have success working at this level and, therefore, should intervene elsewhere. However, I believe that few clients contemplate an overall personality change—most just wish to have a few traits modified. Thus, I would prefer to use the concept of stages on the intrapersonal level with respect to single traits. For me, psychotherapy consists of several sequences of precontemplation, contemplation, action, and maintenance stages, each sequence being terminated when a goal has been reached, a problem solved, a trait changed.

In his case, DiClemente describes which processes of change took place in his clients. However, I missed any clear reference to the therapeutic means by which he got these processes started and maintained. He rarely refers to techniques in his description of sessions but writes at the end of his chapter that a "wide range of behavioral, cognitive, family system, interpersonal, and insight-oriented techniques" was employed. Despite his mentioning action-oriented techniques, he seemed to be quite passive in the sessions. From his case I learned how Antonio and Ann behaved in the sessions, but little about DiClemente's actions and reactions. As he writes, "The pattern of the therapy was dictated largely by the events and initiatives of the client" (p. 175). Most of the responsibility for change was also attributed to the client. However, these are only my impressions and are not intended to be criticisms.

In summary, I believe that the transtheoretical approach as a process theory has to be supplemented by a theory of personality and psychopathology, i.e., by content aspects (see Prochaska & DiClemente, 1982, p. 282). For me transtheoretical therapy is another approach to psychotherapy—a term I use for a subjective way of seeing events that happen in the therapist's office, of organizing and describing one's observations. I believe that each therapist develops his/her own idiosyncratic approach according to his biography, age, sex, personality, image of people, values, training, and employment situation. Each therapist develops a subjective approach to therapy in order to organize information, experiences, and observations, explain events in his office, recognize pathological phenomena, formulate treatment goals and strategies, define his own role, select techniques, and measure his/her success. He does not need to observe all reactions of his client or infer all processes occurring in him—which would be impossible. Thus, he concentrates on a few, e.g., processes, stages, and levels of change.

Therapeutic integration, however, is more for me. It means developing a theory of psychotherapy that brings together the knowledge and experience of all psychotherapists and organizes it. This, then, has to result in a harmonious and interrelated whole. Such an encompassing theory sees man as a biological, psychological, social, and spiritual being embedded in families, networks, institutions, and society. I consider DiClemente's approach a theory of therapeutic change that is of great value to an integrative theory and for research on psychotherapy.

## REFERENCES

Prochaska, J. O., & DiClemente, C. C. (1982). Transtheoretical therapy: Toward a more integrative model of change. Psychotherapy: Theory, Research and Practice, 19, 276–288.

Textor, M. R. (1983). Integrative Psychotherapie. In: Integrative Psychotherapie. Münchner Beiträge zur Integrationsforschung (Vol. 1) (pp. 29–41). Munich: Kurt Schobert Verlag & Schreibbüro.

Textor, M. R. (1985). Integrative Familientherapie. Berlin, Heidelberg, New York, Tokyo: Springer Verlag.

CHAPTER 7

# The Teenage Prosecutor: A Case in Pragmatic Family Therapy

*Richard H. Driscoll*

Conducting psychotherapy involves two related factors: observing and trying to understand, and intervening to promote changes. Any orientation has characteristic ways of proceeding with each of these, and a comprehensive integrative approach must be able to manage both the range of observation perspectives and the range of interventions across the various orientations.

Pragmatic psychotherapy is an eclectic approach that uses ordinary language concepts to structure observations, and a set of procedural guidelines to organize interventions. The cover term "pragmatic" refers, in language analysis, to the social influence of words, and also means emphasizing practical considerations over ideology. The major principles of pragmatic psychotherapy are found in Driscoll (1984) and related readings (Bergner, 1983; Farber, 1981; Ossorio, 1976). A synopsis of the organizing framework precedes the presentation of the case.

**ORDINARY LANGUAGE CONCEPTS**

Ordinary language concepts are used in lieu of concepts based in theoretical formulations. Our ordinary language concepts readily access the wealth of distinctions used in everyday social concerns, and can be used to organize and integrate the various theoretical formulations. Ordinary language is thus the basis of a common language immediately familiar to all, and provides an answer to the problem of separate and incompatible languages among theoretical orientations (cf. Goldfried & Padawer, 1982). Emphasis is on observation and straightforward description of behavioral phenomena using these concepts.

Behavior is formulated here as purposive action, involving cognition, motivation, and competence (Ossorio, 1969). Action is undertaken *in order to* achieve something, although the outcome is not always what one was trying for and there are numerous ways that things can go wrong. One can misperceive things, have conflicting motivations, misunderstand how to make things change, and so on. Awareness of these related aspects of purposive action helps us identify the troublesome factors in those cases when things do go wrong.

The occurrence of behavior is a function of situations and individual characteristics. Some personal problems arise from inhospitable situations, many from maladaptive individual tendencies, and others from incompatible combinations of situations and individual characteristics. Situations and individual characteristics were acquired from past events, the former by social transitions, the latter by learning, maturation, and so on. Psychotherapy attempts to alleviate restrictions in ability to participate in meaningful ways of life, by changing (present) behaviors, situations, and individual characteristics.

## GUIDELINES

Therapeutic interventions are made in order to influence and change our clients. The various interventions available are organized here by the objectives they can be used to accomplish.

A set of intervention guidelines is used to specify the objectives we find important time and again with a broad range of clients. These guidelines were constructed from an analysis of familiar interventions and are an organized composite of the important objectives found in current psychotherapy orientations. Various interventions have been grouped together by the guideline objectives they are used to accomplish, and a variety of overtly dissimilar techniques from separate orientations may be classed together as a means of accomplishing the same objective.

The guidelines are meant to aid in identifying pertinent objectives and in selecting interventions appropriate to the circumstances at hand. The guidelines specify the clinical tasks that might be called for in particular clinical circumstances and suggest ways those tasks might be accomplished. In this way, they serve to guide our choices of therapeutic interventions. The guidelines thus specify the *clinical strategies* or *principles of change* suggested by Goldfried (1980) as heuristic connections between the broader goals of therapy and the specific techniques chosen at any given moment.

There are 26 guidelines covering the broad tasks of maintaining a therapeutic relationship, building on clients' existing strengths, assessing what matters for interventions, clarifying situations and the paths of change, instilling new patterns, and motivating clients. These are listed in an appendix at the end of the chapter, and are referred to in parentheses throughout the case presentation to indicate how they are used in selecting and understanding therapeutic interventions. Since space limitations allow mention of only a few of the connections between these principles and the orientations they integrate, readers are referred to Driscoll (1984) for this information.

## CLINICAL JUDGMENT

Insofar as eclectic practice involves the selection of aspects from various orientations, understanding the clinical judgment by which we make such selections is especially critical. But the considerations involved in clinical judgments are often implicit. As practitioners our attention is primarily on understanding and intervening appropriately, and not on articulating what we are doing. It is noteworthy that eclecticism itself emerged from practitioners' needs for versatility and prior to any formal statement of how selections between orientations were to be made.

But a reliable articulation of clinical judgment is important so that we can critique ourselves, improve what we do, and teach others. The concepts and guidelines of pragmatic psychotherapy comprise an articulation of some of the perspectives that are used implicitly by eclectic therapists. The approach here is to clarify our already existing concepts and clinical competencies, and to build on them. Many of the formulations appear commonsensical, in that they try to appeal to our experience and judgment.

In the following case, I have tried to include sufficient information on the grounds on which I made clinical judgments. The case transcripts are meant to portray the process by which case information is attained and case formulations are made. Information that is missing or ambiguous in the sessions is not provided gratis by an omniscient commentator, but is revealed in the manner that it is acquired in the actual sessions.

The interventions follow from my understanding of the case and from the intervention guidelines. In many instances, other interventions might have been selected that would have been as appropriate or sometimes more so to the circumstances. Ordinary language pragmatism* is a way of grasping and comparing the various alternatives that might be appropriate in particular circumstances, and not a general prescription on which ones to use in any specific instance.

I chose this particular case for the *Casebook* because of the variety of interventions involved. One of the strengths of eclecticism is its versatility, and this case required some revision of my initial case formulation and numerous variations and alterations in my intervention tactics.

---

*As there are other candidates being proposed as common languages not based in ordinary language, the cover term "ordinary language pragmatism" is more descriptive and is preferred now to the "common language pragmatism" title I used originally.

And since one of the clients was a mental health professional, there was the possibility of some additional insights on treatment that might not be otherwise available.

The father called me several months after he heard me speak on family relationships. He was interested in some consultation on what he considered to be family problems.

## SESSION 1

My initial objectives in beginning a first session are to set the clients at ease and make them comfortable with the therapy situation (II-2), to establish an alliance with them (I-2), and to convey that this is a safe and reasonable way to look for solutions to their problems (I-3). It is important to win their confidence quickly, to set the basis for further work, and to improve the probability for their returning. Although there is some attrition in individual treatment, the complexities of couples and family work increase the considerations we must manage to keep clients in treatment.

I generally begin by asking for names and addresses and then for the information necessary to understand the basic relationships between the principals involved in the case. There is Jim, his wife Laura, and his three children from a prior marriage. The father is in his late thirties and the stepmother several years younger. He is a clinical social worker and she an accountant. The daughter, Becky, is 13 and there are sons Tom, age 10, and Robbie, age six. When I ask for the address, one of the boys gives his address and then the father gives his own address and clarifies that the children live with their mother, who is his ex-wife. The boys are adding to the confusion and seem to be enjoying making it a challenge for me to get the relationships straightened out. I make a tongue-in-cheek reference to the amount of confusion in stepfamilies:

Driscoll [to wife]: Do you have a first marriage?
Laura: Yes. This is my second marriage.
Driscoll: But no children. You just wanted to simplify things.
Laura: Right. [laughs] I wouldn't have married Jim if I had wanted to simplify things. [laughs]

While I would ordinarily want to establish a relationship and get some sense of my clients before trying humor, these clients were being playful with each other, and it seemed natural to join in the playful atmosphere. Appropriate humor can help break tensions and make people comfortable with the situation (II-2; Driscoll, in press).

Driscoll: Did everybody get told about why you were coming in?
Becky: No. We just found out. We had no say at all.
Driscoll: Are you here against your better judgment?
Becky: I don't really care. I have gone to a psychiatrist before. It's no big deal to me. I'm just not crazy. I know that.

I was looking for indications that anyone was opposed to being in the sessions. We would want to address any such concerns at the outset, to establish working relationships with the various parties (I-2).

The parents were divorced four years ago, and the father remarried last year. Becky had seen a psychologist (not a psychiatrist) for two or three sessions at the time of the remarriage and seems annoyed at her father for taking her to me rather than to the one she saw before. The father explains that he approves of the other psychologist, but wants someone with more of a family orientation. He and his wife saw a marriage counselor for about a year before they got married, to work out some communication troubles before they became problems. He jokes that if it had not gone well, they probably would not have gotten married. She agrees.

The father and his wife have the children every other weekend plus an additional evening, every other holiday, and for several weeks in the summer. I mention that it is not all that much time and ask if he would want to have more time with them. He says that he is satisfied with the visitation schedule and mentions that work and church take up the other evenings.

The children are bickering among themselves, and I inquire about how they get along:

Driscoll: [to Becky]: Do you fight with your brothers?
Becky: No. Well, I mean we have 10-minute fights. You know how kids are.
Driscoll: You mean sort of *normal* fights.
Becky: Really. We don't kill each other very often [laughing].... We argue, but two minutes later if we can settle it on our own everything is fine.

By labeling the fights normal I am supporting Becky's assertion earlier that she knows she is not crazy, continuing to try to make her comfortable with the situation (II-2).

Father mentions that the rowdiness gets on his nerves when he is driving the car, but that it is not a major issue. I comment that almost everyone has problems with children being rowdy on trips, again to portray such problems as normal (II-2). I do an impersonation of some kids in a car:

Driscoll: Hey, gang. Dad's got the wheel. Now's our chance. Let's get at it.
Laura: You must have kids. Right?
Driscoll: Yeah. Tell me about it.

I was trying to show I was familiar with the issues everyone was dealing with (I-3), and Laura seemed to appreciate my experience.

I ask what some of the more usual problems are that they have together:

Becky: Laura and I get along fine most of the time when we are talking to each other. But when Dad comes into the conversation, everybody gets mad and gets into a fight.

Laura seems to generally get along with all of the children although she occasionally gets angry and sets them straight. Becky says Laura screams at them, but Laura considers that too harsh. We settle for "raises her voice" as a more acceptable label (II-2). She gets over being angry quickly, and does not hold grudges. She mentions that she has been more angry at Jim on occasion than at any of the children.

Driscoll: It is sounding like this thing about the wicked stepmother is all a myth. (I-4).
Father: The problem here is that I am the bad guy.

Laura has also tagged the main problem as Father is the bad guy. So there is a consensus here that the problem is that father is the bad guy. Only when Becky says it, she means that he *is* the bad guy, but when Laura and father say it, they mean that he comes out looking like the bad guy. Many ordinary language words can be used in several ways, and we must be aware of what these people mean when they use them (III-2).

Father: Normally when there is a conflict, there is an [important] value involved. In the last one Robbie had gotten into it with some of his friends and had thrown a rock and broken a taillight on their parents' car. He said that he hated the fellow. But they had been pretty consistent friends for quite awhile, and I think that that was carrying it way too far.

Driscoll: I think all kids say "I hate someone" now and again, and then later on they forget it and get on with things as they were.
Father: Okay. Well, we may have made too big of a deal of that. But we did feel strongly that breaking the taillight was his responsibility. And that is what the fight was about.

I was introducing a standard of normative or usual behavior for that age, to use in judging the importance of Robbie's comment (IV-2). I am noting here how readily the father accepted my comment and went on to his other concern. We learn from how clients react to our interventions (III-4), and the father seems to be willing to readily hear my suggestions and to reconsider his positions.

Father: The argument quickly lined up as "them against us." It started out as the children against me, and that is when Laura came in [on my side] because I am not really that good of an arguer. Laura is pretty good and can articulate her points and make it clear. But I am not as good in conflict as other people are.

An inability to hold his own in an argument could be a critical factor in parent-teenager relationships.

Father: The children were saying that it was not Robbie's fault that he threw the rock and broke the light, because the other girl started the fight and was throwing rocks.
Tom: She likes to start fights, and she knows Robbie has a temper.
Becky: She does. She picks on him and tantalizes him. And Daddy doesn't want to see it.
Tom: She was even throwing rocks at us. After she started throwing rocks at us she ran into the neighbor's garage, and

that's when Robbie tried to throw a rock at her and it bounced and hit the taillight.
Becky: It wasn't directly her fault. But don't you think that she had a lot to do with it? I mean, you called Mom a "damned bitch" long ago and it was because she was tantalizing you. She made you so mad that you screamed "damned bitch" at her.
Driscoll: You used the "rhymes with witch" word?
Father: We don't normally use that language.
Becky: I mean that wasn't completely Dad's fault, because Mom did push him over the edge.
Father: I will take responsibility for what I say.
Driscoll: But hear what she is saying. She is saying that there are times when you are responsible, but not completely or fully responsible, because there are provocations or mitigating circumstances. . . .
Father: But if my ex-wife wants to sue me for slander, then I would not have much of a case. I know that is carrying it to the hilt.
Driscoll: Yeah, but even carrying it to the hilt there, I would say that since you were clearly provoked that you would have a case.
Father: Okay. That's good to know [laughs]. Just in case I ever want to go through that again.

While one orientation holds that you are responsible for your actions and another holds that you are not, our everyday conventions suggest various conditions under which you are held to be fully or somewhat responsible or not responsible for particular things that you do. It seems that father is being too "all or none" here and is in a poor position against Becky and the brothers who are arguing the more appropriate standards for attributing responsibility. The argument Becky made is overtly supportive of father, but the illustration she used of his cursing his ex-wife is a clear violation of his own standards and so makes him squirm. She seems to be exceptional in her mastery of the verbal joust. In clarifying mitigating circumstances, I am in the fortunate position of being able to be supportive of Father while also backing the children's argument (I-2).

The everyday concept of responsibility that I am providing for Father makes allowances for mitigating circumstances and is generally easier to live with than the concept on which he makes his judgments. Your concepts are the distinctions you know how to make, and in clarifying concepts we try to improve on clients' abilities to make appropriate distinctions themselves (IV-2). Concepts are termed "constructs" in Kelly's construct theory and "schema" in Piagetian and cognitive-behavioral approaches.

The conversation continues on the issue of responsibility, and I rephrase and repeat my clarifications. Some reiteration is generally necessary to familiarize clients with any new viewpoint (V-2).

Driscoll [to Becky]: If he were to see your point, would you find it easier to see his point?
Becky: Yes, probably. I have told him before that I would be willing to meet him halfway. . . . He has said to me, "Well, Becky, I guess I am just not a good father, and I just give up." And I will say to him, "Okay, Dad, you have finally got something right." [everyone laughs] What Dad really wants is the easy way out.
Father: No, I don't think so. Although I will say that it takes a lot of energy to stay in there and argue with you.
Becky: I am a good arguer.
Father: I know. [All laugh.]

I mention to father that he may be seeing things as too strictly black or white, but he has another interpretation of the problem:

Father: I used to be very flexible and very easy to manipulate, and that is not as true as it used to be. I think that I have changed in that I am better at making stands. That is a very difficult change for me to make.
Driscoll [to children]: Your dad is saying that he used to be too permissive and would let you get away with too much.
Tom: He still does.
Becky: Oh, he doesn't either.
Father: It should be possible for us to have differences of opinion and for me to still have a little more authority because I am the adult. That is where I am coming from. That is what I am saying.

It is healthy for parents to have an appropriate amount of authority over their children and proper for us as therapists to try to support their authority. I am looking for a firmer sense of how he is mismanaging or otherwise restricted in his exercise of authority.

Becky complicates the matter by painting a glowing portrait of their mother as more lenient and much easier to get along with, while father is impossible. Father sees his ex-wife as too lenient and failing to uphold reasonable standards of conduct. Since the children are with their mother most of the time, she is in a position to have more influence on them.

Becky complains that Father does not trust her, and that she was in trouble with him because he wanted her to sit where he could see her in church and she sat beyond his sight. I interpret this as a concern that the children will appear fidgety and unruly. I give my impression that he is concerned with how the children appear in public:

Father: That is true. I do care how they appear.
Becky: Sometimes I just dress as ratty as I can. I just want my friends to like me for who I am rather than for how I dress. . . .
Driscoll: You are just the opposite of a lot of teenagers, who really can give their parents headaches because they have to wear the right clothes and have the right makeup and the right purses, and they can wind up costing their parents a lot of money. . . . What Becky is saying would be a breath of fresh air if you had been dealing with this other sort of problem.

A stand on neater apparel is often a losing position for parents, and it seems especially so here. Some defiance seems to be involved, and making an issue of dress could elicit further resistance from her (VI-2). In focusing on the opposite problem, I was introducing a comparison to try to temper everyone's concern for casual dress.

Father is also concerned that the boys want to wear punk haircuts and have talked about piercing their ears:

Father: Robbie had trouble in the last school he attended. Maybe this is old-fashioned, but I think that there is a chance that a teacher would react negatively to Robbie because his hair is punk and not give him a chance. And I am concerned about that.
Becky: But, Daddy! Nobody thinks anything about haircuts nowadays.
Driscoll: You really stand up for your brothers, don't you.
Becky: Yeah. You shouldn't have to wear your hair a particular way just to please someone.
Driscoll [to Becky]: What I am hearing is that when Daddy wants you to conform it flies all over you, because you do not want to have to do it any particular way just because everyone else is doing it.
Becky: Well, we are about like everyone else. We are not trying to break any laws of nature here [laughs].

My comment was a simple rephrasing of her position (I-4), but she responded to it with a reaffirmation of normalcy. I am aware of my lack of any working alliance with this youngster. The issue of conforming continues, and father's original concerns seem to have gotten lost:

Driscoll [to Father]: I think that you were concerned about his hair because you would not want him to get on the outs with his teacher.
Father: Right.

My comment is essentially an active listening response again (I-4), although it comes several comments after his original statement. This sort of statement is supportive of Father without alienating the youngsters (I-2). It is clear that everyone wants something from Father:

Driscoll [to Father]: Sounds like you are real popular.
Father: Right. I am popular. That is very important. Even though I am the bad guy, I am popular. The message is "We want you, but damned if you can do anything right. We are going to get you either way." [laughing]

Becky complains about the ways Father treats her when she is with him, and she complains about the time that he spends away from her. She complains that he never gives her hugs.

Driscoll: Sometimes when you give him a hard time, is it not so much that he is a hardnose but that you miss him?
Becky: Yeah. Just because he is not with us enough.
Driscoll: You have been complaining about the things that your dad does, and then you seemed to change a bit and you were saying that what really upsets you is that you miss him.
Becky: It is a combination of things. He bugs me when I am with him [laughs], so I wish he would stop bugging me. And then when he does stop, I wish he could do more with me.

Becky is seeming to be mothering her two brothers, with her arms around one and the other with his head on her lap.

Driscoll: A lot of this is that you are missing your dad.
Becky: Yeah. He didn't even come in and kiss me goodnight. But my little brothers do. I say, "Come here," and they give me a big hug. They are my little support group.

I ask if Father can be more physical with the children and suggest that he might do so (IV-6). He says that that would be no problem and that he would be comfortable with it.

Becky argues that her mother has reasonable standards and that she feels freer around her mother because Mom does not object to how they dress or to occasional cursing. Father feels that the cursing is an indication that he has not done enough or is not bringing them up properly. I invite Becky to focus on the uncomfortableness her father experiences:

Driscoll: Let's look at it this other way. [The cursing] makes your father uncomfortable or it makes him feel like he has not done a good job in bringing you up.
Becky: I never thought of it in that way....

She complains that he seems mad rather than uncomfortable, so I have him talk about how and when and why he is uncomfortable. Initially he does seem more angry than uncomfortable, and I point that out and invite him to show the other side of his feelings. It is an attempt to appeal to whatever concerns Becky might have for her father's feelings (VI-1). The tactic is suggested in the "I" messages in

Gordon's parent effectiveness training. But she does not seem to be affected by his comments, indicating that concerns for his feelings are probably not high on her priorities (III-4). We focus again on Becky wanting more of her father, and she turns the discussion into criticism against Father:

Becky: [My father] doesn't ever criticize me. He has humiliated me before really well, but he has never really criticized me.
Driscoll: Humiliated you? Give me a for instance.
Becky [to Father]: You want me to go into that?
Father: That is up to Richard [the therapist].
Driscoll: I am the only one who is in the dark. I think it would be helpful [to tell it].
Becky: I asked Daddy if I could sleep with him once. Innocently. I mean just *sleep* with him.
Driscoll: Sleep in the same bed.

Simple responses such as these convey that we understand the message and facilitate further responses (I-4).

Becky: Yeah. I mean, I'm no sexual pervert here.
Driscoll: Okay. [Everyone laughs.] We do not want to make any mistakes here.
Becky: I said, "Daddy, is it okay if I sleep with you?" And you acted as if I were some kind of alien here. You made me feel really bad about it. I was just considering it an innocent question. You said, "Becky, you are almost a woman."
Driscoll: You were just wanting to sleep with him for the comfort of it. (I-4, II-2)
Becky: Yeah. But you made me feel awful. What was it you said? You said that some girls, well, have some secret desires for their fathers, and they kind of want to have affairs with their fathers.
Father: No, I don't think that I said that.
Becky: Yeah, you said that. That's what got me.
Father: I did say that I feel like you are beginning to develop sexually.
Becky: But that doesn't mean that I'm a pervert.
Father: And I did say that I think that it is inappropriate. And I will go with what Richard was saying. It is something that I was uncomfortable with.
Becky: Well, you didn't have to make me feel like a total jerk.
Driscoll [to Becky]: Catch this. Your dad is saying something important here. He is saying that he is uncomfortable with it. (IV-1)
Becky: I know. But that's not what he said.
Driscoll: You did not know before that he was uncomfortable. Because all you knew was that he made you uncomfortable. (IV-1, V-2)
Becky: Yeah, he made me feel really terrible....
Driscoll [to Father]: Talk a little more about feeling uncomfortable. I have talked with other fathers who also feel uncomfortable, who ask, "How do you relate to girls who make you feel just a little bit sensual toward them?"

By suggesting that sensual feelings are relatively normal, I was trying to make such issues more acceptable so that he would be comfortable enough to talk about them if they were important (II-2).

Becky: That is when he said, uh, what was that word that you used that I had never heard before?
Father: "Erection?" Did I say, "What if I had an erection?"
Becky: No. You said "ejaculation."
Father. No. I would not have said that.
Becky: You did too, Daddy. I didn't even know what the word meant.
Father: I find it very difficult to believe you, Becky.

Becky: I swear to God.
Father: But. . . .
Becky [interrupting]: [I know] you said that because I had never heard it, and I went home and asked Mom what it meant. And she said, "I have never heard it either, Becky." We couldn't figure out what it was. We had to look it up in a dictionary.
Driscoll [to Becky]: See that he is saying that he is uncomfortable because he doesn't want to make you uncomfortable.

My sense was that something in Becky's argument is not adding up properly but, still focusing on calming the situation, I missed the giveaway clue about having to look it up in the dictionary. I was observing that Father was trying to make amends for whatever ways he hurt her feelings, but that Becky was continuing her case against him and unwilling to let the thing go. She was arguing her position as the victim and so casting him as the perpetrator of sexually improper comments against her. At the same time I felt that Father should have been more circumspect in his comments to her.

Something more than the conventional hour is generally useful for a first session with families, because of the sheer number of individual and relationship concerns. This session goes about an hour and a half, and the animosity over the sleeping-together incident remains unresolved.

I have gotten some sense of the concerns and a good sense of the interaction patterns of the family together. But family interaction creates its own pressures, and, in some ways, restricts the focus of a session. I want to get a better sense of the parents and want to be more directly supportive and affirming of them in their role as parents. The father seems to have gotten the worst of the session, in several places but especially in that last sexual-proprieties interchange. And the lengths of their prior treatments suggest that he is interested in strengthening the bonds with his wife, but maybe not supportive of individual treatment for Becky. I scheduled with the parents only for next week, when Father does not have the children, and schedule the appointment after that for the whole family together. In alternating between whole-family and parents-only sessions, I am trying to reap the benefits both of family interaction and of parent consult approaches. Sessions are a week apart for the first six sessions, and two to three weeks apart for the next three sessions because of the family's busy schedule.

*Impressions*

The specific stands Father has taken here suggest that his standards are too strict or that he is not flexible enough with the children, although his willingness to alter his positions when I suggest he do so indicates considerable flexibility. Although he says that he has not been strict enough with the children, my initial impression is that he is making too many stands on the wrong issues, and thus inviting failures. I surely agree with the consensus that he is not a good arguer. He needs to be more careful on the issues he is willing to do battle on, and to learn better tactics for the ones he does fight on.

Laura was relatively quiet in the session, but seemed sensitive to what was going on. The comments she did make were consistently supportive of her husband.

Becky is quick-witted, loves the verbal joust, and is more than a match for her father. I appreciate her wit and social savvy, and I am sympathetic of her wanting more time with her father. Although I have been supportive of her, my impression is that she does not trust me and that she is eager to do battle with her father.

The sexual-proprieties interchange strikes me as quite pernicious and as something of a reversal of the common child-sexual-abuse issues. It is the daughter here who is pushing for more intimacy, and she was making accusations of sexual improprieties against her father for his somewhat awkward attempts to maintain proper limits with her.

The boys got lost in everything else that was going on, but seemed to be a part of the clear children-against-adults alliances in the family.

### SESSION 2*

I mention that this session should be easier without the youngsters around and offer my sympathies to Jim for the pressure he is under from Becky. I am trying to build an alliance (I-2). Father says he is being somewhat more physical with the children, and that they seem to be getting along better.

We discuss what went on in the last session. Father makes a case that Becky was wrong in her comment about an ejaculation: As an analogy he had said that her brother should not sleep with his mother or he might get an erection. But he maintains that he never used the word "ejaculation." Becky's contention that was the word because Mother had to look it up in the dictionary does not hold together, for their mother would obviously know what it meant.

Being a social worker, the father might be expected to talk about issues that would be easier to avoid. But mentioning having an ejaculation seems too inappropriate, and he seems too concerned with social conventions to have introduced something like that with his daughter. I rate him more credible generally than Becky. Some aspects of assessment are a matter of playing junior mystery detective, and weighing the character and motives of the participants together with the plausibility of their stories.

I introduce the concept of the pragmatics of statements, in contrast to the content. Words are also deeds, and in understanding Becky's comments we should ask, "What is she *doing* by saying those things?" Clearly, she was making a case against her father and placing him in an extremely awkward position. I am thus presenting a critical concept (IV-2) and using it to help the parents better understand the situation (IV-1). Concepts such as these are obvious once they are introduced, but too readily overlooked under ordinary circumstances. My interpretation avoids buying into Becky's presentation of herself as merely a victim (II-4), but confirms the control that she is exercising with her father (II-3).

Moreover, Becky is willing to reach into areas of sexual improprieties and apparently to fabricate to strengthen her case, suggesting an absence of appropriate boundaries and a poor regard for the truth. She is being the prosecutor, and her father is left with the role of defending himself. One can only continue as a prosecutor so long as the opposition continues in the complementary role of defendant, and one of my objectives is to help Father to be something other than the defendant.

Father takes Becky too seriously, and I suggest that he might do better to let her know that he understands her concerns or to joke with her some, but not to tangle on every issue. I use some of the active listening comments I made in the last session as illustrations and suggest some active listening and other responses for him to consider. Most active approaches suggest alternate actions for the clients, and the particular ones we suggest must be geared to our understanding of what will work for the clients in their specific situations (IV-6).

Father is also concerned with the boys, particularly the younger one, and is angry at Becky for dominating the session so

---

*There was no recording on session 2, and the comments here are from notes made immediately after the session.

that other concerns were not heard. Robbie had trouble in school last year and had to be placed in another school which gave more individual attention, where he is now doing well. Father is concerned that the school problems indicate underlying personal adjustment problems of a more general nature. I inquire if there are adjustment problems now, and do not find sufficient indications. If anything, he seems to be relatively well adjusted to the circumstances. I suggest to the parents that he seems relatively well adjusted and mention that we can look into it further if some signs of problems show up later. My aim is to reassure, to keep the focus on the obvious problems, and to avoid introducing uncertainties into areas of apparent strengths (II-5).

## SESSION 3

Father mentions that he felt good about the way things went the last weekend with the children. They walked in the woods together, played soccer, and went shopping. The boys enjoy themselves telling about the weekend activities, and they talk more and seem more comfortable than they had in the first session. They both say that things are fine with their Dad and Laura, and when I inquire specifically, they have no complaints. There is evidence, not found in the first session, that Father and the boys enjoy being with each other.

Becky complains again that Father never hugs her. I focus on the issue of hugs, as a way of moving Becky's concern out of the bedroom and into the arena of public and appropriate physical affection:

Driscoll: We have a hug-me sign here. Would that help?
Becky: No. Because then he will hug me because he sees the sign and it will mean nothing.
Father: I'd like to understand a little better. We went for a long walk and my arm was around you when you didn't ask for it. So when you say I never hug you, I'm not clear if really you want it all the time we are together or what you are saying.
Becky: But that was about the only time you put your arm around me.
Driscoll: You like lots of hugs?
Becky: Yeah. I get hugs from everybody but him. My brothers hug me, my mom hugs me, and everybody else hugs me.

I try to lighten it up:

Driscoll: Is she pretty huggable?
Father: Yeah, pretty huggable.
Driscoll: How would you rate her on a huggable scale?
Father: I would probably put her about in the middle.

Becky complains again that he never hugs her; Father says that he is comfortable moving over and hugging her right now. I suggest that he do that, to see what will come of it (III-3):

Father: Here we go. [ He hugs her.] Is that a good hug? How do you rate that hug?
Becky: It's irritating.
Father [joking]: Oh no. I can't even do a hug right.
Becky: It is a waste of time.

Becky complains that the hugs are too seldom or are only to appease her. She has a hurt and hysterical quality in her voice not present in the first session. Becky says she wants hugs yet refuses to accept the ones she gets, and I try to show her the sense she makes or might make in her contradictory position (II-1):

Driscoll: Even when you do get a hug, it surely doesn't make up for all the times that you have felt neglected by your dad.
Becky: That may have something to do

with it. But I don't get them that often, so there is no point in thinking of it that much.

She appeared interested, but then rejected the idea. Becky is arguing opposite sides against her father, and I try a paradoxical prescription to point out the probable purpose:

Driscoll: Try to get him confused, and then get a couple of steps ahead of him.
Becky: I'm not trying to get him confused. He's already confused enough.

Paradoxical interventions may be used for any of several understandable objectives (Driscoll, 1985), and this one was intended to make an unacceptable pattern conscious to Becky by appearing to support it. But she saw through it, was not amused, and turned it against her father. Perhaps a more elaborately constructed paradox might go somewhere, but I am not optimistic and do not try it again.

I talk with Father more about the importance of staying steady with Becky. He is doing better with her this session, and I compliment him on staying calmer and joshing with her instead of getting defensive. He gets in at least one humorous comeback of his own:

Becky: . . . .I prefer being with my friends or with my mother. [Dad] is an oddball.
Father: Having one strange parent really adds flavor to things. Think of how boring life would be if everybody was the same as your mother. . . .

Becky complains about various concerns with her father. She wants more time with her father, but when her father is available she wants to be with her friends instead. She is sounding quite upset and close to crying during much of the last half of the session. As I actively listen, the focus of her concerns changes and nothing gets nailed down. I mention that the issues she is concerned about were changing.

## SESSION 4

The father asks to borrow the tape from the last session, to try to get a better sense of what was going on. Reviewing a session tape is one way to promote carryover of information from sessions (V-3).

Father: There was a lot of hostility that night after we left here, even from the boys. Becky was saying that she feels like a fifth wheel around the home and was listing things that were more important to her. Tom added money to the list, and he was also angry [at me].
Laura: I was pretty overwhelmed after hearing it. I have been hearing it for two years, but so much was concentrated into an hour that it wore me out.
Driscoll [to Father]: How much was Tom really throwing in? Was he just making a few comments? Both boys seem very supportive of you.
Father: Right. Maybe it was just that he knew what he was doing and it surprised me. . . . Let me share a contrast to that. Becky spent the night with a girlfriend, and there was not any conflict with the boys in the time I spent with just them. It makes me wonder what is going on. I am kind of lost here.

The boys had seemed to be ganging up with Becky against their father. I explain that from an adult that might indicate more, but that children would not be sensitive to how much it hurts when you are already under fire and that they could easily add something simply because that is when there was an opening. The point is to clarify the relationships that he has with the children (IV-1). Father has been seeing them together as a single alliance and needs to separate them into the individuals that they are.

Clients can get hurt in family sessions,

and the parents' comments about being overwhelmed are a reminder that we need to maintain the peace between warring family members and to protect each of them as much as possible. Since I am unable to allay Becky's attacks, it is fortunate I have the alternate sessions to support the parents. I try to support Father by lowering the credibility of specific arguments Becky makes:

Driscoll: My impression is that you are a little sensitive about getting criticized by the youngsters.
Laura: There is the weight of it and the vast quantity of it. It is hard to treat it lightly.
Father: There are three of them at me at once, and it is hard to treat it lightly.
Driscoll: Becky did keep after you the whole session last time.... I mentioned this in the session, but it is really important: The issues that she was criticizing you on were changing during the session. One issue would blend into another. She was complaining that you did not spend enough time with her, and then that she did not get enough time with her friends the weekends she visits you.... My responses were all essentially attempts to clarify for her what she was saying, and she would change a bit each time... I am not sure that we ever really traced it down to a final point, and I am not sure that she has either....
Father: I could see that the way you have of not arguing with her was getting to her feelings. If you keep going with her that way, she eventually has to change.
Driscoll: And if you enter into an argument with her, you may be arguing about something that she does not really care about.

I explain more about actively listening as an alternative to argument and recommend that they use it. But I am not so optimistic as the father is that Becky has to change. I went quite a while actively listening with her last session and saw no signs of anything changing.

Father tried hugging Becky over the last few days and felt that was what she was wanting. She did not respond, but she did not resist either. I mention that when he hugged her in the session she was not gracious about it. I comment that we will have to see whether she really wants him hugging her more and if anything is to be gained by doing that. I thus invite him to collaborate with me to find out whether more hugging is going to do any good (III-3).

One of my main goals is to make Jim more comfortable and adept, and less touchy and defensive, in his role as a father. His defensive responses may be contributing to her tirades against him in several ways. His arguments against her are provocations that she responds to with further anger; she is out to nail him, and his reactions give her the satisfaction of hitting the mark; and his seriousness confirms for her that all this is to be taken quite seriously. To the extent that he can maintain more confidence with her, he could allay some of her continuing accusations. And not fighting with her so much would also make his life easier.

Some of these contributing factors are covered under the behavioral principle of reinforcement, although there are some contrasts as well. Behaviorists might consider that it is the attention that is reinforcing and so tend to recommend no response or isolation. Seeing the contributing factors as they are listed above allows us to consider actively listening, joking, or other responses as plausible alternatives. My impression is that the father does not yet have the confidence here to try something like isolation with her and make it work. As his confidence increases and if other things fail, I might suggest a more authoritative approach.

I suggest that his status as the father is more secure than he considered it to be:

Driscoll: There are some ways in which you can loosen up and let go of some of the power struggle. You do not have to win every argument. You can even give in some things now and then. But the last line is that you always remain the father....

I use an image from animal social behavior to introduce the concept that a youngster should not count as so much of a threat (IV-2):

Driscoll: I heard something which may be just a myth, but it makes a good point. In a wolf pack there is a strict hierarchy of authority. A lower member does not bark at a higher member, get out of line or take his food, or in any way challenge his authority. Or if he does, there is hell to pay. But a puppy can do just about anything he wants. A puppy could growl at the leader, or even snap at him, and the leader might just push him away or walk away himself. The puppy is *ineligible* to threaten the leader's position in the pack. So nothing that he could do is taken as a serious threat, and the leader remains the leader.... I am suggesting that with Becky you need to get to where nothing she can do really threatens your positions as father and stepmother. You need to get the sense that she remains the child and you remain the parents.

The parents ask for some clarifications, but understand the analogy. They mention that there are issues on which they cannot give in, specifically Becky's demands for more time and money. I draw distinctions between those arguments which are mostly hot air and those where something of substance is involved. You can give on the former and not lose anything, but not on the latter. The parents support the principle of real limits to the time the children can have to visit.

There is some benefit from the earlier sessions:

Laura: We practiced what you were working on last session. There were a million things that Becky said [to get at us], and we just made jokes of them or ignored them, and she could not get one thing started. She said [in our last session] that she just ignored us all weekend, but that was not what happened. We did not give her anything to get her teeth into.

And she offers a reasonable interpretation of the continuing anger:

Laura: Becky would like to intimidate us and is used to doing it. I think that she is real mad about it because she has lost her power.

It is common when the parents become firmer for the youngster to escalate her attacks. It is important that parents see this as an understandable stage and not as a failure of the program (I-3).

Father says that he has become more sympathetic to Becky since the first session and feels good about being able to see her position with some sympathy rather than anger. My presentation of Becky has been balanced rather than strictly sympathetic, and his change in attitude may be due to increased self-confidence.

The parents see Becky as trying to be the caretaker for her mother and sometimes for her brothers. They note that Becky often takes the positions her mother has in the arguments between the parents over financial and other matters. Family loyalties are at issue, and I suggest a way of managing them (IV-6):

Laura: There are some fights that don't even involve her, which she enters into just because she has overheard her mother complaining about something.
Driscoll: You might just comment to her

that she is doing that. Say something like "You are taking your mom's fight here. Let your mom fight this one out on her own." Do not treat her as somebody to argue with. Treat her as a noncombatant, no matter what she says. It is the idea of ineligible again. She is a noncombatant, so whatever she says is just kibitzing.

In response to Becky's complaint last session that she was only a visitor, I mention that a 13-year-old is old enough to be by herself and explore whether they can allow more visitation. They see Becky as irresponsible and quite willing to go through their personal belongings and to otherwise abuse any privileges. They agree that it is not her house and that she is essentially a visitor there. It is apparent that they cherish the little time they have alone, and that managing the children can be a full-time responsibility with considerable strains and too few satisfactions. Although additional visitation might help allay Becky's anger (IV-4), the option of adding visitation hours is just not there.

They mention that the problems really began last year when they got married. Becky wanted to be more involved with the wedding and was hurt and angry that she could not be. She refused to visit for several weeks and has still never fixed up her room with any of her personal belongings. Information such as this is interesting, but it need not be a basis of our initial interventions. It may be acquired in later sessions as we try to fill in the missing pieces (III-4).

Father mentions that he has been uncompromising sometimes because he feels that Becky can overwhelm him, and that if Tom and Robbie asked for the same things he would be over the edge. I mention that having someone attacking you that way would easily make you feel you have no room to maneuver (II-1). His explanation helps account for his initial appearance of being inflexible.

## SESSION 5

I was seeing the two boys somewhat as captive observers, but Tom surprises me by mentioning that he likes coming because we talk about what is going on. Becky says she does not like coming, which does not surprise anyone. She comes because she does not want to miss anything. She leads off against Father, but fails to gain the advantage:

Becky: Last time you gave me a "hug-me" sticker. And I really think that if I have to have a "hug-me" sticker, then he may hug me but not because he wants to. I hate fake hugs. . . . And I don't want to be hugged when there are other people around. . . . It is okay in front of my family, but why does he have to hug me in church?
Father: I am being more and more hugging. But I can leave it out at the church. That is no problem.
Becky: Well, why do you always have to be hugging me in public places?
Father: Right. No problem. No hugging in public places. I can handle that.
Driscoll: Is that the response you want?
Becky: I don't know. It doesn't matter any more.
Driscoll: Does your dad hug you enough now?
Becky: I don't even notice.

Father is clearly more adaptable and less combative than in the first session. She is no longer able to best him in the verbal joust. The hugs become a bogus issue, which I was suspecting earlier but could not know for sure until we tried it out (III-4).

Becky complains again about not having enough time with Father, and he tries another angle:

Father: What you don't have is so important that you don't even [enjoy] what you do have.

Becky [sarcastically]: Oh God bless you, Daddy. You give us so much. I mean, you are just so wonderful.
Father: No, I don't expect you to say that. But it would be helpful if we focus on what we do have together. I could live with that a lot easier.
Becky: If we looked at all the good things in life?
Father: I tend to do that. Did you know that about me?
Becky: That would be just like having pollution and ignoring it. If you sit and look at the blue sky, it is just going to get worse.

Becky is arguing for more hugs and more time together, but she does not appreciate what she gets of either one. She is making a case that her dad does not give her anything and were she to appreciate what she is getting she would obviously weaken her case. So the pursuit of her case prevents her from enjoying what she says she is wanting.

The children agree that they are easier on Laura:

Becky: We don't expect Laura to want to see us more. We feel that is dad's responsibility.... We feel we are her guests.

Is this why Becky is so much easier on her stepmother? Standards for expressing oneself are mentioned:

Father: I think I really value expression of feelings. Becky says I don't care about it, but I think I do. Maybe not to the extent that she means....

It is important to gauge how much expression he has allowed, and whether the principles should change. Since he is a social worker, it would make sense that he does value the free expression of feelings.

Becky complains that her dad gets them dinner sometimes before he takes them home, but not other times, and we touch again on her concern for her mother:

Driscoll: Is that a problem for your mom?
Becky: Yeah. Mother never knows whether we are going to eat or not. He doesn't give her any definite time.
Father: Your mom can usually take care of her own issues. I don't think that you need to fight over her issues. If she doesn't like it, then she can tell me and I can deal with it then.
Becky: What bothers my mother bothers me.

The last comment confirms the impression Father offered last session that Becky fights her mother's fights. Father is following the advice I gave him last time in clarifying that it is her mother's fight and not fighting with Becky over the issue.

Becky is close to tears and has come to tears in several sessions when nobody is fighting with her and I am actively listening to what she is saying. So the anger may be a reaction to the uncomfortable sadness, and I try to see if we can go anywhere focusing on the sadness.

Driscoll [to Becky]: I think that much of this is really painful, and rather than try to sort through it all, it is easier to just lash out.
Becky: Well, I just get so tired of it. I try to be decent to him but....

I try to provide a gentle interpretation to Becky that she is actually hurting her father by the things she is saying:

Driscoll: When you are talking about the negative so much it can come across as an accusation. And it can hurt.
Becky: I could care less whether I hurt his feelings or not. I used to care, but he

hurts my feelings all the time. . . .
Driscoll: Since he hurts you, you cannot care that you hurt him [back].
Becky: I'm not sorry. I don't want to hurt his feelings but I feel that I have no choice.
Father: I think that my sadness has been in terms of the children. The saddest time I can remember is when they used to cry when I left them [with their mother].
Becky: You don't care if I cry.
Father: I do care. But I have a harder time relating to your sadness because of your anger.

It is hard to focus Becky on the sadness. She feels justified in her accusations, and I showed her the sense it makes for her to lash back (II-1). This confirms my earlier impression that she has little concern for her father's feelings, and I do not try to appeal again to any concern she should have for him (III-5). This youngster wants to nail him and feels quite justified in doing so.

Father: I'm not sure this family is going to change that much, but I think that just understanding what is going on is helpful. Tonight I found out about the sadness. I knew about the anger, but I did not know about the sadness.
Driscoll: The sadness comes out when there is nowhere to go with the anger. The sadness comes out more here [than at home].

This is an essentially psychodynamic interpretation of one emotion as a cover for another emotion, and it seems to fit well here. I will try to follow it up in a later session, but I am not sure where to go with it. Becky is quite uncomfortable with the sadness, and she does not see me as enough of an ally for me to support her through it.

Father: I feel some responsibility for the sadness. I think that some of your sadness is my fault because of the divorce. I think that the divorce is part of why the sadness is there.
Becky: If only you weren't divorced but you are, so what does that have to do with anything?
Father [to Becky]: I feel sadness that you and I cannot relate in a more fun and more understanding way. I probably have as much trouble accepting you as you have accepting me. You are just better at saying it.
Driscoll: Some of that comes from how much you blame yourself for the problems that are going on.
Father: Yeah, I do that. I would really rather not do that.
Driscoll: It doesn't seem to get you anywhere. Even when you can look and say, "My doing this caused these problems," your spending a lot of time blaming yourself does not make you a better person. You are saying, "I may have messed it up, but at least I care enough to suffer for it." And things just get worse.

Portraying it as self-affirmation through penance shows the sense he makes in suffering for his wrongs (II-1), and from there he can understand the failings of suffering as a means to indicate caring (IV-5). Conducting penance for wrongdoing is one of a variety of purposes that may be involved in self-criticism (Driscoll, 1981, 1982; Driscoll & Edwards, 1983). My objective is to lessen the self-condemnation.

Becky asks what we will talk about in the next sessions and seems uncomfortable with things going on when she is not there. Father had mentioned that he was uncomfortable with anger, and I explain that we will talk about ways that her dad might get more comfortable with anger, how they can be better parents, and things like that.

## SESSION 6

I ask how things are going. Father comments that he felt good about the time he spent with the children on their last visit. They sang Christmas songs together, and he took Becky shopping. He felt he was quite patient with her. Laura comments that Becky can be quite critical in general.

I comment that the critical mood will lessen when she realizes that nobody is reacting the same way to it anymore. I explain to Father that as he has a steadier mood with Becky there will be fewer provocations for her, and she will see that she can no longer control him with her moods. I also suggest that he is the one who will have to make the changes here, because he is the one with the interest and commitment to try something else, whereas Becky wants to have it her way by antagonizing him, and has little motivation for giving that up. I am appealing to his sense of responsibility as a father (VI-1).

Laura says that Jim does get angry and that anyone would get angry in that situation, and asks what he is supposed to do with his anger. One of the things they do now is talk together about their angry feelings and support each other after the sessions and after the children are gone. I support that as a reasonable way to let go of the angry feelings without taking them out on the children (II-5).

I mention that they seem to be having a much better time with the boys:

Laura: We always have a good time with the boys, and nothing ever seems to go wrong.
Driscoll: That's my impression. You don't have problems with [all] three children. The other two are real easy children. You get a warm gleam from them much of the time. Tom said he actually liked being here because he liked seeing what was going on.
Laura: We were watching them play a basketball game. Becky was making all the rules and [the boys] just walked off into the woods and left her because she was so controlling. We were wondering how they would be when they grew up, and I said maybe they would be really adaptable.
Driscoll: I think you missed that when you brought them in and said that you were having problems with them. You are not having problems with the two boys.
Laura: I used to say the children were a problem when it was not the children [together] at all. Now I catch myself when I am doing that.

This is confirmation here that the parents are separating the children in their minds and that the old alliance between Becky and the brothers is no longer solid. It is important to identify the strengths in the family and to separate them from the actual problems.

Father is still inwardly jarred by the accusations, and I offer him a *light-shielding* meditation to inoculate him against their impact (IV-3):

Driscoll: I have something I wanted to run through with you and see if it will help. It seems to make quite a difference for most of the people I have tried it with. I take you into a meditative state or trance state and have you imagine a light and make the light into an actual shield that it is a protective shield with the strength of steel, so that nothing harmful can get through it. And you will see Becky on the other side, and that she will be hurling verbal attacks at you and that they will hit this shield and bounce off and you will realize that they do not hit you.... It is your capacity for self-suggestion that makes it work.... Those with Christian beliefs can imagine that the light is the love of Jesus and that the protection is God's protection....

Whenever possible I try to give information on a procedure beforehand so that the client can give informed consent and does not have the feeling of being tricked into something. This maintains our own credibility and appeals to the client's interests in having some say in the treatment.

I have him close his eyes and relax, and we go through a seven-numbered sequence of breathing in deeply, imaging a color of light, letting the air go, and relaxing. Suggestions are given that he is moving comfortably into a trance state in which he can give himself positive, constructive suggestions, and that he is becoming closer in touch with his "unconscious" mind:

Driscoll: I want you to imagine that Becky is there on the other side of the shield. She is angry and upset and she accuses you of something. Ordinarily, the accusation would come right at you and hit you in the face or in the chest or in the gut. Imagine that the accusation comes hurling at you and it just hits that shield and falls to the ground harmless and loses its force. And you realize here that you have not been hit, and you let go and relax. . . . Imagine she is throwing something again. . . . If you need more protection, you increase the intensity of the light shield. You realize again that you have not been hit and you begin to relax. . . . The shield is something that you can practice at home and take with you. You will feel protected and be calmer while facing the accusations.

After the procedure I ask him what his experience was:

Father: I had the image of the shield clearly in my mind, and I felt relaxed. It was easy to imagine Becky throwing stuff at me, specific things, and [me] not getting at all upset at them.

The shielding procedure is adapted from the familiar relaxation and imagery procedures from behavior therapy combined with light imagery from meditation practices and the power of trance suggestions. Persons ordinarily experience anger and accusation as coming at them and hitting and hurting them, so the image addresses directly the actual experience of being hurt by a verbal attack. The shielding procedure is something I spliced together earlier from available methods and I found to be apparently effective* in brief applications, and so continued using.

Imagining the light as the love of Jesus is an integration of a Christian tradition into an otherwise ordinary mental health procedure. It suggests a bridge to something that matters to the clients with strong Christian beliefs and may make the procedure more acceptable to such clients.

We talk some more about child management techniques. I contend that yelling at Becky increases the tension and conflict because there is so much argument, but that in a calmer atmosphere a very strict statement can go a long way. I am again supporting Father in limiting what he is willing to fight over, so that the stands he does make carry more weight.

## SESSION 7

The children are in a soccer league and enjoy telling me about some of their experiences. Becky mentions that she called

---

*I have used this procedure with perhaps 10 individual clients and once with a meditation group of 12 members. There was clear benefit for most of the individual clients and possible benefit for the others. Ten of the twelve members of the meditation group reported increased calmness during the next week. I ordinarily ask clients to identify any tendencies they have to lash back, and I caution that trying to get even destroys the shielding. The procedure is best used in combination with appropriate assertiveness suggestions.

her father something after he let her off at Mother's house, and he could not do anything about it. He had not heard what she yelled at him, and he refuses her invitation to fight about it. He does not want to know what she called him and contends that what she does when she is with her mother is not his business. Becky resumes complaining that Father is spending time with Laura and leaving her out:

Becky: It just makes me mad because he is going places with her.
Driscoll: And you are feeling left out.
Becky: We are being completely excluded. I don't see why we can't all go as a family and work on our relationship.

Her continual complaints are getting old, and other family members are not taking them that seriously anymore. I have no confidence that the active listening responses such as the one above have any real therapeutic value, but I give them here and there out of habit or simply because I am not coming up with anything else to say. It has become relatively easy to steer the conversations away from her complaints and onto other issues. I mention to the boys that they seem to be holding their own with Becky:

Becky: If I get mad at Tom or Robbie, they gang up on me. But I don't care.

The earlier children-against-adults alliance really has vanished. The issue of standing up for their mother comes up:

Becky: My mother asked Dad a favor to babysit us, and he said no. He is being a real jerk...
Driscoll: You are very loyal to your mom. You stand up for her.
Becky: Yeah....
Driscoll: Does it ever get hard on you doing that? You are fighting your mom's battles. It would be easier on you if you weren't fighting them.

Becky: It would be easier on me if I just stand here and play dead....
Driscoll: You are not doing this whole fight just for yourself. It is a matter of principle for you. And loyalty to your mother....

I continue emphasizing that she is in the fight out of principle and loyalty, to show the sense it makes for her to continue fighting even for a losing cause (II-1) and to acknowledge what are essentially ethical considerations for her action (II-2). Perhaps credited already with being loyal to her mother, she could find a way to ease out of the battle. I press the issue and continue talking with her on this for several minutes. She changes the subject to Dad is a jerk, I change it back, she changes it again, and I allow her to continue with it. She does not acknowledge that my interpretation is of any importance to her.

Family loyalties, such as seen here, are a focus for some family system orientations, and my interpretation is a reframing or positive connotation. I focus on the issue not because I am of one of the family systems schools, but because the conversation revealed that that was what was transpiring in this instance. As a general principle, we should make case formulations not because of an adherence to any theoretical orientation, but because that is what is revealed from the cases themselves.

Becky is a good student in school and is apparently somewhat more stable with other people than with her father. Clients who are in such turmoil when making angry accusations sometimes calm down when the adversary is not present.

I spend perhaps 20 minutes with Becky individually, to try out this remaining possibility. I actively listen and she continues the complaints; she mentions that Dad prefers Laura because she is easier to get along with, and I follow up on this, but she ignores her own insight. I try placing her in charge:

Driscoll: If you were me, what sort of things would you do with your father?
Becky: I would tell him that he is the stupidest person on earth. And he needs five years of counseling.
Driscoll: After five years of counseling, you will be grown. We have to get something [that works] faster than that.
Becky: I could care less. My life can go on without him.

She is on a tear and apparently unresponsive to anything I do. I have the sense that I am relatively interchangeable with her father, and that she is having some of the same emotional reactions to me as she has toward her father. One of the guideline principles is to counter transference reactions such as these (I-2), but I have not found a way to do it. Being with Becky alone for any length of time would wear me out.

## SESSION 8

I ask Jim how he has done with the light shielding. He says that he had forgotten about it and did not practice it. Laura says that he has seemed calmer with Becky since we did the procedure, and she thinks that it did some good. He says he feels detached from Becky, which I suggest might be because some of the turmoil is gone but has not been replaced yet with a positive relationship. He agrees that he has not been so overconcerned about her, but is not sure whether to attribute it to the procedure. Clinical interview assessment can be frequently inconclusive, leaving us with impressions but not clear confirmation.

I review my impressions of my time with Becky individually. I mention that Becky went on and on with the accusations and seemed to have no real awareness of me or of my reactions to what she was saying. I mention that it wore me out to be with her that long, and I do not recommend an individually oriented course of treatment. I believe we can do better with parental management tactics.

Laura mentions that Jim has always been stricter on the two boys than he is with Becky, and he realizes that is so. He now realizes that he would never allow the boys to get away with saying some of the things that Becky says all the time. Laura notes that she is firmer with Becky than Jim is and suggests that is why Becky treats her more respectfully than she treats Jim. I consider this as a good account of why the children are so easy on their stepmother.

Father mentions that he has given Becky too much power over his life. There was a lot of conflict in his family when he was growing up but he never learned to deal well with conflict. He had a sister who fought with him a lot and often got the best of him. Laura mentions that he once called Becky by the name of his sister. He mentions that when Becky calls one of the boys "stupid" or "dummy," it makes him absolutely furious. Such taunts against the boys would be a reminder of what he was subjected to growing up.

So here we see a way the relationships in his own family of origin contributed to the present family patterns. Taunted growing up, he is easily intimidated by smart-mouthed females, and his being easily intimidated contributed to Becky's getting the upper hand in their relationship. The etiology is interesting and useful. It legitimizes his being intimidated by his daughter (II-1), and it helps confirm my impression that his being intimidated is at the core of the problem. Intergenerational family theorists would look for interpretations such as this and focus on them. But notice here that uncovering the origins is not in itself a solution to the problem. Moreover, I have formulated the problem and have been working it for some time now without knowing the etiology. The key factor is that Father was intimidated by Becky, and much of what I have been doing has been to build his confidence with her. The past can be interesting in cases such as this, but is not critical either for the formulation of the problems or for their treatment.

I feel it is time for some stronger measures to control the accusations. I do not have any reservations left that Father would be inappropriately strict with her: I see him as appropriately strict with his boys and unusually lenient with Becky. He seems to have the savvy and confidence to wrangle with her, and she no longer has the support of her brothers against the parents. I mention that the parents must set the standards for what is allowed in their house:

Driscoll: You have to look at your own standards. You can look from one family to another and see that no two have the same standards. But what they have in common is that they all do have standards. You have your choices as to where you can draw the line.

But at the same time I suggest that Becky really has gone beyond what seem to me to be reasonable and appropriate limits. I suggest that Father should make a stand. I outline a child management program and deal with their objections (IV-6):

Driscoll: You need some sort of consequence. For general complaining or for condemning someone you could give her a warning. Like say, "Becky, I don't want you doing that and I want you to stop." And then if she continues she gets a point, and if she gets three points then she has to go to her room for 10 minutes.

Both parents are apprehensive about the flack they expect they will get. Father says he feels that he can do it. I have them practice some of the statements they might say to her (V-2). I mention that if they think it will be hard with a 13-year-old, they could wait and try it with a 16-year-old (VI-1). They vote for trying it now.

I give an illustration where the firmer use of authority was of considerable benefit. I tell of a 16-year-old who accused her mother of not loving her, in order to get her way, and found that Mother buckled under the accusation and gave her whatever she wanted. When she wanted to get out of school, she began complaining that her teachers did not love her, which was a new application of the earlier tactic. The problem cleared considerably when the mother saw through the manipulations and refused to allow the complaints. Illustrations such as this promote confidence in the program (V-1, I-3).

The parents are concerned that Becky is running the boys down too much. I mention that Tom seems to hold his own, and I comment that they could support Tom by complimenting him on holding his own with Becky. I want to support a reasonable alliance between the parents and the boys. Laura is concerned that Robbie is too much like Jim, in that he lets everyone walk over him. Father still has some concern that the children are allied together against him, but sees Becky as the sole instigator.

Father says that he grew up with parents who were very strict and had not wanted to be that way with his children. He had become too lenient because he had not wanted to repeat the pattern of his own childhood. Here again, the past is helping us make sense of the present problems. He had come to see the use of authority as oppressive, and I portray a more balanced concept of authority (IV-2).

They mention that they have been doing more things with the boys when Becky refuses to participate. They come back and say it was really fun, and the implication is that she missed out.

## SESSION 9

The tougher line seems to have done the job, and relatively easily:

Becky: We haven't been arguing lately. Dad and I have gotten along. Everything's okay for the time being. As far as I am concerned he may have given up on me.

In the last week Father called Becky once or twice on smarting off to him and told her she was out of line. He raised his voice to her and told her to stop in a more forceful manner, and she gave up. He says that she has not been making accusations since then, and that they have been getting along considerably better. He once made her clean up her room for smarting off, but he never put her in her room as an isolation technique.

I had prepared the parents for more of a struggle, but she gave in more easily than we expected. She had been receiving little support for her positions for quite awhile now and should have been growing tired of fighting the losing battle.

The parents have gotten what they wanted from therapy and decide to terminate treatment. The family patterns seem to be relatively normal and appropriate ones at this time for a stepfamily. I respect their feelings of completion and agree with their decision. I schedule a final session a month later to ensure that the program continues to work and that no new problems develop (V-3).

## SESSION 10

The family confirms that things are still going well a month after the last session. Father judges that "everyone is doing pretty good," and Laura concurs. Becky goes on a tirade later in the session about the school bus driver being such a jerk, which I tend to consider about normal, although I sympathize with the school personnel who must operate in that sort of atmosphere. She does not lash out once at her father in the entire one-hour session. We terminate the sessions, with the understanding that they will contact me if these problems recur or if there are other problems.

## CLIENTS' IMPRESSIONS

A counseling evaluation questionnaire was completed by each of the family members approximately eight weeks after the last session. The questionnaire asked: "Overall, how much do you feel you benefited from the counseling you received?" and "How much do you feel that [each of the other individuals] benefited?" The responses were on a five-point scale, with 5 = a great deal, 4 = moderately, 3 = some, 2 = none, and 1 = was harmed. The amount of reported benefit is indicated in Table 1, with the respondent on the left

Table 1

| Respondent | Person Rated | | | | |
|---|---|---|---|---|---|
| | Father | Laura | Becky | Tom | Robbie |
| Father: | great deal | great deal | some | some | some |
| Laura: | great deal | moderately | some | some | some |
| Becky: | some | some | none* | some | none |
| Tom: | none | some | none | none | none |
| Robbie: | some | some | some | some | some |

*None is an average: Becky circled some, none, and was harmed.

and the persons being rated listed across the top.

There were three open-ended questions, which are listed here with the comments from those who responded to the questions:

*"What Were the Strengths of the Counseling as You See It?"*

Father: You were easy for all family members to relate to, and therefore freedom to be expressive was established. The mixture of every other week being couple only and the next week the entire family aided communication. Your sense of humor was used effectively. You were direct with me and paradoxical with Becky.

Laura: Alternating sessions: one week family, next week couple. Counselor's relaxed attitude. Everyone seemed to feel comfortable to say what they wanted to.

Becky: Let me scream at Dad.

Tom: Let me play longer.

*"What Were the Weaknesses or Problems?"*

Father: At times I didn't follow the drift of a personal example enough to make it applicable.

Laura: No problems that I remember.

Becky: Telling me to shut up when I got mad. I came there to express my feelings.

Tom: Becky crying or screaming.

*"Please Make Any Other Comments You Feel Might be Appropriate."*

Father: I felt confident in you as a therapist throughout. I felt your ideas and insights and directives were helpful. I did not feel a bias toward any family member but I do feel you communicated the parent-child hierarchy well. I feel I could very comfortably recommend you as a therapist. Thanks for your help.

Becky: It made me mad as something to go there and made me upset so I hated it. I didn't need to put myself in that kind of mood.

In a later conversation, Father adds that through therapy he found the strength to set the limits, and that he feels that was a lot to have accomplished.

These evaluations were consistent with the appraisals the individuals had been making during the course of the treatment, and so were about what I might have expected.

## CONCLUDING COMMENTS

Many themes weave through the course of these sessions. Some were resolved with apparent gains, others seemed to lead nowhere, and still others were resolved satisfactorily but the benefit remains unassessed. One characteristic of the pragmatic approach is the willingness to look into various aspects of a case, find out where they take us, follow up on the ones that hold promise, and let go of the ones that do not pan out. Judgment and experience are obviously involved in telling how far to carry an intervention and when to let it go.

Issues and concerns may be considered for a while in the sessions and then the focus moves on. But we can often benefit from returning to the apparently pivotal factors over and over through several sessions, until they are resolved. My support for the father on parenting approaches took various forms, but was included in several ways in each session throughout the course of treatment. The objective is to familiarize the clients with the new patterns until they take hold (V-2).

Although I usually try to balance individual sessions with the parties on each side of a family conflict, I did not have an individual session with Becky until later in the treatment. Although there were time limitations, I suspect that my early view of Becky as hard to manage made it easy for me to put off trying to fit in an individual session with her. She was as hard to manage in my individual session with her as I suspected she would be, although I cannot tell if she would have been easier to relate to earlier—before I became identified too closely with her parents.

Although my initial impression was that Father was too strict, I came to see him as trying to maintain appropriate authority but too easily intimidated and in need of the skills and confidence to make firmer stands with Becky. My concluding formulation was that, because of his inadequate control, he had allowed Becky to continue in angry and inconsiderate social attitudes toward him. He appeared overly strict and rigid in the first session as he was trying unsuccessfully to regain some semblance of control over the children.

My initial impression of Becky was a positive one of quick wit and social insightfulness, but I gradually came to see her as very out of control and in need of parental management. I would have preferred a resolution in which she felt she was gaining something for the concessions she had to make, but I was unable to arrange such a compromise.

Although I eventually recommended time-outs with Becky, Father never used them but brought her under control by simply raising his voice and demanding that she stop her accusations. His authority was increasing and hers decreasing over the course of the sessions, so that by the end he could get her to stop by merely commanding her to do so. I wondered later if my treating her accusations as an ethical position may have made it easier for her to give them up, although this cannot be confirmed.

Many of my observations and interventions are associated with familiar therapeutic orientations. The active listening responses used for clarifications are from client-centered counseling. The concern for alliances and family hierarchy is found in family systems approaches, as is the focus on loyalties. The specific parenting suggestions used are similar to the assertiveness training and child management recommendations of behavior therapy. There are smatterings of other orientations as well, and the light-shielding technique is a schmorgasborg all by itself.

My observation of Becky's comments as "making a case against her father" is pivotal. I portray it this way because it seems to be the most straightforward description of what she is doing by saying what she says. Note that her comments could also be formulated as "expressing her feelings," which might be preferred in humanistic approaches and which Becky herself prefers. But seeing the comments as "making a case against" recognizes the social influence aspect of her comments and invites us to try to understand their purpose. Although I originally assumed that she was making a case in order to get more affection and time with Father, her later responses and the loyalty issues make another motivation more plausible: She was trying to bring her father to justice for abandoning her and her mother. It can be important to talk about the concerns, but it seems clear that the issues would not have resolved here by allowing her to continue in the role of prosecutor.

In making her case against her father she focused continually on his abandonment and neglect and ignored indications of his concern and love for her. She exaggerated his faults, to the point of apparently fabricating some of her evidence against him. Although hurt is inevitable when parents divorce, her overemphasis on the negatives undoubtedly extended and heightened the hurt she experienced. The viewpoint she argued became a critical aspect of the experience she had of her life. Blindly perpetrating her case against her father, she became also a victim of her own propaganda.

Although there were more immediate and apparent benefits for Father and Laura, I suspect that the benefits for Becky could be quite significant in the long run. Father became more assertive with women, and he and his wife have a more peaceful relationship with the children. But the accusations Becky was committed to were causing continuing turmoil for her as well and could have led to significant social and emotional impairments were they to have continued through her teenage years. Through family therapy she adjusted better to her two-family situation and began to look for some benefits in her relationship with her father.

In conducting psychotherapy, my attention is on understanding the case and on obtaining my intervention objectives, and not on the controversies between theoretical orientations. Observations and interventions are made because they seem to fit in the case, and not because they are associated with any particular orientation. As pragmatists we can borrow freely from whatever is available to fit the requirements of our cases.

Pragmatic psychotherapy is one attempt to organize and clarify what we must actually attend to in the conduct of eclectic psychotherapy. The concepts are the distinctions we use, and the guidelines organize the objectives we seek as we work with our clients.

The breadth of the concepts and guidelines encourages versatility, and there are obvious advantages in having so many options organized into a single integrated approach. We have a range of choices in what to use and alternatives when our initial interventions do not provide sufficient therapeutic leverage. As a pragmatic psychotherapist, I am using aspects of various schools of therapy but am practicing from a single comprehensive orientation.

## APPENDIX: OUTLINE OF GUIDELINES FOR PRAGMATIC PSYCHOTHERAPY*

Guidelines are prescriptions for interventions focusing on major therapeutic objectives and the usual ways to achieve them. Specifying general objectives, the guidelines require clinical judgment on when and how to implement them.

### I. The Therapeutic Relationship

1. *Be on the client's side.* Act in the best interest of the client. Avoid or resolve attitudes and feelings which interfere.

2. *Maintain an alliance.* Act so that the client can see you as an ally. Begin where you are welcome. Be personable and active. Correct misunderstandings, and counter transference.

3. *Maintain credibility.* Show the sense of what you are doing. Show how therapeutic procedures contribute to improvement. Avoid statements that are untrue, and be careful with those that appear naive or false to clients.

4. *Convey an understanding* of the client's position. Share your impressions of the client's feelings and concerns.

5. *Share responsibility* for improvement. Take responsibility in ways that enable the client to take responsibility. Provide what clients are unable to provide themselves, and encourage them to do what

---

*Revised from the listing in Driscoll (1984), pp. 195–199. One guideline is an addition *(address emotional reactivity)*, and the tasks of clarifying factors and of instilling new patterns are now separated.

they are able. Tailor interventions to individual clients.

## II. Affirmation and Accreditation

Identify existing strengths. Treat the client as one who in important ways already makes sense, is acceptable, and is in control.

*1. Legitimize (show the client the sense he or she makes).* Misunderstandings or unusual situations may make sense of puzzling feelings or behaviors. Learning histories can make sense of unusual individual characteristics.

*2. Make it acceptable.* Decriminalize. Interpret characteristics in ways the client can accept. Create a comfortable atmosphere. Use humor. Select acceptable phrasing. Emphasize positives, underplay negatives. Introduce norms for comparisons.

*3. Confirm the client's control.* See the client as someone who is already in control of his or her actions. Show the legitimate reasons clients have for the control they maintain. Show the ways they are successful.

*4. Don't buy victim acts.* A client may present himself or herself as a victim in order to avoid responsibility or to gain sympathy. Interpret and legitimize the reasons for the act. Challenge the ideology that affords special privileges to the sufferer.

*5. If it works, don't fix it.* See strengths as strengths. Avoid introducing uncertainties into areas that are already appropriate and functional.

## III. Assessment

*1. Assess what matters.* Assess what is needed for effective intervention, including areas of strengths. The pivotal factors are those that contribute significantly to the overall problems and that can be readily altered by interventions. Stay with specifics. Omit extraneous information.

*2. Use ordinary language concepts.* Respect conventions of word usage, and avoid overly generalized concepts. Recognize what individual clients mean by the words they use.

*3. Collaborate.* Ask for specifics from clients. Outline plausible interpretations and collaborate on which ones might fit best. Monitor judgment. Recreate key episodes; invite interactions with family or friends.

*4. Learn as you go.* Weave together assessment and interventions. Intervene early, and learn from the reactions. Successes may confirm initial assessments. Use failures to further understand the problems. Begin with the simplest adequate explanation, and elaborate as more leverage is needed.

*5. Don't expect the client to be somebody else.* Realize that problems are often entrenched and may survive your initial or most obvious solutions. Avoid holding clients responsible for what they are unable to do.

## IV. Clarifications

Help the client understand what is happening and how to change things to gain advantage.

*1. Clarify situations.* Identify the client's confusions, and suggest clearer views of the real world. Weigh alternatives with the client, and encourage clients to observe for themselves. Legitimize misunderstandings. Emphasize understandings over misunderstandings.

2. *Clarify concepts.* Introduce and apply distinctions that the client can see and use. Build and elaborate upon concepts that are already familiar. Untangle confounded concepts.

3. *Address emotional reactivity.* Deal with the tendencies to overreact to things as bad, wrong, unmanageable, intolerable, and catastrophic.

4. *Deal with the reality basis of emotions.* Fear and anxiety are related to perceived threat or danger; anger to provocations; guilt to wrongdoing. Deal with the circumstances generating the emotion—not merely with the experience or feeling.

5. *Clarify operating premises.* Look at the means by which the client is trying to get what he or she wants. Analyze the premises that are the basis of impractical attempts, and show how such premises are invalid.

6. *Present alternatives.* Clarify how the client can better get what he or she is after. Deal with objectives, and weigh the risks involved.

V. *Instilling New Patterns*

Take measures to maintain new views and new behaviors.

1. *Use illustrations and images.* Used to present material, a strong image may imprint and hold a concept in the client's mind.

2. *Familiarize (bring it home).* Support, restate, and deal with objections, so that the client may truly assimilate the information rather than merely hear it. Involve clients: have them try on more positive statements and practice new approaches.

3. *Structure carryover* of session gains into the client's everyday life. Make notes for clients to review. Have clients talk to others about key insights, or include family or friends in the sessions. Assign homework activities which maintain the suggested changes.

VI. *Motivations*

1. *Appeal to what matters.* Values change slowly, so that immediate motivations are best changed by appealing to what already matters to the client. Show how your suggestions are ways for clients to get what they actually want.

2. *Avoid generating resistance.* Coercion elicits resistance. When resistance appears, look at what you are saying that the client may see as unwarranted force or pressure. Redescribe interpretations to make them more acceptable, bypass objections, or leave the issue until later.

*Exceptions.* Minimize resistance, unless using it paradoxically to motivate healthy reactions.

## REFERENCES

Bergner, R. (1983). Emotions: A conceptual formulation and its clinical implications. In K. E. Davis & R. Bergner (Eds.), *Advances in descriptive psychology* (Vol. 3). Greenwich, CT: JAI Press.

Driscoll, R. (1981). Self-criticism: Analysis and treatment. In K. E. Davis (Ed.), *Advances in descriptive psychology* (Vol. 1). Greenwich, CT: JAI Press. Reprinted in *Pragmatic psychotherapy.*

Driscoll, R. (1982). Their own worst enemies. *Psychology Today, 16*(7), 45–49.

Driscoll, R. (1984). *Pragmatic psychotherapy.* New York: Van Nostrand Reinhold.

Driscoll, R. (1985). Commonsense objectives in paradoxical interventions. *Psychotherapy, 22,* 774–778.

Driscoll, R. (In press). Humor in pragmatic psychotherapy. In W. Salameh & W. F. Fry (Eds.), *Handbook of humor and psychotherapy—Advances in the clinical use of humor.* Sarasota, FL: Professional Resource Exchange.

Driscoll, R., & Edwards, L. (1983). The misconception of Christian suffering. *Pastoral Psychology, 32,* 1, 34–48.

Farber, A. (1981). Castaneda's Don Juan as psychotherapist. In K. E. Davis (Ed.), *Advances in descriptive psychology* (Vol. 1). Greenwich, CT: JAI Press.

Goldfried, M. (1980). Toward the delineation of therapeutic change principles. *American Psychologist, 35*, 991–999.

Goldfried, M., & Padawer, W. (1982). Current status and future directions in psychotherapy. In M. Goldfried (Ed.), *Converging themes in psychotherapy*. New York: Springer Publishing Company.

Ossorio, P. G. (1969). Notes on behavior description. Boulder, CO: Linguistic Research Institute.

Ossorio, P. G. (1976). *Clinical Topics* (LRI Report #11). Boulder, CO: Linguistic Research Institute.

# Commentary: The Teenage Prosecutor as an Example of Systematic Eclecticism

## Bernard D. Beitman

*Struggle as many of the case authors in this volume might, they remain bound by certain general principles of psychotherapy. Each may wish to clothe his/her presentations in striking theories or durable models, but many of these attempts are more accurately construed as garments synthesized by their own unique life experiences. Varieties of systematic eclecticism are conceptual grids that both express underlying principles of psychotherapy and reflect the author's own life experiences. Richard Driscoll's case and concepts illustrate these points. For the reader, separating the author's own idiosyncrasies from solid, useful, and fresh observations can be a puzzling process.*

### DRISCOLL'S MODEL AS A REFLECTION OF UNIQUE LIFE EXPERIENCES

*The theoretical thrust of Driscoll's approach represents one not uncommon human approach to increasing complexity: "Let's get back to basics." Eclecticism is a reaction against the confusing proliferation of psychotherapy schools. One of the chief confusing elements is the proliferation of terminology often with unacknowledged overlapping meaning. For years, for example, Jerome Frank (1976) has spoken about the demoralization hypothesis and the need for self-mastery, while Bandura (1977) has spoken about self-efficacy. The terms truly have similar meanings yet they have emerged from different professions (Frank is a psychiatrist and Bandura a psychologist) and from within different traditions although both are prominent psychotherapy researchers. Driscoll's response has been to return to "ordinary language concepts" as a way to answer the problem of separate and apparently incompatible languages among theoretical orientations. But, as he states early in his case, "ordinary language words can be used in several ways" and, in my view, can suffer from the same ambiguity as multiple theoretical terms. In addition, who is to decide what is "ordinary" and what is not?*

*The appeal of ordinary language for psychotherapy is its populism. If this view had a slogan, it would be "Let's return psychotherapy to the people. After all that's who it is supposed to serve." Perhaps this attitude has been influenced by the fact that unlike most of the case authors in this book, Driscoll is not on the regular faculty of any university. He has been greatly influenced by Peter Ossorio and the Lin-*

guistic Research Institute of Boulder, Colorado (see Driscoll, 1984, and his case for references). In my view his bows to ordinary language concepts stem from his need to clothe eclecticism in political and philosophical concepts familiar to him.

## DRISCOLL'S CONTRIBUTIONS TO FUNDAMENTAL PRINCIPLES

It is around the term "pragmatic" that the strengths of his contributions begin to turn. Language is not only thought but also deed. Words affect others. There is in speech the intention to influence. He insists that therapists learn to pay attention to the effects of speech as well as its content. Although he is not unique in this regard (e.g., Watzlawick et al., 1967), this crucial aspect of communication needs continuing emphasis in psychotherapy.

His "guidelines" are clarifications, systematizations of basic psychotherapeutic principles. His reference to these guidelines during the case makes them difficult to comprehend since the reader must break the flow of the case by referring to the appendix to grasp the details. His book contains clearer, more easily read descriptions (Driscoll, 1984). The guidelines are written in simple English and are geared toward each of the stages of the psychotherapeutic process. He offers ways to build the psychotherapeutic relationship and places much emphasis on affirming the client's personhood and strengths. During the search for important patterns he reemphasizes the need to collaborate and to learn from unexpected responses to therapist intervention. During change (which he calls clarification) he insists that the therapist sharpen the maladaptive patterns through illustrations and alternatives and also pay attention to the reality basis of emotions. He mirrors cognitive approaches by suggesting that the "operating premises" (also known as schemata and constructs) be analyzed and, where appropriate, declared or demonstrated to be invalid. As faulty attitudes are revealed, alternatives can be clarified and "brought home," a process that resembles psychodynamic working through and cognitive review. Finally, it should be "carried over" or, as behavioral therapists might say, maintained and generalized. He also offers guidelines for dealing with client motivation: "Appeal to what matters" and "Avoid generating resistance." However, he does not mention the therapist's reactions to the client, which may also generate resistance. This omission implies that the pragmatics of human communication apply only to the client's effect on others and the therapist's effect on the client but not to the client's efforts to influence the therapist.

A final important point is made less clear in the case introduction and presentation and more clear in his book. Driscoll acknowledges that he is not able to tell therapists what to do when, but only how to think about what to do when. The unique confluence of the personalities of therapist and client create too many variables for which a single author cannot control. His guidelines contain crucial goals and general ways to meet them. The specifics must be developed by the individual practitioner at the time action is required.

Driscoll's handling of the family members and his comments on the process offer some other ideas worthy of emphasis:

1. Humor may be useful during the engagement stage as well as later in therapy.
2. Responsibility is neither "all or none" but rather may be only partial, depending on the circumstances. People influence each other, and one's own actions may be in part a product of external influence.
3. Therapists are teachers. Driscoll demonstrates that therapists try to convey to clients their own favorite lessons. He tries to show Becky, the teenage prosecutor, and her father how her words influence his feelings.

4. He shows a useful flexibility in scheduling by alternating stepfamily meetings with couple's meetings. He goes for 1.5 hours for the first session.
5. Clients may learn more from watching us than from what we think we are communicating. For example, during an early session, the father saw Driscoll model an alternative way of responding to Becky that could work. In the week before the fourth session the father and stepmother had begun to pull back from the roles Becky was attempting to have them play. This was the crucial change upon which the success of the therapy pivoted.
6. Stalemates need not be prolonged. When he found himself frustrated with his inability to handle Becky individually, he switched back to the family therapy approach. I would have been curious to know in what ways he reacted to her and whether or not this information would have been useful in understanding how the father reacted to her. However, I am uncertain that such information would have improved his handling of the case.
7. Uncovering the origins of a problem is not in itself a solution to the problem. The past can be interesting and illuminating from a theoretical perspective, but Driscoll places much needed emphasis on changes now. Intergenerational theories and psychoanalytic theories can distract clinicians from the practical work at hand by rewarding them for confirming theories.
8. Latent content may be missed without consequence. In session 10, the follow-up session, Becky goes on a tirade about the school bus driver "being a jerk." Driscoll mentions that he sympathizes with the school personnel who must operate in that atmosphere. I believe that she was unconsciously referring to her anger at Driscoll (the "psychotherapist equals school bus driver") and that he was also expressing sympathy for himself for having to operate in that kind of atmosphere. Perhaps this observation is of no use to the conduct of this therapy, but because of my own training and predisposition to see latent content, I mention it. Generally speaking, whether or not therapists are monitoring it, clients do make indirect reference to therapists, and therapy awareness of this can sometimes be useful.

## SYSTEMATIC ECLECTICISM AND INTEGRATION

As Driscoll would probably be among the first to acknowledge, the words we use influence not only the behavior of others but also our own behavior. His calling his approach "pragmatic" implies that others are not pragmatic, just as the term psychodynamic implies that other therapists are psychologically static. In the same way, the term "cognitive" implies that other therapists do not use thinking. Similarly, some writers consider themselves integrationists and others call themselves systematic eclectics. Are the differences between these two groups truly that great? Ultimately these competing labels may meld together into a definition of psychotherapy that is generic and without the implied bias of superiority. Driscoll's work is a reflection of the efforts of many others who in their own ways are adding to a clear, more precise definition of the psychotherapeutic enterprise.

## REFERENCES

Bandura, A. (1977). Self-efficacy: Toward a unifying theory of behavioral change. Psychological Review, 84, 191–215.
Driscoll, R. (1984). Pragmatic psychotherapy. New York: Van Nostrand Reinhold.
Frank, J. (1976). Restoration of morale and behavior change. In A. Burton (Ed.), What Makes Behavior Change Possible? New York: Brunner/Mazel.
Watzlawick, P., Beavin, J. H., & Jackson, D. D. (1967). Pragmatics of human communication. New York: W. W. Norton.

# Commentary: Practicality in Need of a Direction

## Lawrence C. Grebstein

*Pragmatic family therapy is an eclectic therapy emphasizing practicality and clincial utility. This approach emphasizes the use of ordinary language concepts and follows a set of guidelines presumably developed for individual therapy. The author states that this therapy uses interventions from client-centered counseling, family systems approaches, behavior therapy, psychodynamic therapy, and "smatterings of other orientations as well." In addition, I recognized interventions usually associated with several different systems of family therapy, including* strategic *therapy (use of paradox),* structural *family therapy (emphasis on understanding relationships in the family), and* intergenerational *approaches (influence of family of origin on present family).*

The eclecticism in Driscoll's approach is most apparent in the use of technique. The procedural guidelines that form the basis of the approach are intended to represent a synthesis of familiar interventions from a variety of current psychotherapeutic systems. Interventions are chosen "because they seem to fit the case, and not because they are associated with any particular orientation." The author states that he is not concerned with "the controversies between theoretical orientations." Thus, the major emphasis is on finding the therapeutic tactics that best fit the case.

An effective eclectic approach requires the integration of different theories to provide a conceptual basis for the application of different interventions. The issue for the eclectic therapist is not one of competing theories. The task is to integrate aspects of different theories in order to achieve a clearer understanding of a case. The combining of theories is as important for the eclectic therapist as the selection of techniques. A theoretical perspective integrating individual and family level variables is essential in providing a context for determining which interventions "best fit" the situation. A lack of theory creates difficulties both in the application of the guidelines to family therapy and in providing a rationale for choosing particular guidelines at specific choice points in therapy.

Family therapy requires not only an understanding of individual behavior and dynamics but an appreciation of family systems theory and interactions. Because of differences in the developmental stages of different family members, there are often inherent conflicts in the family members' needs, desires, goals, and overt behaviors. Consequently, a careful assessment is often necessary before embarking on a therapeutic course. Driscoll favors the interweaving of assessment and intervention under the guideline of "learn as you go." The combination of therapy and assessment is a well-established procedure within some approaches to family therapy. However, my personal preference is for a more substantial and formal assessment prior to beginning the treatment phase of therapy. In this case, the author begins to intervene at the outset, prior to obtaining a clear or detailed understanding of the presenting problem or the family dynamics. Although the author bases his assessment on his observations of the family interactions, it would be helpful to obtain the family's impression of why they are seeking therapy. In reading the case, it was never clear to me why the family specifically came in for therapy or what the presenting problem was from their point of view.

Some of the guidelines appear more suitable to individual psychotherapy than to family therapy. For example, the first three guidelines for establishing a therapeutic relationship are: "Be on the client's side, maintain an alliance, and maintain credibility." My question is: "With whom?" A major difference between individual psychotherapy and family therapy is that disagreements often exist among different family members with regard to values, acceptable behavior, therapeutic goals, and other issues. Families in harmony rarely present themselves for therapy. In this case, the rationale for the specific interventions used is clear to the extent that particular guidelines are specified. But the guidelines themselves are not easily applied to a family context. For instance, the therapist is sensitive to the interpersonal struggles between Becky and her father and to family dynamics (the breakdown of boundaries and the different alliances). He makes clear therapeutic choices regarding who to support, what behaviors to modify (e.g., helping the father become more comfortable in his role as father), and what tactics to use (e.g., separating the parents and instructing them in child management techniques). However, there does not appear to be any general plan or rationale for why these particular issues are addressed.

A different issue is the importance of theory as a rationale for choosing interventions. It is on this point that I disagree with Driscoll. The author states: "As practitioners our attention is primarily on understanding and intervening appropriately, and not on articulating what we are doing" (emphasis mine). My contention is that by articulating what we do, we achieve understanding and appropriate interventions. The advantage of eclecticism is that it provides the clinician with a large repertoire of tactics and interventions from which to choose. It is important that the clinician have a clear sense of theory to guide the selection of techniques. The author states: "Ordinary language pragmatism is a way of grasping and comparing the various alternatives that might be appropriate in particular circumstances, and not a general prescription on which ones to use in any specific instance" (emphasis mine). What is needed in eclectic psychotherapy is a coherent rationale for deciding on what intervention to use in a specific instance. In my opinion, a delineation of the theory underlying the choice of interventions would strengthen this approach. Theory serves the purpose of providing a rationale for choice. As such, it can often serve a practical purpose in providing a direction for therapy when there appear to be equally viable choice points. This is especially true in family therapy where the presence of several clients simultaneously often leads to interpersonal conflict and/or disagreement or there are a number of different options available.

A major objective of this approach is to make the intervention(s) that best fits the case. In family therapy it can be difficult to decide what constitutes a "best fit" because of the different people involved. The eternal struggle between parents and children, especially teenagers, often labeled as the "generation" gap, is testimony to the differences that exist. Theory can be helpful in deciding whether to focus on a compromise solution, helping the teenager to individuate or differentiate, or to support the parent in setting limits on the youngster. In this case, the therapist made a number of clear choices, but the rationale for the choices is not clear to me. For example, the therapist states that one of his main goals is to make the father more comfortable and effective in his role as a parent. This is based on his formulation that the father's initial rigidity and strictness represented an overcompensation for a loss of control over his children. Becky's competition and rivalry with her stepmother is *an alternative interpretation to explain the conflict between Becky and her father. This view might lead to a very different set of interventions.*

*The issue is not which formulation is correct. It is the nature of therapy for the therapist to continually be faced with situations in which there may be equally good alternatives for both understanding and intervention. Even the most experienced therapist faces uncertainty. The author acknowledges this at one point when he states, following an intervention: "I will try to follow it up in a later session, but I am not sure where to go with it."*

*Clinicians experienced with families will recognize that the emphasis on the use of ordinary language and practical interventions makes good common and clinical sense. This case was handled with skill, sensitivity, and versatility. Because the eclectic clinician faces so many choice points as a result of the spontaneous occurrences in therapy and the diversity of available techniques, it is helpful to have a cognitive map for guidance. Theory provides the conceptual map for organizing the specific formulations and interventions. Without such a map, the rationale for our specific choices can be unclear and the therapy can lack direction.*

CHAPTER 8

# Theoretically Consistent Eclecticism: Humanizing a Computer "Addict"

*Windy Dryden*

## MY UNIQUE BRAND OF THEORETICALLY CONSISTENT ECLECTICISM

Theoretically consistent electics are therapists who have a particular theoretical perspective on human psychological disturbance but are prepared to use particular techniques developed by other therapeutic schools (Dryden, 1984a). In doing so they do not subscribe to the schools' theoretical postulates, but use techniques spawned by these schools for therapeutic purposes consistent with their own orientation. Although I consider myself a rational-emotive therapist (RET) in that I am in basic agreement with the theoretical tenets of RET, I also consider myself "eclectic" in that, in the *practice* of psychotherapy, I select what appears to be best from diverse therapeutic sources, systems, and styles to help my clients. The therapeutic practice of theoretically consistent eclectics is likely to be quite individualistic in that these therapists will draw from the aforementioned sources, systems, and styles what *they*, individually, consider to be best. What guides them in their choices is as yet unknown, and this area would be a fruitful one for research.

Before describing the case I have selected here, I wish to outline the major elements that constitute my own brand of theoretically consistent eclecticism.

*1. Rational-Emotive Therapy: My Theoretical Base*

I am in basic agreement with the ideas of Albert Ellis (1984) concerning the foundations of psychological disturbance. RET posits that although emotions, cognitions, and behaviors are interdependent processes, much human disturbance seems to stem from absolutistic, evaluative cognitions that profoundly affect how humans feel and act. These cognitions, which are often couched in the form of "musts," "shoulds," "oughts," "have to's," etc., are termed "irrational" by RET theory in that they frequently impede people from reaching their basic goals and purposes. One of the major tasks of RET therapists is to help clients change their absolutistic evaluative cognitions to those which are nonabsolutistic in nature. These latter cognitions are frequently couched in the form of "wants," "wishes," "desires," "preferences," etc., and basically help people achieve their basic goals and purposes and adapt constructively when these cannot be met.

RET therapists have invented a whole range of cognitive, emotive, and behavioral techniques that they routinely employ in therapy, but RET-oriented theoretically consistent eclectics, as mentioned above, go further and employ a number of techniques derived from other therapeutic schools to help clients effect a profound philosophical change, i.e., from devout absolute beliefs to nondevout relative beliefs. In my case, I often use methods and techniques derived from Gestalt therapy, transactional analysis, personal construct therapy, behavior therapy, person-centered therapy, and Adlerian therapy, to name but a few. However, and this should be emphasized, I use RET as a guiding framework for the selection of appropriate techniques. In addition, RET helps me decide which techniques *not* to choose (Dryden, 1984b). In the case that follows I attempt to show how I use RET as part of my therapeutic decision making in this regard.

## 2. Therapeutic Alliance Theory

The second major element in my brand of theoretically consistent eclecticism concerns the application of what has come to be known as "therapeutic alliance theory." Although the term "therapeutic alliance" has been in use in the literature for over 50 years, the concept has recently been reformulated by Ed Bordin (1979). Bordin has argued that there are three major components of the alliance between therapist and client: *bonds, goals,* and *tasks.*

Alliance theory proposes that effective therapy occurs when the bonds between therapist and client are strong enough for the work of therapy to be executed. My overriding concern here is to develop a type of bond with a particular client that will enable me to help that person without unwittingly perpetuating his or her problems. There are two important elements here. First, most clients (if not all) come into therapy with implicit (or explicit) preferences for a particular type of relationship with their therapist. Some, for example, seek a formal type of relationship, whereas others prefer one that is more personal and intimate. I seek to meet a client's preferences to the extent that they do not perpetuate his or her problem. As will be shown in the case to be described, the client sought a formal type of relationship with me, which, if offered, would have rendered me a less potent change agent. The second element, the relationship between the client's interpersonal style and his problems, is to be found in the writings of interpersonal psychotherapists (e.g., Anchin & Kiesler, 1982). These theorists argue that clients bring a preferred interpersonal style to therapy and "pull" a complementary response style from their (unsuspecting) therapists, which, in turn, reinforces both their own self-defeating style and their psychological problems. Thus, a client who presents herself as "helpless" in therapy may well "pull" an overly active-directive stance from her therapist, which renders her more "helpless." Thus, I ask myself: "What interpersonal style will enable me to keep this client in therapy [clients' disconfirmed expectations here may lead to premature termination] while at the same time helping him (or her) to escape his (or her) self-imposed vicious cycles?"

Second, the *goals* of the enterprise must be considered. Effective therapy is deemed to occur when therapist and client agree on the latter's goals. Agreement on goals can occur at three levels. First, client and therapist can set *outcome goals*, which represent what the client wishes to achieve at the end of therapy. Second, *mediating goals* can be set. These are the goals that the client needs to achieve before outcome goals can be reached. For example, a client may have to become proficient in a number of social skills before realistically being able to achieve the outcome goals of finding a partner. Finally, client and therapist can set goals for a particular session (i.e., *session goals*). Alliance theory predicts that effective therapy is facilitated by the participants' agreements on each of these goals (where appropriate) and when they both can see the progressive link between the three levels (i.e., session goals ♦ mediating goals ♦ outcome goals).

Third, therapeutic *tasks* must be considered. Both therapist and client have tasks to carry out in therapy. Alliance theory predicts that effective therapy is facilitated when each person: (a) understands what tasks he or she has to execute; (b) can see the relevance of the other person's tasks; (c) is able to execute his or her respective tasks; and (d) acknowledges that the execution of these promotes the attainment of the client's goals. In addition, the tasks must have sufficient therapeutic potency to facilitate goal achievement. Thus, as a theoretically consistent eclectic, I need to know that the techniques I select from other therapeutic schools are sufficiently powerful vehicles to promote therapeutic change. For example, exposure methods may well help clients overcome phobic reactions, but Gendlin's (1978) focusing techniques probably will not.

Finally, a channel of communication needs to be established between therapist and client so that alliance issues can be discussed and problems in the alliance resolved.

## 3. Challenging but Not Overwhelming

The third major feature of my eclectic approach is one that I have developed myself (Dryden, 1985). It is a principle that I have come to call "challenging but not overwhelming." I believe that people learn best in an atmosphere of creative challenge, and I try to develop such an environment for my clients in therapy (Hoehn-Saric, 1978). Conversely, people will not learn as much in a situation that either challenges them insufficiently or overwhelms them. In this respect, Hoehn-Saric (1978) has shown that a productive level of emotional arousal facilitates therapeutic learning. For example, some clients are emotionally overstimulated, and hence the therapeutic task is to create a learning environment that decreases their emotional tension to a level where they can adequately reflect on their experiences. With these clients, I make use of a lot of cognitive techniques and adopt an interpersonal style that aims to decrease affect. This style may be either formal or informal in character. These strategies are particularly appropriate with clients who have a "hysterical" style of functioning. On the other hand, other clients require a more emotionally charged learning atmosphere. Such clients often use "intellectualization" as a major defense and are used to denying feelings (see the case to be described). With such clients I attempt to inject a productive level of affect into the therapeutic session and employ emotive techniques, self-disclosure, and a good deal of humor. These "challenging" strategies are best introduced gradually so as not to overwhelm clients with an environment they are not accustomed to utilizing. However, before deciding on which interpersonal style to emphasize with clients, I routinely gain information from them concerning how they best learn. Some clients learn best directly through experience whereas for others vicarious experiences seem to be more productive. I try to develop a learning profile for each of my clients and use this information to help me plan my therapeutic strategies and choose techniques designed to implement these strategies. Care needs to be taken, however, that the therapist does not use a mode of learning that may perpetuate the client's problems.

I also developed the "challenging but not overwhelming" principle in response to Ellis' (1979, 1980) writings on "discomfort anxiety." Ellis has argued that many clients perpetuate their problems and deprive themselves of learning experiences because they believe that they *must* be comfortable. Thus, a major therapeutic task here is to help such clients challenge this belief and carry out assignments, while tolerating their uncomfortable feelings. Although this is a sound theoretical principle, I have found that it needs to be modified for pragmatic purposes. It may be desirable for a client who is anxious about eating in public to go to an expensive restaurant and challenge her anxiety-creating cognitions in a situation where her worst fears may be realized, but many clients will not do this. When I provide a rationale for homework assignments, I do so in a way that incorporates the "challenging but not overwhelming" principle and contrasts it with gradual desensitization and implosion methods:

There are three ways you can overcome your fears. The first is like jumping in at the deep end; you expose yourself straightaway to the situation you are most afraid of. The advantage here is that if you can learn that nothing terrible will happen, then you will overcome your problems quite quickly. However, the disadvantage is that some people just can't bring themselves to do this and get quite discouraged as a result. The second way is to go very gradually. Here, on the one hand, you only do something that you feel comfortable doing, while, on the other, you don't really get an opportunity to face putting up with discomfort, which in my opinion is a major feature of your problem. Also, treatment will take much longer this way. The third way is what I call "challenging but not overwhelming." Here you choose an assignment which is sufficiently challenging for you to make progress but not one which you feel would be overwhelming for you at any given stage. Here you are likely to make progress more quickly than with the gradual approach but more slowly than with the deep-end approach.

I find that when clients are given an opportunity to choose their own rate of progress, the therapeutic alliance is strengthened. Most clients choose the "challenging but not overwhelming" approach, and only very rarely do they opt for gradual desensitization therapy. When they do so, I try to dissuade them and frequently succeed. In the final analysis, however, I have not found it productive to insist that clients choose a particular way of tackling problems that is against their preferences.

Having outlined the major elements of my eclectic approach, I shall now describe the case I have selected to demonstrate my approach in action.

## THE CLIENT

The client, whom I shall call Eric, was a 31-year-old, white, unmarried man. He was born in the South of England, an only child of Peter and Margaret. His father was a ranking officer in the British Army and his mother did not work outside the home. At the time of treatment, Eric lived alone in a flat in Birmingham and worked as a computer programmer in a middle-sized business institution that manufactures electronic equipment. He was educated at a leading British university and has a master's degree in computer studies.

Eric sought therapeutic help because he

had increasingly come to feel that his life lacked direction and he had recently become concerned about his level of alcohol intake. This was the first time that he had sought help and there was no evidence of any psychiatric history. He enjoyed good physical health.

He initially reported his childhood to be uneventful; he saw his father infrequently because of the latter's Army commitments and described his relationship with his mother as "cordial but rather distant." He was sent to boarding school at the age of 10 where he remained until age 18, when he went to university. He said that he had many acquaintances at boarding school and university, but no real friends. He dated infrequently and reported no intimate relationships with women. He was sexually inexperienced and recently lost his virginity after having sex with a local prostitute. Describing this experience, he said, "It was time, I thought, that I had sex with a woman; I felt a bit stupid being a 30-year-old virgin. I didn't enjoy it and wondered what all the fuss was about." His main interest was in computers. He was fascinated by them and often worked late into the night trying to solve a problem posed by the latest program he was working on. Of late, however, he said, "I can't seem to dredge up the enthusiasm any more."

He was recommended to see me by his local G.P., who gave him the name of a number of therapists in the area. Explaining his choice of therapist, Eric said: "I chose to come and see you because I was attracted by the name rational-emotive therapy. I see myself as basically rational, but there seems to be a breakdown in my logic at the moment. I'm hoping you can isolate the bugs in the system." Perhaps not surprisingly, Eric's language reflected his interest in computers. My immediate impression of this tall, well-groomed man was that he had almost become an extension of the computer he had recently lost interest in. His speech was very precise and his language lacked emotionally toned words. He was almost devoid of affect apart from allowing himself a little laugh when he drew attention to the fact that his surname was the same as a leading computer company.

His expectations for therapy were as follows. He anticipated that we would have an orderly discussion of his life's goals and why he had become "stuck." He further hoped we would find out why he had started drinking more heavily than was his custom. He was pleased that I was not going to ask him to lie on the couch: "I like to see who I am talking to." I was left with the initial impression that here was a man who kept a very tight rein over his feelings from which he had become increasingly divorced. He seemed to employ intellectualization as a major defense in his life. Yet the cracks were beginning to appear. This marked the end of the initial interview, at which time I offered to accept him for therapy. We would review progress after five sessions, which would give him an opportunity to determine whether I was the kind of person who could help him. He accepted this contract.

## THE THERAPY

What I shall do is to give an account of my work with Eric over the 17 sessions I saw him. I will include at various points (a) my thoughts as a therapist, which will help the reader understand my eclectic approach, and (b) verbatim transcripts of our interchanges to illustrate (a) Eric's mode of functioning, (b) two critical incidents, and (c) how I dealt with an incident concerning Eric's resistance to experiencing feelings.

*1. Initial Phase (Sessions 1 to 4)*

Initially I asked Eric to help me understand more deeply his predicament and what he would like to achieve from therapy. He reiterated the theme first raised in the intake session, namely, that he wanted to regain his enthusiasm for his computer interest and was puzzled about what had been going wrong.

Initially I wanted to test my hypothesis that his difficulties lay in the feeling domain, so I decided to ask him to fill out a structural profile (Lazarus, 1981) to test this and to demonstrate to Eric how he saw himself as a person.

*Session 1 Transcript (Client Functioning)*

T: Okay, Eric, now throughout therapy I'll be sharing some hunches with you, and it would be good if you could help us both by giving me honest reactions to these hunches. I see you and myself as a team joining together to figure out what has gone wrong in your life and how you can find a more meaningful direction for you. How does that seem?
C: Fine.
T: Now, human beings have seven basic aspects. These aspects interact with one another to be sure, but I want to understand how you see yourself on these aspects. I want to use a rating scale from 0 to 10, 0 being an absence of this modality and 10 being a high score on it. Now these modalities are behavior, affect, sensation, imagery, cognition, interpersonal relationships, and biological factors.[1] Now taking behavior first . . .

I then spent some time developing the structural profile with Eric (see Fig. 1).

T: Okay, what's your reaction to this profile?
C: What do you mean?
T: Well, can you see anything that might be related to your current difficulties?
C: Mmm. Well . . . I'm not sure.
T: Okay, let me share my reaction. I'm struck by the low scores on affect, sensation, and interpersonal relationships. For example, I wonder if you would benefit from experiencing more feelings in your life. Let's start with that.
C: Feelings? I'm not sure what you mean by that.
T: Well emotions like joy, guilt, happiness, sadness, anxiety, depression, pleasure.
C: Well, I used to get pleasure out of my computer, but the others? I . . . er, I'm not sure. I'm puzzled by that. Aren't feelings biological processes that originate in the hypothalamus or is it the thalamus?
T: [ignoring the temptation to discuss the psychophysiology of emotion]: You seem to be finding it difficult to relate to these emotions.
C: Yeah.
T: Well, is this an area we need to explore?
C: [doubtfully]: I suppose so.

A similar dialogue occurred on the topic of sensations with Eric speculating on their biological origins rather than on his experience. Following is the interchange concerning Eric's interpersonal relationships.

T: Now how about your relationship with people?
C: Well, I've never sought people out.
T: Have they sought you out?
C: No.
T: How do you feel about that?
C: What do you mean?
T [noting the client's puzzled response to another feeling-oriented question]: Well you describe your life as being empty of people. What do you think your life would be like if there were more people in it?
C: It would distract me from my computer work.
T: So you wouldn't like more people in your life?
C: I wouldn't know what to *do* with them.

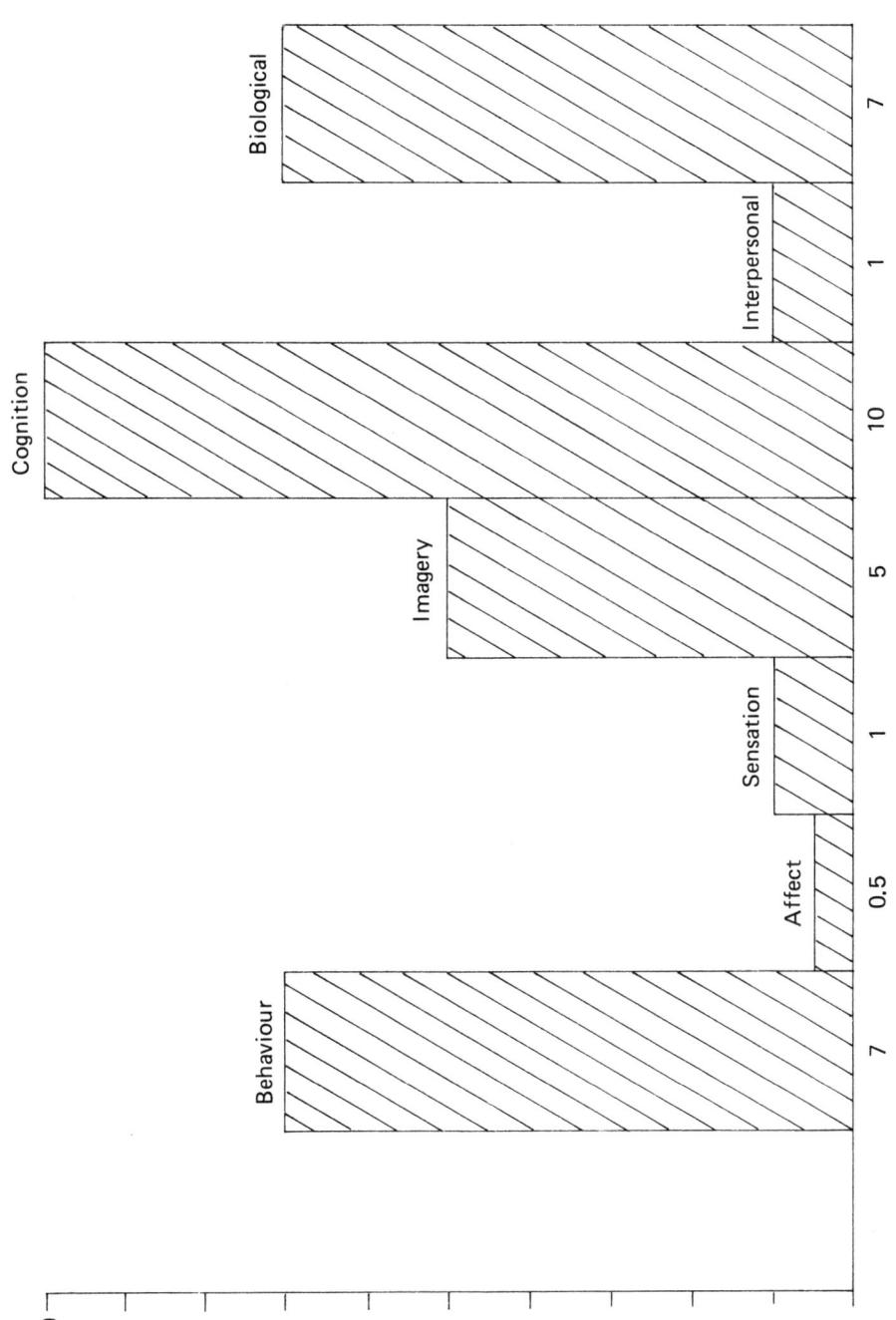

*Figure 1.* Eric's structural profile (session 1).

The above excerpt shows Eric's dilemma. Feelings are alien experiences and people are either an unwelcome distraction or a puzzle. He doesn't know what to *do* with them. I remember experiencing something of a dilemma myself at this point. How can I help this man entertain experiences that are so alien to him?

I decided to share my dilemma in session 2 when we were talking about goals. This was an error since Eric could not relate to what I said to him. However, when I asked him, "Could these areas be the bugs in your system?" he reacted with visible (although transitory) alarm. I remember thinking that I was going to have to use his language to build the bridge between his affectless world and one that held the most promise for him. An investigation into how Eric best learned revealed an overreliance on books, radio, and television. These would clearly be of little relevance in our therapeutic work since these media could well reinforce Eric's detachment and intellectualization. Other learning modes would have to be gradually introduced.

Although I like to set treatment goals early in therapy, I decided to postpone goal setting for a while and work in a less structured way with Eric for two reasons. First, I did not consider that he would benefit from an early discussion about goals since he could not yet relate to issues about feelings, sensations, and relationships. Second, I considered that he would initially benefit more from a more open-ended therapeutic contract. This would help him to widen his horizons and to loosen up a little.

In session 3 we talked about his thoughts concerning his structural profile and the "bugs in his system." He noticed that he tended to drink more at those times he found himself thinking about our sessions. I suggested that he refrain from drinking to experience whatever it was that he might be feeling at those times. I taught him Gendlin's (1978) focusing technique to help him in this regard. This technique is particularly helpful in that it directs clients' attention to their inner sensations and experiences and helps them to articulate what these experiences might be about. In session 4 I helped Eric to attach a feeling label to his experience. He was feeling sad. I helped him to realize that sadness can be a cue that there was something missing from his life, perhaps something else than computers. He nodded imperceptibly in agreement, but wondered what that was. I suggested it was our task to help him find out.

Up to now I would describe my approach to Eric as basically exploratory. I was beginning to "challenge" him to look at his inner experience, but not in a way that would "overwhelm" him and possibly scare him away. The two techniques I used in this initial phase were designed to help both of us move into what was for Eric the uncharted waters of his inner world. Neither of us could see at this stage that the next session would be so critical in the therapeutic endeavor.

## 2. Middle Phase (Sessions 5 to 14)

While reviewing my notes a few days prior to my fifth session with Eric, I noticed that Eric would have his thirty-second birthday on the day of this session. I let my mind wander and experienced a sense of sadness. I pictured Eric on his birthday alone in his flat and guessed that nobody would send him a birthday card. I decided I would buy him a card, which I would give him at the beginning of the session. My decision was prompted by a sense of empathy, but I also reflected on the therapeutic wisdom of doing so. Would he despise me for my open display of caring concern? Would he be affected? What might he experience? Empathy won the day, although I was somewhat apprehensive when I sat down at the beginning of the session. I want to stress that I did not see this purely as a technique. If I did not experience the concern, I would not have given him the card. The following are excerpts from the session.

*Session 5 Transcript (Critical Incident)*

T: Eric, I noticed today was your birthday and I felt that I would like to give you this [handing over the card].
C: [puzzled]: What is it?
T: Why don't you open it?
C [opening the envelope]: Oh! Er...um...I don't know...what to say.
T: You seem agitated.
C [clearly embarrassed]: Yeah... well...that's...a...well...um [bursts into tears].

Eric wept silently for about five minutes and was clearly distressed. I felt both touched and concerned lest this was too overwhelming an experience for him at this point.

T: When was the last time you received a birthday card?
C [distracted]: What?...er...well, let me...see...er...I can't remember.
T: When I decided to buy you the card, I felt kind of sad because I guessed that nobody would have sent you one.
C: Pathetic isn't it.
T: What is?
C: Weeping like a baby over a silly card. Oh! I didn't mean...
T: I know what you mean. How do you feel about weeping with sadness?
C: I feel bloody stupid.

The rest of the session was spent helping Eric to see that he could accept himself for crying and that his sadness was perhaps an indication that some important desires were not being met. However, Eric remained somewhat distracted and I used these strategies to decrease the intensity of his experience (which I hypothesized would have otherwise been overwhelming for him) as well as a method of disputing his irrational belief: "I am worthless if I cry."

Toward the end of the session, I wondered aloud whether Eric would find it difficult to come back next session having expressed some strong feelings. He nodded, and I said that I understood that feeling.

Indeed, Eric did not show up for session 6. I was concerned about him, particularly as he did not call to cancel his appointment. I decided to write the following letter:

Dear Eric,

I was sorry that you were not able to attend our session on Wednesday. My hunch is that you feel embarrassed about our last session. If I am right I can understand you feeling that way. If you recall, I mentioned at our second session that therapy can be difficult at times and there might be occasions when you might not want to come.[2] However, I feel it is important for us to talk about these experiences in person, so I look forward to seeing you for our next session at the same time next week. Please confirm that this arangement is convenient.

Yours sincerely,
W. Dryden, Ph.D.

I received a reply from Eric, thanking me for my letter and confirming that he would attend our sixth session. The following is an excerpt from this session.

*Session 6 Transcript (Critical Incident)*

C: You know, when I got home, I found myself with a whisky bottle in my hand before I even knew what was happening. I remembered what you said about not drinking to see what feelings came up. I was overwhelmed with stomach cramps and I began to cry again. Somewhere at the back of my mind I remembered you asking me if I was worthless for crying. I was able to see that I wasn't and for the first time I let go. I cried and cried. I remembered my father saying things when I was a child like: "Call yourself a boy, stop those tears." I also remembered my mother getting agitated because I was crying and my father was due home soon.

T: Sounds like a lot of hidden feelings came up for you.

C: Yeah. When last Wednesday came, I panicked. You were right, I couldn't face you then. I went to my computer. I realized that I'd been using it as a friend, someone . . . something rather . . . that I could relate to. . . . I also remembered what you said about your challenging but not overwhelming principle. I'd had enough challenge for a while and needed to have a rest. Sorry I didn't let you know.

[And later in the session . . .]

C: I can see more clearly that I do need to get to know about some of those modalities that were low; you know, affect and the others. That's what I'd like to focus on.

At the end of the sixth session I suggested that Eric think about what kinds of experiences he would like to seek out. He came back with the following list at session 7.

- Learn to dance
- Find myself a girlfriend (about time!)
- Go walking in the woods
- Join 18+[3]

Eric devised his own program and followed it through according to the "challenging but not overwhelming" principle with good success. On a number of occasions he chose not to go to an event, using his computer as a kind of anxiety-reduction technique.

Mindful of the importance of using emotively-oriented techniques to help Eric, I employed a number of these methods to help him focus on avoidance behavior.

For example, in session 9, Eric reported that he couldn't be bothered to go to 18+ on club night and spent the evening working on his computer. I decided to use a Gestalt empty-chair technique to dramatize the situation to enable Eric to identify any possible anxieties.

*Session 9 Transcript (Using a Dramatic Method to Uncover the Meaning of Eric's Avoidance Behavior)*

T: Let's see if we can understand whether you were avoiding some important feeling. Now let me explain a drama technique to you. First, can you imagine how you were feeling that night?

C: Er . . . yeah . . . tired.

T: Okay. So one of the players in this play is "Tired Eric." Now another one is your computer. (Can you imagine Tired Eric talking to his computer?)

C [laughs]: Just about.

T: Good. Now, see this empty chair? Imagine your computer on that chair. Got it?

C: Yeah.

T: Now strange as it might seem, I want you as Tired Eric to talk to your computer. And I'll play myself in this. Okay? Right. Okay, Tired Eric, it's time to go out to 18+.

C [as Tired Eric]: I'm too tired.

T [to computer]: Is Eric too tired or might he be feeling something else? Eric, change chairs and answer me as your computer.

C [as computer]: Well, no, he's scared.

T [to computer]: Scared of what?

C [as computer]: Well, he's got his eye on a girl at the club but he's scared she might not want to know him.

T [to computer]: So why don't you tell him to go and face his fears.

C [as computer]: Er . . . because . . .

C [as Tired Eric and changing chairs after

being prompted by the therapist]: I know, because he doesn't think I'm strong enough to cope with rejection.
T [to Tired Eric]: Is that true?
C [as Tired Eric]: No, but why risk it if it's a possibility?

This dialogue helped Eric and myself see that two important beliefs were holding Eric back. One was "I'll only do things if they are certain to work out" and the other was "If I do things and they don't work out, I'm no good." I then helped Eric to dispute these beliefs using traditional RET disputing methods. He considered a more healthy alternative to both beliefs to be "Things won't work out if I don't try. So I'd better increase the chances of getting what I want by going for them. If they don't work out, tough. I'm no less a person." Eric practiced these new beliefs by acting on them. He carried out a number of homework assignments between sessions 9 and 11 which were designed to help him accept himself in the face of failure and to help him work toward goals, the achievement of which could not be guaranteed.

In session 12 it emerged from reviewing these assignments that Eric feared losing control if he experienced strong arousal. His belief here was "If I get excited, I'll lose control and that would be awful." In order to test out the prediction that he would lose control if he experienced a lot of arousal, Eric did several things between sessions 12 and 14. He did a number of shame-attacking exercises (Dryden, 1984b). For example, he went into a large department store and shouted out the time. In addition, in session 13, I got him to sprint up and down on the spot and then do a number of expressive meditation exercises designed to raise his arousal level. Finally he went to a dance-therapy workshop and did a lot of vigorous dance exercises. All these experiences helped him to see that he could get highly aroused without losing control.

By session 14, Eric considered that he had made a lot of progress. He was feeling more in touch with his emotions, the range of which had markedly increased. He gained pleasure from walking in the country and enjoyed experiencing a variety of country odors. He had taken up bird watching and had found a girlfriend who also enjoyed these activities. He had made several friends at the 18+ club and was experimenting with a wide range of activities. His enthusiasm for his computer work had returned, but he spent far less of his recreational time at his computer terminal.

### 3. End Phase (Sessions 15 to 17)

Eric suggested at the beginning of the fifteenth session that he would like to come less frequently and work toward termination. I outlined a number of ways we could terminate our work together. He chose to come twice more at monthly intervals. We spent these final sessions reviewing our work together, and Eric reported that he had maintained the gains he had made in therapy. At the end of session 16, I suggested that Eric might bring to our last scheduled session a written account of what he had achieved in therapy. The following is a verbatim account of what he wrote under the heading, "What I Gained from Therapy."

*What I Gained from Therapy*

I have gained a great deal from seeing you, far more than I thought I would. You have opened my eyes to a whole new world of experience that I was only dimly aware of, if at all. I would say first and foremost I feel a more complete human being. Although I still respect my intellect—or the cognitive domain as the American man who invented those sheets calls it—I have learned to experience and gain respect for the other modalities. I have learned that it isn't unmanly to cry and feel sad. I've tried to discuss this with my father, but perhaps predictably he doesn't understand what I'm talking about. I have learned that it's not so bad to try and achieve something and fail. Indeed, if a person doesn't try, he certainly won't achieve. Obvious now, but I didn't see that before.

I have also learned that control has little to do with feeling strongly aroused. To some degree, looking back, I was using my computer to shield me from life, although of course I didn't realize that then. I guess I was using my computer as a substitute friend and yet it was a bit of a one-sided friendship. I now feel much more a part of the social world. 18+ has helped tremendously in that respect. Before I wouldn't have thought I could have so much fun with others. I didn't even think of life as having fun. Strange isn't it! I still have to force myself to go out occasionally when I feel "tired" but I can now distinguish between genuine tiredness and anxiety.

I've redone those modalities (see Fig. 2) and have enclosed them within. I find the differences interesting. One last thought, I remembered being struck by the name of your therapy before I came to see you—rational-emotive therapy. I was attracted to the word "rational." I must confess that I'm now more attracted to the word "emotive." I hope you find this instructive.

At the end of the seventeenth session, Eric and I agreed to have two follow-up sessions, the first one being 12 months after our last session. However, this has not yet taken place at the time of writing.

*4. Therapist's Summary*

From the point of view of RET, Eric had developed an unsatisfactory life-style partly because he had little experience in the affect, sensation, and interpersonal modalities but mainly because he held a number of irrational beliefs which led him to avoid experiences in each of these areas. Namely he believed:

1. "Experiencing emotions and sensations is extremely dangerous and must be avoided at all costs."
2. "I must be in control of myself. To lose control would be terrible."
3. "I must be certain of achieving something before I try it."
4. "I'm no good if I cry or if I fail to achieve important things."

Adopting a theoretically consistent eclectic view based on my rational-emotive conceptualizations, I decided to emphasize strategies and techniques that were dramatic, affective, and expressive in nature. In doing so I was sensitive to avoid overwhelming the client, but to challenge him gradually at first and later increasingly so as therapy progressed and as he began to make significant gains. Thus I decided to use: (a) *structural profiles* as an assessment tool to help test my hunch about important deficits and to help Eric learn about these deficits, such techniques as (b) *focusing*—to help Eric to identify feelings and articulate what these feelings pointed to; (c) *Gestalt, two-chair dialogue*—to help him identify the meaning behind his avoidance maneuvers; (d) *dramatic meditation* and *dance therapy*—to help him learn that strong affective experiences were not dangerous and did not threaten his sense of control. All these methods were chosen in line with strategies consistent with my RET-inspired formulation and in keeping with my hunches about the importance for Eric of learning to become accustomed to the experiential-affective domain of human functioning.

From the point of view of alliance theory, I was able to develop a well-bonded relationship with Eric. Initially he viewed me as a rather distant "expert" who would

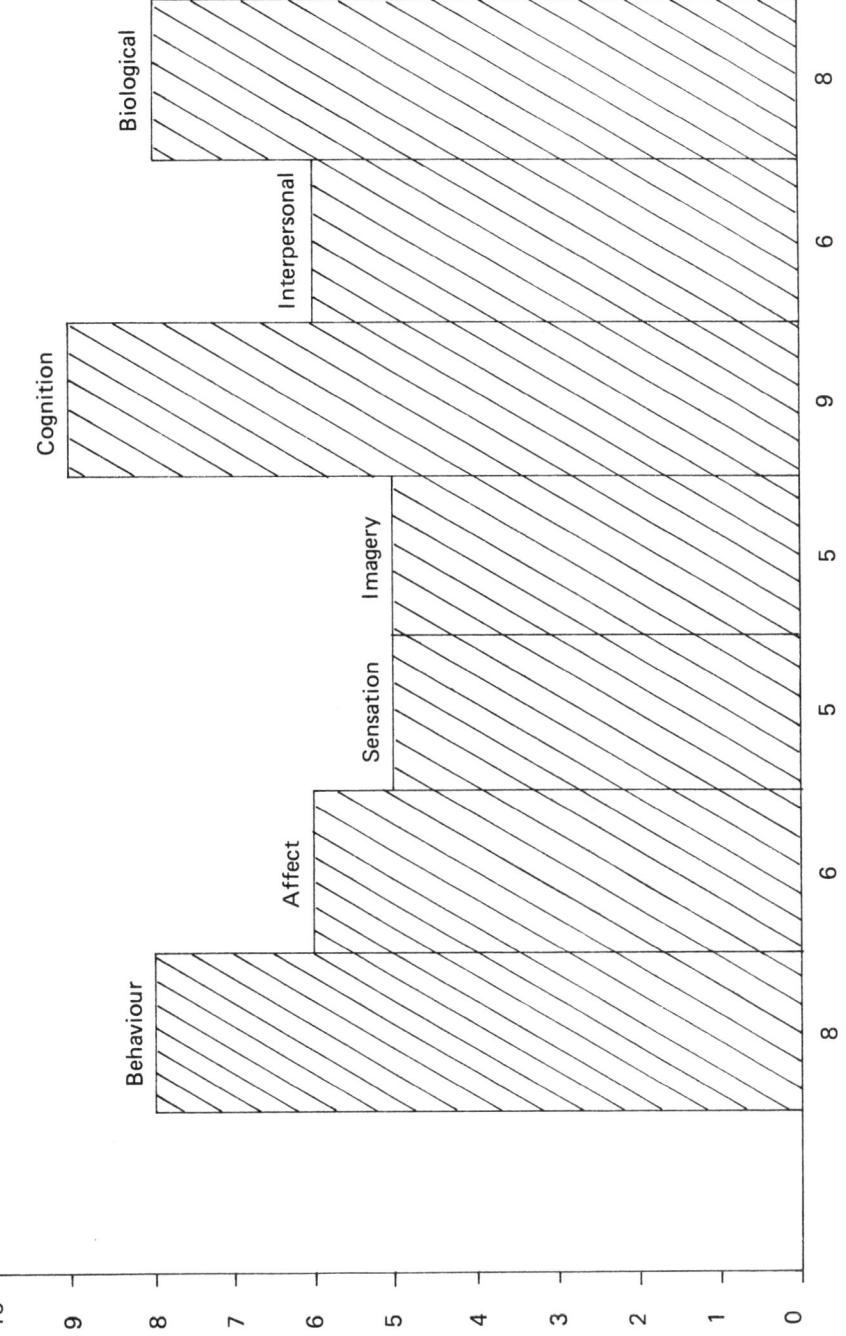

Figure 2. Eric's structural profile (session 17).

help him iron out the "bugs" in his system. The birthday card incident confronted him with the fact that I was also a human being who cared about his plight. This touched a deep cord in him and seemed to help him relate to me in a more affective manner. From session 6 our relationship was characterized by mutual respect and trust. I related to Eric in a moderately warm, informal manner without us both losing sight that we had various tasks to achieve.

With respect to the goal domain, I deliberately refrained from setting concrete goals at the outset of therapy. Initially, Eric wanted to pursue goals which, in my opinion, would have not been constructive for him. He wished to strengthen his intellectualized defences and rid himself of the "bugs" in his system, which he hoped would help him shut out his increasing sense of isolation and dissatisfaction and hence to return to his computer. I did not attempt to explicitly deal with the self-defeating nature of these goals at the outset. I considered that to do this would have been unproductive and might have led to a futile "intellectual" discussion, which I wanted to avoid. There was also evidence at this initial stage of therapy that Eric would not have understood the importance of goals that emphasized becoming increasingly aware of his feelings and the healing aspects of interpersonal relationships. Instead, I sidestepped the issue of goals by showing Eric the importance of looking at himself as a total individual (by using the structural profile) and how he was living his life against this backdrop. To some degree I think that Eric went along with me because he viewed me as an expert who knew what he was doing and because he was not too insistent about meeting his initial goals. Specific goal setting followed Eric's increasing understanding of the importance that the affective, sensation, and interpersonal modalities might play in his life.

As Eric gained this understanding, it was fairly easy to show him that the execution of various tasks could help him achieve his newly discovered goals. The more Eric derived benefit from being able to experience feelings, sensations, and the pleasure of relating to other people, the more he was able to see the sense of the evocative techniques that I suggested to him and how they could help him achieve his goals. Interestingly enough, we rarely had to talk *about* the relevance of therapeutic tasks; I believe he and I developed an implicit and shared understanding about these matters.

Following Bordin (1983), I believe that the repair of rifts in the therapeutic alliance can be most therapeutic. That Eric and I were able to sustain our relationship through the birthday card and the missed-session incidents was, I believe, important for a number of reasons. I consider that Eric learned from these two incidents that the expression of strong feelings (i.e., his feelings) could be tolerated by another person and by himself and that no catastrophe would result. I also think that Eric learned it was possible to talk about relationships with another person with whom he was involved and that rifts in these relationships can be repaired when both people show "good faith."

Applying the "challenging but not overwhelming" principle to the case, I would like to make the following points. First, I attempted to provide a therapeutic environment that was increasingly charged with affect to encourage Eric to develop his potential to use the affective, sensory, and interpersonal modalities. In this sense, I tried to challenge Eric's use of intellectualization as a defense against such experiences without overwhelming him in this regard. The birthday card gift could have been an overwhelming experience for Eric, and to some extent I underestimated the effect that it would have on him. However, it was not a damaging experience for him, and indeed it contained important therapeutic ingredients for change (see the section on "Client Impressions"). Second, I explained the "challenging but not overwhelming" principle outlined earlier, with respect to the execution of therapeutic tasks, and Eric applied it to very good effect in his homework assignments. Indeed, as his own account in the next section shows, Eric has used this principle after therapy ended to maintain and extend his progress.

## CLIENT IMPRESSIONS

Two months after formal therapy had finished, I wrote the following letter to Eric:

Dear Eric,
I hope this letter finds you well. I have been asked by Dr. J. Norcross of University of Rhode Island, U.S.A., to contribute a case study to a book he is editing entitled *Casebook of Eclectic Psychotherapy*. With your permission I would like to write an account of our therapy and would like to request your permission for this. Your anonymity will of course be preserved.

If you agree, Dr. Norcross also seeks to include the client's impressions of his/her therapy experiences. I would be grateful if you could write your impressions according to the following guidelines:
a. What were the most helpful and least helpful aspects of therapy?
b. What were your impressions of two critical incidents in therapy. Here I have selected (a) the session where I gave you a birthday card and (b) the session following the time you decided to miss our scheduled appointment (session 6).

Please feel free to be as candid as you can in your account. I look forward to receiving your reply upon which I will send you a copy of my account.

Yours sincerely,<br>W. Dryden, Ph.D.

I received the following reply from Eric which I present as his verbatim account:

Dear Dr. Dryden,
Thank you for your letter. You have my permission to write about our therapy work. I am pleased to offer my perspective of my therapy experience. I hope that it may be helpful to your colleagues and their clients. I would be interested to see your own account when you have finished it.

### 1. Most Helpful and Least Helpful Aspects of My Therapy

As I look back over the period of my therapy I can think of many helpful aspects but only one or two experiences that perhaps weren't very helpful. So my account is somewhat skewed to the positive. The most positive aspect of the therapy was the fact that you helped me discover the importance of feelings and personal relationships in my life. Until seeing you, I had not considered that these had any place in my life. Indeed, I had not really given these matters much thought. Why this should be so is difficult to say, but I suppose it had something to do with my father's attitudes toward feelings and the fact that my boarding school emphasized the value of hard work rather than the value of relationships between people.

Your suggestion that I refrain from drinking to help me discover what feelings I was hiding from and that focusing technique was particularly helpful in this respect. I also found some of the techniques you suggested that we try out together in our session helpful in aiding me to identify my feelings and some of the blocks I set up to stop me being uncomfortable. In particular, those mediation exercises were good and I still do some of them from time to time.

The other helpful aspects of my therapy were those exercises I did outside your office. I enjoyed immensely the dance workshop you suggested I attend. In fact I have joined a regular dance therapy group which I find valuable in helping me to overcome my tendency to what you called "intellectualization." I didn't like that term when you first used it. I still don't like it but I know what you meant by it. I call it "cutting out."

The therapy helped me to make much better use of outside resources than I would have done without therapy. Therapy helped me to form some important friendships, in particular my relationship with my girlfriend June, which is still flourishing. Therapy was like a release in this respect.

Looking back I think your patience and understanding was very important (I'll mention your concern for me as a person later). Your easygoing manner was good for me although at the beginning, I'm not sure, but I think I would have preferred seeing an older man, one who was more formal in style and dress. I realize now that these things are unimportant though. I also found some of your explanations helpful. Your own principle of challenging but not overwhelming yourself was valuable, and I still use it as a guideline in my life.

Now some not so helpful aspects, although these are minor. First, at the beginning it might have been more helpful if you could have given me a clearer idea about what therapy was like. I was puzzled for about the first three sessions and was not sure what you expected me to do or say. Finally, it might have been more valuable if we could have spent more time talking about my childhood and my experiences at boarding school. I don't know whether that would have been helpful but I think that it might.

## 2. Critical Incidents

I can understand why you selected these two incidents. They stood out for me too. I was shocked when you gave me the birthday card—shocked and very embarrassed that I reacted in the way that I did. Your concern for me hit me between the eyes. I wasn't prepared for it and just did not understand at the time why I reacted so strongly. That experience really made me stop and think about my life. It made the meaning of the first profile I did come alive and helped me to see what I had been missing in life. I was, as you suspected, too embarrassed and ashamed to face you the week after. Your letter helped me to come back. You understood what I was feeling and again your concern was an important fact in helping me to return the following week. To be honest, if you had not written, I doubt whether I would have made the first move.

Coming back after the missed session was very important for me. You helped me feel that I wasn't a weak freak and also by not making too much of my missing the session you gave me important breathing space. Your matter-of-fact reaction gave me the impression that it was no big deal and also helped me think that you would not be shocked or startled by whatever I told you about myself. That attitude has remained with me and is also an attitude I can now apply to myself.

Well, I hope that you find these remarks of use. I'm very grateful to you for helping me in the way you did and am pleased to have had this opportunity to repay you in this small way.

Yours sincerely,
Eric

## NOTES

[1] See Lazarus (1981) for a full description of the structural profile and how to use it in therapy.
[2] I frequently tell my clients that there may be times when they may wish to miss sessions. I do this partly so that I can remind them of the fact if and when the "going gets rough" for them.
[3] 18+ is a national social club for people between the ages of 18 and 30. A number of the members, however, are older than 30. It has branches throughout Britain.

## REFERENCES

Anchin, J. C., & Kiesler, D. J. (Eds.) (1982). *Handbook of interpersonal psychotherapy*. New York: Pergamon.

Bordin, E. S. (1979). The generalizability of the psychoanalytic concept of the working alliance. *Psychotherapy: Theory, Research and Practice, 16*, 252–260.

Bordin, E. S. (1983, February). Myths, realities, and alternatives to clinical trials. Paper presented at the International Conference on Psychotherapy, Bogota, Columbia.

Dryden, W. (1984a). Issues in the eclectic practice of individual therapy. In W. Dryden (Ed.), *Individual therapy in Britain* (pp. 341–363). London: Harper & Row.

Dryden, W. (1984b). *Rational-emotive therapy: Fundamentals and innovations*. Beckenham, Kent: Croom-Helm.

Dryden, W. (1985). Challenging but not overwhelming: A compromise in negotiating homework assignments. *British Journal of Cognitive Psychotherapy, 3*(1), 77–80.

Ellis, A. (1979). Discomfort anxiety: A new cognitive behavioral construct. Part 1. *Rational Living, 14*(2), 3–8.

Ellis, A. (1980). Discomfort anxiety: A new cognitive behavioral construct. Part 2. *Rational Living, 15*(1), 25–30.

Ellis, A. (1984). The essence of RET—1984. *Journal of Rational-Emotive Therapy, 2*(1), 19–25.

Gendlin, E. T. (1978). *Focusing.* New York: Everest House.

Hoehn-Saric, R. (1978). Emotional arousal, attitude change and psychotherapy. In J. D. Frank, R. Hoehn-Saric, S. D. Imber, B. L. Liberman, & A. R. Stone (Eds.), *Effective ingredients of successful psychotherapy* (pp. 73–106). New York: Brunner/Mazel.

Lazarus, A. A. (1981). *The practice of multimodal therapy.* New York: McGraw-Hill.

# Commentary: Reactions from a Multimodal Perspective

## Arnold A. Lazarus and Clifford N. Lazarus

Dryden's "unique brand of theoretically consistent eclecticism" brings to mind an old saying (author unknown): "Originality is the fine art of remembering what you hear but forgetting where you heard it." Although there is perhaps a pervasive desire in most writers to feel that they can contribute something special, something truly novel, it is incumbent upon them to go beyond mere labeling and demonstrate the validity of their contentions. After careful examination, we failed to discern any significant differences between Dryden's "theoretically consistent eclecticism" and Lazarus's (1967, 1971, 1981) technical eclecticism *(except for the more cumbersome verbal construction of Dryden's term!).*

A technical eclectic may draw on numerous techniques from different sources without subscribing to any of the theories or schools that spawned them. Typically, technical eclectics adhere to a testable, empirically derived theoretical base. A theoretical eclectic who borrows divergent notions from different schools of thought may unknowingly subscribe to paradigms that are epistemologically incompatible. Since all enlightened approaches to eclectic psychotherapy are predicated upon consistent theoretical underpinnings, one would indeed expect practitioners to eschew a theoretically labile position. To do otherwise would be an egregious error!

This is not the place to discuss theoretical and metatheoretical distinctions, but it should be emphasized that what Dryden calls "rational-emotive theory" and "therapeutic alliance theory" are readily subsumed by the tenets of social learning theory (Bandura, 1977). In the interests of scientific parsimony, it is wise to avoid superfluous constructs, and it is confusing to introduce synonyms as though they were brand-new terms (e.g., bonds, goals, and tasks). Dryden demonstrates a fondness for catchwords and pithy sayings. "Challenging but not overwhelming" seems to capture the age-old wisdom of applying educational incentives that encourage the student to learn, without making any task seem so formidable that the learner withdraws through intimidation or discouragement. It is the basis of any good desensitization therapy, which, if correctly administered, should proceed at a pace that the client finds consistently "challenging but not overwhelming." To our way of thinking, this adds nothing new to the standard clinical repertoire.

Turning now to his specific case presentation, we are indebted to Dryden for offering a different (better) way of employing structural profiles. Typically, in the practice of multimodal therapy, we have tended to use structural profiles somewhat sparingly in individual psychotherapy (favoring their use more in marriage therapy), whereas Dryden employed the scale very early in the initial session as a springboard for eliciting and addressing the client's depressed scores on affect, sensation, and interpersonal relationships. We were favorably impressed with the manner in which this provided such a rapid and well-focused examination of Eric's most salient response deficits and lacunae. In this procedural context, Dryden can lay legitimate claim to some originality. (The pithy comment by Erasmus in Epicureus seems fitting: "Almost everyone knows this, but it has not occurred to everyone's mind.") It was Thackeray who stated that "the two most engaging powers of an author are to make new things familiar, and familiar things new."

The "birthday card intervention" prior to the fifth session brings to mind Standal and Corsini's (1959) Critical Incidents in Psychotherapy, a book that has made a lasting impression on one of us (AAL). In that book, numerous authors described the serendipitous gains that had accrued when they deviated from standard protocol. Thus, a nondirective therapist in a moment of uncharacteristic emotion says to his client: "I forbid you to sleep with another man!" A Freudian clinician pounds the desk and shouts, "Dammit—look, why don't you just quit this verbal diarrhea!" As Fay and Lazarus (1982) have stressed, dramatic breakthroughs in a variety of clinical problems may follow such unexpected therapist actions as an unsolicited telephone call by the therapist, shedding a tear with a patient, walking out of a session, or other things that are out of character or out of the patient's ordinary experience of therapy. Dryden's description of session 5 falls into this category, and in our estimation, the client's reactions were deftly managed.

The follow-up letter was also clinically astute and sensitively worded, but we take issue with the nonegalitarian flavor of "W. Dryden, Ph.D." writing to "Eric." It is our personal preference to practice parity (unless specific clinical exigencies dictate otherwise), and if we call our clients by their first names, we invite them to address us similarly.

As is well known, it is important to consider the client's specific frames of reference so that he or she can resonate to the therapist's examples. Thus, in session 9, Dryden cleverly incorporated the client's profound interest in computers into his empty-chair dialogue.

It is uncertain how Dryden was able to gain the degree of compliance evident in sessions 12 to 14. The "shame-attacking exercises" that Albert Ellis devised, and which Dryden implemented, have, in our combined experience, proved most difficult to put into effect. The degree of "resistance" that we have characteristically encountered is at odds with the apparent ease with which Dryden persuaded Eric to shout out the time in a large department store, for example.

In essence, Dryden's case illustrates the thoughts and actions of a competent, sensitive, and creative clinician, operating mainly within a rational-emotive therapy framework, with the addition of some techniques drawn from other disciplines. How would a multimodal therapist have proceeded differently? First, in addition to Dryden's perspicacious use of structural profiles (quantitative self-ratings of the client's perceived levels of functioning in behavior, affect, sensation, imagery, cognition, interpersonal relationships, and biological factors), a modality profile would have been constructed. This is a list of specific problems and proposed treatments in each of the aforementioned dimensions. Indeed, the multimodal clinician would have generated a modality profile before the third session, as this provides a "road map" of the desired course of therapy. As Yanis (1985), an eclectic therapist who conducted a retrospective analysis of multimodal therapy concluded, this orientation provides various "maps" that enhance therapy planning and make it less likely that something will be overlooked in assessment. Certainly, by working multimodally, Eric's major criticisms of Dryden's treatment would have been circumvented. Eric wrote that he would have found it helpful to have been given a clearer idea of the treatment trajectory. He also suggested that insufficient attention had been paid to his experiences at boarding school. The multimodal practitioner, when explaining how and why modality profiles are employed, would have avoided the first criticism, since this procedure automatically provides clients with information about treatment plans and processes (see Lazarus, 1981). As to the alleged omission of a potentially significant clinical area (certain childhood experiences), it is hoped that this would have appeared on the modality profile and hence been subjected to clinical scrutiny.

## REFERENCES

Bandura, A. (1977). Social learning theory. Englewood Cliffs, NJ: Prentice-Hall.
Fay, A., & Lazarus, A. A. (1982). Psychoanalytic resistance and behavioral nonresponsiveness: A dialectical impasse. In P. L. Wachtel (ed.), Resistance: Psychodynamic and behavioral approaches. New York: Plenum.
Lazarus, A. A. (1967). In support of technical eclecticism. Psychological Reports, 21, 415–416.
Lazarus, A. A. (1971). Behavior therapy and beyond. New York: McGraw-Hill.
Lazarus, A. A. (1981). The practice of multimodal therapy. New York: McGraw-Hill.
Standal, S. W., & Corsini, R. J. (1959). Critical incidents in psychotherapy. Englewood Cliffs, NJ: Prentice-Hall.
Yanis, M. (1985). The case of Sally: Heuristic questions, speculative answers. In A. A. Lazarus (ed.), Casebook of multimodal therapy. New York: Guilford.

# Commentary: Demonstrating Therapeutic Eclecticism

## Douglas H. Powell

In this elegant report of eclectic psychotherapy, Dr. Windy Dryden neatly outlines his theoretical approaches and concisely demonstrates the application of these concepts in the successful treatment of an isolated computer programmer. Though evidence is accumulating that therapists from a single persuasion often apply a mix of treatment modes, rarely do we find such theoretical eclecticism so clearly articulated.

This example shows both the value and the economy of eclectic psychotherapy. Little doubt exists in my mind that a mental health worker would have a most challenging task attempting to match this outcome using behavior therapy alone. And the economy of Dr. Dryden's approach is staggering. One can only imagine the months and years it would have taken a skilled insight-oriented therapist to achieve the same result—if, indeed, the same outcome would have been possible.

This case clearly illustrates the back-and-forth nature of eclectic psychotherapy. One moment Dr. Dryden had Eric rating himself on the BASIC-ID, and in the next asked him about his reactions to the results and adroitly sidestepped temptations to be woven into his intellectualizing defenses with a skill that an insight-oriented therapist can only admire. Here he had the client focusing on sadness and there he empathized with his loneliness and responded caringly.

Although Dr. Dryden says he considers himself a rational-emotive clinician, his report of his work suggests that he blends in a number of elements characteristic of all successful therapies: taking the problem seriously; forming a therapeutic alliance; providing warmth, humor, and empathy; gently helping the client to understand some of the forces contributing to the distressing symptoms; teaching adaptive means of relieving disabling feelings and thoughts; and encouraging appropriate changes. What seems special about his therapy with Eric is that, in addition to the above, he marshaled an array of specific procedures from other schools of thought for helping the client recognize his problem, confront his emotions, and relieve discomfort—e.g., BASIC-ID profiling, Gendlin's focusing, the Gestalt empty-chair technique, and the shame-attacking exercise. His report leaves little doubt that these ingredients were just as important to the positive outcome—and the speed with which it was achieved—as the more general elements.

It is always helpful for us to have a particular frame of reference when we try to help a client or when trying to explain to our colleagues just what it was we did and why. For me it was easier to follow Dr. Dryden's description of his use of the principles of therapeutic alliance and creating a "challenging but not overwhelming" environment than how the principles of rational-emotive therapy were applied. Partly this may be because the examples and discussion more often emphasize the impact of the first two ideas. It also may be that a frame of reference—how we think about the process of therapy, what meaning we attribute to the client's words and deeds, and what we choose, or choose not, to say and do—is far harder to convey in chapter length than the application of the other principles.

One of the features I liked best about Dr. Dryden's approach was that his blend of direction and open-mindedness created a climate of collaboration which encouraged the client to bring his own ideas, feelings, and reactions into the treatment. The process started early using the BASIC-ID profile so that Eric could recognize what was missing from his life—in his case, affects, sensations, and satisfying interpersonal relationships. This allowed the client to see for himself what the goals of therapy might be. (This also allowed him to see the progress that he made at the termination of treatment.) This collaborative spirit continued in the therapist's willingness to postpone treatment goal setting, a modification of his normal procedure. This open-ended style benefited Eric because he then had nowhere to focus his major defense of intellectualization. This, in turn, allowed the therapy to help him regain awareness of crucial repressed affects.

Even Dr. Dryden's more direct advice had a quality that gave Eric plenty of room to maneuver. The suggestion that he refrain from drinking and use a focusing technique provided an opportunity to discover on his own that he felt sad. Later, in the session following the critical incident, the client was encouraged to think about experiences he might like to seek out and devise his own program according to the challenging-but-not-overwhelming principle.

A nagging problem for me as a practitioner of eclectic psychotherapy is that I am often left with the feeling of incompleteness at the termination of treatment. Either there seems more to be accomplished in the behavioral domain, or far more exploration of the psychodynamic factors contributing to the problem seems in order. On one hand, I know that at some basic level all treatments are incomplete. On the other hand, the techniques at our disposal as eclectic therapists stimulate us to imagine addressing a great many concerns which may increase the degree and durability of improvement. In spite of the remarkable progress made by Eric, this example reinforces my feeling.

For instance, I would like to have heard more about how Eric's attachment to computers evolved. In many ways his history is reminiscent of several cases Turkle (1984) portrayed of computer hackers who were traumatized in early adolescence by interpersonal difficulties with peers. To avoid being further "burned" they turned to computers, creating a safe environment they could control.

The transcript fragments of Eric's case point to problems with a stern father who told him to "stop those tears," but little is mentioned about what his friendship patterns were like in boarding school. One suspects these were unpleasant and contributed equally to his turning away from people toward the refuge of computers. Some support for this conjecture comes from his statement on page 236 that he would have liked to talk more about his experiences in boarding school. Is it possible that the probability of Eric's sustaining the gains he achieved in his treatment would have been enhanced by exploring this area further?

Perhaps the most exciting aspect of this chapter is how much it stimulates creative thinking for the clinician reading it. Dr. Dryden's description of his work provides a well-marked pathway to follow with troubled clients similar to Eric. But this case also encourages us to look within ourselves as well as at our repertoire of techniques to consider what mix of approaches might stand the best chance of relieving the suffering of those who consult us.

## REFERENCE

Turkle, S. (1984). *The second self: Computers and the human spirit.* New York: Simon & Schuster.

# CHAPTER 9

# A Case of Eclectic Family Therapy: "Are We the Sickest Family You've Ever Seen?"

*Lawrence C. Grebstein*

## AN ECLECTIC PERSPECTIVE

The treatment of this case is based on a model of eclectic therapy that emphasizes a brief, practical, and problem-focused approach to treatment. The model, which has been described in greater detail elsewhere (Grebstein, 1986), combines elements of several contemporary systems. These include: the problem-solving focus of strategic family therapy (Haley, 1976), the interpersonal interaction of the structural approach (Minuchin, 1974), the problem-centered orientation of the McMaster Model (Epstein, Bishop, & Levin, 1978), the nurturant and supportive emphasis of Satir (1967, 1972), the experiential orientation of Kempler (1973), and some of the theoretical constructs of family systems theory (Bowen, 1976). The therapist's role is that of a guide who leads the family on its journey to a new destination. The therapist serves as a consultant whose task is to observe, understand, design intervention strategies, and act as a model. The family's responsibilities are to participate actively in the process and to experiment with new ways of relating by practicing agreed-upon homework assignments. Engagement of the family in therapy is perhaps the single most important factor in using this, or perhaps any, model of eclectic family therapy. The effective application of this approach is contingent on the therapist having sufficient life experience, personal flexibility, and a large enough repertoire of intervention tactics and skills to be able to establish personal and professional credibility with the family. Success in the use of this model is not based on the therapist never being wrong or never making mistakes but on his/her willingness to recognize errors, acknowledge them, and correct them.

---

I would like to thank Marion Usher, A.C.S.W., who was a consultant and supervisor on this case, for her helpful suggestions, wise counsel, and personal support.

The approach combines a wide variety of different tactics, which range from the spontaneous, unstructured, and experientially based responses of the therapist to planned and highly structured behavioral techniques, such as modeling and behavioral rehearsal (role playing). The model is based on the belief that an effective eclectic family therapist not only has a large repertoire of specific diagnostic and intervention skills but is able to organize and conceptualize the process of therapy into definable stages and areas of family life requiring alteration. Theory is important in providing the guidelines for obtaining information, its meaningful integration, and the choice of intervention tactics.

A comprehensive assessment precedes the therapy. The assessment includes a detailed evaluation of the presenting problems and major areas of family functioning as described in the McMaster model of family functioning (Epstein, Bishop, & Levin, 1978); a family history using the genogram (Guerin & Pendagast, 1976); and an appraisal of the family's dynamics and organization based on the constructs of structural family therapy (Minuchin, 1974). The formal assessment can be curtailed in some instances. In the case to be presented, extensive information was available from other sources, and the clinical facts of the situation indicated the need for more immediate intervention.

## CASE SELECTION

This case was selected for several reasons. First, it is representative of family therapy referrals in that the presenting problem is a single family member in distress and reporting symptoms. Second, it is a poorly organized, chaotic, and multiproblem family, which requires extensive and diverse interventions, including the use of family, couple, and individual therapy sessions. Third, because of their low level of self-esteem, the family members, both individually and collectively, believe they are beyond help. Thus, the family presents a formidable challenge to the therapist's professional skills and personal level of perseverance. Finally, the parents are in the process of getting a divorce and are battling, both legally and psychologically, for the custody of their children. Consequently, they represent a common referral problem for family therapists.

### Presenting Problem

Mr. W. is a 37-year-old, white male who came to an outpatient psychiatric clinic in a state of acute anxiety and depression following his separation from his wife. They were separated about two months prior to his presentation at the clinic. The couple had been married for 15 years. Mrs. W. left the home to live with a friend, and the children remained with her husband. Mrs. W. was given temporary custody of the children by the court about one month after the separation. Mr. W. was given visitation rights every other weekend, with the children to sleep over one night at his house. It was the awarding of custody to his wife which appears to have precipitated the onset of Mr. W.'s symptoms. Mr. W. challenged the court's decision, and the couple was embroiled in a bitter and nasty custody fight at the time of referral. Prior to his referral, some of the children stated that they did not want to stay with their father, and one child (Jay) was refusing to visit. Mr. W. complained that his wife was keeping his children from visiting him, lying to them, and encouraging them to think poorly of him. After his first visit to the clinic, Mr. W. took a three-week leave of absence from his job as an electrician and was seen for three outpatient crisis intervention visits by a staff psychiatrist. Mr. W. was given a termination diagnosis of episodic depression with the recommendation that he and his children continue in family therapy.

*Family Constellation*

At the time of referral, the family consisted of the following members.

Mr. W.: a 37-year-old white man employed as an electrician in the maintenance department of a private university
Mrs. W.: a 35-year-old white woman employed as a keypuncher by a private computer firm
Betty: a 13-year-old girl entering the eighth grade
Jay: an 11-year-old boy entering the fifth grade (repeating)
John: a nine-year-old boy entering the fourth grade
Penny: a six-year-old girl entering kindergarten

*Previous Problems*

The marriage was a stormy one from the beginning and had deteriorated in the last six years. Mr. W. complained that his wife was a poor housekeeper and poor manager who did not pay their bills. Mrs. W. complained that her husband had been verbally and physically abusive. In the six years prior to their separation, Mr. W. had two violations for domestic assault and battery, one charge of driving while intoxicated, eight traffic violations, and one charge of disorderly conduct (dismissed). Mrs. W. has no arrest record.

The couple has had several prior separations. The first was for a brief period (three days) in which Mrs. W. left and went to stay with the same friend she was staying with at the time of the referral. That separation followed a quarrel and ended when Mr. W. called his wife and asked her to return. The next separation involved a male friend of the family. According to Mr. W., this friend came to live with them at his wife's request and over his objections. The friend was unemployed and in need of a place to stay. After a while, Mr. W. told the friend to either find a job or leave. Mr. W. claims his wife thought he was an inhumane, uncaring, and ungrateful person for this action. Mr. W. claims his wife and this friend would do things together while he was at work and then talk about all the good times they had. When Mr. W. finally kicked the friend out of the house, the friend went into a county inpatient alcohol treatment unit. Mrs. W. allegedly "bragged" to her husband how proud she was of the friend for taking this action. Mr. W. suspected his wife and the friend of having an affair and stated, "They played it cool. They didn't do it when they thought I'd be around." Mr. W. loaned the friend his tools and claimed that many of them were missing when he finally returned them. He also claimed his wife was helping the friend steal things from him, and that she called him a liar when he confronted her with these accusations.

*Family History*

The following information was obtained from the court records based on investigations conducted to determine awarding of custody.

*Father*

Mr. W. is a short, stocky man with a serious and intense facial expression whose speech is occasionally slurred, making his pronunciation of some words difficult to understand. He is an only child who was born in a city and raised in a surrounding suburb. He graduated from high school and attended a technical institute where he learned his current trade of electrician. His father is a 62-year-old retired municipal government civil servant. His mother is a 59-year-old woman still employed in a bank. Mr. W. reports that he has an excellent relationship with his parents, that they do many things together, and have, in the past, gone out for family drives on most Sundays. Mr. W. has been at his present job for about three years. Prior to that, he worked for 11 years as an electrician and refrigeration expert for two private companies.

*Psychological evaluation.* Mr. W. was given a psychological evaluation by order of the court to determine his suitability for custody. The assessment indicated that Mr. W. was functioning in the average range of intelligence, but a huge discrepancy between his verbal and performance scales (performance IQ 55 points lower) suggested both the potential for higher functioning and an organic disability in the perceptual-motor area. Poor performances on the Bender-Gestalt and drawings supported the impression of organic impairment. Projective tests suggested an immature man with poor ego development who is governed by immediate needs for gratification and a tendency to act out his impulses, rather than delay gratification. He has conflicts over aggressive and affectional needs, and his needs for nurturance are unmet. He views others, especially women, as aggressively demanding. Many of his responses to the projective tests were highly personalized, but there was no evidence of reality distortion. The evaluation concluded that Mr. W. is experiencing the anxiety associated with his unmet needs and is described as having the potential for successful adjustment.

*Mother*

Mrs. W. is an articulate, outgoing woman whose attractiveness is diminished by her considerable obesity. She was born in Colorado and moved around quite a bit during her youth because her father was in the military service. Her parents reside in the western part of the United States. Her father, aged 63, is a retired lobbyist, and her mother, aged 63, is a retired secretary. Mrs. W. reports that her father was an alcoholic for about five or six years, but that the onset of his alcohol problem did not occur until after she had left the home. She describes her relationship with her father as follows: "We're two stubborn hard heads, very similar, but I care for him and he cares for me and that's what counts." Mrs. W. describes her mother as a very old-fashioned person who "was always there when I needed her."

Mrs. W. reports that she still cares about her husband and that basically he is a good person but that he has never been a good husband. However, he was a good father until two or three years ago and that is why she stayed with him. She reports that, since he changed jobs, he takes a lot of his frustrations out on the family. For example, he would come home from work and start "ranting and raving and carrying on" for no apparent reason. She stated that she cannot count the number of times he has physically abused her in the last two or three years. Specifically, she says that he has hit her, shoved her against the wall, pulled her around the room by the hair, and thrown her on the floor. She reports that sometimes she fought back and sometimes she did not. Mrs. W. further reports that the atmosphere in the home has been very tense and constrained, that he yelled at her constantly, and belittled her constantly. He would complain that she could not hold a job and could not cook. For example, at the dinner table he would say something like "What kind of slop are you serving for dinner tonight?" and then have two helpings. Mrs. W. reports that she and her husband have not shared the same bedroom for nine years. She states that her husband has a bad back and poor circulation and took up most of the bed. She slept with her daughters on the couch.

Mrs. W. describes her husband as having sleeping problems and dreams about her coming into the room with a knife to try to kill him. She states that she finally left him because she had to get the children and herself out of the house because the children hated their father. She further stated, "He has hurt me so much I'm afraid to be alone with him." She reported that he has only hurt two of the children on one occasion.

Mrs. W. says that she loves her children and that they are the most important things in her life. She is concerned about their welfare and has taken time to help them out and be part of their lives. The court probation counselor had the opportunity to observe Mrs. W. with her children and reports that during that time she was affectionate and complimentary of them. They all seemed relaxed and able to relate to each other comfortably and easily. Mrs. W. feels she is better able to care for her children because she is more sensitive to their needs and is more able and willing to take the time to understand and care for them.

*Psychological evaluation.* Like her husband, Mrs. W. was given a court-ordered psychological evaluation to help determine her suitability for custody. The evaluation indicated that her intellectual functioning was in the average range but that the extreme variability of the subtest scores and her high scores on several subtests (vocabulary, comprehension, similarities, block design) suggested the potential for functioning in the superior range. An unusually high level of anxiety lowered her scores on several tasks (arithmetic, digit span, digit symbol). The psychological report described Mrs. W.'s anxiety in part as a natural reaction to the strain of the custody proceeding. She is described as coping with her uncertainty behind an amiable and carefree facade. The psychological tests portray Mrs. W. as lacking an adequate sense of identity and having strong fears of inadequacy. She does not see herself as a person in her own right and seeks her sense of identity from what others think of her. Her need for approval, belongingness, and a positive response from others is exceptionally strong. She denies expression of her own feelings, particularly self-assertion, anger, and aggression, and this places her under excessive strain. At times her controls are inadequate and she tends to act out impulsively. However, her usual pattern is to intellectualize and express her pain and conflict in the form of abstract ideas. For example, despite the difficulty of her own marriage, she describes marriage as ". . . a bond of loving and caring between two people." Mrs. W. does acknowledge her frustration and on one sentence-completion item indicated that "sometimes . . . I feel like screaming."

The report concludes that Mrs. W.'s inner conflicts and emotional needs may interfere with her parenting skills. Her need for affection may tend to reverse the parent-child roles, thus putting a burden on her children, and her suppressed emotions may take the form of acting out, such as not following through on her responsibilities. The evaluation indicated that her inner turmoil interfered with her ability to detach herself sufficiently to view her environment objectively and impersonally and that she does not depend enough on a practical, common-sense approach. The report concluded that Mrs. W. has the potential to be a capable mother with supervision, support, and counseling.

### Children

*Betty,* the oldest youngster, will be entering the eighth grade. She is an unusually pretty, but overweight, youngster who is vivacious and outgoing. She is a typical 13-year-old with interests in many things, including: gymnastics, having nice clothes, and visiting with her friends. Betty remembers that when she was about five years old, her parents used to fight. This used to frighten her a great deal. As she got older, she began to stand up to her father during parental arguments. She stated that she used to try to help her mother by yelling at her father or trying to calm him down. She described several incidents in which she would cry and beg her father to let her mother up when he had her mother pinned down on the floor. Her father would then tell her to stay out of the fight. Sometimes when she felt helpless and could not do anything to stop the fight or calm her father down, she would leave the house and walk around the neighborhood until she calmed down. Betty reported that she was able to confide in one of her friends who had a similar home situation, and that this was comforting to her.

Betty states that she likes her father when he is not in one of his bad moods. She likes him most when they have company. In her own words: "If we have company, he's really on like good behavior." She does not like the way he yells a lot, stays at work too much, and sits around the house and dictates to the children on how to work. For example, she describes that on many occasions, he would sit watching television and say: "Go get me a Pepsi" or "Go get me something out of the car." He rarely says "please" or "thank you."

Betty describes her mother in more positive terms. She says her mother spends a lot of time with the children, is more fun, tries to take them places, and gives them treats. She says that her mother is fun to be with but that sometimes she loses her temper, yells at the children, and tells them to stay out of her way. If the children do stay out of her way, she gets in a better mood in about an hour. Otherwise, she yells at them more. Betty would like her mother to be able to talk things out better when she is in a bad mood instead of just demanding peace and quiet. Betty says that what she would like more than anything is for her parents to get back together but only if their situation changes. If they are reunited, she would like her father to spend more time at home and be less critical and angry. Betty enjoys her brothers and sister but says that she and Jay fight too much. They fight less frequently since they moved out of the house.

*Jay,* a handsome 11-year-old boy with large expressive eyes, will be repeating the fifth grade. He has had a very difficult childhood and has been referred to the local community mental health center on two different occasions for therapy. The first time he was referred was about five years prior to the present referral, and he was seen in individual psychotherapy weekly for about three months. His mother was seen in collateral therapy with a different therapist for about the same amount of time. An attempt was made to involve the father since Jay's problems appeared to reflect conflicts between the parents and Jay's lack of time with his father. When Jay's therapist left the clinic, a conference was held with both parents and both therapists. The recommendation was that Jay not be reassigned to a new therapist but that the parents continue treatment together. Mrs. W. appeared more interested than Mr. W., and they did not follow up.

At the recommendation of the school, Jay was referred to the mental health clinic for the second time about a year prior to the present referral. The intake report described Jay as a diminutive youngster who gave the appearance of an eight- or nine-year-old. He "sat on a chair, head resting on one arm, eyes downcast with a sorrowful facial expression." He was articulate and talked openly about his worries in an intellectualized manner. He expressed particular concern about losing control of his temper, even though his prior therapy had been helpful to some extent. Jay described mixed feelings toward his father, stating that he wanted to be close and have more contact but also feeling rejected and fearful. He recounted painful and rejecting experiences with peers, especially when he tried unsuccessfully to establish friendships. Jay relates feeling disappointed, hurt, and angry when he found himself alone. In general, Jay's description of his life experiences reflected a sensitive and lonely boy with unmet dependency needs and fears of abandonment. Like his older sister Betty, Jay stated that he would like to bring his mother and father back together again but without all the tension. In his own words: "I love them both, but the way things are going now, I hate both of them." The clinic recommended group therapy in order to help him with his peer relationships and to build on the prior individual therapy, but no group was available at the clinic at the time.

*Psychological evaluation.* Recent psychological testing done in the school indicated that Jay has average intelligence, but there was evidence of anxiety, perceptual and psychomotor problems consistent with a learning disability, and immaturity. In general, his test performance, including interpersonal skills, was characteristic of a younger child and reflected a lowered developmental level. The report recommended placement in a learning disability program.

*John,* a handsome nine-year-old boy with blond hair and blue eyes, will be entering the fourth grade. He was not seen individually but was seen on a home visit with other family members present. He is a quiet boy who does not offer information spontaneously. Both parents report that he has a good relationship with family members and peers and is experiencing little difficulty.

*Psychological evaluation.* John was referred for a psychological evaluation the previous school year because of academic difficulties, even though he was already repeating the third grade. John has average intelligence but an 18-point discrepancy between his verbal and performance (lower) IQ's, and the subtest scatter pattern suggested visual-perception problems. This was supported by his Bender-Gestalt reproductions, which were characteristic of those of a much younger child. It was recommended that John be placed in a program for learning-disabled youngsters.

*Penny,* a pretty five-year-old girl, is pleasant but not verbally responsive in the family context. She was observed with her mother and described as relating easily and affectionately. Penny has not entered school and has not been in any preschool programs.

*Treatment Information*

*Setting.* This family was seen in the outpatient clinic of a psychiatry department in a private medical school located in a large city. Appointments were scheduled for once-weekly one-hour sessions with permission for videotaping and/or observation by colleagues.

*Organization of treatment.* The total treatment of this case consisted of 30 therapy sessions on a once-per-week basis over a period of 10 months. The therapy was divided into three stages: an *engagement* stage, consisting of the first eight sessions and including the intake and assessment procedures; *midphase,* covering the next 16 sessions over a six-month period; and a *termination* period, which included six sessions over the final two months.

*Therapeutic Strategy and Course of Therapy*

Because of the complexity of the case, the poor communication within the family, and the number of agencies and helpers involved, it was important to develop a clear and structured treatment plan. This involved not only therapeutic interventions with the family but coordinating treatment with the court system and another mental health agency where the mother and children had apparently gone for help. Following the initial visit, I contacted the other clinic and obtained their agreement to consolidate the therapy at our clinic. Since the mother and children were not presently being seen, they readily agreed to let us handle the case.

The treatment plan involved both short- and long-term goals. The latter were established after the first three assessment sessions. The following specific therapy goals were formulated.

1. The most important and probably most difficult aspect of treatment was to get all the family members involved in the therapy. One of the children (Jay) refused to attend the initial session and was reported to be unwilling to attend sessions if the father was there. The father refused to attend sessions if the mother was there. Consequently, the first major task in therapy was to find a way for all the family members to attend the therapy sessions.
2. A second major goal was to form an alliance with each member of the family by acknowledging the validity of their gripes and dissatisfactions and emphasizing the importance of each person stating what changes he wanted.
3. To engage the father in individual therapy in order to deal with his problems of alcohol abuse, emotional instability, and other personal issues. The goals of the individual therapy were to diminish his use of alcohol and get him to relate to his children differently so that they would not be so afraid of him.
4. To continually emphasize the importance of having the mother involved in the therapy sessions and to look for ways to bring this about.
5. To point out conflicts and other emotionally upsetting areas and help the family find more reasonable ways of interacting.
6. To identify problem areas in everyday functioning and to use specific behavioral interventions to increase the level of family efficiency and effectiveness in accomplishing the tasks of daily living.
7. To help the family improve its internal communication by using structured exercises to improve their listening and communicating skills.
8. To reduce the level of negative emotion in the family by emphasizing their strengths and positive qualities.

A number of specific interventions from different theoretical orientations were used to accomplish these goals. A chronological summary of the case follows, including excerpts from transcripts of key sessions, to illustrate how the course of treatment actually transpired.

*Initial contact.* The first appointment for the family was scheduled for September 18, approximately three weeks after Mr. W. concluded his three individual crisis intervention appointments and about two weeks after he returned to work following his leave of absence. The session was scheduled for Mr. W. and his children, and everyone attended except Jay, who refused to come. Because of the considerable amount of information that was available through the court records, I dispensed with those intake and assessment procedures concerned with doing a genogram and taking a history and focused on obtaining a clear picture of the current situation. There were two major goals for the first session: (1) to try to get a clear understanding of the problems from each family member's perspective, and, (2) to try to get clues as to how to engage all of the family in treatment. The two youngest children, John and Penny, participated only minimally. They did not initiate conversation at any time and spoke only in response to direct questions from the therapist. Mr. W. attempted to dominate the session with complaints of how he was misunderstood, unappreciated, and betrayed by his wife. He was frequently tangential, volatile, and bordered on irrationality. He was often inappropriate in attempting to bring up his suspicions of his wife's infidelity and other aspects of their sexual relationship in front of the children. Mr. W. presented himself as a frightened, hurt, and angry adolescent who was desperately competing with his wife for his children's affection and loyalty. Betty assumed the role of peacemaker and placator, trying to represent her mother's position and that of the other children, particularly Jay, in a way that would not further alienate her father. It was clear from the discussion that the main areas of conflict were between Mr. W. and the absent Jay, who served as the defender of his mother's honor and whose style of attack was similar to that of his father.

The therapist's interventions were centered around keeping Mr. W. within the bounds of propriety, emphasizing the importance of getting Jay to attend the sessions, and discussing ways in which the family, particularly the children, might get him to come to the next sessions.

*Session 2 (9/25).* Jay came to the second session. Like his father, he is sensitive and easily hurt and attempts to cover his vulnerability with explosive anger and verbal attacks, primarily at the father. In the beginning of the session, both Jay and his father tried to dwell on the past and go over old grievances, conflicts, and mutual injustices. This quickly escalated into nonproductive quibbling, arguing, and mutual accusations of fault and blame. Betty's role was to sit back and criticize both Mr. W. and Jay for their behavior.

It was very clear that the children had aligned themselves with their mother in putting the blame for the family's problems on Mr. W. and his "problems." Betty and Jay both parroted the mother in stating that as soon as Mr. W. gets "treatment for his problems" (which they estimate should take a couple of years), Mrs. W. would be willing to reunite with her husband. Mr. W. clearly resented being cast in this light and was reluctant to acknowledge that he had any adjustment difficulties. In response to the complaints about his verbally and physically abusive behavior, Mr. W. admitted to drinking five or six beers on a daily basis and admitted that he could be difficult to get along with when he was drinking.

The therapeutic strategy in this session was to try to break the impasse created by Mr. W.'s and Jay's mutual hostility and their attempts to have their opinions prevail. Although we were still in the assessment phase, it was clear that unless this hostile standoff between Jay and his father could be put aside, it would be difficult to engage the family and impossible for therapy to proceed. I focused on the mutual hurt that underlied their anger and asked them to state what changes they wanted in the family. Jay stated that he wanted his father to call more often and spend more time with him but not order him around when he was at the father's house and that he wanted his parents to get back together. It was clear that the children were intimidated by their father and hesitant to speak because of his counterattacking style. They also made it clear that they were reluctant to participate in treatment unless he would get individual help. Mr. W. was resistant to individual therapy because he considered the acceptance of individual treatment as tantamount to an admission of guilt for the problems in the family.

Three important clinical issues emerged during this session: first, the significance of the father's abuse of alcohol and the importance of dealing with this and other issues in individual treatment; second, the importance of bringing Mrs. W. into the family sessions so that the children, particularly Betty and Jay, were not put in the untenable position of representing her at the sessions; third, the importance of engaging Jay. I presented these issues directly to the family, using the alcohol issue as a way of trying to engage the father in individual treatment in a face-saving manner. I also explained that it would be necessary to see the family for several sessions in order to do a complete evaluation. Mr. W. refused to allow his wife to be involved, and I accepted this for the present with the clear understanding that her participation was an option for future sessions. We agreed to meet the following week in a split session in which I would see the father alone and the children alone for a half hour each. I also obtained the father's permission to talk with the court social worker to clarify the conditions of visitation since it was hard to evaluate the legitimacy of Mr. W.'s complaints in view of his defensiveness and agitation.

*Contact with court worker.* Prior to the next therapy session, I had two telephone conversations with the court social worker, Ms. C. In our first conversation, she informed me that the conditions of visitation are as follows: Mr. W. can call the children and attend any school activities or sporting events in which the children are involved (e.g., Little League games). He cannot see the children on other occasions without his wife's permission. His wife claims that this is a problem and that he tends to be a "pest."

In a subsequent conversation, Ms. C. told me that Mrs. W. had called with the following complaints. Mr. W. had called his wife stating that a mutual friend of theirs was getting his bank statements, and friends of theirs had reported that while repairing a furnace at their house, Mr. W. was observed talking to the furnace "as if it were a person" and, when a dog came into the basement, he claimed it was a "sign." Ms. C. said there had been other incidents in which he had made claims that turned out to be untrue. She felt that individual therapy for Mr. W. would be helpful.

*Session 3 (10/9).* The following session is the third evaluation session in which I met with Mr. W. and the children separately. The session was one week later than originally scheduled since Mr. W. canceled the previous week. In the first part of the session with Mr. W. alone, the excerpts illustrate his tangential and possibly paranoid attempts to discredit his wife. The second part of the session shows my attempts to engage the children in family therapy by specifically addressing their resistance. In the final segment, I present my recommendations to Mr. W. and the children. Throughout the session, I take an active role in initiating topics and maintaining close control over the interaction. In the following excerpts from the session, certain words (indicated by quotation marks) used by Mr. W. appear to be misspelled. These are not typographical errors but represent my attempt to phonetically reproduce his distortions in using these words.

The session begins with my coming to the therapy room to find Mr. W. already there, slumped in a chair, looking overwhelmed and pathetic.

Mr. W.: I didn't think you were going to be here yet, so I just came in and sat down.
LCG: There's a waiting room down the hall where you can wait if you get here early. Usually I like to get here a little early. Do you want to relax for a few minutes before we begin?
Mr. W.: As long as you're here, let's start.
LCG: What happened last week? I got a message you couldn't make it.
Mr. W.: I had to work, so I couldn't get them here.

LCG: How about the kids, how come they're not here?

Mr. W.: I think they're coming. My wife is bringing them.

LCG: I see. You expect them to be here but they're not here yet. One of the things I wanted to do today was to spend some time with you and the kids alone, so as long as you're here, we might as well get started.

Mr. W.: I don't feel well.

LCG: In what way?

Mr. W.: Physically, achy, tired, cold . . . I ache all over.

LCG: How have things been going in the family since I saw you?

Mr. W.: Pretty good there for awhile. [Mr. W. goes on to complain about a dispute with his wife and the court social worker (Ms. C.) over psychological testing for the kids, that he cannot afford it, and that he found a place where he could get it done for no charge.]

LCG: Have you worked it out with your wife so that she'll bring the kids here?

Mr. W.: There's something about Jay, he won't come unless she brings him. [Mr. W. goes back to discussing his arrangements for Jay's testing and complaining that now that it's possible, Jay will not go through with it and that his wife and the court social worker will not help.]

LCG: Do you feel that Ms. C. and your wife are lined up against you?

Mr. W.: I know that.

LCG: How do you know that?

Mr. W.: First part of July, I had gotten back from Georgia and I was out to where my wife is living. I was going to pick up my nine-year-old boy, John, to bring him back to the house with me. My wife got into one of her little "tenter" tantrums. I thought she was going to attack me. She came running out of the house. I was down in the car. Instead she attacked John.

LCG: When you say "attacked," what do you mean?

Mr. W.: John was sitting in the car next to me. She ripped open the car door, grabbed him by the back of his shirt collar, and literally yanked him out of the car and threw him up on the ground like this [demonstrates]. He was crying and screaming. She was screaming and yelling for him to get into the house if he knew what was good for him. It was bad.

LCG: What was that all about?

Mr. W.: It was about the other guy this other broad is shacking up with. She's spaced out on narcotics all the time.

LCG: You just lost me. What other woman?

Mr. W.: This other woman my wife is living with, V. She takes like 20 "miyorgrams" of Valium a day and 10 "miyorgrams" of . . .

LCG: How did she get involved in this?

Mr. W.: She was out there when her boyfriend, D., showed up. I said something to him, and he said, "Shut up, you son-of-a-bitch." I said I wanted to talk to M. and he said, "She doesn't want to talk to you."

LCG: M. is your wife?

Mr. W.: What started everything off was—me and M. had problems before—when she [V.] came back up here was when M. started talking about leaving me and dumping me.

LCG: I don't understand why your wife was going after John?

Mr. W.: She, D., and V. had stolen other people's property out of my house. They took it and knew it wasn't our property, a brand new mattress, bed frame, and whole bunch of other stuff that didn't belong to us, that belonged to other people. I told them I wanted the stuff back in the house. His attitude was that anything that was in that house he could take when he wanted to take it.

LCG: Again, I don't understand how this relates to your wife going after John?

[Mr. W. continues with a rambling story about how his conflict with D., V., and his wife over the articles taken from the house caused his wife to become so upset that she allegedly attacked John.]

LCG: Now, where did you get the idea that your wife and Ms. C. were working against you?

Mr. W.: I called the county police and they refused to get involved because it was a domestic situation. The police did make a report that I'd called them and what statements I made. I called my parents, and my parents came out to the house and talked to D. and V. The story they got is entirely different. The next day I had John over to the house. In fact, I had all the kids over to the house. I asked John what happened to his shoulder. Why was his shoulder and the back of his head bleeding? Because when I got home—I picked my son Jay up—I was being told that I threw John up against the house, that I was crazy, and that I didn't know what I was doing.

LCG: Who told you that?

Mr. W.: D. and V.

LCG: Now, if I understand things right, somehow the fact that your wife dragged your son got turned around that you did it. Now, how does a person like myself, who's coming in from the outside, figure out what is really going on?

Mr. W.: You couldn't!

LCG: If she were here, she'd tell a different version than you and there's no way to tell which is right?

Mr. W.: Right. Well, my parents were over. No, I had the children over my parents' and I asked John right there, "Well, John, how's your shoulder and neck after your mother yanked you out the car that way?" His statement was: "Well, daddy, I just hit the ground and scraped off an old scab." My father was sitting there and he says: "That's enough, son, don't say anything more" and he called their attorney.... We called Ms. C. and she said: "Well, M. is their mother and she can do what she wants as far as punishing them is concerned. It was perfectly within her right to yank John out of the car. There was absolutely nothing wrong with it. Now everybody loses their cool once in a while" [repeated].

LCG: This is the basis for your feeling that she is taking your wife's side?

Mr. W.: Not only that, but it's been proven in court that six years ago my wife had a man she was shacking up with. Now, Penny, I don't know if she's mine and I don't care. At the time it all occurred, yes, I was very disturbed about it and was for a long time.

LCG: I think you still are because you've brought it up several times in our sessions.

Mr. W.: I wouldn't be if it just happened that one time, but the one thing I didn't know until court was that she kept seeing that same man for six years afterward.

LCG: What I'm saying is that even though it happened a long time ago, a lot of upset feeling is still there.

Mr. W.: Yeah, it's still there to a degree. Yeah, that's not the only person it's happened with. There have been four others.

LCG: I think it would be helpful to not talk about these things in front of the children.

Mr. W.: Yeah, she tells the children that I'm crazy, that I hallucinate, that I can't tell right from wrong, that I cannot provide for them, and that she never went to bed with anybody.

LCG: Regardless of what she tells the children, they have their own eyes and ears. If, in fact, you are a reasonable, kind, and loving father who is not drinking and not blowing up, they are going to see things as they really are, no matter what she tells them.... If you try and counter what she is saying, the best that can happen is that the kids will try to get away from both of you as soon as they can....

Mr. W.: Well, like Tuesday ...

LCG: I'd like to see whether the kids are here yet. [I leave, return with the children, and explain that I want to spend some time with the children alone as we agreed in the previous session. After that, I will see them all together to discuss the next step. The following transcript material is with the children alone.]
LCG: I missed you last week.
John: Thank goodness.
LCG: Thank goodness? I thought you liked coming here.
John: Not very much. She'd [Penny] come back. She just plays.
LCG: Two weeks ago you all said you'd like to talk to me alone. I was wondering what you wanted to talk about?
John: When we say something and he knows it's true, he tries to denounce it. Well, like one time Betty said something and he tries to denounce it and call you something.
LCG: So, if you have a difference of opinion—do you know what I mean by that?—he'll get angry real easy?
John: It's two different stories. Yours is wrong and his is right most of the time.
LCG: That would involve Betty. Betty, can you tell me a little about that? Do you agree with what John is saying?
Betty: Yeah, I guess.
LCG: Do you know what he is talking about?
Betty [in a very soft voice]: No.
LCG: How do you see it? How do you see the difficulty in getting along with your father?
Betty: I don't know.
LCG: I had the feeling, not the first time, but the last time we met that I kind of lost you. Do you know what I mean by that? Is that right? Was my feeling correct?
Betty: Yes.
LCG: Can we talk about that because I don't want to lose you. . . . I didn't think it was something I did or something that happened here. I had the feeling that your body was in the room but the rest of you left. You say now that's right. [Silence] Is it hard for you to tell me?
Betty: I didn't feel like coming.
LCG: I'm trying to find some way to help everybody in the family. I really need your help to do that. For myself, when I don't feel like going somewhere, there's usually reasons for it. Sometimes it helps me to try and figure out what those reasons are. If you could tell me why you don't want to come here, that might help us.
Betty [silence and then barely audibly]: It's a pain!
LCG: Can you tell me more?
Betty: No.
LCG: In what way is it a pain?
Betty: Well. . . . [mumbles something inaudible]
LCG: I didn't hear you. Can you say it again?
Betty: I can't spend time with my friends. I have to do my homework after school, then we eat and leave.
LCG: So one of the things you're upset about is that you have to give up the things you like to do to come here. If you didn't come here, how would things be different? Would you be with your friends?
Betty: Yeah. Every time we come here, everyone is edgy.
LCG: What are you edgy about? Do you know? Jay, what about you? Do you have any idea about what's going on?
Jay: I just feel like there isn't any need in going.
LCG: I have a pretty good picture of the story. Your mother and father have been having trouble for a long time. They've split up. They're in a fight and you guys are caught in the middle.
Jay: Plus my grandparents are trying to do the same thing. They're always debating and they won't ever let us alone.

LCG: One of the reasons you're here alone right now is that it's very important for me to try to understand what's going on with you without your grandparents and your mother and father here. I hope you can talk freely without them here.
John: I just feel that there isn't any need in going because it's not going to help.
LCG: Not going to help what? What needs help?
Jay: A whole lot of things except it's still not going to work.
LCG [with mild annoyance]: I'm getting tired of hearing from all of you that it's not going to work. Maybe it isn't. . . .
Jay: We just go through the same thing again.
LCG: Well, I haven't. Maybe you have and I can appreciate that you've had to do this before. But every time I ask you for some clues or what might help, you can say, "Well, I don't want to bother to answer that because it's not going to work." Well, if it's not going to work, I'm not going to waste my time either. I'd like to know what's not going to work, why you don't think it's going to work, and what needs to be done. You're the only ones who can tell me. Now, I'm starting to think that you guys don't want it to work. Maybe you like something about the way it is. I don't know if that's right or not.
Jay: A little bit.

Following this, the children open up and we discuss their likes and dislikes about the current situation. Jay takes the lead and is the most articulate. They discuss their dislike of the grandparents' attempts to control the situation and the tension and fighting between their parents. In their discussion, Betty disagrees and challenges Jay, and they reenact the struggle going on between the mother and father with Betty defending her father and Jay taking the side of his mother. Jay complains about his father's temper and the fact that they never do things together anymore. They acknowledge that they feel their father has problems. As John so aptly puts it: "His brain is telling him things that are not true." I attempt to steer the conversation away from old material and more toward what changes they would like to see in the family while pointing out the importance of their involvement. I challenge their claim that he's forgotten about them by pointing out that he has not missed any therapy appointments. The session resumes with both Mr. W. and the children together.

LCG: Do you feel that anything has changed in how you relate to each other?
Jay: Not necessarily.
Mr. W.: I don't think so.
LCG [to Mr. W.]: How would you want things to change, if at all?
Mr. W.: Like I was discussing before, a little bit of trust. Some belief in what I say. I'm totally ignored and called a liar.
LCG: So you'd like them to listen to you more. [to kids] Any way of that happening?
Jay: Maybe, maybe not.
LCG: What does he have to do and what do you have to do?
Jay: He has to tell the story right.
LCG: Who decides if it's right or not?
Jay: Actually, who was there and who was listening.
LCG: One of the reasons I wanted all of you to come in together was so I could see and hear what happens and I could tell who's hanging things around. But if only some of you come, I can't do that.
Mr. W.: Well, this weekend, my wife came down . . .
LCG [interrupting]: I don't want to get into that. One of the things I really want to stay away from is rehashing things that go on outside of here for the simple reason that we'll get into the

same thing. Unless your wife is here, I don't want to talk about things unless the people involved are here. What I'd like to do now is give you some feedback about what I see going on.

During the last part of the session, I point out that Mr. W. has to continue with the progress he's made on cutting down on his use of alcohol. The payoff for Mr. W. would be that his kids would want to be around him more. I help the family to negotiate some specific tasks, such as Mr. W. and Jay spending time together with Mr. W. teaching Jay about his work. There is more "yes, butting" from both of them, but I insist on getting them to agree to spend one hour together prior to the next visit. In the same vein, we discussed one activity they could all do together that would be fun. After some negotiating, they decided to take a trip to the country to visit a friend's farm and to pick apples on the way. The session closed with the family's agreement to come in for family therapy and individual therapy (for Mr. W.) on alternate weeks.

*Session 4 (10/16).* This was an individual psychotherapy session with Mr. W., which focused on his excessive use of alcohol, his "short fuse" with regard to expressing anger, and some of his reported "hallucinations." He explained the reports of his "talking to the furnace" as simply problem solving done out loud, similar to reading directions from a repair manual out loud rather than to himself. He denied any delusional or hallucinatory experiences, and his explanation was plausible. The session was also used to obtain more history, particularly to hear "his side of the story" about his marriage, with the goal of reducing some of his anger and frustration. Once again, I raised the option of involving his wife in the therapy, and for the first time he did not reject it outright.

*Session scheduled for 10/23 was canceled*

*Session 5 (10/30).* This session was attended by Mr. W., Jay, and Betty. Mr. W. began by saying he was tired, "strung out," and wanted to quit early so he could have a drink and go home. I ignored these comments and asked how the family had done on the two tasks they had agreed to in the previous session. They did not follow through on either one, and most of the session was spent dealing with the issues between Mr. W. and Jay that prevented their spending time together. Mr. W. had taken the initiative in approaching Jay, but Jay was inaccessible to his father because he was in a bad mood. This was confirmed by Betty. We focused on Jay's anger and the difficulty in dealing with him when he's angry. This included role playing. Like his father, Jay tends to go off the subject and project all the blame for his own anger on to his father's mistreatment of his mother. He was finally able to admit that he is still too angry at his father to be able to share any activities with him. I concluded the session by: (1) pointing out the progress they were making, despite the considerable remaining problems; (2) reemphasizing the importance of bringing Mrs. W. into the sessions so that Jay would not have to represent her; and (3) focusing on Mr. W.'s opening remark about wanting a drink. I complimented him on his progress in not drinking and emphasized the importance of his continuing to abstain. Despite Jay's anger, it was clear that both he and Betty were more engaged than in the previous session.

*Session 6 (11/4):* This was an individual therapy session with Mr. W. The central themes of the session were Mr. W.'s complaints about his wife's infidelity and obtaining more information about their sexual relationship. He claimed their sexual adjustment was good for the first three years of their marriage but then deteriorated when she started making excuses. He stated that she performed oral sex on him but that he did not on her because "I can't stand crowded places and certain smells." His description of his wife's alleged first affair was especially interesting because of what appeared to me to be his clear collusion and simultaneous denial of any responsibility. He described bringing a friend home for lunch on a regular basis. Eventually the situation evolved to where the three of them would drink and watch pornographic movies together. One night, after doing this, he excused himself and went to bed early, leaving his friend and wife alone. Later, he woke up and came down to get a snack and allegedly caught them making love in the cellar. Mr. W. says his wife denied that anything happened beyond some mild petting and was angry at him for "setting her up." He denied any responsibility for what happened and could not see how his actions in any way contributed to what happened. A major purpose of my intervention strategy was to try to elicit some of his feelings (e.g., hurt, rejection), but this was unsuccessful. Mr. W. attributed all their sexual difficulties to his wife.

At the end of this session Mr. W. disclosed that he intended to file for divorce and wanted me to tell his children. I pointed out the inappropriateness of that and discussed briefly with him how he could go about telling them. As the transcript from the next session indicates, he decided to wait until the therapy session to tell them.

*Session 7 (11/13):* This is a critical family therapy session in which Mr. W. informs the children that he has filed for divorce. This provokes a strong emotional reaction on the part of the children and sets the stage for me to insist that Mrs. W. be brought into the therapy. The session begins with a rather lighthearted discussion of the past weekend's activities. Mr. W. tries repeatedly to get Penny's attention by calling her by her nickname ("Hey, Put-Put") and making a clicking sound with his tongue, in much the same way as one would call a pet dog.

Betty mentions that Jay had not participated in many activities over the weekend because of a headache. She does a satirical imitation of Jay, in which she gets on the floor, moaning and groaning. This elicits a lot of laughter and silliness among the children. Jay attributes his headache to something he ate. I ask Jay if his headache is a possible way in which he can avoid doing unpleasant tasks, like going to his father's house, and he agrees with this. Following this, as the following excerpt reveals, Mr. W. makes his announcement.

Mr. W. [in a very soft voice, almost a whisper]: Betty, Jay, John, Penny, I've got something to tell you. I don't know how to tell you or even the right way to tell you. Mother and I have been separated now for six months. I thought maybe things could get a little better. They haven't gotten better. They've gotten worse. So we're going ahead and filing for legal separation and divorce.
Betty [in a soft voice]: When did you do that? [repeats]
Mr. W.: Last week.
Betty: Mom didn't say anything.
Jay: Why didn't you tell us?
Mr. W.: I didn't tell you because I didn't know how to tell you.
Jay [interrupting]: Don't you think we're involved in this?
Betty [in a high voice, fighting back tears]: Jay, he's telling us now.
Mr. W.: I thought things would get a little better but they haven't. They've gotten worse. So I don't know how to tell you or even if I'm using the right words. [long pause] The papers were filed last Wednesday or Thursday.
Betty: Did you file them or did Mom?
Jay: Did you talk it over?

Mr. W.: She knows about it.

LCG: How are you feeling, Betty?

Mr. W.: I told her and she says: "You know I still love you and all that and you've been under psychiatric treatment for six months now and after another year and a half of intensive psychiatric treatment, we'll get back together."

Jay: That's a bunch of shit!

Betty: Well, I think it's time for you and Mom to have some psychiatric counseling down here together.

Mr. W.: Well, Betty . . .

Jay [interrupting]: We've asked Mom, but Betty and she say it's your decision.

Betty: I've already told her that you've been thinking about having her come down here and she said, "Fine, whenever you're ready."

Mr. W.: Well, Betty, after what's happened last week, two weeks ago, the phone calls, it's past that point now. When I talked to Dr. Grebstein last we were still considering it, weren't we?

LCG: Well, as far as I'm concerned, we still are.

Mr. W.: Well, her and I are getting to some agreement . . .

LCG [interrupting]: Before we get into that, Betty, how are you feeling?

Mr. W.: She's feeling hurt.

Betty: No, I'm not.

LCG: Let her talk. I'd like to hear from you. Can you tell your father how you feel? [long silence]

Betty: I don't think you should make the decision . . .

Jay: At least until school is over.

Betty: . . . until you talk it over. [tearfully, but fighting it] Anyway, you have to be separated for a year so maybe things can change.

Jay [belligerently]: What I'd like to know is why . . . before you ever filed . . . you could have talked to us. That's what I'd like to know.

Mr. W.: Because, Jay, and I'm sorry to say this, that really isn't your decision. If I'd talked to you all, maybe I would have hurt you all and maybe I wouldn't have gone through with it.

Jay: Yeah, but don't you think it's going to change our lives. You changed our lives since June and it's not getting any better. And when you do it, you change everybody's lives. [loudly and starting to cry] I'm getting sick of it. Because everybody's just sitting there, just sitting there and cussing everybody out and everything and you don't even think we're involved in it. And that tells me you don't even care a little bit. [crying] We're involved in it as much as you are and you can't tell me we're not. We're sitting here, trying to help everybody and all you want to do is just sit and don't think we're involved and that shows me down deep in my heart that you're not caring.

Mr. W. [very softly]: Jay, you didn't hear what I said.

Jay [interrupting]: Yes, I did.

Mr. W.: You are involved with it.

Jay: You just said I wasn't. You just said we weren't.

Mr. W. goes on to repeat that the situation is just getting worse, and he and Jay get into the following confrontation in which Jay becomes the defender of his absent mother. I try to refocus the session on the children's feelings in an attempt to encourage expression of the hurt and disappointment that underlie their anger.

Jay: . . . You try to avoid Mom every time she's trying to make peace. You keep trying to avoid her in every possible way you can.

Mr.W.: Because I don't want a big hassle like two weeks ago. That wasn't avoiding her.

Penny: Jay, tie your shoe!

LCG: Jay, you sound hurt and angry.

Jay: Yeah, I am.

LCG: You would have liked your father

to discuss it with you before he filed the papers.

Jay: Because I'm sick and tired of everybody else making everybody else's decisions. He could have talked it over with us because we're involved in it and we've got as much right to say what we feel.

Betty: He can tell us, Jay, but it's still their decision.

Jay: It's a little bit ours.

Betty: Well, if they're going to fight like cats and dogs, what's the use of having a marriage?

Mr. W.: That's right and hurting you all even more.

Betty: But still I think the papers could have waited at least until June. . . . [The discussion gets off track into quibbling about legalities.]

LCG [interrupting]: Okay, that's the legality, but what we're starting to deal with here for the very first time is your feelings about your mother and father's separation . . . we're starting to talk openly for the first time and that's important. John, what's your reaction?

John: I think they've been getting along better but I think they should try a little bit harder.

LCG: That's what they should do, but how do you feel about what's happened.

John: I don't like to see them split up because I've seen them married for nine years [his age].

LCG: Can you talk with your father about how you feel?

John: Me and him have been getting along just fine but I don't know about Betty, Jay, and Penny.

I continue to try to get John to talk about his feelings with his father, but I am unsuccessful. At this point, Mr. W. again tries to shift the blame for the most recent escalation of their problems by citing his wife's unreasonable phone calls demanding child support payments with Jay continuing to defend his mother. Once again, I try to bring it back to them.

LCG: Can you two talk that over? It sounds like you haven't finished.

Mr. W.: Yeah, I can.

[I change seats with Jay, asking him to sit next to his father so they can talk more directly and without me between them.]

Jay: Who made the decision about filing papers first?

Mr. W.: Well, I told her what I was going to do and she said: "So what . . . I love you and you've been going to psychiatric treatment and you're crazy. You don't know what you're doing. You're totally insane."

Jay: Why didn't you say that the first time?

Mr. W.: And she says: "After you've been going to psychiatric treatment for two or two and a half years . . ."

Jay: It just changed. It was one to one and a half years.

[They start quibbling over the details of what was said.]

Mr. W. [annoyed]: Jay, everything has been put on me, that I'm the bad turkey and that she is the little goddess. She's not as good as everybody thinks she is or she likes to make everybody think she is. Right now, I am so concerned about you kids, you don't know how concerned I am. Now right now, Dr. "Grekstein" check on this, because we got this guy right up here on the seventh bed ward [referring to the seventh floor of the hospital, which is the psychiatric ward] and I'm griping about this guy on the seventh bed ward who's taking the same narcotics that V. [the woman with whom Mrs. W. is sharing a house and whom Mr. W. blames for giving his wife the idea to leave him] is taking. He tripped out today and tried to kill his girlfriend and tried to kill himself. You cannot take 20 "miyograms" of Valium a day for a year and a half and still have your brains together.

LCG: You're getting away from the point. One of the things it sounds like you're feeling badly about is that you are getting most of the blame for the divorce.

During the next segment, the discussion continues to center around Mr. W.'s role as the "bad guy" in the family, specifically in terms of his being the disciplinarian and having punished the kids, particularly Jay, harshly at times. I get him to admit that he feels badly about this but has never told Jay or the other kids that. Again, I refocus the discussion on the divorce and point out that it appears as if they are all reacting strongly, but are turning off their feelings. I emphasize that it is hard on everyone but it is important to talk about their feelings. Mr. W. again assumes a defensive posture and states that his wife's harassing phone calls at work have been putting his job in jeopardy and he had no choice. I suggest that filing for divorce was his way of getting protection and distance from his wife. An alternative would be to bring her to the sessions and work out an agreement. Betty states that although prior marriage counseling did not work, it might this time, and she wants her father to ask her mother to come. I persist in asking them to express their reaction to the divorce and in the next segment, Jay threatens to leave home.

LCG: How do you all feel about them getting divorced?
Jay: Then they can just lose me.
LCG: How?
Jay [tearfully]: I'll just go to a foster home.
LCG: You're feeling so badly, you'd just like to leave altogether?
Mr. W.: I don't want you to do that, I love you too much.
Jay: I know, but if you love me, how do you sit there and ignore us practically?
Mr. W. [tearfully]: Jay, I just don't sit here and ignore you. I love you but I've got to have something. I can't keep on with the torment, the harassment, these phone calls.
Jay [angrily]: I told you. Get it in writing and it will stop. [shouting] Call the cops or something. You're not doing a damn thing and you know it.
Mr. W.: There's nothing the police can do. There's nothing anyone can do.

A little later in the session after Betty and Jay accuse their father of avoiding their mother, I try to reduce the father's resistance to having the mother come into therapy by pointing out that he is not being appreciated for his efforts. My hope is that he will experience sufficient support from me to risk bringing his wife in.

LCG: It sounds like one of the things that's going on is you two are saying to your dad: "You haven't tried hard enough." And what you're [Mr. W.] saying is: "I've tried harder than anyone knows and no one is giving me any credit for that."
Mr. W. [triumphantly]: That's absolutely right!
LCG: Where we're stuck is right there.

In the last part of this session, Betty and Jay continue to criticize the father for avoiding his wife's invitations. They start quibbling about past history, and Betty finally says: "This is absolutely stupid." Since the session is drawing to a close, I suggest inviting Mrs. W. to the next session so that the children will not be placed in the awkward position of defending her. I make it clear that reconciliation is not a goal. Mr. W. clearly but reluctantly agrees to have her come to the next session but warns: "All I have to be around her for is five minutes and she gets me upset."

*Session 8 (11/20).* This is the first session that Mrs. W. attends. Although the prior session ended with Mr. W. agreeing to having his wife attend, he opens the session by insisting that she leave. The following excerpts illustrate my attempts to maintain control over the session and bring some semblance of order to chaos. The main therapeutic task is to diminish Mr. W.'s rage and prevent the rest of the family from ganging up on him. The session concludes with a change in the therapeutic contract in which they agree to come for three sessions as a whole family. With this agreement, the engagement stage of therapy is concluded and we move on to the midphase stage of treatment.

Mr. W. [as he is removing his coat and taking his seat]: Number one, I'm not going to talk to her because she's not supposed to be down here on this... complex.

Jay: That's the only excuse you've got.

Mr. W.: Jay, knock it off. Number two, when I called her and asked her to come, she said: "Yeah, that was fine and dandy." Saturday, after John's football game—John's team won and everyone was having a good time—waiting for him to get his trophies, she went up and sat in the car, and John and I and the kids were having a good time. They had cakes and pies and things for sale. We had some cookies. There was an old English type of cake. I had one and I took her a piece and I gave it to her. She didn't say anything. About 20 minutes later, I came back and asked how it was. [shouting] "God damn, son-of-a-bitch, it was cold!" Fine, so I left. So then last night, it seems as if somebody decides they would rather have the car busted so somebody poured sand in the engine of the car. So I got out of here today and I took it to the gas station and called her for her to meet me at the house instead of going all the way out there to pick them up. All right. She absolutely knowed she wanted to get me upset and uptight. She deliberately... she never came by the house, she never called or did anything. Now, you [to wife] may get up and you may leave, because I've said...

LCG [interrupting]: Hold it. We agreed last week that she would be invited to the session.

Mr. W.: She voided all that.

LCG: No, she hasn't voided anything. She's here like we agreed. Second of all, I decide who stays in the session and who goes, not you. Now, let's start. [to Mrs. W.] Would you like to respond?

[Mrs. W. tells her version of the "cake story," which is a different version in which she states that she said it would be better heated up. She was careful to not blame him. She denied swearing with: "... part of his problem is that he always thinks I throw in cuss words and I don't, except in the heat of an argument and I wasn't mad at him."]

LCG: Now, one of the problems, you tell me if I'm wrong, is that this is very representative of what happens. That when you two get together, sparks fly. Is that right?

Jay: That's exactly what happens.

LCG: So one of the family problems is how your mother and father can be together without things getting really in an upheaval. Now, [to Mr. W.] you're very upset. What are you upset about?

Mr. W.: I'm upset at the lies, the conspiring, the sneaking, and the thievery...

Mrs. W.: I've already told you, since you told us to get there at 5:15, that we couldn't make it. That we were sitting down to dinner, that we can't make it, and that I would bring them down here to save you the trip.

Mr. W. [nastily]: I said no!

Jay: I was sitting by Mom and you were yelling and screaming.

Mr. W.: Jay, you are lying through your teeth.

Mrs. W.: You were yelling, Jim.

LCG [to Mr. W.]: Let him [Jay] finish.
Jay: See how you're mad now.
Mr. W.: I told her . . .
LCG [interrupting]: You're interrupting again.

The above excerpt illustrates both how I have to take an active role to maintain order and how an attempt to allow Mr.W. the opportunity to express some of his anger backfires when it turns loose his paranoid fantasies and he tries to monopolize the session. The main purpose of the session is to take advantage of Mrs. W.'s presence to try and establish some common goals for the family to accomplish. I ask the children what they would like to see changed. Penny, who has not responded to any of my questions in prior sessions, states: "I want my dad to be friends with my mom!" (Out of the mouths of babes . . .)

The following excerpt comes from later in the session when we are discussing the family's goal of being less angry and having more civil communication.

Mrs. W.: . . . and I have a problem that I have to work out. I'm afraid of him. He's hurt me physically and verbally so much that I want to put some distance between us. I'd be literally afraid to be alone in the same room with him.

Later in the session, I use a mild paradoxical tactic by asking both Mr. and Mrs. W. to go into the observation room together for a few minutes while I talk with the children. Mrs. W. accompanies her husband with no apparent reluctance.

An example of the importance of modeling is given in the following excerpt from Mrs. W., following my pointing out that it's five against one and that I don't believe that Mr. W. is the only problem in the family.

Mrs. W.: What the doctor is trying to do, kids, is—and it's going to be hard—we all have to learn to forget what's happened in the past and start over again. I personally think that's asking an awful lot and that you're going to have to show us how to do it.

As a way of countering the scapegoating of Mr. W. and the family's belief that he alone is responsible for their problems, I ask each person to say one thing s/he would like to improve about his/her own behavior and also to state one thing s/he likes about each of the others. The purpose of this is to take the focus off Mr. W. and to have the family hear that they have strengths. The session appears as if it will end on a positive note. The family agrees to have three weekly family therapy sessions with all the members present and we will reevaluate the progress after those three sessions. Betty then requests that their mother drive them to the appointments to save time. Mr. W. immediately objects because he does not want his wife "wandering around the halls." I suggest a compromise in which Mrs. W. will drive the children to the appointment but I will meet them in the lobby and escort them to the therapy room. Mr. W. accepts this arrangement.

The engagement phase of therapy has now been completed in the eighth session with the inclusion of the mother in the therapy and the establishing of a common family goal.

*Midphase of therapy (11/27 to 5/7).* The midphase of therapy consisted of 16 therapy sessions, mostly with the entire family, but including two appointments with Mr. and Mrs. W., six individual sessions with Jay, and one individual appointment with Mr. W. Generally, the family sessions had a practical, problem-solving focus with the overall goal of increasing the organization and efficiency of family functioning. This phase of therapy is summarized below. Following the inclusion of

Mrs. W. in family therapy, it became clear at the next session that it would be important to defuse some of the couple-related issues, particularly sexual themes, in order to prevent them from creeping into the family sessions. A pattern emerged in which Mrs. W. was able to successfully bait her husband in a pleasant, overtly passive, nonprovocative style. He would respond with enraged attacks against her with accusations of immorality and infidelity. I tried to eliminate this competition for the children by arranging a session for the couple only (12/6) in which we discussed in detail the history surrounding his accusations. In this session, Mrs. W. acknowledged there had been some sexual contact in the first instance but stated it had stopped prior to intercourse. She maintained that this was the only time she had any contact with any other man. Mr. W. made additional accusations about her putting sand in his gasoline tank, which she knew about but denied doing. Mr. W. also admitted to hitting her once. The crux of the session came when he acknowledged that the hurt of being ignored by his wife was what fueled his rage. The session ended with my emphasizing the importance of more reasonable communication in order to keep the children from being caught in the middle. We agreed on better communication as a goal but not with the purpose of reconciling or even being friends.

The next session (12/11) was spent documenting the current problems in the family. These included: the extensive mutual criticism and lack of support or positive comments; the inability of the family members to express their wants and preferences to each other; the need for the children to be more involved in helping with chores and household tasks, particularly when the children visited the father. They were given the homework assignment of making a list of the tasks that needed to be accomplished. The following session consisted entirely of negotiating a specific written contract which listed the responsibilities of each family member with regard to maintaining the household.

The following two family sessions (1/15 and 1/22) focused both on following through on the task orientation and trying to rework some of the relationships in the family. In general, this family can be described as an extremely emotionally deprived family in which there is a pervasive feeling of being unloved, uncared for, and non-nurtured. As a result, the interactions in the family tend to be need-determined, emotionally charged, and chaotic in the sense of violating the usual boundaries. For example, one of the two oldest children, especially Betty, will often act as a surrogate parent. Mrs. W. will treat Mr. W. like a petulant child, indulging and patronizing him. Mr. W. will attempt to become authoritarian to reestablish his power and self-respect.

Three main therapeutic interventions were used. First, the problem-focused task orientation was introduced to bring greater order to the household and to serve as a metaphor for establishing some semblance of emotional order. A second and parallel therapeutic intervention was to continually point out their destructive interactions to them and stop them from occurring within the sessions. The third major intervention was to use role playing, behavioral rehearsal, modeling, cognitive restructuring, and other learning-based interventions to help the family learn new and more positive ways of resolving conflict and relating to each other.

It was necessary to have one crisis intervention appointment with Mr. W. (2/5) after he learned his wife had moved out of her friend's house and taken an apartment. The children missed a weekend at his house, and since he did not yet know his wife's new address, he reacted with panic and rage. This was enhanced by his wife's alleged statement that, according to the court social worker (Ms. C.), she did not have to inform him of her whereabouts but only had to bring the children to therapy. In addition, he related that his job might be in jeopardy and that he had strong feelings for another (married) woman. He appeared agitated, out of control, and possibly decompensating. I tried to be supportive and raised the possibility of a psychiatric consultation for medication if things did not get better. He expressed great reluctance to follow through on this recommendation.

Following the cancellation of two appointments because of snowstorms, I met with Mr. and Mrs. W. alone to discuss their concern about a deterioration in Jay's behavior. Their increased communication had been accompanied by a decline in Jay's behavior. Specifically, he was in greater overt conflict with Mr. W., including swearing at him, was vandalizing property at home, and had beaten up his younger brother John pretty badly. On the one hand, Mr. and Mrs. W. worked surprisingly well together in their mutual concern for Jay, but at the same time, Mr. W. erupted with accusations of blame at his wife for not letting him discipline Jay. I supported the legitimacy of their concern for Jay and obtained their permission to contact his school.

Mr. W. also mentioned that he had been fired and attributed the reason to politics and a personality clash with his boss rather than any negligence on his part. When I raised the possibility of his drinking contributing to his job loss, his wife came to his defense and supported his point of view! After this session, I had a supervision consultation with a colleague, and we decided I would see Jay in individual therapy to supplement the family therapy.

A school consultation indicated that although Jay was academically weak, he was not in danger of repeating the grade. His teachers did report a noticeable decline in the quality of his peer relations, which had never been particularly good.

Recently, he had been picking on other kids and been acting "obnoxious."

I saw Jay for five individual therapy sessions in which we focused on his hurt and anger at his father, his isolation from his peers, and his anxiety in approaching a girl he liked. As with the family, the individual sessions were fairly structured, problem-focused, and used a combination of cathartic-expressive techniques, role-playing specific situations (such as asking his girl out), and modified play therapy tactics (taking him to a gym where he could punch his anger out on a heavy bag). Jay noticed in punching the heavy bag that he hurt his hand. He had the spontaneous insight that when you express anger in an uncontrolled way, you may end up hurting yourself! The individual therapy went very well. He was able to admit that as his father changed (became less "bossy"), this was hard for him to handle. Also, Jay's peer relationships improved, and he approached the girl he liked with the result that she went out with him. As is often the case with adolescents, as soon as he had a girlfriend, his perceived need for and motivation for therapy diminished. We discontinued therapy after six sessions at his request.

The family sessions during this period focused on increasing communication by having the family practice listening skills and how to state their own points of view more directly. We worked on solving other instrumental problems, such as more effective ways of discipline. Because of their different styles, the parents had never been able to agree on issues such as discipline. Instead they had battled over how to punish the children and blamed each other for their mutual lack of effectiveness. A main theme of the family therapy was to help them develop increased parenting skills.

Despite the earlier agreement that reconciliation was not a goal of therapy, it was clear that Mr. and Mrs. W. were less adversarial in their interactions. However, just when it appeared that they might be getting closer, something would erupt. For example, Mr. W. got his job back and invited his wife to go out and celebrate. She refused, putting him in a rage. On another occasion, he announced that he was going to be filing a separate tax return, and this upset her. The family and the couple clearly had a pattern suggestive of not being able to tolerate prosperity. Just as soon as the situation would calm down, someone would do something to cause an uproar. At one family session (5/7), Mr. W. blew up and walked out of the session. When he returned, I pointed out how this type of emotional overreaction contributed to his family's perception of him as unreasonable and "having problems." I also emphasized how the use of alcohol lowered his level of emotional control (during his absence, Mrs. W. revealed that he had been drinking prior to the session).

*Termination phase (5/14 to 7/9).* These final six sessions focused on reviewing the progress to date, continuing to work on increasing communication effectiveness within the family, consolidating the gains made, and planning for the future. Sessions were decreased to one every other week. In a couple session (5/14), Mr. W. mentioned his uncertainty about following through with the divorce. When his wife balked at the idea of an immediate reconciliation, wanting more time to work things out, he got angry and started talking divorce again, as if to punish her. The family agreed that, although they needed to continue to work on issues such as household tasks and communication, they were able to function better on their own and the time for termination had arrived. One final problem to be solved was the dispute about what to do with the house in the event of a divorce. The children felt strongly that they wanted to keep the house since it was their home. The issue was resolved when Mr. W. agreed to buy out his wife's share of the house and keep it. The negotiations that led to this solution occurred in the therapy sessions.

The following segment from the final therapy session illustrates the family's progress. The session opens with the father's criticism of Jay and John for dismantling a bike, for violating a house rule that they could not use his tools when he was not there to supervise, for not "owning up to it," and for not doing their household jobs. Jay responds by complaining about the way his father handles problems and expresses his pessimism about the family's chances for the future. Early in therapy, this situation would have quickly erupted into a hostile exchange between Jay and his father with the rest of the family taking sides. Now, the topic is discussed more calmly, without raised voices, and without personal recriminations or attacks.

Mrs. W.: But Jay, you're going to have that [problem] the rest of your life. Wouldn't you rather work it out here rather than having all that hurt and frustration build up?
Mr. W.: I think if we could get this . . .
LCG [interrupting Mr. W.]: Wait. Jay, do you want to respond to your mother?
Jay: No [looking at the ceiling and appearing very blasé and disinterested].
Mrs. W. [kiddingly]: We need more than a shrug, kid.
Betty: I don't know. In ways we need it [therapy] and in ways we don't.
Mrs. W.: We need to establish new goals and work on them.
LCG: Betty, in what ways do you feel you need it and in what ways do you feel you don't?
Betty: I don't know . . . with the bikes and jobs and that, there's still bitter feelings about that.

LCG: What do you see as the family still having to work on?
Betty: Getting along, I guess. Well, we've been doing pretty good, but still . . .
Mrs. W.: But we're in two separate places. That's not getting along when you're in two separate places.
Betty: There's still a lot of smart comments that go back and forth.
Mrs. W.: Yes, but part of that has to do with your age group.
Betty: Mom, I'm talking about you and Daddy too!
Mrs. W.: I'm talking about everybody.
Mr. W.: I have to agree with that.
Betty: When I try to be civil, Jay starts something. When Jay tries to be civil, I start something. It's always going back and forth.
Mrs. W.: Don't you think that could be worked on?
Jay: We've tried it. It's just going to go on for as long as we're living in the same place. You can't stop it.
LCG: That's true, you can't, and to some extent, it's natural among families that have kids almost the same age.
Mr. W.: But it can be decreased. The main thing is whether it's kidding or in a harassing mood or it has gotten to avengeful period.
LCG: What do you two as the parents in this family think about the kind of teasing, kidding, and commenting that goes on among the kids? Do you think it's overdone?
Mr. W.: Yes, I think it's considerably overdone. Sometimes it starts out as kidding and is this vengeful "I'm going to cut you to ribbons" type of thing and I guess they get part of that from me and Marsha [his wife]!

This excerpt reveals that the family members are able to discuss their problems and shortcomings more reasonably than before and can acknowledge responsibility for their own contributions to the problems.

*Client Impressions*

The following excerpt from the final therapy session illustrates that even though problems continue to exist for the family, they handle them much better. We also get the family's appraisal of the effects of therapy.

John: . . . I think it's helped us a whole lot. Everybody has gotten a whole lot of problems solved out, and if we could do it another year we'd get them all out.
LCG: What problems do you see as being solved? What kinds of changes can you see?
John: My mother and father aren't fighting a lot. Us kids are not fighting a lot.
LCG: So there's less fighting.
John: Right. My father is cutting down on his drinking. He's not bickering.
LCG [to Penny]: How are things for you in the family? [silence]
Mrs. W.: Oh, come on, Penny.
Mr. W.: Speak up.
Penny [in baby talk]: I don't know.
LCG: Do you like it better in your family than you used to?
Penny: I don't know.
Mrs. W.: Now we don't fight, right?
Jay: Pretty much, but the arguments between you and Dad have been pretty heavy.
John: But they don't fight. They just argue.
LCG [to Jay]: Is that painful for you?
Jay: A little bit.
LCG: Do you see that as the way it's been all along or do you see changes?
Jay: They're getting progress but it really hasn't changed much.
[Later, at the very end of the session, Mr. and Mrs. W. reflect some empathy for the therapist when they comment in a good-natured manner:]
Mr. W.: This has become kind of an interesting, challenging case.
Mrs. W.: Never in all his years has he [LCG] seen anything quite like it!

*Therapist Comments*

After 30 therapy sessions spread over 10 months, this family shows signs of changes for the better but also the existence of unresolved problems. On the negative side: (1) the father still continues to bring up new issues and problems at inappropriate times (like in the last five minutes of the final session); (2) Jay continues to be angry, resentful, and provocative toward his father, albeit in more subtle ways; (3) the sense of futility and pessimism, although diminished, continues to exist; (4) the family's level of self-esteem is still low.

From the standpoint of positive changes, the following appear to have occurred. (1) The emotional tone with which the family deals with problems and disagreements is more moderate, calm, and less acrimonious. (2) The boundaries in the family have shifted, resulting in a different pattern of subsystems. The authority for decision making has been restored to the parents, who now support each other better, and the children have been removed from their roles as pawns and victims of a parental power struggle. (3) The father shows fewer signs of psychopathological behavior. Specifically, he is drinking considerably less, is less paranoid, is in much better control of his temper, and is more willing to accept responsibility for his part in the family's turmoil. For example, with regard to his being upset with the kids for "fixing" a bike and making it unsafe to ride, he says: "I'm not going to yell at anybody, scream at anybody, or spank anybody. But if you did it, tell me." He also can admit that had he bought certain parts and fixed it himself, as he promised, the situation would not have arisen. (4) There is less blaming in the family. (5) There is less secrecy and more open discussion.

With this family, as with many difficult clients, two different challenges were presented to the therapist. First, there was the task of devising and implementing a treatment plan that would be effective in alleviating the presenting problems. Second, there was the often more difficult task of counteracting the sense of futility and hopelessness that results from a chronically low level of self-esteem and long-term pattern of poor adjustment. This point was most poignantly described by Jay during one of our individual therapy sessions. We were sitting on a park bench on a beautiful spring afternoon when he turned to me and asked: "Are we the sickest family you've ever seen?"

Treating the multiproblem case, whether it be a family or an individual, requires personal resources, such as patience, commitment, and a high level of frustration tolerance, as well as technical knowledge. I often felt like giving up on this family and more than once felt uncertain, impotent, helpless, and incompetent. With this family, there was often the danger that I would get pulled into the cross-currents of their disputes and might drown by trying to save one person while another one pulled me under. It is important for the therapist to maintain a sense of empathy, tolerance, allegiance, and loyalty to all the family members. This was difficult. At times the behavior of a given family member could be obnoxious, attacking, insensitive, cruel, or alienating in some other way. When this occurred, the family evoked in me the very negative emotions that they engendered in each other and that I was trying to help them overcome. My professional goal was to try to be aware of the feelings and to find ways of coping with them and expressing them so that I could serve as a model for the family. This was easier to hope for than to accomplish. More than once, I felt like jumping into the fray and yelling like the rest of them. It required great personal restraint and the helpful consultation/supervision of a wise and sensitive colleague to help me cope effectively with my own feelings of frustration and anger.

Eclecticism is especially well suited for cases such as this one because it provides a wide repertoire of specific tactics to cope with the many problems presented by the family. In this case, the following approaches were used. Kempler's (1973) advocacy of the experiential use of self gave me the permission and encouragement to share my own feelings with the family, helping me to discard burdensome emotional baggage. Satir's (1972) emphasis on nurturance provided the impetus to seek out the family's strengths and to use these as building blocks for growth. Minuchin's (1974) concepts of boundaries and subsystems were used to recognize the dysfunctional patterns of family structure. The problem-focused approaches of Haley (1976) and the McMaster model (Epstein, Bishop, & Levin, 1978) were useful for helping the family to become more functional in practical and instrumental tasks. My knowledge of learning theory and behavioral therapy was important as a source of ideas and techniques for teaching the family how to communicate and relate to each other better. Finally, Bowen's (1976) constructs were helpful for giving me the distance I needed both to perceive the family with dispassion and to help me understand their own emotional "stuck togetherness." The eclecticism was both deliberate and incidental. At times, tactics were intentional and carefully planned in conjunction with a colleague. At other times, my therapeutic behavior was spontaneous and intuitive.

There are risks to using an eclectic approach. A potential pitfall is that the therapist will jump too quickly from one type of intervention to another in an attempt to counter the family's habitual self-defeating behavior. When combining techniques and/or theories representing different orientations, they must be integrated in such a way as to provide continuity and a cohesive approach. Sometimes this means trying to integrate approaches that on the surface appear incompatible. For example, two of the family therapy approaches that I use in my eclecticism are those of structural family therapy (Minuchin, 1974) and family systems therapy (Bowen, 1976). Minuchin (1974) emphasizes the importance of joining the family so that the therapist can bring about change from within. Bowen's approach advocates just the opposite, which is to avoid being drawn (triangulated) into the family. In this approach, therapeutic effectiveness is achieved by having sufficient emotional distance from the family so that the therapist can work from the outside. In working with this family, I tried to do both. Initially, I attempted to join the family in order to establish credibility and to engage them. At the same time, I tried to remain sufficiently distant from the family to keep from being embroiled in their disputes and to have enough leverage to initiate change from the outside. Although practically it was like walking a therapeutic tightrope at times, the eclecticism provided the flexibility to combine the "best of both worlds."

Change with a family such as this one is slow and requires consistent, deliberate, and repetitive work. The therapy is time consuming, requiring as much or more time in reflection, reviewing videotapes, and consultation as it does in the actual therapeutic contact. Goals must be limited and realistic. Although I used and attempted to integrate techniques, theory, and therapist styles from a number of family therapy approaches, it is important to emphasize that my basic stance was a cautious and conservative one. I proceeded slowly and carefully. I am suspicious of approaches that use more extreme tactics and promise dramatic changes. There are no easy solutions for hard problems in therapy. Eclecticism provides greater resources for the therapist to use. It does not provide magic.

# REFERENCES

Bowen, M. (1976). Theory in the practice of psychotherapy. In P. Guerin, Jr. (Ed.), *Family therapy: Theory and practice.* New York: Gardner.

Epstein, N. B., Bishop, D. S., & Levin, S. (1978). The McMaster model of family functioning. *Journal of Marriage and Family Counseling, 4,* 19–31.

Grebstein, L. (1986), An eclectic family therapy. In J. C. Norcross (Ed.), *Handbook of eclectic therapy.* New York: Brunner/Mazel.

Guerin, P. J., Jr., & Pendagast, E. G. (1976). Evaluation of family system and genogram. In P. J. Guerin, Jr. (Ed.), *Family therapy: Theory and practice.* New York: Gardner.

Haley, J. (1976). *Problem-solving therapy.* San Francisco: Jossey-Bass.

Kempler, W. (1973). *Principles of Gestalt family therapy.* Oslo, Norway: A. S. Joh. Nordahls Trykkeri.

Minuchin, S. (1974). *Families and family therapy.* Cambridge, MA: Harvard University Press.

Satir, V. (1967). *Conjoint family therapy.* Palo Alto, CA: Science and Behavior Books.

Satir, V. (1972). *Peoplemaking.* Palo Alto, CA: Science and Behavior Books.

# Commentary: The External and Internal Context of Eclectic/Integrative Family Therapy

*Alan S. Gurman*

I congratulate Dr. Grebstein for his overall success with this very complex, difficult, and personally demanding family case. Though I think I might have done some things differently from Grebstein (e.g., limit initial goals to basic structural aims of strengthening generational boundaries in the W. family; insist that Mrs. W. get involved earlier in the course of therapy; hold sessions with different subsystems for different purposes), I have no fundamental disagreement with the general aims or thrust of his work with the W.'s. His detailed and honest description of a family treated with an eclectic style of therapy does provoke me to consider the context in which such eclectic work arises. In this commentary, I will offer some thoughts about both the external (professional) context and the internal (personal) context of such family work.

## THE EXTERNAL CONTEXT OF ECLECTICISM/INTEGRATIONISM

In the last few years, at least in the United States, there has arisen a groundswell of enthusiasm for the development and refinement of eclectic and integrative approaches to marital and family therapy, and some observers in the field have gone so far as to call the decade of the 1980s the "decade of integration" (Gurman, 1980). To Americans, this movement is rather new, though in continental Europe and Great Britain integration has been the dominant motif for quite a long time. Perhaps this has been because so many of the so-called "major models" of marital and family therapy have been "imported" from across the Atlantic Ocean and, therefore, have not been so marked in Europe by proselytizing and by the narcissism that predictably accompanies such proselytizing. In addition, the professional entrepreneurship so common to family therapy in the United States does not seem to characterize the field in Europe.

Several integrative family therapy models have been proposed in the last few years, bringing together strategic and behavioral methods (Spinks & Birchler, 1982), strategic and structural methods (Stanton, 1981), and behavioral and psychodynamic methods (Feldman, 1982; Gurman, 1981;

Pinsof, 1983). We may consider why eclectic/integrative efforts such as these and Grebstein's are happening at this time, and why not very much until recently. I believe there are five major reasons for this growing interest in integration in the family field. First, it seems simply to have been the case that it was not until the late 1970s that each of the dominant schools of family therapy had firmly established itself and attracted a critical mass of adherents and followers. Second, it was also not until the late 1970s that significant numbers of us began to take very seriously the need for competing therapies to document their effectiveness through carefully designed empirical research (Gurman & Kniskern, 1978). And, as has generally been the case in individual therapy, there have been two main trends in this research: First, the outcomes of very few of the alternative marital and family therapies have ever been investigated (Gurman, Kniskern & Pinsof, 1986), and second, and perhaps more tellingly, when such research has been done, it has generally not confirmed the superior effectiveness of any given method (Gurman & Kniskern, 1978).

A third factor in the emergence of this eclectic/integrative movement is that the field seems to have come to an abrupt halt in terms of the development of genuinely new methods of therapy. Perhaps there are just no really new and different ideas waiting to be created. But more likely is that the many thousands of mental health professionals who constitute the fifth and sixth generations of family therapists, and who are currently receiving training in family therapy, are simply already overwhelmed by the diversity of models and methods and are struggling just to catch up with and keep up with what has already been proposed, developed, and promulgated.

Fourth, in the United States more than in any other country, there has been relentless effort to establish marital and family therapy as a new profession, independent of the traditional major mental health disciplines of psychiatry, psychology, and social work. In this effort, the 13,000-member American Association for Marital and Family Therapy several years ago succeeded in establishing an influential national commission to develop standards and criteria for the curricula used to train family therapists in dozens of training centers. This process has probably increased the homogenization of training, especially in degree-granting institutions, with a major pedagogical thrust being to expose students to the broad range of views in the field.

A fifth reason for the emergence of eclecticism/integrationism in the field is that the integrative movement in the field of individual psychotherapy has been strong for quite some time, as illustrated by recent efforts to bring together behavior therapy and psychodynamic psychotherapy (e.g., Wachtel, 1977). As much as family therapists may yearn to dissociate themselves from individual therapists, the broader field of psychotherapy is an open system, and family therapy will necessarily be influenced by developments in this broader professional context.

## THE INTERNAL CONTEXT OF ECLECTICISM/INTEGRATIONISM

Beyond issues of the clinical management of therapy with the W. family lies a matter that is more fundamental to Grebstein's case study, and that extends beyond the arbitrarily punctuated boundary of the field of psychotherapy known as family therapy. That issue is the distinction between eclecticism and integration. Grebstein used the terms interchangeably. That is noteworthy because the two do not seem to me to be the same animal, and I would submit that eclecticism is usually an untenable clinical position.

*Eclecticism Versus Integration*

*Though philosophically complex debates are heard at times regarding the distinction, or lack thereof, between eclectic and integrative therapists, differentiating between them is really quite simple. You merely listen to how they describe what they do. Eclectic therapists add together techniques and strategies that derive from different models of therapy. Eclectic therapists say things like "I choose the technique that fits the problem best," or "I choose from different theories; with some types of problems, I use Theory A, with other types of problems, I use Theory B, etc.," or, "I select from the available techniques in the field on the basis of research and my own clinical experience."*

*This seems to be precisely what Grebstein has done: his therapeutic approach includes a bewildering array of family therapy models and techniques: strategic, structural, problem-centered, behavioral, psychodynamic, client-centered, humanistic-experiential, and Bowenian. I think that most family therapists would agree that it is simply impossible to operate out of a consistent theoretical framework that is true to the major premises of all eight (!) of these approaches. In addition to some fundamental incompatibilities among these methods at a conceptual level (Gurman & Kniskern, 1981), there is the more per-*plexing *problem of personal coherence in the face of conceptual divergence. Psychotherapists "choose" theoretical orientations in a manner that is probably not too different from how we choose our marriage partners, i.e., both on the basis of overt qualities of the theory (partner) that we identify as attractive,* and *on the basis of covert qualities of the theory (partner) of which we are unaware, or to which we at least pay little conscious attention. The choice of a theoretical orientation is ultimately a very personal statement of self. Choosing to be an eclectic or integrative therapist is also a profound statement of self. But how many of us can tolerate having multiple selves? For example, some family therapy methods require a detached distance, whereas others require enormously warm immediacy; some place a premium on concreteness, whereas others demand openness to intuitive exploration, etc., etc. When a therapist selects a technique, he/she also selects a world view that goes with it. Some world views just do not go together. And most of us cannot tolerate behaving with extremely different selves (e.g., close/distant), because at least one of these selves will be a false self. And, I would suggest, our patients are sensitive to presentations of false selves. It is for reasons such as this that I believe eclecticism is usually untenable. Perhaps the only way to survive as an effective eclectic therapist is to provide a degree of personal caring and involvement that overrides these difficulties, so that one's personal mission diminishes the salience of technical factors. It is just such a quality of dogged dedication that comes through in Grebstein's work with the W. family.*

*In my view, the overall positive outcome Grebstein achieved with the W. family is attributable to his deep involvement and active caring rather than to eclectic elegance. There may be quite a lot of therapists who are able to do effective family therapy without articulating their (eclectic) theoretical base. And although such a state of affairs is just fine for the clients of such therapists, it is not sufficient for the advancement of the field as a whole. The field as a whole will profit less from eclecticism than from theoretical and technical integration. Integration, in contrast to eclecticism, involves, indeed requires, the careful and systematic elucidation of the principles by which apparently incompatible views are brought together. Likewise, it requires clear principles by which clinical practice is guided and clear principles by which specific interventions are se-*

lected. Integrative therapists select techniques and strategies because they share internally consistent theoretical foundations; i.e., they "make sense" vis-à-vis one another. Integrative therapists may "translate" concepts from school to school, they may incorporate a given school's assumptions within another school, or they may identify more neutral, non-school-dictated premises that the approaches have in common. But in any case, the bringing together of apparently disparate ideas is coherent. In contrast to the eclectic therapist, who chooses a technique or theory to fit the patient, the integrative therapist chooses techniques or theories in a way that fits him/herself as well as the patient. Requiring oneself to articulate the principles of a personally acceptable integrative therapy, rather than allowing it to remain implicit, forces a therapist to define him/herself as a therapist. Thus, integrative therapy is inherently more self-referential, recursive, and circular than eclectic therapy; in a word, it is more systemically sensitive and, therefore, more in keeping with the major tenets of all approaches to family therapy.

Since the ultimate integration in any method of psychotherapy is the **personal** integration of oneself-as-healer and one's method of healing, setting forth explicitly the principles of any integrative therapeutic approach is essential.

## REFERENCES

Feldman, L. B. (1982). Dysfunctional marital conflict: An integrative interpersonal/intrapsychic model. Journal of Marital and Family Therapy, 8, 417–428.

Gurman, A. S. (1980). Behavioral marital therapy in the 1980's: The challenge of integration. American Journal of Family Therapy, 8, 86–96.

Gurman, A. S. (1981). Integrative marital therapy: Toward the development of an interpersonal approach. In S. Budman (Ed.), Forms of brief therapy. New York: Guilford.

Gurman, A. S., & Kniskern, D. P. (1978). Research on marital and family therapy: Progress, perspective and prospect. In S. Garfield & A. Bergin (Eds.), Handbook of psychotherapy and behavior change (2nd ed.). New York: Wiley.

Gurman, A. S., & Kniskern, D. P. (1981). Handbook of family therapy. New York: Brunner/Mazel.

Gurman, A. S., Kniskern, D. P., & Pinsof, W. M. (1986). Research on the process and outcome of marital and family therapy. In S. Garfield & A. Bergin (Eds.), Handbook of psychotherapy and behavior change (3rd ed.). New York: Wiley.

Pinsof, W. M. (1983). Integrative problem-centered therapy: Toward the synthesis of family and individual psychotherapies. Journal of Marital and Family Therapy, 9, 19–35.

Spinks, S. H., & Birchler, G. (1982). Behavioral systems marital therapy: Dealing with resistance. Family Process, 21, 169–187.

Stanton, M. D. (1981). Marital therapy from a structural/strategic viewpoint. In G. P. Sholevar (Ed.), Handbook of marriage and marital therapy. New York: Spectrum.

Wachtel, P. (1977). Psychoanalysis and behavior therapy. New York: Basic Books.

# Commentary: Eclecticism or Responsiveness?

## Stephen Murgatroyd

### INTRODUCTION

The central tenet of family therapy is that the experience of distress and the means by which distress is maintained are functions of the structure and communication patterns within families. As Minuchin (1974, especially pp. 129-130) makes clear, "the therapist . . . regards the identified patient merely as the family member who is expressing, in the most visible way, a problem affecting the entire [family] system." The goal of therapy is, therefore, to affect the family system in such a way as to reduce the distress of the identified patient (in this case Mr. W.) without transferring the symptoms to another family member (Murgatroyd & Woolfe, 1985).

In commenting on a case report, it is important to recognize that the focus of family therapy is different from individual therapy. Family therapy is focused on interactions and relationships not simply on the identified patient. Minuchin and Fishman (1981), Murgatroyd and Woolfe (1985), Treacher and Carpenter (1984), Barker (1981), and many others have described a variety of techniques that can be used to affect family communications and dynamics. What is not readily available is an integrative framework within which therapists' decisions about appropriate interventions or the framework within which dilemmas are resolved can be understood. That is, there is an absence of an integrative model of eclectic family therapy. Grebstein's contribution to this volume must therefore be reviewed as an illustration of an eclectic method using some integrative approach.

## THE CASE OF MR. W.

Family therapy is practiced in a variety of settings. These include child guidance clinics (Treacher & Carpenter, 1984), residential care services for children (Minuchin et al., 1967), probation and aftercare services (Johnson, 1974), general medical practices (Dimmock, 1984), hospitals (Procter & Stephens, 1984; Treacher, 1984), and family therapy centers. In all these settings, cases such as that of Mr. W. are not unusual—indeed, the multiple-problem family is a frequently discussed and written about phenomenon. The particular difficulty of getting and keeping family members working together in therapy and of meeting individual needs at the same time as forming therapeutic alliances with other family members are very common issues.

## THE THERAPEUTIC PROGRAM

Grebstein makes clear the often neglected point that the identified patient often needs help in his or her own right (Minuchin, 1974). It seems clear that Mr. W. needed help within the framework of both brief therapy and crisis intervention. Mr. W.'s own resistance to individual therapy once family therapy had begun is also commonplace. What is surprising is that the therapist or the family did not confront this reluctance more directly.

From a British family therapy point of view, I am interested in the extent to which this therapeutic intervention with the family is "layered." Grebstein works with such a variety of layers within the family (e.g., Mr. W., the children, Mr. and Mrs. W., Jay) that the maintenance of a clear perception of the therapist's alliances by family members must have been difficult. What this layering suggests, however, is that the therapy was far more responsive than strategic. This is also suggested by the length of therapy, which (at 30 sessions), by British standards, is long.

To elaborate, the therapist points to the dilemma of making alliances with subgroups and individuals, on the one hand, and the family on the whole, on the other. The difficulty lies in sustaining meaningful relationships throughout the family while at the same time offering help when it is needed. The impression given in the case study (which may not fully reflect what actually happened) is that the family determined the behavior of the therapist. This is seen most clearly in the layering of the therapist's work. A strategic intervention might have addressed more directly the desire of the family to compartmentalize the work that needed to be done.

What is also clear is that the interventions described by Grebstein derive from a therapeutic base but are not a clear part of a strategy or hypothesis-testing program. As described, the therapy seems to be driven by the behavior of family members rather than by a strategic understanding of the meaning of this behavior for the family. This may be a harsh criticism, but it is my reading of the case as presented.

The case, though interesting, tells us little about eclectic psychotherapy. The therapeutic endeavor seems to be best described by the phrase "if it works it is appropriate" rather than by reference to some integrative framework. The process seems to drive the strategy.

Dryden (1984) offers a classification of eclectic therapy types. These include: (a) theoretical eclecticism, in which a person adheres to one particular school (e.g., strategic family therapy) but is prepared to use other techniques as and when they are appropriate; (b) structural eclecticism, based on the work of Murgatroyd and Apter (1984, 1986), which sees reversal theory as an integrative diagnostic and therapeutic device; (c) combination eclecticism, which seeks to integrate two or more therapies at a high-order theoretical level; (d) existential eclecticism, similar in many senses to the therapy recommended by Greenwald (1973); (e) technical eclecticism, as developed by Lazarus (1981); (f) systematic-persuasive eclecticism, in which a wide range of variables are used to help the therapist plan a systematic treatment strategy; (g) integrationism, best represented in the writings of Garfield (1982); (h) developmental eclecticism, in which theory is relegated to second place in preference to action—see Robertson (1979); (i) transtheoretical eclecticism, developed at Rhode Island and involving a stage understanding of therapy as a series of stages that need to be integrated and managed (see Prochaska and DiClemente, 1982); and (j) haphazard eclecticism, which is probably the single most frequently practiced form under the name of eclectic therapy.

In seeking to classify this case, the developmental category appears the most appropriate, for it is clear that the case involves a simple developmental sequence each stage of which requires different therapeutic skills to be applied to separate parts of the process of therapy. Theoretical issues are secondary to practice, and the nature of the therapy is driven by a concern for social awareness and reality testing (Egan, 1982). Although I regard this as a theoretically weak form of eclectic practice, it nonetheless has proven effectiveness and attracts a substantial body of support. Its weakness is that it is not readily replicated as a practice form by others. It depends too much on intuition.

These comments should not detract from the complexity and difficulty associated with multiple-problem families. It is not surprising that Grebstein felt, on more than one occasion, "like giving up" and "uncertain, impotent, helpless, and incompetent." Many of us would too. What strikes me about this is: what is it that he learned from his work that will be beneficial to him and communicable to others when Mr. X. and his multiple-problem family arrive for therapy in three weeks' time? I am not sure how much the case adds to our understanding of eclectic practice, other than demonstrating the fact that it is often more difficult than many imagine.

## REFERENCES

Barker, P. (1981). Basic family therapy. London: Granada.
Dimmock, B. (1984). Developing family counselling in general practice settings. In A. Treacher & J. Carpenter (Eds.), Using family therapy. Oxford: Basil Blackwell.
Dryden, W. (1984). Issues in eclectic practice. In W. Dryden (Ed.), Individual psychotherapy in Britain. London: Harper and Row.
Egan, G. (1982). The skilled helper—A model for systematic helping and interpersonal relating. Monterey, CA: Brooks-Cole.
Garfield, S. (1982). Eclecticism and integrationism in psychotherapy. Behavior Therapy, 13, 610–623.
Greenwald, H. (1973). Direct decision therapy. San Diego, CA: Edits.
Johnson, F. (1974). Hooking the involuntary family into treatment: Family therapy in a juvenile court setting. Family Therapy, 1, 79–82.
Lazarus, A. A. (1981). The practice of multi-modal therapy. New York: McGraw-Hill.

Minuchin, S. (1974). *Families and family therapy.* Cambridge, MA: Harvard University Press.

Minuchin, S., & Fishman, C. (1981). *Family therapy techniques.* Cambridge, MA: Harvard University Press.

Minuchin, S., et al. (1967). *Families of the slums: An exploration of their structure and their treatment.* New York: Basic Books.

Murgatroyd, S., & Apter, M. J. (1984). Eclectic psychotherapy—A structural phenomenological approach. In W. Dryden (Ed.), *Individual psychotherapy in Britain.* London: Harper and Row.

Murgatroyd, S., & Apter, M. J. (1986). A structural phenomenological approach to eclectic psychotherapy. In J. Norcross (Ed.), *The handbook of eclectic psychotherapy.* New York: Brunner/Mazel.

Murgatroyd, S., & Woolfe, R. (1985). *Helping families in distress—An introduction to family focussed helping.* London: Harper and Row.

Prochaska, J. O., & DiClemente, C. C. (1982). Transtheoretical therapy—Toward a more integrative model of change. *Psychotherapy: Theory, Research and Practice, 19,* 276–288.

Procter, H., & Stephens, T. (1984). Developing family therapy in the day hospital. In A. Treacher & J. Carpenter (Eds.), *Using family therapy.* Oxford: Basil Blackwell.

Robertson, M. (1979). Some observations from an eclectic therapist. *Psychotherapy: Theory, Research and Practice, 16,* 18–21.

Treacher, A. (1984). Family therapy in mental hospitals. In A. Treacher & J. Carpenter (Eds.), *Using family therapy.* Oxford: Basil Blackwell.

Treacher, A., & Carpenter, J. (Eds.) (1984). *Using family therapy.* Oxford: Basil Blackwell.

# CHAPTER 10

# Functional Therapy: A Case of Training

## John Hart and Joseph Hart

### BACKGROUND

Functional therapy is a historically based eclectic orientation derived from the general functional psychology of William James and the clinical functionalism of Pierre Janet. Unlike most other contemporary eclectic approaches, functional therapy began as an eclectic orientation. (For a critique of functional therapy as an eclectic therapy see Patterson, 1986.) William James was the great synthesizer of the early 1900s, hospitable to a range of psychoanalytic and behavioral, philosophical and experimental methods and ideas. James' style of eclectic synthesis was not inclined to look for a single overarching theory but to evaluate the potentials of many theories. The hallmark of Jamesian functionalism was an emphasis on consciousness as the central concern of psychology. Concerns about accessing subconscious contents and modifying behavior followed from his central concern—to learn as much as possible about each individual's "stream of consciousness" (see Hart, 1981; James, 1950).

Functional therapists pay attention to both personality characteristics and moments of consciousness. A "reactive personality" is one that operates with little awareness; a "responsive personality" is one that functions with a high level of awareness and responsivity. The overall task of therapy is to help clients become more responsive and less reactive. The shifting of personality functioning from reactivity to responsivity entails: (1) becoming more aware of reactive moments (i.e., of happenings that appear as gaps in consciousness), (2) feeling and showing those automatisms within the safety of the therapeutic encounter, and (3) beginning to experience the real-life possibilities of an expansive personality existing in nondefensive, open, responsive moments.

It is important to note that a reactive personality can be either adapted or socially maladapted. From the phenomenological point of view, both adaptive and nonadaptive reactivity are impediments to development. The first clinical and experimental demonstrations of reactivity in the history of functional therapy were made by Trigant Burrow (see Hart, 1983, Chapter 5, "The Iconoclastic Eclecticism of Trigant Burrow," and Burrow, 1953). Burrow's psychophysiological experiments provide the first evidence for defensive versus nondefensive experiencing and patterning in the clinical-experimental literature.

A modern theorist who has made full use of the James-Janet ideas about the subconscious is Ernest Hilgard. In his book *Divided Consciousness* (1977), which attempts to revive the James-Janet theory of dissociation, Hilgard argues that a failure to recognize the difference between dissociated mental contents and repressed mental contents can lead to therapeutic errors. Dissociated contents are directly accessible to consciousness, but repressed contents are only indirectly accessible through derivatives such as dream symbols and interpretations (*ibid.*, pp. 248-255). Hilgard points out that Janet used the term "subconscious" to avoid the undesirable implications of the term "unconscious." For both James and Janet the subconscious or subliminal was an accessible psychic process. The most direct means of access was by attending to "gaps" in consciousness and by subjectively staying with "felt tendencies" to fill those gaps. This method is essential in almost every session of functional therapy. The modern humanistic-existential theorist Eugene Gendlin has devised a specific training method to instruct clients in this form of inner attending called "focusing"; the focusing method is taught to all clients who participate in functional therapy. (See Gendlin, 1981, and Gendlin, 1962.)

All the techniques of functional therapy that will be illustrated in the case sessions (focusing, work with personality dynamisms or styles, and work with dynamics of expression) are intended to help clients move from automatic reactivity to awareness, and from closed functioning to open functioning.

## TRAINING GROUP FOR FUNCTIONAL THERAPY

The training case format was chosen to illustrate functional theory and methods for a number of reasons. Most important, within the training, a variety of eclectic techniques are used by the trainer in every group. The training also shows an important philosophical stance of functional therapy, i.e., that therapists need ongoing training and therapy to maintain their own best therapeutic personality. (For contemporary case illustrations of functional therapy with clients rather than trainees, see Hart, 1983, and Hart 1986. Famous historical cases within the functional tradition include those of Prince [1957], Janet [1929], and Taft [1933/1962].)

The training program is similar to the model training therapy program in the text *Modern Eclectic Therapy: A Functional Orientation to Counseling and Psychotherapy* (Hart, 1983). Each training group generally consists of a demonstration and explanation followed by a simple exercise in which the trainees take turns role playing a therapist and a client. One or more of the trainees then presents a case problem or issue that relates to the training exercise; the case problem might then be role-played or simply discussed. Each training group session usually lasts two hours once a week.

The training group takes place in the suite of offices occupied by Hart and Associates on Wilshire Boulevard in West Los Angeles. (A less specialized, eclectic therapy training program, which includes instruction in Jungian, psychodynamic, humanistic, and cognitive behavioral approaches as well as functional therapy, is available at the Counseling Center, California Polytechnic University, Pomona,

California.) The office in which the training group meets is a large rectangular room that comfortably seats eight people. The office is decorated in contemporary fashion with large couches. A swivel chair is used by the training therapist. On one wall is a large drawing stand used for teaching purposes. The room has one wall of glass windows located at tree level giving the room a dramatic forestlike appearance. The other offices in the suite are available for use in one-on-one role-playing exercises.

Trainees must have completed or be enrolled in at least a master's-level degree program and be currently in practice or interning in a human services agency with a caseload of individual clients, families, or groups. Participants are expected to make a 9- to 12-month commitment to the training group.

The intent of the training group is to teach the functional orientation to counseling and therapy. Most of the trainees are attracted to and interested in the practical applications of the therapy, but they are also attracted by the philosophical attitude conveyed in the training.

All participants are clearly aware that group support and encouragement of other participants is expected. Although criticism is certainly appropriate, the general tone at all times is encouragement and support. In order to grow and change and develop their therapeutic personalities, trainees need to know that if they try something new or different, they will be supported and guided. Therapists in training tend to be cautious and careful to the point of timidity. Frequently, participants are being trained and supervised in their agency setting where they are experiencing so much criticism that they have become intimidated to the point of becoming passive listeners, afraid to interact and take chances with their clients.

Personality fitness for therapists is a concept crucial to the training. The idea is that therapists need to be fit in order to practice most effectively. Their own personalities must be in shape, with good endurance and resilience in order for them to do fine therapy. Consequently, to develop a more "fit" personality, regular and consistent personality exercise must be maintained. Individual therapy, of course, is one means of achieving personality fitness; the training group is intended to be another form. Marston (1984) has made an argument that "the overall effectiveness of psychotherapy as a profession should be determined in part by the endurance of therapists in their careers and the consistency of their performance over time" (p. 456). The training experience emphasizes personality fitness for the trainees as a means of enhancing endurance and consistent therapeutic quality.

The therapists in training are encouraged to try out new styles of working that stretch and exercise their personalities and also to become aware of the strengths, weaknesses, and limitations of their styles. Through homework exercises they try to develop approaches that can add to and strengthen their personality styles. The approach could be compared to fitness and skill training for athletes or to the practice of exercises by musicians. The same approach is used with clients in functional therapy.

## INTAKE AND ASSESSMENT PROCEDURES

As stated earlier, a major purpose of the training group is to focus on the therapists' personalities in order to help them learn about their special problems in working with clients. Since most client situations begin with some sort of assessment and intake procedure, the training group begins the new training year with a discussion of assessment within the functional model. Next, there is an assessment of each trainee. The trainees have an opportunity to role-play both therapist and client.

Two methods will be discussed here: the life satisfaction and happiness chart and the personality pyramid graph.

*Life Satisfaction and Happiness Chart*

This is a simple exercise using paper and pen. Each trainee is given a large watercolor pad and two different colored marking pens. They are instructed to draw a large rectangle on their paper. The left vertical line is numbered from top to bottom 5-4-3-2-1. The bottom horizontal line is numbered left to right 0-5-10-15, and so on, up to 65.

The vertical line is for ratings of levels of life satisfaction and happiness, with 5 representing extremely happy and 1 representing very unhappy. The horizontal line represents age.

The trainees are instructed to draw in, first, their parents' lifeline and, next, their own. When doing their own, they are instructed to note any significant events or people around the dips and rises in their charts. The trainer then presents his own life chart. The trainer sets a tone and a level for the depth of sharing that can be elicited in doing the chart. Each trainee then discusses with the group his or her own life chart. The trainer guides each trainee through eliciting pertinent history, significant events, memories, and impressions from the life charts. (Note that the trainer is doing with the trainees, in these first training sessions, what the trainee therapists will be doing with their clients in early sessions.)

Following each chart presentation, the other trainees are asked to formulate clear descriptions about their colleagues and to include characterizations of the strengths and weaknesses and the significant events and people who shaped the person's life. They are instructed to look for the beliefs and life philosophies that emerged from each individual's family background and life events. They also pay special attention to the attitudes and responses made by the person to stressful life events. The trainees' shared self-assessments develop a sympathy and understanding within the training group for each group member.

Graphing and telling about one's life is an experiential means for trainees to learn about functional diagnosis and assessment. Learning to assess others by assessing one's own intrapersonal and interpersonal skills is centrally important because, as Patterson (1984) has pointed out,

... consistent positive findings regarding the elements of the therapeutic relationship are encouraging. This is particularly so in view of the lack of consistent findings in the area of (developmental) psychopathology. The research on the effectiveness of the relationship over a wide range of client conditions or problems provides a basis for a therapy which does not depend on identifying specific causal pathological factors. This suggests either that the specific content of the client's disturbance is unimportant, or that the cause of much, if not most, psychological disturbance is related to the absence of good human relationships, or deficiencies in such relationships. It is also possible that improvement in the client's relationships springing from the therapeutic relationship leads to improvement in other areas of the client's life [p. 438].

Functional therapy places more emphasis on Axes IV and V of DSM-III, than Axes I and II; the concern is more with appreciating the person's strengths, weaknesses, potentials, and levels of functioning than with symptoms or personality psychopathology.

*Personality Dynamics Assessments*

For this exercise, the trainees are given poster paper and pencil. They are again instructed to draw a large rectangle. The vertical line is green—marked top to bottom 5-4-3-2-1. On the horizontal line they write "Expression-Activity-Feeling-Clarity-Contact."

They prepare graphs for each of the following life areas: work, play, friendship, sex, and intimacy. These graphs are used to picture the individual trainee's personality functions in different life areas. In functional terms, they illustrate personality strengths and weaknesses and life area accomplishments and deficiencies.

*Integration of Assessment and Therapy*

As with any clients, the trainee therapists are limited and/or constricted in their functioning by their personalities. Even though case problems and issues are the training focus, it soon becomes clear to trainees that their own personalities must be considered. Just as acceptance of personal responsibility is crucial to client change, so is it crucial to each trainee.

Trainees find themselves upset with their clients because the clients are not compliant, receptive, and welcoming of their interventions, suggestions, insights, and directions. They find themselves rejecting clients who are "cold" and who have difficulty with relationships and then diagnosing them as being "incapable of having relationships."

The trainees are shown that it is up to them to create a relationship with someone who has low skill levels. After all, tennis instructors do not complain about people with poor backhands who come to them for help about their strokes. Nor do dance instructors fret about nondancers wanting to learn to dance. A critical assumption, then, is that clients are doing what they know how to do best with their personalities. It is up to a therapist to help a client become what he or she could be.

## A SAMPLE TRAINING SESSION

The following group session included Marvin and two other trainees, Carole and Donald. The intent of this training session was to extend the trainees' learning about assessment and about the possibilities for active involvement in early sessions with clients. The trainees are introduced to a way of thinking about their work which will be an ongoing emphasis in the group, viz., that the therapist's personality limits are crucial determinants of what can happen between therapist and client.

Marvin has completed his M.A. degree in psychology and is working full-time in a drug rehabilitation agency. The clients of the agency are court referred and are generally "hard-core," low-income drug users. Marvin is developing his bilingual skills and is responsible for one Spanish-speaking group.

Marvin is a strongly built man with dark hair and a brown complexion. His demeanor and bulky size can be imposing; however, he has warm, expressive eyes, a ready laugh, and a playful sense of humor. He supported himself through undergraduate and graduate school as a mechanic, carpenter, and helper in a children's home. He is a dedicated sort of person who tends toward depression at times.

Marvin's father was an alcoholic physician. Marvin was well off enough to attend prep school as a youth, where he was a good athlete and popular among his classmates. He is more ill at ease with women than with men. In the training sessions he shows himself as an honest person who is willing to work hard and expose his feelings in order to learn. He has received personal counseling for many years and is currently in therapy with a woman Gestalt therapist. Marvin has participated in this functional therapy training group for more than a year. In addition to his regular work at the agency, he sees two or three private, low-fee clients.

Marvin lives with a roommate who is also in the mental health field. The roommate has a regular woman friend, but Marvin does not; he dates infrequently.

Dating is an area of his life he would like to improve. His goal is to eventually develop a permanent relationship.

In one training exercise the trainee therapists were instructed to do nothing more than listen attentively and ask questions. The therapist's aim in this clarity exercise is to notice when the client role player is seeming to drift or gap or be somewhere else and to bring it to his awareness. In a clarity exercise the trainees are trying to develop awareness in themselves that they can eventually use to further their clients' awareness. This requires that they be alert to subtle differences in the dynamics of expression.

The trainer chose Marvin to demonstrate the exercise:

T.: How are you doing, Marvin?
M.: Oh, fine [laughs nervously].
T.: And what are you thinking about?
M. [laughs loudly—but clearly stiffens]: Oh no! I want to leave now.
[Trainees all laugh sympathetically.]
M.: I want out because I'm probably thinking something awful about myself. [Gap]
T.: What do you think after that?
M.: I don't like myself. I think I'm bad. [Gap]
T.: What's that?
M.: I feel lonely [rushing] I don't want to say it because I think it's bad to feel lonely.
[Gap]
T.: What's there?
M.: I'm confused.
T.: "Lonely." Is that a thought or the way you're experiencing your life? Put your hand out in front of you. One hand is the experience of being lonely. The other hand is the thinking judgment "I'm a bad person. It's bad to feel lonely."
[T. claps his own hands together harshly and loudly.]
Clap your hands like this, Marvin. Really hit that lonely hand with the other.
[Marvin claps his hand against the other.]
Again. Again.
[Marvin is tearful and very affected.]
T.: What if that hand was a child—someone you loved? What if instead of judging it and thinking it was bad you reached out to someone? Reach out to C. [other group member] with that lonely hand.
[Marvin reaches to C. C. gently holds his hand.]
What is that hand saying, Marvin?
M.: I'm lonely. [begins to cry] I feel so lonely. [crying]
T.: How does that hand feel now, Marvin?
M.: Good!
T.: How is C. treating that lonely hand?
M.: Good.
T.: How else?
M.: Softly . . . gently.
T.: That's right! It's not bad to feel lonely; it's just painful, particularly if we put an old meaning on that feeling. Right? When you're lonely and need contact with other people, your old reaction from your past is to move away and think badly of yourself.

Being responsive to that feeling moves you toward contact and people. Our feelings can guide, Marvin. If you touch a hot stove, you move away fast. Right?
M.: Right.
T.: Lonely is a guide too; only, sometimes when we grow up, we learn to move the wrong way and not trust our feelings or think they are bad. A lonely feeling is telling you what?
M.: I want to . . . I need to be with someone.
T.: Right. The feeling is mostly you, but, if an old thought comes in and says, "Lonely is bad," then you'll get stuck and keep feeling distant emotionally. What about a lonely client?
[Marvin claps loudly.]
Are they bad?
M.: No. [laughing]
T.: What do they need?

[Marvin reaches his hand out. T. takes Marvin's hand, they laugh.]

T.: You could all see when we started what were the thought or thoughts that stopped Marvin and made him react in his usual way. But by sharing the thought out loud and then the judgment and then exaggerating the judgment by clapping, he became aware of how he was feeling. Then, in choosing another movement like reaching out to C., you could see how tentative and vulnerable he was. New movements are difficult, they make your clients feel vulnerable too.

You can also see how your own beliefs about loneliness or other feelings could easily influence your sensitivity to a client. If we aren't able to deal with something in our own emotional life, it is going to be a black hole in our awareness; we will react blindly in our sessions with our clients. I liked seeing that movement today, Marvin, and your courage in relating what you were thinking about yourself.

[Marvin receives group support and compliments.]

For Marvin, this was the beginning of an important phase of his training. He began to learn about the harsh judgments he had about his own feelings and about how they affect his responsiveness and movement. Later training sessions with Marvin will illustrate how his client's feelings and confusions could directly impinge on his therapeutic effectiveness. For now, let us consider another training exercise that introduces another trainee.

In a second training exercise, the trainee is Carole; she recently completed her M.A. degree in counseling psychology. Carole is an attractive woman in her early forties, who in her thirties had a very successful career in the fashion industry.

She is recently divorced. She is the child of two functional alcoholics and has been the sole caretaker at times of her extremely self-destructive mother. The second career in counseling is an exciting new addition to her life. She is very serious and dedicated in her approach to education. She has been involved in personal therapy for several years and works as a training therapist at an inpatient facility for chronic schizophrenics.

She tends to have a straightforward, do-the-direct-thing kind of working style. She is quite composed in appearance, but the composure sometimes masks an uptight, frightened person who wants to do right and do well and yet constantly expects ridicule or abuse. She is socially charming and skilled, but has some difficulties with personal contact and closeness.

These problems are illustrated in the following training session. In this group, four trainees were divided into pairs for a role play of expressive style.

The therapist role player is to identify the client's style of expression and then to show how it works both for and against the person. The intent here is for the trainee therapists to become skilled at identifying styles or patterns shown by their clients. These patterns are typical modes of expression in a client's personality repertoire that might be functional in some settings or in the past, but may not be appropriate or functional in the present. Clients are shown how the styles operate automatically, and by bringing this to their attention an opportunity is created to choose a different way of responding and expressing oneself.

The training therapist instructs the trainee to:

1. Explain and instruct the client regarding style.
2. Identify for the client, in a positive way, the manner in which the style functions—ways that work for and against.

3. Then, working with the client, identify a new style or alternative means that could be chosen.

In this session Marvin worked with Carole. These transcripts are from C.'s training notes and personal therapy tapes.

[M. listens to C. talking about a conversation with her close friend who is having a potluck dinner party. The friend says she didn't invite C., assuming that she wouldn't be interested.]
C.: I just pretended that my feelings weren't hurt. I didn't say anything. I just let it go by as though I really wasn't interested. I don't know what part of me invites people to do that to me. Uh-oh! [M. and C. laugh as C. is aware of what she is saying.]
M.: How would you describe that style?
C.: Anything anybody wants to say to me is okay. Nothing anyone can say bothers me.
M.: Try giving it a label.
C.: How I feel about it and how I act or talk don't match . . . it could be a "That's OK" style. "I won't say anything."
M. [Explains and discusses with C. how that style developed in her childhood and how it was necessary and worked for her survival in that environment but isn't working effectively for her now.]: What would be a new style?
C.: I could say: "What did you say?" It would give them a second chance.
M.: What about giving you a chance?
C.: I realize I'm so automatic with that stuff. I don't want to say anything, do I? I want them to.
M.: What if you said how you felt to your friend? How did you feel?
C.: Hurt.
M.: And . . .
C.: Left out.
M.: What if I were your friend and you could change your style and . . .

C. [interrupts]: . . . If I said how I felt, I would start to cry and I always feel like shit after I cry.
M. [Stops. He's stuck. He looks around . . . ]: I don't know what to say to her now.
T.: She just went back again to her old reaction. It stops her feelings. It's a stopper.
C.: If I got this sad, I couldn't talk!
T. [directing Marvin—standing behind him]: Tell her, "You are sad and you are still talking."
[M. follows through with direction.]
C. [starting to cry]: I wouldn't have the strength.
T.: Another stopper. [He directs M. to say, "You are talking and you are sad and you can see you have the strength."]
[M. follows through.]
T: Tell her to say it louder.
C. [loudly and feelingfully through tears]: I don't think I'm strong enough to talk and cry!!
T.: You see, Marvin, you can counter her old belief system, those stopper thoughts that shut off her feelings and support her old expressive style, by having her say the old thoughts with her new expressive style. Marvin, have her say strongly, "I can take care of my feelings!"
[M. instructs Carole in the new expressive style.]
C. [laughing and crying]: I can take care of my feelings—I can take care of my feelings.
M.: What could you tell your friend if you could take care of your feelings?
C.: My feelings got hurt. Don't leave me out I would like to come to . . .
T.: Can you see how that sort of expressive style—"I won't say anything"—is strongly supported by her thoughts—"I'll feel like a shit if I cry" and "I'm not strong enough, I can't respond"?
C.: You know I see how I teach people to think that nothing they say bothers

me ... that I don't care. [Shaking head] I'm so powerful. It's so automatic.

T.: This little exercise is an important reference point for you to counter that old style and belief. [Turns to M.] What do you like doing the most today?

M.: I liked the role playing.

T.: How did you do?

M.: I think I did well.

T.: I can't hear you.

M. [louder]: I did really well!

[Rest of group applauds.]

T.: You want to keep reminding yourself, in order to remind your clients, to match the expression to the feelings. If you don't, the doubts creep in. To follow up this session with a client, write down on a poster, "I let it go by." These are C.'s own words. Write it down in your notes, then you can keep working this with the client. When they are letting things go by without responses, it will be the same old style with likely the same strong old beliefs and thoughts stopping them from being able to express and respond. This style session is very important for you and the client. See what you have learned about each other and yourself in this exercise.

M.: I can see where I would believe the "stopper" thought and then stop too.

T.: Yes.

C.: To let things go by that personally affect me and then feel bad about what someone is doing to me is the story of my life. This is like the core of me.

T.: It isn't your core, it is a passive shell that leaves the sensitive, responsive, inside person to get hurt.

[C. cries.]

T.: What's that? I can't hear you.

C.: I feel sad.

T.: Strongly sad?

C. [laughing and crying]: Yes! Strongly sad.

T.: There's the core. You see, with this exercise, there can be a new reality. An awareness or perspective on what's possible to experience and express. You don't look like you feel like shit.

C.: No, I don't.

[Group laughs.]

*Commentary*

This brief transcription does convey how the trainer and the trainee worked with both a specific expression dynamic and a particular personality style. When the client expressed herself more loudly she was varying a dynamic of expression, much as an actress would to convey a different feeling. By varying the expressive dynamic the client could become more easily aware of the rigidity of her typical personality style and of the meanings connected to her automatic way of reacting. Every defensive style of reacting exists within a narrow band of expression dynamics; by changing those dynamics the client goes beyond the band of reactivity to allow, first, awareness and, second, responsivity to emerge. The session also shows how rapidly dissociation or gapping can occur; fortunately, Carole, with Marvin's help, was just as rapidly guided to become aware of the dissociative reaction "I just pretended that my feelings weren't hurt" and then to develop a new way of responding from her feelings.

## GETTING HELP

In this training group, Marvin begins the group by asking for some help with one of his clients. He describes the difficulties he is experiencing working with a young woman whom he describes as "depressed, negative, and continuously resistant."

He goes on to describe how she seems to thwart his every effort. Whenever he tries to involve her in any sort of experiential exercises, she responds with "I can't" or "It won't work." Marvin says she is so difficult for him that he just feels like giving up.

T.: How does she look when she's sitting in front of you, Marvin?
M.: She looks . . .
T.: No, you be her—just sit and hold your body like her.
M.: Well, she . . .
T.: Say "I."
M.: I'm all slumped over and I'm looking down and I'm sighing and I don't really look at you.
T.: What is it like?
M.: I'm just all bound up here. I'm not going to move or talk.
T.: Okay. Let's change places. Now you're the therapist and I'm your client. Now how are you sitting?
M.: I'm leaning back and my head is down and I'm . . . my hands are behind my head.
T.: Okay. Now lean back a little more—head down more, just exaggerate it a bit.
M.: Okay.
T.: All right, is this how you get?
M.: Yes—this is it.
T.: Now who do you remind yourself of right now—what's your experience?
M.: I'm just like she is! I have just the same energy and dead hopeless feeling.
T.: So who's teaching whom?
M.: She is—
T.: Right, Marvin, she's training you to be like her. [Explains to the entire group.] It's important to be aware of how powerful your clients' personalities are. She may sound sad, depressed, nonfunctional in many ways—which she is—but she is strongly that way. She is creating her reality in the room and within Marvin. What are you starting to think about with her Marvin?
M.: I can't do anything.
T.: And what is it she's always saying?
M.: "I can't do anything." Oh no!
T.: "Oh no!" is right. She's the Zen Master of "I can't" and she's converting you. The longer you sit there that way, the stronger she'll seem to you. Instead of trying so hard and so hopelessly to try to get her to do what she can't, why don't you try to show her how strong she is at this. Get up and just walk around in here and describe out loud what she is good at.
M. [standing up and moving around]: I can see you're good at being depressed.
T.: How good, Marvin?
M.: Really good—I mean great.
T.: Good enough to get you depressed.
M. [louder now]: Yes! Good enough to make me depressed. You're great at being depressed.
T.: What else?
M.: You're invincible at being resistant and saying you can't do anything. You're amazing. You've convinced me I can't do anything.
T.: Louder!
M.: I can't do anything!
T.: All right. Now that you're moving around, you seem much clearer about everything. It's important for you to maintain some movement—actual physical movement, Marvin. Otherwise you begin to stop and get depressed yourself in the sessions with her. Does "I can't do anything" remind you of something and someone?
M.: Yes, my father and his drinking.
T.: Good clarity, so it's important to be able to move—now what if you could show your client how good she is—how strong this "I can't and won't" style of personality functioning really is. On the board, you could show her the strength of that way of functioning and then the little and big ways that it is working against her. Then, when you next encounter that form of resistance with her, you can point out to her how she's "doing it again." She's the best. She's showing her strength whenever she's saying, "I can't." The key to this,

though, is you. If she can convince you that she can't, then she is essentially teaching you rather than you helping her. All right?

*Commentary*

This was a critical session for Marvin's training. It was a dramatic illustration for him of the powerful influence of a client's personality. For Marvin, the quiet, passive acceptance of his client's reality could be counteracted by maintaining a vigorous, active, playful interactive mode that accepted the client's strength rather than trying to take it away, while maintaining his own independent activity level. In follow-up, Marvin reported that the training allowed both himself and his client to view "can't" and "won't" from a new perspective and enabled his client to move toward a wider range of more effective functioning and living. Just as it is important for clients to actively bring therapeutic movement from their sessions to movement in their lives, so is it crucial that therapists in training bring the movement they make in the training sessions to their work with clients. By actually getting up out of the chair, physically moving, and vigorously engaging the client, Marvin was able to avoid the nonresponsive pattern that contributed to his believing that the client was hopeless.

This session is a good illustration of functional therapy's insistence that the therapist examine his or her own personality functioning within the session. In this training instance, Marvin was capable of matching his own expression, activity, and clarity level to those of the client. The feeling experience in his session with the client was close to his own family experiences with his alcoholic father. By consciously using movement, Marvin can maintain his own present reality and function effectively in his work with this client.

This is further illustrated with Marvin in another training group session with another of his clients with whom he had similar difficulties.

## A FOLLOW-UP TRAINING GROUP

Marvin begins by saying that he feels like he "missed something" in his last session with V. She had entered in a low mood, saying that she had again begun seeing a man she had "swore off" some time ago. She said she was "confused" and wondered whether Marvin felt that "it was OK" that she take up with a man who was physically and emotionally abusive with her. Marvin suggested doing a sentence completion exercise to help her with her "confusion." She was apathetic and resistant during the exercise and then after the exercise. Marvin remarked, "Her affect kept going down and down and . . . I went down with her."

T.: Could someone role-play his client?
C.: I'll do it.
T.: Okay. Now Marvin, just go ahead and listen to her describe going back to this abusive guy and how confused she is and then go ahead with the sentence completion exercise—and Carole, just kind of go along but be depressed and sort of blaming and then criticize what Marvin is doing.
[C. & M. role-play.]
T.: Okay. Freeze! Marvin, don't move! All right, group, where is he?
C.: He's depressed.
D.: He's slumped down and she's abusing him.
T.: Right—you're right. Marvin, you were missing something last session—you! You were missing. Let's send out an APB missing person report and get back! She's a victim and now you're the victim.
M.: I've seen this position before. [laughing cynically]

T.: You sure have—physically and psychologically. So what do you need to do?
M.: Get up and move.
T.: Good start. Try this. Let's get your own clarity back—talk as if you could say anything you want to your client. Do the role-play but you talk—say what you see—that is what clarity is about.
[M. begins talking.]
T.: Loudly, Marvin, very dramatic. There's no victim here. Act like everything you say is THE TRUTH—be a television preacher.
M.: You want me to tell you what to do. [even louder] You want me to say it's OK to do what you feel bad about. You want me to be responsible. I won't do it! I won't be responsible! You don't want to be clear about this. You don't want to be responsible. You want to stay confused and be a victim and have it be someone's fault!
[T. and group clapping and cheering.]
T.: All right. Marvin is clear, if I draw a bullseye and a big target on the board [draws target] where are you hitting?
M.: In the middle—right on.
T.: Right. Where were you before?
M.: Way off target.
T.: Why?
M.: I wasn't saying what I could see and sense.
T.: And then what happens?
M.: I'm a victim. I get confused and depressed.
T.: Okay, all. I want you to get up and shoot bullseyes while you work. Go for clarity. Say what you see. Your homework is, at least two times every session, hit the center of the target—that's clear awareness.

*Commentary*

This group showed Marvin falling back into the personality patterns of expression, activity, feeling, and clarity that had caused him problems. As with clients, the problem process stays constant; it just has different content at different times. This particular episode was helpful in showing Marvin the importance of expressing what he sees and knows with his clients. If he shuts up and isn't direct, he becomes confused.

This session also shows the positive aspects of breaking old roles or images. When given "permission" to say or talk to the client any way he wanted to (rather than from the image of the quiet, compassionate, empathic counselor), he was also capable of a much clearer understanding of the client as well as the restrictions of the role he had adopted. Even experienced therapists are often surprised at the role they have allowed themselves to assume with a client and experience real difficulties altering dysfunctional roles. The functional approach emphasizes the advantages of consistently being responsive rather than attached to a reactive role, even a positive one such as guide, teacher, coach, counselor, or therapist.

Each session includes a follow-up for the trainee therapists to take to their work. Change requires practice in order to become a part of a trainee therapist's repertoire. By giving Marvin a homework exercise to be clear and confrontative in his sessions with clients and by attaching that new role image to the imagery of shooting bullseyes, the trainer is trying to give Marvin something he will be able to hold in consciousness and use. That will be essential if Marvin is to integrate this side of himself into his work. The practice of doing it under pressure in the training group will enable him to have the confidence to try it on his own. Having to exaggerate it beyond the extremes of nearly any real session will effect the feeling "If I can do that, I can do anything." The role-playing tasks are supported by the group and the trainer but are still very difficult. They need to be difficult to put a demand on the trainee's personality so that there is an "exercising" of the personality. As a consequence of this sort of exercising, the trainees can develop awareness of the strengths and weaknesses of their own personalities in action. Only the action or expressive mode provides a chance to choose responsivity over reactivity, which, of course, is the same choice that the trainees as therapists will offer their clients.

## ANOTHER TRAINING EXAMPLE

Donald is 50 years old and recently remarried. He has completed his M.A. degree and an internship and presently is working part-time in a counseling agency to earn hours toward licensure. Counseling is a second career for him; he has a Ph.D. and is a tenured professor at a major university. Although he had a successful academic career, Donald has always been interested in psychotherapy and prefers to make therapy his career focus now.

He grew up in a middle-class home where he had a rather "cool and distant" relationship with his parents. He was a good student. Although he has a very pleasant and likable personality, he feels that his childhood affected his ability to fully experience his feelings. He has been personally involved in psychotherapy as a client throughout much of his life with an emphasis on abreactive modalities. He is an active and willing participant in the training group.

In this example he is shown asking for some help with his work with a client named Robert. He describes Robert as a withdrawn individual who has low motivation, few skills, and no friends, whose only strong interest is in plants. He lives alone in a small guest house. Donald feels that his client is not being responsible in his work or seriously committed to change in the therapy. He can't involve him in looking at alternatives to his behavior and is concerned that perhaps he is "too difficult." Donald states that he has been trying to understand his client but feels that Robert "blocks out" any form of intervention.

T.: Okay. We need a volunteer to roleplay.
M.: Okay.
T.: All right, Marvin, Donald will work with you and you just block him out and withdraw.
M.: No problem [laughing].
D.: I'd like to follow up on last week's session with you.
M.: Um.
D.: I've suggested you look into taking that class—look over here at me.
M.: Oh, okay.
D.: Let me show you something. Let me show you how you are acting in here. First of all, you aren't looking — remember our talk about contact and the importance of eye contact with people?
M.: Uh . . . yeah, I think so.
T.: Okay, okay, enough—you're too good at this, M. All right D., what's going on?
D.: I just can't get through this. He just doesn't seem interested enough.
T.: Are you?
D.: What?
T.: Interested.
D.: In what?
T.: Him. You seem involved in what you are trying to teach him. But are you interested in him?
M.: I feel like he just wanted to show me something.
D.: I guess that's what I'm doing. He's so frustrating.
T.: Switch places with Marvin. Marvin, you communicate like Donald but not out loud. Nonverbally convey the posture and gestures. Donald, you just slouch down like your client and watch.
[M. goes through nonverbal imitation of D.]
T.: All right, very good. What's that like, Donald?

D.: I'm just talking down to him. I'm trying to teach him something I know and he doesn't.
T.: How was it being your client?
D.: I felt unimportant.
T.: And how much contact do you experience coming from the therapist?
D.: I don't feel he's interested in me.
T.: Come sit over here next to your client.
[D. sits next to Marvin.]
T.: All right, put yourself in his world. Put yourself in his place. See the world his way. What is it like?
D.: Well, my world is . . . lonely. No one notices me . . . even my therapist doesn't notice me.
[Begins to be sad. Speaks tearfully.]
T.: What do you care about?
D.: What?
T.: What do you care about the most? What are you most interested in?
D.: Plants.
T.: Plants. Now Donald as the therapist. What are you interested in?
D.: Plants.
T.: Right—why?
D.: Because he's interested in plants.
T.: What else?
D.: Because that's something he really cares about—it's him. It's a way to make contact with him.
T.: For who?
D.: For me to make contact with him—to show him I care.

*Commentary*

This example was included because it makes a basic point very clearly —therapists must not overfocus on techniques. Even effective techniques will not work when they are used without close contact between the therapist and the client. Sometimes caring but inexperienced co-counselors or paraprofessionals are more effective than experienced but overtaxed professionals. It is desirable for therapists of all levels of experience to be reminded that human caring is a necessary condition for therapeutic change. Donald was able to take what he learned from this training session into his next meeting with Robert and relate to him personally and caringly rather than just as a teacher-technician.

## TRAINEES' IMPRESSIONS

The following comments were supplied by the trainees in response to an invitation to answer these questions: How would you evaluate your training group experiences? What parts of the training were especially valuable for you? And what are your criticisms of the training?

*Marvin's Comments*

My reasons for being in the group are: I'd like to continue to improve my skills as a therapist. I like the trainer's approach and orientation. I'd like to learn as much about the functional approach as possible. Also, I feel comfortable with the group, and that is important to me.

The group is very supportive. Definitely has "home court" feeling. The trainer gives suggestions and works with us in very noncritical or maybe I should say "nonhostile" manner, very supportive and encouraging yet also direct in talking about our dynamics. Another positive strength is the information about functional theory and different techniques or viewpoints offered by me or others. A weakness is I haven't heard much about working with couples or families mostly because I haven't had that many couples and families as clients. I would like to focus on the functional approach with couples and families in the future.

Through my almost two years in the training group I've definitely developed an awareness of my movement/activity with clients in sessions and especially in groups. At times I forget, yet I'm definitely more aware of my posture and of the need for changing it when stuck or tired. Also, I've gained confidence in expressing myself and my thoughts/opinions to clients. In addition, I've grown confident in myself with groups. I feel stronger and I'm more aware of using my body activity to be more effective in the group.

One of the main sessions that has affected me was my very first session, which focused on me standing up from my chair and moving. I still remember and use this to help myself adopt a different role or posture when I get stopped by the client's behavior or problem. Another critical session was one where I was working on getting angry with T.J. and realizing that, beneath this, I do care about my clients and can express that or get in touch with that.

*Carole's Comments*

My overall impression of the training group is that sharing the experiences of being a therapist with other therapists is critical to developing into a first-rate counselor. Realizing my own issues and learning to recognize my own instinctual material—how I'm feeling as I listen to a client—are paramount in the therapeutic setting. To switch over from worrying about how I'm feeling, i.e., negative, and letting that feeling overwhelm me, to instead realize that what I am feeling as a reaction to the client is valid. When I recognize these feelings as valid, I therefore realize that this is the way most people would react to the client. This is best described as seeing and feeling the client's PROCESS versus content analysis.

This gift we have of feelings, intuition, or instincts is the part of the therapist that needs fine tuning. In training this was demonstrated endlessly; each and every time I sat amazed at how WE need to continually retune and become reaware of this V.I.P. aspect. The group also enabled me to move from the spot of wanting to be right (perfect), never making mistakes, to feeling more open, more able to share, and thus able to HEAR nondefensively.

For example, I walked away feeling that not only is it OKAY to need help and training, but, in fact, that simply by attending this group I was demonstrating my eagerness and forthrightness in wanting (desiring) to become an excellent therapist versus just an average one.

Personally, when taking this training group when I did, during a developmentally heightened period in my personal growth, I was still under the impression that therapy was MAGIC. By this I mean I had still not fully arrived at total adult awareness. (A secret plot was underway to get me well, but OTHERS were knowledgeable about the system.) Not till I started my own career as a therapist was I able to leave the cocoon of mystery and realize that NO MAGIC existed, that in fact the magic questions disappeared when I welcomed my self to the land of REALITY. At this point many of my defenses faded, and as an adult living in reality land, I am now able to feel and know what is happening in a therapeutic exchange.

I feel that a good therapist should always have either a group or a class like this throughout his or her career to BOUNCE OFF OF OR TO HELP STAY ON TRACK OR TO HELP JUDGE their own CENTEREDNESS with people or a person trusted to KNOW enough about his or her system, so old stuff, etc., is picked up easily by that person. HEY CAROLE, HERE'S THAT BLOCK. DO YOU HEAR OR FEEL IT? "I SEE IT."

Here's a quote from my supervisor's letter of recommendation: "Carole has always been very willing to share herself in supervision and understands the importance of self-examination for a therapist." There's no question in my mind that the training gave me the example, role model, and understanding of this process.

## Donald's Comments

When I first joined the group, the members were working on "activity," one of the five dynamics. I discovered my typical "activity" style is "driven." Somewhere inside I knew that about myself, but identifying it in this way in the group felt like a revelation nonetheless. I had all sorts of thoughts I carried around constantly, that I called into play whenever I might have relaxed to enjoy the moment.

This characteristic style of mine was consistent with styles I was able to identify in the other dynamics: for example, my "clarity" style is to stay "one step ahead" of everyone as much as I can, and my "contact" style is to be a "fortress" around others.

In the training group I chose new styles to develop as alternatives to my old characteristics. My favorite was a new "contact" style of "lean forward." By consciously identifying these, I was able to practice, model, even exaggerate a new style like "lean forward" enough to create the experience of a "lean-forward" approach in my ordinary life, and in my counseling work. "Lean forward" had definite spillover effects in other areas of my life and in other personality styles, such as my "activity" and "expression" and "contact."

One specific episode that affected me more than any other was a lesson I learned during the time the group was working on "contact" as a personality dynamic or style. I presented a difficult case that I was dealing with in my counseling, of a client who was extremely bright and extremely scattered. This client liked to cross back and forth over the line of what seemed to me to be reality, and I was experiencing considerable frustration making and staying in contact with him. While I was working on my lean-forward style, the trainer also helped me give up my effort to stay "one step ahead" of him, and just be with him, and, in effect, allow him to lead me. In subsequent experiences with this client, I was able to put this into practice, with the result that the client and I developed an entirely new connection and personal bond. This alone proved more helpful to this client than all my prior efforts with him.

## CONCLUDING COMMENTS

It should be apparent by now that functional therapy is more closely aligned with the humanistic-existential mode of therapy than with the psychoanalytic-behavioral mode; there is more concern with existential issues than with clinical issues and more emphasis on understanding and contact than with diagnosis and treatment. Because the field of psychotherapy has become so dominated by the medical model (because of pressures from insurance companies, pressures from licensing and certification boards, and the rivalries between various competing professional groups), the existential approach is of lesser influence now than it was in previous decades. However, hegemony is not proof and influence is not truth. It remains to be seen whether people are most helped with problems of living and personality conflicts by regimens of treatment or by the same kinds of human effort that are required in art, education, politics, and religion. Here is a test: If a therapist truly believes that ideas such as "love," "faith," "hope," "courage," "will," and "destiny" are useless and irrelevant in the practice of therapy, then that therapist is a candidate for the "doctor-patient" orientation; therapists who believe that these are real and necessary ideas, rather than mere words, will be inclined toward the "counselor-client" orientation.

Let's expand this argument with a few commonplace observations and several speculations.

First, it is important for therapists to keep in mind that there are many more people who do not suffer from psychopathological disorders than there are who do. Even when the big-number psychopathologies are considered, such as schizophrenia and depression (which may turn out to be chemical disorders best treated within the medical framework), in general, most people in the population are not clinically disturbed.

Second, people can suffer from depressive feelings, confusion, anxiety, conflict, frustration, indecision, stress, and other problems of living without being clinically abnormal.

Third, people can benefit from help, but "getting help" and "getting treatment" are very different activities. The state of mind of a patient and the state of mind of a client are necessarily different (at least within traditional, rather than holistic, medicine). The authentic help that a counselor or psychotherapist can offer is much more like what is offered by a priest, a friend, or (sometimes) a teacher than it is like the treatment given by a medical doctor. To change a person's personality, beliefs, feelings, attitudes, and actions so that he or she can more effectively and more fully live is not the same as setting bones, doing appendectomies, or prescribing pills.

Personal change requires a change in awareness, understanding, and responsibility—it cannot be done to the person. Vital change can only be brought about with the person and by the person—it is a process of discovery and growth, not a treatment process.

We speculate that the current ensnarement of therapists in the false medical model will lead to two possible outcomes (which, perhaps, have already come about). One, the field of therapy will be divided into clinical practitioners, who follow the medical model of diagnosis-treatment plan-prognosis-treatment evaluation, and nonmedical counselors, who follow the humanistic model. Or, two, psychotherapy and counseling will be more definitely separated, with psychotherapists modeling physicians and counselors taking a nonclinical approach. Of course, real life is more complicated than these logical divisions—in some states counselors are already pushing for licensure so that they will be able to receive insurance reimbursements in the same ways that physicians and psychologists (who are generally licensed under state medical boards!) are reimbursed. Counselors who move in the direction of licensure will inevitably be pressured to conform to the medical model, just as psychologists have. From an insurance company's point of view, unrealistic specificity, which can be entered neatly onto forms, is better than realistic open-endedness. Human problems, existential issues, personal conflicts, and self-development are very difficult to fit into reimbursement schedules.

We further speculate that genuine eclecticism in the field of therapy will not emerge until the dominant medical model is supplanted. It would require that therapists be born in the nether regions of the Amazon or New Guinea jungles to avoid some degree of eclecticism in their practices today. There have been too many contributors to therapy's store of ideas and methods in the last one hundred years of Western culture for any contemporary therapist to be anything but eclectic. But there are broad schools of thought that are almost fundamentally incompatible, such as the medical-clinical versus the humanistic-existential. William James sought to maintain the dialectical tensions between "tough-minded" and "tender-minded" evaluations, between philosophy and religion, and between science and art. That is the kind of effort that is required for true eclecticism; it is an eclectic attitude of mind incompatible with medicalism.

In a recent, significant social-psychological study of American life by Professor Robert Bellah and his colleagues (1985), the place of therapy in our culture was recognized as serving an important, widely accepted function parallel to that of the manager: "The therapist, like the manager, takes the ends as they are given; the focus is upon the effectiveness of the means" (p. 47) and "Compared to the practices members of a traditional family, church, or town share over a lifetime, the therapeutic relationship leaves us with relatively little to do together except communicate, and much less time in which to do it. In this, the therapeutic relationship resembles many other relationships in our complex functionally differentiated society, particularly in professional and managerial life" (p. 123).

The problem with this circumscribed kind of relationship, which is based on a doctor-patient or manager-employee model, is that it provides for no other moral standard than that of utilitarian individualism or expressive individualism: "The question is whether an individualism in which the self has become the main form of reality can really be sustained. What is at issue is not simply whether sef-contained individuals might withdraw from the public sphere to pursue purely private ends, but whether such individuals are capable of sustaining either a public *or* a private life" (p. 143).

To put some of these questions of the profession's identity into perspective, we will quote from the comments of another of our trainee therapists, Jason:

In my lifetime, which is now nearly 50 years, I have only needed the services of a physician or hospital a few times and each time those services were performed quickly and skillfully. I count four times in all: once when I was sick with pneumonia at age two, once when I had a bad cut at age ten, once when I was 35 and broke my arm, and more recently when I was about 47 for allergy treatments. I don't count my birth because I believe the doctor was there more for my mother than for me—I could have been born without his help but I definitely needed hers. At this rate, if I live another 20 years, maybe I'll need a physician another dozen times at most, even if I accelerate the number of visits due to the accumulated wear and tear on my body machinery. (I'm not counting dying since, as with my birth, I think I can probably do it better without a doctor's assistance.)

Now compare the number of doctor's visits, about 16, to the number of times I expect to need counseling help from a therapist or friend. I would estimate that I've had at least 20 sessions a year, on average, since I was 20 years old. That is 30 times 20, or 600 sessions. If I live another 20 years and need counseling help at the same rate, that will amount to 600 plus 400, or 1,000 total sessions in my lifetime. Look at the comparisons: 1,000 therapy sessions to 16 physician's treatments, or a ratio of better than 60 to 1. I suppose that someone could say that the medical visits should be weighted more heavily because, in some instances, they were dealing with life-threatening and painful illnesses. However, some of the counseling sessions were lifesavers too, and all of them helped me improve the quality of my life. From that standpoint the counseling sessions may have contributed as much to my physical health as did the medical treatments; it is well known that quality of life contributes to longevity.

I find it ludicrous to apply the medical model to evaluate counseling. Even from the standpoint of the raw numbers, there is no viable comparison—the number and kinds of counseling help that I needed far exceeded the number of doctor's visits that I needed. It doesn't make sense to evaluate them with the same yardstick. Both medical treatment and counseling are personally important to me, I want access to both kinds of help. But they are such different kinds of life events that it is not even close to say that we should not compare "apples and oranges"—it's more like "fruit and aspirins" or "words and medicines." The words-medicines equation is a seductive form of psychobabble that misleads both therapists and clients.

Functional therapy is a philosophical-psychological orientation to helping people, not a medical-managerial orientation. This emphasis has been true from the beginning of the functional approach in the works of William James. The scholar Professor Eugene Taylor makes the point that

James' theory "implies a therapeutic method allied as much with therapy and religion as with experimental medicine and psychology: one based ultimately on understanding of the patient's problem followed by self-help, rather than on professional diagnosis by classification followed by impersonal treatment" (Taylor, 1982, p. 12). In the 1901–1902 Gifford Lectures, which formed the notes for his book *The Varieties of Religious Experience*, James stressed the need for a tolerant attitude toward the boundaries of consciousness and human nature. In *Varieties* he sought to explore "... the true record of great-souled persons wrestling with the crises of their fate ..." (James, 1958, p. 23). He concludes the book with this famous passage: "The whole drift of my education goes to persuade me that the world of our present consciousness is only one out of many worlds that exist, and that those other worlds must contain a meaning for our life also ..." (*ibid.*, p. 391).

The wider questions of therapy, for the functional therapist, are: How open can people be? What are the varieties of consciousness? What are the consequences of more openness, more consciousness, and more responsivity? What are the personal and social consequences of failing to achieve more openness? To what extent can reactivity be replaced by responsivity? These are questions that require a very broad model both for the professional helper and for the client who comes for help in the discovery of personal answers to essential questions; that is what we try to convey to both our trainees and our clients.

## REFERENCES

Bellah, R. N., Madsen, R., Sullivan, W., Swidler, A., and Tipton, S. (1985). *Habits of the heart: individualism and commitment in American life*. Los Angeles: University of California Press.

Burrow, T. (1953). *Science and man's behavior*. New York: Philosophical Library.

Gendlin, E. (1962). *Experiencing and the creation of meaning*. New York: Free Press.

Gendlin, E. (1981). *Focusing*. New York: Bantam.

Hart, J. T. (1981). The significance of William James' ideas for modern psychotherapy. *Journal of Contemporary Psychotherapy, 12,* 88–102.

Hart, J. T. (1983). *Modern eclectic therapy: a functional orientation to counseling and psychotherapy*. New York: Plenum.

Hart, J. T. (1986). *Functional eclectic therapy*. In J. Norcross (Ed.), *Handbook of Eclectic Therapy*. New York: Brunner/Mazel.

Hilgard, E. R. (1977). *Divided consciousness*. New York: Wiley.

James, W. (1950). *The principles of psychology*. New York: Dover.

James, W. (1958). *The varieties of religious experience*. New York: Mentor, New American Library.

Janet, P. (1929). *The major symptoms of hysteria*. New York: Macmillan.

Marston, A. R. (1984). What makes therapists run? A model for analysis of motivational styles. *Psychotherapy, 21,* 456–459.

Patterson, C. H. (1984). Empathy, warmth, and genuineness in psychotherapy: A review of reviews. *Psychotherapy, 21,* 431–438.

Patterson, C. H. (1986). *Theories of counseling and psychotherapy* (4th ed.). New York: Harper & Row.

Prince, M. (1957). *The dissociation of personality*. New York: Meridian.

Taft, J. (1962). *The dynamics of therapy in a controlled relationship*. New York: Dover. (Work originally published 1933)

Taylor, E. (1982). *William James on exceptional mental states: The 1896 Lowell lectures*. New York: Charles Scribner's Sons.

# Commentary: Present-Centeredness and the Client-Therapist Relationship

## Hugh C. H. Koch

A "responsive personality" is one, according to Hart and Hart, that functions with a high level of awareness and responsivity, as opposed to operating with little awareness, i.e., a more reactive approach. One of the most direct means of access to this "responsivity" is by training and shaping up the inner attending process called "focusing," a central technique in Functional Therapy (Gendlin, 1981). As the authors suggest, to be able to use this technique therapist trainees themselves have to develop this awareness so that they can eventually use it to further their clients' awareness. This self-awareness on the part of the therapist involves examining his/her own personality functioning within, as well as outside, the therapeutic session.

Currently, most therapeutic schools are developing awareness of basic personal and interpersonal "nonspecific" factors, which may well account for much of the so-called "success" that therapists and clients achieve together. The mere fact of establishing a relationship based on listening and sharing is fundamental. Encouraging a structure or "container" for personal or emotional problem solving via regular meetings or regular session formats can itself be very reassuring and facilitative. In addition to these fundamental factors, of which there are several more documented (Meyer & Chuser, 1970), this idea of focusing presented in Hart and Hart's chapter is also well known to the psychoanalyst, the cognitive-behaviorist, and the humanist-existentialist. However, I feel it is the interpersonally oriented therapist who perhaps can offer an additional slant on this focusing process when he/she confronts the reality which each client sets up in the therapy room with the therapist. This reality may be partly what Ryle (1975) calls "metaphorical," i.e., an "as if" relationship based on fantasy, desire, or transferential feelings, or it may well be a very personal and real, in the proper sense of the word, relationship based on an adaptive or maladaptive interaction between two people, the client and the therapist.

When listening carefully to clients, the therapist picks up feelings within himself toward his clients—feelings of intimacy, attraction, antipathy, coolness. He notices that he feels "impelled," or, as Kiesler (1982) puts it, "pulled," to respond in a certain way to the client. In one situation, he wants to solve the problem and give advice. In another, he wants to hold back and wait for the client to react. These inner engagements on the part of the therapist are elicited at the beginning by the client's nonverbal and verbal behavior. To be fully aware of the client-therapist relationship and then to be able to confront the meaning and behavior occurring in it, which I feel is one of the most powerful therapeutic techniques, these "impact messages" or "countertransference" feelings must be identified and focused upon. These impact messages, as Kiesler (1982) calls them, refer to all internal events a therapist experiences and all the overt behaviors he shows in his session with a client where the client-therapist relationship is the focus. They include direct feelings (e.g., angry, bored, cautious), action tendencies (e.g., I must give advice here; I must be careful with him), cognitive attributions (e.g., the client wants me to do the work; I'm going too fast for him; she wants to be in control), and, last, fantasies (e.g., I wonder what a sexual relationship with him would be like; I'd like a good row with her).

Impact messages are multidimensional—they include a complex mixture of positive and negative feelings. They are important to share with the client because not only will these messages be elicited by the client's distinctive interpersonal style in therapy but they may well occur when he/she repetitively engages other significant persons in his/her life. Unless confronted and understood, those transactions which are "disordered" or "dysfunctional" continue to cause havoc in the client's (as in all our own) relationships.

There is insufficient space here to elaborate on how the therapist confronts relationship issues with clients. For this the reader is referred to Kiesler's (1982) excellent text Handbook of Interpersonal Psychotherapy. However, I would like to briefly describe a more precise scheme for understanding the variety of "meaning frames" that represent the dyadic options the therapist has in responding to the explicit or implicit meanings of clients' statements.

Any client statement or behavior has relationship, as well as content, meanings, which can be divided into a client-client component (how the client sees himself, expresses feelings about and evaluates himself) and a client-therapist component (feelings and thoughts the client has toward the therapist). Both relationship aspects are communicated not only by the statements the client makes, but also by the nonverbal behavior accompanying the words.

As a recipient or participant in the dyad, the therapist can be aware of two corresponding aspects of relationship messages, the therapist-client meaning and therapist-therapist meaning. Therefore, following any comment or action by the client in a session, the therapist has four options:

1. To respond to the explicit content of what the client has said
2. To respond to one of the four relationship aspects (CC, CT, TC, TT) just outlined
3. To change the subject
4. Not to say anything

Which option is taken depends on the therapist's personal judgment as to which would help the client most at that particular time. It will also depend on what has gone before and on the therapist's own model of what is useful in therapy.

Figure 1 shows how a client's statement "I don't think talking will help" can be focused upon by the therapist listening to the variety of internal messages or impact messages he receives from the statement.

It should be clear from this that the therapist is very much a participant in the client's interpersonal world and that both a real and metaphorical relationship is established in therapy. The client inevitably has feelings and thoughts about the therapist. It is essential and very useful to conceptualize what these impact messages are and how they can be acknowledged and clarified. According to Gendlin (1981), "Without detailed vocabulary about what we do inwardly, we cannot talk to each other or train new therapists" (p. 375) and "if the patient does so and so, I find it helpful to do so and so" (p. 375). Kiesler has offered, via this interpersonal model, a clear and most useful elaboration of how to focus carefully and productively on the client's behavior as it relates to one of the most important aspects of therapy—the client-therapist relationship.

Hart and Hart have provided a service by illustrating these themes in their training program.

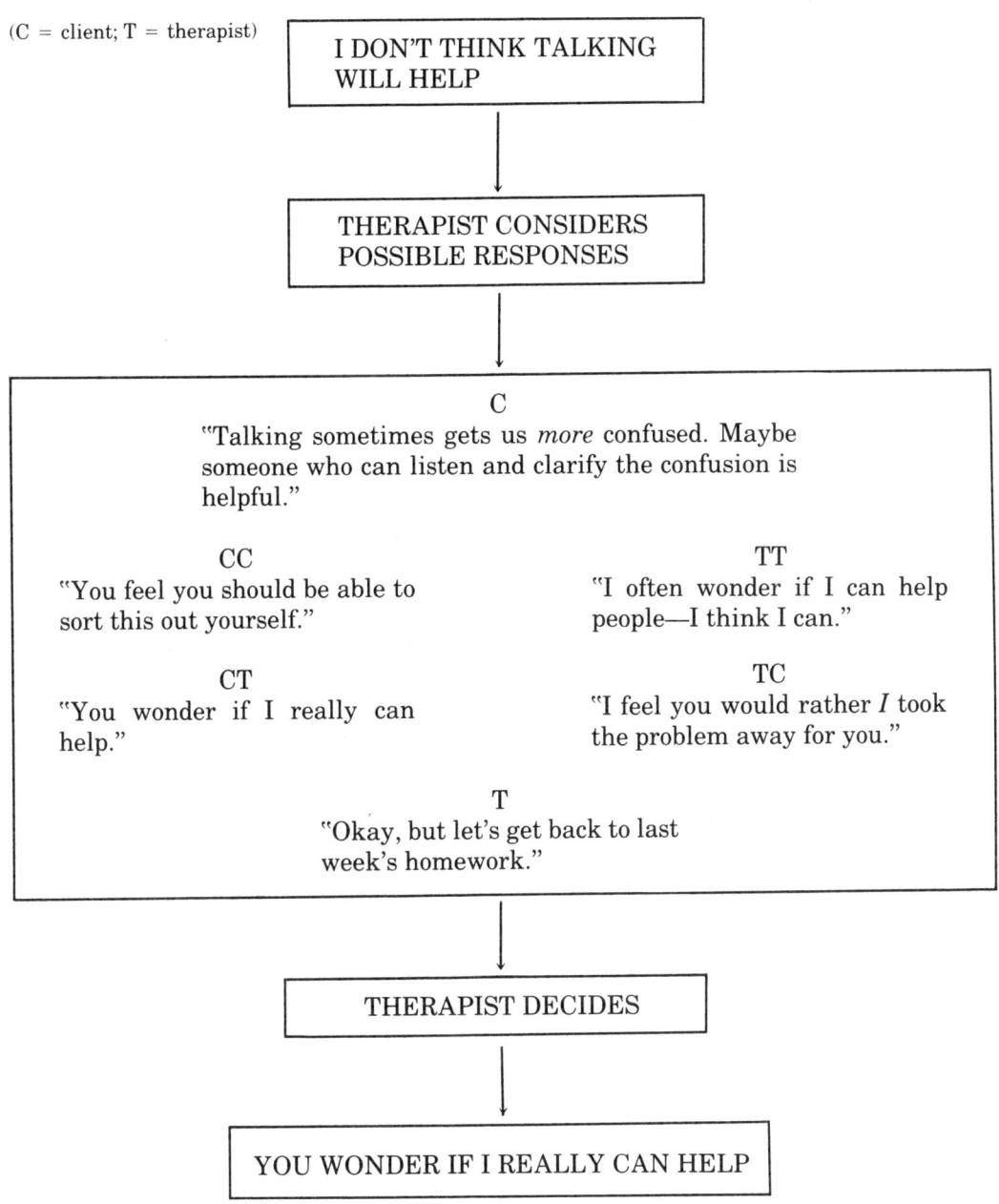

Figure 1: An example of relationship meanings in psychotherapy.

## REFERENCES

Gendlin, E. T. (1981). Focusing. New York: Bantam.

Kiesler, D. J. (1982). Confronting the client-therapist relationship in psychotherapy. In J. C. Anchin & D. J. Kiesler (Eds.), Handbook of interpersonal psychotherapy. New York: Pergamon.

Meyer, V., & Chuser, E. S. (1970). Behaviour therapy in clinical psychiatry. London: Penguin.

Ryle, A. (1975). Frames and cages. The repertory grid approach to human understanding. London: University of Sussex Press.

# Commentary: Therapist, Heal Thyself First

## Malcolm H. Robertson

Drs. Hart and Hart conduct a psychotherapy training program that is: (1) experiential (learning by doing); (2) based on the theory of functional therapy; (3) eclectic (encompassing theoretically diverse interventions); and (4) philosophically committed to developing a therapeutic personality through ongoing training and therapy.

My understanding of the authors' approach is that a therapist's self-awareness and self-change, in response to a client's interpersonal style, is a necessary condition for client change. In relating to a therapist, a client frequently replicates interpersonal problems that characterize significant relationships outside therapy. Instead of being controlled by what a client is or is not doing in the relationship, a therapist responds as if a client were capable of a more spontaneous and self-disclosing interaction. This strategy is consistent with a familiar principle of interpersonal problem solving, i.e., to change another person, change oneself first and in the direction one wishes the relationship to be. Therefore, the task of a therapist is to show rather than to tell a client, to respond actively rather than passively to a client's behavior.

A slightly different conceptualization is that a therapist responds to a client's behavior with recipathy, a term coined by Murray (1938). Recipathy is a therapist's self-awareness and self-disclosure of what is called forth or evoked by the client's behavior in the session. The therapist uses his or her own personal reactions to encourage a client to experiment with a different style of relating both within and outside therapy.

Although the authors state that trainees learn to do therapy by taking turns as therapist and as client, the main thrust of the chapter is personal growth gained in a client role. Trainees learn how to change clients by first learning as clients how to change their own behavior. As clients, trainees are taught how to increase self-awareness and how to use the increased self-awareness to relate more effectively as therapists. The learning experience is directed by a therapist/trainer who explains, demonstrates, and models how new awarenesses, if transformed into action, may result in therapeutic change. Once trainees have discovered how to modify personality dynamics that block critical awareness of self and others, and to express the new awareness in thought, feelings, and actions, they are ready to assume a therapist role in which they learn and practice specific therapy techniques.

I agree with the authors' training philosophy because of my conception of therapy as an educational process, and because of my belief that therapists teach clients more effectively and convincingly when they teach from experiential knowledge rather than from conceptual knowledge. In comparing their training program to the one I conduct at Western Michigan University, I place more emphasis on specific skill training in the therapist role and less emphasis on personal growth acquired in the client role. On the other hand, the close attention that the authors give to a trainee's personal growth, especially the experience of being in therapy as a client, has strong support in the literature on eclectic psychotherapy training (cited in Robertson, 1986).

Hart and Hart draw an interesting parallel between the fitness and skill training of therapists and that of artists and athletes. I am reminded of Strupp's (1978) comment that "a fine therapist closely resembles a painter, novelist, or composer" (p. 317). Like an accomplished artist or athlete, an accomplished therapist must maintain fitness, i.e., a high degree of psychological responsiveness and expressiveness, and must hone his or her technical skills by continued performance, as well as by arranging for periodic coaching and consultation. Although likening a therapist to a performing artist or athlete might be opposed in some circles, the commitment to upgrade or at least maintain clinical skills through continuing professional education has become an integral part of professional life.

## ADDITIONAL COMMENTS

I would describe the authors' psychotherapy approach as an example of technical eclecticism. That is, client problems and goals, and the therapist-client relationship, are conceptualized within a single theoretical orientation (existential-humanistic), although specific techniques may be selected from other theories on the basis of perceived relevance to client problems and potency for implementing therapy goals. There is at least an implicit acknowledgment of the efficacy of tailoring interventions to clients' personality styles and problems. In addition to empathy, relational immediacy, Gestalt awareness tasks, and therapist self-disclosure, which I subsume under an existential-humanistic orientation, other interventions, such as contracting, cognitive restructuring, role playing, and psychodynamically based interpretation, may be used at a therapist's discretion.

To support their conclusion that the training program translates into improved therapist performance with clients, the authors cite a number of positive evaluations given by trainees. However, the reader is not presented with direct evidence of transfer and generalization of learning from the training role to the therapist role, a limitation that this program shares with so many others that fail to establish competency-based criteria. The authors would strengthen their conclusion if they provided excerpts of therapy sessions that demonstrate changes which the therapist trainees have made as a result of the training sessions. Another omission is how the authors' program prepares trainees to do eclectic group, marital, and family therapy.

In contrast to traditional psychotherapy training, the authors do deal directly and decisively with the trainees' personality dynamics and blindspots. On the other hand, at least in the chapter, development of relationship skills and intervention strategies is not given as much emphasis as I believe it deserves and receives in the literature on eclectic training (Robertson, 1986).

Relatedly, diagnostic competence seems to be downplayed, partly in the authors' assertion that most clients are not clinically disturbed and do not suffer from major psychological disorders. The fact that a large majority of clients are not clinically disturbed is useful base rate data. However, a therapist's clinical decision about the presence or absence of psychopathology in a particular client still requires diagnostic acuity.

To conclude, I commend Hart and Hart for training psychotherapists by means of personal and professional growth experiences rather than by formal didactic presentations, for their commitment to developing a therapist's personhood, and finally for their concrete illustrations of how to assist trainees to overcome personality dynamics and developmental experiences that limit therapeutic effectiveness.

*For some psychotherapy trainers the chapter will reinforce their commitment to experiential eclectic training, and hopefully it will encourage others to follow suit.*

**REFERENCES**

Murray, H. A. (1938). *Explorations in personality.* New York: Oxford Press.

Robertson, M. (1986). Training eclectic psychotherapists. In J. C. Norcross (Ed.), *Handbook of eclectic psychotherapy.* New York: Brunner/Mazel.

Strupp, H. H. (1978). The therapist's theoretical orientation: An overrated variable. *Psychotherapy: Theory, Research, Practice, and Training, 15,* 314–317.

CHAPTER 11

# Depression and Structural–Phenomenological Eclectic Psychotherapy: The Case of Gill

*Stephen Murgatroyd*

### INTRODUCTION

The classification of depression has been and will continue to be a controversial matter. Kendell (1976) has observed that not only are those not directly involved in the classification debate extremely confused, but it is now also the case that those most intimately involved are increasingly unsure of their ground.

Rumke (1960) has identified 13 forms of depression. However, much more common are classifications involving one (Lewis, 1938), two (Pollitt, 1965), three (Overall et al., 1966), four (Paykel, 1971), or five (Blinder, 1966) depressive etiologies. Almost all of these multiple classifications draw a distinction between type A depressions (endogenous/psychotic) and type B depressions (reactive/neurotic). In this chapter a case study is presented of a person experiencing a type B depression.

Of these two major depressive types, type B is less well differentiated than type A. Indeed, most of the debate about classification clusters around: (a) the distinction between psychopathological and nonpathological depressions of the neurotic-reactive kind; and (b) the extent to which reactive depressions are conditioned responses to given social situations as opposed to a cognitive-affective state, which is largely independent of social cues (Foulds & Bedford, 1976).

Classical behavioral formulations of depression have sought to address this last issue. All six major "classical" formulations of depression —[(a) reductions in the quality of reinforcement (Lazarus, 1968); (b) reduced frequency of reinforcement (Hersen et. al., 1973); (c) the loss of reinforceable behavior (Ferster, 1973); (d) the loss of reinforcer effectiveness (Costello, 1972); (e) aversive control (Moss and Boren, 1972); and (f) learned helplessness (Seligman, 1975)]—assume that depression is "a consequence of the reinforcement contingencies of which the individual's behaviour is a function" (Eastman, 1976). Individuals are seen to be responding in a depressive way to social and personal situations—they pursue what Lazarus (1968) has called an "extinction trial." Until relatively recently, affective and cognitive factors did not overly intrude into these behavioral formulations.

More recently, cognitive-behavioral explanations of depression have emerged which give emphasis to the importance of the phenomenological experience of the person in maintaining the depressive responses to internal and external cues. Of particular importance in this respect is the work of Ellis (1962), Beck (1976), and Meichenbaum (1977). The essence of this position is that depressive actions are maintained by irrational thoughts and inner monologues that cue the individual to experience actions and the social world in a depressive way.

The development of the cognitive-behavioral school of behavioral analysis has a further implication, important for our purposes here. When a person's belief system and irrational thoughts are seen to cue and trigger behavioral responses, then it is necessary to ask questions about the experiential bases of these beliefs and thoughts. Mandler (1975) observes:

Whenever a search of appropriate action systems indicates that because of past experience or the generalized evaluation of personal competence, no actions are available that will achieve desirable ends then helplessness and hopelessness will result. These means and ends need not be associated with the avoidance of aversive events, *they may just as well relate to the unattainability of desirable states* [pp. 211–212, my emphasis].

Mandler implies that we need to have an understanding not only of the persons' behavior but of the origins of this behavior in experience. To do this, we need a comprehensive theory of motivation and metamotivation.

The theory of psychological reversals, developed by Smith and Apter (1975), refined by Apter (1982) and enhanced by Apter and Smith (1985), provides an appropriate theory of motivation and experience for understanding a great deal of depression. What is more, this same theory provides the rationale for structural phenomenological eclectic psychotherapy (Murgatroyd & Apter, 1984, 1985).

The theory is based on the assumption that an individual's actions have specific motives, but that these motives are not sufficient in themselves to explain either the action or the way in which the person experiences that action. To have such an understanding it is necessary to understand the metamotives a person has for his actions. In this context, metamotives are the motivational states within which the person experiences specific motives for action. To use an analogy from literature, a novel is one form of metamotivational structure within which words are written; the stream-of-consciousness poem is another. Although the actions of writing may appear similar between the person who on one day writes poetry and on another works on a novel, they are in fact "driven" by different values, assumptions, and beliefs. The same action (writing) carries different meanings in these two instances. There are two important features of this example: (a) the same action can be undertaken for different motivational reasons; and (b) individuals can change their motives for action such that the same action can be undertaken for oppositional and different affect.

This is not the place to elaborate the detail of this theory (but see Apter, 1982; Murgatroyd, 1985a; Murgatroyd & Apter, 1985). What is important to recognize here is that a person can become depressed not only because of a specific reaction to a specific cue (reactive depression) but because of failure to achieve changes in the metamotivational state. For example, Mike is a serious and hard-working executive who finds his work demanding and intellectually strenuous. He experiences work in a *telic metamotivational state*—as something serious, to be planned for, and in which arousal has to be avoided if effectiveness is to be achieved. When he is not working, he likes to be outgoing, arousal seeking, and here-and-now oriented—he seeks out experiences characterized in this way since he is seeking to reverse into the *paratelic metamotivational state*. This reversal between two major metamotivational states (telic to paratelic and, at a later time, back again) constitutes a major feature of Mike's inconsistent metamotivation. Mike is typical of most people—he seeks such motivational inconsistency in order to maintain sanity. When, for whatever reason, he is unable to achieve an appropriate reversal or he reverses inappropriately, or he behaves appropriately for the state in which he finds himself but inappropriately for the social conditions he is experiencing, then some kind of distress occurs. The extent and nature of this distress depend on the nature and duration of the "barrier" to reversal. In some individuals the resultant affect can be anxiety; in others, depression may occur.

Apter (1982) offers a formulation of depression that takes this model a little further. He identifies four types of depression: (a) *anxiety depression*, in which depressive experiences are layered with anxiety; (b) *apathy depression*, in which the person is unable to produce arousal or activate an affective state other than depression and lethargy; (c) *overexcitement depression*, which occurs rarely in the case of mania when the person feels unable to escape from a state of chronic overexcitement and experiences depression along with this feeling—Apter (1982, esp. p. 251) observes that this form of depression occurs also when a person "is unpleasantly overwhelmed by strong sensations of all kinds which he feels he cannot avoid"; and (d) *boredom depression*, in which the person is unable to attain either the excitement or level of activation he desires.

The first two of these depressive types relate to the telic metamotivational state. They occur because the person is "locked" into a state that is serious, arousal avoiding, and planning orientated and either cannot achieve the satisfactions of this state or is unable to exit from this state into its opposite. Anxiety depression occurs because the person experiences excessive arousal in this state and cannot reduce it or reverse into a paratelic state to experience this arousal differently; apathy depression, in contrast, occurs because there is so little arousal that the person cannot activate the behavior and affective tones "required" by the telic state. The third and fourth of the depressive states identified here relate to the paratelic metamotivational state—arousal seeking, a here-and-now orientation, and high intensity of experience. Depression occurs in this state when the affective needs of the state are not satisfied or when the appropriate level of arousal and hedonic tone cannot be achieved. Overexcitement depression occurs when the person feels trapped in a sensation-seeking state, and boredom depression occurs when the person is aware of the needs he is seeking to fulfill in the paratelic state but is unable to discern appropriate ways of achieving these needs.

This formulation of depression has many implications for treatment strategies, not all of which can be examined here. Indeed, the intention of this chapter is to focus exclusively on a case of apathy depression experienced by a 28-year-old single person called Gill. The point about the Apter (1982) model is that it emphasizes the need to understand the phenomenology of the person and the structure of that phenomenology (in terms of metamotivation) if the depression is to be treated.

The remainder of this chapter will examine the way in which a person experiences both actions and motives in a depressive frame. In addition, the procedures used to promote a change within the telic state and reversal to the paratelic state will be described. Throughout the therapy with Gill detailed transcripts from videotapes were made available to both the therapist and Gill, and these will be used at several points to illuminate procedures and document the images and experiences that characterized this work. In the final section some written reactions of Gill to this chapter are provided together with some extracts from letters to indicate the nature of subsequent progress and her own evaluations of therapy.

## THE BASIS OF REFERRAL

Gill was referred for psychotherapy through a self-help group that specialized in the depressive and phobic problems in a particular community with which I have had considerable involvement. The referral occurred because of the concern within this group about the severity of Gill's depression. She had had no psychiatric or medical history that was relevant to her current state, according to the referral information I received—which Gill later confirmed. She was then 28 years old, unmarried, and not currently involved in relationships with males. Though in the past she had had many relationships, some lasting over three years, she claimed now to no longer need either the intellectual, emotional, or sexual fulfillment that such relationships had given.

By any standards, Gill was middle class. She was an assistant manager for a group of stores selling clothes and cosmetics. She earned an income that rivaled that of most women in business of her age (app. £8,000—a considerable income for a woman, or a man, in Britain). She owned a house, which she had inherited from her parents, and a sports car. She was always well dressed and attractive. She had received a college education in business studies up to the age of 21.

Gill was the only daughter of Sam and Mary. Sam had died when Gill was 20 and he was 68 years old. Her mother had died when Gill was 24 and she was 56 years old. Gill said that the discrepancy between her parents' ages had not bothered her, though at the time of referral she was somewhat preoccupied by the fact that both her parents had died of coronary heart disease, which for her meant that she too was at risk. She ruminated on questions about the effect that she had had on her parents' life; in particular, she spent some time reflecting on the fact that her parents "had not expected to have *any* children—then I came along and they wanted another but never managed it." She said that she had never "envied those with brothers or sisters or both" and that she had been "quite happy" as a child.

## PRESENTING ISSUES

The following extract indicates the nature of the presenting problem as seen by Gill in the first session.

P: I am just going through the motions of being alive and around. Inside I feel empty, lost, and without purpose. I have no energy . . . [silence for 18 seconds] I just can't find anything that . . . [silence for 11 seconds]
T: You say you have no energy and you let your speech drift off into silence. What other forms does this lack of energy take?
P: I forget what I am doing sometimes . . . quite often in fact . . . [silence for nine seconds] I won't make decisions

... I am relying on others at work to do more and more of the work ... and even small things (like shopping or going out) become things that I am unable to make decisions about. It's like having a black hole inside me that wants to engulf me and take me over. The only response I can have to this is to feel engulfed and overwhelmed, and yet continue to ... well ... just exist.

This presentation of self was offered in a monotone. Though the language appears firm and clear, it was expressed without a feeling of firmness or clarity. The timed pauses actually seemed to be more substantial than the numbers indicate.

In the first session I was able to establish: (a) that Gill was normally a serious person—she liked things to be planned and to be clear, she did not like spontaneity or practical jokes or unforeseen circumstances—she was "at her best" when she "knew just what was going to happen"; (b) she sought out relationships with others that were largely undemanding of her—a good relationship was one in which "both knew where we were going and what it was we wanted from each other—if that was sex, that was fine ... if it was intellectual stimulation, that was fine ... as long as I *know where I am*"; (c) that her expectation of her own development was that she would simply continue to experience the social world as she had always done and that she had "passed the period of changes" (her expression); and (d) that her current depression and inability to engage the social world or to obtain satisfactions from her actions was a sustained and painful experience that was both unique and extreme for her. Though she superficially appeared to be coping with her work, close inspection of her work behavior and performance would, she claimed, reveal that she was currently not working to the benefit of the company and she felt "helpless" to do anything about it. She was sleeping badly and not able to eat properly—she claimed to have lost 18 pounds in weight in seven weeks.

My detailed notes, arranged under the headings suggested by Lazarus (1976), of the presenting issues are given here:

*Behavior.* Gill is not sleeping or eating well, she is losing body weight rapidly. She speaks in monotone and behaves in routinized ways. She has disengaged from social behavior and has not engaged in relationship building for some time. She presents a coping image to the world but does not behave as if she is coping in her own judgment. She finds holding a sustained personal conversation difficult, though is succinct in her language use.

*Affect.* Gill presents as if she is devoid of affect. Her monotone shows no anxiety or energy. She talks about her depression as if she was incapable of ever having experienced excitement. Any pleasurable affect in the past has been planned *(telic)* and deliberate—she now does not seem to have the energy or the "will" to engage in such planned activity. She presents her emotions as having been drained into a black hole. The overwhelming impression was of apathy (passionless existence; lack of interest or desire) layered with considerable pain and self-pity.

*Sensation.* Gill does not present herself as bored—she does not operate from a sensation-seeking or frustration mode—she is clearly apathy depressed in terms of her extreme telic orientation. She is not trying to do anything that will raise her arousal; she seems to be seeking to maintain her arousal at the lowest possible level *(arousal avoidance is extreme)* while expecting that this will lead to affective satisfaction. It is as if satiation of this state has occurred but that the reversal that normally follows satiation has failed to materialize. This leaves her with a sense of depression both about the state and about the experience of satiation.

*Imagery.* Gill uses two images in her

self-presentations about her depression: (a) feeling as if she is being engulfed and overwhelmed by a black hole, which she finds immensely depressing, and (b) feeling trapped under the weight of her own depression. Occasionally, she refers to her state as "the drained coconut" or as "the sapling tree that cannot leaf." Clearly, the most powerful image is that of the black hole. (A subsequent analysis of the transcript of this first session shows that she used this image 26 times in 58 minutes to describe her depressed state.)

*Cognitions.* Gill had difficulty in identifying her own self-talk and cognitions. One was clearly evident: "There is nothing I can do about the way I feel, it's just how it is supposed to be." I explored with her the idea that "she had passed the period of changes," which seemed to constitute another belief. She said that she felt no different now than when she was 18 (apart from the depression) and that she certainly did not feel that she wanted to change. When pressed to express this as a single belief statement, she simply said, "Change is what happens when you're younger; when you get to my age you are how you are." This seems to me like another version of the irrational belief that unhappiness is a function of events outside the control of individuals.

*Interpersonal.* Gill has poor interpersonal skills, according to her behavior during this session. She has had relationships in the past (some of which have lasted up to three years), but these have to be planned and purposive. She cannot have casual relationships (she says) and needs to have a clear agreement about the parameters of a relationship before she feels comfortable.

*Drugs.* Gill is not seeing a doctor at this time and only takes an occasional pill (paracetamol or Anacin) when she has a headache.

Toward the end of this first session I asked Gill to complete the *Telic Dominance Scale* (Murgatroyd, Rushton, Apter, & Ray, 1978) and the Leeds Depression Inventory (Snaith, Bridge, & Hamilton, 1976). These revealed that Gill was extremely telic (a score of 13 on seriousmindedness, 11 on both planning orientation and arousal avoidance—highest score possible on any subscale = 14) and chronically depressed. We contracted for eight sessions of one and a half hours. A clear part of this contract was that Gill would complete homework assignments. At the end of the first session I asked her to keep a visual diary of her experience between appointments (which were weekly). This diary would involve her trying to capture her experience in drawings and words so that she could discuss these with me. I also asked her to bring photographs of herself that represented the way in which she thought of herself before she became depressed. I felt that these requests would provide me with more insight into Gill's phenomenological field while creating some arousal in Gill. Creating arousal was important for therapeutic progress—a part of her depression related to the experience of extreme low arousal. Gill now writes that "these requests challenged me: It was as if I was being asked to go into the black hole and confront it.... I found this very disturbing, but somehow managed to complete the tasks that I had been assigned."

In discussing this case with a colleague as part of my own supervision arrangements we explored the difference between apathy depression and boredom depression. What was clear about Gill was that she was a very serious and planning-oriented person and that her depression was very well described by the item on the Leeds Scale concerned with apathy ("I have lost interest in things") rather than the item concerned with boredom ("I am restless and can't keep still"). She made several statements about not having the "energy" to "invest" in her plans for the future or the patience to start new activities or relationships. She seemed both depressed and apathetic about her depression. She was a clear case of apathy depression. What made this clearer was the description of boredom depression provided by Apter (1982, esp. p. 251) as having its origins in the paratelic state. Gill did not seem to have residual arousal that she was able to activate so as to become more spontaneous, action oriented, and sensation seeking (these being the qualitative features of the paratelic state)—she was not bored.

This hypothesis about Gill's presenting problem guided my thoughts about initial treatment goals. The first task was to encourage her to understand her depression in motivational terms. The second task was to encourage her to identify her motivational experiences and their structure. The final task was to facilitate a change in the way in which she experienced her own motivation and actions. Almost all of these would require Gill to experience higher levels of arousal than was the case at this first session. I intended that her arousal levels should provide a major focus for the process of therapy. I also decided that at the next session I would seek to explain the motivational theory in which I was working and to relate this theory to her depression.

## SESSIONS 2 TO 4

I have grouped the second, third, and fourth sessions together since they form a natural developmental segment of the work with this client. This segment can be characterized by the phrase "exploration and exaggeration" for reasons that will soon become clear.

Gill presented at the second session in a more distressed and depressed state than at the first. She said that the homework assignment I had set had caused her "a lot of pain" and that if therapy was going to make her more and more depressed, she was not sure that she wanted to continue. She said that she had become angry by the fact that I was "making her" go into the black hole and that I was "making her" depressed. She also said that she had undertaken the homework tasks with considerable reluctance and had only been able to complete them by using the "insomnia" time that was available to her—"it was one way of trying to get me distracted enough to sleep." She created an extension to one of her images—the homework had "been like an insecticide sprayed on me as a leafless sapling."

I used these statements to congratulate Gill on a clear identification of her symptoms and to encourage her to reveal more of the inner workings of her experience, since this was a central part of the process by which her depression could be affected. In addition to giving her symptoms a positive connotation (see Minuchin & Fishman, 1981, esp. pp. 33–34), I also reinforced her use of her "insomnia time," arguing that it was a constructive use of time she would otherwise have wasted and that, even though it made her angry, this was more constructive a use of her time than being depressed. This last comment is a variant on Haley's ordeal therapy method in which time "wasted" in negative emotional experiences has to be compensated for by the completion of behavioral tasks (Haley, 1974).

Providing two positive connotations for statements that Gill anticipated would be received negatively seemed to promote some arousal in her. She looked startled and confused. She had expected me to be angry as she had been. Here is some dialogue from this session, which illuminates the impact of positive connotation and reinforcement:

P: You mean to say that you are *pleased* that I was *angry*?!
T: No, I am pleased about two things—your ability to be clear and precise in un-

derstanding just what is happening to you and the fact that you were something other than depressed. I am also pleased now to hear that your voice is reflecting your feelings and that you are completing sentences that describe precisely the way you are feeling.

P: This is something else! [Sits upright in chair, moves forward, and begins to gesticulate by pointing a finger] I do not like being angry and I do not like being depressed I just want to be me—we'd better understand this before we go much further.

T: Gill, am I right in seeing that you are aroused right now? Am I right in seeing you aroused and feeling that this is making you anxious?

P [hesitantly]: Yes, yes you are . . . I suppose I am feeling aroused . . . and upset.

T: Gill, please help me. I want you to focus on arousal and what happens to you when you experience arousal. I want you to describe what is happening to you now that this arousal is around. Do it quickly, Gill, before this arousal goes away. Tell me, what's this arousal like?

P: Well [sits more forward on the chair—on the edge] . . . I feel my heart beat a little faster and I can feel the blood pulsing in my neck [puts left hand to her neck] . . . I also feel my thoughts beginning to move a little quicker, as if I could get out of control if I don't watch it . . . I feel I have to do something, say something or do something so that I stay in control. . . .

T: Gill, I want you to notice something. When I asked you what happens when you experience arousal, you described your feeling that you needed to control that arousal so that you could control your experience. This is another good insight into your experience, Gill, and I am grateful for your clarity. It shows me that your feeling of depression is about overcontrolling your experience of arousal.

P [flash of anger appears to produce this statement]: What's this? Instant diagnosis!

T: Thank you for sharing your anger with me, Gill. It shows that you can get aroused quickly and that you can show that arousal to others. Is that what happened right then . . . you got angry?

P: [moves back into chair and looks directly into my eyes for the first time during these first 20 minutes of the session; pause for nine seconds; voice is quiet and hesitant]: Yes, yes that's right. [pause for 12 seconds] I am sorry that I was angry with you.

T: I am happy that you can be angry with me, Gill. I am also happy that you were angry . . . it shows me that you do become aroused and that you experience arousal in a particular kind of way.

P: Yes, but it always makes me upset. . . .

This interchange was a critical lead into two features that dominated the first session: (a) the fact that her arousal was experienced as something unpleasant indicated that arousal was being experienced in the telic state and was therefore being suppressed; and (b) we had established the focus on here-and-now issues for therapy rather than past or future issues.

The remainder of this session was spent explaining the nature of reversal theory, with the emphasis being placed on the way in which arousal is experienced differently in the telic and paratelic metamotivational states (arousal is felt as unpleasant in the telic state and as pleasant in the paratelic state). I asked Gill to work through the meaning for her of the curve shown in Figure 1. She clearly identified herself as at the extreme end of the telic curve—beyond relaxation and in a state of apathy. She related her drawings and photographs of herself to this figure and was able to further confirm that she was to be located in apathy at this time and on the telic curve "when I'm not this bad." She claimed to recognize few, if any, paratelic experiences.

In exploring this diagram and its meaning for her—a basic way of enabling us to share a language about arousal and its link with experience—I emphasized some of the features of the telic state that are of particular importance in understanding the nature of depression. These are summarized in the list given here which I worked through with Gill:

*Means-Ends.* In the telic state you attempt to complete tasks, to meet essential and imposed goals that you see as unavoidable; you are acting to achieve ends and are not that interested in the processes by which these ends are achieved provided that the process is not overarousing; you are reactive rather than initiating.

*Time.* In the telic state you prefer planned and purposive activity; you like to know where you are going; you therefore constantly look to the future and see yourself more in future time than the present, here-and-now time; your life always points beyond where it is to where you see yourself; you prefer events to have high significance in terms of this plan, though you recognize that your plan will modify itself in the light of experience.

*Intensity.* In the telic state you prefer low arousal—high arousal is experienced as anxiety, which is often expressed as frustration, anger, or agitation; you are generally realistic, not risk taking, and you seek out situations in which the things you experience will have a low emotional intensity rather than a high intensity; you work hard to create "safe" environments.

Gill claimed that these observations described her experience of the social world well, and she was able to connect to many features of the description. She further connected her photographs to these items.

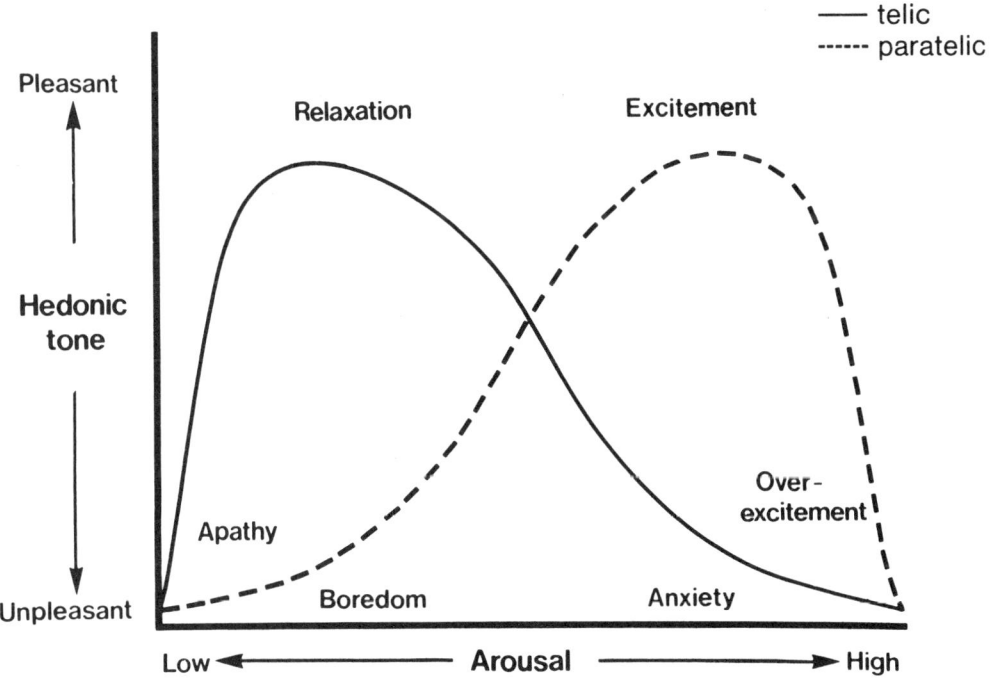

*Figure 1*

She showed herself dressed conventionally, doing conventional things, and minimizing the interest in photographs that could have had interesting features. She also discussed the quality of her relationships with men as being about safety and planned relationships. At the end of the second session I asked Gill to make a note in a notebook I had provided her of all the feelings that she experienced between this session and the next appointment. I asked her to be diligent and encouraged her to be explicit. I reminded her of her skills in self-observation (further positive reinforcement of her symptoms) and asked her to attend to the features of the telic state we had just explored; means-ends, the experience of time, and the intensity of her experience.

The third session built on this foundation and used her "feelings diary" to connect her experience with the model represented in Figure 1. Of particular importance to this period of continued explanation was her realization that the experience of arousal in telic terms was only one way of experiencing motivation and emotion and there were alternatives. The following is an extract from her feelings diary:

*Tuesday*: Annoyed at how late the postman is becoming and at the fact that no one has written to me anyway. Felt numb for most of the morning. Felt a pain in the base of my back—put it down to stress after the therapy session. Felt sad about being so depressed and then felt depressed about being so depressed.

*Wednesday*: Felt tired and exhausted as soon as I awoke. Felt weak and limp and a little better. By 7:30 A.M. I wanted to scream with the pain of being so depressed. Then I slowly began to feel angry: thought about this in terms of what we'd talked about—angry is aroused, isn't it, and that's what's wrong, I am not aroused enough! (Does this mean I am getting better?)

*Thursday*: Couldn't get out of bed today and felt miserable. Thought a lot about this paratelic idea and tried hard to remember when I had let myself go. I recalled an incident when I was eight and was running wild in a field and got beaten for it and a sex thing with a girl and a boy from school when I was eight and felt guilty . . . but nothing else. By noon I was too tired even to be depressed. By 4:00 P.M. I was fitful and somber. Slept. Felt tired when I awoke. Felt bitter about another wasted day. Felt bitter about having to keep this diary. Felt bitter about everything.

The diary read as a kind of intellectual diary—feelings had become intellectualized and her emotions relegated to a set of standard statements that had literary merit. Her apathy was apparent as well as her bitterness. I felt that the diary indicated the operation of a second pair of metamotivational states outlined in reversal theory—the negativism and conformity pair (see Apter [1982], esp. pp. 220–223). In particular, there is a high degree of "self-negativism" displayed in the diary material (and in the earlier drawings). Apter (1982) defines self-negativism in the following way:

If the self polarizes into the "I" and "me," then it is possible for the "I" to see the "me" as external to it in some way, and to see its requirements as coming "from outside." Therefore under these conditions the "I" can, when the negativistic state is operative, act negatively against the "me." This will be referred to as self-negativism (p. 220).

There are a number of ways in which self-negativism can arise, but the most appropriate in this case is to regard it as a form of retroflection (Perls, Hefferline, & Goodman, 1973). Gill has substituted herself for her environment and acts against herself rather than those things in her environment which she would really like to react against. This observation adds a new element to my hypothesis—Gill is highly telic, satiated in this metamotivational state, and depressed because she cannot achieve a reversal to the paratelic state or achieve the satisfactions of the telic state, and now it is clear that she is also self-negativistic.

Once again I congratulated her on the clarity of her own understanding of her symptoms and on the diligence with which she had completed her homework task. I said that in this third session I wanted her to enable me to see and feel the kinds of experiences she had written about and that I wanted to use some drama work to achieve this. I explained that the way in which I wanted her to behave was risky for her—she would get aroused—but that this was all part of the therapy. The essential task was for her to portray, in as detailed and as elaborate a way as possible, the emotions she had recorded in her diary. I further observed that this way of working is derived from the work of Keith Johnstone (1981) and will involve her in having to improvise; I pointed out that this would not be too difficult since I wanted her to improvise being herself as described in her diary. At first she did not take me seriously. She asked, "Is this for real?" and I observed that her diary was for real, but this was to be an enactment of her feelings. After some considerable persuasion, she agreed to "try this stuff" but did so with the feeling that it would not work.

I began by asking her to act out the scene in her diary in which she describes waking and feeling angry (see the Wednesday entry). To make matters easier for her I said that I would play at being a servant—I intended to use this role to engage in some paradoxical interventions. Each time she offered a scene I (as the servant) complained that it was not depressed and exhausted enough—she did not really look like she was about to scream or that she was in pain—and I asked her to work harder and harder at being depressed. After five or six tries at this scene the following encounter (with us both out of our role play) occurred:

P: Shit! It's me that knows what it's like to be me. I am the one that gets fucking depressed not you . . . so will you just stop badgering me and stop making me so fucking angry! God, it's awful and I'm paying for this . . . charade!

T: You keep saying you're depressed, but you never show the depth of your depression.

P: What more do I have to do, for Christ's sake [shouting] . . . cut my fucking wrist! Slit my throat! Would that make you happy? God, everyone always has plans for me and I never get to be myself.

T: And what would being yourself mean, Gill?

P: Oh . . . not having to take responsibility all the time . . . being, well, being the me I was never allowed to be as a child.

Through the use of a dramatized paradoxical intervention (Riebel, 1984; Coleman Nelson, 1962) in this third session I was able to achieve: (a) a display of negativism toward me, which highlighted this feature for both patient and therapists; (b) a high level of arousal in Gill, which she experienced initially as anger and subsequently as exhilarating (as she herself reports below); and (c) a new statement of her experience of the social world, which seemed *for her* to encapsulate her depression. This session was to prove critical in her therapy, as we shall see. What was also critical was the attempts I made to ensure that she left this session in a state other than one of anxiety and anger. I did this by using a quick relaxation method (Murgatroyd, 1985b) and by talking her down and building an agenda for our next meeting. This session ran for two and a quarter hours.

I did set Gill a homework assignment. It was to write a letter to me that should arrive the day before our next scheduled meeting. This is the letter she wrote:

Dear Stephen,
I have thought a lot about the last session. You really got me angry! So angry that I didn't

have time to be depressed!! For the first time in five months I felt as if I had grown some foliage. I hope you will not be angry with me when we meet tomorrow—it all just poured out of me. I felt so angry at being directed and forced to be something that I don't want that I just had to scream at you. (Do you know that I have never used those words before with another person present?)

After I left the session, when you'd taught that quick relaxation method, I was still quite high. I felt like I could be me for a while. Since then I have become more depressed. I think that what is happening is that I am feeling that it is okay to be me when I am pushed to be by you, but that I can't keep it up when I am out here. This is something I would really like to talk about when we meet.

One other thing, I would like to explore just where this thing about everyone else having plans for me comes from. I have not thought that way since I was around 14 or 8 and I am not sure what it means for me now.

Anyway, don't be angry with me.

Gill

My objectives for the fourth session were discussed with my colleague and supervisor following the receipt of this letter. Both of us felt that the fourth session would shape the direction of the therapy that followed. I felt strongly that the essential task was to continue to generate arousal which Gill could experience in a variety of different ways, the point being that the experience of arousal as anger, excitement, or frustration might induce either a shift in the telic state such that Gill would become more adept at handling the social world or a reversal into the paratelic state, which would certainly lead to a lifting of the depression. My colleague, however, felt that the issue of control ("everyone has plans for me and I never get to be myself") was so central to her experience of the social world and her self-evaluation that I should focus exclusively on this feature in the fourth session. I decided to combine both perspectives and to use some challenging and confronting techniques to do so.

When Gill arrived for the fourth session she looked a little more alert than usual. I noticed that her voice had far more modulation than had been the case during her normal conversation on previous sessions. I began by thanking her for her letter and explained that, far from being angry, the last session had produced some important material for us to work on. She agreed, noting that she had identified an issue in her letter to me which she felt was important and about which she had been thinking carefully. I said that I had observed that, but that I wanted her to engage in some more work first. I said that I had listed on a piece of paper six features of Gill which I would like her to look at. These were: (1) Gill the worker—efficient and enthusiastic; (2) Gill the daughter—alone and unsure; (3) Gill the planned relator; (4) Gill who has never said "fuck" with someone else present; (5) Gill the frustrated; and (6) Gill who can only be angry or depressed. I asked her to throw dice and talk for five minutes about whichever feature of Gill the dice indicated. I made clear that after five minutes I would ask her to throw the dice again and repeat the process. My aim in using this technique (developed from Luke Rinehart's *The Dice Man* [1972]) was to provide a frustrating opportunity for Gill to talk about different features of herself so that we could explore the meaning of her social world and her motivation while at the same time increasing her arousal. I assumed that the uncertainty inherent in the procedure would be arousing as well as the fact that some of the content would generate arousal in its own right. Gill was persuaded to comply. The dice was thrown and landed on 3. Here is a transcript of the next few minutes:

P: Hmm . . . well, when I was small mother used to always brief me on how to behave when we went anywhere. If I went to someone's house then I was expected to behave in a certain way and was always rewarded when I did so. If I didn't do what she expected then I was punished—not physically... perhaps I wouldn't have things I wanted or perhaps mother would become ill or something like that, but I knew when I had to behave. After father died it became more and more important to her that she knew just what I was up to. I used to plan my day and tell her about my plans and then she would check on my progress. When I went to college I was still living at home—mother used to plan my work and my time and my money and I just learned how to do it from her.

T: So your mother shaped your behavior, Gill. Tell me about your relationships with others.

P: Well, I found that on my first date this boy was, well what we call "keen"... he kept feeling my breasts when we were dancing and making suggestions. I could feel myself getting worked up and I didn't know what to do... I was all confused and I hate that... I told you, I like to know just where I am.... So I decided that my relationships with men and with my friends (some of whom would drop their pants for anyone!) should be careful and planned.... You'll not believe this, but I once wrote out a list of how to be with a boy... you know, date 1 holding hands and kissing with mouth shut; date 2 holding hands and kissing with mouth open; date 3 kissing with mouth open and letting him touch my breasts outside my clothes... and I actually kept to that schedule... it looks funny looking back at it....

T: ... but it is the kind of plan your mother would have expected?

P: Yes, well... no... I mean, she wouldn't have expected me to... well, you know... Anyway, since then I have been careful about the way I relate to others, and...

T [interrupts]: It's time to throw the dice again, Gill.

Gill was clearly frustrated by having to curtail her exposition, but complied. The dice this time took her to item 5. Before she began to speak I reminded her that she only had five minutes. She got angry:

P: Now look, I have waited a week to tell you about this and you tell me we only have five minutes! What in hell's name is going on here?

T: I am listening, Gill, you have four and a half minutes.

P: Typical! Typical! All my life I have had to plan to get what I want and well over half the time I get frustrated by other people. Now it's you! You sit there pontificating and telling me to do this and to do that and then I get pushed around. Well, I am not having it with you or anyone else, I am just through with it [begins to cry]... I can't go on any longer.

T: You still have time to tell me something about it, Gill.

P: I haven't got time! I haven't! It would take over this whole session to tell you about my frustration, about the way I have screwed up my career and about the way my mother manipulated me and about how I feel trapped.... I haven't got time and now it's too late. It's too late here and it's too late for anything, I am trapped.

T: ... and whenever you feel trapped like this, you get angry and then you start to get depressed, is that right, Gill?

P: Oh, we're back to the instant diagnosis again are we!

T: I asked a question, Gill...

P: I heard you, for Christ's sake, I heard you! Well... [calming down] I suppose so... I suppose you're right... [wiping her eyes and beginning to take control of herself]... if I am not angry then I am depressed... and recently, well until I started seeing you, I have just been depressed . . . it was as if I couldn't even be bothered to get angry anymore . . . that's how depressed I was.

T: Time to throw the dice again, Gill.

P [looking defiant and on the edge of tears]: I'm sorry, I can't go on with this . . . it's too much . . .

T: What you are saying is that you won't go on with this, is that right, Gill? It's not that you can't go on with this, it's that you don't want to, isn't it, Gill?

P: I don't want to go on with this . . . no.

T: Are you clear about what it is that you *do* want, Gill?

P [sobbing]: . . . No . . . I don't know where to start. . . .

T: Are you missing your mother's guidance, Gill?

[At this point Gill cries for about two minutes continuously.]

This interchange provided a further element for my hypothesis about Gill. The hypothesis can be thought of as having the following components: (a) Gill is a highly telic person who plans ahead and seeks to avoid arousal; (b) Gill has planned ahead and sought to avoid arousal for so long that she is satiated within this metamotivational state (*telic*) but appears unable either to shift within this state or to achieve a reversal into another state; (c) this failure to achieve a reversal or a shift is the source of her depression, which in turn is producing a degree of self-negativism; (d) the self-negativism is in itself arousing, and this leads her to experience anger as the learned alternative to depression—increasing the number of anger incidents in therapy appears to be revealing more about the underlying dynamics of Gill's life; (e) the self-negativism and the depression are both related to her current frustration to perceive future goals and her consequent feeling of entrapment; and (f) in the past, her failure to perceive new goals and tasks has been something which others gave attention to, but now she has no one to provide new goals or purposes for her and this too adds to her feelings of depression. The consequence of this interpretation for Gill is that she will continue to alternate between depression and self-negativism or anger while she persists in her feeling of pointlessness. The consequences for therapy are that it is time to choose between seeking out new goals that make sense to Gill and restore the satisfactions of her telic orientation or seeking to promote some reversals between the telic and paratelic states. Given that our contract was for a brief therapeutic intervention (only eight sessions), I felt that the first of these therapeutic options was the most appropriate for Gill. It is also the option most likely to be attainable.

I ended the fourth session of her therapy by sharing my hypothesis about her depression and negativism and by drawing her attention once again to the importance of goals in her life. I observed the role her mother had played historically in the development of goals and how the need for goals had so permeated her life that she had lost the ability to relax in the telic state or to see goals in the context of change and development occuring throughout adult life. I pointed out that her essential reason for depression was that she had achieved the goals she had set herself and was now empty of goals. She needed more if she was to continue to develop as a person. What is more, she needed to feel that she "owned" these goals—that they were genuinely from within her—and that they were not imposed from outside. To recognize and own some new goals would enable her to feel satisfaction in itself, even before she began to work on achieving the goals.

Throughout my exposition of this interpretation, Gill remained motionless but very attentive. At the end of the exposition she said simply, "*The black hole has a white star and the leaves are growing.*" The hypothesis appeared to be accurate. I asked her to consider what goals were important for her and to give thought not to *how* she could achieve them (or to the problems associated with them) but to just *what* the goals might be. She agreed to come to session 5 with some goals.

So far the therapy with Gill had used explanation, interpretation, and paradoxical intervention using drama and a dice-based confronting strategy. All these therapeutic tools were intended to increase arousal, to create a need for Gill to experience that arousal and interpret it for herself, and to facilitate the release of negative and positive emotions. Another way of saying this is that a variety of methods were employed to test a hypothesis that in itself was derived from the theory of psychological reversals. The next stage of therapy would require the use of other strategies.

## SESSIONS 5 TO 8

I had decided that the goal of therapy was to restore active coping in the telic metamotivational state—achieving reversal was a goal for a therapeutic contract with Gill other than the one under which I was now working. This meant that I needed to facilitate: (a) the identification of goals and tasks and the ownership of the significance of these; (b) the restoration of relaxation; and (c) the removal of self-negativistic responses to arousal. All these therapeutic tasks derive from my understanding of reversal theory. I shared these observations during a routine supervision session. My colleague agreed that these tasks were appropriate for Gill given the way in which the therapy had developed. He suggested that some form of relaxation training may be appropriate, since he felt strongly that Gill needed to be taught that relaxation was a realistic alternative to depression once goals had begun to be worked on and she felt that arousal was low.

Gill arrived at the fifth session 15 minutes early. She looked much more confident than she had been on the previous two occasions and her conversational tone was normal and her voice modulated appropriately during conversation. Gone was the outward portrayal of apathy and depression. Before I could begin the session, Gill took command:

P: Right now, before we start, Stephen, I have something to say. On the last two occasions we have met you have pushed me into a corner and I have become angry and been very upset. So angry that I swore at you and that I have cried. Since I saw you last I have decided that I am old enough to be able to deal with the kind of anger that you generated, and I want you to know that I am not going to even start playing any of your games this week. Is that clear?

T [smiling, and humorously]: Perfectly, ma'am.

P: What I am going to do is to talk to you about what I have decided to do . . .

Gill then outlined three goals she had decided were appropriate for her. The first was to sell the house her mother had left her—"too many memories and too much pain . . . in any case, I need the money and do not need a four-bedroom house . . . also, I think a two-bedroom apartment is much more manageable. . . ." She had already placed the property in the hands of a real estate company. The second goal was to work toward opening her own business—"After all, I have virtually run the one I work for and I am qualified in business. . . . I am sure that I can manage. . . ." Her final goal was by far the most ambitious, at least to me—"The next thing is that I am going to stop being so miserable about myself. . . . I've wallowed in self-pity and pain for too long." She looked pleased with herself. The session progressed as follows:

T: Do you mind if I speak now?

P: Of course not, I haven't shocked you?
T: Why should you shock me.... No, I am pleased that you have taken my advice to identify goals so seriously, though I do hope that you haven't moved too quickly in seeking to implement them. Remember, I asked you to look at *what* the goals might be not *how* you might achieve them. But no, what strikes me, Gill, is this... where has all this energy come from? When you first came here it was like looking at and talking to a China doll whose batteries were flat! Now I feel that I am receiving messages from a ghetto blaster!
P [laughs]: ... I don't know where this energy is coming from, I only hope it can last [looks serious]. It will last, won't it?
T: That is up to you and the way in which events unfold.... None of what you have mentioned sounds easy and all will be challenging....

It is obvious from these extracts that the tone and focus of this session are markedly different from those of sessions 1 to 4. What is more, at no time in this session did Gill show any signs of anger, apathy, depression, or fear. Instead, the session was characterized by calmness, occasional amusement, and a kind of certainty that had not been evident before.

Toward the end of the session I suggested that some activity intended to release energy and, at the same time, to promote relaxation would be beneficial. I indicated that I felt that Gill had a reserve of energy which remained underutilized and that a particular form of dynamic meditation (Rajneesh, 1983; Murgatroyd, 1985b) would be a valuable skill to develop. I gave some instruction and provided her with a tape especially made for the meditation, which involves shaking, dancing, swirling, and total relaxation. I asked her to engage in this activity each evening for the remainder of the therapy and to regard this as a task that I attached importance to on her behalf. She agreed to undertake the meditation, but not on these terms. She said, "I do have energy and I will try your suggestion ... if I like it I will continue, if I don't I will return your tape in due course." I began to suspect that she had been to an assertiveness training course since I saw her last!

In many ways, this was a remarkable session. It marked an abrupt change in Gill, which can only be accounted for by events outside the therapy. One of these, I learned later, was her decision to finally get rid of her mother's belongings and clothes (except for photographs and jewelry), which had remained in the house since her death. Another was the decision of her company to reduce the number of stores in the area—Gill felt that one of these was a viable business concern that she could make profitable if the overheads were reduced. These two events were significant for Gill. She later wrote about them:

...What the therapy did at this stage was make me more sensitive to events outside me. I felt that the therapy challenged me and led me to want to find a challenge. Both the decision to break my ties (which were still very physical—clothes and furniture) to my mother and the decision to become a business entrepreneur were the result of looking for a challenge. I am not sure, looking back, whether the therapy I had had (which hurt like hell for the first few sessions) made me want to prove something to Stephen ... but I certainly wanted to prove something to myself.

This letter (written to a friend, and shown to me by Gill for the purpose of completing this case study) makes clear that she had made her mind up to work with some goals and tasks that she felt she owned. By session 5, then, a major task of the therapy had been achieved.

The sixth session was spent discussing her reaction to the meditation technique I had asked her to try. She said that she at first found it strange. The technique is physically very demanding. It begins with the person shaking for 15 minutes, followed by 15 minutes of dancing, then 15 minutes of relaxation, and then 15 minutes of swaying and gently rocking. The audiotape I had provided is a tape of music specially recorded for this purpose. Gill had completed this meditation each day for seven days. She said that "it gave me so much energy and I felt so calm that I have enjoyed the sensation of relaxation more than anything else I have experienced in the last five or six months." She said that the use of an hour a day for the purpose of deliberately trying to relax while at the same time using a lot of energy had had a kind of purging effect. We explored the meaning of "purging" for her—she made clear that it involved, at least at this stage in her life, "getting rid of all the feelings of being destructive to herself," which I saw as a statement about actively seeking to rid herself of her self-negativism. I used this observation to explore with her the idea of retroflection and the objects in the social world which she really felt negativism toward. It became clear that the objects were largely her own lack of spontaneity and her feeling of a lack of direction in her employment and in her social life. The session ended by me asking whether she needed further sessions. We agreed that she should come in the next week and that the eighth session would be a month after the seventh—a follow-up session.

The seventh session was a detailed exploration of her emotional experience of being active again. She made clear that the plans and tasks she had set herself had a high level of ownership for her and that she was "restored." I asked her how she dealt with frustrations and uncertainty and with the need to be more spontaneous, now that she was running her own business (she had bought her store). This is her reply and the exchange that followed:

P: I have given this some thought. I think I am more willing to take risks, somehow. One reason is that I really feel, perhaps for the first time, that I am doing things which I planned and I decided upon. Almost everything else I have achieved was under the direction of my mother. I hadn't realized just how significant that was for me, until I decided that it was time I made my own mind up. Now that I have sold the house, sold her things, started on my own as far as work is concerned and started to relax for the first time in my life (at least it feels like that), I am much more able to take each day as it comes. So, I think I am slowly being able to live an easier life, though it is hectic.

T: Gill, can I ask you something. Did you attend your mother's funeral?

P [looks mournful and a little hurt at this question]: No . . . no . . . I didn't. . . . I made all the arrangements and made sure that all the practical things had been taken care of . . . but on the morning itself I . . . I . . . just collapsed and couldn't face it . . . that was four years ago . . . I have felt guilty about it since . . . .

T: But now you feel that you have attended to the burial as well. Is that what the sale of her clothes and possessions was about, Gill?

P: Yes, yes, I think so. I had wanted to feel as if I was no longer dependent on her. You see, I had achieved all the ambitions she had for me . . . I had got what she wanted . . . but somehow this left me feeling empty. Now, well, what I feel now is that I have my own plans. . . . I mean, I am grateful for the guidance and help and love my mother gave me . . . don't get me wrong . . . but now I feel, well, I am on my own . . . and I should enjoy it.

T: You are no longer willing to feel guilty about having plans of your own?

P: That's it. [smiles] You know me very well, don't you, Stephen?

As is often the case with depression of this type, unresolved issues were at the core of the depression. In this case, the loss-grieving process (see Murgatroyd & Woolfe, 1982; Parkes, 1972) had not been completed, and grief and locus of control issues had remained unresolved for Gill. I used this observation to begin the discussion with Gill about the impact of the termination of therapy. She said that, though I had provided a trigger for her to snap out of her depression, she felt that she had achieved a great deal on her own and was feeling capable of overcoming any difficulty about termination. In any case, she said, we were seeing each other in a month's time and this would provide a basis for her rehearsing life without therapy.

A month later Gill arrived promptly for her final session. She said that she could only stay for an hour (the session was planned to be an hour and a half), but that she thought this would be adequate. She explained that she had been extremely active since I last saw her. She had moved house, her business was beginning to work in a way that she found acceptable, and she had started to go out with a female friend—Jenny—whom she had met through the community group that had referred her to me. They met each Friday and went to a yoga class and then on for a drink. She said that she had enjoyed Jenny's friendship and had not felt that it needed to be something that was controlled and planned. One of the things that she had learned in therapy, she said, was that even careful plans about what would happen can come to nothing if the other person does not fully share the plan or the need to plan. She referred particularly to session 4 in this discussion.

I asked her to review her therapy. She said that the most critical experience was being forced to realize that the only alternative to depression that she could produce was anger. She particularly identified with the feelings of negativism, which she felt she was strongly directing toward herself. She realized that this must be some kind of displaced anger or hostility. It was only later that she realized that this anger was directed at her mother. The other thing that she felt was important to her was having some features of her personality recognized in the beginning (session 2). For her, knowing that the work we completed was grounded in something she herself could understand ("it wasn't all mumbo-jumbo and black magic") meant that she was willing to trust me when I asked her to do some drama work or the dice work.

After an hour of this discussion and evaluation, the session ended, and my contact with Gill was over—at least so I thought.

Three months later Gill wrote to me—a kind of thank you and evaluation letter. Here is the text:

Dear Stephen,
It is some time since my last session. It occurs to me that I did not really thank you. When I came to you I was very depressed and so exhausted that I felt near to the point at which life would seem pointless—you made me feel that there was an explanation for how I felt and that I could overcome the depression.

You challenged me in a number of ways. I understand now that you were trying to get me back on the telic curve (I hope that's the right term); at the time, though, I thought you were cruel and hard on me. I kept hearing my mother say that "nice" people are always kind and considerate and that your behavior meant that you were not a nice person. So, I thought bad thoughts about you. But then I started to think about the way I had always been controlled by mother and about the way in which I felt that, even though she was dead, she still controlled me.

The one thing I have given a lot of thought to since we met (we've been very busy at work) is why I did not go to her funeral. It seems to me that I was afraid of seeing her being cremated and knowing that, from that moment, I was on my own. I think a lot of the anger I had was about knowing that I was free from her influence and yet not knowing what to do with my freedom. You helped me find this issue, so I have to thank you for that.

One more thing. I do really want to thank you for the meditation. I still do it each day (unless something else has happened). It gives me such a tranquil feeling and it's so reliable that, well, I think you should tell all of your clients to do it!

So, thank you, Stephen. If you ever need any cosmetics let me know.

Gill

This was my last significant contact with Gill. Though there appear to be many unresolved issues in her life that she may one day wish to discuss, Gill is certainly not currently depressed.

## CONCLUDING COMMENTS

This case study indicates the way in which a body of theory about the person and about the structural impact of therapy (Murgatroyd & Apter, 1984, 1985) can be used to provide a rationale for eclectic therapy. In my work with Gill I used a variety of techniques from paradoxical intention to meditation as devices for changing the way in which Gill experienced arousal. In terms of her depression, changing both the level of her arousal experience and the way in which these experiences were interpreted by her was critical to the change in her phenomenal field. These interventions were derived from my understanding of her presenting problem in terms of the theory of reversals and in terms of my understanding of the likely impact of these therapeutic interventions on both her arousal and motivational systems. Reversal theory thus guided my hypothesis about Gill and my assumptions about the impact of therapy on Gill.

Other cases using reversal theory have been published (Blackmore & Murgatroyd, 1980; Murgatroyd, 1981; Murgatroyd & Apter, 1984, 1985) which illuminate the way in which the theory of psychological reversals offers a framework for eclectic practice. The case reported here illuminates some limited features of the eclectic model—the other reported case illuminate different facets of this approach. It is hoped that the case of Gill illuminates the nature of structural phenomenological eclectic practice.

## REFERENCES

Apter, M. J. (1982). *The experience of motivation—The theory of psychological reversals*. London: Academic Press.

Apter, M. J., & Smith, K. C. P. (1985). Experiencing personal relationships. In M. J. Apter, D. Fontana, & S. Murgatroyd (Eds.), *Reversal theory—Applications and developments*. Cardiff: University College Cardiff Press.

Beck, A. T. (1976). *Cognitive therapy and the emotional disorders*. New York: International Universities Press.

Blackmore, M., & Murgatroyd, S. (1980). Anne—The disruptive infant. In S. Murgatroyd (Ed.), *Helping the troubled child—Interprofessional case studies*. London: Harper and Row.

Blinder, M. G. (1966). The pragmatic classification of depression. *American Journal of Psychiatry, 123*, 259–269.

Coleman Nelson, M. (1962). Effects of paradigmatic techniques on the psychic economy of borderline patients. *Psychiatry, 25* (2), 119–134.

Costello, C. G. (1972). Depression—Loss of reinforcement or loss of reinforcer effectiveness? *Behavior Therapy, 3*, 240–247.

Eastman, C. (1976). Behavioural formulations of depression. *Psychology Review, 83*, 277–291.

Ellis, A. (1962). *Reason and emotion in psychotherapy*. New York: Lyle Stuart.

Ferster, C. B. (1973). A functional analysis of depression. *American Psychologist, 28*, 857–870.

Foulds, G. A., & Bedford, A. (1976). Classification of depressive illness—A re-evaluation. *Psychological Medicine, 6*, 15–19.

Haley, J. (1974). *Ordeal therapy*. San Francisco: Jossey-Bass.

Hersen, M., Eisler, R. M., Alford, G. S., & Agras, W. S. (1973). Effects of token economy on neurotic depression—An experimental analysis. *Behavior Therapy, 4*, 392–397.

Johnstone, K. (1981). *Impro—Improvisation and the theatre*. London: Macmillan.

Kendell, R. E. (1976). The classification of depressions—A review of contemporary confusion. *British Journal of Psychiatry, 129*, 15–28.

Lazarus, A. A. (1968). Learning theory and the treatment of depression. *Behaviour Research and Therapy, 6*, 87–89.
Lazarus, A. A. (1976). *Multi-modal behavior therapy.* New York: Springer.
Lewis, A. J. (1938). States of depression—Their clinical and aetiological differentiation. *British Medical Journal, 2,* 875–878.
Mandler, G. (1975). *Mind and emotion.* New York: Wiley.
Meichenbaum, D. (1977). *Cognitive behavior modification—An integrative approach.* New York: Plenum Press.
Minuchin, S., & Fishman, H. C. (1981). *Family therapy techniques.* Cambridge, MA: Harvard University Press.
Moss, G. R., & Boren, J. H. (1972). Depression as a model for behavioral analysis. *Comprehensive Psychiatry, 13,* 581–590.
Murgatroyd, S. (1981). Reversal theory—A new perspective on crisis counselling. *British Journal of Guidance and Counselling, 9,* 180–193.
Murgatroyd, S. (1985a). Introduction to reversal theory. In M. J. Apter, D. Fontana, & S. Murgatroyd (Eds.), *Reversal theory—Applications and developments.* Cardiff: University of College Cardiff Press.
Murgatroyd, S. (1985b). *Counselling and helping.* London: British Psychological Society and Methuen Books.
Murgatroyd, S., & Apter, M. J. (1984). Eclectic psychotherapy—A structural phenomenological approach. In W. Dryden (Ed.), *Individual therapy in Britain.* London: Harper and Row.
Murgatroyd, S., & Apter, M. J. (1985). A structural phenomenological approach to eclectic psychotherapy. In J. C. Norcross (Ed.), *The handbook of eclectic psychotherapy.* New York: Brunner/Mazel.
Murgatroyd, S., & Woolfe, R. (1982). *Coping with crisis—Understanding and helping people in need.* London: Harper and Row.
Murgatroyd, S., Rushton, C., Apter, M. J., & Ray, C. (1978). The development of the telic dominance scale. *Journal of Personality Assessment, 42,* 519–528.
Overall, J. E., Hollister, L. E., Johnson, M., & Rennington, V. (1966). Nosology of depression and differential responses to drugs. *Journal of the American Medical Association, 195,* 946–950.
Parkes, C. (1972). *Bereavement—Studies of grief in adult life.* London: Tavistock.
Paykel, E. S. (1971). The classification of depressed patients—A cluster analysis derived grouping. *British Journal of Psychiatry, 118,* 275–288.
Perls, F., Hefferline, R. F., & Goodman, P. (1973). *Gestalt therapy—Excitement and growth in the human personality.* Harmondsworth: Penguin. (Originally published in 1951 in the U.S.)
Pollitt, J. (1965). Suggestions for a physiological classification of depression. *British Journal of Psychiatry, 111,* 489–495.
Rajneesh, B. S. (1983). *The orange book—The meditation techniques of Bhagwan Shree Rajneesh.* Rajneeshpuram, Oregon: Rajneesh Foundation.
Riebel, L. (1984). Paradoxical intention strategies—A review of rationales. *Psychotherapy, 21,* 260–272.
Rinehart, L. (1972). *The dice man: A novel.* London: Granada.
Rumke, H. C. (1960). *Psychiatrie* (Vol. 2). Amsterdam: Scheltema en Holkeman.
Seligman, H. E. P. (1975). *Helplessness.* San Francisco: Freeman.
Smith, K. C. P., & Apter, M. J. (1975). *A theory of psychological reversals.* Chippenham, England: Picton Publishing.
Snaith, R. P., Bridge, G. W. K., & Hamilton, M. (1976). The Leeds Scale for the self-assessment of anxiety and depression. *British Journal of Psychiatry, 128,* 156–165.

# Commentary: Why Not More Phenomenology and Less Structure?

## Joseph Hart

*The task of commenting on this chapter is not an easy one because I found much to admire, several features of the approach I did not like, and much to question. To put all of these impressions and thoughts together in a few pages will be difficult—perhaps the best way to do it is the direct way.*

### WHAT I LIKED

*The therapist managed to blend a variety of techniques in truly ingenious ways. His use of a "feeling diary," role-playing, photographs of the client and her relatives, homework assignments, paradoxical interpretations, meditation instructions, and* the teaching of the theory to the client were all combined into an effective and innovative professional approach. I thought that his use of the dice technique to teach role flexibility and enhance feeling expressiveness beyond the client's usual boundaries was especially impressive. (I had read the novel **The Dice Man** several years ago but Murgatroyd's is the first therapeutic application that I have heard about.) I believe it is extremely important that therapists draw widely from the arts and the culture at large in our search for techniques and ideas and not confine ourselves to whatever is currently normative and accepted within professional circles.

The author described sessions 2 through 4 as focused on "exploration and exaggeration." His willingness to encourage emotional expressiveness that took the client outside her typical meanings and feelings was impressive. All too often clients spend weeks and months talking about themselves from emotional ruts simply because therapists pay more attention to the content of their talk than the style. Murgatroyd showed a real deftness in directing Gill to attend to the ways in which she expressed herself as well as what she said. By attending to the theatrical side of the communications, the therapist was able to challenge, directly, the long-established, restrictive meanings that Gill had attached to being angry, depressed, and aroused.

## WHAT I DISLIKED

Most of my problems with this chapter were with the theory that seemed to be guiding the therapist; in other words, I was concerned not with what he did (which in most instances I found desirable) but with his explanations. Part of my difficulty with the author's explanations is undoubtedly due to my own unfamiliarity with structural phenomenological psychotherapy. My own training and reading have included the study of phenomenological and existential theorists such as Rollo May, Medard Boss, and Eugene Gendlin, but I find their emphases to be quite different from those of Murgatroyd and his colleagues. For one thing, the emphasis is often on attending to the phenomena as they are and noticing changes that emerge. In contrast, Murgatroyd typically imposes meanings and changes on the client's experiences, basing these impositions (or interventions) on structural theory. One hopes that the theory is awfully good and complete—if it is not, there are real dangers of prescriptive phenomenology, i.e., teaching the client to have the experiences and meanings that fit the theory. By and large, that is what Albert Ellis does in his rational-emotive therapy. Although a certain amount of prescriptive phenomenology is required in any kind of therapy, it is well to be cautious; the therapist should certainly, in my view, be more of a follower than a leader when exploring the client's inner world.

My second caveat relates to the author's failure to do anything with the symbols presented by his client. He does report them but does not say anything about how they were discussed. The central symbol Gill used to describe herself in the first session was "having a black hole inside me that wants to engulf me and take me over." She interpreted later sessions of the therapy as forcing her to confront the black hole. Finally, she reported a new image of the black hole, with a white star and growing leaves. This symbolism deserves more attention. Within many therapeutic approaches Gill would have been encouraged to relate to the symbol, through dialogues and drawings or paintings. Because this kind of phenomenological work does not seem to fit within Murgatroyd's telic theory and methodology, the wider meanings of the symbolism remain unexamined for Gill. This seems to me to be a real loss in the client's therapeutic experience because she has lost not only the oppportunity to know herself more deeply through understanding her special symbols but also the opportunity to learn a process of symbolic working through that she could have used creatively in the future.

**FURTHER QUESTIONS**

I have been stimulated by Mr. Murgatroyd's chapter and will certainly read several of the references he cites about the work he and his colleagues have done. When I read those works, I will be extremely curious to see how they relate to phenomenological, teleological, and existential theorists who have very much influenced my own thinking.

First, I am curious to know how the telic conceptualizations of Apter and Murgatroyd relate to those of Joseph Rychlak. For decades now, Rychlak has been arguing, against the mainstream, for the necessity of telic theorizing in psychology. How would Apter and Murgatroyd relate structural phenomenology to Rychlak's rigorous humanism? (see Rychlak, 1968 and 1977.)

Next, I would like to know how structural phenomenology relates to Gendlin's experiential psychotherapy. Specifically, how would structural phenomenologists make use of Gendlin's technique of focusing? Focusing is a method that teaches clients how to pay attention to what they are experiencing and to communicate the changes that occur in their experiences. For Gendlin a certain level of focusing skill is considered prerequisite to phenomenological therapy. (Consult Gendlin, 1962, 1979, 1981.)

Finally, I would like to evaluate how structural phenomenology relates to various classical positions within psychology and psychotherapy. What does structural phenomenology have to say about theories of the unconscious and the subconscious such as those of Freud, Jung, James, and Janet? How does structural phenomenology relate to the ideas of religious phenomenology found in Buber? How does structural phenomenology relate to humanistic psychology as found in the works of Rogers and Maslow?

I suppose all these questions relate to one general question: what is the scope of structural phenomenology? That is a question that is too large to be evaluated within the scope of a commentary, or even a chapter.

**REFERENCES**

Gendlin, E. (1962). Experiencing and the creation of meaning. New York: Free Press.
Gendlin, E. (1979). Experiential psychotherapy. In R. J. Corsini (Ed.), Current Psychotherapies (2nd ed.). Itasca, IL: F. E. Peacock.
Gendlin, E. (1981). Focusing. New York: Bantam.
Rychlak, J. (1968). A philosophy of science for personality theory. Boston: Houghton Mifflin.
Rychlak, J. (1977). The psychology of rigorous humanism. New York: Wiley.

# Commentary: Is There Truth in Psychotherapeutic Packaging?

## Robert N. Sollod

Murgatroyd's "reversal theory" approach to psychotherapy, as illustrated in the case of Gill, provoked an odd array of thoughts and feelings. First, I was thrown off by the ostensible underpinnings of the theory, which purported to be not only structural but also phenomenological as well as eclectic. A great admirer of the ideas of Levi-Strauss, Piaget, Heidegger, Husserl, and Binswanger, not to mention a variety of leaders in developing eclectic psychotherapeutic integrations, I was at first prepared for an intellectual tour de force, in which the essential structure of human experience would be first elucidated and then therapeutically transformed. I was also pleased to see that this new theory did not purport, at least in its packaging, to be scientific—as have so many other psychotherapeutic theories that were anything but scientific (Sollod, 1982).

What Murgatroyd has presented in this case illustration, however, seems to me to be less phenomenological in method and spirit than what he desires it to be. It is, rather, an approach that reduces human experience to a relatively dichotomous labeling system, although using newly invented terms. In my view, Murgatroyd's therapeutic method is no more or less phenomenological than that of a psychopharmacologically-oriented psychiatrist who asks patients how they feel and concludes whether they are depressed based, in large part, on their self-reports. The term *structural* apparently refers to the use of the newly invented labels "telic" and "paratelic," which constitute, according to the theory, a very large part of human experience. Much of the psychotherapeutic process consists of teaching the patient to label his experiences using these terms. Telic and paratelic states are also referred to as "metamotivational"; perhaps the title could have included this term: e.g., "An Eclectic, Phenomenological, Structural, Metamotivational Theory."

There are some therapeutically relevant hypotheses and insights indicated in Murgatroyd's case and in his theory (Murgatroyd & Apter, 1985), which I will present below—in plain English:

1. Normal people are sometimes serious and sometimes playful.
2. It is not good to be serious or goal-oriented all the time. ("All work and no play makes Gill a sick girl!")
3. It is not good to play all the time either.
4. It is best to be calm and relaxed when engaged in goal-oriented behavior and to be more excited when playful.
5. The therapist should help a person to be serious and playful at the right times, to be calm when goal-oriented and more playful when excited.
6. Whatever the therapist can do to facilitate these goals is encouraged (eclecticism?).
7. A good way to tell whether clients have been playful or serious is to ask them (phenomenology?).

This psychotherapeutic approach does seem, as indicated by Murgatroyd and Apter (1985), to have some useful applications. It is not clear what is added by calling it a structural, phenomenological theory, when it has more to do with labeling of play and work states and assessing high and low arousal. I prefer to call Murgatroyd and Apter's approach "work and play psychotherapy."

The case history does illustrate an important use for theory—that it gives the therapist something to believe in, something to be interested in, as well as something to do. Such sincere therapist belief and optimism have been demonstrated to be an important placebo in outcome research. In addition, the client is given a relatively nonthreatening structure within which she can recount major events in her life, express feelings, and initiate new behaviors. No doubt the packaging of Murgatroyd's approach will attract the attention and encourage the involvement of other therapists and investigators for whom the terms "structural," "phenomenological," and "eclectic" are appealing. What more can one ask of a theory?

The case history indicates not so much the effectiveness of Murgatroyd's approach but rather the importance of therapist encouragement, a caring relationship, and the efficacy of catharsis. Gill's case also *illustrates conventional Freudian dynamics in mourning and depression. Gill's depression appears to result from an intrapunitive reaction to the loss of her mother. In the course of therapy, she grieves, gets in touch with her angry feelings, and becomes mobilized in dealing with her own life. Discussion of such psychodynamics is a notable lacuna in an otherwise wideranging eclecticism. If anything, the case supports Wachtel's (1977) integrative psychodynamic approach, in which action and insight reinforce one another.*

*The case of Gill illustrates a major fallacy in the development of new psychotherapeutic approaches—the classic* post hoc, ergo propter hoc *fallacy. The psychotherapeutic version is "If a therapist informed with a given psychotherapeutic approach works closely with a patient and the patient improves, then the theory is demonstrated [invalidly, we hasten to remind the reader] to be true."*

*There are valid psychotherapeutic roles for some of the concepts of reversal theory and related psychotherapeutic techniques. It is hoped that a more modest and appropriate theoretical superstructure can be developed for this theory. In addition, carefully conducted outcome research, in which various ingredients of therapeutic impact are explored, is clearly a necessity. The intriguing concepts of reversal theory, as presented in the case of Gill, do not appear to be comprehensive enough to constitute a new psychotherapeutic school. It is quite possible, however, that some of the ideas and methods presented in this case will be found to be effective. They might be used selectively with certain clients or integrated into other, more comprehensive psychotherapeutic approaches.*

## REFERENCES

Murgatroyd, S., & Apter, M. J. (1985). A structural phenomenological approach to eclectic psychotherapy. In J. C. Norcross (Ed.), Handbook of Eclectic Psychotherapy. *New York: Brunner/Mazel.*

Sollod, R. (1982). Non-scientific sources of psychotherapeutic approaches. In P. Sharkey (Ed.), Philosophy, religion and psychotherapy. *Washington, DC: University Press of America.*

Wachtel, P. (1977). Psychoanalysis and behavior therapy: Toward an integration. *New York: Basic Books.*

CHAPTER 12

# Spontaneous Insight Associated with Behavior Therapy: The Case of Rex

## *Douglas H. Powell*

A widely recognized—but little discussed—phenomenon among clinicians using behavior therapy is the client's spontaneous recognition of psychodynamic factors associated with symptom formation. These insights frequently are accompanied by powerful new affects and thoughts. Often, these events are difficult to anticipate during the diagnostic phase of the treatment process.

Lazarus (1981) writes of this occurring in the case of a 32-year-old male with multiple problems, including anxiety attacks, hypochondriasis, and chronic dependence on his mother. While proceeding with the desensitization process, the man was asked to imagine coping with anxiety by becoming ill while alone in a strange city. Lazarus describes a powerful moment when the client recollected an unconscious memory.

At this point the client started hyperventilating, sobbing, retching, heaving, and panicking . . . a "forgotten memory" . . . evoked a full-blown abreaction. When he finally calmed down, he recounted vivid memories of an event that took place when he was seven years of age. He was in a hospital after a tonsillectomy and was coming out of the anesthetic, when he could barely make out some people hovering around his bed. His mother was talking to someone about his frail and sickly make-up. "I hope he lives to see 21," she declared. (pp. 24–25)

As therapy progressed, the client recognized that he internalized this statement and became the fragile person his mother assumed that he was.

Kuhlman (1982) tells of behaviorally treating a married, 23-year-old, male business student who failed four examinations in a row. During the assessment interview the client—an unusually rigid and nonintrospective individual—was unwilling to discuss his personal life, could recall almost nothing about his early years, and wondered why this was relevant anyway. Not surprisingly, little important information was uncovered as to what intrapsychic conflicts might be fueling his problems. Following several muscle relaxation exercises, Kuhlman and the client constructed a fear hierarchy relevant to the test anxiety problems. At a point midway through the construction of the hierarchy, Kuhlman encouraged the client to visualize a scene with his wife before an examination. Eventually, the scene was written this way:

I'm downstairs at breakfast. My wife asked what I'm doing today and I tell her I have a math exam. "Well," she says sarcastically, "you'd better do well on this test or else." Now I feel anxious with some angry feelings as well, but I don't let on. Still her sarcastic threat has triggered a loss of self-confidence. (p. 90)

When the client was asked what "or else" meant, he denied it had any significance or that his marriage was in any way related to his text anxiety.

In the next meeting the client said he had been thinking about his marriage and had begun to consider that it might be part of the problem. He went on to talk about his in-laws—with whom he and his wife were living—their control of him, and his feelings he could not compete successfully with both his wife and father-in-law. When the implications of this were pointed out to the client, he acknowledged them but didn't wish to pursue them further.

A week later the client reported that he had taken the examination and obtained a "B." He also began a discussion with his wife about separating, but showed little interest in exploring his marital problems.

Other evidence accumulating from both the laboratory and clinical practice suggests that a significant minority of individuals treated with behavior therapy experience unanticipated, upsetting feelings, thoughts, and other discomfort. Heide and Borkovec (1983) documented evidence of anxiety reactions in 5 of 14 men and women practicing relaxation training in their psychological laboratory. In addition, 31% of their subjects who received progressive muscle relaxation, and 54% of those who were given relaxation, reported increased tension. These findings are consistent with the second author's previous reports of the unintended effects of behavioral treatment (Borkovec & Grayson, 1980; Borkovec & Sides, 1979; Borkovec & Hennings, 1978.)

Clinicians Jacobsen and Edinger (1982) reported that two of their patients developed severe anxiety or muscle cramps as side effects of muscle relaxation. In addition to increases in anxiety, scattered reports have appeared noting other effects of behavioral treatment with relaxation or systematic desensitization. These include depression, depersonalization, obsessive thinking, and impulsive fantasies (Fitzpatrick, 1983; Rickles, Onoda, & Doyle, 1982; Marks, 1971; Lazarus, 1963).

What is so intriguing about these scattered case and laboratory findings is that the behavioral treatment was applied to achieve another result. The affective changes, symptom alteration, or insights into the psychic origins of the presenting symptoms emerged unbidden, without prompting from the therapist. Furthermore, the potential for these unexpected developments was anticipated neither by the initial assessment of these clients and laboratory subjects nor in previous psychotherapy.

These reports are consistent with my clinical experience using behavior therapy to alleviate target symptoms. A substantial minority of clients react with unexpected changes in affect, cognition, or action. The paradoxical effects, noted by Heide and Borkovec, occur: One woman experiences bouts of anxiety while trying to relax and another is overcome by sadness; a junior faculty member becomes terrified by dreams following the process of relieving headaches by self-hypnosis and imagery and finds himself becoming furious. Then we observe acute distress leading to sudden insight as Lazarus' case suggests: During autogenic training to relieve cold hands, a graduate student starts sobbing quietly as she recollects a painful memory about a sister favored by her parents; a senior staff assistant, treated with EMG and imagery for a long-standing inability to use the right hand for writing because of a psychogenic tremor, recalls with considerable emotional upheaval the moment she lost the use of that hand at age 13 after she punched her mother.

Not all insight is attended by psychic discomfort: A 36-year-old scientific researcher receiving progressive muscle relaxation for back spasms begins to note that he tenses up in particular situations—going to the laboratory and coming home to the woman he lives with; a law student given a range of behavioral treatment for compulsive picking and hair pulling, recognizes how unhappy she is at the thought of being a lawyer.

Finally, behavioral changes occur which are striking to those close to the clients: The colleagues of an admissions officer treated with hypnosis, relaxation, and imagery for bruxism wonder whether he has taken a course in assertiveness training; a friend, who has not seen a nurse for a year given biofeedback and relaxation for stomach pains, comments that she seems different, more businesslike, and tougher.

All of these patients, and many like them, were given psychotherapy along with behavior therapy to help them understand the reasons for their distress. This is not such a radical notion. Behavior therapists point out that they are indeed responsive to unintended distress or spontaneous insights generated during the course of relieving target symptoms. In the process, they may use a range of psychotherapeutic techniques to assist the client in consolidating new awarenesses (Walker, Hedberg, Clement, & Wright, 1981).

My experience suggests that behavior therapy can promote sudden awareness into factors connected to the presenting symptom. Or treatment can lead to a recognition of upsetting affects associated with the disorder. I believe the therapists employing behavioral treatment may have a unique opportunity to assist their clients by responding to these new, unanticipated developments by integrating psychotherapy into the overall therapeutic program. This can help them in understanding these spontaneous cognitions and emotions as well as consolidating the material to produce better mental and physical health.

## THE CASE OF REX

The case of Rex illustrates the emergence of spontaneous insight into several of the dynamic factors associated with his presenting symptom—performance anxiety—during a short period of successfully treating this problem behaviorally. At his initiative there followed nine meetings for psychotherapy in which an effort was made to help him understand some of the intrapsychic forces contributing to the onset and maintenance of his performance anxiety. Follow-up meetings several months later helped him consolidate these gains.

Rex was selected as someone to illustrate this particular theoretical perspective for three reasons: (1) his treatment was coincident with the need for me to have a case to present in this *Casebook*; (2) the course of integrated therapy was representative and neither particularly unusual nor dramatic; and (3) after reading all the materials describing the book, he was willing to participate.

Rex came to the mental health clinic because he had severe inhibitions about public speaking. He felt this to be a massive handicap because he was a first-year doctoral student at the Kennedy School of

Government and had aspirations for a political career. In addition, he worked part time for a nonprofit, lobbying organization. This required him to speak 20 to 30 times a year.

At our first meeting he had been taking propranolol regularly for more than two years to control his anxiety. Previously, he used Valium for a decade. Even with medication, his symptoms when he spoke or thought about it were heavy perspiration, pounding heart, and muscle tension. In class, his powerful dread of talking in class caused him to remain silent. This upset Rex for two reasons: (1) he wanted to engage in classroom discussion to impress his professors as well as other students; and (2) because his classes use the case method, which invites discussion, his grades were dependent on how much and how well he spoke in class.

Rex said that he was bothered enormously by this symptom because he felt such a disparity between the way he would like to present himself and the way he currently observed himself. Also, he experienced this as his body out of control, perversely betraying him, frustrating his wishes.

He reported that he had had considerable previous treatment. Further details of Rex's biography and personal style are stated below, excerpted from a larger autobiography written by him at the termination of therapy in May 1985.

The oldest of three sons, I was born in a suburb of St. Louis, Missouri, in 1947. My mother did not attend college and my father completed only a two-year business program, but both were well-read, culturally and politically aware people. My father formed his own travel agency company and was moderately successful. By the time of my college graduation, however, my father manifested signs of acute and chronic alcoholism. My mother's health deteriorated sharply during my mid-teens, when she became afflicted with muscular dystrophy. She died in 1984.

I remember my early childhood as a happy and secure period. I was intensely competitive at an early age, eager for adult approval, and shattered by occasional teacher criticism. Until 16, I sustained an almost unbroken record of high achievement, became recognized as a popular student leader, and generally enjoyed life.

Complications ensued at about the time my mother's disease was diagnosed, a time when my father's alcoholism also may have begun to emerge. During my junior year in high school, I gradually neglected my schoolwork, experienced conflict with some teachers and administrators, and became more alienated, confused, and depressed.

My father arranged for me to see a psychologist for a few weeks, but I stopped shortly after starting. I remained an extremely erratic student for the remainder of high school. The emotional focus of my life became a girl, Karen, whom I met late in my sophomore year. When Karen finally "ended" the relationship one year or so after high school graduation, I took an overdose of over-the-counter sleeping pills to express my despair and helplessness. Other incidents of rage and self-inflicted damage to myself and my possessions took place during late adolescence.

I began to see another psychologist at this point, largely on my own initiative, but paid for by my parents. Issues were primarily related to my perfectionist tendencies. This work, sustained for more than one year, enabled me to return to night school to perform quite effectively and to eventually gain admission to Washington University in St. Louis, from which I later graduated Phi Beta Kappa and summa cum laude in 1971.

By the time I entered graduate school, however, I faced another period of crisis. The University of ―――― graduate program I entered was populated with equally accomplished people, and I could no longer rely on academic excellence as a source of personal distinctiveness and well-being. I felt very threatened by failure and almost immediately sought assistance at the university's counseling center. For approximately seven months I met weekly with a female psychologist. We worked on approval-seeking behavior and the awareness and expression of feelings. With her help, I got through the academic year and completed the two-year program on schedule. Yet, life at ―――― was largely an unhappy and anxious time for me, and I left without feelings of accomplishment or pride.

After graduate school I was offered a job as a community worker on a church staff in ———, where I worked with imagination, effectiveness, and a greater sense of congruence than in any of my previous jobs. I strengthened my relationship with a woman who became my wife while working at the church. This relationship was and remains, a happy, fulfilling, and intimate match.

This period was not trouble-free, however. I also was using tranquilizers to get me through the more frequent public speaking required of me professionally. I began to see a psychiatrist and continued to work with him for about one year, after which I left ——— for a foundation job in ———.

In ——— I arranged to see a psychologist with whom I made really significant progress. In a sense, this therapy involved a recapitulation of every important issue previously raised. When we terminated after two years, I believed I had concluded formal treatment. I had become more confident, with a far greater sense of ease, expressiveness, and efficacy. While in ———, I achieved greater professional notice and made the leap forward to parenthood. Two daughters were born in 1980 and 1982.

I left in 1983 to accept a job in ———. My life here has been exceptionally happy and productive. Increasing this sense of growth and personal gratification was my admission to the Ph.D. program at Harvard.

The one down side of the Harvard experience has been dealing with the lingering public-speaking issue. I have felt handicapped, almost victimized, with a disability I could not fully understand or control without medication. My frustration derives from my own basic sense of competence, from my conviction that I have something to say and can say it in an articulate, persuasive, even forceful manner when I am not inhibited with performance anxiety. This desire to better understand and deal nonmedically with this public-speaking anxiety prompted me to see Dr. Powell.

## THE COURSE OF TREATMENT

Rex was seen by me at the Harvard University Health Services, a comprehensive health maintenance organization serving a population of about 40,000 individuals.

In all, I saw Rex 14 times from December 1984 through May 1985. We then met for eight follow-up sessions in the fall. The first meeting was devoted to diagnosis. During sessions 2, 3, and 4—scheduled approximately biweekly—a behavioral treatment plan was discussed, implemented, and modified as needed. Rex responded positively to this therapy. By the fifth contact, he was essentially symptom-free. Three weeks later, Rex came to my walk-in clinic to discuss his progress and exhibited interest in seeing me on a more regular basis. At this time I discussed with him the possibility of his being a case for this book. There followed nine further sessions until our termination in May 1985. "Pause" was a more correct term than "termination" as I saw him again in the fall of 1985 at his initiative.

The remainder of this section will be devoted to discussion of the four phases of the treatment process—diagnosis, behavior therapy for performance anxiety, the integration of psychotherapy, and follow-up Excerpts from interviews 1, 6, 7, 8-12, and 14 are included to illuminate significant moments in our work together and the nature of the client-therapist working relationship.

*Diagnostic Phase*

*Session 1*

T: What brings you in to see me?
P: Well, basically it's a very specific sort of problem. Since coming here to work and starting school, I have been made reaware of my difficulty in public-speaking situations and felt the frustration and demoralization of feeling so ill at ease in these situations, which are now fairly common or frequent, that I felt that I needed some consultation on how to better understand what I'm ex-

periencing and how to better manage those situations.

T: What kinds of problems have you been having, specifically?

P: Well, essentially it is a tremendous amount of anxiety in these public-speaking situations. In any situation where I'm presenting myself orally, there is a high probability that I would feel such a lot of undue anxiety before the experience that it makes me uncomfortable and may interfere with the quality of the presentation, at least initially.

T: What kinds of symptoms?

P: Symptoms like perspiration, stage fright kind of things, the dry mouth or almost a kind of feeling shaky, or feeling, almost in its worst manifestation, a paniclike symptom of shortness of breath. The intensity of any given episode, it varies. Racing heart, the whole continuum. Again, these symptoms are not absolutely predictable and that's kind of a puzzling feature of this in some ways.

T: How does this affect you in a classroom situation?

P: Well, it may make me hesitant to speak at all in situations where class participation is a requirement. My own life experience over 38 years of being intelligent and extremely articulate in situations where I'm not inhibited in this way—and on many such situations—makes it particularly frustrating for me to perform, to present myself in a less than adequate way. I tried using tranquilizers to calm myself down. I ultimately rejected the dependency on the Valium, for example, to see me through those situations. I really felt unfree in a certain way, and dependent. I then discovered propranolol and found that a far more acceptable way of medicating the problem. However, it doesn't completely dampen down the symptoms of discomfort. So, I feel very, very vulnerable. It is a very extreme sort of vulnerability that I've worked on in conventional kinds of talk therapy. And despite all the concentration and effort, I've not been able to get a handle on the problem.

T: What would you like to happen if this therapy were successful?

P: Well, I would like to be able to feel some significantly greater sense of control and assurance about public-speaking situations, or situations where I'm presenting myself even to small groups. It's not that I want to eliminate tension altogether because I think that often it fuels good performance in whatever context. I want to know going into those situations, that some disaster is not going to befall me, that I'm not going to unravel in front of an audience, that I'm going to be able to present my ideas, my thoughts, or myself, uncontaminated by what I regard as an enormously excessive and completely unwarranted anxiety.

T: Have you had any experience of unraveling?

P: I have had one experience where I was speaking to a professional group of about 15 people in a small room and quite by surprise, with the suddenness of a panic attack, had this anxiety well up and had to interrupt my presentation. It was the worst nightmare one can imagine in a situation like this. That this could happen reinforces the sense of doubt that compounds the problems of going into the next situation.

T: Tell me a bit more about the impact of this anxiety, or whatever, in the classroom situation.

P: Well, uh . . .

T: Now, you're talking about a case method pretty much, are you not?

P: What typically will happen is that I'll formulate an idea, an opinion and feel inclined to voice and then go through a sort of rehearsal, on my own, about expressing that opinion, begin to be quite self-conscious about my role participation in the class. When I go into the mode of preparing to participate, it's as if I'm going on a stage, that I am the lead actor in a role.

T: An actor.

P: I know that there are 15, 75, or 100 out there in the class and no one is really performing in a lead role. Yet, I transformed that into a kind of dichotomous situation in which I'm the performer and everyone else is the audience and is a critical, scrutinizing audience to boot. So, by the time I'm called on, if I can sustain my desire to go through this and get recognized to speak, I've got a feeling that all eyes shift to me. My heart's pounding, and I feel very unnatural . . .

T: Almost an opening-night mentality.

P: Opening-night mentality. In a class, if I can get around to making the second comment, there's a good chance that I'll feel significantly more relaxed. But the opening-night mentality is exactly an excellent metaphor because that is precisely how I feel going into these situations. Though my interpretive comments about a case may be only 1 of 35 comments voiced in the course of an hour and a half, it feels much, much more momentous to me. The funny thing about it is that it's a somewhat variable experience. If I am able, for some reason, to feel at ease and feel that there is no critical dimension to this classroom situation, that things are basically alright for me regardless of what I say or whether I say anything or not, I can hold forth and feel fine.

T: If there were just you and the professor in the class, do you think you'd feel the same amount of anxiety?

P: No, I wouldn't feel the same amount of anxiety. Although, if I endow even another individual with this critical, judgmental, powerful kind of critiquing role capacity, I can make myself uncomfortable and significantly less at ease.

Yet, what I do is even transform that situation, at least momentarily, into one in which I'm double clutching onto some sense of it.

T: You have to perform. Have you explored this problem in previous therapies?

P: Um huh. . . . During my last therapy I explored it with some concentration and, I would say, to some good effect. However, not with any sense of mastery. I felt better able to handle myself, but I also felt still uncertain. . . .

The balance of this first session, and part of the second, were consumed with history taking, covering much of the ground summarized in his autobiographical statement.

My impressions of Rex were that he was a charming, energetic, and troubled man. He exhibited an intense, extroverted, optimistic personality style with a number of histrionic traits evidenced in his autobiography. He brought considerable resources to the treatment process —motivation for relief, willingness to work, a flexible defensive structure, verbal facility, intelligence, and a history of positive experiences in psychotherapy. The down side seemed to me to be that his positive, outgoing style might cover significant underlying issues; that his active life might preclude his following the demands of this type of therapy; that psychotherapy of any sort might occasion significant regression; and that his five experiences with previous treatment had little effect on his presenting symptom even though Rex believed that the therapy had been valuable.

From my perspective it seemed that previous insights had not led to a reduction in his symptoms, especially in new and challenging situations. I wondered whether successful treatment of his performance anxiety might result in his being able to achieve new insights into the psychological origins of the problem.

On the basis of this initial appraisal, it seemed appropriate to focus the initial phase therapy on the target symptom of performance anxiety with the recognition that it might be appropriate to integrate psychotherapy into the process, depending on his response to the behavioral treatment.

*Behavior Therapy*

Sessions 2 to 5

Sessions 2 and 3 were devoted to describing and practicing the treatment techniques we would use to relieve anxiety and increase the frequency of his classroom participation. The first was a modified, abbreviated version of systematic desensitization. After developing a capacity to put himself in a state of relaxation, Rex was asked to imagine an increasing hierarchy of anxiety-producing classroom situations. As he felt the first twinge of tension, Rex was taught to evoke the relaxation state. He was instructed to practice this on a daily basis.

By the third meeting, Rex reported that he used the approach successfully prior to his speaking in public. He had yet to talk in class, but felt optimistic. At this point, Rex was taught a second technique aimed at the classroom inhibition. He was asked to observe opportunities to speak in class. When he saw such an occasion, he was encouraged to record it by making a small circle in the margin of his notes. After cautioning him to try to avoid feeling that he must speak in class, or say something significant, I asked him to draw a line through the circle if he found himself taking one of these opportunities to participate in discussion.

Three weeks later in our fourth meeting, Rex not only was able to observe opportunities to talk, but was beginning to participate more in class. This was helped, he thought, by the continuing systematic desensitization. His classroom participation during this period, excerpted from his notes, is shown in Table 1.

The data presented in Table 1 show a relatively modest improvement through March in both the recognition of opportunities to talk and the taking of these opportunities to participate in the class discussion. By April Rex felt sufficiently confident about controlling his performance anxiety that he was able to end the recording process.

No effort was made to analyze these patterns since it is my feeling that if the technique is effective from the client's point of view, it remains better unexplored for the moment. It is interesting to note that Rex's subjective sense of improvement was far in excess of the objective merits of the data, especially in class B. This seemed in keeping with his subjective, impressionistic personality style. Also, it is true that the record may not reflect the quality of his remarks and the response of his professors and classmates.

Two negative developments were that he was beginning to be driven by the desire to improve his record of classroom participation each day and week. I suggested that he stop recording his classroom performance. He gave this up with no difficulty. Also, Rex had some trouble in meeting his own performance expectations when he had to speak spontaneously. He had been interviewed by a radio station with another student and found that he had initial difficulty responding to the questions because he was not prepared for them.

Though on the whole Rex felt his performance anxiety had diminished markedly, he still felt that somehow he was not meeting his own expectations. He "knew" from his previous therapies that this was because he had internalized a powerful and demanding father, whom he could never satisfy. I noted, but did not respond to, this invitation. Instead, I suggested that we continue to focus on Rex's behav-

TABLE 1
Rex's Notes on Opportunities to Talk in the Class

| Date | | Opportunities Taken |
|---|---|---|
| *Class A* | | |
| February | 8 | 000 |
| | 15 | 000 000∅ ∅0 |
| | 22 | 0∅ |
| | 27 | 0∅∅ 000 |
| March | 1 | 000 000∅ |
| | 6 | ∅00 000 000 |
| | 8 | 000 000 |
| | 13 | 000 000 000 ∅00 |
| | 20 | 000 000 00 |
| | 22 | 000 ∅∅0 000∅ |
| April | 3 | No record |
| | 5 | No record |
| | 10 | 0∅∅ |
| | 12 | No record |
| | 17 | 000 ∅ |
| | 19 | 0∅ |
| | 24 | No record |
| *Class B* | | |
| February | 4 | 000 000 00 |
| | 6 | 00∅ 0∅∅ |
| | 11 | ∅00 00∅ 00∅ |
| | 13 | 0 |
| | 25 | 000 |
| | 27 | ∅00 0 |
| March | 4 | 000 000 |
| | 6 | 000 |
| | 13 | 000 |
| | 18 | 000 |
| | 20 | 000 000 |
| April | 1 | No record |
| | 8 | 00∅ |
| | 10 | ∅∅∅ |
| | 15 | No record |
| | 17 | ∅ |
| | 22 | No record |
| | 24 | No record |

*Note*: Circles indicate opportunities to talk. Lines through circles indicate speaking in response to the opportunity.

ior and meet in six weeks to examine his progress.

Three weeks later Rex came into my walk-in clinic. He said that he wanted to tell me that he had progressed from saying virtually nothing in class to being one of the leaders. However, he still had physiological signs of stress—especially high heart rate and heavy perspiration. We discussed what some of the reasons might be for these continuing stress reactions. We touched on his recognition of his own extremely high ambitions for himself and a tendency to cast any performance situation into heroic terms: the stakes were very high, a kind of academic superbowl in which he had to do well, to vanquish or be vanquished.

He had been noticing this tendency for the past month or so as he was recording opportunities to talk in class. He always thought it had to do with his powerful and demanding father, but now he was not so sure. It was at this moment we discussed meeting regularly. From March through May 1985, we scheduled almost weekly appointments.

*Integration of Psychotherapy*

Session 6

In this meeting we focused on the origins of his high ambition. Previously, Rex had thought this stemmed from a desire to please his father, a man whom Rex remembered saying that it did not matter how well he did as long as Rex did his best. That put no ceiling on how hard he should try or how well he should do. But since doing the behavioral work, this was less clear. At this point, I shared with Rex a hunch that had been growing in my mind since the fourth meeting. This comment and related events seemed to have a significant impact on the direction of therapy—though not quite in the way I anticipated.

T: I have been thinking about your description of your father as a powerful and admirable man whom you felt that you could not satisfy. Yet, you have also described him as an alcoholic, unstable, and often indifferent. I wonder how much of your perception of him is real and how much is illusory. I wonder how strong he really was. What do you think?

P: I don't know. He was a singular figure for me. There was no one with whom to compare him except the other boys' fathers. He was clearly a lot smarter and more cultivated than the fathers of the boys I knew. So, he just loomed very large for me. I remember him being pretty affectionate in my early days and fun to be around. Later on, he was significantly less predictable and my expectations began to change. I wanted, in some ways, more from him as kind of a sponsor, or a parent, or a friend, or whatever, and it just wasn't there.

T: What was your actual relationship like with your father in the early days and as you grew through adolescence?

P: I think I have mentioned to you that my mother was a very passive person so that all of my focus as a child, or much of it, was on my father and was on him almost in a reverential way. Also, it was made known to me at an early time that he had had lung surgery relating to tuberculosis and that one and a third lungs had been removed. He'd spent a year and a half in a sanitorium. And therefore, he was a frail individual. I can remember my mother stressing to me during certain play situations when I was about 6 or 7 years old, and there were other kids playing, that I had to keep an eye on my dad. That if we played too roughly with him, he could overextend himself and lose his breath and collapse.

T: Lose his breath.

P: Yeah. He jut didn't have enough wind. He would become winded. And my understanding at the time was that the consequence of him becoming winded could be quite severe. Although she never said he would die, I felt that this great man, my father, could be overtaken by my play.

T: You had to be careful, otherwise . . .

P: I also had the impression, which was not entirely untrue at the time, that my father was a very principled and ethical man, that he was a very self-sacrificing person. He was a person of enormous patience. He, you know, he seemed to me, of course from the child's uncritical standpoint, to be an affectionate man. He sang to me, read stories to me, was probably more involved with me as a child than a typical father was at that time, and was a gentle man, in many ways. He would tell me, at certain points when I was entering school and competing or expressing myself in schoolwork or sports, that he couldn't do—he could never have done what I was doing, that I had already outperformed him by those early years. I had a sense that he was a, you know, titanic figure in terms of intelligence and moral stature. But frail, physically. . . .

T: Vulnerable?

P: Yeah, a certain degree of vulnerability. Also an intensity. I had an intensity early on about competing that would be a puzzle to any observer or any nonprofessional observer. As a nine-year-old in fourth grade, I contracted chicken pox and had to be taken home from school, and threw a tantrum when I got home. I felt quite bereft when I discovered that I could not make up the math and spelling tests that would be taken during two weeks that I was not there, and therefore, I could not sustain my role of stars on the charts on the front wall of the classroom.

T: You had to have those gold stars.

P: Right across the line, and not miss one. And the same thing sort of translated into sports.

T: How does that connect with your father?

P: I think at some points he seemed to try to cure my intensity, which was baffling to me. I would study fairly hard and late into the evening because I had tests coming up and I could remember him coming in and telling me I had to go to bed. This ran counter to some of the messages that I had gotten before.

T: How so?

P: My dad prohibited me from playing Little League baseball, which he thought was excessively competitive and parent-dominated. He thought that parents became overly involved in watching their children play, and he didn't want me to be subjected to that kind of pressure. Later I had a chance to observe my father when he did permit one of my younger brothers to play Little League baseball. And my father, particularly, stood on the foul line shouting at my brother, who was a pitcher, and instructing him after every single pitch about how to adjust his form or follow through, or whatever. So, clearly, looking back on it, although he claimed to be uncontaminated by competitive instincts himself, his tendency to project onto his kids was so intense that his fear may have been that he couldn't have controlled himself, going to a Little League game where I was performing.

T: It would have been too difficult for him to hold back the intensity?

P: Yes. And I guess on one other point, one of the earliest experiences I had in observing him around competition. He was very involved in following the St. Louis Cardinals when they were the underdogs. And I remember sitting with him in a room watching the games on TV and seeing him hold his hands together, sort of lace his fingers together and sort of shuffle his thumbs and become red in the face and get terribly, terribly worked up as these games went down to the final inning. And I can remember the Cardinals losing sometimes and going to bed crying myself, because I felt that there had been a significant setback or defeat for him. Somehow, he would never interpret that experience for me as a child the way I would for my children now. It was a colossal, almost a moral, confrontation between one team and the rest of the world. I felt that there were some very major issues at stake, and it is ridiculous, but that is how I observed him making meaning for me of an event.

T: So, the times you saw your father exhibit heightened emotions—anger, depression, whatever—were around sports. . . .

P: Well, no, politics too. If we watched a political convention together, I saw the revulsion with which he viewed a person like Richard Nixon and sensed again that in that political arena there was something very significant at stake. So the times that I saw my father exhibit heightened emotion in sports or around intellectual or political issues, there appeared to be something very significant at issue there, and again, those situations were never really interpreted to me as a child. I just observed the meaning my father made of them.

T: How does this influence you now?

P: My way of entering into, initially, situations in a classroom or speaking before certains kinds of audiences, has a lot to do with how I view what is at stake there. I really just feel I handicap myself enormously by bringing certain kinds of unclarified values, assumptions, or expectations or perceptions to bear in those contents.

T: Where is your father in this?

P: Well, he may be within me. He was there occasionally, in ———, when I was driving just after the birth of my second daughter, to address a fairly large audience of foundation executives and trustees. . . .

T: Yes.

P: On the way there, I realized that my father wouldn't have felt entitled to be in that room with those trustees and executives. He would have felt unworthy or incapable, or something like that. So, you know, in my little inner dialogue talking back to him, I tried to tell him that he was entirely worthy to be in that room. Then, it was very sad for me. In fact, I wept as I drove over there because I felt how sad it was for him not to feel that sense of worth.

T: How about the recognition of your sense of loss?

P: How about . . . meaning what?

T: To some degree, you might have been experiencing loss of the idealized father. The tears might have been for yourself.

P: I think that is very possible. [weeping] Even talking abut it now, it is a situation that I feel a lot of emotion about. I just felt, in some ways, sorry for him. I think driving to the speech was a situation where I felt sorry inside for him, but, as you say, maybe I am sad for myself.

T: Yes.

P: You know, it's been a shock to me to realize that he wasn't the sort of figure I had imagined.

Father's fragility, and the early awareness that Rex had to be careful not to overtax him, provided some support for the hypothesis of his vulnerability. So, too, did Rex's description of his excessive, emotional outbursts around Little League games, the St. Louis Cardinals, and politics convey a sense of an inadequate man living through others, investing them with heroic stature. Rex's recognition of his father's inadequacy was powerfully communicated when he broke down weeping while talking about the fact that he was now functioning in a world that his father could never be a part of.

Yet, this interview also shows another dimension to their relationship prior to adolescence—a warm, caring, highly supportive bond. As we shall see later, it was when this contact was eroded by his father's drinking and instability—as well as his mother's illness—that Rex's problems began in earnest.

In this sixth session we began to examine the reality of Rex's perception of his father and made some progress in recognizing his father's fragility. Then between these meetings, as sometimes happens, an unexpected event occurred, which furthered this recognition. Rex received a deposition from a family lawyer vigorously contesting his mother's will, which left her money and possessions to the children.

## Session 7

P: I was struck by our conversation about this notion of the illusion of a strong father.
T: Let's talk about that.
P: That's a really critical thing, and, ironically, we had this session scheduled just a few days after I got a transcript of a deposition that my father had given relating to an estate settlement involving my mother, a contested estate settlement. I didn't bring it, but I may bring it simply to convey to you some sense of my father.
T: That would be very interesting, I think.
P: Although the transcript wasn't particularly interesting reading and was, some places, very choppy and incoherent, it felt very devastating for me to have a written text, a sort of written record of my father's deception and lack of focus, lack of memory, lack of analytical ability, all packaged for me. It made me feel, initially, very sad, like a . . . you know, as if I'd been punched in the stomach. And there was nothing . . . I could have wept over it.
T: That was upsetting.
P: In any case, going back to this illusory, the issue of the illusory father . . . I was looking over my notes from my last therapist. I used the word "benevolent" to describe him. That's not quite the same as "idealized" or "illusory."
T: Not quite.
P: But somehow, I think . . . I think when it got to be a teenager, my father just wasn't there anymore.
T: Not like before.
P: It was just kind of a cold and remote situation. The main point is that although I felt that he was a basically good guy in most ways, he was less and less able as a father to an adolescent to meet my needs. So I began to look to a particular coach or a teacher, or I began to almost take on the identity of certain types of people I read about. I was particularly drawn to the scholar/athlete types. I would read these articles about them in sports magazines. Although I lacked any details by which to model myself after them, I tried to almost build my character around those people. My frames of reference began to be less and less those of my father who, I am almost certain, was less attentive to what I was experiencing than he used to be. Even my accomplishments were less noteworthy to him. I could not imagine going and telling him that I had any confusion about sex, that I thought about drinking a beer, and drank a beer at the football game, that I lost some money. I just kind of wrote him off. He was not a person I felt comfortable going to. Increasingly I would rely on the mentor, the English teacher, the track coach, my girlfriend, or her parents.
T: Did they get invested with the same?
P: They got invested with the idealized parent virtues. I felt comfortable going to them. They seemed compassionate

and intelligent. They were genuine mentors or sponsors of mine. I would be looking for that relationship. With that I could work wonders. I remember getting an F in a history class because I was caught cheating on a term paper. The teacher, who was a young, attractive guy, told me that he would almost forget the first quarter's grade and see what I could do the second quarter. He was a very demanding teacher and I almost got a perfect score the second half of the quarter because I had a defined task. I felt he was rooting for me and I felt that there was a chance of scoring a noteworthy success. What I could not live in was this limbo state of uninvolvement and unrecognition, which really kind of characterized where I was with my father.

T: Uninvolved? Unrecognized? How so?

P: Well, I think it has taken me a few years as an adult to learn this stuff. If you had an independent conversation with my father today and asked him what he was proudest of in me, he would probably recall a race I won in high school. That to him is worth calling forth in conversations now. It is as if nothing happened between that time in 1963 and the present, despite the fact that my academic record in college was way more significant than that race. He is not aware of those things. He'll remember my winning. But I was living in a kind of emotional desert between the events of that time. We were close. When I was competing in high school and was racing about every week, I felt pretty close to him then. After the season ended, we were adrift again. Then, as time went on, I became increasingly aware of his alcoholism, his behavior....

During this and the following five sessions, Rex began to perceive the association between his disintegrating relationships with his father and a sick mother, and a growing pattern of disorganization and impulsive behavior. Several excerpts from these meetings follow.

*Sessions 8 to 12*

P: While I was in high school, I had no clue that he had a problem with drinking whatsoever. I just knew that as a junior and senior, I had a lot of restless energy and anger, I was prone to playing pranks or being mischievous, I was running away from school and....

T: I would like to hear a bit more about that.

P: When I was in junior high school, I followed all the rules. I was considered an exemplary person, not just an achiever. But when I got into high school, particularly as a junior, I began to feel that that was less satisfactory. I increasingly tested the limits. I would just stop doing school work and instead of getting A's, I began getting D's or F's and get progress reports sent home. Things of that sort. I began to miss more days of school, cut more classes, and then I got to a point where I think I was feeling very desperate about where I was going to be. A friend of mine, almost on the spur of the moment, decided to take his father's truck and we drove to New Orleans. It came at a time when I was class president. In reality, had anybody intervened for me, I probably could have pulled that semester out of the fire academically and gotten back on track but I was....

T: No one was there?

P: I really had no emotional reference points. One expectation of mine subconsciously might have been that someone would come in and actively intervene for me or take my part, or whatever, and sort of shepherd me through a process and exhibit some affectionate love on a consistent basis. What in reality happened was that my father would either send me off to a psychologist, which he did once in high school, and I had a big burst of strong academic and athletic achievement while I felt connected to that. Or he would simply talk to me or question me in the most tedious and infuriating way, as if I had failed him and was infected by some kind of malaise that was my own making. He had a habit of stacking coins while we talked. He would just stack his coins, fumble with his keys, and kind of hold me captive in a way until he felt he had elicited all the information he wanted in one of these question-and-answer sessions. I just felt it was a form of persecution. I felt such rage sitting there listening to him question me under those circumstances.

T: Tell me some more about running away. How long were you away?

P: I was only away three or four days. Anyway, when I came back, I found I had really wiped out the semester. I had gone too far. I had lost the student office and so forth. At that time the school year was winding up and there was an assembly for our class. I dressed up in a suit and tie and wrote something out that I wanted to say to my classmates. When I got to the auditorium, the school advisor would not let me go on stage to make this presentation. So, off to the side in this auditorium I flung my notebook down the hall. I walked up to one of the main buildings and proceeded to punch my hand through the window in the school, and I have little patches on my wrist today that testify to that. I mention that because that marked, in some ways, the beginning of an intensification of this whole downward spiral. I had other episodes of breaking windows or breaking things that were of value to me. Just really turning up all that anger, just really continuing to sort of increase the volume of this anger. I would get into really just damaging myself.

T: How so?

P: I broke trophies that I had won. These were really hard-earned. I didn't have a whole library full of trophies, so the ones I had that I broke, I was breaking something very dear to me. I would just smash them. Like an Old Testament prophet, I was in a complete rage. I would be really kind of desperate.

T: Did you ever hurt yourself further?

P: It is embarrassing to mention it, but I can remember taking a knife and just poking it into skin, not creating anything requiring stitches but little gouge marks. Not repeatedly, it would just be one gesture of exasperation.

T: So you were really upset.

P: Oh, yeah. I just didn't know where to turn.

T: When you think back on those days, they sound extraordinarily painful because of where you were and all of that. You describe it as though it were a gradual process. I am wondering if something might not have set you off for that run to New Orleans.

P: It's hard for me to recall. I know that the exact, specific precipitating event was that I had missed a whole day of school and felt that some of my teachers would call home....

T: How were things at home at that point. Do you recall?

P: My mother's physical problems increasingly limited her. She was obviously the first person I saw when I got home. I can remember one day saying to her as she sat on the couch, "Why don't you ever ask me what has happened for me during the day?" I got really angry, and she burst into tears. So I would feel in a kind of rage and feel the guilt about making her cry and I would just go back into the bedroom. I really do not remember any substantial interaction with my dad around areas of importance to me in my life. I just remember it being a kind of wasteland, not a whole lot going on. Unless something

extraordinary was happening, a race I was running, there wasn't a lot going on.
T: So unless you were performing in some way, winning, there was not much between you and your father. And it was different earlier?
P: Much different. Much better.
T: Because?
P: The main thing is that I felt myself, at least as a child, in a kind of symbolic relationship almost with him. It was as if he commissioned me to go out and do some of these things. By a fairly early age, I internalized this. So, whether he was literally saying one thing to me or not, I brought my own feelings to these experiences. A teacher might be the surrogate parent, or whomever I was relating to. All they had to do was push some button with me and I was there—I would perform for them. That is kind of how it was.

These excerpts reveal the change in Rex's relationship with his father and mother. He moved from a rich, almost symbiotic, connection with his father to an emotional desert. This was complicated and exacerbated by his mother's deteriorating condition due to muscular dystrophy. In this context, Rex began to recognize the meaning of his own aberrant behavior during this period, as the following excerpt illustrates.

P: From 11 to 12 on I wasn't getting much guidance whatsoever. I was operating on some of these myths or assumptions that I had formed earlier about my father and about what a person ought to do in any given situation. I was really inventing these things or picking them out of literature or films or wherever I was getting them, church or. . . .
T: You weren't getting much from home.
P: Because I wasn't getting much emotional contact back, I shifted gradually to a more extreme failure mode, I think. Later on, I got into this in my junior year at high school. And that just brought out—I mean he would ask me questions and give me these long lectures and so forth, which would be absolutely tedious and infuriating for me. There was never a meeting of the minds and emotional connection at all, which particularly amazes me now because I have young children and I really have daily contact with them. I know pretty much how they feel every single day. I don't think he knew how I felt at all for long stretches of time.
T: There was no awareness. . . .
P: None. . . . He wasn't cruel or abusive or anything in a direct sense, but he just wasn't involved. I could go through a whole semester practically flunking out when things were going bad for me, and he wouldn't have a clue about this because he would never ask and never know what I was doing until the reports started to come back and then he would be kind of outraged. But he would never express the outrage in a way such as, "Goddamit, what the hell is going on?" or even something softer but equally direct. I just felt kept at arm's length. Essentially, I tried two modes. The one mode that worked initially for me, which was the success mode, seemed to be what he wanted of me and that worked for a while, but then when that seemed to be the status quo, that's when I tried being bad. But that didn't work either. [Weeps silently]

Though we didn't discuss it further at this moment in treatment, it seemed obvious to both of us that Rex's tears were for the father he lost sometime around the beginning of adolescence. Achievement could not win him back and neither could being a bad boy. My thought was that he coped with this loss during the high school years in a number of ways: (1) finding a series of surrogates to please by being alternatively good and bad; (2) looking for contemporary role models to emulate; (3) acting out his anger toward his father and numerous self-destructive episodes; and (4) creating an illusion of his father as someone who cared about his success, someone he felt driven to satisfy. We touched on all of these issues to some degree. A dream that we discussed in session 11 opened the way to recognizing his angry feelings.

P: I had this dream the other day that seems important. I had gone to some event with a date. We are out late. We pull in the driveway. I am kind of beginning to present in my mind what my explanation for being late, and so forth, is to my father. He comes out. My dad approaches me, and as I am about to launch into my explanation, he begins to tell me that in the course of pulling into the driveway himself, in his own car, he had an accident. He holds up one of his hands, and the fingers of the hand are basically cut off at the first knuckle—a bloody stump. He is very calm trying to tell me that it was a minor accident of some kind, but his hand is mangled. I remember, in the dream, holding my head in my hands and saying, "Your hand has gotten so mangled over the years," and just feeling very demoralized about this last catastrophe. I think that is pretty much where the dream ends. I have not had a dream about my father for an awfully long time. I am sure our work is kicking up some stuff, and the fact that it was almost a kind of amputation of a hand—it is something I can't fully understand—but it felt in some way significant.

T: In what sense?

P: In some ways, it is true to life. My father, as an alcoholic since I have moved out of the house, has had a number of bizarre accidents, I must say. He'll try to separate two dogs fighting near his house and end up getting all scratched or gouged up. He falls from time to time and ends up requiring stitches in an emergency room. It is somewhat in character that he would have an accident like this. It is somewhat in character that he would display the injury almost as a source of curiosity—almost detached fascination. There is almost a self-mutilating quality to these accidents. This was a mutilation, not another term I am trying to come up with. I think in a way I have felt that each of these revelations about his character has been a display of an inner mutilation that I have had to come to terms with over a period of time.

T: Which hand was it?

P: I was trying to remember this. I was tempted to say right hand because of the symbolic. I'm not really sure. It may have been the left hand because he was facing me and I think he held it up.

T: Left hand, right hand?

P: I'm right handed. The other thing that struck me about the dream, or the feeling I have from it, is this feeling of personal devastation. I feel shocked, but also it was almost the accumulative effect of this, which is referred to when I say, "Your hand has gotten so mangled over the years." It is a combination of anger and sadness. In the dream there was a similar feeling of incredulity mixed with anger. It seemed like a very, very critical wound for me. It didn't look like something that could be fixed. I didn't know what he was going to do with his hand, but it was a mess.

T: Anything else?

P: Right. One of my fantasies . . . I think that his business is virtually gone. I honestly don't know how he is going to live out his life economically. He does have a lover with whom he lives, who

is a teacher. They have a house that's paid for, but it is a pretty sorry picture financially. I don't know how it is going to work out. Over the last several years, he has receded to become less alive—literally less alive and less alive for me. Although in a focused context like this, his existence moves up a little more vividly and the dream obviously reemerges. . . .
T: Damaged?
P: Right. Right.
T: Could you have had anything to do with it?
P: With his hand in this dream? Not the way the dream. . . .
T: I know about now. I'm wondering about that temporal period.
P: In my actual life, could I have had anything to do with his own destruction?
T: Or did you on some level?
P: Well, it's important for me to remember that early on my charge was that this guy's fate was in my hands. In a certain sense, that if I was playing with him and overtaxed him, he could collapse. I was responsible for him. He couldn't do it. My sense was that if left to his own devices, he would play too hard and he would kill himself, basically. So, I had to monitor how easily he was breathing because of his tuberculosis.
T: So, his life was in your hands?
P: Right. I felt that he was physically frail. I was told that it was worse for him to get a chest cold. You can't evaluate these things when you're a kid, but I felt that he was a noble spirit, a fine mind encased in a fragile body, and that he was vulnerable—he had vulnerability.
T: Did you ever feel angry at him and not be able to express it?
P: By the time I was about 15 or 16, when it was time to use the car. At that time, he was more inclined to speak more sharply, lay down the law a little bit more. I would react to that. I would feel angry. By the time I was a junior or senior, we had a couple of, at least one physical contact where he would shove me across the room. I remember when I was trying to make up ground in a class—this class I had gotten an F in—and I was trying to get the grade up as high as I could and I had an exam coming up the next day and I knew I was missing one set of notes. I was attempting to leave the house at about—it was late—9:00 or 9:30 P.M. to get some notes to review before the test, and he insisted that it was too late to go out and he shoved me back down into the chair. I am sure I burst into tears at that point. I was bereft, angry, humiliated, and so forth. My reaction was to feel just outraged. It was just a terribly snarled-up period of time in terms of how we would communicate. It was just miserable.
T: It sounds very tough. What do you do when you know you can hurt somebody?
P: It just lays you out, totally lays you out. When he got mad at me when I was a teen-ager, I was bereft, angry, humiliated. I was crying and feeling outraged. It was just miserable.
T: Yes.
P: I turned a lot of rage and anger on myself. No question about it. My previous therapy dealt with this.

I didn't feel particularly pleased about my response to the dream. Just why I became so obsessed with whether the injury occurred to his father's left or right hand remains a bit of a mystery to me. Otherwise, we seemed to be out of rhythm during this encounter, perhaps both working too hard to try to distill what we both believed to be important, symbolic material in the dream. As frequently happens in the course of therapy, however, when we fumble with what seems to be an important issue, other chances present themselves. Here is an excerpt concerning the dream from the next meeting.

*Session 12*

P: When we stopped last time, one of the things we had talked about was this dream. I made a couple of notes after our session because you had said you might want to return to this dream and also you were wondering about the associations that might happen.
T: Let's return to that dream if you're comfortable with that.
P: Basically, this dream had to do with my father's hand being maimed, disfigured in some kind of bizarre way. After the session, I was thinking about my associations with the hand. The two or three associations I had are biting the hand that feeds you, give me a hand, the right hand of God. There were two or three quick reactions, and there may have been one or two others. I think there are a lot of obvious symbolic references to the hand, and those are three. The parent is the person who feeds you, or is supposed to, both physically and psychologically. This is set, not only against the context of our work, but against the point of this estate settlement in St. Louis in which I am, for the first time in my life, formally in an adversarial relationship with my father. He is on one side and I'm on the other. Unless there is a compromise settlement, one of us will win and the other will lose.
T: Where are you now?
P: I find myself taking almost an uncharacteristically hard line.
T: Do you have any further associations to the dream other than....
P: Not really, as we talk about it now. I guess I'm struck by some feeling of guilt, almost irrational guilt, with the fact that my father has his hand injured. I had nothing to do with causing it, but as I'm talking about the dream, I feel some guilt—some responsibility.
T: In the dream. What might that be?
P: Well, the thing that I felt uneasy about in the dream was that I got separated, that I separated myself from my father. I guess if I had thought it through, I might have imagined that had I stayed with him, he wouldn't have had this injury. That it happened because he went his own way and by the time I reconnected with him, something had already gone wrong. In fact, if I had linked that up to actual realities, obviously, very early on I did have a sense of some responsibility in certain situations for protecting my father's health while we were playing or having games. My mother gave me the very strong impression, as I said earlier, that if I overtaxed him he would collapse. So, there have been different points in which I have felt responsible for him and I think that's part of it in the dream situation too.
T: What else?
P: Well, I think guilt, and outright expressions of anger were very much frowned upon or discouraged. I think they were felt almost to be morally wrong. There was never any discussion of this, but it was as if really direct anger was almost a transgression, it was irrational.
T: As a youngster, what were your feelings about what might happen to someone if you got very angry?
P: I think that initially I probably, as a youngster, didn't have any terribly complicated feelings about that. I just directly expressed the anger. A lot of it, I remember, would be associated with competitive situations.
T: What about anger toward your parents?
P: I guess I am sure that there would be a physical punishment with some withdrawal or there would be very, very strong disapproval. I think that there was no feeling that that was at all appropriate or accepted. What would happen, even though I've never tested it too often, I suppose I may have felt that my parents would be less friendly to me or less kindly disposed to me for a period

of time, I don't know.
T: Did your anger have the power to hurt people?
P: Well, I don't know. I just can't be clear enough about it. I remember one incident in which my mother and father had one of their few arguments. My mother may have thrown something at my father and started crying. His response would be to be wounded or abused by the anger. Anger was not, after a certain age, a young age, was not part of my emotional repertoire by and large. I thought that I was a real nice guy, a person who never had conflicts with anybody. As a kid, I can remember one incident where another person was accusing me of something. My response was to be extremely angry, but what I did was bang myself on the head with a little toy gun.
T: How about now?
P: I am much more readily able to call forth anger correctly. I still . . . I guess I have some lingering feelings about the desirability of expressing anger. Some part of me would rather not. But, it doesn't take too long for me to be aware that I am feeling angry and to let that feeling, in some measure, come into play. It is not a buried feeling anymore.

In the last session, Rex and I talked about the course of treatment. Two issues that were on my mind were how this therapy compared with previous treatment in his thinking and the extent to which the positive effects would be durable.

## Session 14

T: What are your feelings about this experience compared with previous therapies, if it is possible to summarize, or even compare them?
P: I think my therapies have been effective. I have had a bond with the person with whom I was working.
T: Certainly, by everything you've said, I'm led to believe that previous therapies were highly effective by the standards I know of.
P: Right. They were . . . I suppose a lot of it has to do with timing. This therapy has been a very, very focused and intense kind of process as far as I'm concerned.
T: Compared with. . . .?
P: Compared with experiences that were more open-ended. For example, I never imagined that I would be able to continue to work with you beyond a couple of months or so. I knew we had to get something done quickly, and I was assured that we would get something done. I also brought in a presenting problem that was very ripe for a solution. I had no ambiguity about wanting to deal with it compared with previous situations where I might have not even been sure initially what the issues were. By and large, I've been fortunate in identifying very strong people as therapists and working pretty much without reservation with them without some kinds of resistance or defensiveness or whatever.
T: What have your feelings been about our relationship and what we've been doing?
P: In terms of idealization, I think that as our work progressed, my sort of affection for you increased significantly. There was a sense, because I was on the firing line, testing out our methods of a real partner experience here. That meant a lot to me. No question about it. Early on, I wasn't sure whether you would ever really get to know me in a personal sense or whether I would be just another one of a number of clients or students rotating through this office. It made a significant degree of significance to me to feel personally linked to you in this work. There is no doubt that that attachment, that bond, is something that I still feel very strongly. Al-

though it rises and falls, I am expecting more out of this than I might have originally. I am going deeper into it than talking about a particular behavior and a behavioral strategy for dealing with it. I feel like I'm in it deeper emotionally.

T: Deeper than what?

P: We're looking at a whole range of issues instead of simply the phenomenon of public presentation. Because we've widened the focus, I feel much more exposed, more vulnerable, more wounded in a sense, having to recapitulate quite raw, unhappy past experiences....

T: Well, we have about 10 minutes left. I guess I'd like to think back to the beginning of our work together and think about the question of the extent to which this work has met your expectations, what you see beyond this.

P: Well, I would have to say that this work has met or exceeded my expectations.

T: In what ways?

P: In the sense that we've been working with almost a perfect kind of laboratory—that being the classroom and the case and so forth. Results from our work almost had to be manifested or I would have suffered some consequence, either lowered grades or at least temporarily reduced self-esteem, or something like that. After years of disappointment in trying to address this problem in some systematic way, this has been the first time that I felt some substantial measure of control in the way I approached this public-presentation thing. I've charted my participation in class so that I have a complete record of the frequency of participation and opportunities for speaking. And I've gone from almost zero participation, or very episodic participation, to very regular participation in almost every class and sometimes multiple comments per class. In fact, my impression is that in one of the classes I have come to be regarded as one of the more thoughtful contributors to class discussion.

T: I wonder how durable you imagine the results of this work might be. I'm not fishing for compliments. I'm just curious.

P: I expect the results to be very durable. Obviously, I've had a problem that has afflicted me for 15 years or so. So, I've been aware that it has been most acute in the last 10 years or so.

T: I think we noticed it in your junior year or one of those years from an earlier session.

P: Right. Right. And there have been some false starts and some disappointed hopes in attempting to deal with that problem, but I've never had such a dramatic turnaround before, as has taken place in the few months of our work. I'm also very drawn to certain kinds of exercises, methods, or techniques that have a kind of specificity. Those sorts of approaches appeal to me, and I like using them and incorporating them into my daily routine, and so I feel good about what we've done and what I've done individually and look forward to the gratification that comes from continuing to use it and benefit from it. So, I really feel . . . I never had the benefits of previous therapies erode or reverse when they've really taken hold, and the work that I concluded in 1982 is just as valid for me now and has not slipped away, and I don't expect this to slip away either.

T: What do you think next fall is going to be like?

P: Well, I really have confidence in the enduring effects of this method and I'm going to try to work with them. There are areas that I would like to continue to explore, and I've talked about the desire to enhance the technical approaches with some additional insight or understanding, and I may want to come back to you.

## CLIENT IMPRESSIONS: MAY 1985

Following are Rex's written impressions of his treatment:

Treatment can be divided into two phases. First-phase sessions, scheduled at two- to three-week intervals, imparted, refined, and reported on desensitization/behavioral modification approaches to the problem presented. These sessions were cordial but brief (usually less than 45 minutes) and somewhat impersonal. Again, emphasis was placed on *techniques* of proven effectiveness rather than on developing an interpersonal context for the therapeutic relationship. I was struck by the economy of these early sessions, but was reassured by Dr. Powell's confidence in the methods I was to implement. On the negative side, I worried that student volume at the University Health Center dictated a certain assembly-line quality to care. I wondered whether Doug was really engaged in our work, whether he was relating to me as an individual.

As sessions progressed, a second treatment phase began. This phase featured three developments. First, Doug's techniques did *work* (although some setbacks were occasionally experienced), and I developed an increased sense of confidence in, and gratitude toward, him. Second, Doug began to reveal more of himself and divulged some similarities in our backgrounds, which created a much greater sense of intimacy and collaboration. Third, we began to augment behavioral strategies with discussion of what Doug called the "existential" issues. Sessions were scheduled more frequently, usually lasted the conventional 50 minutes or longer, and were much more wide-ranging in terms of topics covered. I began to cry during one of the phase II sessions, indicating the greater intensity and trust of the work at this point. I began to refer to treatment as a joint venture (our work) rather than as something I was pursuing alone. Also, I began making postsession journal entries recapitulating important points. Although treatment began in January 1985, I did not make my first journal notation until March. During the second phase of treatment, such entries were common, again attesting to the more complex texture of these sessions.

I initiated the discussion of "existential" issues in the hope of enhancing behavioral techniques with insight. This effort has laid the groundwork for additional understanding, but has produced less dramatic or conclusive results than the behavioral work. This technique-oriented work was perfectly suited to my situation because it had a focused, almost surgical, quality that quickly produced relief. I remain confident, as we wind down our work, that the talk-oriented therapy will contribute significantly to my healing and growth process. It is important to me that this work culminate in some new understandings because the review of past personal history has reinflamed some very painful psychic wounds.

## THERAPIST IMPRESSIONS: MAY 1985

My overall sense of the treatment process with Rex is that it was both successful and incomplete. I believe that he shares some of these feelings. Perhaps that is not surprising considering we met only 14 times and the academic year has a way of bringing premature termination to clinical work. At the time I did not know whether he would return in the fall.

With respect to the therapy itself, I enjoyed working with Rex. Like many students in settings such as these, he is bright and exhibited considerable verbal facility, which lubricated the therapy process. I was bothered occasionally by his extraordinary verbosity and psychological mindedness. The first made it hard to keep him on a track which seemed productive. His self-interpretations were sometimes at odds with mine. However, I did think he responded well to my directional comments.

On the plus side was his strong positive transference, especially toward the end of the behavior therapy phase of our work. But even in the beginning there were many times when Rex picked up words or concepts very quickly that I used. Also, he was used to feeling positively about previous therapists, and he was relatively faithful about carrying out behavioral exercises necessary for a successful outcome.

Also on the plus side were my sympathy for his problem and confidence that I could help him. Though I do not recall telling him this, I am a former stutterer who experienced great frustration around speaking in classes, had an alcoholic father, was an athlete, and had a high school career paralleling Rex's. He obviously sensed this shared experience in my remarks. As I had successfully treated a number of Harvard students with performance anxiety with this and other behavioral techniques, his presenting problem did not cause me excessive concern. That confidence apparently transmitted itself to Rex.

As to the treatment itself, I am always struck by the economy of behavior therapy in alleviating symptoms. Within two months his performance anxiety was sharply reduced. We might have stopped there but for the fact that he began to recognize that his present anxiety was driven by several intrapsychic forces. Rex's first spontaneous insight was becoming aware of his tendency to cast every situation into heroic terms in which he had to perform well. As the therapy progressed, it became apparent that this tendency was rooted in the desire to attract his father's affection. This is why "doing well" in any performance situation never alleviated the anxiety the next time. No matter how well he performed, the emotional desert between them remained in his unconscious. The vain hope of reconnecting with his father through his achievements caused him to continue to keep expecting more and more of himself.

The second spontaneous insight, which emerged very quickly, was his becoming aware of his illusion of father's competence and ambitions for him. According to Rex, it was not until our work together that he realized that he himself had created the image of the powerful father who continually demanded that Rex excel. In fact, the father was increasingly indifferent from early adolescence onward. Rex created this image in order to remain connected to his father.

Whether these insights would have surfaced during a course of psychotherapy, it is difficult to determine. My experience is that they were not likely to have come up so early and may not emerge at all. They surfaced initially in the context of the behavioral practice and our discussion of his reactions to it. Also, I had the feeling that psychotherapy with Rex would be a wide-ranging enterprise, covering an enormous territory. It was doubtful whether there would have been sufficient focus on any specific material for these insights to emerge as significant issues. They had not in the past.

## POSTSCRIPT

Rex and I resumed contact in the fall. We met biweekly until terminating the week prior to Christmas.

By the end of the first month, Rex believed that his problems speaking in class—and elsewhere—were behind him. Now that he felt more comfortable about entering into discussions he could choose *not* to speak without becoming uncomfortable. This was a vastly different experience than believing he could not talk without embarrassing himself.

A relatively small event opened the way for further understanding of the origins of Rex's tendency to transform the mildest competition into an Olympic struggle. The event was Rex's comment in passing that he had just finished a letter to his father and enclosed a newspaper report of an address he had given to a group of Boston executives.

As we discussed why he wanted to send the clipping to his father, Rex again went over his desire to obtain his father's love through his achievements. At this point I recalled his father's earlier comments that Rex recounted in the spring: by the time Rex was an early adolescent his father told him that Rex had already exceeded him. Remembering his mother's cautions about his father's frailty, I wondered whether Rex's continual bombarding of his father with his achievements might have been—and might continue to be—a sublimation of both normal competitive instincts as well as aggressive impulses deriving from years of frustration. This seemed to hit home.

The remainder of our sessions dealt with one form or another of his aggressive feelings. Numerous dreams occurred involving his father: in one his father was mangled; in another the family station wagon, usually driven by his father, went out of control and crashed on the freeway.

Toward the end of our work together, Rex had two dreams in the same week about expelling something noxious and ugly inside him. The first involved trying to vomit something up but not being successful. In the second dream he was sitting on the toilet after defecating. When he tried to wipe himself, he spread the fecal material rather than being able to clean it away.

As he followed his associations to these dreams, Rex concluded he seemed to be trying to rid himself of his anger by expelling it in some way. But plainly this was not working. Shortly, Rex recognized that a key message in these dreams is that he did not want to totally purge himself of his aggression. He wanted to use this energy, integrating this force into his personality.

Indeed, in the previous week, Rex recalled making a presentation and being provoked by a prickly member of the audience. Rex handled the confrontation with humor, which diffused the badgerer. This was the first time he had ever been able to do this. This was the first time, Rex mused, that he didn't worry that his anger might have lethal consequences.

Rex's case illustrates a crucial point about integrated therapy—namely, the power of insight-oriented treatment to maintain the improvement achieved by behavior therapy. As Birk and Brinkley-Birk (1974) pointed out, psychotherapy aims at helping people make sense of things whereas behavioral procedures assist them in changing their actions to live more comfortably in their world.

Behavior therapy integrated with psychotherapy does create a sharpened attention as well as an intensity which can arouse considerable emotions. Garfield (1980) may be correct in saying the therapies that have greater potency to change behavior also possess a higher probability of causing emotional upset than milder, but perhaps less effective, procedures.

Rex's case, and others like his, reinforce the notion that clinicians employing behavior therapy will do well to maintain an ongoing diagnostic vigilance and be prepared to modify the treatment accordingly. Although it's true that only a small percentage of patients treated with behavior therapy are likely to want to explore emotional issues that emerge, this does happen in a significant minority of cases.

In spite of a complete history and behavioral diagnosis, in spite of extensive anamneses and psychological testing, I have been unable to anticipate with many clients the quality or the force of unconscious material that is associated with presenting behavioral symptoms. These feelings, thoughts, and experiences were not accessible prior to the application of behavior therapy. I believe that clinicians using behavioral techniques—and perhaps those working in psychological laboratories as well—need to be especially alert to changes across the client's affective, ideational, and behavioral repertoires as well as attentive to new perceptions or distressing symptoms. These changes present an opportunity for insight-oriented therapy, which may not have been possible without the behavioral intervention.

## REFERENCES

Birk, L., & Brinkley-Birk, A. W. (1974). Psychoanalysis and behavior therapy. *American Journal of Psychiatry, 131,* 499–509.

Borkovec, T. D., & Grayson, J. B. (1980). Consequence of increasing the functional impact of internal emotional stimuli. In K. Blankstein, P. Pliner, and J. Polivy (Eds.), *Assessment and modification of emotional behavior.* New York: Plenum.

Borkovec, T. D., & Hennings, B. C. (1978). The role of physiological attention-focusing in the relaxation treatment of sleep disturbance, general tension, and specific stress reaction. *Behavior Research and Therapy, 16,* 17–19.

Borkovec, T. D., & Sides, J. K. (1979). Critical procedural variables related to the physiological effects of progressive relaxation: A review. *Behavior Research and Therapy, 17,* 119–126.

Fitzpatrick, M. M. (1983). A modified behavioral psychotherapy approach in the treatment of a schizophrenic adolescent. In H. Fensterheim and H. I. Glazer (Eds.), *Behavioral psychotherapy.* New York: Brunner/Mazel.

Garfield, S. L. (1980). *Psychotherapy: An eclectic approach.* New York: Wiley.

Heide, F. J., & Borkovec, T. D. (1983). Relaxation-induced anxiety: Paradoxical anxiety enhancement due to relaxation training. *Journal of Consulting and Clinical Psychology, 51,* 171–182.

Jacobsen, R., & Edinger, J. D. (1982). Side effects of relaxation treatment. *American Journal of Psychiatry, 139,* 952–953.

Kuhlman, T. (1982). Symptom relief through insight during systematic desensitization: A case study. *Psychotherapy: Theory, Research, and Practice, 19,* 88–94.

Lazarus, A. A. (1963). The results of behavior therapy in 126 cases of severe neurosis. *Behavior Research and Therapy, 1,* 69–80.

Lazarus, A. A. (1981). *The practice of multimodal therapy.* New York: McGraw-Hill.

Marks, I. M. (1971). Phobic disorders four years after treatment: A prospective follow-up. *British Journal of Psychiatry, 118,* 683–688.

Rickles, W. H., Onoda, L., & Doyle, C. C. (1982). Task force study section report: Biofeedback as an adjunct to psychotherapy. *Biofeedback and Self-Regulation, 7,* 1–33.

Walker, C. E., Hedberg, A., Clement, P. W., and Wright, L. (1981). *Clinical procedures for behavior therapy.* Englewood Cliffs, NJ: Prentice-Hall.

# Commentary: Some Combinations and Guidelines in Insight and Behavior Therapy

## Kalman Glantz

*Most of the various hybrid forms of therapy that combine behavioral interventions and insight-oriented exploration can be classified, I believe, under four headings:*

1. *behavior therapy which is used to provoke insight, by creating a situation that forces a client to discover, and subsequently discuss, an old pattern;*

2. *behavioral interventions which are suggested by particular discoveries made by a client during an exploration process;*

3. *relaxation exercises which are used to facilitate recall and/or reduce the fear of self-exposure;*

4. *insight-seeking exploration which is used to consolidate or enhance insights*

that arise spontaneously following a set of behavioral interventions.

For several reasons, the fourth combination may well be the best place to start for behavior therapists who have not already integrated psychodynamic exploration into their work. Opportunities arise frequently; most people want to talk with an informed, sympathetic listener about what they have learned and/or accomplished. No detailed planning is necessary; therapists don't have to set out in advance to use insight during a particular case. Finally, special techniques for overcoming resistance can be dispensed with, since the client is already eager to talk.

The case presented by Douglas Powell is an excellent example of type 4. Dr. Powell designed several behavioral interventions. These interventions were not specifically designed to provoke insight, nor were they based on the client's insight into the roots of his problem. The interventions were successful, but the client expressed a need for something more. Dr. Powell, unfettered by ideology, was able to respond effectively.

## INSIGHT THERAPY AND EMOTIONAL CONTACT

What Rex, the client, needed in this case was significant, for it points clearly to one of the major advantages of eclecticism over a strict behavioral approach. Rex explicitly states that during the behavioral phase of the therapy, he was concerned about Dr. Powell's degree of commitment to him as a person. He wanted a relationship with the therapist; he didn't want to be an anonymous "case." He wanted to feel that he was understood.

Rex's desire points to the emotional basis of insight oriented therapy. Such therapy, however cognitive or analytical, involves the sharing of the client's story. This sharing creates what might be called kinship ties between client and therapist. These ties provide clients with inclusion and acceptance, which are critical factors in the recovery process.

The desire to have a relationship with the therapist is akin to the desire to be treated as an individual in the family, at school, at work, and elsewhere. It is a simple human desire, one that will be found in just about everyone who enters therapy. It should not be explained as a manifestation of childhood attitudes toward parents and other authority figures.

The value of "relationship" was neglected in behavior therapy during the years when energy was being invested in the overthrow of the dogmas of psychoanalysis. But that time is past. Contemporary ideas about development and the origins of psychopathology provide a perfectly adequate framework for behavioral interventions. There is, therefore, no further need for behavior therapists to shun psychodynamic exploration. By using an eclectic approach, they can meet each client's need for affiliation and recognition, no matter which techniques they rely on most heavily to bring about change.

## THE NEED FOR MEANING

In addition to their need for contact, people have a need for meaning. Powell cites various references in the literature to show that spontaneous insights occur frequently during the course of behavior therapy, but such references are hardly necessary. Can it be otherwise? Insights happen spontaneously all the time; they are bound to leak into even the most rigid behavioral setting.

Neuropsychology is making it increasingly clear that it is in the nature of the human brain to observe itself, draw conclusions, and form models of its surroundings (e.g., O'Keefe & Nadel, 1978). These models then affect the response of the organism to future stimuli. It follows that anything which affects the model may affect future behavior. Can one therefore really separate insight and behavior change? To arbitrarily exclude the intellectual dimension from therapy is to work with a truncated conception of the human mind.

## SOME GUIDELINES FOR ECLECTIC THERAPY

Powell's handling of this case demonstrates several principles that are worth noting. He keeps interpretation to a minimum. He asks questions that elicit specific information. He often uses the (Rogerian) technique of simply feeding back statements that the client has made. He makes his most crucial interventions on the basis of contradictions in what the client actually says (e.g., father is powerful but tubercular, alcoholic, and weak), not on presumed characteristics of the patient's mind. In fact, it seems to me that he handled the psychodynamic phase of the treatment more or less as an extension of the diagnostic phase of behavior therapy. All this should be reassuring to those behavior therapists who might feel that psychodynamic exploration is unfamiliar ground, or whose idea of it derives from one of the more arcane, esoteric traditions.

Powell's handling of Rex's dream is a good case in point. Most of the time, he simply asks for more information. The first time he introduces something new into the discussion of the dream, he does it with a practical question: "Could you have had anything to do with [your father's injury]?" In other words, avoiding complex, symbolic interpretations, he brings the client back to his own role in the situation. Again, this intervention was clearly based on something Rex had specifically stated, namely, that his mother had warned him about tiring his father out.

## THE VALUE OF AN ECLECTIC APPROACH

This case makes it clear that any time one is combining techniques for behavior change with insight-oriented therapy, one acquires a good deal of freedom with respect to interpretation. In the eclectic approach, a change in behavior does not depend on any particular insight (since one can always use behavior therapy to bring about change). Therefore, therapists don't need to wait around for some particular insight to surface in order to move things along (as, say, a psychoanalyst might wait for a patient to discover his oedipal desires). Eclectic therapists can just take whatever comes to the surface, help the client to understand the material in his or her own terms, and establish emotional rapport.

Powell's handling of this case demonstrates the value of having an eclectic approach to the various schools of insight-oriented therapy. So many interpretations of what caused Rex's performance anxiety seem to hover over this transcript! There is fear of failure (father will be critical), and fear of success (father will be outdone and thereby shamed). There is fear of being "like father" (weak), and fear of being "unlike father" (going beyond him). One could say that Rex's father might have been too dominant or too important in this child's life, but one might also think that he may have been too weak—unable to provide support during critical periods. Which of these factors, or which combination, is at fault? The answer isn't known and probably cannot be known. Dr. Powell's willingness to work without making any single interpretation of behavior the focus of all his interventions provides valuable insight into the factors that lead to success in eclectic psychotherapy.

## SOME ADDITIONAL POSSIBILITIES

For the sake of illustration, it might be helpful to point out some opportunities this case presented for combining behavioral interventions and exploration more directly, had there been a need to do so. I will briefly note two possibilities that occurred to me.

a. The relaxation technique that Rex learned could have been used during the exploration phase to help him reexperience aspects of his relationship with his father.

Rex himself didn't seem to have much trouble making emotional contact with the events that apparently shaped his life, perhaps because of his previous experience with psychotherapy. But with clients who aren't in such close touch with their past, relaxation is a valuable tool.

b. Guided fantasy could have been used to help Rex experience his fear of destroying the image of a strong father. (For example: "Imagine yourself as a high-school student telling your father that you had already outdistanced him intellectually.")

Here again, Rex himself was able to get in touch with his feelings by himself, but another client with similar problems might require a little push to really perceive the inhibition.

## CONCLUSION

In my view, cases such as this make it clear that behavior therapy bears no essential, theoretical connection to the principles of behaviorism. The techniques of behavior change developed over the years remain perfectly usable even if one believes, for example, that Rex's problems with his father stemmed from oedipal longings, or that Rex's performance anxiety was due to an innate, genetically determined need for a father who would be a source of strength and love. Hopefully, theory will soon catch up to the progress that clinicians have made in their day-to-day work.

## REFERENCE

O'Keefe, J., & Nadel, L. (1978). *The hippocampus as a cognitive map.* New York: Oxford University Press.

# Commentary: When Is Behavior Therapy Enough?

## George J. Steinfeld

The case of Rex raises some interesting clinical and ethical dilemmas for those of us who practice within an eclectic or integrative framework. In Dr. Powell's opening remarks, he states that clients frequently become aware of psychodynamic factors associated with their symptoms while participating in behavior therapy. I, too, have witnessed this phenomenon. However, the issues in question refer to how we explain these occurrences theoretically and how to deal with them in an ethically responsible and clinically appropriate manner.

My theoretical explanation is simple and, of course, may be wrong. I explain these phenomena by referring to factors such as "perceived" similarity between current stimuli and past events. These past, emotionally charged events have been deposited in our nervous systems as memory traces. We remain unaware of these memories. The current stimuli, by virtue of their perceived similarity to the past stimuli, arouse the memory trace and bring it totally or partially into awareness, along with the associated thoughts, images, and feelings. This cognitive process is spelled out in the literature on perceptual processes, along with the specific mechanism for the arousal of the trace, e.g., the Hoffdung function (Rock, 1962).

In developing a treatment plan with

clients, it is important to establish goals and spell out the means by which these goals will be reached. This fosters a more egalitarian relationship, demystifies the therapeutic process, and helps prevent subtle and more obvious power plays by the therapist. Mutual responsibilities should be spelled out, as well as potential side effects and/or consequences of successful treatment.

As noted by Powell, it frequently happens that relaxation training aimed at reducing stress, or used during the process of systematic desensitization, actually increases tension in the client. My first experience with this happened many years ago. I was treating a woman for agoraphobia and was trying to relax her using the standard procedure of the day. The more she practiced, the more anxious she became. She kept saying, "I'm freaking out," when she did her relaxation at home and in the office. Since that time I have come to believe that relaxation, or the feelings associated with a nontension state, were anxiety arousing for a number of reasons.

With Sharon, relaxation stimulated feelings of vulnerability, associated with unresolved business in her family of origin. She also "misinterpreted" her relaxation response. This new "positive" feeling was perceived to be "ego alien," that is, not fitting Sharon's view of herself as an emerging "calm" person. She frequently stated, "I've been nervous all my life." She seemed to be "comfortably uncomfortable" with her tension-filled "freaky" nature, since this was part of her self-image.

In fact, Sharon's case stimulated my recall of a story by comedian Buddy Hackett. He had grown up with a constant heartburn as a result of his mother's cooking. When he entered the Army, his heartburn went away. On discovering this, he rushed to the infirmary, frightened that, since "the fire went out" of his chest, he would freeze to death. He had adapted to the pathology of his mother's cooking as all children adapt to the "craziness" of their families. The change to the "normal" (healthy) condition made him uncomfortable, again pointing to the positive aspects of any symptom and the potential risks of removing it (the side effect of change).

A case presented by Arnold Lazarus also highlights the importance of establishing clear treatment goals and honoring the contract. Lazarus was presenting a case at the psychoeducational clinic at Yale, and I had come over from a nearby child guidance clinic because I had been interested in behavior therapy for a number of years and was familiar with Lazarus' work from the literature. The case presented was of a woman who sought treatment for a phobia because she, too, was familiar with Lazarus' contributions to behavior therapy and because traditional therapy was not helpful. A fairly straightforward systematic desensitization procedure was outlined and accepted as the treatment of choice in the early 1970s. During one of the early interviews, however, Lazarus, being the broad-spectrum therapist that he was (and still is), pursued some clinical material related to her relationship with her husband that appeared relevant to her phobia. At the end of that session, Lazarus felt good about the many "insights" they had derived from the session. However, at the next session, the client was very upset, and I believe correctly so, and chastised Lazarus. She had sought him out for treatment of her phobia through a behavioral approach, and because she felt him to be the best person for the job. She saw no relevance between her problem and its relationship to her husband, and she was angry. Was she appropriate, defensive, resistant? They had not negotiated pursuing relationship issues. It violated her expectations, and she felt disappointed, ripped off, and disrespected.

As you can see, I never forgot this incident, and since that time, I have witnessed personally, and indirectly, the seductive nature of psychotherapy. It has led me to my position that we need to establish clear treatment goals and make known the relevance of procedures to those goals. I also realize, despite these concerns, how easy it is to get sidetracked and seduced by "interesting" clinical material, thereby lengthening therapy, and not giving clients what they are paying for. We have the ethical responsibility to discuss these possibilities with the client.

Although my personal experience testifies to the clinical findings that there are negative effects in the form of emotional discomfort as well as undesired (and undesirable) "insights" during behavior therapy, we have the ethical responsibility to discuss these possibilities with the client. These side effects can then be monitored by both therapist and client during the therapy process. "Strategically," this would increase the client's "perceived expertise" since the side effects were predicted as possible outcomes, but more important, it would tend to alleviate the anxiety if mild discomfort should arise. These feelings would then be open for discussion. If "insights" spontaneously occurred, the client and therapist could negotiate whether the client wanted to explore their "possible" relevance to the treatment goals.

A related issue has to do with the entire question of what it means to be "relevant" when we are talking about "insights" of the relationship between psychological events. Human beings have the capacity to relate or connect everything, the more metaphorical the better, in analytically oriented therapy, and some forms of indirect hypnosis of the Eriksonian variety. We therapists can create traps for ourselves and our clients by making interpretations and creating relationships that exist in our heads, and then trying to convince the client of them. In attempting to convince clients of the clinical relevance of the material, of our "insights," we have always reserved the right to call clients "resistant" if they fail to agree with us. If they agree "too" readily (whatever that means), we call them overcompliant. They, of course, have to accept our interpretive insights in just the right ways for us to think well of them and make ourselves feel good about our creativity and clinical intuitions. Man, can we create a lot of nonsense, and I feel, iatrogenically, create a lot of suffering.

A question that helps me out of this kind of trap is "so what?" Very often, there is no "necessary" relationship between our "insights" into the dynamics of the problem and the symptoms and goals in question. In these cases, and I believe this was the case with Rex, there was no relationship between historically related material and the effects of behavior therapy. Dr. Powell would, I firmly believe, have been equally successful without the added psychotherapy. He did an excellent job when he worked directly with the client and his phobic reaction. He and Rex collaborated well in helping the client desensitize the public-speaking anxiety. It was brief, to the point, both effective and efficient. This meets the criterion of a fair exchange in therapy. The client gets what he paid for, and, in this sense, it was ethically responsive to the needs of Rex.

As I see it, one problem here was not with the behavior therapy, although other approaches might have been taken. For example, my preference would have been cognitive-behavioral therapy, focusing on anticatastrophizing and "awfulizing" cognitions associated with the anxiety, and on "decontaminating" Rex's unrealistic expectations (from his parent ego state), his fear of failure (child ego state), and his irrational equation of his behavior with himself as a person. I might also have been less efficient than Powell, since I might have explored, with Rex's permission, other factors associated with his anxiety, e.g., nutritional, hormonal, and might have sent him for a physical examination. I might even have wondered, again with his permission and understanding, how the anxiety is beneficial.

Personally, I am not convinced of the

*necessity for psychotherapy in this case. It was not needed for the treatment of his phobic reaction to be effective. The case material was interesting, as it generally is when we deal with people's lives. And we can, in fact, perceive relationships between past events and symptoms. But because we perceive them does not mean they exist in a causal way to the symptoms, nor do we have to explore them to be effective with the problem in question. Because the focus was vague, we have no behavioral indicators of when therapy was to end, and this created the potential for "interminable psychotherapy." As Woody Allen has stated, "I've been in therapy for 20 years . . . I'm getting better . . . now I can eat without a bib."*

*Rex came for something, but he was unclear, and the therapist helped with the unclarity. Rex stated that he thought his public-speaking anxiety had something to do with his "powerful and demanding father, but now he was not sure. It was at that moment we discussed meeting regularly" (p. 334).*

*How would Rex know whether his anxiety was, in fact, related to his relationship with his father? Did Rex merely want to "understand" his father, or the relationship between his father and the symptom; or did he want to change? It was not clear what he wanted beyond change in his anxiety reaction, and how he would know he had "understood" (developed "insight"). In other words, I believe it would be ethically acceptable if Rex was unsure of the relationship between his experiences with his father and the symptom and wanted to explore these connections. The mistake was not in doing this work, but in Powell and Rex not agreeing on how they would know if, and how, the historical events were related to his public-speaking anxiety, and in not establishing clear criteria for termination.*

*A related concern is that by doing analytical therapy, we may propagate the myth that insight leads to behavior change. I have no strong evidence that this happens; the reverse seems to be equally true, namely, that behavior change leads to insight. I am also aware that looking into history for "causes" for current behavior can, if we are not careful, foster the "blaming" position of the "victim," rather than helping the client accept the proactive position of self-responsibility. No matter what Rex's parent did, or didn't do, which impacted on him in a negative way, it's regrettable. It is Rex himself, as an adult, who continues to induce his own anxiety by holding onto "irrational" expectations and demands on himself and others. His anxiety also has consequences for himself and others, a payoff for him, but this was not discussed in the case presentation. What are the advantages of his symptom? This is a useful question, whether we are doing behavior or dynamic psychotherapy.*

*Exploring personal history is interesting, but its relationship to the NOW is always problematic. As Ram Dass often says, "Wherever we look, we find what we are looking for." If the client is willing to buy his or our interpretation, and it helps alleviate suffering, so be it. I don't know what Rex was looking for, and how he would know when he found it. Maybe the best thing we can do for Rex is to help him stop looking. The summaries by both Rex and Powell indicate that they, too, question the usefulness of the psychotherapy. My own summary is that Powell did good work, particularly in the behavioral realm. I would have preferred that he and Rex be more clear about their treatment goals and that precautions and side effects be discussed more openly. "Be careful of what you ask, you just might get it" might be an opening statement we make to all of our clients.*

## REFERENCE

Rock, I. (1962). A neglected aspect of the problem of recall: The Hoffdung function. In J. Scher (Ed.), *Theories of mind* (pp. 645–659). New York: Free Press of Glencoe.

# CHAPTER 13

# Radical Eclecticism: Case Illustration of an Obsessive Disorder

*Malcolm H. Robertson*

**PERSONAL BACKGROUND**

To paraphrase the title of a motivational film of a few years ago, "who I am is where I've been." And in the beginning, about 30 years ago, I was pretty much like everyone else, a psychodynamically oriented clinician. The first bend in the road came during my doctoral study, during which I was trained in a loose merger of neoanalytical and learning theory, as set forth by Neal Miller, John Dollard, Joe Shoben, and others of that era. After graduation and for the next 10 years, I cultivated this hybrid form of psychotherapy, but basically my energies went into doing what one does to make one's mark as an academician.

Then I had two impactful experiences, both of which were peripheral to my professional ambitions, but in retrospect had pivotal significance for my career as a psychotherapist. The first was participating in one of those "touchy, feely" marathon group encounters so popular at the time; the other was a six-month stint overseas as a Peace Corp "shrink." I'm not sure, but I think what happened is that I belatedly started to define myself in terms of my experiences rather than in terms of a set of externally defined values. To come to the point, as a psychotherapist I opted to become present-centered, feeling oriented, with a focus on learning by doing. Concurrently, my academic priorities shifted from teaching and research to community consultation, training students to do psychotherapy (rather than to learn to talk about it) and, on the side, teaching myself to do the kind of psychotherapy that I sensed I was cut out to do.

My self-taught program led me from workshop to workshop, from institute to institute, like a wandering therapist in search of the therapeutic grail. At a point about 10 years ago, I simply burned out trying to imitate and emulate the master therapists whom I had observed. I had to admit to myself that I was never going "to pull the rabbit out of the hat," as they so deftly demonstrated time and again to spellbound audiences. At this juncture I decided to ask myself the questions which for so long I had asked of others. What is it you do? How do you do it? Why do you do it?

## RADICAL ECLECTICISM

Radical eclecticism is an atheoretical approach. Selected interventions from current systems are applied sequentially to foster therapeutic movement in the client, or two, at the most three, specific interventions are integrated and applied as a single intervention unit in order to effect change in thought-feeling-action patterns (Robertson, 1979). It is atheoretical in that interventions are organized not according to a formal theory base, but around the objectives or goals they are designed to help the client reach (Barker, 1984). The therapist selects interventions that clinical judgment and experience suggest are therapeutically potent for the presenting problem. Radical eclecticism differs from synthetic eclecticism, which I would describe as a synthesis of current concepts and principles for conceptualizing client problems and therapeutic outcomes. It differs from technical eclecticism (a term coined by Arnold Lazarus), which I would characterize as a polymethod/single-theory approach. And it differs from systematic eclecticism, which I understand to be an integration of concepts, change strategies, and specific interventions from several major systems into a new conceptual framework.

To develop and maintain a therapeutic relationship, I rely on interpersonal interventions, most of which are derived from person-centered psychotherapy (Egan, 1982). Examples are empathic reflection of explicit and implicit feelings, needs, values/beliefs, and goals; confrontation to identify conflicts and inconsistencies; therapist self-disclosure of personally or professionally relevant experiences; relational immediacy, i.e., communicating about the therapist-client communication or about the overall relationship; clarifying/summarizing; giving information directly, or indirectly, e.g., metaphors, images; and selective probes. I have found these interventions helpful: (1) to explicate problems and generate alternatives for the client to consider, and (2) to develop a therapeutic relationship that differs from the client's social/personal relationships, which so often maintain and perpetuate rather than challenge or change well-established, albeit maladaptive, interpersonal behaviors (Roberston, 1979).

To give clients a different perception of their problems, I use two neutral terms: (1) themes, e.g., recurring feelings, needs, thoughts/beliefs, actions, and (2) issues, e.g., thematic feeling of anger, thematic need for approval, thematic belief in subordinating one's needs, thematic unassertiveness. Following the identification of themes and issues, specific changes are planned with the client. Based on the literature and my experience, structured interventions are selected to implement the planned changes, e.g., relaxation/positive emotive imagery to relieve thematic anger, cognitive restructuring to suggest alternative ways to satisfy a thematic need for approval, Gestalt two-chair dialogue to challenge a thematic belief in subordinating one's needs, behavior rehearsal to develop assertive actions. An important component of the intervention work is to discuss with the client the immediate impact of the intervention and, if positive, to plan how the positive outcome may be used outside the session.

Additional features of my approach are: present-centered with an emphasis on emotions; flexibly structured with an agenda tailored to the client, the session, and the stage of therapy; tentative time limits correlated with progress reviews; and contractually based with between-session assignments. My therapeutic role is fourfold: interpersonal model, conceptualizer of information, change agent, and "professional" friend. I use the early stage (first session or two) of psychotherapy to develop a collaborative relationship, to gather and conceptualize information, to formulate therapeutic goals, and to begin formal intervention work. The middle stage consists of applying and evaluating interventions, planning between-session practice, and attending to impasses that arise within or outside the sessions. In the termination stage sessions are less frequent, difficulties in transferring and maintaining changes outside the session are addressed, and a self-help program and follow-up contacts are planned.

Several of my personal and professional values are reflected in the therapeutic relationship. The relationship is an egalitarian, collaborative partnership in which client and therapist have their respective responsibilities, are mutually self-disclosing, and are willing to confront and negotiate differences that arise during the course of therapy.

Although radical eclecticism does not have a formal conceptual framework, clinical decision making is guided by three assumptions. One is that psychotherapy is a reflective learning-by-doing for both client and therapist. The client learns by trying out unfamiliar behaviors within and outside the sessions and by evaluating the outcome in relation to his/her goals. The therapist learns how to change a particular client with a particular problem by conducting both planned and improvised interventions and by being modified by feedback from the client. A second assumption is that increasing clients' awareness of self and others creates a readiness to make and implement new decisions about how to live their life. A third assumption is that assessment and change are ongoing, interactive processes in psychotherapy, in which seeking therapy is the first (but hopefully not the last) change. Relatedly, clients are always in a process of change, part of which may be a response to their experience in psychotherapy (Efran & Lukens, 1985, p. 72).

The author limits his practice to adults with mild to moderate problems of living who are referred by colleagues. Instead of doing diagnostic testing beforehand, I rely on information gained in the first session or two. Based on an abbreviated version of an assessment strategy developed by Hulse and Jennings (1984), I assess strengths and limitations on the following client variables: expectation of and motivation for therapy, cognition, affect, behavior, health, current and past interpersonal relationships, developmental maturity, and communication style. From this information a tentative intervention strategy is drawn up to implement therapeutic goals and is later modified in response to client progress or lack of progress. The decision to use a group, couple, or family modality, concurrent with or in place of individual therapy, may be made at any point in the course of therapy. Generally, I use a group modality if I believe the client would benefit from peer support and peer confrontation, and from having a miniature social situation within which to try out new interpersonal behavior. A marital or family modality is utilized if significant others have problems closely related to those of the primary client and are willing to participate in conjoint therapy.

At present, I do not have an ongoing research program for radical eclecticism, which, in addition to other limitations, precludes determination of the contribution of each intervention to therapeutic progress. I do conduct a psychotherapy training program in individual, group, couple, and family therapy, in which graduate students are trained in radical eclectic psychotherapy (Robertson, 1984).

The remainder of the chapter is a presentation of radical eclectic psychotherapy with a client whom I saw for nine sessions over a four-month period. He is similar to other clients who are referred by colleagues.

## THE CLIENT

The client, who will be referred to as Steve, is in his early thirties, has been married for nine years to the same wife of approximately the same age, and has two pre-school children. He has a terminal degree in a health service field. His primary employment is administration, with secondary employment in clinical service and teaching. His wife, who will be referred to as Sandy, has a B.A. degree and is presently a full-time homemaker.

*Motivation.* Steve sought psychotherapy in order to make his life more balanced, i.e., by eliminating his workaholic behavior and by investing more time and energy in his marital and family relationships. He commented, "My work is taking over my life and I have to do something about it immediately."

*Expectation.* He expects that psychotherapy will be helpful, will require active effort on his part, and that change will be gradual.

*Cognition.* He is mentally alert and intact. His thoughts are organized, lucid, and convergent rather than divergent. A major cognitive theme is self-appraisal of professional performance.

*Affect.* Emotionally he is restrained, even inhibited, though his feelings are congruent with his thoughts, but not always with his actions, e.g., sometimes he "goes through the motions" or acts contrary to his feelings.

*Behavior.* He comes across as accommodating and compliant. He reports that he generally tries hard to do what he believes others expect of him and has trouble saying no. Overall, his actions suggest that he feels ill at ease in interpersonal situations.

*Health and physical appearance.* He is of average height and slender stature, and his facial expression is serious, earnest, with a constrained smile. His health and medical history are satisfactory.

*Past interpersonal relationships.* Steve is the oldest of five children of parents of mixed ethnic and religious backgrounds. His mother was a nurse and his father was in the same health profession as Steve. The family moved frequently, partly in response to the vicissitudes of his father's professional life. Although compatible, the family was not close or demonstrative. His mother was the primary parent and household manager and also contributed to the family income. The father, frequently absent from the home, was on the periphery of his marriage and his family. Steve stated that he has always been studious, achievement-oriented, and somewhat isolated socially. His social/recreational life was curbed partly because of family moves, and partly because, as he was the oldest child (and probably because of his accommodating nature), his mother leaned on him for assistance in managing the home and taking care of the younger children. His father died unexpectedly when Steve was in his first year of professional training. His mother and brothers live in other parts of the country; three siblings are in professions and one is in a skilled trade. Steve began dating his wife during their senior year in college and they married shortly thereafter.

*Current interpersonal environment.* His life is centered primarily in his profession and secondarily in his family. His social/recreational life is limited mainly to friends and activities connected with his church. He reports being under considerable pressure at work to meet his self-imposed standards, and under pressure from his wife to devote more time to her and to family activities. Because of the stress and strain of parenting, their sexual relationship lacks the frequency and quality that it had in the earlier years of marriage.

*Communication style.* Steve's speech is deliberate, thoughtful, and laconic; he listens well, chooses his words carefully, and is a responder rather than an initiator.

*Developmental maturity.* Steve is above the norm with respect to professional identity, career development, and intellectual maturity; he is at the norm in terms of providing dependable financial support for his family and in parenting responsibilities; and he falls short of the norm in terms of marital and social adjustment.

*Additional information.* Steve suffered a moderate depressive episode during his third year of professional training, for which he did not seek professional assistance. Two years later, he had psychotherapy for three or four months for "general coping problems," and he described the therapy as "somewhat helpful." My diagnostic impression is obsessive personality with moderate anxiety and depression.

*First Session Summary*

I gave Steve some administrative forms to complete and to return at the next session. I discussed confidentiality and obtained permission to tape the sessions. I explained the procedure that I would follow if I wished to use any part of the therapy material for professional publication. I told him that I preferred weekly sessions, but the frequency could be negotiated as we went along. I described my professional style as informal, suggested that we use first names, and encouraged his feedback on what I was doing and how I was doing it. In the following tape excerpt I explain my approach.

My approach is straightforward. I find out what the client wants to change and then use the sessions and between the sessions to work toward those changes. I use a formula, awareness plus decision plus action equals change. That is, I help the client to become aware of what he is thinking and feeling, and how he is acting, and then what thoughts, feelings, and actions he wants to change and how to go about it. I also find that in making changes, it's helpful for clients to change what they are in the habit of attending to or not attending to . . . so let's see first of all what you want to change, and why . . . what you'll gain from it, and what you'll have to give up, because with most important changes you have to give up something as well as get something.

In the remainder of the session, I focused on what changes Steve wished to make, what was happening in his life that made the changes desirable or imperative, and what the changes would entail. I used empathic responding to identify important feelings, needs, values, and goals; clarification to specify and particularize his comments; confrontation to underscore discrepancies, conflicts, and obstacles to change; self-disclosure to draw him out; and relational immediacy to comment on how we seemed to be communicating and how I experienced him at a paticular moment. Thematic feelings included: feeling controlled by his work, feeling anxious about success, and feeling guilty about shortchanging his family. Thematic needs included professional recognition and achievement and fulfilling expectations of others. Thematic thoughts included being prepared and being on top of problems. Thematic values included professional accomplishment and family loyalty. Thematic actions were those of trying harder, pleasing others, and getting bogged down in details.

The session closed with an agreement that we would work together to reduce his anxious preoccupation with his job, and to become more available emotionally and conversationally to his wife and children. In preparation for the next session, I decided to use a behavioral prescription because (1) it was relevant to the identified problems, (2) he was cooperative, and (3) he was a "doer." He agreed to set aside the last hour of his work day "to put the day to rest," by reviewing what had been positive and negative, readying himself for the next day rather than doing so at home, and then planning what nonjob activities he would do at home in the evening.

Following is an excerpt from the second half of the session. I use relational immediacy to change the question-answer exchange to a more spontaneous expression of his concerns; self-disclosure to check out additional feelings; confrontation to emphasize the conflict between needs and actions; and imagery to convey an additional perception of the problem.

T: Could you talk about the problem in a freewheeling way. I'm concerned that my questions are not drawing you out. I'm feeling a need to back off and let you express yourself in your own style . . . you. . . .

C: Okay, maybe I can describe what happens . . . I get home from work and these problems are still there, and then I'm still trying to hash these problems out and situations at work, and I'm . . . difficulty in thinking . . . my wife and kids ask me questions and I answer them and I'll ask them questions, and soon as I ask these questions . . . and I don't hear their answers . . . and it stays that way throughout the evening and night. I can't seem to break away from it . . . been going on for about a month . . . gotten to the point where I can't stay asleep. I wake up around four or five. The only other time was when I had a major depression when I was a junior in ——— School, and that's a signal things have gone too far. Also I'm not able to enjoy doing things at home, like working in the yard, just talking to my wife. I can't seem to listen to her. I know it's important for her sake and for mine and I just couldn't do it . . . you . . . so it's obviously a major problem now and something needs to be done.

T: There are some similarities to that period in ——— School.

C: Yes, things haven't gone well at work. I rush around from one thing to another . . . can't sit back . . . can't get organized like I did before, and I get discouraged and this interferes with ability to solve problems.

T: You want to be able to be there for your wife when she needs you, to be there, but on the other hand, you can't do it.

C: Right.

T: You can see her, but you can't reach her.

C: And I feel that way about my children, like I'm there in body but not in spirit.

T: But I hear you say you really want to be.

C: Right. The problem is I don't know how to get there.

T: How to overcome that distance between where you are and they are.

C: Yeah.

T: As you talk, it almost had a dream quality . . . the image I have is of someone in a field . . . you can see people and start going toward them, but like in a dream you try and can't and you don't really move.

C: Yeah.

T: Like being impotent. You can't do what you want to do.

[C: doesn't comment.]
T: If I were in your situation I would feel out of control. You withdraw from where you are and you feel unhappy with the place where you are withdrawing to.

After the session, I felt satisfied with what we had accomplished and optimistic about being able to work with Steve. I was also conscious of how I had had to struggle with a similar problem of balancing career and family life, and of my successes and failures in trying to work out a satisfactory balance.

*Second Session Summary*

My objective was to explore similarities and differences between his work/family life now and in the past. I used empathic reflection, confrontation, clarification/summarizing, and selective probes to obtain the following information.

He enjoys his present job more than the previous ones, but feels more frustrated now because he can't leave the job at his office, and he is not as successful as he wishes to be. He is conflicted about the job preoccupation that he experiences at home. On the one hand, he feels relieved that he can plan and ready himself for the next day, yet he feels guilty about doing it at home, and also feels controlled by the rumination because he can't stop or diminish nagging worries. He also disclosed that he is away from home more than he should be, because of his secondary employment of teaching and clinical service. He drew a parallel between a period during his professional training when he worked hard, felt dissatisfied with his performance, and would come home to assume household responsibilities because his wife was ill during the pregnancy of their first child, and his current life in which he works hard, feels dissatisfied, and returns home to relieve his wife who is emotionally exhausted from 10 hours of child care. He acknowledged recurring, depressive feelings, though not as strong as the depression he had during his training. He noted that since childhood "I have always been a worker at home," especially helping his mother with his younger siblings. He identified a long-standing need to anticipate and be prepared for problems that threaten to overtake him. He stated that, like childhood, his present life is characterized by an incessant drive to achieve and to be prepared for any and all problems, which in turn restricts his social/recreational life.

Midway through the session, I decided to use an imagery intervention in order to help him verbalize issues concerning his self-definition as a person. My rationale was that imagery would elicit reactions of which he was now only marginally aware, and that he would respond well to imagery because of his verbal skills and introverted personality. Following a brief relaxation exercise, I had him visualize, as vividly as he could, first a tree and then a house near the tree. After five minutes of visualization, we discussed the experience and made connections between the imagery and his current life. The intervention was not as productive as I had expected it to be. It revealed personal traits which he felt he lacked, but which he had the potential to develop given a less stressful work and home environment.

I gave him three assignments to do before our next session. The first was not to struggle against the intrusive thoughts. I explained that, paradoxically, struggling against an unwanted thought often strengthens the thought. At the same time, I instructed him to look around the house for something to attend to sensorily, as this might counteract the intensity of the rumination. The second assignment, which was based on his suggestion, was an extension of the first-session assignment of "putting his work day to rest." He would go to a nearby library on his way home and spend 15 to 20 minutes reading his favorite newspaper columnist. The third assignment was to draw his family of origin and bring the drawing to our next session. The purpose of the drawing assignment was to examine how unpleasant experiences of the past are influencing his present life.

After the session, I sensed that he left feeling unfinished, as if he were ambivalent about saying something more. I made a mental note to use relational immediacy in the next session if I sensed the ambivalence. I noted that even with strong verbal skills, he seemed to have difficulty in this session and in the previous one in talking spontaneously and in elaborating on personal issues.

*Third Session Summary*

Steve reported that he had gone to the library twice during the past week, and found it helpful in putting his work day to rest and in preparing emotionally for the transition to his role as husband and father. I stressed the importance of making the library interlude an integral part of the passage from job to home.

He then presented his family-of-origin drawing that depicted a holiday scene in which family members were gathered together for the holiday meal. He guessed he was about 10 at the time. By using empathic reflection, clarification, selective probes, and relational immediacy, and sharing my perceptions of the drawing, I centered his attention on what was happening in the scene that distressed him then and now. The following excerpt is noteworthy insofar as it marked the first time that he displayed significant, affective arousal. He was visibly moved as he recounted the unhappiness that accompanied holidays. The source of the unhappiness was mainly the behavior of his father, who suffered from manic-depressive episodes.

T: What was your mother's role in the family?
C: Well, she was, you know, continually working . . . keeping things going.
T: Well, she was continually working . . . and then what wasn't she doing?
C: You mean, like spending time with us?
T: Okay, with you, and when your dad was there, what was his role?
C: Well, he was . . . physically but not psychologically . . . he was there but. . . .
T: What do you remember of this time when he was there physically but not psychologically?
C: Whenever we'd eat supper . . . he'd eat through his supper . . . then put his head on his hands . . . and wouldn't talk.
T: What was going on?
C: Well, [long pause] he was a manic-depressive.
T: That must have worried you.
C: Well, yeah.
T: As a child, it must have been scary . . . what's wrong with Dad now . . . what did I do . . . did I cause it.
C: Well, it was just the way things were when he was home.
T: What did your mom do?
C: Keep up a front.
T: Like a buffer . . . her part was to protect him . . . to be a buffer . . . to spare him the commotion at home.
C: Yeah, that was pretty much it.
T: You knew not to make demands on him.
C: Yeah, right.
T: How old were you when you found out he was a manic-depressive?
C: I guess about 10.
T: How did you know that?
C: Well, my mother told me he was ill.
T: What that connects for me is the theme of uncertainty . . . father who is ill . . . the kind of illness that's not like a physical illness . . . uncertainty about

what is going to happen ... how will he be today ... tomorrow ... will he be home and how will he be if he does come home?

C: Well, [long pause] there were certain periods when he never came home ... other periods he'd come home but just not be available psychologically to us.

T: Sounds like your mom tried to provide the consistency that he couldn't.

C: Yeah.

T: Do you remember worrying about your dad when you found out he was ill?

C [long pause]: Ah ... ah ... I remember worrying because we were told that he wasn't going to be able to work, or might not be able to work anymore.

T: That would do it ... there again is the uncertainty.

C: Yep, yes.

T: So your mother became the one you could count on and depend on. If someone was going to keep the family together, it would be her.

C: Right.

T: Everything pretty much depended on her.

C: That's right.

T: When doing the drawing, did you get any kind of memory or association as you were doing it?

C: Nothing that hasn't occurred before ... Christmas was a very unpleasant time ... always has been ... and always since then ... not as bad now as it used to be.

T: How do you mean that?

C [long pause]: Well, it was a very unhappy time. I'd often wonder why other people enjoyed Christmas and I didn't.

T: How come they and not me.

C: Yeah. I had some resentment about that.

T: You feel resentful ... and sad also ... perhaps a lot of sadness.

C: Yeah.

T: And you've had to work through the sadness and resentment.

C: I feel bad right now.

T: I know that ... it's still a living memory ... sometimes you have to deaden those feelings, but you don't deaden them completely ... and they come back at you.

C: Yeah. I guess so.

Steve elaborated on his resentment of having to assume a caretaker role in the family because of his father's frequent absences and impaired functioning when he was at home. Connections were made between his caretaker role as a child and his caretaker role as an adult, both at work and at home. I pointed out the vulnerability he felt as a child in response to the uncertainty surrounding his father's illness, and the vulnerability he feels now in response to ever-present uncertainty, and to the pressure to anticipate, to be prepared, and to be in control of whatever may befall him.

As the session drew to a close, we shifted to the resentment he presently feels in functioning as a caretaker, especially at home. He agreed with my observation that he and his wife are more like compatible business partners. Each is busy as a caretaker for the children; both are suffering from caretaker role fatigue; the relief from the caretaker role is achieved separately rather than together; and the result is a lack of an intimate, sharing relationship. No assignment was made other than to allow time to process what had come up in the session, and to explore how his current lack of fulfillment is related to experiences of the past.

*Fourth Session Summary*

Because of Steve's cancellation, the fourth session took place two weeks later. My objective was to respond further to the material of previous sessions and to formulate some therapeutic suggestions. To summarize, I pointed out how the anxious rumination at home, and the emotional distance from the family, signaled a lack of balance in his life. I emphasized the importance of making some specific, modest changes in order to intervene in the rumination and emotional distancing. I raised the possibility that he was focusing his strong sense of responsibility on keeping bad things from happening instead of making good things happen. I suggested that at work he delegate more responsibility, enlist support from others in dealing with problems, scale down his expectations of what he thought he and others should accomplish, and schedule some brief, winding-down periods. When at home, I suggested that he engage in activities with his children that he enjoyed doing instead of accommodating to what they wished to do.

After the session I wondered if I had been too directive, even "preachy." I felt a mounting pressure to get back to the changes we had agreed to work on, and to encourage him to experiment with alternative ways of relating to his job and to his family. I decided against an earlier plan to use a Gestalt two-chair dialogue to address unfinished elements in the relationship with his father. He seemed unresponsive to working on that issue, and I sensed that an experiential intervention might stiffen rather than relax his resistance to exploring strong affective reactions. Because of the time-consuming procedure, I chose not to use systematic desensitization to relieve the anxious preoccupation. I also thought that a cognitive restructuring intervention might reinforce thinking rather than acting. If direct suggestions and behavioral prescriptions did not impact sufficiently, I decided I would use behavior rehearsal to experiment and practice alternative behaviors. I also recalled a remark he made as he left the session, to the effect that he was going "to wait on his marriage for the next couple of years." I wondered if the real reason for seeking therapy at this time was to deal with a decision to remain in his marriage.

*Fifth Session Summary*

Much of this session had to do with bringing me up to date on what had happened during the previous three weeks when he was out of town much of the time. He reported that he and his wife had talked at length about how to schedule more time together away from or at least out of the presence of the children. He had discovered that he could spend some of his parenting time doing what interested him, and that also appealed to his children, e.g., outdoor activities, cabinet making. He stated that he was delegating more responsibilities at work, was taking nonworking lunch breaks, and was enlisting the assistance of others in coping with job problems.

I brought up the comment he had made in the previous session about a time period for his marriage. He clarified the remark by stating that in two to three years he would not be as busy professionally as he is now, and therefore he could invest more of himself in the marital relationship. I cautioned him about the risk of waiting too long to restore the intimacy that he and his wife had had before the arrival of the children. I shared a comment which Cliff Sager had made at a workshop, that sometimes it is too late for a husband and wife to recover intimacy, even though both are committed to do so. I also told him of my struggle with the same issue of shortchanging my marital relationship, because of a drive to establish a productive career, and because of the parenting demands generated by three preschoolers.

Later in the session, I used relational immediacy to point out the difficulty he was having in responding to the session focus. I found myself asking many questions in response to frequent silences, like priming the pump, yet he seemed unable or unwilling to stay engaged conversationally. The following is an excerpt of that exchange.

T: I just want to check out with you about how our communication is going . . . it could be what you mentioned about things going pretty well for you now, and there's not the pressure to focus on problems. On the other hand, I'm wondering if I'm the kind of person you find you can relate to conversationally . . . because with some people it's easier to talk to and with others it's hard. Some persons we click with and others we don't. Anyway, I'd like to check this out with you in terms of how you and I click or don't click.
C: That's a . . . hard question to answer . . . 'cause the kind of issues we talk about . . . I don't talk about with others—I won't. Some people I'm very good friends with, I'll not even talk about personal issues with.
T: Yeah. One thought I had was that I might remind you of someone you found it hard to be at ease with.
C: Well, the kind of issues we talk about . . . I've always had trouble talking about those . . . and that was true for the other therapist I saw.
T: Okay. I just wanted you to feel free to suggest any changes I could make that would make it easier for you to talk with me . . . but it sounds like it's the personal issues rather than my style.
C: That's pretty much it.

Steve then commented that his problems were not pressing now, and that some headway had been made. He suggested a "maintenance schedule" of biweekly sessions in case the positive trend did not last. He reiterated the point in the above excerpt that it was hard for him to self-disclose, especially about feelings. After the session, I thought about the possibility of using an imagery exercise next time to deal with the impasse concerning self-disclosure of feelings. Briefly, the exercise is one where the therapist first shares his/her imagery of the therapeutic impasse (likens it to something removed from therapy) and then translates the imagery into the therapy situation, at which point the client follows suit (Klagsbrun & Brown, 1984).

*Sixth Session Summary*

Steve reported that the positive changes at work were still in effect, and that he was doing fairly well at home in controlling the intrusion of work-related thoughts. He also mentioned that he was taking his lunch breaks at home, and with one child in kindergarten, he and his wife had found some time for quality conversation. He had decided not to accept any more part-time teaching. He was also considering how he might spend less time in administration and more time in service work. The latter was more stimulating intellectually and more satisfying emotionally, and also allowed social interaction with colleagues "who are more on my wavelength" than are his colleagues in administration.

Near the end of the session, he commented that although he had initiated psychotherapy, he did so as much in response to pressure from his wife as in response to his concerns. She had asked him repeatedly to cut back on his work, and to be more communicative with her. For reasons I am unsure of (and I still am), I decided to do a brief monologue with his wife as if she were sitting in the chair next to him. The following is an excerpt of that monologue.

T: Sandy, what could you do or change that would make it easier for Steve to be emotionally available to you? He has to become more available emotionally, and how could you facilitate that . . .

what could you do or not do that would bring him closer to you?

Afterward, Steve inquired about the possibility of my seeing them as a couple. We decided that I would see his wife alone next week, and then we would schedule two or three conjoint sessions. Because of the change in our plan for the subsequent sessions, I decided to postpone using the imagery exercise I mentioned in the previous session summary.

*Seventh Session Summary*

Sandy came willingly to the session. My agenda was twofold: (1) to learn what progress she had observed in Steve, and (2) to assess the role of the marital relationship in Steve's workaholic behavior and emotional withdrawal at home. She reported that the sessions seemed helpful to his adjustment at work and to the time he spent with the children, but the problem with which she was most concerned, their marital communication, had not improved perceptibly.

She is an intelligent, articulate person, affable, and on the surface unflappable. She described her family of origin as closely knit and demonstrative. She noted her weight problem and reported considerable anxiety and stress over child management issues. She appreciated their compatibility, but she was disappointed in Steve's lack of interest in relationship-focused conversation, as well as his lack of interest in conversational interactions with other couples. She valued his deep conviction about life, his calm, rational problem-solving approach, his willingness to make personal sacrifices for what he believed in, and his acceptance of her criticism of their lack of communication. In talking with her, I relied mainly on empathy, personal/professional self-disclosure, clarification, selective probes, and occasional confrontation of her conflicting feelings and needs.

*Eighth Session Summary*

My purpose was to observe their interaction and to make a few specific suggestions to improve their relationship and their parenting, which they could try out during the next four weeks when the family would be out of town.

I presented the idea of how a marital-relationship problem is sometimes converted into a parent-management problem, because the former is too threatening to confront. They did not think this idea fit them, and they emphasized that indeed they were faced with two very strong-willed children who preempted most of their time and energy.

The following suggestions were made and accepted by both. First, they would take a firm, united stand with their children on bedtime. Second, they would arrange more family activities outside the home, as both reported much less stress in dealing with their children outside the home. For example, they agreed that since dinnertime was especially stressful, they would take the family out to dinner more often, at least during the week. Third, they would identify positive conversational topics that they had in common and would make an effort to pursue these topics. Fourth, when she became overstressed with the children, she would tell Steve what she needs from him, which in most cases is to be listened to rather than to have the problems solved (as Steve often believed he had to do). Fifth, a blend of symptom scheduling and contingency contacting was suggested, whereby they would agree on a time period when Steve could engage in his job ruminations, and then another time when he would be available for you-and-me talk. The following excerpt reveals a recurring problem in their interaction, and how it might be partially resolved.

T: What do the two of you need to nourish your relationship—to enhance it?

H: Spend more time together... by ourselves.

W: There are times when [inaudible]... it's a comforting attitude I need [inaudible]... sometimes I don't need you, but it's nice to know when I do that you'll be there... not so much that you're doing anything, but that you're there.

T: How do you react to what Sandy just said?

H: Well, it's [inaudible]... a thing... like things are just fine with you, and then....

W: I think... it's a sense I don't want to burden you with what's going on in me... maybe it's like you're one of the kids and I don't need any more problems [laughs].

T: I think a couple of things are operating at these times. I do experience you being protective of Steve. Also, because he hasn't been there emotionally for you, you think "I have to do it myself... I don't know if he will be able to step in... he's preoccupied and maybe it's all up to me"... so it's partly protective and partly feeling you're going to have to handle it without him anyway.

W: I think so... [inaudible]

T: So what do you need from him?

W: [inaudible]... it's nice to have someone there... just like holding hands, like getting a backrub... [inaudible]... like the other night when I needed solace, comfort, [inaudible]... and you teased me [laughs]. I was scared, totally scared—no ability to go to sleep... I tried to talk myself out of it... for awhile... but not for long. I was panicky.

T: That's the way it is with an anxiety attack.

W: Is that so?

T: Then you came downstairs.

W: Oh, I was having trouble breathing, feeling very uncomfortable, so I decided to go downstairs and see what you were doing. [inaudible]

H: You said you were nauseous.

W: Oh, yes, and you said, "Oh, you're always nauseous about something"—and this really ticked me off.

H: You said you were nauseous from [inaudible]... you get nauseous easily, and I meant it seriously.

W: I think you said something about you're always nauseous.

H: Well [inaudible].

W: I went back upstairs... and you came up later. I tried to lay down in bed and the breathing became more difficult.

T: When you came downstairs, what did you need from Steve?

W: I think... just physical closeness... warmth... just [inaudible]....

T: So you didn't need a solution—just some physical contact.

W: Yeah.... Yeah... [inaudible].

T: Like you just wanted to regress—just curl up.

W: Yeah [laughs]. Yeah [laughs]. After the anxiety went away, I had this intense desire to go into the kids' room and get that big teddy bear [laughs]... I almost did, but I didn't want to wake the kids, and I thought it might disturb you because you were asleep by then.

T: So, Steve, you're saying we need to spend more time together, and Sandy, you're saying there are times when you just need to feel Steve's physical closeness and support.

W: Yeah, that's pretty much it.

T: You're not looking for a problem solver—it can be Steve just being there... and if Steve realizes that he doesn't have to solve any problem or come up with any answers, that will take pressure off him. I think you need to make it clear at those moments just what you do need from him.

W: [inaudible]

H: So I did come around and say something about having a backrub—I had no idea that was what you wanted earlier.

T: I think that is a good example of what Sandy and I talked about last week, and what Steve and I talked about earlier. He needs to be there for you, and you need to tell him what you want, and it may be nothing more than just sitting next to you or being quietly supportive.

W: I think it's good that Steve sees these attacks I've been having lately . . . to what extent I'm overdrawn . . . you're seeing my limits . . . how overwhelmed I am . . . he realizes my need, and as a result I have more freedom to say "Help!"

*Ninth Session Summary*

Both reported that the vacation trip had been stressful in terms of the children, but they concluded that their stress was a function of the circumstances of the trip. They reported a modest improvement in their conversational relationship, and in coping with the children since returning home. We agreed that this session would be our last, and that they would contact me about future sessions, alone or together, if they so desired.

*Follow-up and Client Impressions*

I sent Steve the following evaluation form six weeks after our last session. Six months later I sent him the tape excerpts for review and for permission to use in this chapter and included a one-page evaluation form to assess different components of the therapy and my overall style. He authorized use of the tape excerpts, but did not complete the six-month evaluation form, because of his vague memory of the sessions and his current preoccupation with some critical issues at work.

*Psychotherapy Evaluation*

1. What in particular was helpful?
   Focusing on ways to divert attention from work-related activities
2. What in particular was unhelpful?
   Not sure any of it was unhelpful
3. What would you have liked more of?
   Perhaps more focus on dealing with my fundamental attitudes toward work and appropriately prioritizing it in my life
4. What would you have liked less of?
   —
5. To what extent did you receive what you expected?
   I expected to receive help in breaking the "hold" that my work held over me in terms of my preoccupation with it. The therapy did accomplish this for you.
   At last, here it is. Hope you're doing well.

## CONCLUDING COMMENTS

My overall evaluation of the therapeutic work is mixed. Steve had made some progress in terms of coping with job stress. He was less anxious about his ability to manage people and to handle the politics of his job. Relatedly, at home he had gained a modicum of control over job-related preoccupations, insofar as he was able to reduce the frequency and duration of his ruminative thinking. A commitment to improve the marital relationship had been established, and he was more willing to implement suggestions which he and his wife negotiated.

Belatedly, I had become aware of the magnitude of Steve's problem in initiating and maintaining personal communications within and outside the therapy sessions. I regretted that I had not given this problem a central focus in our sessions. In retrospect, I can see that my failure to achieve, at least a partial resolution of the problem, set limits on how much positive influence we had on each other. In addition, if unresolved, the problem will continue to be a source of dissatisfaction for his wife.

With a few exceptions, I believe that I was consistent in demonstrating radical eclectic psychotherapy, which I described earlier in the chapter. I selected interventions I judged to be therapeutically potent for Steve's two presenting goals of relieving the anxious preoccupation with his job and being more available emotionally and conversationally to his wife and children.

At various junctures, I used imagery, the family-of-origin drawing, interpretation of past experiences on present functioning, paradoxical directive (not to struggle against the intrusive thoughts), and conjoint marital sessions. However, I was surprised by how much I relied on behavioral prescriptions and the interpersonal interventions of empathy, confrontation, relational immediacy, self-disclosure, clarification/summarizing, and selective probes. In hindsight, I wish that I had used behavior rehearsal to address Steve's problem in initiating and maintaining personal communications, first with the focus on conversations outside therapy and later with the focus on our communication. To do so, we would have had to agree on a goal of improving communication skills. The interpersonal interventions, even relational immediacy, were not sufficient to modify Steve's communication style. Again in hindsight, I would have started conjoint marital sessions in the middle rather than in the late stage of therapy, with one or two sessions that included the children.

Consistent with my approach, the sessions were primarily present-centered with an emphasis on feelings, and contractually arranged with respect to within-session agenda and between-session assignments. I made a conscious effort to fit the interventions to Steve's stated goals and personality. I still believe that he would not have responded well to a Gestalt intervention or to protracted attention on earlier developmental experiences. Consistent also with my approach was the progression of therapy tasks from early to middle to late stages of therapy.

I thought that we developed an egalitarian and collaborative relationship, e.g., use of first names, negotiating goals and tasks, mutual feedback. The three assumptions to which I referred earlier, learning by doing within and outside therapy, increasing client's awareness of self and others, and blending assessment with intervention, were evident at least in terms of the agreed-upon goals.

Finally, I am persuaded that radical eclecticism is a viable example of eclectic/integrative psychotherapy insofar as interventions are tailored to a client's problems, personality, and environmental resources. I am equally persuaded that radical eclecticism needs an explicitly stated conceptual base, a systematically developed intervention strategy to decide which technique to use for a problem at a particular stage of therapy, and a program of research that addresses both process and outcome variables.

## REFERENCES

Barker, R. L. (1984). *Treating couples in crisis.* New York: Free Press.

Efran, J., & Lukens, M. D. (1985). The world according to Humberto Maturana. *The Family Therapy Networker, 9*(3), 23–28, 72–75.

Egan, G. (1982). *The skilled helper.* Monterey, CA: Brooks/Cole.

Hulse, D., & Jennings, M. L. (1984). Comprehensive case conceptualization in counseling: A visual integrative technique. *Professional Psychology: Research and Practice, 15,* 251–259.

Klagsbrun, J., & Brown, D. (1984). Getting the picture: The use of imagery to clarify therapeutic impasses. *Psychotherapy: Theory, Research and Practice, 21,* 254–259.

Robertson, M. (1979). Some observations from an eclectic therapist. *Psychotherapy: Theory, Research and Practice, 16,* 18–22.

Robertson, M. (1984). Teaching psychotherapy in an academic setting. *Psychotherapy: Theory, Research and Practice, 21,* 209–212.

# Commentary: Radical Eclecticism as Directive and Structured

## Sol L. Garfield

This case report provides an interesting and frank account of one psychotherapist's approach to working with patients. Although the report naturally focuses on the therapeutic interactions with one patient, the reader gets some feel for the general approach that Robertson uses. It also illustrates that you can't really tell what a psychotherapist actually does in therapy by the designation used to describe or categorize his or her form of therapy. In the final analysis, one has to be informed about the actual operations of therapy. Being able to observe the therapy is, of course, the optimum way to know what actually takes place. This, however, is not always possible, and a case description with verbatim excerpts is a reasonably good substitute.

There are a number of items in the case report that I found to be of interest. There did appear to be quite a strong directive thrust to the therapy described despite the author's emphasis on the therapeutic relationship, the interventions derived from "person-centered psychotherapy," the mention of empathic reflection of feelings, therapist self-disclosure, and "relational immediacy." It was interesting to me also that how we use language has a clear impact on others. For example, the author at one point states: "I used relational immediacy to point out the difficulty he was having in responding to the session focus" (p. 365). I did not believe that relational immediacy could or should be used simply as a technique—it seemed to make the relationship sound insincere, forced, or manipulative. However, as the author uses it, the term simply means that the therapist pointed to difficulties the patient had in communicating in the therapy session. At the same time, I would view empathic responding as more of a personal quality or style and not as a technique (p. 360).

A number of other aspects were of interest to me, and I can comment on only a few of them. Although the therapist clearly has some general scheme for conducting therapy and, as indicated, exhibits a somewhat directive stance, he refers to the relationship as egalitarian. Clearly, this is his view and represents his value system in this situation. However, as long as one individual is in the socially superior role and is being paid for his services, I do not believe the relationship can be truly egalitarian. For example, in the second session, the therapist used confrontation, clarification/summarizing, selective probes, an imagery intervention, and a relaxation exercise, and also gave the client three assignments to do before the next session. This appeared to me as something other than egalitarian, but I am making no value judgment as to its goodness or badness. In the final analysis, the therapist does have the responsibility for conducting therapy, and this is a responsibility he/she must acknowledge.

I myself, do not tend to use imagery very much, but I wondered about its use in the present case. What rationale was provided to the client for its use? How were connections made between visualizing a tree and a house and the client's current life? Such information would have made these interventions more meaningful.

It is also of interest that despite a cancellation after the third session, some reflective doubts on the part of the therapist during the fourth session, and a three-week interval before the fifth session, the client in the fifth session "commented that his problems were not pressing now, and that some headway had been made. He suggested a 'maintenance schedule' of biweekly sessions in case the positive trend did not last" (p. 366). Two possible hypotheses come to mind. The client has received some help from therapy and wants to keep it going; also, the weekly sessions are too much for him and he would prefer to have them more widely spaced.

I was surprised, as apparently was Robertson, that he decided to carry out the pseudomonologue with the client's wife, and in essence shifted the focus from the client to the wife. This led to the therapist arranging to see the wife for the seventh session and subsequently to see the husband and wife together for the last two sessions. There is no reason not to see the wife, although there are some possible dangers in suddenly shifting the focus (or responsibility) onto the wife, particularly in what appeared to be a sudden decision. I may have preferred to discuss this further since the issue was brought up toward the end of the therapy session. On the other hand, the decision to see both individuals together was a reasonable one and probably should have been initiated sooner, as the therapist himself has stated. On the basis of the eighth session, it does appear as if the wife may have more personal difficulties than was apparent in her interview during the preceding session.

I believe that I would have tended to reflect the wife's "panicky" feelings more and to have her express her feelings more fully. In many ways she has carried responsibilities without being able to have the strong support of her husband. She verbalizes the continuing problem as one of marital communication; it is that but also something more than that.

Finally, I would note that Robertson felt that he had relied on too few "structured interventions" and wished he had tried some Gestalt interventions, as well as behavioral rehearsal. As indicated earlier, I received the impression that he was quite directive and actually used structured interventions, although, again, these terms may have different meanings to different individuals. I would have used somewhat less structured and directive procedures, and perhaps these are some of the differentiating criteria for radical eclecticism and just plain eclecticism. In any event, Robertson does reveal honestly and openly how one therapist functions and that decisions frequently are made quickly and sometimes spontaneously. Later, the therapist may conclude that he might have done something differently. It is good that he attempts to appraise his work, and he is not alone in thinking, "I might have (or should have) tried something else."

# Commentary: Perspectives from an Interpersonally Based Behavioral Therapist

## J. Kevin Thompson

First, a few words about my own particular, emerging, psychotherapeutic approach—a position from which I will comment on Dr. Robertson's excellent presentation of radical eclecticism. During the past two years, along with Donald Williams, I have evolved an interpersonally based behavioral psychotherapy (Thompson & Williams, 1985; Thompson & Williams, in press). This approach emphasizes that the prior establishment of a positive client-therapist relationship is necessary for the maximal usefulness of behavioral techniques. This relationship is fostered by the creation of an accepting therapeutic environment by the therapist, who attempts to communicate to the client Rogers' three crucial therapist variables—genuineness, empathy, and unconditional positive regard.

Robertson's case nicely illustrates his facile use of a variety of techniques, chosen from various orientations. He uses Rogerian procedures (reflection, clarification) and other interpersonal techniques (relational immediacy, self-disclosure). He uses behavioral strategies (behavioral rehearsal, homework tasks, directive interventions) and cognitive approaches (cognitive restructuring, imagery). Finally, he also tosses in a Gestalt technique (empty chair) and a psychodynamic procedure (projective drawing).

Of primary importance, and most impressive to me, is the fact that Robertson's madness has method. In each of the instances with his client, he supports the use of his chosen psychotherapeutic gambit. For example, if he feels the need to alter the session from a question-answer style to one that focuses more on the client's immediate feelings, he readily uses relational immediacy to increase the client's spontaneous expression of his concerns (p. 361). On the other hand, if the client seems resistive to an experiential intervention, he is adept at transferring to a specific behavioral approach (p. 365).

I believe that the case presentation by Robertson nicely illustrates how a therapist may alter the style and content of psychotherapy, based on the immediate needs of the client. However, to the extent that this case is typical of the radical eclectic approach (and I am forced to generalize based on this chapter), I have a major problem with Robertson's psychotherapy.

I am concerned that many clients will not feel a specific, focused, direction of therapy when confronted with the myriad number of things happening in Robertson's radical eclectic approach. My experience is that starting and stopping a variety of tasks, especially within a short psychotherapeutic time span (nine sessions for Robertson's case), usually leaves the client in a state of confusion. Insight into the dynamics of a problem may occur quite rapidly, especially if the therapist acquires adequate information from the client and feeds the content of this information back to the client in an easily interpretable form (as I believe Robertson does). However, change in behavior patterns and belief systems proceeds ever so slowly, especially when the problem is one based on "personality" disorders. (Robertson labels his case an obsessional personality. According to DSM-III, the diagnosis would probably be "compulsive personality." I might also label the individual "type A".)

This is the case with Robertson's client. After the first session, the client is given "homework" to use the last hour of his workday "to put the day to rest" (p. 361). The efficacy of this plan is not discussed by Robertson, but he assigns further tasks to the client at the end of the second session, including: (a) distraction—for intrusive thoughts; (b) relaxation—the client is asked to read at the library; and (c) to "draw his family of origin" (p. 362). At the third session, the drawing is discussed, and Robertson notes that the client made two trips to the library; however, the distraction assignment is not discussed. These assignments are discontinued at the end of session 3—instead the client was encouraged to "process what had come up in the session" (p. 364).

In the subsequent sessions Robertson does a host of things, including: offering a variety of suggestions aimed at reducing workaholic behaviors and ruminations (session 4); dealing with the client's marriage and lack of self-disclosure (sessions 5 and 6); interviewing the client's wife (session 7); and seeing both parties in therapy (sessions 8 and 9). Although some of these issues are followed up, in general, many issues are touched on, but none are given adequate attention and none are resolved at the time of termination. In many ways, I feel that I've read nine sessions of an initial assessment—and now have sufficient information to conceptualize the case and choose an appropriate intervention.

I think that this concern is especially relevant given the client presented by Robertson. We are dealing with a fairly typical case of the compulsive workaholic who has ignored emotional needs (of self and significant others) and, instead, focused on productivity. One of the most important factors in treating these cases is to get the client to challenge their beliefs regarding what is worthwhile (work, success, etc.) and what is not (free time, verbal communication, intimacy, etc.). In addition, the relationship with these clients is extremely important; the therapist must demonstrate that he/she accepts them unconditionally—otherwise, these clients will spend much of therapy simply trying to please the therapist, in their perfectionistic, compulsive drive to be error-free. Therefore, these clients need a good deal of time in therapy—time spent focusing on a few basic issues, including a strong focus on specific strategies to break compulsive behavior and an emphasis on the client-therapist relationship.

I realize Robertson's presentation of his procedure is constrained somewhat by the limitations of presenting any psychotherapy within the confines of one client and one short chapter. I applaud any attempt to focus on behavior, cognitions, and affect in a single therapy. As it is presented in this book, however, I feel that radical eclecticism must deal with the issues raised in this commentary if it is to evolve into a widely accepted psychotherapy.

## REFERENCES

Thompson, J. K., & Williams, D. E. (1985). Behavior therapy in the 80's: Evolution, exploitation, and the existential issue. The Behavior Therapist, 8, 47–50.

Thompson, J. K., & Williams, D. E. (in press). An interpersonally-based behavioral therapy. In M. Hersen, R. M. Eisler, & P. M. Miller (Eds.), Progress in behavior modification. New York: Academic.

# CHAPTER 14

# A Marital Triangle: How Open Can We Be?

*George J. Steinfeld*

## INTRODUCTION TO THE TARET APPROACH

The present case discussion focuses on a couple's attempt to resolve some very thorny issues involving two problems that can destroy marriages—physical abuse and infidelity. This case is formulated and treated from my integrative therapeutic approach known as the TARET systems.

My interest is in holistic health and psychotherapy. I have worked with clients of all ages, in varied settings, and in most modalities. My concept of holistic health on the individual level is consistent with a systems model of family functioning. The family, like the individual, is conceived to be *whole*, more than the sum of the interacting parts, with its own uniqueness in structure and process. Each member interacts with others, affecting and being affected by them; the family unit is seen as a part of even larger systems, also having interactional effects. At the center, however, remains the person, the seat of all psychological events, living in his world as a function of his level of consciousness (level of awareness). The problem for me has been to find ways to characterize the relationships between the uniqueness of the person and his family as a unit, and the relationships between the family members, without losing sight of both the smaller unit (the interacting parts of the person) and the larger social community systems.

My search for concepts and methods that can describe these interactional processes on the intra- and interpersonal levels has not been easy, and I have used and subsequently discarded a variety of personality theories. Currently, to help organize all the information that is gathered while working with people, the clinical theories of transactional analysis, rational emotive, and social learning theories are combined within a holistic family systems framework. More formally, it is a cognitive-behavioral systems approach to intrapsychic and interpersonal relations. It is called TARET systems (Steinfeld, 1980). TARET systems integrates transactional analysis (TA), rational emotive therapy (RET), and systems thinking.

Given this framework, how can we understand the presenting problems of John and Jane? John's abusive behavior and his infidelity, and Jane's anxiety regarding his abusive potential and her conflictual feelings about John's affair, need to be understood within this holistic family systems framework. This means that their cognitive-affective-behavioral responses are affected by their genetic-biochemical factors, past learning histories, current perceptions, which reflect current stresses, models of the world, and themselves, values and spiritual beliefs, family of origin, and their future hopes. All of these manifest themselves in their verbal and nonverbal behaviors, subtle and obvious, which affect one another in a never-ending series of transactions, which feedback on themselves and others who are part of their world.

The TARET model employs a levels approach. That is to say, clients can choose to work specifically on behavioral changes in themselves or the relationships between members of the family (level 1). They can choose to work on understanding the historical and current cognitive and emotional antecedents and consequences for the behavior in question (level 2). Or they can choose to work on discovering the deeper meaning of their lives, struggling with the relative nature of reality, their existential predicaments, and their spiritual selves (level 3). The current case describes primarily the first two levels of work, although we touch on level 3 in the final phases of treatment. The case was selected because the couple wanted to participate in taping sessions, and the problems presented represent struggles that many couples face in a variety of constructive and destructive ways.

*Change,* as opposed to *understanding* ("insight"), is the primary goal, and contracts are developed in which the client and the therapist are responsible for their respective parts in the therapeutic process. Awareness, self-control, and the development of prosocial personal and relationship-enhancing responses also lie at the heart of the approach. Thus, the TARET model is primarily a cognitive therapy, with affective and behavioral responses important insofar as they help alter the basic cognitive structures of the client. In this regard, I take my lead from Ellis (1962, 1977), Beck (1976), Meichenbaum (1977), and other cognitive therapists, including Berne (1961). In regard to the systems aspects of the model, the author has been most influenced by the M.R.I. approach to brief treatment (Watzlawick et al., 1974; Fisch et al., 1982), as well as the work of Bowen (1978), Haley (1976), and, of course, Bateson (1972, 1980), who was quite aware that the punctuation of the learning process is based on cognitive operations in the mind of the observer. It was Bateson's writings that provided the link between a theory and functioning of a family and the cognitive operations.

My search for concepts that are applicable to individual and family relationships led me to the work of Piaget, and his concept of *decentering,* as the bridge between intrapsychic and interpersonal functioning (see Steinfeld, 1978). In terms of family therapy, the cognitive-behavioral-systems model is an attempt to integrate different approaches. The client is helped to develop options that can be translated into behaviors whose effects are likely to be in his "enlightened self-interest," and not repetitively self-defeating. Clients are conceived to be either "ignorant," in that they do not know what to do under stressful conditions, or "well intentioned," but often full of "hubris" (i.e., the prideful demand to be "right" even in the face of solutions they have attempted in vain). In this sense, clients have become addicted to a set of beliefs, feelings, and behaviors that are closely linked to their self-concept, that is, who they think they are or should be (Steinfeld, 1978). Therapists can be similarly addicted when we continue to operate in ways that are not very useful. In this model, therapy is collaborative with the goal of helping clients take responsibility for their lives and become their own therapists.

As Bandler and Grinder (1975) make clear, when people come to therapy they feel "stuck"; they cannot find a way out of their psychological prisons. These clients have learned to block themselves from seeing options and possibilities that are open to them, since these are not available in their model of the world. What is called for, then, is cognitive therapy which increases awareness, expands consciousness, and opens up new approaches to solving their problems in living. In coming to understand how some people continue to cause themselves pain and anguish, it is important to realize that people are fallible human beings and not bad, sick, or crazy. They are, like everyone else, making the best choices from those of which they are aware, choices that come from their own particular models of themselves, others, the world, and the universe.

It should be clear by now that the cognitive-behavioral systems model is based on a perceptual learning foundation, which has been spelled out elsewhere (Steinfeld, 1975), and a developmental notion that families, like individual systems, go through a series of evolutionary stages. One of the cornerstones of the model is the idea that there is a distinction between an event, as perceived or experienced (seen, heard, touched, etc.), and the interpretation of that event which guides subsequent behavior. The basis for the interpretation of any event is the "sets" or underlying cognitive structures to which the event is assimilated and accommodated. It should also be clear that groups do not perceive anything, that families have no "rules." All we have are individuals thinking, feeling, acting, and reacting as a function of past experience and expectations in consistent ways. These patterns appear "rule-governed" from the perspective of the observer who punctuates and gives meaning to the events in ways that are similar or different from the family. "Wherever we look, we find what we're looking for" (Ram Dass, 1976).

In this regard, a systems approach differs greatly from both RET and the TA/Gestalt model, which focus primarily on intrapsychic changes. Holistic therapists need to be aware of the implications of personal change for the entire social system of which the person is a part—affecting and being affected by the myriad of persons in his life. It is irresponsible for a therapist to facilitate change on a psychological level without regard for the effects of these changes on others (and thereby on the client). This is why it is important for a therapist, before accepting a contract, to discuss with clients the possible long-term disadvantages of personal change. Not only is this strategically useful (Watzlawick et al., 1974), but it sets the stage for helping the client move past his egocentric position toward a more "mature" awareness of the reciprocity involved in human relationships.

## THE CASE OF JOHN AND JANE

### Referral Information

John, 48, a middle manager for an international corporation, and Jane, 30, a sculptress, were referred to me because of my experience of working with men who were violent in their relationships. The setting was my private practice; frequency of sessions was once a week. After four sessions, John felt he could not work with the previous Employee Assistance Program therapist. The therapist told me that she felt he "needed" someone with my experience. My hunch was that both the therapist and John felt intimidated by one another. Although I didn't know why this might be so, my hypothesis was that she might have been anxious about his directness and his violent potential, and he might have been uncomfortable about her assertiveness. Actually, he later said that it was her lack of directness that bothered him because he wasn't sure she could deal with him, or if he could learn anything from her.

My goal during the evaluation period is to get a sense of how each views the problem, what form it takes, what has been tried to alleviate the problem, and to establish a treatment contract. This takes about four sessions; following the first couple session, I give each a questionnaire, which I use during the second and third individual interviews, to explore historically relevant material, their future hopes and fears, and any areas that failed to emerge during the initial interview, or to get further data on areas I sensed were avoided during the couple's first session. This is especially important with cases of violence, since it often is the case that women feel intimidated by their abusive partners and may not share what they really feel and think in his presence. I generally see the man first for the individual session to alleviate his anxiety about what may emerge with his wife in her private session, and to reinforce the idea that he is not "mad or bad," that his anger and abuse are learned behaviors, that they can be unlearned, and that, because of our conditioning histories, many men suffer from similar problems. The fourth session is used to bring things together, establish our treatment contract, and prioritize the treatment goals.

The following pages summarize the first 13 sessions. Although all sessions were tape-recorded, the first 13 are not available because Jane requested access to them for personal listening but failed to return them. Parts of the last four sessions are given verbatim and will comprise the second part of the chapter. The richness of the first 13 sessions is therefore lost, and it is clear that I am selecting certain aspects of the data to present, based on my formulation of the problems, and my own needs at the time of writing this chapter. The quality of the interactional pattern between the three of us is a little clearer in the last four sessions.

*Evaluation*

*Session 1.* After brief introductions and some small talk, we moved into the referral issues, current perceptions of the problems, and how they thought I might help. Jane focused on John's angry outbursts and his threats to throw her out, both of which scared and intimidated her. John agreed to the long-standing anger problem, which had gotten him into trouble in his social relationships and on the job. Regarding the latter, his angry confrontational approach had kept him from advancing in his career. He wanted to learn techniques to handle his angry feelings in nonthreatening ways. Jane not only wanted to reduce her anxiety with John, but wanted to be more "expressive with him," socially, and with her family of origin. No tissue damage had occurred.

I began thinking of the learned roles of persecutor, victim, and rescuer (Karpman's triangle) (Karpman, 1968) as we explored their relationship. How did family-of-origin issues and learned patterns fit together within their marriage? Their relationship history was described, including their previous marriages, prior affairs, and triangles. John described his bout with alcoholism, which he was winning, having been dry for more than eight years. The second issue was John's current affair. After they met, and began thinking of a long-term relationship, an open marriage was discussed. Jane was interested, but felt that she could only handle it after their marriage had solidified. Nine months later he was ready and acting it out; she wasn't. She still wanted a 1:1 committed relationship, whereas he wanted the option of an affair. She couldn't trust him regarding a commitment because of both his affair and his violent tendencies, which could easily destroy the relationship. Trust issues were explored. Jane could not have an affair because, at this time, she wasn't sure she wanted it, and because John couldn't handle it. It was unfair to her, a theme that emerges throughout the treatment process.

My first objective was to negotiate a nonviolence contract, to which John readily agreed. We continued to explore reasons for both the violence and the affair. Both were related to his feeling neglected and threatened with abandonment. These feelings were associated with Jane's previous and current relationship with her lover, although she stated that her current relationship with this man was not a sexual one.

At the end of the first session the issues were beginning to take shape. He wanted an open marriage; he was a sexual person and "needed" lots of sex and affection and physical contact, all of which his current lover gave him. He was threatened by Jane's previous lover still being in the picture, and her emerging success as a sculptress, and he felt that she would leave him when she was economically able to. She claimed she did not want an affair at this time; perhaps later she would be able to deal with it. She was nonsexually involved with her previous lover and could not have an affair and tell John, as he had told her, because this would threaten him and he would or could be violent around this issue. She was anxious and mistrustful of him. He wouldn't give up the affair; she wouldn't give up her "friend," nor could she really be affectionate toward John because of how she was feeling. Both were not getting what they said they wanted. They had tried talking about the situation, to no avail. Jane had been in therapy for four years and still saw her therapist occasionally. I was searching for both script issues from their family of origin and cognitions that were creating their affective and behavioral patterns. I liked both of them after the first session.

*Session 2.* I saw Jane alone and reviewed her life history questionnaire. Again she focused on her fear of John and detailed her reasons. Her vulnerability also had a history, stemming from a birth defect, a series of operations, her small, somewhat deformed body, and other issues, namely, her financial dependency on John. She felt she was generally nonassertive. She was unclear about her role in the flareups between them. I explained again my belief that each person was responsible for the quality of the relationship and his own behavior. She was not responsible for his threats and his violent gestures, he was. She confirmed that John was not drinking at this time and was a member of AA, and she attended Alanon meetings for emotional support and to learn how to cope with an alcoholic. When conflict escalates, she is able to control its intensity by crying... "he walks away when I cry." In many violent relationships, tears could provoke the abuse. It was becoming clear that John's anger and threats were reactive, stemming from anxiety, and not "instrumental" with the purpose of dominating and controlling Jane (although it had this affect as well and this needed to be explored with John). We went over her development, her family of origin, sexual history, and current sexual feelings. John was described as a gentle lover; she was orgasmic, but not penile-vaginally. He felt this was a problem, she did not. She had body image problems, but she acknowledged that John was accepting and caring and was not affected by her stature. John wanted more sex; at this time, she was not initiating sexual contact. She was able to describe the positive aspects of the relationship. She confirmed that an open marriage was discussed, but that she wanted sexual exclusivity at this time. She wanted therapy to help her overcome her fears of John, her general feelings of vulnerability, in pursuing ways of becoming financially independent, so that she could, if it ever came to that, leave John if they couldn't resolve their differences. "I want to grow up."

*Session 3.* John had already begun to read the books I recommended (i.e., Ellis, *How to Live With and Without Anger, A New Guide to Rational Living,* 1977). His agenda included the reasons for his affair with Mary—his sexual "needs," his feeling inadequate with Jane because she was not orgasmic penile-vaginally, his feeling threatened by the ongoing relationship with her past lover, fear that she'll leave when she was financially secure, anger at her withdrawal from him, and general lack of affection. His sexual history included references to his father, who was a "skirt chaser." He had affairs in his previous marriage. His current lover, older than he, satisfied many of his "needs," physically and emotionally. They do things together and she is a very loving and accepting person. He had told Jane because he values honesty, dislikes having to lie, and prides himself on telling the truth and being direct. He described his parents' divorce when he was 10, and his feeling of guilt because his mother had to marry a man she did not love to take care of them. He has rescue fantasies regarding his mother and several of the women in his life, including Jane. He was concerned and sad over the possibility that he may never be able to make a commitment to one woman. He was confident that he could learn to control his anger and his threats, because he gave up drinking. I labeled both addictions, which he understood and accepted. I described the TARET model, and it made sense to him. He also knew his anger was manipulative at times and was aware of the hollowness of his victories with Jane. He described its history in his family of origin, at college, and at work. His mother had mentioned that his father had hit her. He saw his father as an angry, military man, short in stature, and needing to prove his masculinity through sexuality and his violence. He was easily aware of the similarities between himself and his father. I focused on the differences. I raised the possibility of the fear of closeness—what would it mean to him if he was committed to one woman? He hadn't thought much about that, but added, "Jane accuses me of being incapable of a committed relationship ... of being open and loving and maybe it's true." It was said with sadness. I wondered if the same were true of Jane at some level.

*Session 4.* The purpose of this session was to pull observations and reactions together and to finalize our contract. John and Jane had monitored their thoughts and feelings, as I had suggested. John discovered his ambivalence with Jane, saying yes, and then resenting her. When John was angry, Jane sometimes stated, "You'll get over it," to which he felt discounted. John felt used by Jane, that he rescued her, and will eventually be discarded when she no longer needs him. This leads to anxiety and anger; the sound of his voice is scary to her; she withdraws, and the marital dance continues. Trust issues were evident in his feeling that she will leave:

John: I'm not sure she'll stay.
T: What do you mean, John?
John: She'll leave me one day.
T: Say more.
John: I'll drive her away ... if I'm unable to control my anger and continue to threaten her, I know I'll drive her away.
T: Anything else?
John: When she's financially independent, she'll leave ... I'm expendable.

Jane validated some of what John felt,

but added that she did not want to leave John at this time. She did not feel John would leave her even though he had a lover. In describing their experiences, John was more concrete; Jane had more difficulty putting her feelings into words. "When I feel special and important, I feel secure with John." I tried to get her to describe how she'll know she is special and important to him. Even when he does what she asks, she never knows whether she can trust it . . . "is he laying a trip on me . . . manipulating me?" We discussed how she could know what is "real" and what's a manipulation. She wanted to be "seen and heard" by John and "touched by him." His behavior was not an indication of his caring. The "be spontaneous" paradox started to emerge as a relationship trap. "If I'm clear about what I want, and John gives it to me, I get what I want, but I can't trust that he's giving it to me because he wants to or because he's manipulating me to get what he wants. . . . If I'm unclear, I may not get what I want, but if I do, if John gives me what I say I want, especially if I don't actually say it, then it's spontaneous."

The session ended with a reaffirmation of the contract—the elimination of violence and the exploration of relationship issues, especially whether Jane wanted to be in a relationship in which her spouse was having an affair. I suggested two tasks: to keep monitoring their interactions and to use the TARET model, which we had gone over; and for both of them to think about the pros and cons of being clear in asking for what they want from one another. It appeared that John had little problem with asking and was more able to see the relationship as an exchange of services. Jane had more romantic notions, at least as she presented during these sessions. My not confronting the disadvantages of what each was asking for early in the treatment may have been an error that haunted us later.

## Treatment

*Session 5.* The interactional monitoring continues. No violence had occurred. Honesty as a value in the relationship was discussed. My focus was on "choice" being the issue, not necessarily expressing or not expressing themselves. The choice needed to be based on what each wanted to achieve at any moment in time, evaluating ways of getting what they wanted, as separate from what they "needed," while also respecting what the other wanted. We kept focusing on the consequences of their behavior, in an effort to increase responsibility and choice. TARET was discussed in more detail, separating "wants and needs . . . cause and effect." In line with the latter, the focus was on the intent of messages and their effect, with each person being responsible for the congruency in the sending and responding to one another. Both continued to claim that the relationship was "sound" in many ways, but that John's womanizing could destroy it. The "self-fulfilling" aspect of John's behavior was discussed in regard to his family of origin. Was he in fact driving Jane away? Was Jane living out her victim's role? My task to them was to think about their relationship in regard to any "scripty" messages from their families of origin. At this time, levels 1 and 2 of the TARET model were being employed—focusing on behavioral change, with exploration of the cognitive antecedents, historical and current, to the behavior in question.

*Session 6.* We continued working on priority 1, John's anger, and explored its history, its costs, and its benefits. John validated Jane's feeling that it sometimes is used to control her, yet his anger distances him from her. I focused on its alienating effect on Jane and himself. Using the examples they had brought in, we discussed, in more detail, how messages were sent and received, the relationship between their perceptions, interpretations, feelings, wants, and behaviors that get played out in their marital patterns. Each was "sensitive" to the different aspects of the sent message; John responded to her tone of voice, Jane to his tone and his facial gestures. He scared her, and he playfully said that the next time he got angry, he would draw an angry face on a paper bag and put it on his head to help her not to be afraid of him. We discussed other ways in which he could keep from creating further anxiety in Jane when he got angry. We had further discussions of the expectations that each had for the other, letting themselves and each other down; their family of origin as creating much of the basis for their unrealistic expectations was clarified.

Much of the session explored what was behind John's anger and her fear. My hunch at this time was that they were playing out a victim-persecutor game, each being the reciprocal of the other. They were not in touch with the reciprocal part of themselves; namely, John was not aware of the pain regarding the loss of his father, and the softer aspects of himself, including wanting a close relationship with men. Jane was not aware of her anger at being born crippled, some of the ways she was treated as a child, and felt in touch with the victimized part of herself, but not with the controlling aspects of her behavior. In my work I look for ways in which people are denying the reciprocal parts of themselves, believing that by owning and balancing the various aspects of ourselves we can become emotionally healthy, accepting of our total selves as fallible human beings, and empathic to others. Owning our entire selves facilitates, in my thinking, truly accepting, nonjudgmental beliefs about ourselves and others, and the relative nature of reality.

*Session 7.* What emerged in this session was that each wanted unconditional love and acceptance. They were looking outside for what could only come from within. In this regard, we explored their families of origin, Jane doing most of the talking. The difference in the way her mother and father expressed their love to her was discussed, Jane feeling that her mother was more conditional than her father. It was clear that she was looking for the unconditional love from John that she had experienced with her dad; we discussed the four stroking patterns: conditional, unconditional, positive, and negative. Jane's mother was perceived to be less honest: "You can catch more flies with honey." My thoughts were that John was perceived to be more like her mother, with his manipulations, and that she chose not to see these aspects of herself. Differentiation from her mother was the goal of her previous therapy, especially around her not having a child. The doctors had told her that her body couldn't handle the birth process. She had a tubal ligation, feels all right about that decision, feels that through sculpturing she uses her creativity to "give birth" to things, so that having a child is not as important as it once was. The session focused on how each was both similar and different from their parents. An exercise I encouraged them to do was to list all the qualities they perceive in themselves, and which they perceive in their parents. They can note the similarities and differences, as well as which are positive and negative to themselves; further, they can accept the positive, and use therapy to modify those aspects of themselves they are uncomfortable with. Differentiation from one's family of origin is thereby facilitated, as we focus on the observable aspects of their "personalities."

The session ended with my giving them the additional task of monitoring their stroking pattern in their relationship, and noting how these are similar and different from the stroking patterns—the giving and receiving, the kinds of strokes—from the interactional patterns that existed in their families of origin.

*Session 8.* Pursuing the theme of the previous session, Jane felt that she could give and receive unconditional love and acceptance if John stopped threatening her with ending the relationship and throwing her out when he got angry. He had not been violent or threatening since therapy began. She also wanted him to end the relationship with his lover, and to do more things together. Although he had been caring this past week, she still didn't trust him—was it because he cared, or because he wanted her to act in ways that were satisfactory to him? Thus, even though they were more sexually active this week, and he was loving in his behavior, she was mistrustful: "Does he mean what he does?" Jane was struggling with the separation of behavior from its motivation, fearing manipulation, that she would be set up to care, only to find at a later time that he was still bullshitting her and exploiting her for his own ends. John readily acknowledged his desire for reciprocity in behavior; this still did not feel right to Jane. As we pursued these issues, her anger emerged: "Why should I give him anything?" Power and control issues emerged as defenses against their feeling vulnerable with one another. Although I pursued trying to get specific behavioral indicators of her concepts, Jane found this hard to do. Words could not explain it, and I tried getting her to picture ways that could describe her feelings. Finally, John, in an angry outburst, said, "We're picking at shit . . . I don't feel I'm insensitive . . . and I feel attacked by you [Jane]." I focused on his interpretation of what Jane was struggling with, his misreading it as an attack, the hurt underlying his anger, and his frustration and feelings of inadequacy at not being able to please her. This was clearly John's issue and connected with his feelings of sexual inadequacy in regard to Jane not being orgasmic penilely.

Despite his hurt and angry feelings, he still would not give up his lover. I was still uncertain as to whether Jane couldn't trust him because of his behavior (anger, threats, lover) or was projecting her own hidden agenda regarding trust and honesty issues. The conflict escalated during the session. She decided that she wouldn't have sex with him anymore, till he gave up his lover; he was feeling deprived of sex and closeness. At the peak of his anger, he yelled, "She wants me to cringe and crawl . . . and apologize . . . she's trying to control me."

I pointed out to John and Jane that they were both feeling anxious about being manipulated and controlled. The session ended on a very pessimistic note regarding the viability of the relationship. John was angry and wondered whether he could ever feel close to Jane; she was fearful and angry. I suggested to them that, since they both knew what the other wanted, they imagine apologizing for the hurts they inflicted on each other, forgive themselves and the other, and, via a small, almost insignificant gesture (not words), start to overcome the breach in the relationship. Both had expressed deep hurt and anger, had regressed to painting general portraits of one another. As they left, I, too, was wondering if they wanted to, or could, heal themselves and the relationship.

*Session 9.* Jane's hurt and anger continued to increase at John and me. She felt I cut her off during the last session and was able to express it to me directly, albeit a week later. She had been experiencing her anger more of late, as well as her sense of betrayal, her own feelings of inadequacy in relation to John wanting a lover. No, she realized that she could not accept this relationship, even though she had been trying. I, as I had done often, expressed that I felt it would be hard for anyone to accept a triangle. She had wanted to see if she could work within this framework, and she was realizing that she could not. In her own anger, she wanted to have her own lover, felt John couldn't handle it, and would regress to threatening her again. She was getting stronger and more determined to show him that she would not die if the relationship ended.

They agreed to my suggestion that Jane could have the choice of an affair. If John asked her whether she had a lover, she could say "yes" or "no." But whatever she said, John would know that she was lying half the time. He agreed not to discuss his lover in her presence. This agreement gave her the power and freedom she needed, without feeling threatened. He could continue his affair for the time being, while they worked on other aspects of their relationship. They would see whether developing the positive aspects of the relationship could make things work out for them.

We also explored, at this stage, the positive and negative aspects of the triangle. Jane was able to acknowledge its positive qualities . . . she could use it to avoid sex and physical activities she did not like, and couldn't do, but his lover could, and his lover could give her the time she needed for herself. On the negative side, it tapped into her fear and insecurities regarding abandonment, interfered with intimacy and the safe feeling she wanted, fed mistrust and anxiety, and robbed her of the "sense of usness" she wanted. Although we had worked out an agreement that gave her power and relieved the threat, the session ended in sadness for everyone. We had covered much this session. All I did was let them know I would give this session much thought, as I knew they would.

*Session 10.* Jane's anger continued to increase, and she was more expressive as she was becoming more secure. John could hear her, and wouldn't threaten her when she became angry with him. Jane was still ambivalent. Intellectually, as an enlightened and independent woman, she felt she "should" be able to deal with John's affair. Emotionally, she couldn't. It still hurt, and she felt like a "jealous bitch." John wanted full acceptance and love, despite his lover, yet realized this was a lot to ask of anyone. He couldn't accept it if the reverse were happening. This was a tough test for Jane. If she could love and accept him with his lover, this would mean she really loved him, and he would be lovable. Jane, for the first time, discussed, in detail, a three-year triangle she had been involved in. This gave her a family, with love and acceptance, but she felt used as well. I wondered about triangular relationships in her family of origin, mother-father and her. Jane discussed her past and her ambivalence regarding the triangle, and John mentioned, for the first time, "maybe" he could give up his lover and entertain thoughts of a committed, sexually exclusive relationship. Despite (or because) of our heated sessions, he had been feeling closer to Jane over the several weeks. Jane was still hurt and angry and withholding sexually.

I confronted both with what they wanted to be the foundation of their relationship. Was it honesty? If so, they needed to be careful of what they asked, they just might get it. Were they prepared for total honesty in their relationship? Both were confused at this time; they were struggling with defining the basic values they wanted to underlie their relationship. Jane was finally able to ask for time while she worked out how she could be close again. The session ended with some clarity. She would not ask about his lover; he would not mention her; more important, they would think about a committed relationship and what it would mean to both of them. At this stage of therapy, John "appeared" more honest than Jane in being able to state what he thought and felt. However, there was a quality of *"de besten ligen ist die emmess"* (the best lie is the truth) in John. (My mother used to say this; it appears she had great insight.)

*Session 11.* Several weeks elapsed, and John and Jane were feeling good about the relationship; they were getting along extremely well. Anxiety and anger had decreased. John was appreciative of Jane's efforts at home, and she was more relaxed. She had agreed to accept John's lover as a fact, although she did not like it. She was coping well, and they were doing fine at this time. She was still uncertain as to what she wanted regarding a monogamous relationship. She was less angry, and when she did express her vulnerability and her anger, John's accepting response helped her feel less threatened. Now she was aware of her fear of abandonment and the sense that perhaps she wasn't lovable. "How could someone really love me?.... How could I be sure they won't leave me?.... I feel with John as I did as a child."

She related a host of memories related to her hospitalizations, especially her mother telling her that the nurses said that Mom couldn't come if she couldn't control her child. A flood of related memories came, leaving her with a sense that she could not express her real feelings without the threat of being left. She had felt like an object ... powerless ... vulnerable ... with people making decisions about her and her body when she was a little girl. Her early decision seemed to be: "Don't feel, don't express, or you'll be left." She also learned to suppress her sexuality and angry feelings ... nurses stuck her with needles, no one explained anything to her ... she was a frightened child and much of this remained in her. John listened as Jane used the session to describe these early experiences, her feelings of vulnerability, her mistrust, her anxiety about expressing her feelings and the ultimate self-blame: "I always wondered what I did to deserve what happened to me." My job during this session was to listen, to facilitate the owning of her feelings, and to help her to differentiate the past from the present.

*Session 12.* Now it was John's turn. He discussed themes of honesty and trust. Being tactful is perceived as not telling the truth. His father was direct and tactless. "I have a reputation of being brutally frank." We discussed Mead's concept of the "me" and the "I," with John sorting out where he was coming from regarding the honesty issue. In business, he doesn't play politics, and this has interfered with his career. The rewards, however, have been self-respect and the respect of others. As he feels more secure with himself, he has less need to "beat people over the head." His Unitarian church affiliation, with Jane, is useful to him spiritually, and he feels calmer of late. He has been using the RET model at home and at work. He is less defensive, and he feels less threatened. Jane has been better able to express her anger, and he has been better able to accept it. Jane has been better able to own the "right" to be angry, and vengeful. John was moving toward not needing to be angry and owning more of his vulnerability. John was feeling more guilty regarding the relationship with Jane and his lover. My focus is usually to help people move from guilt to regret and to own their responsibility for change. Jane was still struggling with what she wanted. Sometimes, she could even tease him about his lover: "Sometimes I wake up swinging." John is more accepting of her hurt and anger, and when she asks for something she needs, he generally gives it to her: "I'm starting to feel more important to him." At times, she still wondered whether he was manipulating her. They were talking more specifically about what they wanted, giving each other more, but there was still an uneasy quality to their relationship. Jane was still ambivalent about the monogamous relationship, still trying to live within the triangle. They were both struggling as the year came to an end.

*Session 13.* As we moved into the new year, several weeks elapsed between sessions. We reassessed our original contract. Anger and anxiety had markedly decreased, but communication and relationship traps were still present. John's hurt and anger emerged again. He was feeling deprived of love and affection, but Jane wasn't "buying into it." She stated, "He wants too much from me now . . . he can take care of himself."

They were feeling stuck again. John was wondering whether Jane really loved him or was staying because of her economic dependency . . . he was aware that his rescuing her was also his emotional downfall. He felt embarrassed, but "admitted" that he liked kissing, hugging, and touching Jane: "Jane makes fun of women who flirt, kiss, and stroke their men." Jane felt uncomfortable engaging in this behavior. John claimed to give physical stroking freely, whereas Jane was perceived to be somewhat repulsed by this: "I don't ask for it as much as I would like, because I know Jane doesn't like to give it." Jane claimed that she didn't like kissing at this time. "I'm staying, but I'm angry . . . I like snuggling, but kissing is too intimate for me . . . I can't kiss now . . . I don't feel I can trust John."

John felt that Jane was reneging on their agreement: "When we first came here we were in a bad way . . . violence . . . then for a few months, things were okay . . . now I feel we're apart . . . cut off . . . and I don't want to kiss . . . to be intimate with John." Jane was feeling confused and trapped, as was John. She was not ready to end the relationship, but was not ready to accept John's desire for an open marriage.

The power relationship was also shifting. I tried to reframe John's dilemma to help reduce his anxiety and his resentment. As Jane was becoming more economically independent, if she decided to stay, it would mean that she really loved him and didn't "need" him. John was willing to struggle with this idea and my suggestion for him to use the marriage as a vehicle to work on himself. He could continue to give to Jane the caring he felt like giving, but without attachment to getting much back from Jane at this time. Jane was sorting out her feelings. He could learn patience and feel good about himself. We discussed the difference between suffering as "grace" (as a way toward emotional growth) and as a "virtue" (which could lead to self-righteousness and anger). I shared the belief that "suffering is optional" . . . they had a choice.

Jane at this point was beginning to wonder about her own level of guilt. Was she, in fact, purifying her soul (through suffering) by staying in this uncomfortable relationship? Though she was feeling more economically powerful with her new job, she still felt confused about what she really wanted, with John, at this stage of her life, and what specifically was unsatisfactory in her relationship . . . his "fucking" another woman, his "caring" for someone else, his intimacy with his lover, his closeness relative to theirs, her fear of losing John, his time away from her. . . .

I made no value judgments regarding her decision to stay or leave the marriage. I did, however, share my experiences that I had never seen a triangle that "worked" when affection and specialness were at stake. I had worked with "swingers," where different sex partners were acceptable and even added to the relationships. However, when "caring" came into play with one of the spouses, the triangle broke down. In my experience, sexual exclusivity was a value for most, but not all, committed relationships. The decision was up to them to work out the basis for their relationship. In general, I feel comfortable sharing my experience and my self with my clients. Feedback from them indicates they find this useful, as is my "leading without pushing." I struggle with trying to maintain this balance. I generally answer all questions directly, asking its relevance to them. I try to establish an egalitarian relationship with my clients, although some prefer to put themselves in a one-down relationship to the "doctor." I challenge them on this because I have found that people feel and do better when they function from their adult ego states. My experience in a therapeutic community for drug addicts in a prison setting reinforced this idea.

This session ended with both John and Jane feeling badly about what had transpired; he was feeling deprived and angry; she was feeling confused and ambivalent regarding the relationships, what she was willing to give to it.

*Session 14.* John and Jane had celebrated their third anniversary and things were going well. I wondered how it got that way since they were both "hot" at the end of the last session.

John: Depressing is the word I would use.
Jane: Right!
T: I almost called, but decided not to rescue . . . I felt that you guys could work it out. I'm still interested in how it got to be better.

(The audio transcripts that follow have been slightly modified because of lack of clarity of recordings.)

John and Jane describe how they worked on their relationship by *not* discussing the previous session. Instead, they became absorbed in their individual lives. As they did things for themselves, they started to feel better about each other. Jane expressed her feeling of appreciation for John, his understanding and accepting her anger regarding a ski trip that he was planning with a mutual friend. He was sensitive to her feelings, and she said, "Good, great, someone is finally hearing the things I'm coping with."

At this time in their relationship, both are feeling that they are sensitive to one another; Jane is more open in expressing her anger, communication is flowing, and problems are getting resolved. Jane is not as threatened as she is doing more for herself and is feeling more independent. This is not to last very long, as the session moves into more of the feelings generated by triangles. They wanted to discuss the problem of jealousy, something both had experienced and which got in their way. John described how he felt when he thinks about Jane being "playful" with her past lover. What bothers him is her intimacy with him, not the sex act itself. John feels envious when he thinks that someone has something he feels he lacks in a relationship with Jane. Going further, John felt that jealousy had to do with the potential loss of Jane to someone who has more to give than he does on the spiritual, intellectual, and physical levels. Jane will feel this lack and eventually leave him. In terms of their sexuality, John claimed not to feel threatened and jealous if he believed Jane's sexual life with him is equivalent to her sex with her lover. If he feels that her lover is "better," he would feel the threat and, thus, jealousy. It makes him feel inadequate to imagine Jane has something with someone else that she doesn't have with him. Jane not being orgasmic penile-vaginally is threatening since he feels that she could be orgasmic with someone else, and this is important to him. It was not that important to her. John's feelings continue to emerge. He feels that Jane perceives him as forcing her to have sex and emphatically states that this is something he does not want. He wants to let her know he wants sex and wants her to make her own decision once she has information about what he wants.

We then focused on Jane's feelings about jealousy and sexuality, attempting to clarify the thoughts and feelings about these issues. Jane related to jealousy as loss, and to her anger as what she perceives is unfair in the relationship. She's also threatened and jealous when she feels she'll lose her special place with John. When this is felt, she gets angry and has thoughts of ending the relationship. We continued to discuss fear, anxiety, and how angry they feel over the triangles that have intruded into their marriage. This is followed by the next exchange....

John: ... what I think the immediate reward is. I mean we fabricate these ... we ... I fabricate these feelings in myself to create pain and anxiety in myself, but what's the reward? I'm sure there's some immediate reward that motivates me to do that. I could think of some long-term scenarios and historical reasons for me to feel that, but I can't understand why I fabricate it. My parents were divorced over relationships my dad had with women, and that was really painful. But why do I recreate that? ... that's an interesting question.

Jane: Could I just toss this thing in here that's sort of related to what John's saying? And it's a feeling I have that's just generated from me. But sometimes I have this feeling that John is reenacting something that his father got, and now I've been cast in the role of, in this situation, his stepmother. And almost testing me to see if I'm gonna do for him what his stepmother did for his father. Now that's....

John: That may be pretty accurate.

Jane: But that's coming from me and based on things John has said.

John: That might be pretty accurate.

T: Can you go over that some more because I'm not sure I understand.... "John is reenacting something that his father got—I'm cast in the role of the stepmother."

Jane: Oh, okay ... in other words, coming from me, what I see is, John's father divorced his mother, married another woman and continued to fuck around and this woman stayed with him through the end and John told me, and has said on occasion to me, and they really care for one another now, and he got it out of his system, and it's okay, and, and so I have thought to myself, I am now, not that I'm in a stepmother role, but I'm in the role of that woman who stood by the man who fucked around and all of that. Yeah ... and that would mean a woman who does that, who sticks around despite that, okay, is, what? Is really proving what?

John: That she loves me.

T: Yeah ... yeah ... yeah, this is the thought that came to me as I was listening to Jane. What are the reasons for this extramarital affair? There is John, in a sense testing the strength of this relationship: "How much you really care about me, and if you really care about me, you'll hang in there." I didn't put it into a past relationship. That was a thought. Because you said, "I really don't feel that she cares." You said that a number of times and this is an ultimate test, you know. Because if she doesn't stay, which is very hard for her, it's a really tough test, I mean if this is a test, it's a tough one. Not too many people are going to make it through this one. If she doesn't, if she says, "I can't deal with it," which is what we struggled with the last ... few sessions ... you were concerned about whether or not that was happening, okay, "Will she leave me when she gets independent?" And you know ... that is one of the things you fear, and yet it's almost if you're creating the condition where that could happen. You almost push her, and if she leaves, what will you say to yourself? What's the payoff in that way? If Jane leaves, what will you say to yourself?

J: I knew it all along.
T: I knew it all along, yeah ... I knew what?
J: I knew that she didn't love me enough all along and that she wouldn't last.
T: Which is a very interesting conclusion to come to.
J: I don't see where the reward is for me.
T: What will that show you for yourself?
J: I'm not worth loving.
T: Okay ... now the question is ... no I think the issue is, because you said it a number of times, you said it on the phone, you said it here, having to do with questions, of "whether I am lovable. Am I somehow lovable and can I in fact love?" Those two questions concern you.

The implication is that John has some early "not okay" messages stored in his child ego state since he has to put women through this severe test. It also has the quality of the reenactment of the oedipal triangle in which John outdoes his father. This is validated by another example in which John wants to "show off" to his father that he can have two women with both wanting him and loving him while each knows about the other woman.

To pursue the historical antecedents, their current cognitive sets, and their potential consequences, the following task was suggested:

T: If you would like to, both of you, ask yourselves the question: "Where do you think you're gonna end up in your life?" If we hypothesize that there may have been some scripty messages that you took in, you may want to take a good look at them ... especially if there are "not okay" messages.... These can be changed if you like ... if you have some irrational ideas about not being okay, these can be modified. I want to add that I feel all "not okay" feelings are irrational, when these apply to evaluations of the self. In other words, a child has some painful experiences and translates them into a personal "bad" feeling, usually based on feedback he's getting from "irrational" grownups who give the kid "mad or bad" messages just because he isn't living up to their unrealistic expectations.... The kids take it in ... believe it ... start to own the shit ... and live it out.... They live out their lives like that ... I think that's irrational and destructive.... Some of these ideas could lead you to project some outcome ... what's gonna happen to such a not okay person or persons.... Do you understand?

[John and Jane state that they do.]

T: Let's take a look at these messages, these irrational ideas, these future projections ... so we can say.... "Wait a second ... slow down ... these outcomes are based on some irrational assumptions" ... we can reframe them ... we can change your personal history ... its meaning ... so that these experiences don't mean the same things they mean to the "little kid" in you thinks it means.... The little kid may be leading you to play out your life in certain destructive ways.... Maybe we can modify that.... Do you understand what I'm asking you to do?

John: Right ... almost ... we're gonna create a mental projection of where we will end up, either personally or as a couple, with those "not okay" scripts we're carrying around in ourselves ... so we can work on those scripts ... and modify the interpretation of our personal history ... our experience ... so we can create a new personal history ... so we can end up feeling okay with a different projection

of the outcome . . . constructive . . . not destructive. . . .
T: That's great, John. . . . You've been doing the reading . . . [playfully] you're definitely corporate presidential material. . . .

The rest of the session is spent reviewing the issues related to separating interpretations of messages between one another in light of their expectations. We further discussed how they both wanted validation from one another, and how each is hurt by their responses which do not meet their expectations.

Jane was still angry when she left. I suggested that they continue to monitor their interactions in light of what we had been discussing, to get in touch with their expectations, trying to separate adult from child ego states, and furthermore, to continue to realize they had options, which, if exercised, might lead to different outcomes where they get what they want in the short run, as well as in their long-term outcomes, in and out of the relationship.

*Session 15.* John started by talking about his aunt in California who was dying, but had to move into this subject by preceding it with an intellectual discussion related to the irrational ideas behind various emotional states. The mood quickly changed as he expressed his guilt for not going out to see her while she was alive and well. The impression was clear that John was struggling with grief and potential loss of a loved one, but when I asked him about it, he said: "That doesn't really bother me." The session waxed philosophical for a while, but later, when questioned again as to his feelings, he expressed the desire to tell his aunt that he loves her and misses her and "stuff like that."

T: She sounds kind of special. . . . What do you admire about her? . . . What will you miss when she dies? . . .

John: All her independence, and her "they can kick me but they can't whip me" attitude.

[This is dealt with for a short time, before Jane expresses her own feelings that she is feeling heavily weighted in relation to "us" (the marriage). We pursue this in some detail, as Jane continues to express deep concern about the relationship.]

Jane: I think we're running on the same tracks . . . parallel, but I don't think we're crossing over too much.

She continues to discuss her unhappiness in the relationship with John, adding that she doesn't know what she really wants . . . her new job and her projects are taking all of her energy right now.

Jane: I don't feel John, and I don't feel real close to one another. . . . I feel sort of distant and unattached . . . I feel guarded. . . .

[I try to clarify what Jane feels—the difference between unattached, distant, guarded. It's difficult going, so I pursue what Jane's ideal is.]

Jane: My ideal is a very loving, secure, comfortable relationship . . . one that has some joy in it . . . and no pain. . . . It's an ideal . . . no pain. . . .

Clearly Jane is struggling to sort out the way she really feels, what she wants, what is idealistic . . . what is realistic to expect with John or any relationship. . . . Jane goes on to say that when they were away for the weekend, it was very good . . . they were feeling close . . . but coming back to reality was difficult. I try to point out to Jane that sometimes we are not very clear about what is important. I relate it to the process of dying . . . when it happens, suddenly we become clear about the stuff we were caught up in and realize what really is important. . . . I continue to discuss how we allow ourselves to get trapped by the "stuff" of life, our ego attachments. I ask,

"What kinds of things do you allow to get in your way of feeling good?" As we continue to discuss these issues, I notice that John is uninvolved and rather tense. I decide to say nothing, waiting for him to say what he feels. Finally, he expresses his anger . . . his not wanting to hear for the umpteenth time all of the problems that Jane is unhappy about. He feels that Jane has her job, her sculpture, and "she's got a place to run." He comments that he doesn't want to give any more in the session . . . and that Jane and I should work alone. He's depressed and doesn't want to get into Jane's disappointment with the relationship.

T: Is there anything we can offer you now, John?
John: No . . . I can take care of it myself. . . . Well . . . I'm sitting here feeling an awful lot of loss and what do you and Jane get into . . . all the shit about what's wrong with the marriage again. . . .

He doesn't want to talk anymore and withdraws, as Jane continues to discuss her reading of Edward Albee works, which deal with sex, love, and marriage . . . as well as existential issues. . . .

I try to relate these to the existential issues brought up in the session, especially being alone on one's path . . . how we are alone yet need to reach out and connect with someone (relating to the feeling Jane expressed earlier regarding parallel tracks). . . . We go on to talk about the issue of bonding which Jane brings up, bonding with others. . . . Jane can relate to this . . . we struggle with the feeling that although we may not feel the bond all the time, it doesn't mean the bond is broken . . . people can reconnect. I describe my work with incestuous families where many bonds have been broken, yet in some cases, through hard work, the connections can be reestablished. . . . The session ends with Jane reflecting on how important it is to connect with something larger than the self. I relate this to John's reconnecting with his dying aunt . . . an important part of his earlier life. . . . I raise the question of how they can connect with other other, while still being on their own path. I give them the task of trying to create some images that would represent their current dilemma, and to change some part of their images to represent a way out relevant to the issues of connecting.

*Session 16.* Both had not followed through on the task, and we spent some time discussing issues of responsibility for the client and the therapist. I let them know my thoughts about the concept of resistance, that it is not useful as it was traditionally used because it implied "blaming the victim." I mentioned that the concept of counterresistance is equally applicable in relation to therapists. Resistance is better conceived of as a relationship issue. This moved us into a discussion of the reciprocity involved in all relationships.

T: Let's apply these ideas to our relationship here, and to relationships in marriages as well . . . the question that I feel is important to ask is "what am I doing or not doing that is facilitating or not facilitating the direction that we all want to go in?" You come here for service. I'm paid to provide it. If I'm not doing my job from your perspective you tell me. I listen . . . we work it out . . . if I continue without considering what you told me, you have the right and the responsibility to fire me. The same processes applies to marriage and the family, but it's clearly more complicated. It's hard to fire a spouse, or a parent or a kid . . . but psychologically we can cut loose . . . but if you stay, you can ask, "What is it that I'm doing that may be contributing to the way my partner is behaving toward me?" I think if you ask those kinds of questions, you begin to see the reciprocity in all relationships, as well as the need to differentiate....

John: At least you're in the analytical mode, instead of anger and blaming .... disowning responsibility ... you're challenging your assumptions ... whatever you call it ... debating ... debating your assumptions....

T: Yes ... there could be a danger here too if we're not careful ... you might wind up blaming self ... which, of course, is equally destructive ... the issue is responsibility without guilt.

[John moves to connect with the previous session.]

John: Well, in our last session ... if you remember our last session ... I was really down in the dumps.... Carrie had a lot to do with it ... I was feeling bad not seeing her before she died ... but of course what we were talking about was pretty grim too ... Jane leaving ... she can't stand this and that ... I think that what we were talking about ... but after I made the decision to see Carrie, I felt a hell of a lot better ... and I grieved for her ... I've seen her ... I've done what I needed to do and what I can reasonably do....

[There's some additional talk about his aunt and the family.]

T: Are you okay now?

John: Yeah ... yeah....

Discussion moves to their "attachment" to concepts of themselves, who they think they are, which aspects of themselves they identify with. John relates to his intelligence, with the idea of "dumbness" being a big one for him. It would be hard for him to think of himself as dumb and still feel good about himself, still feel lovable. Jane's identification was in the areas of creativity, being approved of by her family, and being a "good" person. Through work on herself, she feels that she can accept that she will never be famous, and that she has done "some very not nice things." Still, she claims to feel okay about herself. What images do they want to project to one another? John relates to wanting to be confident and capable (part of the rescue fantasies) and able to communicate with Jane. He admires her creativity and respects her for her intensity and dedication to her art. Jane validates John regarding his intellect and his creativity, and they ask me about my attachments.

T: Yeah, I'm always thinking ... my fear of Alzheimer's relates to that. I drive my wife nuts: I wake up in the morning, we're having coffee, she's trying to wake up, and I'm into my ideas about this and that, her eyes aren't even open and I'm talking concepts.... Fuck off, George....

Our discussion moves to the concepts of polarities and complimentarities, and Jane states that she is attracted to intellectual people to complement her creativity and emotional parts. John talks about how he is trying to balance those parts of himself that involve being alone, with their being together. He's comfortable sharing time with Jane, and enjoys time with his lover ... being alone is hard for him (we do not at this time get into the anxiety that is associated with being "alone"). Jane is feeling okay now that she has other outlets, namely her work, and wants to spend quality time with John. She rejects the idea of a lover ... "it's too dangerous." Going further ... "it's a dangerous game ... it would be regressive ... putting the relationship back a year.... Right now I'm doing okay ... if I started an affair, things would go downhill fast.... I'm not willing to take that risk." Her anger at the "unfairness" in the relationship is still there, and thinly veiled.

T: You said he can do something that I can't.

Jane: I mean he will not give me something I give him. So I can't do what he's done ... he has a lover knowing I'm not leaving him because of this other woman ... I don't have that luxury.

I pursue the feelings related to "he can do something I can't do" and "he won't give me what I give him," to see if they are familiar. Did she ever experience these feelings in prior relationships, in her family of origin, or as an adult. At this point I'm wondering whether the "intensity" of her feelings is related to past unresolved feelings about herself and others, added to the current "injustice" and unfairness in her relationship with John. Jane acknowledges her envy of men and their power in our society, but doesn't connect with past feelings. We return to the triangle.

T: Well, it seems that there are two elements. . . . First, that "I don't want to deal with John's reaction to my having a lover," and second, "I don't want that kind of relationship."

Jane: Actually, when I imagine having a lover, I say to myself, in a fantasy, too bad, I'm sorry you're in pain buddy, fuck you. . . .

T: Now you know how I feel. . . .

Jane: Now you know ... welcome to the ... club ... you know ... all that kind of real angry, screw-you feeling, it's too bad you're in pain. And that's a real indication to me of real anger on my part about what's going on here.

T: That, and then there's another piece of. . . .

Jane: Then there's another piece. . . .

T: Which is what you've been saying, you want to have a one-to-one relationship with someone.

Jane: Mhmm ... I want a relationship and it doesn't necessarily exclude what John is doing, but I want the bonded, committed relationship; if he wants to go out and fuck around, I'll deal with that, but I'm not gonna deal with it when he's out fucking around and I'm still not getting what I feel and need inside the relationship. That's my bitch.

T: So, the issue is, if you could feel that bonded, committed closeness ... and John gives you what you want, then maybe the affair is manageable. John, you want that closeness from love too, and sometimes you have not felt that we've talked about it the last time ... what could you do to get that ... anything happen, did you ... think about it?

Jane: Yes, as a matter of fact, I went home and thought about what you said and decided that I really was gonna go ahead with trying to do some things for John, but I also recognized that it would have to be things that could be comfortable for me too. I said, well, you can get out the black garters and you can do the whole thing, and I thought, no I'm really not up to that ... that would be too far for me to go ... but I did much more ... I cleaned the house and prepared a nice dinner ... and for 24 hours everything was fine. . . .

Everything went well until Jane mentioned what she was doing. At this point Jane reports that John said he was going skiing with his lover. She felt that he moved away, just as she was moving toward him (the pursuer-distancer dance). To her, she did what he wanted, and he pulled back. His perception was that he moved away when she wouldn't share time with him. She felt as if she were "slapped in the face" and was left feeling that he "could never do enough ... it's never enough ... it's never fucking enough." John said that he had appreciated the meal, but felt manipulated by Jane, as if she were saying, "You owe me ... I can't be here emotionally ... but wait ... and be available when I'm ready." Jane and John were stuck—she was feeling hurt, angry, and inadequate ("not giving enough"); he was feeling manipulated ... waiting for her to get around to him. But John also adds, regarding Jane's feeling, that he induces that feeling of "it's never enough."

John: That's what Amy [his first wife] used to say about me.

I point out that both play a role in the trap. John feels that nothing is enough, yet he feels manipulated by Jane. Jane buys into that feeling and that expectation of John's, feeling inadequate, hurt, angry, and resentful ... but that is her issue ... she doesn't have to feel bad ... the question remains how to identify and get out of these emotional traps. ...

T: John, you often feel that Jane doesn't give enough ... in this situation, you felt on call, as if you were being manipulated. ... Jane, you felt as if he wants too much from you, but no matter what you give, it's never enough. How can we work with these feelings ... not giving or getting enough, and feeling manipulated ... how can we get past these feelings? ...
Jane: Could you go over that some more?
T: I think you need to separate the issues. John's behavior indicating to you that what you do is not enough is his issue. Your issue of "I can never do enough," that belongs to you. If you could get clear on what's enough for you, that you're doing things for you for clear reasons, John may or may not accept that. If John doesn't feel that it's enough, that's regrettable, it may be negotiable ... but you could still feel okay about yourself and you wouldn't have to be angry ... a little disappointed, maybe, but you wouldn't have to be angry about it ... your intense anger may come from another place. ...
Jane: I don't understand when you ask, "How can you work on those pieces?" I can answer that: "How can I work with him myself?" I don't understand how to work with John. ...
John: You don't have to solve my problem. My feeling manipulated is for me to work on. ...
T: ... although there might be certain things that you can request of Jane, the basic work on feeling manipulated is yours, John.
Jane: Right. Okay. I can say to you, I know what to do within myself, to get past that. ...
T: To get past the. ...
Jane: It's never enough ... but I don't know if that's enough to straighten out what's going on between him and myself. When I say I know how to work on that, what I'm saying is that I know I do enough, I've known all along I do enough, your saying I get angry. I think I'm frustrated because I'm trying to prove to myself and the evidence is there.
T: I'm trying to prove to myself what?
Jane: I'm trying to prove to myself that I do do enough and so extend myself some more and then. ...
T: And then you feel hurt and rejected and put down when John doesn't appreciate all that you have done, and it hurts you and then you get angry. It's that issue. Not laying that expectation on John that he has to appreciate. ...
Jane: I didn't lay it on him, I didn't lay ... he's just hearing it now. ...
T: But, you ... you got angry. ...
Jane: Sure.
T: Okay, so that's what I mean. ...
Jane: Okay. Yeah.
T: "He should" have appreciated all that I have done. ...
John: More than that ... I should have behaved in a certain way. ...
T: In response to that. ...

John: In response to it . . . I should have been content to stay home and wait for Jane to make her time available to me.

T: Okay. That's what you hoped for, expected, and wanted. That would have been an indication to you that. . . .

Jane: What I want . . . wanted and still want . . . is something that I don't feel I'm getting in the relationship. John's going skiing is sort of neither here nor there. I mean I keep. . . .

T: What could he have done that would have made you feel that you got what you wanted from John?

Jane: In truth, right now . . . nothing. Nothing. I'm not willing to. . . .

T: No, at that moment. . . .

Jane: At that moment?

T: What could he have done? Which would have symbolized to you what you say you need from him?

Jane: At that moment he could have said, "Okay, I'll spend . . . you know . . . just hang out here and work" . . . you know, he says about all the work he never gets to. And we'll be in the house together.

T: That's what you would have wanted from him. . . .

Jane: Right . . . that's what I wanted. . . .

T: . . . and that would have meant to you that gee, John. . . .

Jane: That would have really said, gee, he was really happy to be home and so he would have been happily home but didn't necessarily need me to entertain him or be his companion because I had something else to do.

T: Could we . . . 'cause I promised myself that I'm gonna be on time because what happens by the fourth hour is it's 11:30 and . . . but I would like to pursue this if . . . okay, the task is to go inside yourself and to ask yourself, "What would I need from my partner, not to feel badly like I sometimes do with him or her, okay, and how can I work on myself, while at the same time making my messages clear to my partner that I would prefer rather than demand it, from one another. So that we can help each other with that."

Jane: I'm leaving here feeling great now. [sarcastically said]

T: Good. . . . No, I know it doesn't feel good to you, Jane, but . . . we'll continue next time.

*Session 17.* We pick up where we left off in the previous session.

Jane: And you said, you know, what you were saying, does that, is that tied into your past? And when I got home and I realized I was angry at you, because that was too easy a reason. I thought, you know . . . come on guys . . . that's just too easy . . . I mean it's a part of it, sure . . . but it's so much a part of my makeup we can't really use it. What I thought you were saying to me was that this is tied to your feeling sorry, being a cripple, that whole routine of I can't do what he can and. . . .

T: "You can't do enough. . . ."

Jane: No it's different from I can't do enough. It's what I thought I heard from you was the question of whether I can't do what he can? In other words. . . .

John: You can't do what other people can. . . .

Jane: Right . . . right. . . .

John: Because I'm handicapped. . . .

Jane: Because I'm handicapped. Like something I slip into or it's a way of perceiving what was going on with John and saying to myself I can't do it too. Now, you may not have been saying that to me, but that's what I read, and part of why I got pissed.

John: No. He doesn't say anything until he tries to get you to say the right thing. [Rescue attempt.]

T: I don't know what the right things are. What are you talking about?. . . .

Jane: So anyway. . . .

T: Because the theme. . . . Because the theme was that you guys seemed to be struggling with... as I listened to you... was John's sense of being manipulated, that was his issue... and your issue was the not doing enough thing... it seemed to me, well, we can listen to it [the tape] again, maybe you can even take the tape home with you....

Jane: Yeah, I'd like to take the tape home and listen to it.

T: Now what I thought was that you had an overreaction, or what I assume to be an overreaction, to your feeling that you "can never do enough to please him."

Jane: Yeah, well that's also part of it.

T: And that's why I was asking whether or not your overreacting was due....

Jane: ... tied....

T: ... to some old business of never being able to please someone... to do enough to please someone.

Jane: Okay. Well then, I misread or misheard, but I thought I was hearing you say that I can't do what John can, and okay, so we got some crossed signals.... And the other part of it was that I was angry because... and this I didn't realize until later on... I just felt, he feels manipulated! Jesus Christ....

T: He feels manipulated. What should I say?...

Jane: Yeah, I feel manipulated too. I'm the one who *is* manipulated.

[At this point I bring them back to the task we left off with at the end of last session. John recalls part of it; Jane was so angry that she forgets the assignment.]

T: Yeah. There are two parts. What can you do, John, because the feelings of manipulation were real, and it was your issue? If you feel manipulated, that's your issue. Okay. Then what can you do for yourself that you can alleviate feeling manipulated—and then, maybe, something you can request of Jane to help you in that process even though it's your issue?.... Jane, your issue was the not doing enough... that feeling seems to me... we seemed to say that John may say "you're not doing enough," but you don't have to buy into that. Your buying into it, is your issue. And....

Jane: I don't buy it....

T: You don't buy into it.... Then what is it that you do....

John: What's the issue....

T: So what is it that you can do to keep you from feeling like there's more that you can do, okay, and what is it that John can do that will give you what you want?... which is always the issue because you're always wondering or saying that John isn't giving you what you say you need. Your question always is, "What can he do?" So last time you went through a thing in your head and the outward work, okay, to provide something that you felt was for John and the hope that he would give you back what you needed; John misread it and, from your point of view, things didn't work as well as you would like. The question is, what is it that John can do to feel connected with you emotionally, which is what you want from him, without your feeling, "I could never do enough"? And that's the question that I was wondering about.

John: Okay, well, basically the way to not feel manipulated is to make up your mind on what you want to do and then do it. Regardless of what the other person does. This is one approach. It is in essence you give yourself more independence and you don't let the other person define what allowable behavior for you is, I mean you decide it, you take charge of it and you decide what allowable behavior is, and you do it. That's one. That's what I can do for myself. I've done that. Jane may not like it, but I do it. Jane... what Jane can do to keep me from feeling manipulated is basically not make what she does conditional on what I do. Or not make her behavior conditional on what

I do. For example, she cleans the house, but expects me to stay home because she cleans the house, that's making the work that she does conditional on what I'm going to do so I feel manipulated. What I'd like is . . . you know I clean the house and cook meals because I love you and because I want our relationship to work and because I like a clean house and I like a good meal with you. That's fine, that's not making it conditional on my behavior. Now she says, now I've done this so you've got to stay home and not see Mary, that's making it conditional.

Jane: I, uh . . . I want to defend myself about that Saturday. In fact there are a couple of things I want to say, I mean that episode of my doing something for John. I realize the anger stems from what we talked about, partly came out of that episode. I don't feel that I manipulated you at all because what I did I didn't even do this consciously, but I realized it afterward; maybe if I had told you before I did anything, in other words, if I had said to you, I'm gonna be nice to you for the next 24 hours and you can't go out with Mary. But I didn't do that. After 24 hours I said, "Okay, this is what I've been doing." I don't think I was manipulating you, I think I was just disappointed.

[Jane describes how she feels set up by John.]

Jane: I'm not your mommy. You know I feel like a mommy to you. "Can I go out and play?" Remember, I even said that to you, when you were sitting there and you were pissed at me because I said, please don't, and you needed to ask me . . . to say no. Okay, okay. But you put me in the position of "can I" and I said no. The thing is I know when you are lying, I can see right through it. Most of the time I know. But I don't want to be in that position. I don't want to be asked. I don't want to know. . . .

T: You don't . . . if he asks. . . .

Jane: And I say no . . . and he gets pissed . . . and then he goes anyway. . . .

T: Then you're the bad guy. . . .

Jane: So I wind up being mad and he goes anyhow. . . .

T: You're the bad guy and he is like a . . . deprived child and he gets mad at you and does it anyway, and then you really get mad because you were set up to be asked and then it doesn't hold anyway.

Jane: Right . . . right. . . .

John: That makes sense . . . in fact, it sounds like it's consistent with the first thing I said. The way I feel not manipulated is taking charge of what I do and not asking permission.

Jane: I said to you tonight, and I feel and have felt since the impact of Mary in our lives, the one thing that I feel better about is that there's a lot more looseness in our relationship. I don't feel obligated to get home and cook supper or be there at a certain time, or go away. You're doing and I'm doing what we want, and that's one of the things that's okay about this. Some of the pressure is off of me.

T: Pressure for what?

Jane: To be there.

John: Perform as a wife.

Jane: To perform as a wife, yeah. . . .

John: You don't like the concept of being a wife anyway. . . .

Jane: I never have. . . .

T: Well, it has a certain connotation. I mean, if you have a connotation, it depends on what wife means, to perform as a wife. It has a certain image . . . every wife or husband has a certain image of what those words mean. So you have a certain image of wife . . . when you hear it, you don't like it as applied to your own ideal self, but that's not what wife necessarily means . . . one of the things we're struggling with is how can we define husband and wife in more creative terms, so that you can be a "husband

and wife" without the negative aspects of husband and wife that you both carry around. See, that's a piece of being manipulated. If we identify with the role, we manipulate ourselves ... we just got trapped by our concepts ... learned ideas about who we think we are. ...

As we discuss issues of manipulation, we move into the areas of power and control. We discuss negotiation versus manipulation, and how these get worked through in their relationship ... how they work out times being with and away from each other. Jane is sensitive to John asking for what he wants, and then still doing what he wants, despite what she feels.

John: Well, in our institution of marriage, we are institutionalizing the process whereby we both have a lot of freedom. I mean I have some freedom to go with Mary or some other playmate, and you have the freedom to go and do whatever you want to do during that time period. ...

Jane: Or when I choose, pal. ...

John: Or when you choose, right, and then when you choose.

Jane: It's not gonna be set up at convenient times for you.

John: Well, if we were going on vacation together, it might be, we might want to coordinate our schedules. ...

Jane: We might want to. ...

John: Well, we wouldn't want to deliberately antagonize each other. ...

Jane: We might want to do that too. ...

John: I figured we might want to. ...

T: Deliberately, deliberately as a payback or deliberately for one's own benefit.

John: Deliberately, for payback or a little bit more. ...

Jane: I'm not sure of that John.

T: Well that's the question, you know ... do you want to have that freedom of time, which feels good to you and that makes me feel good with John? Do you want that because it feels good to you or because you think, "fuck you, John"?

Jane: Well, both probably. The time thing really does feel good to me. But I am afraid, and with respect to what I was talking about last week, if I were to start a relationship with someone, John would be in there manipulating and bitching and carrying on, claiming I don't have enough time for him, and you'd be going to go away for a weekend and leave me home. I play out all these scenarios.

T: Well, that's in a sense what you're saying too ... you're worried John's gonna say some of the things you are saying ... because you have said what concerns you about John's relationship with this other person, it's not necessarily the threat that she poses, or the time that they do certain things you *don't* want to do, but that you want certain things from him. And when you're not getting those things, it starts to upset you because you feel deprived. And when John wasn't feeling he's getting what he needed from you, he might feel deprived and then hurt and angry. The question is, when you start to feel that way ... like you're not getting what you want, you're not getting the closeness that you want ... how do you let each other know that, in a way that is not restrictive, constricting, and not manipulative? How do you ask for those needs to be considered in a way that still gives each other the space that you both claim you want?

Jane: I don't know. I know that I don't know.

John: ... ask each other for time ... ask her to do things. We can go to a matinee one Saturday or Sunday.

T: Would you say that you are better, do you think you're better at asking for what you want than you think Jane is? You think she can ask like you can?

John: I wouldn't say either one of us was really that good at asking for what we want emotionally. I ask for more specific things, like I want to go to a movie, do you want to do this, want to do that, but Jane's pretty good at that when she's not busy. Lately she's been so busy that I felt like she couldn't make any commitments at all.

T: But when you ask for specific things, are you asking for specific things or are you asking for those specific things which represent something emotional that you want from Jane?

John: Well, I don't say specifically, hey, I'm lonely . . . well, sometimes I say, hey I miss you, I miss us, it's not often. . . .

Jane: That's rare. . . .

John: That's rare . . . usually I'll say something like want to go to a movie. . . .

T: If you do . . . if you are feeling like you're missing the contact . . . and if you are feeling that, what would get in the way of your saying that?

John: I think we do say it, I think we're both missing contact . . . we haven't had it for a long time.

Jane: I think Mary right now is the biggest reason, it's more a feeling of, hey, I'm not going to show him I'm vulnerable if he's doing this to me. I think the truth is that I don't really want to get a boyfriend, but out of pride, at this point, I'll show you my power. But I don't believe in power games in relationships. But there's just enough anger floating around in me and stuff for me to say, "All right, okay, I'll show you. . . ."

John: What's good for the. . . .

Jane: What's good for the goose is good for the gander.

T: I think you've been saying that from the very beginning, Jane, and that's not your preference. Your preference is for something else.

Jane: Something else. . . .

T: Something one to one. I want a one-to-one relationship with John, I want that to be our primary relationship, but I also want my time alone. That would be your ideal somehow. Negotiating your own space in the context of a one-to-one relationship with John.

John: Well, why don't we talk about getting rid of Mary. I've proposed that, I've talked it over with Mary.

T: You have?

John: Mhmmm . . . I told Jane we talked it over . . . I told Mary that I thought the marriage was bad . . . things were getting so bad that either give her up, give up the relationship with Mary or give up the marriage. And she agreed. I also said I didn't want to do it until after the Killington trip. . . .

Jane: So, I said fuck that. . . .

John: I can understand. . . .

Jane: My response was not all that John wanted it to be.

John: How about shit! Little bowel movements there. . . .

T: . . . cocky-duty. . . .

Jane: Cat cocky.

T: Well, what about that idea . . . I mean. . . .

John: I'm trying to give her what she wants. . . .

Jane: Well, I got a lot to say about that too. . . .

T: Okay, let me hear. . . .

Jane: First of all, *I don't buy it. I don't believe it.*

T: Oh. . . .

Jane: I don't believe it.

T: What don't you believe?

Jane: Oh, I believe that John will sincerely try for a while, and the first time I say I don't want to have sex with him he'll say, "For this I gave up Mary. . . . For this! Who needs this?" . . . and then he'll go and find somebody else, it'll be Mary and I won't know or it'll be somebody else and I won't know, so what I'm saying is I think that John would lie to me and just keep it under a hat, fooling around down the road.

T: Is that your perception of John, or of any relationship. . . .

Jane: Both. . . .

T: That if a person doesn't give the other what he wants, the other person, the other person is going to hurt her?

Jane: No. I don't think it has to be that way. I believe that there are some people who don't do that, but I really am convinced, and this . . . to come back to this last week again, I felt when I left last week that you didn't get it. That John didn't want closeness even though he did say that when we were together last week, and John and I got it, like "come on George". . . .

T: Well . . . say that to me again. . . .

Jane: Okay, what I'm saying to you is that. . . .

T: I may get it or maybe I'm operating in a completely different world from reality . . . but the reality for you is . . . go ahead. . . .

Jane: What I felt was and feel is that really John is much more contented with the situation as it is set up now with Mary and me, and a lot of distance between both of us and doesn't really want that closeness that I want. And to push him into something that is monogamous . . . I don't think he's all that enthusiastic about it. I think he's doing it to save the marriage maybe, or talking about it to save the marriage, or to give me the feeling that I'm safely in a monogamous relationship. But my sense is that that's not really what he wants.

T: Let me raise another question to you. That may be valid, maybe you and John can even agree that that's valid. I'm not saying you *are* agreeing with that, but I'm trying to say that . . . what if I raise the opposite? That in fact John does want that and you don't . . . even though you pretend that you do . . . there's also anxiety attached to that, and in fact, probably there is . . . I can ask that question . . . I can ask, then, just to turn things around, okay, I'd rather make a statement because my question is not answerable right now. The question is only answerable when one gives a lot of time to it to sort through, and I, my suggestion is, that there are parts of all of us that want both, that want and don't want.

Jane: Yep. I agree. I know it.

T: You know. And we all struggle with that. I think every relationship that I've seen, including my own, and that everyone else struggles with, do I want that committed relationship, one to one, total vulnerability. Sometimes you want it, it seems to me, and sometimes you don't want it.

Jane: Well, I agree with you about that, and when I say that John doesn't want closeness, when I think of that, I think that on a certain level he doesn't want closeness. Down deep, he might.

T: And down beneath that he. . . .

Jane: Might not. . . .

T: There's another part . . . I don't know if it's down beneath, or side by side, or aspects of, or parts of, or fantasies about, you know that raise anxiety . . . but maybe, a generalized question around that issue is "What are the advantages and disadvantages? What are the pros and cons? What are the dreams and fears that get connected to a one-to-one relationship?"

Jane: It's a big thing. . . .

T: It's a biggy because we generally don't think about it; when we have it, we sometimes don't want it; when we don't have it, then we want it . . . let me give you an example.

[I share a case of a client who is struggling with similar issues.]

John: Did he marry this other lady?

T: Well, he's living with her now and . . . packed up his suitcase and walked out and. . . .

John: Sounds familiar. . . .

T: And living with this person, and even though he has a marvelous relationship, he doesn't know whether or not, what's gonna happen, because there were some certain aspects of his other relationship, that despite his uncomfortability was not totally uncomfortable for him. For a long time it was comfortably uncomfortable ... now it's the reverse. ...

Jane: Some stuff he was getting.

T: Some stuff he was getting, which we talked about, and then there was stuff that he wasn't getting, and now, here is this marvelous relationship with a lot of interaction, a lot of give and take, a lot of sex ... but he doesn't have some other things that he had with his wife ... so be careful of what you want, you just might get it. ... So, these forces operate ... something to think about. ...

John: It sounds like a full-time fucking profession, George ... [very loud laughter]

We continue to discuss the polarities of experience ... what we want and what we fear, the roles of victim and persecutor in relationships and in ourselves ... issues of the fair exchange in marriages ... what we feel we give and what we get. ... Jane discusses her feeling of holding back from John because of her mistrust of him and her vulnerability. I ask if she ever surrendered emotionally to anyone. She describes several people in her life whom she felt totally safe with, including an incident with John on a boat when he saved her life. At that moment in time, she completely let go and placed herself in John's hands. He rescued her.

T: I'm struggling with this question of surrender and commitment and the pros and cons of that kind of relationship. I wonder if you can think about it, either metaphorically, I don't care how ... with people or nonpeople. Some people deal better with images of animals. ... If you could depict this experience of both pros and cons of this relationship with animals, or other objects, or nonhumans based on past experience, or what you imagine could be the pros and cons of having this kind of relationship ... a committed, surrendered relationship ... use your creative imagery that would help you get in touch with that part of you that wants it, and that part of you that doesn't ... that maybe is afraid of it ... the goal would be to overcome the fears associated with this kind of relationship.

[Both John and Jane claim they understand what I'm asking them to do, as the session ends.]

## EPILOGUE

Several weeks after the last session, Jane moved out of the bedroom, stating that she was angry, needed space, and didn't want to be involved with John sexually. She also terminated therapy. She did both without any discussion. I, of course, discussed this with John when he showed up without her, going over his thoughts, feelings, what he wanted to do now for himself, what he felt it meant regarding the relationships, did he want to continue in therapy, or wait until Jane came to some decision.

He wanted to continue therapy. Since this would require a switch in the therapeutic contract from the relationship being the client to John, I called Jane to check things out with her, what she wanted, expected, what she was feeling, etc. Jane said she wanted time and space to think about what she really wanted. She also requested the tapes since we were recording the sessions, claiming she wanted to go over them to see what had happened and to help her understand the issues more. She picked them up a few days later, and did not want to discuss the situation further. (She ultimately failed to return the tapes to me.) When I confronted her directly about the nature of the therapy, she denied being upset or angry. However, things did not "smell" right, and I felt there were certainly unresolved issues between us.

John, as he stated, continued to see me. He reported that although they were living under the same roof, it was feeling more and more that they were going their separate ways. Occasionally, they would get together to talk about their relationship, for dinner, and for lovemaking. John stated that at times Jane would initiate sex by coming to his room during the night. He accepted the offer, but it made little sense, and he didn't feel it meant any change in their relationship.

This arrangement went on for a couple of months. Then, over a long weekend, Jane moved out, again without notice. She left no forwarding address or telephone number, although John could certainly contact her since he knew where she worked. She informed him that she was filing for divorce. They had been moving in this direction, so that neither of us was shocked, but we were surprised that she had said nothing of her intentions. Further reflection made it less surprising. This was her style, and she was, in all likelihood, scared of John's response if he knew what she was planning. I called her at her office, with John's permission, and arranged for a follow-up session by phone a few days later. I was up in the air and wanted some understanding of her thinking and what she was going through emotionally. Jane told me she was surprised that I had called, that I was interested (which surprised me), and wondered if I were going to charge her for the session (which I wasn't since I initiated the call). She stayed on the phone for a long time, sharing a great deal of information and feelings with me. Basically, she reiterated that she wanted a monogamous relationship and couldn't deal with John's having a lover. I wondered why she had chosen this time to end the marriage, when John was starting to entertain the idea of a commitment, and she said that she could not trust him. He had never been faithful, and she didn't feel he could carry out the commitment, and it was too painful to try.

Did she have any feelings about our work that she wanted to share, I asked. All she could say was that it helped her clarify her real feelings. Why hadn't she shared her movement toward her final decision? She was fearful of John's reaction and needed protection. Therefore, she told no one except for a few friends who helped her move when John was away on a trip. She said that she would get back to me so that she could go over the process again when her life became more settled. There was no mention of the tapes. I doubt that I will see either Jane or the tapes, and am left with the uneasy feeling that there is a good deal of unfinished business between Jane and myself. Did I miss some vital aspects of the relationship based on countertransference issues? Was Jane acting out with me some unresolved transference issues? Was it as she claimed? I have presented the material to colleagues; they have as many opinions as there are people, and their reactions are as much a projection of their own ideas and feelings as what the "data" indicate ("wherever we look we find what we're looking for").

Meanwhile, John continues to come to therapy for the purpose of developing a "deeper" understanding of his feelings and behavioral patterns. In addition to discussing how the divorce is going, he is getting in touch with all of the losses he has experienced in his life. Since Jane has moved out, John has lost a close aunt, a father surrogate has died, and the meaning of friends and relationships has emerged as a therapeutic issue. The scripty quality to John's womanizing has also taken form. "Mom used to say that I wouldn't be ready to settle down till I was through 24 women.... Well, George, I've counted them all ... and it's been 24 counting Jane ... maybe I'm ready." Then, a few minutes later, he would counter, "It's 24 depending on when I start counting ... maybe I still have a few to go." Thus, John's mother may have given him the injunction prohibiting a commitment until he experienced two dozen close relationships that didn't work out, and his father may have taught him how to do this through his own behavior, and his message that "we Joneses have always chased the mossy bush."

Nevertheless, John has been experiencing his loneliness and isolation more and more. This despite his continuing to be involved with his previous lover, who is older than he is, and his beginning a new sexual relationship with a woman much younger than he. Both are married, and I've wondered whether John is setting himself up to get hurt physically. We continue to explore his feelings about himself, his divorce, his sexuality, his conflictual feelings regarding a commitment to one person, his fears (loneliness, financial problems, aging body—"will I wind up like my father," who has had a long-term relationship with a woman, being married for the past 20 or so years). I've encouraged him to reconnect with his two children, women in their twenties whom he loves but who have not been the subject of much conversation in our sessions till now. I also want to pursue the meaning of sexuality in his life.

Unresolved issues with his father still crop up. In one session, as he was angrily disparaging his father for what he did to the family, John suddenly broke down and sobbed ... and through his tears, he said, "That son of a bitch ... no matter how I hate him ... I still always wanted to be close to him." This surge of emotion surprised him, as have other "softer" feelings of sadness, tenderness, and guilt. John recently wrote a poem to Jane describing his feelings. Poetry has always been a way for him to express parts of himself he could not express directly. It seems appropriate to end this chapter with his thoughts as he moves through the divorce process:

these are harsh times
when it seems that the only thoughtful
    words
that flow between us
are lawyers' letters with copies to. . . .

yet for all the fear
and bitterness and losses that we are
    counting
I still yearn
to see you, hear you, and sense your presence

there are softer words
that should be spoken if only I could dismiss
some vanity and pride
and take off this facade of strength

words like
I feared your loss so much
that I could never admit your importance to
    me
and so made the loss I feared happen

other words like. . . .
I tried to hold on to the free spirit
that I loved
and the holding turned freedom into escape

it is somehow easier
with time and distance between us
to admit those vulnerabilities that I could
    not speak of
when we were close enough to touch

I who tried to appear knowing
did not know how to learn from you
nor could I patiently teach you the little I
    knew
without vain pride rearing his ugly head

I who wanted to be thought of as competent
had so little control of the child-driven tapes
    inside me
that I helped to destroy
the relationship that could nurture that child

I who wanted to enjoy the rest of my life
with someone I wanted to die with
inflicted more pain on both of us
and left more scars that take precious time
    to heal

for this and more
I am truly sorry
yet with all this to grieve for I can still say
I am glad to have known you.

John

My question still remains: "Do you really mean it, John?"

*John's Notes on the Therapy Process*

Therapy started pre-George, with several sessions with Paula. She wanted Jane and me to negotiate an agreement. We did ... an open marriage for me and total freedom for Jane (if she had the courage to take it). Paula didn't think the agreement would work. She was right. She died three or four months after we switched to George, in a car accident, at the age of 35. So much for the spiritual influence of therapists ... poor Paula, I don't think she wanted to die.

We interviewed two therapists, including George, and picked him. He seemed smart, had a sense of humor, didn't view his profession as a sacred cow, and appeared goal oriented. I thought he would force us to think, read, do homework, set goals, check our progress, give us insights, be proactive, and do it in a way that had some fun in it so the work wouldn't seem too hard.

I feel I've flunked therapy again.... My goals were: (1) learn to control my anger so I did not scare Jane with it, and (2) work on the relationship with Jane [implied was the desire to improve a faltering marriage], to determine what kind of relationship we could have in the future. Creativity was encouraged. Possibly we succeeded. After about 6 months of therapy, I suggested a divorce to Jane, after a very angry argument. A little while later, Jane moved out of the bedroom and then quit therapy and moved out of the house. She took the therapy tapes with her. We both got lawyers. We are now fighting it out. She's not at the house, so I have no one to be angry with. I don't miss the anger, and only occasionally miss Jane. In a perverse way we accomplished the therapy goals.

Still, I feel like I've flunked therapy because:

- I have few if any new insights into my behavior.
- I haven't motivated myself to change much of anything (except a tendency to fall in love and get overcommitted too soon; and this seems to be a result of a painful divorce, not what we discussed in therapy).
- I'm not sure I've really learned to control the anger ... it's just that the frustration went away.
- I haven't taken any action yet to do the things George thinks I should do. He's not this directed, but I think I can detect his bias, e.g.,
get more spiritual
get more involved in AA
quit using two relationships at a time to avoid intimacy
give up the relationship with married women
learn to love myself.

I still haven't written much about the process, only my perception of the results and a scorecard for my performance.

Therapy seems like a catch-22 system to me. If you are really committed to change yourself, you will; but if you don't change enough, then you were not really committed enough. The therapist must strike a balance between progress and client satisfaction. If he pushes too hard, he'll end with very few clients because most of us don't want to change anyway. It is easier not to push at all, or very little; in that way you collude with the client to let them think they are really doing something about their problems ... they are partially satisfied, and you have more clients. The process seems very open, undirected and non quantitative to me. It's hard for this ex-engineer to believe that it ever leads to much.

We talk about the work of therapy, and we make an issue over it. I guess I haven't "worked" enough because I have no sense of accomplishment.

George has cast doubt on my sincerity with his "Do you really mean it?" comment after my poem to Jane. I, too, doubt my sincerity toward her. At times I would like to see her dead . . . at other times I miss her presence, of a person, but I'm not at all sure the person is her (sometimes, almost anyone will do), and sometimes, I long for a chance to start again with Jane and am truly sorry for the loss of our relationship. If sincerity must equal consistency, then I am guilty of insincerity, but when I wrote the poem, the feelings evolved as it was written.

It's hard to talk about the therapy process because it doesn't seem to have much structure . . . doesn't seem to be much more than George and I getting together and talking about intimate things, like I do with some friends.

Over the years, I have learned that I have little to hide, and a lot to gain, by being "open" and loving. I may have learned a lot of this through the following "therapy" situations: two sensitivity training labs; three therapists in the past; several one-to-three-day workshops in the AA program, a very close Unitarian minister friend, women who have loved me and taught me that the sensitive side of me is what they really value. . . .

Oh, George . . . it is hard to write about the therapy process with you when I view most of life as therapy. I can't hide from the pain of life, and I seek the grief that helps heal the pain, and I seek the friends who will listen, and I seek the love that will soothe. . . . Possibly there is a better way but I don't know how to see it yet. . . .

*Jane's Notes on the Therapy Process*

In early December, Jane agreed to join John and me for a session, during which we discussed what had transpired during the previous months prior to the divorce, which had just been granted. John admitted to doing some things during the divorce process which infuriated Jane. She called me to express her feelings. She also agreed to write her thoughts about the therapeutic process. These follow:

December 29, 1985

Dear George:

Here are my thoughts on the therapy process, which I promised you a zillion months ago. This year has left me depleted—hence the holdup.

I enjoy therapy. I see it as the process of learning about my internal world, which has always been more real to me than the outer one. So I start from a positive position. For me, therapy is an internal restructuring of the ways in which I understand.

When I began the counseling sessions with you I was looking for help with my relationship with John, and privately I was struggling over the labels Susan (my therapist) had assigned to John ("somewhat psychopathic, a person with an impulse disorder"). Her ability to predict what John would do after we married was uncanny because it turned out that she was correct most of the time. (She warned that he would stop treating me fairly once we were married, that he would turn me into a mother figure, etc.) I had resisted what she said, choosing to marry John, only to find it happening right in front of me. Susan was the one who encouraged me to seek marriage counseling (but later she felt that you did not see the full picture about John). You were suggesting that there was indeed hope if we could be more honest with each other. While I agreed with the idea, I wasn't (and still am not) sure what is possible for me with John.

I wanted the sessions with you to somehow disprove or change what I was indeed living with. But I felt as though I had two therapy philosophies warring with each other and I was caught in the middle.

In the end I turned to Susan, because I did not feel, in this area of my life, that I could see clearly enough on my own. I allowed myself to believe what she was saying, that John is a deeply troubled person and that there was no hope for the marriage straightening out. Also I was at the point of a breakdown. (I do not use the word lightly.) I was in trouble and the only thing I could think of was to get away and stop the pain.

It has been a lifetime habit of mine to not speak up for my needs and then flee when I'm unhappy. I'm aware of this, but I lost my ability to believe that the marriage could change swiftly enough for the pain to stop. I know it's a problem that I create, but I just felt too uncertain and desperate about this situation to be patient.

All of this, George, is really background for who I was when I walked through the door over a year ago. What we did in those sessions was good, but it seemed to skim over the surface of the situation. I was in extraordinary pain, but did not feel safe enough to get out what was truly happening in the depths of me. I was too scared of what John was pulling when we were not in the safety of those sessions. I was complaining about John and Mary, but uncertain in my soul who this character was that I had tied myself up with, and deep down inside I felt so utterly rejected. It was, in short, too late for me and I used the sessions as a staying mechanism till I could flee.

As much as I would like to, there is no point in saying, "if only." There is only now.

I have seen John a couple of times since the last blowup. As you predicted, I have softened. I'm afraid I always do, and I am not sure it is a good quality. It seems to lead me into trouble and does not often generate a like response from the outside world. Perhaps I ask kindness from unkind people. I don't know.

I do see that John has remained in therapy with you far longer than with anyone else. And he does seem better, less driven to manipulate the moments we are together. But then I don't know if those moments are real or the enactments of someone who is psychopathic in nature.

The way he is treating me now, the responses he is giving me are what I want to hear. They are good, really good, maybe too good and that's how I was drawn in before. I care about John and I care about what happens to him and I am pleased that he has remained with you. I see that as the best proof of the process at work.

I felt the sessions with you had such wonderful moments, and I felt then, "If only I was married to someone who wasn't quite so warped, this would really help." I think you are good at what you do. You bring an element of gentleness to the therapy that is comforting and reassuring. It gave me hope, even though that hope was confusing and frustrating. I would not have bothered to write to you, except that I really believe in that gentleness and patience you hold out. It broke through my shield of being so defended and forced me to take a look at my "flight mechanism." I struggled over the question, "Is this one more excuse? Am I afraid of intimacy or is this more than I can handle?" In the end I was blinded by too much pain and opted to get away from that.

Now, after six months of living alone, the worst of the pain has receded. What's left is manageable. I can see John and not flip out over slights, and I have learned to set limits on what I will tolerate. I will call the police or whatever, if he goes too far. I would like to see something good happen between John and myself, and I am willing to try again and to try to not flee.

However, this is also an old game of mine, usually based on the fear of taking on the other parts of my life. So while I say I would like to work on my relationship with John, I am being cautious with myself to find out what that truly means (also to consider what, if anything, John wants and is capable of). At the same time, I am trying to face those other parts of me that I have avoided for so long.

Writing this letter to you has been good for me. I've enjoyed it. It's really the first time I've sat down to write in months. I thank you for that also, since I know this effort at writing leads back to the other writing. I hope it will offer you some insights. It's raised a lot of thoughts for me and I would enjoy hearing your reactions.

Thanks for your help. I hope to see you again.

A healthy and prosperous new year to you and your family!

Sincerely,<br>Jane

## REFERENCES

Bandler, R., & Grinder, J. (1975). *The structure of magic* (Vol. 1). Palo Alto, CA: Science and Behavior Books.

Bateson, G. (1972). *Steps to an ecology of mind.* New York: Ballantine Books.

Bateson, G. (1980). *Mind and nature.* New York: Bantam Books.

Beck, A. (1976). *Cognitive therapy and the emotional disorders.* New York: International Universities Press.

Berne, E. (1961). *Transactional analysis in psychotherapy.* New York: Grove Press.

Bowen, M. (1978). *Family therapy in clinical practice.* New York: Jason Aronson.

Dass, R. (1976). Talk delivered at Omega Institute, New York.

Ellis, A. (1962). *Reason and emotion in psychotherapy.* New York: Lyle Stuart.

Ellis, A. (1975). *A new guide to rational living.* Englewood Cliffs, NJ: Prentice Hall.

Ellis, A. (1977). *How to live with and without anger.* New York: Readers Digest Press.

Fisch, R., Weakland, J. H., & Segal, L. (1982). *The tactics of change: Doing therapy briefly.* San Francisco: Jossey-Boss.

Goodman, D., & Maultsby, M. S. (1974). *Emotional well being through rational behavior training.* Springfield, IL: Charles C Thomas.

Haley, J. (1976). *Problemsolving therapy.* San Francisco: Jossey-Boss.

Karpman, S. (1968). Script drama analysis. *Transactional Analysis Journal, 7,* 39–43.

Meichenbaum, D. H. (1977). *Cognitive behavior modification.* New York: Plenum.

Steinfeld, G. J. (1975). *A theoretical basis for rational emotive therapy.* New York: Institute for Rational Living.

Steinfeld, G. J. (1978). Decentering and family process: A marriage of cognitive therapies. *Journal of Marriage and Family Counseling, 4,* 61–70.

Steinfeld, G. J. (1980). *TARET systems: An integrative approach to individual and family therapy.* Jonesboro, TN: Pilgrimage Press.

Watzlawick, P., Weakland, J., & Fisch, R. (1974). *Change: Principles of problem formation and problem resolution.* New York: W. W. Norton.

# Commentary: Marital and Treatment Triangles

## John F. Clarkin

*We are treated here to an experienced therapist dealing with two very difficult and frequent themes of troubled intimate relationships: aggression and triangulation involving sexual infidelity. The therapist's theoretical eclecticism involves transactional analysis, cognitive/behavioral, and systems approaches to such situations. But, of course, his clinical acumen goes beyond that, in the way he structures a supportive atmosphere and helps the couple frame their difficulties. This is not an easy case. I hope my comments, which will focus mainly on areas of uncertainty in order to further an eclectic orientation, will not detract from the overall expertise of the therapist's approach.*

### ASSESSMENT AND DESCRIPTION OF THE CASE

*It is not clear what information in the assessment process led to the specific combination of intervention format and techniques described by Steinfeld. Is Steinfeld a cognitive systems behaviorist who applies this approach to all cases of marital interaction involving violence, or only under specific situations which were not totally detailed? When would he not use this approach? To advance eclecticism as an articulated approach, such is needed.*

*We do not get much of the history of the relationship, though time is spent in obtaining histories of each individual. This* apparently helps Steinfeld in understanding earlier "scripts" as they influence current interaction. We are not given the diagnoses of the two individuals, nor are we given enough clinical data to make our own. This lapse is probably related to a typical bias of systems therapists, who eschew individual diagnoses. The individual diagnosis on the male client may have been important for treatment planning, as he has a past history of alcoholism and one would wonder what associated personality traits.

## FORMAT

The author has an interesting set format for intervention with couples who exhibit potential or actual violence. Session 1 is a joint one, followed by sessions 2 and 3 which are held individually with each spouse. Session 4 is a conjoint session used to summarize problems and goals and form a treatment contract. Subsequent sessions are conjoint ones. The conjoint treatment ended abruptly upon Jane's initiation, and subsequently the therapist saw John alone.

A key issue in recommending the particular format (who comes to the sessions) of treatment, in this case individual therapy for either or both or couples therapy format, is to assess whether or not the problem behaviors are under the control of the relationship interaction. In his assessment of the violent behavior on the part of the male client, by session 2 the therapist had determined that this behavior was reactive, stemming from John's anxiety, rather than instrumental in dominating or controlling Jane. Of course, one could ask what Jane does that precedes John's anxiety. At any rate, a functional analysis of the key behaviors must be done to determine whether interactional patterns are controlling or largely contributory to the occurrence of the behavior. In most situations, when a chief complaint concerns the relationship pattern, conjoint treatment format is indicated.

## THERAPEUTIC ALLIANCE

The therapeutic alliance is central to all therapies, and we can ask: (1) what was the nature and tenor of the alliance established here; (2) what was the contribution of each of the three participants; (3) how did the alliance contribute to the outcome? The therapist reports that he liked both clients, but does not say what he found likable. The therapist discussed more specifics with John in the early evaluation sessions, showing possibly a greater like and interest in John. One would expect that the triangles formed by John, his lover, and Jane, and Jane, her former lover, and John, might be replayed in the therapy. In the therapeutic triangle formed by Steinfeld, John, and Jane, it appears that the first two were seen as a collusive pair by Jane, who bolted without explanation from both the therapy and the relationship with John.

The therapist suggests that there might have been some unresolved alliance issues between himself and Jane. I agree, and one can only wonder as to what strategies and techniques, especially in the early sessions, could have been used to foster a better alliance with her. Did the male therapist need a female cotherapist? Would a husband-and-wife therapy team model some interpersonal commitment for John and Jane?

The therapist says that he values and tries to establish an "egalitarian" relationship with his clients. Does this mean equal rights but different roles for therapist and client? The therapist seems to take the role of a caring teacher, who by definition knows more than his clients at least about interpersonal behavior and its causes. Behaviorally, he calls his patients by their first names, and shares some of his own personal experience with them, behaviors *that could be seen as building an "egalitarian" relationship.*

## STRATEGIES AND TECHNIQUES

*Strategies and techniques mentioned by the therapist or labeled in the actual transcript by this commentator include: (1) negotiation of a nonviolence contract, (2) exploration of current and past feelings of anger and violence, (3) searching for "script" issues from the family of origin, (4) instruction and teaching (e.g., recommending books, instruction in the TARET model, and Mead's concept of me and I), (5) interpretations (e.g., fear of closeness), (6) assignment of tasks (e.g., to monitor thought and feelings, think about pros and cons of communicating clearly, thinking of current behavior and scripts from the past, listing ways they are like and different from parents, monitor their stroking pattern, separate adult from child ego states), (7) reframing, and (8) sharing of the therapist's own experience.*

*In order to compare this intervention to some outside standard, we will use Beutler's (1983) classification of techniques based on their goal of insight enhancement, emotional awareness, emotional escalation, emotional reduction, behavioral control, and perceptual change. There was some use of insight enhancement (interpretations to John about his fear of intimacy), some fostering of emotional awareness, some emotional reduction via contract and exploration of feeling around violence, and some induction of behavioral control via teaching and homework tasks of monitoring. The main emphasis was on perceptual change through the teaching of transactional concepts.*

*Since this is a brief therapy, the focus of the intervention (how the focus is formulated and pursued) is of central importance. It appeared to this reader that the issue of violence was handled initially and rather easily. Subsequently, the central focus became the sexual exclusivity of this relationship, which overtly the female wanted and the male did not.*

*Of particular interest was the way the therapist, who has years of clinical experience with violence in family settings, structured the treatment at the beginning with a contract to control this behavior. This contract was laid out in the beginning sessions, was reassessed and renewed in later sessions, and seemed quite effective. Once the behavior was thus controlled, the therapist explored feelings and cognitions around the behavior.*

*Why didn't the therapist use a comparable contract around behavior that breaks the boundaries of the couple's sexual exclusivity? One could argue that John would have never accepted such a contract, as he wanted to continue his sexual liaison with a second woman and made that clear. By raising the issue, however, the therapist could have even indicated this kind of contract would be a goal in the treatment. I wonder whether it is possible to explore the meaningful cognitive and emotional aspects of a couple's relationship when one partner is sexually active with a third party. This therapist may have accepted a situation that precluded or limited his ability to explore in any depth the interaction between Jane and John.*

*The author's notion that one must proceed through various levels of intervention is clinically useful. However, we do not get a sense of what levels to approach when, and what signals the need to shift to another level. Gurman (1981) has described what he calls an integrative marital therapy and provides guidelines for sequencing of intervention, which I find helpful.*

## ACHIEVEMENT OF MEDIATING AND FINAL GOALS OF TREATMENT

*The outcome of the therapy can be assessed in terms of the accomplishment of the mediating and final goals of the inter-*

vention. Was this a successful outcome, and what criteria could be used to assess it? One level of assessment is the patients' satisfaction. John seemed satisfied that he had established a relationship with the therapist that enabled him to discuss his problems and life issues. Jane seemed less satisfied, was angry at John and probably the therapist early in the therapy, and ended the therapy and the relationship without prior discussion.

Was the problem that was central to the focus of the brief treatment solved? The answer to this is complicated, as the two patients probably had different goals in the treatment. As reported by Jacobson et al. (1984), often the happiness of one spouse is increased through marital treatment while that of the other is not. At the beginning of treatment, John had several female relationships and had several at the end of treatment. From a behavioral view, he did not change. Apparently, Jane came to the realization that John would not join her in an exclusive relationship and, having realized that, was able to leave the relationship.

Did symptoms decrease? The interpersonal violence attributed to John apparently decreased. Since we do not have a baseline of the behavior prior to intervention, it is not clear whether the intervention was effective. It may, however, have been effective in preventing future violence or in reassuring Jane so that she could behave more freely.

What were the mediating goals of the treatment as articulated by the therapist? As articulated by the theory, I think the mediating goals included a contract to control violence, increased perceptual awareness by each partner of their interactional patterns, and how these patterns were influenced by their "scripts" from the past.

## THERAPIST RATIONALE

*In order to approach the case without preconceptions and to assess the congruence of techniques to rationale, the present commentator read the session-by-session transcripts before returning to read the author's rationale and theoretical orientation. The therapist describes his orientation as a cognitive behavioral systems approach to intrapsychic and interpersonal relations. The therapist's TARET orientation utilizes the conceptualization of transactional analysis and rational emotive therapy with systems thinking. The essence of the approach is a cognitive one, says the therapist, with the goal of teaching the client a system that will help him increase his awareness of internal processes linked to behaviors.*

*It seems to this reviewer that there is consistency between the therapist's stated orientation and his behavior in the therapy hour (basic, but not always found to be the case). As noted above, an analysis of the sessions indicates that the therapist spent much effort in perceptual change techniques. In this particular case, however, it is not clear that the patients' cognitive expansion by focus on scripts from family of origin or monitoring between sessions was helpful in solving their specific interpersonal dilemma.*

*The conceptualization of scripts, for my taste (and it may only be a matter of taste, unrelated to outcome), is quite simplistic when compared to an object relations approach (Dicks, 1967). I do not think such "genetic interpretations" will have much impact unless they are preceded by interpretations of the current interaction patterns between spouse and spouse, and spouse and therapist.*

*Is this an integrated approach to therapy? On the theoretical level, Steinfeld combines cognitive, transactional analysis, and systems thinking. Why did he choose these theoretical systems to integrate rather than others? Around what principles are these theoretical stances integrated for Steinfeld? Of course, much ink has been spilled over such questions and little practical value has come from it. Of much more interest and value is the at-*

tempt at practical, clinical eclecticism in order to form an approach tailored to the individual case or client. Do the data from the assessment lead to an integrated approach for this case? At key choice points in the therapy, why is one type of intervention used as opposed to another? The ultimate criterion (in addition to outcome data) for any eclectic or integrated system is whether or not it can be taught to others. What are the principles of action in this system? When does one utilize strategy A as opposed to strategy B? If these principles with clinical illustration can be enunciated, they can be taught to others. Steinfeld's approach (like that of the rest of us) is partway there.

## REFERENCES

Beutler, L. E. (1983). Eclectic psychotherapy: A systematic approach. *New York: Pergamon Press.*
Dicks, H. V. (1967). Marital tensions. New York: Basic Books.
Gurman, A. S. (1981). Integrative marital therapy: Toward the development of an interpersonal approach. In S. H. Budman (Ed.), Forms of brief therapy (pp. 415–457). New York: Guilford Press.
Jacobson, N. S., Fallette, W., Revenstorf, D., Baucom, D., Hahlweg, K., & Margolin, G. (1984). Variability in outcome and clinical significance of behavioral marital therapy: A reanalysis of outcome data. Journal of Consulting and Clinical Psychology, 52, 497–504.

# Commentary: Is it Possible to Make a Happy Marriage of Cognitive-Behavioral and Family Systems Approaches?

## Michael A. Westerman

This case presentation represents an ambitious undertaking on two counts. The case appears to have been a very difficult one. In addition, Steinfeld has set for himself the difficult goal of integrating diverse theoretical perspectives. Although discussion of the case runs the risk of stumbling over a number of pitfalls (e.g., misusing the benefits of hindsight, misunderstandings about what went on given that any case presentation can provide only a limited amount of information), the case material raises interesting issues, and several important points emerge from a consideration of what transpired. I believe that the approach taken in this case was limited in several notable respects at the level of clinical practice, and that these limitations reflect problems in the theoretical goal of integrating cognitive-behavioral and systems approaches.

There were many positive points about the approach taken. For example, the therapist recognized that both John and Jane contributed to their marital difficulties even though the presenting problems, John's abusive treatment of Jane and his infidelity, might have led to an exclusive focus on John's role. In addition, there was an appreciation of the role played by conflictual motives. The presenting problems did not simply reflect John's moving away from (or against) Jane but more complex processes that included a wish for closeness and fears about being unlovable on John's part and a similar conflict in Jane. Also, in certain respects the therapist engaged the couple in useful discussions of the interpersonal dynamics that played a crucial role in their difficulties. An example is the discussion in session 16 about how John responded when Jane made a special effort to clean the house and prepare a good dinner as her way of trying to change her approach to the relationship.

These features of the therapeutic approach represent real strengths, but what theoretical perspectives do they reflect? At least in broad terms, it is possible to see the influence of the systems perspective. This is reflected most clearly by the therapist's appreciation that both John and Jane contributed to the marital difficulties. Other than this very general (albeit extremely important) idea from systems theory, the theoretical perspective that seems to figure most prominently in the positive aspects of the case is one that supposedly does not play a significant part in the TARET system. The influence of a psychodynamic orientation can be seen quite clearly, especially in Steinfeld's understanding of the conflictual nature of Jane's and John's motivations.

Can we find in the actual clinical work the influence of the theoretical orientations that, in addition to systems theory, are supposed to be present? This question can be answered in the affirmative with respect to transactional analysis, which provided the therapist with a useful language for labeling certain interpersonal phenomena (e.g., the "pursuer-distancer" pattern identified in session 16). However, I believe that it is not possible to discover a role played by the cognitive-behavioral perspective when one considers the positive aspects of the case material. On the other hand, the influence of a cognitive-behavioral approach appears prominently when one considers limitations in the work that was done.

This approach provided a general perspective that was reflected in many ways in the work. This perspective focuses on how an individual thinks about his/her life and the world. Unfortunately, it contributed to making the therapeutic process overly reflective or abstract. This made it difficult for both John and Jane—but especially Jane—to stay involved in the work. Also, it appears to have been very difficult for the couple to make use of those parts of the sessions that were most strongly characterized by this problem. Indeed, the focus on how one thinks about things was especially likely to appear once an issue was identified, at which point it took the form of exhortations about how one should think about certain issues, feelings, events, etc. I have suggested elsewhere (Westerman, 1986) that the cognitive-behavioral approach frequently leads to these kinds of problems, and that it may even be more prone to these failings than is true for traditional forms of insight-oriented therapy.

The influence of this perspective can be seen in another and even more important way. The cognitive-behavioral approach focuses on processes in the individual, not primarily on interpersonal relationships. As noted above, at a number of points constructive work was done on the interpersonal dynamics in the marriage. This involved discussions of events that took place between John and Jane outside the therapy situation. However, the approach taken was much less successful when it came to dealing with in-therapy occurrences of problematic interpersonal processes between husband and wife. For example, an exchange took place in session 17 that appears to have been the mirror image of an interaction discussed in session 16. As noted above, there was a discussion in session 16 about an incident that occurred at the couple's home regarding how John responded when Jane made an attempt at changing her behavior toward him. There was a crucial juncture in session 17 when John tried to change (he opened the question of ending his relationship with Mary) and Jane rebuffed him. The therapist appears to have been much better able to deal with the extra-

*therapy events as compared to the in-therapy occurrence. I believe that this limitation in responding to in-therapy processes reflects a view of the therapeutic exchange between husband, wife, and therapist as a third-person enterprise in which three individuals "collaboratively" (see Steinfeld's introductory remarks) engage in thinking about extratherapy phenomena.*

*The issue about how interpersonal phenomena were handled also includes questions about the therapeutic relationship. The most obvious points here concern the relationship between the therapist and Jane. I suggested above that it was especially true in Jane's case that the abstract quality of much of the therapeutic work led to difficulties in her becoming involved in the treatment process. But it would be a mistake to view this simply as a poor fit of styles. This mismatch of styles should be viewed in terms of a larger framework that includes therapeutic relationship issues. Specifically, Jane may well have experienced the therapist's suggestions that she think about certain issues in a particular way as demands that she was unable to meet. She may have felt that she could "never do enough" for the therapist in much the same way that she felt she could "never do enough" for John. In her marriage, this feeling reflected her sense that she was unworthy (deformed) and also a deep resentment about not being accepted as the person she is. There is good reason to suspect that the resentment played a powerful role working against cooperative involvement in her relationship with the therapist just as it did in her relationship with her husband. It is important to note that when the therapist turns to the question of his relationship with Jane in the Epilogue he resorts to the psychodynamic concepts of transference and countertransference, not to cognitive-behavioral concepts.*

*The relationship between the therapist and John also warrants consideration. Here, there was a match of styles in that*

*John was in many respects quite ready to engage in discussions "in the analytical mode" (session 16). But again, this match needs to be viewed in a larger framework. John's active participation in the sessions may have reflected a wish to gain the therapist's acceptance rather than straightforward cooperation with the therapeutic process. The abstract, reflective parts of the therapeutic exchange gave him an opportunity to pursue this objective, but this motivation could not provide the basis for real change in his relationship with Jane.*

*The case material also offers considerable evidence that the issue of a relationship triangle, which was the presenting problem that proved most recalcitrant to treatment, was replicated within the therapeutic context. In the therapeutic context, John had a positive (at least overtly) relationship with a third party with whom he appeared to be more ready and able to establish a constructive exchange than he was with his wife. Jane was once again left out. I believe that an adequate understanding and response to the issue of a therapeutic triangle was the single most important thing missing in this case. Interpersonal processes involving relationship triangles are well recognized—in fact, they are put on center stage—in the systems perspective (e.g., Haley, 1977; Westerman, in press). What got in the way of an adequate appreciation of this crucial feature of the in-therapy process in this case was the cognitive-behavioral perspective with its focus on individuals thinking about extratherapy events.*

*It should be noted that it is one thing to recognize therapeutic relationship phenomena and another thing to decide how to intervene. In particular, once one recognizes that a particular process is taking place, it is an open question whether the best way to respond is by making observations along these lines to the couple. The view that responding to a problematic process must involve pointing it out/explaining it/interpreting it itself re-*

flects central commitments of the cognitive-behavioral perspective. In my opinion, though such strategies might have been of some use in the present case, other ways of responding would have been more helpful. In particular, the most useful strategy for avoiding a therapeutic triangle would have been the appropriate tuning of the therapist's responses on a moment-to-moment basis. The therapist could have established greater balance in his stance in terms of the direction of his attention and an even-handedness with any comments that might have been construed by either Jane or John as "blaming."

A final comment concerns another feature of the therapist's response to a therapeutic relationship issue. Steinfeld appears to have been well aware of many appearances of resistance on the couple's part, especially in terms of their frequent failure to work on homework assignments. Nevertheless, it is not clear from the case material how and, indeed, whether he attempted to respond to this resistance in some way. One idea that has been the subject of considerable theoretical attention within the systems perspective (e.g., Watzlawick, Weakland, & Fisch, 1974), which has now received empirical support (Kolko & Milan, 1983; Westerman, Frankel, Tanaka, & Kahn, in press), is the view that paradoxical interventions are useful in cases involving high levels of resistance. Although I do not think I would have employed what might be called a "molar" paradoxical intervention in the present case (e.g., prescribing continued infidelity on John's part), homework assignments based on "small scale" paradoxical strategies might well have been useful. For example, for one assignment the therapist might have urged both husband and wife to decide on something each really wanted the other to do and then experiment with some new strategies for "getting the other to come across." This paradoxical frame, which emphasizes "getting" or "taking" in a relationship, might have served as one useful strategy for helping John and Jane move away from their self-defeating patterns of making requests to what would actually be more considerate and noncoercive ways of getting their needs met.

But my main point here does not concern the pros and cons of paradoxical interventions. What paradoxical approaches clearly reflect is the readiness on the part of systems-oriented therapists to identify and respond to resistance. There are many other ways to respond to resistance. In the approach taken in the present case, however, little therapeutic attention appears to have been directed to this concern. I believe that once again this reflects the influence of the cognitive-behavioral perspective. Although some therapists working within that approach have shown some interest in resistance (e.g., Meichenbaum & Gilmore, 1982), the underlying philosophical commitments of the cognitive-behavioral approach point away from such concerns. The model of an individual thinking about the world suggests an ethics of individual choice (it's up to the patient whether he/she wants to change) and not an ethics of interdependence (what the therapy can do to open up new alternatives for the patient even though he/she is likely to work against this opening up at first) as is true for the systems perspective (Westerman, 1986).

Is it the case that there is no way to bring together these perspectives so that the strengths of the cognitive-behavioral perspective can be employed to enhance a systems-oriented approach to a marital/family problem? I imagine that there is one way of doing this that would work. It should be possible to integrate specific cognitive-behavioral interventions within the context of a systems approach in a way that would lead to an overall improvement in effectiveness (for example, interventions modifying self-talk might be useful in certain cases). The points that I have made above, on the other hand, suggest that there are fundamental disparities in the two perspectives at the level of basic orientation.

*The present case reflects an attempt to forge a therapeutic approach that reflects both basic orientations. Viewed in this way, I believe that the attempt to integrate the two approaches is ill conceived because the general perspective of the cognitive-behavioral approach involves ways of looking at things that detract from the systems perspective. Perhaps the most important point that emerges from consideration of this case is that it is critically important to keep in mind that therapeutic orientations involve underlying, basic commitments, not just a set of techniques, and that these basic commitments must be taken into account when one tries to develop an eclectic approach (cf. Messer & Winokur, 1984; Westerman, 1986).*

## REFERENCES

Haley, J. (1977). Toward a theory of pathological systems. In P. Watzlawick & J. Weakland (Eds.), The interactional view. New York: Norton.

Kolko, D. J., & Milan, M. A. (1983). Reframing and paradoxical instruction to overcome "resistance" in the treatment of delinquent youths: A multiple baseline analysis. Journal of Consulting and Clinical Psychology, 51, 655–660.

Meichenbaum, D., & Gilmore, J. B. (1982). Resistance from a cognitive-behavioral perspective. In P. L. Wachtel (Ed.), Resistance: Psychodynamic and behavioral approaches. New York: Plenum Press.

Messer, S. B., & Winokur, M. (1984). Ways of knowing and visions of reality in psychoanalytic and behavior therapy. In H. Arkowitz & S. B. Messer (Eds.), Psychoanalytic therapy and behavioral therapy: Is integration possible? New York: Plenum Press.

Watzlawick, P., Weakland, J., & Fisch, R. (1974). Change: Principles of problem formation and problem resolution. New York: Norton.

Westerman, M. A. (1986). Meaning in psychotherapy: A hermeneutic reconceptualization of insight-oriented, behavioral, and strategic approaches. International Journal of Eclectic Psychotherapy, 5(1), 47–68.

Westerman, M. A. (in press). Systematic investigation of "triangulation": A family level explanation of marital discord-child behavior problem associations. Journal of Social and Personal Relationships.

Westerman, M. A., Frankel, A. S., Tanaka, J. S., & Kahn, J. (in press). Client cooperative interview behavior and outcome in paradoxical and behavioral brief treatment approaches. Journal of Counseling Psychology.

# Name Index

Allen, W., 355
Anchin, J.C., 222
Andrews, G., 46
Apter, M.J., 274, 302, 303, 310, 319, 322, 323
Arizmendi, T.G., 55
Arkowitz, H., 6

Bandler, R., 377
Bandura, A., 215, 237
Barker, P., 273, 357
Barlow, D.H., 7
Bateson, G., 376
Beck, A.T., 20, 302, 376
Bedford, A., 301
Beitman, B.D., 4, 6, 13, 14, 16, 19, 20, 47, 49, 50, 215
Bellah, R.N., 292
Berger, L.S., 8
Bergin, A.E., 93, 98
Bergner, R., 186
Berne, E., 376
Beutler, L.E., 4, 13, 14, 21, 53, 56, 58, 63, 64, 91, 133, 135, 151, 152, 409
Binswanger, L., 323
Birchler, G., 269
Bishop. D.S., 242, 243, 268
Blackmore, M., 319
Blinder, M.G., 301
Bloom, S., 97
Bonime, F., 8
Bonime, W., 8
Bordin, E., 222, 234
Boren, J.H., 302
Borkovec, T.D., 326
Boss, M., 321
Bowen, M., 242, 268, 376
Brady, J.P., 4
Brammer, L.M., 4
Brehm, J.W., 56, 152
Brehm, S.S., 56, 152
Brown, D., 366
Brownell, K.D., 7
Buber, M., 322
Budman, S., 97
Burlingame, G.M., 14, 92, 98, 103, 129, 131
Burrow, T., 277
Bushway, D., 103
Butcher, J., 97
Burns, B.J., 13
Butler, S.F., 7

Carpenter, J., 273
Chevron, E.S., 134
Chuser, E.S., 295

Clark, H.B., 7
Clarkin, J., 4, 5, 14, 16, 132–135, 151–155
Clement, P.W., 327
Cohen, L.H., 7
Coleman, J., 96
Cooper, S., 7
Corsini, R.J., 238
Costello, C.G., 302
Coyne, J., 51
Crago, M., 55
Cummings, N.A., 28

Dahlstrom, L.E., 61
Dahlstrom, W.G., 61
Dass, R., 355, 377
Davanloo, H., 134
Derogatis, L.R., 61
Dewey, J., 11, 14
Dicks, H.V., 410
DiClemente, C.C., 4, 5, 13, 14, 29, 50, 51, 129, 158, 161, 179–185, 274
Dimmock, B., 273
Dimond, R.E., 5
Dollard, J., 356
Dowd, E.T., 8
Doyle, C.C., 326
Driscoll, R., 4, 8, 13, 154, 186, 187, 189, 203, 215–219
Dryden, W., 13, 14, 49, 91, 92, 221–223, 231, 237–241, 274

Eastman, C., 302
Edwards, L., 203
Efran, J., 358
Egan, G., 49, 99, 274, 357
Elliott, R., 7
Ellis, A., 179, 221, 224, 302, 321, 376
Epperson, D., 103
Epstein, N.B., 242, 243, 268
Erickson, M., 21
Everly, J., 55
Eysenck, H.J., 5

Farber, A., 186
Fay, A., 238
Feldman, L.B., 13, 269
Ferster, C.B., 301
Feyerabend, P., 15
Fisch, R., 376, 414
Fishman, C., 273
Fitzpatrick, M.M., 326
Follette, W., 28
Foulds, G.A., 301
Fox, R.E., 14

Frances, A., 4, 14, 16, 132–135, 151–155
Frank, J.D., 95, 215
Frankel, A.S., 414
Freud, S., 8, 9, 14, 15, 21, 322
Fuhriman, A., 92, 103, 109, 111, 113, 114, 120, 129

Garfield, S.L., 4, 5, 94, 96, 274
Gelso, C., 96, 97
Gendlin, E.T., 223, 240, 277, 295, 296, 321, 322
Gilbert, P., 91
Gilmore, J.B., 414
Glass, G.V., 94, 134
Goldfried, M.R., 3, 5, 15, 47, 159, 187, 196
Goldman, R., 7, 97, 130
Goldstein, A.P., 4
Gomes-Schwartz, B., 135
Goodman, P., 310
Gordon, S.G., 7
Gotlib, I., 51
Grayson, J.B., 326
Grebstein, L.C., 13, 218, 269–271, 274
Greenberg, L., 7
Greenwald, H., 7
Grinder, J., 377
Guerin, P.J., Jr., 243
Gurman, A.S., 7, 14, 269–271, 409

Hackett, B., 353
Haley, J., 179, 242, 268, 376
Hariman, J., 5
Hart, J., 295, 296, 298, 299
Hart, J.T., 4, 13, 276, 277, 295, 296, 298, 299
Harvey, R., 46
Havens, R.A., 5
Healy, J.M., 8
Hedberg, A., 327
Hefferline, R.F., 310
Heide, F.J., 326
Heidegger, M., 323
Heitler, J., 98
Held, B.S., 4, 6
Hennings, B.C., 326
Hersen, M., 301
Hilgard, E., 277
Hoehn-Saric, R., 223
Hollon, S., 22
Howard, K.I., 134, 135
Hughes, S., 159
Hulse, D., 358
Husserl, E., 323

Jacobson, N.S., 410
James, W., 276, 277, 292–294, 322
Janet, P., 276, 277, 322
Jayaratne, S., 4
Jennings, M.L., 358
Johnson, D., 96, 97
Johnson, F., 273
Johnstone, K., 311
Jung, C.G., 322

Kahn, J., 51, 414
Karoly, P., 46
Kelly, G.A., 21
Kempler, W., 242, 268
Kendall, P.C., 4
Kendall, R.E., 301
Kessler, L., 13
Kiesler, D.J., 222, 295, 296
Klagsbrun, J., 366
Klar, H., 134
Klein, D.F., 46
Klerman, G.L., 134
Kniskern, D.P., 270, 271
Kolko, D.J., 414
Koss, M.P., 13, 97
Krasner, L., 93
Kuhlman, T., 325, 326
Kuhn, T.S., 15
Kurtz, R., 4, 94

Lambert, M.J., 93, 94, 98
Larson, D., 6
Lazarus, A.A., 4–6, 8, 15, 237–239, 274, 301, 302, 325, 326, 353, 357
Lazarus, C.N., 237
Lessler, K., 14
Levin, S., 242, 243, 268
Lewis, A.J., 301
Lin, T.T., 61
Loew, C.A., 6
Lorion, R., 96
Luborsky, L., 7, 97, 113, 134, 135
Lukens, M.D., 358

Mahoney, M.J., 179
Malan, D.H., 28, 97, 98, 130, 135
Mandler, G., 302
Mann, J., 7, 97, 130
Marcus, S., 8
Marks, I.M., 326
Marmor, J., 4, 6
Marston, A.R., 278
Mash, E.S., 46
Maslow, A., 322
Masters, J.C., 179
Maultsby, M.C., 6
May, R., 321
McConnaughy, E., 49, 50, 159
Mead, G.H., 409
Meichenbaum, D., 179, 302, 376

Messer, S.B., 6, 11, 129, 415
Meyer, V., 295
Milan, M.A., 414
Miller, N., 356
Miller, T.J., 95, 134
Millon, T., 55, 63
Minuchin, S., 242, 243, 268, 272, 273
Morrow-Bradley, C., 7
Moss, G.R., 302
Murgatroyd, S., 273, 274, 302, 311, 316, 318, 319, 321–323
Murray, E.J., 6
Murray, H.A., 298

Nadel, L., 350
Nash, J., 13
Nelson, C., 311
Newman, C., 3
Norcross, J.C., 4, 5, 7, 9, 13, 15, 94

O'Keefe, J., 350
Onoda, L., 326
Orlinsky, D.E., 134, 135
Ossorio, P.G., 186, 215
Overall, J.E., 301

Padawer, W., 186
Palmer, J.E., 4
Papp, P., 7
Parkes, C., 318
Parloff, M.B., 7, 93
Patterson, C.H., 276, 279
Paul, G.L., 93
Paul, S.C., 92, 103, 129
Paulson, M.J., 61
Paykel, E.S., 301
Pendergast, E.G., 243
Perls, F., 310
Perry, S., 4, 5, 14, 16, 132, 134, 151–155
Peterfreund, E., 7
Piaget, J., 323, 376
Pinkerton, R.S., 28
Pinsof, W.M., 129, 270
Pollitt, J., 301
Powell, D.H., 13, 239, 350–355
Prince, M., 277
Prochaska, J.O., 4, 5, 7, 13, 15, 29, 49–51, 94, 129, 158, 159, 161, 179, 184, 185, 274
Procter, H., 273

Rabkin, J.G., 46
Raimy, V., 48
Rajneesh, B.S., 316
Reid, W., 97
Rice, L.N., 7
Rickels, K., 61
Rickles, W.H., 326
Riebel, L., 311
Rimm, D.C., 179
Rinehart, L., 312

Robertson, M., 4, 13, 274, 298, 299, 357, 358, 371–374
Rock, A.F., 61
Rock, I., 352
Rockwell, W.J., 28
Rogers, C., 322, 373
Rosenak, C.M., 7
Rosnick, P.B., 14, 132, 151–155
Rounsaville, B.J., 134
Rumke, H.C., 301
Rychlak, J., 322
Ryle, A., 295

Safran, J.D., 4
Sager, C., 365
Sargent, M., 7
Satir, V., 242, 268
Schafer, R., 7
Schontz, F.C., 7
Schutz, W.C., 61
Seligman, H.E.P., 302
Sherwood, M., 11
Shoben, J., 356
Shostrum, E.L., 4
Sides, J.K., 326
Sifneos, P., 97
Simon, R.M., 6
Singer, B., 97
Sloane, R.B., 134
Smith, D.S., 4
Smith, K.C.P., 302
Smith, M.L., 46, 94, 134
Sollod, R.N., 323
Spence, D.P., 7, 8
Spinks, S.H., 269
Standal, S.W., 238
Stanton, M.D., 265
Steffen, J.J., 46
Stein, N., 4, 5
Steinfeld, G.J., 13, 14, 376, 377, 407, 408, 410, 412
Stephens, T., 273
Strong, S.R., 21
Strupp, H.H., 7, 14, 135, 299

Taft, J., 277
Tanaka, J.S., 4, 14
Tarte, R.D., 7
Taube, C.A., 13
Taylor, E., 293, 294
Terdal, L.J., 46
Textor, M.R., 183
Thackeray, W.M., 238
Thompson, J.K., 373
Thorne, F.C., 4, 15
Treacher, A., 273
Turkle, S., 241

Ullman, L.P., 93

Velicer, W., 49, 50

Wachtel, P.L., 4, 6, 15, 95, 129, 270, 324
Wadden, T.A., 7

Walker, C.E., 327
Wanerman, L., 7
Warman, R., 103
Waskow, I.E., 93
Watzlawick, P., 179, 216, 376, 377
Weakland, J.H., 179
Wedding, D., 7
Weiner, I.B., 5
Weissman, M.M., 134
Welsh, G.S., 61
Westerman, M.A., 11, 412–415
Williams, D., 372
Wilson, G.T., 16
Winokur, M., 415
Wolberg, L., 97
Wolfe, B.E., 93
Woods, S.M., 4, 6
Woolfe, R., 273, 318
Wright, L., 327

Yanis, M., 238
Yates, A.J., 6
Young, D., 97